Commentaries on
Early Jewish Literature
(CEJL)

Edited by
Loren T. Stuckenbruck
and
Pieter W. van der Horst · Hermann Lichtenberger
Doron Mendels · James R. Mueller

Walter de Gruyter · Berlin · New York
2003

Dale C. Allison, Jr.

Testament of Abraham

Walter de Gruyter · Berlin · New York
2003

⊗ Printed on acid-free paper which falls within the guidelines
of the ANSI to ensure permanence and durability

Library of Congress – Cataloging-in-Publication Data

A CIP catalogue record for this book is available from the Library of Congress

ISBN 3-11-017888-5

Bibliographic information published by Die Deutsche Bibliothek

Die Deutsche Bibliothek lists this publication in the Deutsche
Nationalbibliografie; detailed bibliographic data is available in
the Internet at < http://dnb.ddb.de >

Printed in Germany
Cover Design: Christopher Schneider, Berlin
Typesetting: Readymade, Berlin
Printing and binding: Hubert & Co, Göttingen

For John Matthew

In remembrance of so many stories read together, including this one

Preface

Several years ago, I read some of the Pseudepigrapha to my children, who were then 6, 8, and 10. They hated *Joseph and Aseneth*. They liked the *Testament of Job*. But they loved the *Testament of Abraham*. Their delight in the latter, and a later request to hear it again, solidified my conviction that the *Testament of Abraham* is a wonderful story with potentially wide appeal. So when an invitation came to write a serious commentary upon the book, I eagerly accepted. As things have turned out, two years spent working on something other than the New Testament, my usual focus, has been both very enjoyable and very profitable; and I modestly hope that my efforts herein will contribute not only something to the academic understanding of early Judaism but that they might also help others to appreciate more a very entertaining and humane book—one which, in a better world, might have made it into the canon.

It remains for me to thank the following people: James H. Charlesworth, who first introduced me to the *Testament of Abraham* during graduate school at Duke University; Loren Stuckenbruck, who asked me to contribute to the series, Commentaries on Early Jewish Literature; Pieter van der Horst, the editor for this volume, who kindly read through the manuscript and offered learned suggestions for improvement; Claus-Jürgen Thornton, who expertly hastened the book through the publication process; Anita Johnson and the staff of the Barbour Library at Pittsburgh Theological Seminary, who diligently obtained sometimes obscure, hard-to-get publications; Kathy Anderson, my much-appreciated secretary, who happily helped me with a million things, both large and small; and my wife, Kristine, and our children, Emily, Andrew, and John, who display constant love and—like the author of the *Testament of Abraham*—good humor.

Dale Allison

Contents

Abbreviations

The following list consists of abbreviations used in this volume. In the book, these usually follow *The SBL Handbook of Style* (ed. by P. H. Alexander et al.; Peabody, Mass.: Hendrickson Publishers, 1999). For reasons of space, however, the abbreviations used for biblical and other ancient sources, as well as technical abbreviations, are not included in this list; these likewise correspond to those abbreviations suggested in the *Handbook*. Ancient sources not mentioned in the *Handbook* are given abbreviations in an analogous form. In any case, the full titles of all ancient writings are provided in the Index of References.

ABD	D. N. Freedman (ed.), *The Anchor Bible Dictionary* (6 vols.; New York: Doubleday, 1992)
ABRL	Anchor Bible Reference Library
AGAJU	Arbeiten zur Geschichte des Antiken Judentums und des Urchristentums
AGJU	Arbeiten zur Geschichte des antiken Judentums und des Urchristentums
ALGHJ	Arbeiten zur Literatur und Geschichte des hellenistischen Judentums
ANET	J. B. Pritchard (ed.), *Ancient Near Eastern Texts Relating to the Old Testament* (3rd ed.; Princeton, N.J.: Princeton University, 1955)
ANRW	W. Haase and H. Temporini (ed.), *Aufstieg und Niedergang der römischen Welt* (95 vols.; Berlin/New York: de Gruyter, 1972–)
AOAT	Alter Orient und Altes Testament
BAGD	W. Bauer, W. F. Arndt, and F. W. Gingrich, *A Greek-English Lexicon of the New Testament and Other Early Christian Literature* (2nd ed., rev. F. W. Gingrich and F. W. Danker; Chicago, Ill.: University of Chicago, 1979)
BAR	British Archaeological Reports
BASOR	*Bulletin of the American Schools of Oriental Research*
BD	*Book of the Dead*
BE	*Bulletin Épigraphique*
BETL	Bibliotheca Ephemeridum theologicarum Lovaniensium
BGU	*Ägyptische Urkunden aus den (K.) Staatlichen Museen zu Berlin. Griechische Urkunden*
BHM	A. Jellinek (ed.), *Bet ha-Midrasch* (6 vols.; Leipzig: C. W. Vollrath, 1853–77; repr. Jerusalem: Wahrmann, 1967)
Bib	*Biblica*

BJS	Brown Judaic Studies
BS	M. Schwabe and B. Lifshitz, *Beth She'arim: The Greek Inscriptions* (New Brunswick, N. J.: Rutgers University Press, 1974)
BZNW	Beihefte zur Zeitschrift für die neutestamentliche Wissenschaft
BZRG	Beihefte der Zeitschrift für Religions- und Geistesgeschichte
CBQMS	Catholic Biblical Quarterly Monograph Series
CCGS	Corpus Christianorum. Series Graeca
CE	*Chronique d'Égypte*
chap(s).	chapter(s)
CIG	*Corpus Inscriptionum Graecarum*
CIJ	*Corpus Inscriptionum Judaicarum*
CIL	*Corpus Inscriptionum Latinarum*
CMC	*Cologne Mani Codex*
CPJ	*Corpus Papyrorum Judaicarum*
CRINT	Compendia rerum iudaicarum ad Novum Testamentum
CT	A. de Buck, *The Egyptian Coffin Texts* (7 vols.; Chicago: Chicago University Press, 1935–61)
CTA	A. Herdner, *Corpus des tablettes en cunéiformes alphabétiques découvertes à Ras Shamra-Ugarit de 1929 à 1939* (Paris: P. Geuthner, 1963)
DDD	K. van der Toorn (ed.), *Dictionary of Deities and Demons in the Bible* (2nd ed.; Leiden: Brill, 1999)
Dict. Bib. Suppl.	*Dictionnaire de la Bible. Supplément* (Paris: Letouzey & Ané)
Ecclus	Ecclesiasticus
ECLS	Early Christian Literature Series
EG	*Epigrammata Graeca*
FoiVie	*Foi et Vie*
fol., fols.	folio(s)
fr., frags.	fragment(s)
Gr.	Graecus
HO	Handbuch der Orientalistik
HSCP	*Harvard Studies in Classical Philology*
HSS	Harvard Semitic Studies
HTR	*Harvard Theological Review*
HUCA	*Hebrew Union College Annual*
IG	*Inscriptiones Graecae*
IGA	*Inscriptiones Graecae antiquissimae*
IGRom	*Inscriptiones Graecae ad res Romanas pertinentes*
JBL	*Journal of Biblical Literature*
JE	*Jewish Encyclopedia*
JECS	*Journal of Early Christian Studies*
JIGRE	W. Horbury/D. Noy, *Jewish Inscriptions of Graeco-Roman Egypt* (Cambridge: Cambridge University Press, 1992)

JIWE	D. Noy, *Jewish Inscriptions of Western Europe* (2 vols.; Cambridge: Cambridge University Press, 1993–95)
JJS	*Journal of Jewish Studies*
JNES	*Journal of Near Eastern Studies*
JQR	*Jewish Quarterly Review*
JSHRZ	*Jüdische Schriften aus hellenistisch-römischer Zeit*
JSJ	*Journal for the Study of Judaism*
JSNTSup	Journal for the Study of the New Testament Supplement Series
JSOTSup	Journal for the Study of the Old Testament Supplement Series
JSP	*Journal for the Study of the Pseudepigrapha*
JSPSup	Journal for the Study of the Pseudepigrapha Supplement Series
JSS	*Journal of Semitic Studies*
JTS	*Journal of Theological Studies*
LSJ	H. G. Liddell, R. Scott, and H. S. Jones, A Greek-English Lexicon (9th ed.; with rev. supplements; Oxford: Clarendon, 1996)
LXX	Septuagint
MAMA	*Monumenta Asiae minoris antiqua*
MT	Masoretic Text
NovTSup	Novum Testament Supplements
NT	New Testament
NTS	*New Testament Studies*
OGI	*Orientis Graeci inscriptiones selectae*
OT	Old Testament
OTL	Old Testament Library
P. Bod.	*Papyrus Bodmer*
P. Fay.	*Papyrus Fayyum*
P. Lond.	*Papyrus London*
P. Oxy.	*Papyrus Oxyrhynchus*
P. Chester Beatty	*Papyrus Chester Beatty*
PG	J.-P. Migne (ed.), Patrologiae cursus completus. Series Graeca (Paris: Migne et al., 1.1857–167.1866)
PGM	K. Preisendanz, *Papyri Graecae Magicae* (2 vols.; Leipzig: Teubner, 1928–31; repr. Leipzig and Munich: Saur, 2001)
PSI	*Papiri Greci e Latini* (Pubblicazioni della Società Italiana per la Ricerca dei Papiri Greci e Latini in Egitto, Florence)
RAC	*Reallexikon für Antike und Christentum*
RB	*Revue biblique*
RecLng.	Long recension (of the Testament of Abraham)
RecShrt.	Short recension (of the Testament of Abraham)
RGRW	Religions in the Graeco-Roman World
RHR	*Revue de l'histoire des religions*
RSR	*Recherches de sciences religieuses*
SAC	Studies in Antiquity and Christianity

SANT	Studien zum Alten und Neuen Testament
SB	*Sammelbuch griechischer Urkunden aus Ägypten*
SBLDS	Society of Biblical Literature Dissertation Series
SBLEJL	Society of Biblical Literature Early Judaism and Its Literature
SBLSCS	Society of Biblical Literature Septuagint and Cognate Studies
SBT	Studies in Biblical Theology
SecCent	The *Second Century*
SEG	*Supplementum Epigraphicum Graecum*
SFSHJ	South Florida Studies in the History of Judaism
SHR	Studies in the History of Religions
SJLA	Studies in Judaism in Late Antiquity
SJT	*Scottish Journal of Theology*
SNTSMS	Society for New Testament Studies Monograph Series
SHAW	Sitzungsberichte der Heidelberger Akademie der Wissenschaften
SVTP	Studia in Veteris Testamenti Pseudepigrapha
TA	*Testament of Abraham*
TDNT	*Theological Dictionary of the New Testament* (10 vols.; Grand Rapids, Mich.: Eerdmans, 1964–76)
Theod.	Theodotion
TLZ	*Theologische Literaturzeitung*
TQ	*Theologische Quartalschrift*
TS	Texts and Studies
TSAJ	Texte und Studien zum Antiken Judentum/Texts and Studies in Ancient Judaism
TT	Society of Biblical Literature. Texts and Translations
TTPS	Society of Biblical Literature. Texts and Translations. Pseudepigrapha Series
TU	Texte und Untersuchungen zur Geschichte der altchristlichen Literatur
UT	Ugaritic Texts
UUÅ	Uppsala Universitets årsskrift
VT	*Vetus Testamentum*
WBC	Word Biblical Commentary
WUNT	Wissenschaftliche Untersuchungen zum Neuen Testament
ZNW	*Zeitschrift für die neutestamentliche Wissenschaft*

INTRODUCTION

The *Testament of Abraham* (hereafter *TA*) first came to the attention of western academics with the publication, in 1892, of the critical edition of M. R. James. In contrast to the meager report in Gen 25:7–10, the book imaginatively recounts the dramatic and humorous circumstances of Abraham's death. When the day for the patriarch to depart this life draws near, God sends an angel, the Commander-in-chief Michael, to tell the philanthropist to set his affairs in order and otherwise prepare to die. When the archangel descends and greets the virtuous man, the latter fails to recognize his heavenly visitor, although he was one of three angels who, under the oaks of Mamre, announced the birth of Abraham's beloved son, Isaac (Genesis 18). The earthly host shows such hospitality to his mysterious houseguest and is so good-natured and pious that the angel cannot bring himself to deliver his message. Excusing himself, Michael returns to heaven, from which God sends him once again to tell Abraham that his end is near.

Going back to Abraham, Michael eventually reveals his true identity and his mission. Abraham, however, refuses to co-operate. The man who, in the biblical tradition, is the paradigm of submission to God's will here disobeys his lord. Eventually, the patriarch proposes a bargain: he will relinquish life if he is first shown all the creation. God agrees, and Abraham travels upon a cloud to behold the world. But God, who is far more compassionate than the sinless saint, has to bring the tour to a premature halt when the patriarch begins calling down death upon the people he espies sinning.

Abraham is next taken to the place of judgment, where he witnesses the post-mortem weighing of souls and learns compassion for sinners. Upon returning to earth, however, he reneges on his deal and again refuses to give up his soul. At this point, God retires Michael and, in his place, commissions Death to take the patriarch's life. Although Abraham likewise refuses to co-operate with this new visitor, his obstinance does not matter. Death, after revealing his terror and decay, manages to trick him and draw forth his soul anyway. And so the book ends, with Abraham never having composed a will or accepted his own death.

I. The Greek Texts

The Testament of Abraham exists in two very different Greek recensions.
Witnesses to the Long Recension (hereafter RecLng.)[1]

A Paris, Bibliothèque Nationale, Fonds grec 770, fols. 225v–241r; dated 1315. James privileged this manuscript, which Schmidt prints as the best representative of RecLng., although he corrects lacunae and other clear errors, usually with the assistance of A's closest relatives (see below).[2] A is in a collection that contains a version of the *Dormitio Mariae*, a book with many parallels to *TA* 20.

B Jerusalem, Library of the Armenian Patriarch, Holy Sepulcher 66, fols. 256r–276r; 15th century. This is also bound in a collection with a version of the *Dormitio*.

C Oxford, Bodleian, Canonicianus grec. 19, fols. 128v–144v; 15th century. C "came from Venice with the rest of the Canonici MSS. and may have been copied there direct from E, to which it shews the closest similarity, only differing here and there by accidental omission, and more frequently by an increased tendency to itacism."[3]

D Paris, Bibliothèque Nationale, Fonds grec 1556, fols. 22r–32v; 14th century.

E Vienna, Theol. grec. 333 (formerly 337), fols. 34r–57r; 11th century. The oldest RecLng. witness; see the edition of Vassiliev.

F Paris, Bibliothèque Nationale, Fonds grec 1313, fols. 32v–37v; 15th century. The text ends in 5:2.

G Istanbul, Library of the Patriarch Panaghias 130, fols. 140r–153r; 17th century (not used by James). The title of G, like that of L, attributes *TA* to Chrysostom.

H Andros, Zoodochos Pigi Monastery 9, fols. 65v–81r; 16th century (not used by James). The title credits *TA* to the monk Hesychias.

I Ankara, Library of the Turkish Historical Society, Gr. 60, pp. 267–320; 16th century (not used by James).

J Montpellier, Bibliothèque de la Faculté de Médecine, Gr. 405, fols. 61r–83r; 15th–16th century (not used by James, although he knew of its existence).

---

[1] Scholars have, following James, labeled the long recension A, the short recension B. This is confusing as the letters represent manuscripts in both recensions, so I have preferred RecLng. and RecShrt. for the long and short recensions respectively.

[2] James, *Testament*, 1: "the best MS of the Longer Recension which I have used." Schmidt, *Testament*, 29, finds *homoioteleuton* in A 2:7–8; 4:1; 7:7; 8:8; 9:8–10:1; 10:9; 11:1–2, 3, 6; 12:7; 13:9; 14:6; 16:3, 6; 17:14 (bis); 19:13–14; 20:6.

[3] So James, *Testament*, 3.

K   Jerusalem, Library of the Greek Patriarch, Saint Saba 373, fols. 405r–411v; 16th century (not used by James). The text is fragmentary and has this order: 1:1–2:4; 7:8–8:11; 11:5–19:4; 2:5–6:5.

L   Venice, Marcienne, Gr. VII, 39 (coll. 1386), formerly Nanianus CLV, fols. 359r–378v; 16th century (not used by James). Like G, this makes Chrysostom the author.

M   London, British Museum, Addit. 25881, fols. 366r–378r; 16th century (not used by James).

N   Athos, Monastery of Panteleimon 631, fols. 49r–67v; 17th century (not used by James). Chaps. 19–20 are abbreviated, and the language is modernized.[4]

O   Jerusalem, Library of the Greek Patriarch, Saint Saba 492, pp. 33–44; 18th century (not used by James). The beginning of the text is mutilated; it starts at 7:7.

P   Bologne, University Library of Bologna 2702 (formerly 579), fols. 129r–152v; 15th century (not used by James).

Q   Athos, Monastery of Constamonitou 14, pp. 358–91; 15th century (not used by James).

R   Patmos, Monastery of Saint John 572, fols. 186v–193v; 16th century (not used by James). This is mutilated after Isaac's dream. It contains a unique conclusion, based upon Ps.-Cyril of Alexandria, *Hom. diversae* 14. Schmidt's edition prints the Greek text of this ending (fols. 190r–193v) on pp. 170–73.

S   Athens, Faculty of Modern Greek and Byzantine Philology cod. Sp. P. Lambros 10, fols. 110r–150v; 17th century (not used by James). The Greek is modernized. See Agouridès' edition.

T   Therapnes, Monastery of the Holy Forty Martyrs 53, fols. 102r–121v; 18th century (not used by James).

U   Andros, Monastery of Saint Nicholas 8, fols. 37v–43v; 18th century (not used by James).

V   Meteora, Monastery of the Transfiguration 414, fols. 44v–56v; 17th century (not used by James). The text is mutilated and the order is as follows: 1:1–3:10; 16:5–20:10; 4:9–8:5.

W   Sinai, Saint Catherine's Monastery, Gr. 431, fols. 80v–94r; 15th century (not used by James). Schmidt did not have access to this manuscript when constructing his critical apparatus.

Schmidt has established, largely on the basis of common omissions, that RecLng. contains three subgroups. A G H I K N and B F J Q W (the latter agree in omitting 19:14–20:5) have the longest text. C E P V and D L M represent a shorter text: they omit 5:11–6:8; 8:6–8; 13:10–14; 14:11–12; 17:7–8; 19:4–6; and 19:8–16. D L M further skip 17:4–8. These omissions are clearly secondary; that is, the longest text is older. O S T U, which are

---

4   See Schmidt, *Testament*, 26.

from the 17th and 18th centuries and are in modern Greek, contain most of the omissions common to C E V P and D L M and represent an even shorter text, which again is secondary.

In addition to the witnesses just listed, some manuscripts remain unedited. Three represent RecLng.: Cluj, Library of the Romanian Academy ms. 364, pp. 5–60 (17th century); Chios, Public Library, ms. A, collection of K. Amantos, fols. 44v–67r (17th century); and Berlin, Deutsche Staatsbibliothek, Gr. 320 (Graec. quart. 22), fols. 65r–80v (15th century; lost during World War Two). Two additional manuscripts are of unknown affiliation: Sinai, Saint Catherine's Monastery, Gr. 1936, fols. 193r–211r (17th century), and Sinai, Catherine's Monastery, Gr. 1937, fols. 32v–88v (17th century).

Readers interested in studying the variants to *TA* must consult Schmidt's apparatus, which renders James' edition obsolete. The present commentary generally restricts its annotations to variants that significantly alter the sense or that illustrate an important tendency in the textual tradition, particularly the tendency to shorten *TA*, which bears on the issue of how the recensions developed; see p. 20.

The translation of RecLng. herein closely follows Schmidt's critical edition, which means that it usually translates A. I have, however, occasionally judged that A contains a younger and inferior reading, in which case I have translated another variant and usually noted the departure from A in the textual notes.

Witnesses to the Short Recension (hereafter RecShrt.)

A Paris, Bibliothèque Nationale, Fonds grec 1613, fols. 87v–96v; 15th century. James thought this the best witness to RecShrt., but he had access only to A B and C.

B Paris, Bibliothèque Nationale, Supplément grec 162, fols. 106v–114v; 14th century. This modern Greek text breaks off at 13:15.

C Vienna, Hist. gr. 126, fol. 10v–18r; 14th century. 13:8–14:6 is missing. This shows occasional knowledge of a RecLng. reading. Michael is a στρατιώτης in 2:4 (cf. RecLng. 2:2, 4) and Adam is the πρωτόπλαστος in 8:12 (cf. RecLng. 11:9–11; 13:2, 5).

D Milan, Ambrosienne, Grec 259 (D 92 sup.), fols. 115r–118v; 11th century (not used by James).

E Milan, Ambrosienne, Grec 405 (G 63 sup.), fols. 164r–171r; 11th century (not used by James). This is the basis for Schmidt's critical edition of RecShrt. fam. E. It contains more Semitisms and fewer late words than other members of RecShrt. and is likewise closer to the Coptic and Slavonic. It is clearly the best RecShrt. witness, as Schmidt has demonstrated.[5]

---

5   Schmidt, *Testament*, 10–14.

F   Meteora, Monastery of the Transfiguration 382, fols. 123r–130v; 15th century (not used by James).

G   London, British Museum, Addit. 10014, fols. 38r–39v; 16th century (not used by James). The text breaks off at 4:9.

H   Athens, Society of History and Ethnology 254, fols. 215r–221r; 16th century (not used by James). The manuscript ends at 7:10.

I   Athos, Monastery of Koutloumous 176, fols. 106v–112v; date: 1438–1439 (not used by James). The ending (14:6–7) of I is close to RecLng.'s ending (20:8–15). 7:15–9:4 is missing.

B F G constitute a family sufficiently different from A C D E H I that Schmidt prints two RecShrt. texts, with B and E as the primary witnesses. The present translation of RecShrt. consistently renders Schmidt's edition of RecShrt. fam. E.

II. The Other Versions

Coptic

The oldest copy of *TA* is a fragmentary fifth-century Sahidic papyrus, unfortunately yet unpublished, held by the Institut für Altertumskunde of the University of Cologne.[6] It is reportedly close to the complete Bohairic text in Vaticanus Copt. 61, fols. 148v–163v (dated 962), which I. Guidi published in 1900.[7] There are translations of this latter manuscript into English, French, and German.[8] The Coptic, although abridged, is for the most part close to RecShrt. Schmidt characterizes it is as "une adaptation plutôt qu'une traduction."[9] In a few places the Coptic agrees with RecLng. against RecShrt. Abraham's vision of the heavenly judgment is told in the first person singular, as in RecLng. 12:1–3 and (perhaps) 11:4–5; and in the Sahidic papyrus, Death has the faces of a basilisk and a panther, as in RecLng. 19:14.

Arabic

Of the several Arabic manuscripts, only Bibliothèque Nationale de Paris Arabic ms. 132 fols. 2r–10v (dated 1629) has been published, and that just in part.[10] There are perhaps half a dozen additional unedited manuscripts.[11] W. E. Barnes supplied a partial English translation of ms. 132 for James,

---

6   Cornelia Römer and Heinz J. Thissen, "P. Köln Inv. nr. 3221: Das Testament des Hiob in koptischer Sprache. Ein Vorbericht," in *Studies on the Testament of Job* (ed. Michael A. Knibb and Pieter W. van der Horst; SNTSMS 66; Cambridge: Cambridge University Press, 1989), 33–34.

7   Guidi, "Il testo copto del Testamento di Abramo."

8   MacRae, "Coptic Testament"; M. Chaîne, in Delcor, *Testament*, 186–213; Andersson, "Abraham's Vermächtnis."

9   Schmidt, *Testament*, 40. J. T. Milik, *The Books of Enoch: Aramaic Fragments of Qumrân Cave 4* (Oxford: Clarendon, 1976), 105, gives no reason for his idiosyncratic judgment that "the oldest, and the original, text is preserved in the Coptic recension."

10   Zotenberg, *Manuscrits orientaux*.

11   Details in Delcor, *Testament*, 17, and Schmidt, *Testament*, 42–43.

and Delcor's commentary appends a French translation by Marius Chaîne and Philippe Marçais.[12] The Arabic derives from the Coptic.[13]

Ethiopic

There are two Ethiopian versions of *TA*, one Falasha, one Christian.[14] They are closely related, the Falasha perhaps being derived from the Christian text.[15] The latter is attested only by the fragmentary Bibliothèque Nationale de Paris Ethiopic ms. 134, fols. 1r–5r (15th century). Aaron Zeev Aešcoly has edited this and supplied a French translation.[16] The Falasha is known from several manuscripts. Conti Rossini and Aešcoly have published critical editions of Bibliothèque Nationale de Paris Ethiopic ms. 107, fols. 20v–26r (19th century), the latter with a French translation, and Leslau has translated the same manuscript into English.[17] A second Falasha manuscript is Cambridge University Library Ethiopic 1878 (19th century), which Maurice Gaguine edited for his 1961 Manchester Dissertation.[18] This dissertation also discusses and prints variants from other Christian manuscripts for which there are no modern printed editions. According to Leslau, "there is no doubt that Arabic was the source of the Ethiopic translation … . The very close correspondence between the two texts, as well as the words copied from Arabic, such as *'atal*, 'tamarisk,' or misunderstood expressions such as *qirn*, 'enemy,' instead of *qarn*, 'ray,' is adequate proof of dependence."[19]

[12] James, *Testament*, 135–39; Delcor, *Testament*, 242–52.

[13] See Schmidt, *Testament*, 43, who argues that the Arabic is closer to the Bohairic than to the Sahidic. James did not recognize the priority of the Coptic over the Arabic.

[14] For a list of the manuscripts see Denis et al., "Testament" (2000), 185–87.

[15] So Leslau, *Falasha Anthology*, 94–95 ("almost certainly").

[16] Aešcoly, *Recueil de textes falachas*, 66–75. There is a second French translation by Marius Chaîne and André Caquot in Delcor, *Testament*, 221–24.

[17] Conti Rossini, "Nuovi appunti sui Guidei d'Abissinia"; Aešcoly, *Recueil de textes falachas*, 49–67; Leslau, *Falasha Anthology*, 96–102.

[18] Gaguine, "Falasha Version." Delcor, *Testament*, 19–23, summarizes some of Gaguine's conclusions. Gaguine raises the possibility that one Ethiopic manuscript, which attributes its contents to Frumentius, that is, Abba Salama, a fourth-century bishop of Axum, whom Athanasius consecrated, might be correct, which would mean that *TA* was translated into Ethiopic in the fourth century.

[19] Leslau, *Falasha Anthology*, 95.

Slavonic

According to Émile Turdeanu, the Slavonic witnesses, which go back to a translation of the tenth century or earlier, fall into four families. He labels these S1, S2, S3, and S4.[20] S1, represented by seven witnesses, is the most important, and its best witnesses are mss. P (Moscow Public Library 27, collection of P. I. Sevast'anov, fols. 1r–6r; 13th century; Middle Bulgarian) and T (Trinity Saint Sergius Monastery Moscow 730, fols. 2r–10v; 16th century; Russian Church Slavonic).[21] Donald S. Cooper and Harry B. Weber have translated P into English and filled its lacunae with readings from T.[22]

S1 and S2 are closely related to RecShrt. E. Schmidt thinks they derive from a near relative of that manuscript.[23] Cooper and Weber, however, note that there are also agreements with B F G and other RecShrt. witnesses against E, so "the relationships involved are more complex than the simple grouping of the Church Slavonic texts with E would indicate."[24] S3 and S4, which are shorter than S1 and S2, likewise belong to the RecShrt. family.

Romanian

TA was popular in eighteenth- and nineteenth-century Romania, and it is represented by about two dozen manuscripts in the Biblioteca Academiei Române in Bucharist. Moses Gaster produced the first edition of the Romanian in 1886 (with an English translation). He used three witnesses, one fragmentary. Nicolae Roddy's critical edition, published in 2001, now supersedes his work. Roddy takes into account almost all of the known Romanian witnesses. Like Gaster, he too supplies an English translation.

Three of the Romanian manuscripts represent RecShrt. and go back to a Slavic prototype related to Turdeanu's families S3 and S4. This means that they are inferior witnesses to RecShrt.[25] The remainder of the Romanian manuscripts belong to RecLng., and Roddy bases his critical edition upon these. Both Schmidt and Roddy show that the longer Romanian is in fact most closely related to Greek manuscripts D L M. Roddy further

---

[20] Turdeanu, *Apocryphes*, 202–38.
[21] For P see Polívka, "Die apokryphische Erzählung"; for T see Tixonravov, *Literatury*, 79–90.
[22] Cooper and Weber, "Slavonic Testament."
[23] Schmidt, *Testament*, 33–36.
[24] Cooper and Weber, "Slavonic Testament," 304.
[25] Turdeanu, *Apocryphes*, 28–29, 32–33. Text in Petriceicu-Hasdeu, *Cărțile*, 189–94.

argues that "the Romanian version was copied [at the beginning of the 17th century] from a single prototype which had entered the region north of the Danube through one of a number of Wallachian monasteries. There it was transformed in more ways than a simple translation before it was disseminated throughout Romanian-speaking regions."[26]

---

[26] Roddy, *Romanian Version*, 18–19.

III. The Relation of the Two Greek Recensions

James, the first editor of *TA*, thought that RecLng., which is almost twice the length of RecShrt., "presents us with what is on the whole the fullest, clearest, and most consistent narrative. Its language, however, has been to some extent mediaevalised"; RecShrt., by contrast, is "an abridgement whose language is on the whole more simple and original than that of A. It omits much, and in several places adulterates the narrative .... It is not an abridgement of A."[27] James nonetheless thought that, in a few instances, RecShrt. is probably more primitive—elements of Isaac's vision in chap. 7, for example, and Abraham's anxiety about being too large to squeeze through the narrow gate in 9:1–3. Perhaps most students of *TA*, including Box and Sanders, have accepted James' conviction about the fundamental priority of RecLng.[28]

Turner, focusing on the linguistic data, argued instead for the relative priority of RecShrt.[29] On his view, both its vocabulary and syntax show it to be for the most part a pre-Christian translation of a Hebrew original. He dated the original Greek text behind RecShrt. to the second century BCE, and he thought it came into being shortly after the Hebrew RecLng., while also a translation from Hebrew, is later and for the most part secondary. Although it derives from a text written 70 BCE – 70 CE, its present form must be, given the vocabulary, later than the fifth or sixth century CE.[30] Yet Turner acknowledged that, at some points, RecLng. is more primitive. In RecShrt. 6:1–2, Isaac asks Abraham to open the door, after which he

---

[27] James, *Testament*, 49.

[28] Box, *Testament*, xii–xv; Sanders, "Testament," 872. Cf. Colafemmina, *Testamento*, 9. Box finds RecShrt. original in several particulars—the tamarisk tree with 300 branches (3:2), Michael's ascent for prayer at sunset (4:4), the removal of Abraham's soul "as in a dream" (14:6). He also believes that RecLng. has "amplified" the description of Death (chap. 17).

[29] Turner, "Testament," 48–100, 194–257.

[30] Turner later retracted some of his opinions in correspondence with Sanders, including his claims about a Hebrew original; see Sanders, "Testament," 873, n. 14. For a later statement of his more nuanced views see Turner, "Testament" (1984), 393–96.

arises (ἀνέστη) and opens the door. In RecLng. 5:8, Isaac asks Abraham to arise (ἀνάστα) and open the door, after which, in 5:9, Abraham arises (ἀναστάς) and opens the door. According to Turner, RecShrt. presupposes the fuller request in RecLng.[31] Given that this is not, for him, an isolated instance, that he finds other places where the two recensions seemingly supplement each other, he judges that RecLng. is based not upon RecShrt. but rather upon a Greek text antecedent to RecShrt., and that RecShrt. is actually a shortened version of something longer.

Schmidt has also argued, in accord with Turner's linguistic observations, for the relative priority of RecShrt.[32] He stresses the importance in particular of ms. E, which has support from the Coptic and Slavic and is the oldest Greek witness to RecShrt. He further contends that there are certain Egyptian ideas in RecLng. alone whereas both RecShrt. and RecLng. show points of connection with Iranian religion. His explanation for this is that RecShrt. is closer to the hypothetical original than RecLng.: Palestinian circles influenced by Zoroastrianism produced something close to RecShrt. in the first century while RecLng. represents a revision made in Egypt during the second or early third century.[33] The Bohairic, moreover, may represent a stage intermediate between the two Greek recensions.[34]

Nickelsburg, in dialogue with Schmidt, has urged that RecLng. is "more artful" than RecShrt.; it has "shape and plot, and out of these, a discernible point to make" whereas the shorter is "a potpourri of incidents, elements, and characters, with little evident structure, plot, and relationships among the characters."[35] Furthermore, items integral to RecLng. appear also in RecShrt., where they have no obvious *raison d'être*. While Abraham's

---

[31] Turner, "Testament," 255.

[32] Schmidt, "Testament," 115–24; "Two Recensions."

[33] Already Box, *Testament*, xxviii–xxix, had a similar view: "the story in its original (Hebrew) form probably grew up in the first half of the first century A.D. ... This probably formed the basis of a free Greek version, which was embellished with some special features (e.g. in the description of the Angel of Death) which owed their origin to Egypt (Alexandria)." Schmidt may not be right in his generalization about the absence of Egyptian elements from RecShrt., for Enoch as the heavenly scribe appears only in RecShrt., and his functions are reminiscent of the scribe-god Thoth, who records the outcome of the postmortem assize. Further, RecLng. may have some Iranian elements unique to it; see on 17:8.

[34] Given, however, that RecLng. and RecShrt. sometimes agree with each other against the Bohairic, this last proposition seems problematic; see George W. E. Nickelsburg, Jr., "Eschatology," 63.

[35] Nickelsburg, "Eschatology"; "Structure and Message." The quotation is from p. 93 of the latter. For Schmidt's response to Nickelsburg see "The Two Recensions."

request to see the whole world is part of a delaying tactic in RecLng., it has no motivation in RecShrt. And whereas, in RecLng., the soul singled out in chap. 11, with its good and evil deeds balanced, becomes an opportunity to teach Abraham a lesson about mercy, in RecShrt. the soul enters and exits the story without contributing to the wider plot. Nickelsburg describes RecShrt. as in part "the result of a clumsy process of oral transmission, in which the storyteller(s) badly garbled the tradition."[36]

Ludlow contends that RecLng. gives us "the best sense of the original comic, parodic tale."[37] RecShrt., by contrast, lacks the whimsical elements typical of the original story.[38] Like Nickelsburg, he notes that some of the narrative elements common to both recensions have a clear function only in RecLng. Michael's tears, for example, turn into stones (or a stone in RecShrt.). Only in RecLng., however, does this miracle play any further role in the story: when Abraham seeks to persuade Sarah that he knows Michael's true identity, he brings forth the stones, which he has hidden (6:7). RecShrt. nowhere returns to the metamorphosis, so the miracle is not integrated into the surrounding story. Again, in RecLng. it is precisely Abraham's refusal to follow Michael that leads to God sending Death. In RecShrt., where Abraham does not resist Michael, Death's advent has no rhyme or reason. RecShrt., then, seems to presuppose something like RecLng., where Death comes because Michael fails.

One of Ludlow's contributions is to observe that there are contacts between RecLng. and both families of RecShrt., B F G as well as E. This entails that there is no simple linear relationship between the three families. This fact, among others, leads Ludlow to posit the following analysis:

$$E$$
$$\nearrow$$
$$RecLng. \rightarrow Proto\ RecShrt.$$
$$\searrow$$
$$B\ F\ G$$

---

[36] Nickelsburg, "Structure and Message," 93.

[37] Ludlow, *Abraham*, 180. See the whole discussion, pp. 152–80, and note the generalization on pp. 119–20: "Recension A focused on a 'cause-effect' type plot as part of its comic strategy: to show Abraham's cunning and stubbornness advancing the events of the story. Recension B seems to have more disconnected episodes (particularly in the second half) because it adapted these events from Recension A but without the same narrative context."

[38] Cf. Gruen, *Diaspora*, 183: RecLng. "is the fuller, the more absorbing, the more coherent, and—by far—the funnier."

In the judgment of the present writer, when all is said and done, James's judgment, which holds RecShrt.'s much shorter story line to be secondary, is sound. Yet the issue remains very complex.[39]

1. One need not, in theory, regard either recension as prior. It is conceivable that an earlier *TA* was shorter than RecLng. and longer than RecShrt., that neither is more faithful to the hypothetical original. One should also keep in mind the good possibility that, in one or more particulars, neither recension preserves the original. There may be sections in which both have moved away from an older text. One place where this seems likely is in the judgment scene in chap. 11; see pp. 239–41.

2. Although the two recensions typically recount the same events with different words, there is enough overlap in vocabulary to show that they go back to the same Greek exemplar. They cannot represent independent translations of a Semitic *TA*; see pp. 86–88 and 149–51.

3. As James observed, and as Turner's dissertation establishes at length, the language of RecShrt. is more Semitic and less ecclesiastical than RecLng.[40] RecLng. is not, however, devoid of Semitisms. The following are among the more obvious:

ἄγγελος κυρίου: 6:1; 7:12
ἀμήν: 2:12; 8:7; 14:5; 18:10; 20:2, 15
ἄρχομαι, pleonastic: 5:9; 7:2
δοξάζω τὸν θεόν: 15:5
ἐκ γὰρ τῶν τριῶν ἀνδρῶν οὗτός ἐστιν ὁ εἷς ἐξ αὐτῶν (resumptive pronoun): 6:5
ἐν ῥιπῇ ὀφθαλμοῦ: 4:5
καὶ ἰδού: 2:1
πάντας τοὺς υἱοὺς τῶν ἀνθρώπων: 2:4; 4:3 (cf. 16:6: τοὺς υἱοὺς τῶν ἀνθρώπων)
προσώπου + genitive following ἀπό, ἐκ, πρό: 2:1; 9:5; 12:9, 12; 15:11, 14
ῥῆμα = *res*: 13:8
σπλάγχνον of tender emotions: 3:9; 5:10, 14
τάδε λέγει κύριος ὁ θεός: 8:5; 9:4, 7
χερουβίκος: 9:8; 10:1
ψυχή = "person": 2:3, 12
verb often placed first (or immediately after the copula): 1:1, 2, 3, 4, 7; 2:1, 2, 4, 8, 9, 10, 12; 3:1, 4, 5, 6, 7, 8, 9, 10, 11, 12; etc.

For full discussion of these and other possible Semitisms readers may consult Turner's lengthy discussion.

---

[39] See esp. Kraft, "Recensional Problem."
[40] Turner, "Testament," 48–107, 195–249.

Turner himself at one time urged that the two recensions are translations of a Hebrew work, to which RecShrt. is more faithful. This is very far from certain. Not only does Raymond Martin's statistical work fail to establish a Semitic origin for either recension,[41] but one can scarcely exclude the possibility of a redactor who, because he grew up speaking Hebrew or because he was immersed in biblical Greek, introduced Semitisms. Certainly scribes sometimes introduced Semitisms into New Testament texts.[42] As for the supposed Hebrew original, Sanders has observed that, while RecShrt. can easily be translated into Hebrew, "it is the classical Hebrew of the early narrative sections of the Bible that emerges, not any form of late Hebrew as known from the late canonical books, the Dead Sea Scrolls, and rabbinic literature."[43] And because there are Greek works that imitate LXX translation Greek—Luke's infancy narrative comes to mind—but no later Hebrew texts that emulate classical biblical prose, it seems best to infer that *TA* was composed in "Semitizing Greek."[44]

4. The Greek of RecLng. is, without question, on the whole later than the Greek of RecShrt. One must indeed suspect the following words and phrases, found in RecLng. but not RecShrt., of being Christian and/or medieval:

ἀβάστακτος meaning "intolerable" is rare outside of Christian sources; see on 17:17

ἄγγελος ... ὁ ἐπὶ τὸ πῦρ ἔχων τὴν ἐξουσίαν echoes Rev 14:8; see on 13:11

ἅγιος ἅγιος ἅγιος + ὁ + characterization of God appears in Rev 4:8 and later Christian texts; see on 3:3

ἀδελφοί μου ἀγαπητοί is a New Testament and typically Christian expression; see on 20:15

ἀμέτρητος after ἔλεος is a patristic idiom; see on 14:9

ἀμήν and ἀμήν, ἀμήν, prefatory, come from the Jesus tradition; see on 2:12 and 20:2

ἀμὴν γένοιτο is common in Christian texts, beginning with *Prot. Jas.* 13; see on 2:12

ἀμόλυντος with moral application is characteristically Christian; see on 11:12

---

41 Raymond A. Martin, "Syntax Criticism." His conclusion is that "net frequencies do not put either recension in the translated or the original Greek ranges of the scale, though Recension B is just a little shy of falling into the translated Greek range." For criticism of Martin see Kraft, "Recensional Problem," 133–35. Box, *Testament*, xxviii, already opined: "it must be confessed that the Greek does not read like a translation."

42 Sanders, *Tendencies*, 190–255.

43 Sanders, "Testament," 873.

44 So too Delcor, *Testament*, 32–34.

ἀναίσχυντον πρόσωπον has its closest parallels in late patristic texts; see on 16:1

ἀνύμνησις does not appear otherwise until the sixth century CE; see on 20:13

ἀνυπόφορος is typical of Byzantine writers; see on 19:6

ἡ ἄνω βασιλεία has parallels in patristic but not Jewish Greek texts; see on 7:7

τῶν ἄνω δυνάμεων qualifying Μιχαήλ is popular with Christian writers; see on 9:3

ἀξιωθῶμεν τῆς αἰωνίου ζωῆς at the end of a book is standard for Christian hagiography; see on 20:15

ἀόρατος πατήρ is a Christian expression; see on 9:7

ἡ ἀπάγουσα εἰς τὴν ζωήν comes from Matt 7:14; see on 11:10

ἡ ἀπάγουσα εἰς τὴν ἀπώλειαν comes from Matt 7:13; see on 11:11

ἀπὸ μηκόθεν appears often in Epiphanius and is characteristic of later Greek; see on 2:2

ἄχραντος, of a voice, occurs in Severianus Gabalensis and Photius; see on 20:13

δοξάζοντες τῷ πατρὶ καὶ τῷ υἱῷ κ.τ.λ. ends countless Christian books; see on 20:15

ἐν ἀληθείᾳ θεοῦ λόγου is a Christian idiom; see on 20:2

δέησις καὶ εὐχή seems to be Byzantine; see on 14:6

δέσποτα παντοκράτορ in direct address to God may have only Christian parallels; see on 8:3

καὶ δεῦρο ἀκολούθει μοι is from the Jesus tradition; see on 20:3

δευτέρα παρουσίᾳ has no Jewish parallel but is popular in Christian writers; see on 13:6

δι' ἄκραν ἀγαθότηταν has parallels in Theodore the Studite and Maximus the Confessor; see on 14:14

δικαίους καὶ ἁμαρτωλούς is typical of patristic sources; see on 13:3

δοξολογία is rare in non-Christian texts; cf. Sophocles, Lex., s.v., and see on 20:13

εἴ τινος τὸ ἔργον κατακαύσει is from Paul; see on 13:12

εἴ τινος δὲ τὸ ἔργον τὸ πῦρ δοκιμάσει ... σώζεσθαι comes from 1 Cor 3:10–15; see on 13:13

εἰσερχομένας διὰ τῆς στενῆς πύλης is influenced by Matt 7:13–14; see on 11:7

ἐκφοβεῖν τὴν ψυχήν may have only patristic parallels; see on 16:5

ἐν ἁμαρτίᾳ διάγοντας has its closest parallels in Tit 3:3 and Chrysostom; see on 10:13

ἐνδόξου ... παρουσίας is typical of Christian writers from the second century on; see on 13:4

ἐνδοξότης is a late word, most common in Justinian; see on 16:4

ἔξωθεν τῶν πυλῶν may be confined to Byzantine sources; see on 11:4

ἔπεσεν ἐπὶ τὸ στῆθος αὐτοῦ κλαίων derives from John 13:25 and 21:20; see on 20:6

ἐπουράνια πνεύματα may be attested only in Christian writings; see on 4:9

ζηλόω + πολιτεία is characteristic of Christian hagiography; see on 20:15

ζυγάς appears to be late and exclusively Christian; see on 12:18

τὸν θάνατον βλέπειν, unlike "to taste death," is likely a Christian idiom; see on 19:10

τὸν θάνατον τοῦ ἁμαρτωλοῦ ἕως οὗ ἐπιστρέψαι belongs to a Christian textual tradition; see on 10:14

ἡ τοῦ θανάτου δρεπάνη has precise parallels only in Christian texts; see on 4:11

τοῦ θανάτου πικρὸν ποτήριον seems to be a Byzantine expression; see on 1:4

θαῦμα θαυμάτων appears only in Christian sources beginning with Hippolytus; see on 7:10

ὁ θεὸς καὶ πατήρ, unqualified, is common in patristic writers; see on 20:12

θεοΰφαντος meaning "divinely woven" is known from patristic texts after the fifth century; see on 20:10

θρόνος φοβερός is Byzantine; see on 12:3–4

καθέκαστον is common in Byzantine literature; see on 9:3

καθότι ἔθος is known elsewhere only in late Scholia; see on 2:2

καθυπουργέω is rare until patristic times; see on 12:17

κἄν τε ἀγαθὸν κἄν τε πονηρόν is most common in patristic sources; see on 6:8

κατῆλθε ... ὁ ἱδρὼς ... αὐτοῦ ὡσεὶ θρόμβοι αἵματος belongs to a Jesus typology; see on 20:5

οἱ κλέπται ... κλέψαι καὶ θῦσαι καὶ ἀπολέσαι is from John 10:10; see on 10:5

κρῖναι τὸν κόσμον is Christian apart from *Sib. Or.* 4:184; see on 13:4

κρίσις καὶ ἀνταπόδοσις is characteristic of Christian writers, not Jewish Greek texts; see on 10:15

ὁ κριτὴς τῶν ἀπάντων καὶ θεός in 20:3 is a Christian appellation for the divinity; see on 14:2

λυπέω καὶ ἀδημονέω are also co-ordinated in Matt 26:37 and several Church Fathers; see on 7:5

μάταιος κόσμος is a common Christian idiom; cf. Rom 8:20 and see on 1:7

μέγεθος + ἀγάπης is a patristic idiom from the fourth century on; see on 17:7

τὰ μέλη τῆς σαρκός is known from Ps.-Justin and fourth-century Christian texts; see on 20:5

μετὰ σπουδῆς καὶ πολλῶν δακρύων has its closest parallels in the Fathers; see on 14:12

ἡ μνήμη τοῦ θανάτου appears in Christian writers beginning with Origen; see on 4:6

μοναὶ τῶν ἁγίων recalls John 14:2 and later texts dependent on it; see on 20:14

μύρισμα is rare outside late patristic texts; see on 20:11

νεονύμφους ὀψικευομένους is a Byzantine combination; see on 10:3

ὁδός ... πλατεῖα καὶ εὐρύχωρος comes from Matt 7:13–14; see on 11:2

ὁδὸς στενὴ καὶ τεθλιμμένη comes from Matt 7:13–14; see on 11:2

ὀδυρομένη πικρῶς has close parallels only in Christian texts; see on 20:6

οὐ θέλω ἀπολέσαι ἐξ αὐτῶν οὐδένα is influenced by John 18:9; see on 10:14

οὐ λύπη οὐ στεναγμός following "Abraham's bosom" is liturgical; see on 20:14

ὀψικεύω is otherwise unattested until the seventh century; cf. Sophocles, *Lex.*, s.v., and see on 20:12

πανευπρεπής is rare outside of patristic texts; see on 2:4

πανθαύμαστος of a saint is clearly Christian; see on 11:8

πανίερος becomes common only in Christian texts; see on 1:2

πανόσιος is a late, patristic word occurring in John Climacus and Photius; see on 13:2

τὰ πάντα ἐν πᾶσιν appears only in Christian literature; see on 13:14

πανώλεθρος describes Death in Eusebius, Theophylact Simocatta, and Ps.-Chrysostom; see on 18:1

πλῆθος ἀγγέλων at the death of a saint is a typical Christian motif; see on 20:10

πληροφορέω meaning "inform" seems unparalleled prior to the fifth century CE; see on 1:6

πόθεν καὶ ἐκ ποίας has precise parallels only in patristic sources; see on 2:5

προσπίπτω + οἰκτιρμοῖς + genitive pronoun has late patristic analogies; see on 14:10

προσυπαντάω is unattested before the third century CE but is common after that; see on 2:2

σπλάγχνα + κινέω with figurative sense is common after the fourth century; see on 3:9

στολὴν λαμπροτάτην has parallels in the *Gospel of Peter* and other Christian writings; see on 16:6

ταλανίζω means "vex" in Chrysostom and the *Acts of Xanthippe*; see on 20:5

τελείωσις meaning "death" is found in Lampe, s.v., and Sophocles, *Lex.*, s.v., but not LSJ, s.v.; see on 20:11

τιμιώτατε πάτερ is a typical Christian idiom; see on 2:3

τὸ τέλος ἐγγύς, καὶ φοβερὰ ἡ ἀπόφασις, καὶ ὁ λύων οὐδείς is a Christian proverb; see on 13:7

τρισάγιον ὕμνον appears first in the fourth century; see on 20:12

ὑφαπλόω, active, is first attested in the *Acts of John*; see on 4:2

φωτοφόρος is a popular patristic word beginning in the fifth and sixth centuries; see on 7:3

τὰς ψυχὰς τῶν ἁμαρτωλῶν occurs only in Christian texts; see on 10:15

The Christian contribution to RecLng. is not, against Delcor, "superficial."[45] Christian scribes did not treat the work as though it closed with Rev 22:18–19.[46] Ginzberg was wrong to assert that "apart from some late Christological additions made in a few manuscripts by copyists, there is not a single Christian interpolation found in the whole book."[47] One cannot delete a line or two here and there and suppose the remainder to be Jewish. There are indeed entire chapters, 11 and 20 for instance, where the Christian influence is so thoroughgoing that one has little hope of precisely reconstructing a Jewish original.

---

[45] Delcor, *Testament*, 66. Cf. Turner, "Biblical Greek," 221: "superfluous and superficial."

[46] There is even evidence of an original pseudepigraphon in the first person; see on 12:1.

[47] Ginzberg, "Testament," 96. Cf. Coleman, "Phenomenon," 332–33.

5. RecShrt. also contains some late words and ecclesiastical expressions; see, for example, p. 279. Christian hands have left neither recension alone.

6. One reason for supposing that RecLng., despite its later Greek, contains ancient material absent from RecShrt. is that the textual tradition of RecLng. shows a very strong tendency toward deliberate abbreviation. This same tendency is also visible in RecShrt. and in the versions; thus the long Romanian is an abridged version of RecLng. while the Bohairic and fam. BFG are shorter than RecShrt. fam. E. Significant additions, by contrast, are met with infrequently. Even RecLng. ms. A, which has the fullest text, sometimes abbreviates; see especially the textual notes to chap. 14. There are, to be sure, many mistakes and omissions that must be due to carelessness, such as *homoioteleuton*. Time and again, however, words, phrases, sentences, and even whole sections are omitted, and yet the remaining text is intelligible. The inference is inevitable: scribes shortened our book. So a partial explanation for RecShrt. is to hand. The opposite view, that RecShrt. grew into RecLng., has no support from the textual tradition.

Schmidt, in his edition, offers an overview of major omissions common to different members of RecLng.; see the opposite page. Of these, only one—10:12–11:4—seems clearly accidental, for all the other omissions leave a comprehensible text. The omission at the end of chap. 13, moreover, begins where the RecShrt. parallel ends, and this may well imply that more than one scribe felt the last part of that section fit for excision. Similarly, the abbreviated ending in RecLng. ms. N recalls the sudden and rushed conclusion of RecShrt., and again one suspects that similar motives explain the parallel.

7. RecShrt. seems secondary vis-à-vis RecLng. in at least the following places:
- RecLng. 1:1 gives Abraham far more than the 175 years Genesis gives him; RecShrt., failing to appreciate that *TA* is humorous fiction, has removed the contradiction by not giving his age.[48] It thereby detracts from the set up: surely the man who has outlived everyone else should be willing to die.
- RecLng. 2:11 explains Michael's refusal to ride an animal; RecLng. offers no explanation; see p. 87.
- In RecLng. 3:2, the cypress sings, "Holy, holy, holy," which is almost certainly older than RecShrt. 3:3's single "Holy"; see p. 105.
- Abraham's premature knowledge of his own death in RecShrt. 3 diminishes both the dramatic tension and the humor of the first part of the book; see pp. 105–106.

---

[48] Cf. the marginal note at the beginning of RecLng. W: οὐ γὰρ ἔζησε 905.

Classification of the Manuscripts of the Long Recension

		A	I	G	H	N	K	B	Q	J	W	F	E	C	P	V	D	L	M	O	S	T	U	Rm
3:7-4:11	ὅτι – θαλάσσης	+	+	-	-	-	-	+	+	+	+	+	+	+	+	+	+	+	+	I	I	+	+	+
5:11-6:8	Σάρρα – πονηρόν	+	+	+	+	+	+	+	+	+	+	+	-	-	-	I	-	-	-	I	I	+	-	-
8:6-8	ὁ διαλύσας – μοι	+	+	+	+	+	+	+	+	+	+	+	-	-	I	I	-	-	*	*	*	-	*	-
10:3-8	καὶ ἁπλῶς – πορνεύοντας	+	+	+	+	+	I	+	+	+	+	+	+	+	+	I	-	-	-	+	+	*	+	*
10:12-11:4	πᾶσαν – δεσπότου	+	+	+	+	+	I	-	-	+	+	+	+	+	+	I	+	+	+	+	+	+	+	+
13:10-14	ἐν δικαιοσύνῃ – δοκιμάζονται	+	+	+	+	+	+	+	+	*	+	+	-	-	-	I	-	-	*	*	*	*	*	-
14:11-12	οὓς ποτε κατέπιεν – δυνάμεων	+	+	+	+	+	+	+	-	+	+	+	-	-	-	I	*	*	*	*	*	*	*	*
17:4-8	λέγει – ἔλεον	+	+	+	+	+	+	+	+	+	+	+	+	+	+	+	-	-	+	+	+	+	+	-
17:7-8	καὶ τὸ μέγεθος – ἔλεον	+	+	+	+	+	+	+	+	-	+	+	-	-	-	I	*	*	+	+	+	+	+	*
19:4-6	ἕως – πάντων	+	+	+	+	*	+	+	+	+	+	+	-	-	-	I	-	-	-	-	-	-	-	-
19:8-16	ὅτι – παραλόγως	+	+	+	+	*	I	+	+	+	+	+	-	-	-	*	-	-	-	+	+	-	*	-
19:14-20:5	Καὶ ἁπλῶς – αἵματος	+	+	+	+	*	I	-	-	-	-	I	+	+	+	+	+	+	+	+	+	+	*	+

+   sequence attested

-   gap in sequence

*   witness presents a gap larger than that considered here

I   witness mutilated

Rm Romanian version

– Although we see in RecShrt. 3:6–9 preparations for the washing of Michael's feet, and while 6:13 refers to the act retrospectively, RecLng. alone recounts the actual foot washing.
– In RecLng. 4:5, Michael professes a need to urinate; in RecShrt. 4:4–5, he must leave to worship God. A pious hand has removed the irreverent humor; see p. 131.
– God tells Michael, in RecShrt. 4:15, to eat whatever Abraham serves, an imperative that links up with nothing before or after. In RecLng. 4 the archangel is concerned about the problem of eating human food, so the command has a context that gives it meaning; see p. 132.
– In RecLng. 6, Sarah figures out what is going on before her husband, whom she has to instruct. In RecShrt. 6 Abraham is not so clearly less astute than his wife; see p. 161.
– The inclusion of the general resurrection and 7,000 years of world history in Michael's interpretation of Isaac's dream in RecShrt. 7 is from a Christian hand; see p. 176–77.
– Abraham's refusal in 7:12 and elsewhere to accept death must be original; RecShrt., in which the patriarch does not resist God's decree, depicts a more conventional Abraham better suited to pious emulation. RecLng. alone explains why, in both recensions, Abraham fails to set his house in order or make his testament, as God orders him to do at the beginning; see p. 177.
– Abraham's request to see the whole world is a scheme to put off death. In RecShrt. it serves no such purpose; cf. above, pp. 13–14.
– In RecLng. 10–14, Abraham slays sinners, then sees their judgment, then regrets his actions, then asks God to undo what he has done—a sensible sequence. In RecShrt. 8–12, Abraham first sees the judgment and then strikes down sinners, a sequence which fails to instruct either the reader or Abraham; and RecShrt. 12 has no real connection with what comes before or after. This is why the Coptic, a member of the RecShrt. family, omits chap. 12; see p. 14. Moreover, the failure to record the resurrection of sinners is theologically motivated: "it seemed imprudent to tell men that, though cut off in the bloom of their sin, they might yet escape punishment through the intercession whether of Abraham or of other righteous men."[49]
– While the introduction of the soul whose good and evil deeds are balanced in RecLng. 11 turns into a lesson on mercy, in RecShrt. there is no coherent link with the rest of the narrative, and RecShrt. 9:8's reference to evenly balanced deeds links up only with the judgment scene in RecLng.; see p. 260.[50]
– RecShrt. 12:14–16, which feels so abbreviated, harmonizes with the Bible in having Sarah die before Abraham; RecLng. 20, in which she is alive when her husband goes, contradicts Genesis; see p. 311.

---

49   James, *Testament*, 47.
50   Note also Nickelsburg, "Eschatology," 56–57, 63.

- RecShrt. 14:2–4, which feels truncated, implies that Death has several heads, as RecLng. details, but RecShrt. describes only two; see p. 338.
- The advent of Death in RecLng. 16 makes sense, because Abraham has heretofore refused to co-operate with Michael. Death's coming in RecShrt. has no motivation; cf. above, p. 14, and see below, p. 323.

RecShrt. seemingly reflects not only a desire to abbreviate but also a piety eager to polish Abraham's character so that he is the obedient figure of Genesis. Some Christian scribes were further concerned to reduce contradictions with the Bible and did not appreciate, as Ludlow has shown, most of *TA*'s humor. One understands their pious mentality. *TA* was, as the works with which it is typically bound show, read as Christian hagiography, and leaders of such services could easily have seen parts of *TA* as potentially unedifying, especially as the text calls readers to emulate Abraham (RecLng. 20:15). How can one imitate a man who refuses to obey God? One recalls how the Chronicler polishes the images of David and Solomon. Some of the manuscripts, not unexpectedly, contain critical marginal comments from later ecclesiastics. A hand in the margin of RecLng. ms. A attributes the story to heretics (ἔστιν ὑπὸ αἱρετικῶν συντεθεῖσα, ἣν οὐκ ὀφείλεις ὁ ἀναγινώσκων πιστεύειν). In ms. I we find the remark that *TA* is false, and a marginal note in Q declares the book to be nonsense (φλυαρίαις). The margins of W are full of negative comments— *TA* is mythical, heretical, unbiblical, nonsensical, etc. It is no mystery that *TA* does not exist in Latin and all but disappeared from the West: it was unable to overcome ecclesiastical censure.[51]

8. Despite the many places where RecShrt. seems secondary, there are a few instances where it *may* be more original. These instances make a shorter list than the previous one and are on the whole less significant, having to do with details here and there, not the basic structure or plot of the story:

- RecShrt. 8 has fewer points of contact with Matt 7:13–14 than does RecLng. 11; see p. 241.
- RecShrt. is less pessimistic than RecLng. 11:11, which allows only one in 7,000 to be saved, a numerical estimate out of accord with the spirit of the presumed Jewish original; see p. 241.

---

[51] Robert A. Kraft, "The Pseudepigrapha in Christianity," in *Tracing the Threads: Studies in the Vitality of Jewish Pseudepigrapha* (ed. John C. Reeves; Atlanta: Scholars Press, 1994), p. 69: "Latin Christianity tended to oppose the (public) use of non-canonical religious literature and to identify it closely with heterodoxy." He adds: "But as the threat of 'the old heresies' waned, and as hagiographical traditions became more and more important to orthodoxy, the Greek churches came to accept and rework certain types of pseudepigraphical literature in great quantity."

– Only in RecShrt. 9 is Abraham anxious about whether he can pass through the narrow gate to heaven; this sort of comedic relief is characteristic of RecLng. and any presumed Jewish ancestor; see p. 259.
– Enoch's presence at the judgment as divine scribe in RecShrt. 9–11 might be original; see pp. 259–60.
– RecShrt. 14:6 has Abraham going to heaven in a chariot; see p. 388 for the possibility that this is ancient.

9. Three episodes in RecLng. but not RecShrt. seem to grow out of the Hebrew text of Genesis. See the commentary on 3:3 (the prophetic tree probably depends upon an exegesis of Gen 21:33); on 6:5 (the resurrection of the consumed calf can be found in Gen 18:8); and on 17:13 (Death's faces are likely inspired by Gen 23:3). The discovery of such dependence upon the MT is consistent with at least parts of RecLng. deriving from a Jewish environment.

10. As others have observed, there are fascinating parallels between RecLng. and traditions about the death of Moses. They may be catalogued as follows:

	Abraham in RecLng.	Moses in Jewish sources
God asks a heavenly being— in some texts Michael and then later (the Angel of) Death—to take the saint's soul to heaven	1:4–7; 16:1–6	*Sifre* Deut. 305; *Tanḥ*. Beraka 3; *ARN* A 12; *ARN* B 25; *Deut. Rab.* 11:10; *Petirat Moshe* (*BHM* 1:127–128; 6:75); cf. *Tanḥ. B* Beraka 2
saint is sitting when the heavenly being arrives	2:1; 16:7	*Deut. Rab.* 11:10; *Petirat Moshe* (*BHM* 6:75)
saint asks the heavenly being about his identity and who sent him	2:5; 7:10; 16:10, 14; 17:4; 19:4	*Deut. Rab.* 11:10; *Petirat Moshe* (*BHM* 1:127–128; 6:76)
a supernatural voice predicts the saint's death	3:3	*Petirat Moshe* (*BHM* 1:125, 128; 6:76–77; etc.); cf. *Deut. Rab.* 11:10
saint refuses to co-operate	7:10–12; 15:10; 16:16; 19:2–4; 20:4–5	*Sifre* Deut. 305; *Tanḥ. B* Beraka 2; *ARN* A 12; *ARN* B 25; *Deut. Rab.* 11:10; *Petirat Moshe* (*BHM* 1:127–128; 6:76–77)
declaration of saint's sinlessness	10:13	*Deut. Rab.* 11:10

the heavenly being returns to heaven to report on what has happened	4:6–11; 8:1–12; 15:11–15	*Sifre* Deut. 305; *ARN B* 25; *Deut. Rab.* 11:5, 10; *Petirat Moshe* (*BHM* 1:128; 6:76)
heavenly being is sent again	4:7–5:1; 8:4–9:1	*Sifre* Deut. 305; *Deut. Rab.* 11:5; *Petirat Moshe* (*BHM* 1:128; 6:76)
to take the saint's soul, heavenly being has a sword or sickle	4:11; 8:9, 10	*Deut. Rab.* 11:10; *Petirat Moshe* (*BHM* 1:127, 128; 6:75)
God instructs the saint that all human beings must die	8:9 n	*Sifre* Deut. 339; *Deut. Rab.* 10:8; *Petirat Moshe* (*BHM* 1:118)
the saint asks for a favor from God before he dies	9:3–6	*L.A.B.* 19:14; *Deut. Rab.* 11:8
saint has a vision of all the world and/or heaven before he dies	10:1–14:15	*L.A.B.* 19:10–16; *Sifre* Deut. 357; *Mek.* on Exod 17:14
saint protects himself from (the Angel of) Death by using the divine name	17:11	*Deut. Rab.* 11:5; *Petirat Moshe* (*BHM* 1:127, 128)
(the Angel of) Death puts on a fearful appearance	17:12–13	*Deut. Rab.* 11:10; *Petirat Moshe* (*BHM* 1:127, 128; 6:75).
saint's spirit is weak	17:19; 18:8; 20:7	*Petirat Moshe* (*BHM* 6:77)
saint dies by a kiss	20:8–9	*ARN A* 12; *b. B. Bat.* 17a; *Tg. Ps.-Jn.* on Deut 34:5; *Deut. Rab.* 11:10; *Petirat Moshe* (*BHM* 1:129; 6:77)
saint's soul goes to heaven	20:12	*Deut. Rab.* 11:10; *Petirat Moshe* (*BHM* 1:129)
angels bury his body	20:11	Philo, *Mos.* 2.291; *Tg. Ps.-Jn.* on Deut 34:6; *Deut. Rab.* 11:10
angelic praise after saint's death	20:12–13	*ARN B* 25; *Deut. Rab.* 11:5

That there is a relationship between *TA* and the complex of legends about Moses' death—particularly the version represented by *Deut. Rab.* 11:10 and *Petirat Moshe*—is obvious.[52] The direction of dependence is also obvious. The relevant traditions about Moses are widespread and naturally grow out of biblical texts[53] whereas those about Abraham are mostly confined to *TA* and do not, for the most part, have any genesis in Scripture. Loewenstamm is correct: "the post-biblical legends concerning Moses' death are deeply rooted in ancient myth, whereas no such roots may be ascribed to the treatment of the patriarch's death in the Testament of Abraham"; again, the "traditions concerning Moses' death are more ancient and even more meaningful than their parallels in the Testament of Abraham."[54]

How does this bear upon the recensional problem? RecShrt. displays far fewer parallels to the traditions about Moses' death than does RecLng., but its dependence upon those traditions remains patent. God's request that Michael get Abraham's soul, the subsequent giving of this same assignment to Death, Abraham's request to see the world before he dies, and his vision of heaven and earth in response to that request are clearly borrowed from Mosaic legend—just as the *Greek Apocalypse of Ezra* borrows from the same when it has its hero resist death.[55] Now we may in theory imagine *TA* gathering additional parallels to traditions about Moses as time passed, but

---

[52] See esp. Chazon, "Moses' Struggle," and Loewenstamm, "Testament," 219–25. In his otherwise excellent study, Ludlow, *Abraham*, 50–54, underrates the parallels with Moses. Reducing them by observing certain differences does not persuade. One might as well pile up the dissimilarities between *TA* and Genesis 18—Abraham is near death in one case but not the other; three angels show up in Genesis but only one in *TA*; the angel cries in one scene but not the other, etc.—and then claim that *TA* does not replay Genesis 18. But it does.

[53] E.g., Deut 3:23–29 records a disagreement between God and Moses regarding the lawgiver's future. Deuteronomy foretells Moses' death again and again (cf. *Deut. Rab.* 11:10; *Pesiq. Rab. Kah.* Suppl. 1:20; *Petirat Moshe* [*BHM* 1:120], counting ten instances), which might imply that Moses was stubborn in accepting the decree. Deut 34:1–4 gives Moses a vision right before he dies. Deut 34:6 (MT: "he buried him"; LXX: "they buried him") lacks a subject and so opens itself to speculation about who buried Moses. Deut 34:5 ("Moses died there ... יהוה עַל־פִּי) could be construed as death by a kiss. The antiquity of the dispute between Moses and God over the lawgiver's death is guaranteed if, as seems likely, the legend of the debate over his body, already attested in the first century (cf. Jude 9), grows out of it; see Kugel, *Traditions*, 886.

[54] Loewenstamm, "Testament," 219 and 224 respectively. Contrast Kohler, "Apocalypse," 592.

[55] See Allison, *New Moses*, 64–65, and Chazon, "Moses' Struggle," 158–62.

the Mosaic elements in RecLng. alone do not strike one as secondary additions. They rather impress one as part and parcel of an organic whole which they largely structure and for which they supply details throughout. The upshot is that the Mosaic parallels are more than consistent with the primary character of RecLng.

11. While the complexities and ambiguities disallow constructing a defini- tive genealogy, perhaps the following is not too far from the truth:

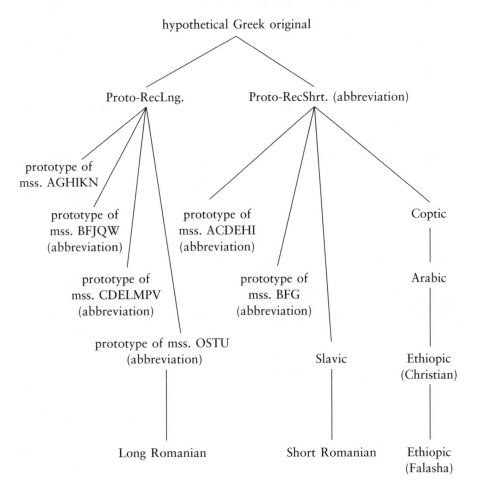

hypothetical Greek original

Proto-RecLng.   Proto-RecShrt. (abbreviation)

prototype of
mss. AGHIKN

prototype of   prototype of   Coptic
mss. BFJQW   mss. ACDEHI
(abbreviation)   (abbreviation)

prototype of   prototype of   Arabic
mss. CDELMPV   mss. BFG
(abbreviation)   (abbreviation)

prototype of mss. OSTU
(abbreviation)   Slavic   Ethiopic
                                                                      (Christian)

Long Romanian   Short Romanian   Ethiopic
                                                                      (Falasha)

IV. Jewish or Christian?[56]

James characterized *TA*, which has come to us through Christian channels, as Christian. Craigie concurred, assigning the book "to a Jewish Christian, who for the substance of it drew partly on older legends, and partly on his own imagination."[57] Few have agreed. Kohler and Ginzberg—the latter of whom felt "not the least room for doubt as to its Jewish origin"[58]—argued long ago that the text is full of Jewish ideas, Jewish idioms, and Jewish lore and so must be Jewish.[59] Subsequent work has only added to the Jewish parallels. One nonetheless cannot establish the non-Christian origin of a text by showing how full of Jewish elements it is. The Gospel of Matthew contains many Semitisms, and most of the book has parallels of one sort or another in Jewish literature. Similarly, the rabbinic corpus often illumines the Pauline letters. Matthew and Paul, to be sure, are overtly Christian whereas *TA*, apart from obvious scribal additions, is not. But Christian compositions do not always wear their faith on their sleeves. The Epistle of James and the *Sentences of Sextus* are Christian texts, yet they are nearly void of plainly Christian elements.

The present writer's judgment is that, while many have underestimated the Christian elements and too quickly assumed that there must have been a Jewish original behind the extant versions of *TA*, it nonetheless remains

---

[56] For the methodological issues involved with determining the Jewish or Christian character of texts see Marinus de Jonge, "The so-called Pseudepigrapha of the Old Testament and Early Christianity," in *The New Testament and Hellenistic Judaism* (ed. Peder Borgen and Søren Giversen; Peabody, Mass.: Hendrickson, 1997), 59–71; also Robert Kraft, "Setting the Stage and Framing some Central Questions," *JSJ* 32 (2001), 371–95.

[57] Craigie, "Testament," 183. Cf. Emil Schürer, review of James, *TLZ* 8 (1893), 281: "Es ist eine recht alberne christliche Dichtung, für welche eine jüdische Grundlage nicht nachweisbar ist." He repeated this judgment in *Geschichte des jüdischen Volkes im Zeitalter Jesu Christi* (4th ed.; Leipzig: J. C. Hinrichs, 1909), 3:338. Contrast the updated volume of Schürer edited by Vermes, Millar, and Goodman, *History*, 3/2:763: "The work should be accepted as Jewish even though the more particular elements of Jewish piety are not stressed."

[58] Ginzberg, "Testament," 95. Cf. Kaufmann, "Testament."

[59] Kohler, "Apocalypse"; Ginzberg, "Testament."

overwhelmingly probable that a non-Christian Urtext underlines our two recensions. The telling point is not the overwhelming number of verses whose language or thought has Jewish parallels but rather the places that have no Christian parallels and indeed clash with what we otherwise know of Christian beliefs. The soteriological optimism that evidently character-ized an earlier form of our work (see p. 239) does not seem at home in the church—which is presumably why the recensions have countered it and why the book was never popular in the West. Even universalists such as Origen and Gregory of Nyssa would have had trouble with a prayer that brings unbaptized sinners into eternal life in an instant, without some purgation through post-mortem suffering (see p. 300). One further fails to find any Christian parallel for the idea, expressed in 14:15, that retribution in this life can cancel retribution in the next. Some Jews, by contrast, did teach that earthly suffering atones and brings redemption in the world to come.

Two further considerations encourage positing a Jewish exemplar. First, given that the LXX was the Bible of the early church, one may doubt the Christian origin of a book containing legends, wholly unattested in Chris-tian writings, which derive from reflection upon the Hebrew Bible (see above, p. 24). Second, it is suggestive that a book concerned above all with death and the life thereafter nowhere even so much as alludes to the resurrection of Jesus or his salvific descent into hell.

As to the sort of Judaism *TA* might represent, the book, unlike *3 Maccabees* and *Joseph and Aseneth*, fails to take a defensive stand over against pagan society or to speak against assimilation to the pagan world. It neither indicts idolatry nor teaches the superiority of Judaism. It is rather, as Kohler noted, consistently cosmopolitan.[60] Despite its focus on Abraham, the book has almost nothing to say, even indirectly, about the Jewish people. Apart from 13:6, which may be from a Christian hand, Israel plays no role. Indeed, the reformulation of God's foundational promise in Gen 22:17 has no reference to the land; nor do the stars and sand represent the number of Abraham's descendants, that is, the multi-tude that is Israel, but his own physical possessions and wealth, which are beyond counting (1:5; 4:11; 8:5). The soul's destiny in the afterlife, more-over, appears to be wholly independent of one's religious affiliation (chaps. 11–14). Descent from Abraham and membership in the covenant made with him are unrelated to the salvific scheme. There is further no interest in Jewish law, only generalized ethics. While Wills goes too far when he

---

[60] K. Kohler, "Apocalypse," 603.

urges that *TA* satirizes traditional Jewish values, from which it is alien-
ated,[61] one could nonetheless ask of the book, "Then what advantage has
the Jew" (Rom 3:1)? There is no Sabbath, no circumcision, no Torah
observance.[62]

That *TA* does not exalt Judaism over its pagan rivals is consistent with
the book borrowing from Greco-Roman mythology and betraying no
anxiety in doing so; see on 3:11 and 6:6–7. It is also consistent with the
borrowed materials not serving any obvious theological or apologetical
agenda. They are not woven into the story in order to demonstrate that
Homer plagiarized from the Pentateuch and so to prove, in the manner of
Aristobulus, that the Jewish tradition is more ancient, more authentic.
There is also no sign that they are self-consciously inserted to show off the
author's knowledge of the non-Jewish world, or to encourage some sort of
dialogue with it. They rather seem to be there simply because they help
make a good story even better. The synthesis of traditions—Turner rightly
thinks that "tolerance and syncretism" characterize our work[63]—is evidently not the product of an attempt to integrate two separate worlds, as
though our author were akin to Ezekiel the Tragedian. They instead seem
to reflect an environment in which the biblical world and Greco-Roman
mythology had already been integrated. John Barclay's characterization of
Philo equally suits *TA*: "There is no hint of a tension between 'Greek' and
'Jewish' values, no fundamental struggle to reconcile the Jew and the Greek
within him."[64] Gruen is right: *TA* reflects "an attitude that transcends
sectarianism and dismisses barriers between Jews dwelling abroad and
their pagan neighbors."[65]

None of this, it should be emphasized, is to deny that RecLng. and
RecShrt. are, in their present forms, Christian. Indeed, the writing of a
verse-by-verse commentary has brought home to the writer just how much
Christian hands have revised the language and content. To illustrate:
against many, removing 20:15 or 20:14–15 as secondary does not eliminate the ecclesiastical contributions to chap. 20, which is rather Christian
from beginning to end. One can certainly make an educated guess about
the older Jewish ending, but we cannot recover it. The situation here as

---

[61]   Wills, *Novel*, pp. 245–56.
[62]   This by itself is reason to doubt, against Kohler, Delcor, Schmidt, and others, that
       TA is close to Essene circles. Other objections in Sanders, "Testament," 875–76;
       Turner, "Testament," 167–75.
[63]   Turner, "Biblical Greek," 221.
[64]   Barclay, *Mediterranean Diaspora*, 161.
[65]   Gruen, *Diaspora*, 193.

throughout *TA* is reminiscent of the *Testimonium Flavianum* or the *Testaments of the Twelve Patriarchs*: one senses both a Jewish original and a Christian revision, but it is often impossible to know exactly what belongs to which. The scribes that passed down *TA* felt perfectly free to add, subtract, and rewrite, and they did this over hundreds of years. We do not have the knowledge or ability to undo their work. What they started with is gone. The upshot is that the texts in our hands are Christian, and any use of them to add to our knowledge about ancient Judaism must proceed with caution.

V. Local Origin

James, in his critical edition, succinctly offered eight arguments for an Egyptian origin:[66]

1. Origen is the first to mention *TA*.
2. *TA*'s Michael resembles Tobit's Raphael, and Tobit was probably written in Egypt.
3. The depiction of Death has its closest parallels in Christian writings from Egypt.
4. Abraham's tour of the world has parallels in *4 Ezra*, *Pistis Sophia*, the *Apocalypse of Zephaniah*, and a homily wrongly attributed to Macarius, and the latter three are from Egypt.
5. The wrapping of Abraham's soul in a cloth has a close parallel in the *History of Joseph the Carpenter*, an Egyptian work.
6. The weighing of souls, which our book features, is prominent in Egyptian mythology.
7. The idea of recording angels also appears in the Coptic *Apocalypse of Zephaniah*; more importantly, there are parallels in the Egyptian *Book of the Dead*, where souls are weighed.
8. *TA* was translated into Arabic in Egypt.

Most of these arguments are feeble. James did not show that Origen knew our book, and modern scholarship commonly assigns Tobit not to Egypt but to Palestine. Abraham's tour of the world does not have a specifically Egyptian background but grows out of the lore surrounding Moses (see p. 210), while the wrapping of Abraham's soul has parallels in numerous Christian works, many of them not from Egypt (see p. 399). And the place of translation need not, obviously, be the place of composition.

James' third point does, however, carry some weight, for while the personification of death points to no particular region, Abraham's vision of Death's faces does indeed have close relatives in Egyptian texts. But James' strongest points are 6–7, which together amount to this: the closest parallels to the post-mortem judgment as *TA* depicts it are in Egyptian

---

[66] James, *Testament*, 76. Cf. Turner, "Testament," 177–85, with the same conclusion. Rosso Ubigli, "Testamento," 41, rightly states that scholarly opinion is nearly unanimous on this issue.

sources. This is indeed the case. As one works through chaps. 12–13, again and again one comes back to Egyptian ideas and Egyptian texts; see the commentary on 12:6–7, 8, 9, 10, 12; and 13:2. It is probably this fact that has moved so many to suspect that *TA* originally comes from Egypt.[67]

One can add to James' list several additional facts consistent with an Egyptian origin:

– The strange tale of the prophesying tree in RecLng. 3:1–3 recalls above all Ps.-Callisthenes, *Hist. Alex. Magn.* rec. α 3.17, according to which two large cypress-like trees, speaking in a human voice, foretold the death of Alexander the Great. Ps.-Callisthenes may come from Egypt. It certainly underwent revision and was popular there.
– The only other ancient text in addition to *TA* 3:1–3 to associate Abraham with a plant of praise is Philo the Epic poet in Eusebius, *Praep. ev.* 9.20.1, and Philo wrote in Egypt.
– *TA* represents, as argued above, a cosmopolitan Judaism happy to make good use of Greco-Roman myths, and just such a Judaism did exist in Egypt.[68]
– Egyptian Christians in particular were fond of "the bosom of Abraham (and Isaac and Jacob)," an expression that appears at the end of *TA*; see on 20:14.
– Erich Gruen has observed the many similarities *TA* shares with the *Testament of Job* and the fragments of Artapanus.[69] All three are Greek diaspora texts that entertain with humor, wit, and irony, and they do not expound the biblical text but rather find in it inspiration for their own fictional creations. Although his case cannot be presented in detail here, the present writer finds it convincing: the three texts do show similar rhetorical postures. This matters for us because Artapanus almost certainly wrote in Egypt, and the *Testament of Job* is most often assigned to the same place. So perhaps the literary similarities reflect the same diaspora environment, namely, the Jewish community in Egypt, and perhaps Alexandria in particular.
– Turner's dissertation, with its extensive word statistics, shows that, despite the presence of later Greek, both recensions share much vocabulary with several books often reckoned to come from Egypt, including Wisdom, 2 Maccabees, *3 Maccabees*, and *4 Maccabees*.[70]

While it is going too far to affirm that "everything points to Egypt as the probable provenance of the book,"[71] it is true that at least several things point suggestively in that direction. Furthermore, *TA* was, as the following pages show, particularly popular among Coptic Christians.

---

[67] Janssen, "Testament," 198–200, is idiosyncratic in urging a Palestinian provenance.
[68] Barclay, *Mediterranean Diaspora*, 103–80.
[69] Gruen, *Diaspora*, 182–212.
[70] Turner, "Testament," 205–49.
[71] Turner, "Biblical Greek," 221.

VI. Date

Given the fifth-century dating of the Sahidic, a Greek version of *TA* must have been in circulation in Egypt before then. There are, however, very few references to it in early times. The *Synopsis sacrae scripturae* 75 of Ps.-Athanasius, from perhaps ca. 500, lists a book known as "Abraham" (PG 28.432B).[72] But this could be the *Apocalypse of Abraham*, which was certainly in circulation by then, or some other lost work associated with the patriarch. More promising is *Apos. Con.* 6:16:3, which speaks of an apocryphal book or books τῶν τριῶν πατριαρχῶν. The three patriarchs must be Abraham, Isaac, and Jacob, and as the testaments assigned to them circulated as one collection at some point in time (as in the Coptic, Arabic, and Ethiopic), one guesses this was already true in some quarters when the *Apostolic Constitutions* was compiled in the latter quarter of the fourth century. It is also possible to find allusive references to *TA* in Priscillian, *Fide et de Apoc.*, ed. Schepss, pp. 45–46,[73] and Epiphanius, *Pan.* 39.5,[74] as did James, but the evidence is dubious.[75]

---

[72] On the *Stichometry* of Nicephorus, which follows Ps.-Athanasius, see James, *Testament*, 7–11.

[73] "Quid est quod Tobi sanctus futurae vitae ad filium praecepta dispones, cum quid custodiret ediceret, ait: nos fili prophetarum sumus; Noe profeta fuit et Abraham et Isac et Iacob et omnes patres nostri qui ab initio saeculi profetaverunt? Quando in canone profetae Noe liber lectus est? quis inter profetas dispositi canonis Abrahae librum legit? quis quod aliquando Isac profetasset edocuit? quis profetiam Iacob quod in canone poneretur audivit? Quos si Tobia legit et testimonium prophetiae in canone promeruit, qualiter, quod illi ad testimonium emeritae virtutis datur, alteris ad occasionem iustae damnationis adscribitur?" Even if this assumes knowledge of a book connected with Abraham, nothing points to *TA* in particular.

[74] βίβλους δέ τινας συγγράφοντες ἐξ ὀνόματος μεγάλων ἀνδρῶν, ἐξ ὀνόματος μὲν Σὴθ ἑπτὰ λέγοντες εἶναι βίβλους. ἄλλας δὲ βίβλους ἑτέρας ἀλλογενεῖς οὕτω καλοῦσιν. ἄλλην δὲ ἐξ ὀνόματος Ἀβραάμ, ἣν καὶ ἀποκάλυψιν φάσκουσιν εἶναι, πάσης κακίας ἔμπλεως.

[75] See James, *Testament*, 12–28. Delcor, *Testament*, 74–76, also finds in Priscillian a witness to *TA*, but he doubts James' conclusions regarding Epiphanius. Delcor further suggests a reference to *TA* in the prefatory letter to Palladius, *Hist. Laus.*, Preface 7:2: "Even those who wrote down the lives of the fathers, Abraham and those in succession, Moses, Elijah, and John, wrote not to glorify them, but to help their readers." It is unlikely that the *Koran's* two mentions of a book of Abraham (53:36; 87:18–19) concern *TA*; see Bowley, "Compositions of Abraham," 218–19.

If the explicit testimony is disappointing, we can learn more from the ancient texts that appear to depend upon *TA*:

– According to Birger Pearson, the *Coptic Enoch Apocryphon* catalogued as "Pierpont Morgan Library. Coptic Theological Texts 3," which Pearson assigns to fifth-century Egypt, "seems definitely to be influenced by [*TA*] Rec. B, but also shows some lesser degree of influence from Rec. A."[76] Parallels include a continuous post-mortem judgment, Enoch's role as scribe, and the weighing of good and evil deeds.

– Scholars have regularly dated the *History of Joseph the Carpenter* to the fourth or fifth century, and an Egyptian origin seems overwhelmingly probable, even if the Sahidic and Bohairic go back to a Greek edition.[77] The text reminds one of *TA* in numerous ways. There is an angelic announcement of death (12). Michael escorts souls to heaven (13, 23). Personified Death and his minions bear a frightful appearance (13, 21). Joseph, like Abraham, is distressed and anxious about death (13, 17). Joseph's soul exits through his mouth (19). When the saint dies, a multitude of angels appears, and his soul is wrapped in shining garments (25). And there is a book with his sins in it (26). Not one of these motifs in and of itself suggests a literary relationship; but their high number does.[78]

– The *Discourse on Abbaton*, which Budge edited, attributes itself to Apa Timothy of Rakote, a fourth-century Archbishop. Among its numerous parallels to *TA* are Abraham's hospitality (fol. 4b), Death's hideous appearance (fol. 5a), Adam seated on a throne (fol. 13a), the seven heads of Death that continually change shape (fols. 22b–23a), and Death's hideous appearance to sinners but pleasing appearance to saints (fols. 24b, 27a–b). Dependence upon *TA* seems inescapable.

– A. Henrichs, one of the editors of the *Cologne Mani Codex*, has raised the question of whether a contributor to *CMC* knew a Syriac version of *TA*. See the commentary on 3:4. Even if one agrees with Henrichs, the dating of the materials *CMC* incorporates is a vexed issue. Beyond that, one fails to see how, if there is literary dependence, we can establish its direction. Perhaps *TA* knows *CMC* or a miracle story that went into it.

– The *Apocalypse of Sedrach* draws heavily upon both *4 Ezra* and legends about Moses' death. In chap. 14, however, Sedrach, for whose soul

---

[76] Pearson, "Pierpont Morgan Fragments," 255.

[77] Morenz, *Geschichte*, 108–12.

[78] James, *Testament*, 34, further observes that there are numerous parallels between the *History of Joseph the Carpenter* and the *Testament of Isaac*. This is consistent with the two testaments circulating together from an early time and the *History* drawing upon them both.

the Son of God has come, entreats Michael to pray with him that God will
have mercy upon the world. The scene strongly recalls chaps. 14–15 of *TA*,
where Abraham asks Michael to pray with him for sinners. One suspects
the one was the inspiration for the other. This does not, however, help us
much in dating *TA*, for the *Apocalypse of Sedrach* could have been composed anywhere between the second and sixth centuries CE.

– Nag Hammadi's *Apocalypse of Paul* (V,2 17:19–24:9) "almost certainly," according to George MacRae, depends upon *TA* or a source
common to both: "Among the main points of contact between the two,
comparing especially the Coptic version of T Abr, are the following: the
role of the angels, the whipping of the soul, the singling out of one soul,
the soul's protest, the mention of the book, three witnesses who speak in
turn, the charge of murder, the mention of night by the third witness, the
casting down of the soul."[79] These are impressive parallels, and when one
also adds, which MacRae did not, that both judgment scenes follow an
account of the seer having a vision of the whole world, it seems that the
Apocalypse of Paul may indeed presuppose *TA*. Given, moreover, that the
Nag Hammadi library is dated to the mid-fourth century, there is reason
to suspect that either a Coptic version of *TA* or a Greek ancestor of the
Coptic was in circulation by the third century.

– The *Testament of Isaac* and the *Testament of Jacob*, both of which
circulated in Coptic, are relevant. The latter, which seems to be thoroughly
Christian, imitates the former, which may go back to a Jewish original; and
the latter shows definite knowledge of *TA*. 2:1, for example, speaks of
Michael as the one sent to take Abraham's soul, and 2:13 (Isaac will upon
death go "from confinement to spaciousness") matches RecShrt. 7:11
(Abraham will upon dying be taken "from a narrow place to a wide
place"). Further, *T. Isaac* 6:12–13 broaches the issue of what happens
when one does not write a testament, as happens to Abraham in our
book.[80] Unfortunately, scholarship does not appear very confident in dating the two later testaments. It is possible that both are as late as the fourth
century and depend not upon a Greek version of *TA* but upon a Coptic
translation. Yet it is perhaps a bit more likely that at least the *Testament
of Isaac* goes back to a Greek text composed no later than the third
century.[81]

---

[79] MacRae, "Judgment Scene," 285.
[80] See further Delcor, *Testament*, 78–79. Note esp. *T. Isaac* 6:12–13.
[81] See further H. F. D. Sparks, "1 Kor 2 9 a Quotation from the Coptic Testament of
      Jacob?," *ZNW* 67 (1976), 269–76; also Delcor, *Testament*, 42–47.

– James thought that Origen knew *TA*. His complex and circuitous reasoning led him to propose that when Origen, *Hom. Luc.* 35, speaks of good and evil angels contending for the soul of Abraham, he is confusing something from *TA* with something from the lost ending of the *Assumption of Moses*. [82] The argument, to my knowledge, has convinced no one.[83] Perhaps Origen knew a story from a book now lost. Or perhaps he wrote "Abraham" when he should have written "Moses" or "Amram." There is scarcely need to posit knowledge of *TA*.

– The *Visio Pauli* likely depends upon the *Testament of Abraham*. This book, which first appeared in some form in the third century or even late second century,[84] opens with Paul, raised to heaven, reporting creation's complaint against humanity. The sun, the moon, the stars, the sea, the waters, and the earth in turn confess how offended they are at the ungodliness they behold, and they implore God to let them execute judgment (3–7). In each case a voice comes and declares, "All these things do I know, for my eye sees and my ear hears; but my long-suffering bears with them until they turn and repent. But if they return not to me, then I will judge them all" (4; variations in 5–6). Although the vindictive, violent judgments of Moses, Elijah, and Elisha play no role here, the *Apocalypse* begins with a bird's eye view of human sins (including theft, murder, and adultery) very reminiscent of *TA* 10. This is followed in turn by a request for judgment, which is answered by a divine voice declaring God's long-suffering desire that the wicked change. The narrative's structure seems to derive from *TA* (although there is also influence from *Apoc. Elijah [C]* 1:3–7). Further, "until they turn and repent" (Arnh 4: *quoadusque conuertantur et peniteant*; P 4: *adusque conuertentes peniteantur*; cf. 5–6) echoes "until he turns and lives" (RecLng. 10:13: ἕως οὗ ἐπιστρέψαι καὶ ζῆσαι; the abbreviated Greek version of the *Visio* [ed. Tischendorf, p. 36] has: ὅπως ἐπιστρέψωσιν). Additional parallels—angelic ascension for prayer at sunset (*Vis. Paul* 7–8; RecShrt. 4:4–5), newly-departed souls worshipping God (*Vis. Paul* 14; RecLng. 20:12), a soul protesting its innocence convicted by an angel reading its sins in a book (*Vis. Paul* 17; RecShrt. 10:4–16), "Enoch the scribe of righteousness" (*Vis. Paul* 20; RecShrt. 11:3), "the river Ocean" in heaven (*Vis. Paul* 21, 31; RecShrt. 8:3)—entail that the *Apocalypse* was familiar with something closer to RecShrt. than RecLng.

---

[82] James, *Testament*, 14–26.

[83] Cf. its early rejection by Emil Schürer, review of James, *TLZ* 8 (1893), 279–81.

[84] J. K. Elliott, *The Apocryphal New Testament: A Collection of Apocryphal Christian Literature in an English Translation* (Oxford: Clarendon, 1993), 617, suggests that Origen already knew it.

– Some have suggested that the New Testament betrays knowledge of *TA*. Kohler took *TA* to be the source of Matt 7:13–14.[85] E. M. Sidebottom claimed that John 5:27 (God "has given to him authority to execute judgment because he is the Son of man") depends upon Abel's role as judge in *TA* 12–13.[86] Fishburne argued that 1 Cor 3:10–15 reflects the judgment scene in *TA*.[87] But it is *TA* that depends upon Matthew, not vice versa (see pp. 239–41), and the parallel with John 5:27 amounts to little. The similarities between 1 Corinthians 3 and *TA* RecLng. 13 are due to Christian contributors to the latter; see on 13:12–13. More interesting is the argument of Troy Martin regarding 1 Pet 3:6: "Thus Sarah obeyed Abraham and called him lord. You have become her daughters as long as you do what is good and never let fears alarm you."[88] Martin observes that Sarah calls Abraham "lord" again and again in *TA* but only once in Genesis, where the term does not connote obedience (18:12); that Sarah is in *TA* the mother of the elect (RecLng. 3:6 and chap. 7 in both recensions); and that fearlessness is a major theme of *TA*. Yet Genesis also depicts an obedient Sarah (cf. esp. 12:10–20, where she sleeps with Pharaoh at her husband's command); and Sarah's status as the mother of the elect, so commonplace for the rabbis (e.g. Tg. Neof. 1 on Deut 33:15), already appears in Isa 51:1–2; and while the characters in *TA* should not fear death, they hardly do so (7:12; 15:4–5, 10; 16:16; 19:2; 20:4–7). So Martin's case is uncertain. The New Testament shows no clear trace of *TA*.[89]

The external evidence strongly suggests that some form of *TA* was already in circulation by the third century. Is there any way to establish how far before that it came into existence? The document alludes to no external political or religious event. Yet if, as already argued, the book originated among Egyptian Jews, then one should date it before A.D. 115–117. This is because the revolt of those years left Egyptian Jewry, especially in Alexandria, decimated, and thereafter Egyptian Jewish literature almost dries up.[90] It is "only at the very end of the third century or the beginning

---

[85] Kaufmann Kohler, *Heaven and Hell in Comparative Religion* (New York: Macmillan, 1928), 80.

[86] E. M. Sidebottom, *The Christ of the Fourth Gospel* (London: SPCK, 1961), 94–95.

[87] Fishburne, "I Corinthians III.10–15."

[88] Martin, "1 Pet 3,6."

[89] Against Chrys C. Caragounis, *The Son of Man: Vision and Interpretation* (WUNT 38; Tübingen: Mohr-Siebeck, 1986), 91–92, there is no reason to suppose that *TA* polemicizes against Paul's doctrine of justification by faith or that Abel's place at the judgment is a deliberate Jewish counter to Jesus.

[90] The papyri also reflect great changes: "CPJ has some 50 documents of the period 117–337, as against nearly 450 for the Hellenistic and Roman periods to A.D. 117."

of the fourth that the first new burgeonings of Jewish life were to appear in the provincial cities of Egypt."[91] The conclusion is all the more sure because *TA*, which "is pervaded by a broad, philanthropic and humanitarian spirit,"[92] reflects no hostility between the Jewish and Gentile worlds. In the words of Gruen, "only ethics, not ethnics, matter"; *TA* suggests "self-assurance and comfort" in the Greek-speaking world as well as "a secure confidence" in its own traditions that "allowed for manipulation, merriment, and mockery."[93] This is hard to imagine after the revolt in the early second century.

Two final considerations support a relatively early date. First, Jewish books that Christians adopted are, as a rule, no later than the second century CE.[94] Second, Turner's linguistic researches show that both recensions of *TA*, despite their late features, bear "a strong syntactical and lexical resemblance to the language of the Septuagint and the New Testament."[95] This is more than consistent with positing an original composed somewhere near the turn of the era.

As for a *terminus a quo*, RecLng. knows the LXX, as this commentary reveals throughout.[96] So RecLng. in anything like its present form must have come into existence after the LXX established itself, which means one cannot hazard a date before the second century BCE. The same conclusion holds for the prototype of RecShrt., as RecShrt. too depends upon the LXX, as one can see at a glance:

So E. Mary Smallwood, *The Jews under Roman Rule: From Pompey to Diocletian* (SJLA; Leiden: Brill, 1976), 406, n. 66. If William Adler, "Apion's 'Encomium of Adultery': A Jewish Satire of Greek Paideia in the Pseudo-Clementine Homilies," *HUCA* 64 (1993), 15–49, is correct to assign the Apion section of the Ps.-Clementine Homilies to a second-century Jew of Alexandria, then its controversial tone reflects a time later than *TA*.

[91] Joseph Mélèze Modrzejewski, *The Jews of Egypt: From Rameses II to Emperor Hadrian* (Philadelphia and Jerusalem: Jewish Publication Society, 1995), 217. See further Christopher Haas, *Alexandria in Late Antiquity: Topography and Social Conflict* (Baltimore/London: Johns Hopkins, 1997), pp. 91–127.

[92] Box, *Testament*, xx.

[93] Gruen, *Diaspora*, 222. Josef Schreiner, *Alttestamentlich-jüdische Apokalyptik: Eine Einführung* (Munich: Kösel, 1969), 72, thinks that the emphasis upon hospitality reflects a time of peace.

[94] So Denis, *Introduction*, 36. Cf. Schürer, *History*, 3/2:764. Although Delcor, *Testament*, 47–51, has argued that *TA* polemicizes against the *Testament of Job* and so must be later, his case is unmade.

[95] Turner, "Biblical Greek," 220.

[96] See also Turner, "Testament," 195–204.

| RecShrt. 2:8 E | ἐκ τοῦ οἴκου τοῦ πατρός σου ... | εἰς τὴν γῆν, ἣν ἄν σοι δείξω |
| LXX Gen 12:1 | ἐκ τοῦ οἴκου τοῦ πατρός σου | εἰς τὴν γῆν, ἣν ἄν σοι δείξω |

| RecShrt. 2:9 E | οὐκέτι κληθήσει | Ἀβράμ, ἀλλ᾽ ἔσται τὸ ὄνομά σου Ἀβραάμ |
| LXX Gen 17:5 | οὐ   κληθήσεται ... Ἀβράμ, ἀλλ᾽ ἔσται τὸ ὄνομά σου Ἀβραάμ |

RecShrt. 12:7 E	ἄνοιξον	τὴν γῆν	καταπίη	αὐτούς
RecShrt. 12:7 B F G	ἀνοιχθήτω ἡ	γῆ καὶ	καταπιέτω αὐτούς
LXX Num 16:30	ἀνοίξασα ἡ	γῆ	καταπίεται αὐτούς
LXX Num 16:32	ἀνοίχθη ἡ	γῆ καὶ	κατέπιεν αὐτούς

RecShrt. 12:4 E	κατέβη πῦρ ἐκ τοῦ οὐρανοῦ καὶ κατεφάγεν + object
4 Βασ 1:10b	κατέβη πῦρ ἐκ τοῦ οὐρανοῦ καὶ κατεφάγεν + object
4 Βασ 1:12b	κατέβη πῦρ ἐκ τοῦ οὐρανοῦ καὶ κατεφάγεν + object

What then of the dates of RecLng. and RecShrt. as they have come down to us? There is no simple answer. Christian hands, as the textual variants show, continued to revise the texts over time; and we do not know, for instance, whether RecShrt. is due primarily to one redactor, whether Jewish or Christian, or to a series of small changes made over time. We can guess, however, that RecShrt. was largely in place no later than the 3rd century CE. The Coptic, which goes back to at least the fourth century, presupposes something close to it, as does the *Apocalypse of Paul*, itself no later than the third century. Furthermore, while Turner dated James' B text to the third century, on the ground that it contains a dozen words unattested until then,[97] Schmidt has observed that ms. E, which James did not use, contains only four words not attested before the turn of the era— σωματικῶς (8:2), συντομή (4:12), ληθαργέω (10:15), and ἀροτριασμός (2:1).[98] Moreover, σωματικῶς appears in Philo, *Her.* 84, and Col 2:9, συντομή in Aquila (Isa 28:22), and ἀροτριασμός in *T. Job* 10:5. So it is quite possible, even likely, that RecShrt., in something very close to its form in ms. E, had already appeared by the second century.

RecLng. in its current form is another story. Turner found several words that do not appear elsewhere until the fifth or sixth centuries. The present commentary uncovers even more late features and confirms that RecLng. as we have it is medieval. This author's impression is that the basic work is early Byzantine, with a few later touches. Yet one must keep in mind that scribes clearly revised the text as they copied it, and many of the ecclesiastical words and phrases must be secondary, so the medieval features hardly prevent a much earlier date for a close ancestor of our RecLng.

---

[97] Turner, "Testament," 49–54a, 245–49; "Biblical Greek," 222.
[98] Schmidt, "Testament," 1:118.

VII. Genre

The Greek manuscripts of *TA* use several words to describe it:

διαθήκη = "Testament," so RecLng. A A margin E I; RecShrt. A D H; cf. RecShrt.
   I: διάθεσις
διήγησις = "Narrative," so RecLng. H J; cf. RecLng. I (20:15): ἡ διήγησις τοῦ βίου
διήγησις and διαθήκη, so RecLng. B Q; cf. RecShrt. B F G: διήγησις of a διαθήκη
λόγος (= "Account"), so RecShrt. C; RecLng. L*; cf. RecLng. G: λόγος περὶ παλαιᾶς
   ἱστορίας and Abraham's διαθήκης
ἀποκάλυψις = "Apocalypse," so RecShrt. A
βίος = "Life," so RecLng. I (20:15): ἡ διήγησις τοῦ βίου

The versions likewise show diversity. The Coptic calls our book, together
with the *Testament of Isaac* and the *Testament of Jacob*, "The Departure
from the Body of our holy fathers" (cf. the Arabic and the Ethiopic),
although the threefold collection is clearly a collection of testaments. The
Slavonic, like RecShrt. A, labels the work an "Apocalypse" or "Revelation" about Abraham's death and testament. The Romanian calls it a
"Life" (*Vita*) written according to "revelation" (*apocalipsis*).

Moderns also disagree on what genre *TA* represents. Kohler called it
"The Apocalypse of Abraham."[99] John Collins, affirming that *TA*, which
has no farewell discourse, is "not a testament but rather the story of
Abraham's death and the events leading up to it," categorized chaps. 10–
15 as an "apocalypse," and that of a particular sort: "Otherworldly
Journey with only Personal Eschatology."[100] Others have thought that,
despite its peculiarities and the absence of paraenesis, "testament" remains
the best categorization, and modern collections of intertestamental writings typically entitle our book "The Testament of Abraham."[101] Denis
categorizes *TA* as "un midrash hagiographique de Gen., 25,5–10 … avec
une apocalypse."[102] Dean-Otting calls it a "kind of romance or adventure

---

[99] Kohler, "Apocalypse."
[100] John J. Collins, "Introduction: Towards the Morphology of a Genre," *Semeia* 14
(1979), 1–20. He places the *Greek Apocalypse of Baruch* and the *Apocalypse of
Zephaniah* in the same category.
[101] Cf. Janssen, "Testament," 195; Schmidt, "Testament," 1:40–43.
[102] Denis et al., *Introduction*, 173.

story" as well as an "Egyptian fairytale."[103] Kolenkow observes that it is
like the Hellenistic νέκυια, a journey to heaven that moves the seer to
repent.[104] Wills has suggested that we read *TA* as a "satirical novel, written
in the form of a mock testament."[105] According to Gruen, the story "draws
on various genres but belongs to none"; it is "a mélange that represents
primarily the inventiveness of its creator."[106]

Several observations are in order. The first is that the diversity of
opinion among both ancients and moderns is proof enough that *TA*'s genre
is not obvious, and it is not clear how important the issue is for interpretation. Second, many books from antiquity are hard to categorize because
they mix genres. Job, the Qumran Pesharim, and Philostratus' *Vita Apollonii*
are examples. So there is nothing odd in holding that *TA* "draws on
various genres but belongs to none." In line with this, a few of the ancient
titles put *TA* into two genres at once. Finally, the command that Abraham
set his house in order comes at the beginning of the book and is repeated
again and again, which sets up hearers to expect a testament. Further, that
the second half of the book is an apocalypse well suits the testament genre,
for testaments often contain apocalyptic visions. The problem is that
Abraham never does make his testament.[107] So *TA* is a parody.[108] This is
why it is so full of comic elements (see below) and why it looks like and
does not look like other testaments. Perhaps one should call it an "anti-
testament."

---

[103] Dean-Otting, *Heavenly Journeys*, 175, 215.

[104] Kolenkow, "Genre." Abraham's education thus becomes the paraenesis.

[105] Wills, *Novel*, 256. On p. 255 he comments: "it is merely the shell of the testament
or the apocalypse that is taken over." Cf. Eckhard von Nordheim, *Die Lehre der
Alten I. Das Testament als Literaturgattung im Judentum der hellenistisch-römischen
Zeit* (ALGHJ 13; Leiden, 1980), 149–50: *TA* is a "Roman" with apocalyptic
elements.

[106] Gruen, *Diaspora*, 191. Wills, *Novel*, 254: *TA* "leaps beyond the expected generic
associations."

[107] Nothing is to be said for Box's speculation, *Testament*, xi, that *TA* may have
contained some testamentary elements in an earlier form.

[108] So also Gruen, *Diaspora*, 191, and Ludlow, *Abraham*, 17–28.

VIII. Structure

George Nickelsburg has offered the following outline of TA:[109]

Part I	Part II
Chapter	**Chapter**
1. God summons Michael: "Go down ... to my friend Abraham and speak to him concerning his death, so that he might put his affairs in order"	16. God summons Death: "Go down to my friend Abraham and take him and bring him to me"
2. Michael leaves and goes to Abraham, who sits at Mamre	Death leaves and goes to Abraham, who sits at Mamre
Abraham sees him and rises to meet him	Abraham sees him and rises to meet him
Michael to Abraham: "Greetings, most honorable father, righteous soul ... true friend of the heavenly God"	Death to Abraham: "Greetings, honorable Abraham, righteous soul, friend of God the Most High"
Abraham returns the greeting, notes Michael's glory and beauty and says, "Teach me from what road your beauty has come"	Abraham returns the greeting, notes Death's glory and asks "From whence has your glory come to us?"
Michael replies elusively regarding his mission	"I speak to you the truth. I am the bitter cup of death"
———	Abraham contradicts Death and then refuses to follow him
2–3. They go to Abraham's house, conversing	17. They go into Abraham's house; Death is silent
The talking tree: a hint	———
Isaac and Abraham wash Michael's feet	Abraham is sullen and inhospitable
4. A room is prepared for Michael	
Michael returns to heaven	Death stays

---

[109] Nickelsburg, "Structure and Message." Cf. idem, *Introduction*, 249–51, and Díez Macho, *Introduccion*, 277.

5. Abraham and Michael go to their beds	Abraham goes to bed and orders Death to leave
5–7. Isaac has a dream, which Michael interprets; the angel reveals his identity and mission	Abraham asks, "Are you Death?" and the two discuss different sorts of death
7. Abraham refuses to go	————
8–9. Michael ascends and returns	Death stays
9. Abraham asks to see all the world	"Show me your savageness"
10. Abraham sees the world and calls down different deaths upon sinners	Death unmasks himself and shows Abraham different kinds of death; servants die
11– Abraham sees post-mortem judgment; 13. Michael explains everything	

14. They pray for the dead and the dead are revived	18.	They pray for the dead and the dead are revived
	19.	Further delays and another refusal; Death explains his various faces
————		
15. Michael returns Abraham home; Sarah, Isaac, and servants rejoice	20.	Isaac, Sarah, and servants mourn
Michael tells Abraham to prepare for death; Abraham again refuses to follow Michael returns to heaven		Abraham suddenly dies; Michael takes his soul to heaven

Nickelsburg observes that both main sections end the same way: Abraham is on his bed, surrounded by his family (chaps. 15, 20). He further notes that Abraham's refusal, which moves the plot forward, explains both the similarities and the differences between the two symmetrical segments. Michael's failure leads to Death's advent, and because their missions are the same, Part II replays Part I. But because Death is altogether different from Michael, there are striking contrasts: Death the destroyer does not act like meek Michael. Thus "each of the two parts has its own pace and tone, corresponding to its relative place in the development of the plot. Part I is lengthy and rambling, and it has more than its share of humorous touches … . When Michael fails in his mission, we move to Part II, where a totally different pace and tone pervade. The divine messenger is 'merciless, rotten Death.'"[110]

This is a very helpful analysis, and one cannot but agree with it. In fact, one can add a few more parallels between the first and second sections:

---

[110] Nickelsburg, "Structure and Message," 86.

Michael in chaps. 1–15	*Death in chaps. 16–20*
stands before God, 4:5; 8:1; 15:11	stands before God, 16:3
is bright as the sun, 2:4	is bright as the sun, 16:10
is handsome above all the sons of men, 2:4	is more beautiful than the sons of men, 16:6
identifies himself with ἐγώ εἰμι, 7:11	identifies himself with ἐγώ εἰμι, 16:11

In one respect, however, Nickelsburg's outline is incomplete. It fails to expose the fact that chaps. 1–15 are themselves highly repetitious: the same sorts of things happen again and again. Nickelsburg's first section actually consists of a series of four parallel episodes: 1:1–4:5; 4:5–7:12; 8:1–9:6; 9:7–15:10. Each episode opens with a conversation in heaven between Michael and God in which the latter instructs the former regarding Abraham. And each ends with Michael's failure to carry out his orders and his ascension to heaven for further guidance. In between each descent and ascent is the interaction between the archangel and the patriarch, and here too there is repetition or resemblance.[111] For instance, if in chap. 7 Michael interprets Isaac's dream, in chap. 13 he interprets Abraham's vision of the judgment. Perhaps, then, it is helpful to envisage *TA* as do the following two pages.

---

[111] There is a parallel with Revelation, where the narrative moves back and forth between heaven and earth, and where different series of events are parallel (e.g. the seven trumpets and the seven bowls).

1:1–4:4	4:5–7:12	8:1–9:6
Introduction: Abraham's character and situation, 1:1–3		
	Michael ascends and stands before God, 4:5	Michael ascends and stands before God, 8:1
	Michael reports what has happened, 4:6	Michael reports what has happened, 8:1–3
God tells Michael what to do; "Go down to my friend Abraham," 1:4–7	God tells Michael what to do; "Go down to my friend Abraham," 4:7–11	God tells Michael what to do; "Go to my friend Abraham," 8:4–12
Michael descends and meets Abraham, who is sitting; Abraham rises and greets Michael; the two exchange greetings; Abraham questions Michael and they converse, 2:1–2	Michael descends and meets Abraham, 5:1	Michael descends and meets Abraham, 9:1
the two journey to Abraham's house; a tree prophesies Abraham's death, 2:9 – 3:4		
Abraham and his family host Michael, 3:5–4:4	Abraham reclines on his couch and hosts Michael; Isaac is present, 5:1–4	
Abraham weeps; Isaac weeps; Michael weeps, 3:9–12	Isaac has a dream and becomes afraid; Abraham weeps; Michael weeps; Sarah weeps, 5:5–14	
	Sarah identifies Michael, 6:1–8	
	Isaac recounts his dream and Michael interprets, 7:1–11	
	Michael identifies himself with ἐγώ εἰμι, 7:11	
	Abraham refuses to go with Michael; "I will not follow you," 7:12	Abraham asks to see the whole world before he dies, 9:2–6

9:7–15:10	15:11–16:16	16:17–20:15
Michael ascends and stands before God, 9:7	Michael ascends and stands before God, 15:11	[[Death does not leave]]
Michael reports what has happened, 9:7	Michael reports what has happened, 15:12–15	
God tells Michael what to do; "Go down," 9:8	God calls Death and tells him what to do; "Go down to my friend Abraham," 16:1–5	
Michael descends and meets Abraham, 10:1	Death descends and meets Abraham, who is sitting; Abraham rises and greets Death; the two exchange greetings; Abraham questions Death and they converse, 16:6–15	
		the two journey to Abraham's house, 17:1
		Abraham reclines on his couch and does not host Death, 17:2–5
Abraham sees the world and slaughters sinners; God stops him, 10:1–14		servants die, 17:18
Abraham sees the judgment and Michael interprets, 11:1–14:14		Abraham sees Death's faces; Death interprets, 17:6–19 + 19:1–16
	Death identifies himself with ἐγώ εἰμι, 16:11	Death identifies himself with ἐγώ εἰμι, 17:5
Abraham invites Michael to intercede with him for a soul whose good and bad deeds are balanced and for the slain sinners; they pray; the souls are saved, 14:1–15		Abraham invites Death to intercede with him for the slain servants; they return to life, 18:1–11
		Abraham asks one last question and begs Death to go away, 20:1–5
Abraham returns home; his family and servants celebrate, 15:1–5		Abraham's family and servants mourn his coming departure, 20:6–7
Abraham refuses to go with Michael; "I will not follow you," 15:6–10	Abraham refuses to go with Death; "I will not follow you," 16:16	
		Conclusion: Abraham's death, ascent, and burial, 20:8–15

IX. Literary Themes and Leading Ideas

1. *The compassionate God of all.* The God of *TA* is tolerant, merciful, and long-suffering, and he gives people the freedom to act as they wish. When they behave wrongly, as Abraham does in chap. 10, God seeks to set things right—in Abraham's case by stopping his violence and then later, in response to prayer, bringing the untimely dead back to life. God is not only extraordinarily patient with the great saint, but also loves sinners. As 10:14 so memorably puts it: "I made the world, and I do not wish to destroy any of them. Rather I delay the death of a sinner until he turns and lives." The one place that God's compassion and even good humor seem deficient is in chaps. 11–13, which condemn the mass of humanity to perdition. But the disquieting estimation of 11:12—"For among seven thousand is scarcely to be found one soul saved and undefiled"—must be, like much of the rest of those chapters, from a later Christian hand. 11:7 and 10, which report on "many" entering into life, and 14:15, which says that those requited while they live on earth will not be further requited in death, surely give us a better sense of the consoling Jewish original.

TA's God is clearly the Jewish God of the Old Testament. Yet our text is not concerned with the Jewish people as such. Nor does it mention specifically Jewish practices such as circumcision and Sabbath-keeping. The land of promise is not emphasized (although note 8:5; 20:11). The eschatology is about the individual, not the nation. And the judgment is according to good and bad deeds in general, not works of Torah in particular. None of this is reason to imagine that our book was ever intended for non-Jews—although, given Abraham's fame in the Gentile world,[112] perhaps we should not dismiss that possibility. The book does, however, seemingly reflect a Judaism interested in broad religious ideas rather than the traditional markers of Jewish identity.[113] *TA*'s God is clearly the God of all humanity, and the relevance of specifically Jewish practices and beliefs, while perhaps assumed, is unspoken—a circumstance that probably made the book congenial to Christians.

---

[112] Bowley, "Compositions of Abraham," 215–38.
[113] See further Sanders, "Testament," 877–78.

2. The Bible. Although the book reflects many exegetical traditions, *TA* is hardly midrash. Nor, despite the fact that the biblical silence concerning Abraham's testament makes its story possible, is it really interested in interpreting Scripture. It is, nonetheless, intertextually rich. Sanders' comment that "almost nothing of the Old Testament appears in the Testament of Abraham except the obvious references to Abraham in Genesis"[114] needs correction. *TA* regularly refers to, quotes, and otherwise borrows from Genesis and other parts of the Tanak and traditions parasitic upon them:

1:5 quotes Gen 22:17
3:3 quotes part of Isa 6:6 and grows out of MT Gen 21:33
3:6 refers to Gen 26:3
4:2 presupposes a legend associated with Gen 21:33
4:6 uses the language of Job 1:1, 8; 2:3
4:9–10 borrows from a traditional interpretation of Gen 18:8
4:11 quotes Gen 22:17
5:3 quotes Gen 22:17
5:13 echoes Gen 14:12
6:4–6 summarizes the episode in Gen 18:1–15
6:5 depends upon a fanciful reading of MT Gen 18:8
7:2–9 transforms Gen 37:9–10
7:6 borrows from LXX Ps 26:7
8:5 quotes Gen 22:17
8:6 refers to Gen 18:1–15 and its outcome
8:7 quotes from Gen 22:17 and uses the language of Exod 20:2 = Deut 5:9; Isa 44:6; etc.
8:9 presupposes the story in Genesis 2–3
9:4 quotes LXX Ps 19:5
9:5 borrows from *Pr. Man.* 4; 1 Kgs 2:16, 20
10:6–7 uses the language of 2 Kgs 2:23–25
10:8–9 uses the language of Numbers 16
10:10–11 uses the language of 2 Kgs 1:9–12
10:14 repeats a refrain from Ezek 18:23, 32; 33:11
13:2 refers to the story in Gen 4:1–16
13:8 applies the principle of Deut 19:15
15:15 names Job and uses the language of Job 1:8; 2:3
17:13 depends upon an exegesis of MT Gen 23:3
20:14 uses a phrase from LXX Ps 117:15

Such a list hardly exhausts the ways in which *TA* engages Scripture. In its first half especially, *TA* constantly reworks Genesis. Chaps. 1–8 weave dozens of words and phrases from the LXX story of Abraham, especially

---

[114] Sanders, ibid., 879.

from chaps. 18 and 22, into its narrative, and the structure of chaps. 1–4 largely imitates the book of Job; see pp. 128–29.

Despite the keen knowledge of and interaction with Scripture, *TA* does not promote a canon-centered piety. Not only are central scriptural themes conspicuously absent—"the theological/ethical ideals of the Testament are more humanitarian than biblical"[115] (see above)—but the story itself does not follow the Bible. *TA* makes its main points not through exegesis but through a new, imaginative narrative. Further, *TA* does not scruple to contradict Genesis itself, as when Abraham lives to be 995 (see on 1:1), or when Sarah is alive at his death; see on 20:6. Beyond such blatant contradictions is the implicit theological criticism of the behaviors of Moses, Elijah, and Elisha; see on 10:11. So while it regularly echoes and finds inspiration in the Bible, *TA* feels perfectly free to go its own way. It does not make Scripture the last word but creatively exploits it for novel ends.

3. Death and Judgment. The central issue in *TA* is Death. The focus on Abraham is ultimately incidental. The patriarch is not, so to speak, his biblical self but rather everyman, the human being faced with death, who is, no matter how pious, anxious about quitting this life.

Janssen has argued that *TA* reflects the typical stages that human beings pass through when confronting death, as documented by Elizabeth Kübler-Ross in *On Death and Dying*: denial, anger or resentment, bargaining, depression, acceptance.[116] This is an intriguing proposal. Abraham certainly does engage in denial. He also bargains with God and becomes finally depressed. That he is ever angry or resentful, however, is less clear (Janssen reads this into 7:12). More importantly, the patriarch never, despite Janssen's reading of chap. 20, comes to terms with his own death, which is why he never makes a testament. *TA* really has as much or more in common with Ernest Becker's *The Denial of Death*, for Abraham is denial incarnate. He is all too slow to recognize Michael and fathom his mission. Then he refuses to co-operate with him. Then he makes a deal on which he reneges. Then he delays the inevitable by quizzing Death about multiple matters. And when slipping away at the end, he is still telling Death to depart. Indeed, at his dying moment he is fantasizing about getting well; see on 20:8–9. So from beginning to end Abraham runs from reality. He never comes to terms with the fact that his death is at hand.

---

[115] James D. Newsome, *Greeks, Romans, Jews: Currents of Culture and Belief in the New Testament* (Philadelphia: Trinity Press Intl., 1992), 375.

[116] Janssen, "Testament," 197–98. Cf. Jean-Claude Picard, *Le continent apocryphe: Essai sur les littératures apocryphes juive et chrétienne* (Instrumenta Patristica 36; Turnhout: Brepols, 1999), 91, n. 38: *TA* is "une sorte de psychodrame."

Although *TA* candidly displays the human denial of death, it does so with humor and sympathy, and it is ultimately optimistic, at least for all those whose bad deeds do not exceed their good deeds. Abraham may, like the rest of us, fear death, but wisdom recognizes that the world is ultimately "futile" (1:7) and that leaving it is, for the saved, to exchange suffering, grief, and groaning for peace, fervent joy, and eternal life (20:15). Death has hideous faces, but they soon fade. *TA* copes with death-related anxiety by teaching that death is not the end but instead the beginning of a better existence.

4. Humor and Irony. Despite the somber topic and the serious theological questions that it addresses, *TA* is in the end "more entertainment than instruction."[117] The light-hearted parody of testamentary literature is full of irony, and "the humor ... is deliberate and persistent, no mere marginal presence."[118] Like the first half of the *Apocalypse of Abraham* and parts of the *Testament of Job*, the text moves us to laugh. It does this largely through irony, through the disparity between its picture of Abraham and that of the Bible and subsequent tradition. From Genesis on, Abraham is a paradigm of faith, obedience, and sagacity. In *TA*, which mocks naive genuflection before scriptural heroes, the patriarch does not exercise much faith in God or display obedience. He does not even show much sense: it takes him, despite a talking tree and tears turning into jewels, a ludicrously long time to figure out what is going on, and even then he refuses to face the inevitable. The man who interceded for Sodom and Gomorrah also acts against character by slaughtering sinners in chap. 10. So the Abraham of *TA* is not the revered Abraham of tradition but his all-too-human opposite. His confrontation with mortality turns him unexpectedly into an obtuse, stubborn old man who exercises not the blind obedience of Genesis 22 but self-centered defiance.

The other characters also breed irony and laughter. Michael, the Commander-in-chief of the heavenly hosts, is not really much of a commander: Abraham has him flummoxed. Nor can he figure out what to do when sitting at table with the patriarch, although this is something he has already done. Similarly, it is ironic that Sarah and Isaac, who divine Michael's identity almost instantly, are faster on their feet than their husband and father, whom they call "lord." And then there is Death, whose hideous appearance reflects anxiety about human mortality. He initially shows up in a brightly shining robe, more beautiful than the sons of men. Abraham

---

[117] Gruen, *Diaspora*, 192.
[118] Gruen, *Diaspora*, 187. See esp. Ludlow, *Abraham*, passim.

greets him—the very thing he is running from. The patriarch, moreover, gets him to answer questions and, in effect, to perform for him in chap. 17. Death even ends up praying for the resurrection of people he has killed— a truly remarkable role reversal.

The irony and humor that run throughout *TA* are one way of approaching its chief subject, death. We can run from death, or we can philosophize about it, or we can give it a religious interpretation. But we can also respond with mirth, by combating its sadness with its opposite. In one respect, *TA* addresses death a bit like some Woody Allen films. It is of course far less cynical, but it wraps its teachings about the somber mystery of death in an often amusing tale.

5. *Christian readings.* The original Jewish *TA* was designed (i) to entertain and (ii) to reinforce a platonic-like optimism about the world to come. But Christians must have heard something else. Just as later interpreters of Canticles read the book against its original intention and made their own interests its subject matter, so Christians must have found new meaning in their revised versions of *TA*. In RecLng. and RecShrt., with their expanded focus on post-mortem judgment, the upshot of the assize is dismal. Far more are damned than are saved. This casts a shadow over the whole book, especially RecLng., where there are 7,000 damned for every 1 saved. This statistic, even when rightly regarded as exaggeration for paraenetical emphasis, makes for a much more serious work, as do the other revisions to chaps. 11–13. Hearers of *TA* might very well have come away worried about the judgment, about their fate and the fate of their loved ones. Such people would no doubt have taken the virtues outlined in chap. 1 to be imperatives for themselves, not part of the ironic set up for an Abraham who cannot live up to his billing. In line with this, TA circulated in collections of serious hagiography, alongside such works as the *Martyrdom of Andrew*, the *Martyrdom of Barbara*, and the *Martyrdom of Philip*. Evidently later readers laughed less than earlier readers.

X. Bibliography

Editions

Aešcoly, Aaron Zeev, *Recueil de textes falachas. Introduction. Textes éthiopiens (édition critique et traduction)* (Travaux et Mémoires de l'Institut d'Ethnologie de l'Université de Paris 55; Paris: Institut d'ethnologie, 1951).

Agouridès, S., "Διαθήκη 'Αβραάμ," *Δελτίον Βιβλικῶν Μελετῶν* 1 (1972), 238–48.

Conti Rossini, C., "Nuovi appunti sui Guidei d'Abissinia," *Rendiconti della reale academia nazionale dei Lincei,* Classe di scienze morali, storiche e filologiche 5/31 (1922), 221–40.

Gaguine, Maurice. "The Falasha Version of the Testaments of Abraham, Isaac and Jacob: A critical Study of Five Unpublished ms.: with Introduction, Translation and Notes" (unpublished University of Manchester Ph.D. dissertation, 1965).

Gaster, Moses, "The Apocalypse of Abraham. From the Roumanian Text, Discovered and Translated," in *Transactions of the Society of Biblical Archaeology* 9 (1887), 195–226; reprinted in *Studies and Texts in Folklore, Magic, Mediaeval Romance, Hebrew Apocrypha, and Samaritan Archeology* (New York: Ktav, 1971), 1:92–124.

Guidi, I., "Il testo copto del Testamento di Abramo," *Rendiconti della reale academia dei Lincei,* Classe di scienze morali, storiche e filologiche 5/9 (Rome, 1900), 157–80.

James, Montague Rhodes, *The Testament of Abraham: The Greek Text Now First Edited with an Introduction and Notes* (TS 2/2; Cambridge: Cambridge University Press, 1892).

Petriceicu-Hasdeu, Bogdan, *Cărţile poporane als Românilor în secolul XVI* (reprint ed.; Bucharist: Editura Didactică şi Pedagogică, 1983), 189–94.

Polívka, G., "Die apokryphische Erzählung vom Tode Abrahams," in *Archiv für slavische Philologie* 18 (1986), 112–25.

Roddy, Nicolae, *The Romanian Version of the Testament of Abraham* (SBLEJL 19; Atlanta: Scholars Press, 2001).

Schmidt, Francis, "Le Testament d'Abraham: Introduction, édition de la recension courte, traduction et notes" (2 vols.; Doctoral Thesis, University of Strasbourg, 1971).

—, *Le Testament grec d'Abraham: Introduction, édition critique des deux recensions grecques, traduction* (TSAJ 11; Tübingen: Mohr-Siebeck, 1986).

Stone, Michael E., *The Testament of Abraham: The Greek Recensions* (Missoula, Mont.: Scholars Press, 1972) (reprint of James' Greek text).

Tixonravov, Nikolaj, *Pamjatniki otrečennoj russkoj literatury*, vol. 1 (reprint ed.; London: Variorum Reprints, 1973), 79–90.

Vassiliev, A., "Mors Abrahami," in *Anecdota Graeco-byzantina*, vol. 1 (Moscow: Moscow University, 1893), 1:lvi–lix, 292–308 (RecLng. ms. E).

Zotenberg, Hermann, *Manuscrits orientaux. Catalogue des manuscripts éthiopiens (Gheez et Amharique) de la Bibliothèque Nationale* (Paris: Imprimerie nationale, 1877), 200–203.

Translations and Commentaries

Agouridès, S.C., "Διαθήκη Ἀβραάμ," in *Τὰ Ἀπόκρυφα τῆς παλαίας διαθήκης* vol. 1 (ed. S. C. Agouridès; Athens: Theological School of the University of Athens, 1972), 238–48.

Andersson, E., "Abraham's Vermächtnis aus dem Koptischen übersetzt," *Sphinx* 6 (1903), 220–36.

Barnes, W. E., "Extracts from the Testament of Abraham," in James, *Testament*, 135–39.

Box, G. H., *The Testament of Abraham: Translated from the Greek Text with Introduction and Notes* (London: SPCK, 1927).

Chaîne, M., "Traduction des Testaments faite sur le Texte Copte Bohaïrique," in Delcor, *Testament*, 186–213.

Chaîne, M. and P. Marçais, "La Transmigration des Pères Vénérables Abraham, Isaac et Jacob," in Delcor, *Testament*, 242–67.

Colafemmina, Cesare, *Il Testamento di Abramo: Introduzione, traduzione e note* (Collana di Testi Patristici 118; Rome: Città Nuova Editrice, 1995).

Cooper, D. S. and H. B. Weber, "The Church Slavonic Testament of Abraham," in Nickelsburg, *Studies*, 301–26.

Cousin, Hugues, *Vies d'Adam et Eve, des patriarches et des prophètes* (Paris: Cerf, 1980).

Craigie, W. A., "The Testament of Abraham," in *Ante-Nicene Christian Library*, vol. 9: *Additional volume containing early Christian works* (Edinburgh: T. & T. Clark, 1897), 183–201.

Delcor, M., *Le Testament d'Abraham: Introduction, traduction du texte grec et commentaire de la recension grecque longue, suivi de la traduction des Testaments d'Abraham, d'Isaac et de Jacob d'après les versions orientales* (SVTP 2; Leiden: Brill, 1973).

Janssen, Enno, "Testament Abrahams," *JSHRZ* 3/2 (1975), 193–256.

Leslau, Wolf, "The Testament of Abraham," in *Falasha Anthology: Translated from Ethiopic Sources with an Introduction* (Yale Judaica Series 6; New Haven: Yale University Press, 1951), 91–102, 176–80.

MacRae, George, "The Coptic Testament of Abraham," in Nickelsburg, *Studies*, 327–40.

Piattelli, Elio, "Testamento di Abramo," *Annuario di Studi Ebraici* 2 (1964), 111–22.

Rießler, Paul, "Testament des Abraham," in *Altjüdisches Schrifttum außerhalb der Bibel* (Heidelberg: F. H. Kerle, 1966), 1091–1103, 1332–33.

—, "Das Testament Abrahams: Ein jüdisches Apokryphon," *TQ* 106 (1925), 3–22.

Rosso Ubigli, Liliana, "Testamento di Abramo," *Apocrifi dell'Antico Testamento*, vol. 4 (Biblica Testi e studi; ed. Paolo Sacchi et al.; Brescia: Paideia, 2000), 15–101.

Sanders, E. P., "The Testament of Abraham", in *The Old Testament Pseudepigrapha* (2 vols.; ed. J. H. Charlesworth; New York: Doubleday, 1983–85), 1:871–902.

Schmidt, Francis, "Le Testament d'Abraham," in *La Bible: Écrits Intertestamentaires* (ed. A. Dupont-Sommer and Marc Philonenko; Paris: Gallimard, 1987), 1647–90.

Turner, Nigel, "The Testament of Abraham," in *The Apocryphal Old Testament* (ed. H. F. D. Sparks; Oxford: Clarendon, 1984), 393–421.

Vegas Montaner, Luis, "Testamento de Abrahám," in *Apócrifos del Antiguo Testamento* (vol. 5; ed. A. Diez Macho; Madrid: Ediciones Cristiandad, 1987), 5:439–527.

Wittlieb, M., "Testament Abrahama," in *Apokryfy Starego Testamentu* (ed. R. Rubinkiewicz; Warsaw, 1999), 87–103. [[Unavailable to the author.]]

Secondary Literature on TA

Allison, Dale C., Jr., "Abraham's Oracular Tree (*T. Abr.* 3:1–3)," *JJS* 54 (2003), 1–11.

—, "Job in the Testament of Abraham," *JSP* 12 (2001), 3–19.

—, "Rejecting Violent Vengeance: The Background of Luke 9:52–56," *JBL* 121 (2002), 459–78.

Aranda Pérez, G., "Apócrifos del Antiguo Testamento," in *Literatura judía intertestamentaria* (ed. G. Aranda Pérez, F. García Martínez, and M. Pérez Fernández; Estella: Editorial Verbo Divino, 1996), 368–71.

Calvert, Nancy Lynn, "Abraham Traditions in Middle Jewish Literature: Implications for the Interpretation of Galatians and Romans" (unpublished Ph.D. Dissertation, University of Sheffield, 1993), 236–61.

Charlesworth, James H., *The Pseudepigrapha and Modern Research with a Supplement* (Chico: Scholars Press, 1981), 70–72, 270–71.

Chazon, E., "Moses' Struggle for his Soul: A Prototype for the *Testament of Abraham*, the *Greek Apocalypse of Ezra*, and the *Apocalypse of Sedrach*", *SecCent* 5 (1986), 151–64.

Coleman, G. B., "The Phenomenon of Christian Interpolations into Jewish Apocalyptic Texts: A Bibliographical Survey and Methodological Analysis" (unpublished Ph.D. Dissertation, Vanderbilt, 1976), 52–54, 324–33.

Collins, John J., *The Apocalyptic Imagination: An Introduction to Jewish Apocalyptic Literature* (2nd ed.; Grand Rapids: Eerdmans, 1998), 251–55.

—, "The Genre Apocalypse in Hellenistic Judaism," in *Apocalypticism in the*

Mediterranean World and the Near East: Proceedings of the International Colloquium on Apocalypticism, Uppsala, August 12–17, 1979 (ed. David Hellholm; Tübingen: Mohr-Siebeck, 1983), 541–44.

—, *Between Athens and Jerusalem: Jewish Identity in the Diaspora* (2nd ed.; Grand Rapids: Eerdmans, 2000), 248–51.

Dean-Otting, Mary, *Heavenly Journeys: A Study of the Motif in Hellenistic Jewish Literature* (Judentum und Umwelt 8; Frankfurt am Main: Peter Lang, 1984), 175–224.

Delcor, M., "De l'origine de quelques traditions contenues dans le Testament d'Abraham," in *Proceedings of the Fifth World Congress of Jewish Studies* (ed. P. Peli; Jerusalem: World Union of Jewish Studies, 1969), 1:192–200.

Denis, Albert-Marie, "Le Testament d'Abraham," in *Introduction aux Pseud-épigraphes grecs d'Ancien Testament* (SVTP 1; Leiden: Brill, 1970), 31–37.

Denis, Albert-Marie et al., "Le Testament d'Abraham," in *Introduction à la Littérature religieuse judéo-hellénistique Tome I (Pseudépigraphes de l'Ancien Testament)* (Turnhout: Brepols, 2000), 173–99.

Díez Macho, Alejandro, with Maria Angeles Navarro and Miguel Perez Fernandez, *Apócrifos del Antiguo Testamento, Vol. 1: Introducción general a los Apócrifos del Antiguo Testamento* (Madrid: Ediciones Cristiandad, 1984), 276–79.

Ellul, Danielle, "Le Testament d'Abraham: Mémoire et source d'imaginaire, la pesée des âmes," *FoiVie* 89 (1990), 73–82.

Fishburne, Charles W., "I Corinthians III.10–15 and the Testament of Abraham," *NTS* 17 (1970) 109–15.

Frey, J.-B., "Abraham (Testament D')," *Dict. Bib.* Suppl. vol. 1 (Paris: Letouzey et Ané, 1928), 33–38.

Ginzberg, Louis, "Abraham (Testament of)," in *JE* 1 (1904), 93–96.

Gruen, Erich S., *Diaspora: Jews amidst Greeks and Romans* (Cambridge, Mass./ London: Harvard University Press, 2002), 182–212.

Harrington, Daniel J., "Abraham Traditions in the Testament of Abraham and in the 'Rewritten Bible' of the Intertestamental Period," in Nickelsburg, *Studies*, 165–71.

Kaufmann, J., "Abrahams Testament," *Encyclopaedia Judaica*, vol. 1 (Berlin, 1928), 561–65.

Kohler, Kaufmann, "The Pre-Talmudic Haggada II. C—The Apocalypse of Abraham and its Kindred," *JQR* 7 (1895), 581–606.

Kolenkow, Anita Bingham, "The Angelology of the Testament of Abraham," in Nickelsburg, *Studies*, 153–62.

—, "The Genre Testament and the Testament of Abraham", in Nickelsburg, *Studies*, 139–52.

—, "What is the Role of Testament in the Testament of Abraham?", *HTR* 67 (1974), 182–84.

Kraft, R. A., "Reassessing the Recensional Problem in the Testament of Abraham," in Nickelsburg, *Studies*, 121–37.

Kuhn, Peter, *Offenbarungsstimmen im Antiken Judentum* (TSAJ 20; Tübingen: Mohr-Siebeck, 1989), 110–14.

Loewenstamm, Samuel E., "The Testament of Abraham and the Texts concerning the Death of Moses," in Nickelsburg, *Studies*, 219–25.

Ludlow, Jared Warner, *Abraham Meets Death: Narrative Humor in the Testament of Abraham* (JSPSup 41; Sheffield: Sheffield Acadamic Press, 2002).

MacRae, G., "The Judgment Scene in the Coptic Apocalypse of Paul," in Nickelsburg, *Studies*, 285–88.

Macurdy, G.H., "Platonic Orphism in the *Testament of Abraham*", *JBL* 61 (1942), 213–26.

Maguire, Henry, "The Depiction of Sorrow in Middle Byzantine Art," in *Dumbarton Oaks Papers Number Thirty-One* (Washington D.C.: Dumbarton Oaks Centre for Byzantine Studies, 1977), 122–74.

Martin, Raymond A., "Syntax Criticism of the Testament of Abraham," in Nickelsburg, *Studies*, 95–120.

Martin, Troy W., "The TestAbr and the Background of 1 Pet 3,6," *ZNW* 90 (1999), 139–46.

Munoa, Philip B., III, *Four Powers in Heaven: The Interpretation of Daniel 7 in the Testament of Abraham* (JSPSup 28; Sheffield: Sheffield Academic Press, 1998).

Nickelsburg, George W. E. Jr., "Eschatology in the Testament of Abraham: A Study of the Judgment Scene in the Two Recensions," in Nickelsburg, *Studies*, 23–64.

—, *Jewish Literature Between the Bible and the Mishnah* (Philadelphia: Fortress, 1981), 248–53.

—, "Review of the Literature," in Nickelsburg, *Studies*, 9–22.

—, "Stories of Biblical and Early Post-Biblical Times," in *Jewish Writings of the Second Temple Period: Apocrypha, Pseudepigrapha, Qumran Sectarian Writings, Philo, Josephus* (CRINT 2; ed. Michael E. Stone; Assen/Philadelphia: Van Gorcum/Fortress, 1984), 59–64.

—, "Structure and Message in the Testament of Abraham," in Nickelsburg, *Studies*, 85–93.

—, ed., *Studies in the Testament of Abraham* (SBLSCS 6; Missoula, Mont.: Scholars Press, 1976).

—, "Summary and Prospects for Future Work," in Nickelsburg, *Studies*, 289–98.

Pearson, B., "The Pierpont Morgan Fragments of a Coptic Enoch Apocryphon," in Nickelsburg, *Studies*, 227–83.

Piattelli, Elio, "'Il Testamento di Abramo' (Testo apocalittico del I secolo dell' E.V.)," *Annuario di Studi Ebraici* 2 (1964–65), 111–22.

Reiser, Marius, *Jesus and Judgment: The Eschatological Proclamation in Its Jewish Context* (Minneapolis: Fortress, 1997), 123–29.

Sanders, E.P., "The Testament of Abraham," in *Outside the Old Testament* (ed. M. de Jonge; Cambridge: Cambridge University Press, 1985), 56–70.

Schmidt, F., "The Two Recensions of the *Testament of Abraham*: In Which Way Did the Transformation Take Place?", in Nickelsburg, *Studies*, 65–83.

—. "Le monde à l'image du bouclier d'Achille: sur la naissance et l'incorruptibilité du monde dans le 'Testament d'Abraham,'" *Bulletin de la Société Ernest-Renan* 22 (1973), 14–18 = *RHR* 185 (1974), 122–26.

—, "Traditions relatives à Abraham dans la littérature juive hellénistique," *École Pratique des Hautes-Études*, Section Sciences religieuses 80–81/3 (1971–73), 321–23.

Schürer, E., *The History of the Jewish People in the Age of Jesus Christ (175 B.C.– A.D. 135)* (3 vols.; ed. Geza Vermes, Fergus Millar, and Martin Goodman; Edinburgh: T. & T. Clark, 1987), 3/2:761–67.

Turdeanu, Émile, "Notes sur la tradition littéraire du Testament d'Abraham," *Silloge bizantina in onore di Silvio Giuseppe Mercati* (Studi bizantini e neo ellenici 9; Rome: Associazione Nazionale per gli Studi Bizantini, 1957), 405–10.

—, "Le Testament d'Abraham en slave et en roumain", *Oxford Slavonic Papers* 10 (1977), 1–38; reprinted in *Apocryphes slaves et roumains de l'Ancien Testament* (SVTP 5; Leiden: Brill, 1981), 202–38.

Turner, Nigel, "The Testament of Abraham: A Study of the Original Language, Place of Origin, Authorship, and Relevance" (Doctoral Thesis, University of London, 1953).

—, "The *Testament of Abraham*: Problems in Biblical Greek," *NTS* 1 (1954–55), 219–23.

Visotzky, Burton L., "The Conversation of Palm Trees," in *Tracing the Threads: Studies in the Vitality of Jewish Pseudepigrapha* (ed. John C. Reeves; Atlanta: Scholars Press, 1994), 205–14.

Ward, Roy Bowen, "Abraham Traditions in Early Christianity," in Nickelsburg, *Studies*, 173–184.

Wills, L. M., "The *Testament of Abraham* as a Satirical Novel," in *The Jewish Novel in the Ancient World* (Ithaca/London: Cornell University Press, 1995), 245–56.

Other Literature (cited more than once)

Allison, Dale C., Jr., *The New Moses: A Matthean Typology* (Philadelphia: Fortress, 1993).

Barclay, John M. G., *Jews in the Mediterranean Diaspora: From Alexander to Trajan (323 BCE – 118 CE)* (Edinburgh: T. & T. Clark, 1996).

Barr, James, "Seeing the Wood for the Trees? An enigmatic Ancient Translation," *JSS* 13 (1968), 11–20.

Bowley, J. E., "The Compositions of Abraham," in *Tracing the Threads: Studies in the Vitality of Jewish Pseudepigrapha* (ed. J. C. Reeves, SBLEJL 6; Atlanta: Scholars Press, 1994), 215–38.

Brandon, S. G. F., *The Judgment of the Dead: An Historical and Comparative Study of the Idea of a Post-Mortem Judgment in the Major Religions* (London: Weidenfeld & Nicolson, 1967).

Erffa, Hans Martin von, *Ikonologie der Genesis: Die christlichen Bildthemen aus dem Alten Testament und ihre Quellen*, vol. 2 (Munich: Deutscher Kunstverlag, 1995).

Forman, Werner, and Stephen Quirke, *Hieroglyphs and the Afterlife in Ancient Egypt* (Norman, Okl: University of Oklahoma Press, 1996).

Fossum, Jarl, *The Name of God and the Angel of the Lord: Samaritan and Jewish Concepts of Intermediation and the Origin of Gnosticism* (WUNT 36; Tübingen: Mohr-Siebeck, 1985).

Ginzberg, Louis, *The Legends of the Jews* (7 vols.; Philadelphia: Jewish Publication Society, 1942).

Goodenough, E. R., *Jewish Symbols from the Greco-Roman Period* (11 vols.; New York: Pantheon, 1953–64).

Green, Arthur, *Keter: The Crown of God in Early Jewish Mysticism* (Princeton: Princeton University Press, 1997).

Gregg, Robert C., and Dan Urman, *Jews, Pagans, and Christians in the Golan Heights: Greek and Other Inscriptions of the Roman and Byzantine Eras* (SFSHJ 140; Atlanta: Scholars Press, 1996).

Griffiths, J. Gwyn, *The Divine Verdict: A Study of Divine Judgement in the Ancient Religions* (SHR 52; Leiden/New York/København/Köln: Brill, 1991).

Hamann-Mac Lean, Richard, and Horst Hallensleben, *Die Monumentalmalerei in Serbien und Makedonien vom 11. bis zum frühen 14. Jahrhundert* (Gießen: W. Schmitz, 1963).

Hannah, D. D., *Michael and Christ: Michael Traditions and Angel Christology in Early Christianity* (WUNT 2.109; Tübingen: Mohr-Siebeck, 1999).

Horst, Pieter van der, *Ancient Jewish Inscriptions: An Introductory Survey of a Millennium of Jewish Funerary Epigraphy* (Kampen: Kok Pharos, 1991).

Johnson, Gary J., *Early-Christian Epitaphs from Anatolia* (TT 35, ECLS 8; Atlanta: Scholars Press, 1995).

Kugel, James L., *Traditions of the Bible: A Guide to the Bible as It Was at the Start of the Common Era* (Cambridge: Harvard University Press, 1998).

Lattimore, Richard, *Themes in Greek and Latin Epitaphs* (Urbana, Ill.: University of Illinois, 1962).

Loewenstamm, Samuel E., "The Death of Moses," in Nickelsburg, *Studies*, 185–217.

Mach, Michael, *Entwicklungsstadien des jüdischen Engelglaubens in vorrabbinischer Zeit* (TSAJ 34; Tübingen: Mohr-Siebeck, 1992).

Mader, Evaristus, *Mambre: Die Ergebnisse der Ausgrabungen im heiligen Bezirk Râmet el Halîl in Südpalästina 1926–1928*, 2 vols. (Freiburg im Breisgau: E. Wewel, 1957).

Morenz, Siegfried, *Die Geschichte von Joseph dem Zimmermann* (TU 56; Berlin: Akademie-Verlag, 1951).

Müller, C. Detlef G., *Die Engellehre der Koptischen Kirche: Untersuchungen zur Geschichte der christlichen Frömmigkeit in Ägypten* (Wiesbaden: O. Harrassowitz, 1959).

Naveh, Joseph and Shaul Shaked, *Amulets and Magic Bowls: Aramaic Incantations of Late Antiquity* (Jerusalem/Leiden: Magnes/Brill, 1985).

—, *Magic Spells and Formulae: Aramaic Incantations of Late Antiquity* (Jerusalem: Magnes, 1993).

Richardson, Emeline, *The Etruscans: Their Art and Civilization* (Chicago/London: University of Chicago Press, 1964).

Rohland, Johannes Peter, *Der Erzengel Michael: Arzt und Feldherr. Zwei Aspekte des vor- und frühbyzantinischen Michaelskultes* (BZRG 19; Leiden: Brill, 1977).

Sanders, E. P., *The Tendencies of the Synoptic Tradition* (SNTSMS 9; Cambridge: Cambridge University Press, 1969).

Stichel, Rainer, *Studien zum Verhältnis von Text und Bild spät- und nachbyzantinischer Vergänglichkeitsdarstellungen* (Byzantina Vindobonensia 5; Wien/Köln/Graz: Böhlau in Komm., 1971).

Strotmann, Angelika, *"Mein Vater bist du!" (Sir 51,10): Zur Bedeutung der Vaterschaft Gottes in kanonischen und nichtkanonischen frühjüdischen Schriften* (Frankfurter Theologische Studien 39; Frankfurt am Main: J. Knecht, 1991).

Theissen, Gerd, *The Miracle Stories of the Early Christian Tradition* (Philadelphia: Fortress, 1983).

VanderKam, James C., *Enoch: A Man for All Generations* (Columbia, S.C.: University of South Carolina Press, 1995).

Wenger, Antoine, *L'Assomption de la T.S. Vierge dans la tradition Byzantine du VIe au Xe siècle: Études et documents* (Paris: Institut français d'études byzantines, 1955).

Wright, Benjamin G., *A Multiform Heritage: Studies on Early Judaism and Christianity in Honor of Robert A. Kraft* (Atlanta: Scholars Press, 1999).

Zandee, Jan, *Death as an Enemy, according to Ancient Egyptian Conceptions* (Leiden: Brill, 1960).

COMMENTARY

Chapter 1:
Abraham's Virtues, Michael's Assignment

Bibliography: Schmidt, "Testament," 2:124, 136. Turner, "Testament," 108–10.

Long Recension

1:1. Abraham lived the measure of his life, nine hundred and ninety-five years, and all the years of his life he passed in quietness, meekness, and righteousness. The just man was altogether very kind to strangers. 1:2. For he pitched his tent at the crossroads of the Oak of Mamre, where he welcomed all—rich and poor, kings and rulers, the crippled and the helpless, friends and strangers, neighbors and travelers. These the pious and all-holy, righteous, and hospitable Abraham welcomed equally. 1:3. But even upon this one came the common and inexorable bitter cup of death and the uncertain end of life. 1:4. So the Master God called his archangel Michael and said to him: "Go down, commander-in-chief Michael, to my friend Abraham and speak to him concerning death, so that he might put his affairs in order. 1:5. For I have blessed him as the stars of heaven and as the sand by the shore of the sea. He has a prosperous life with many things and is exceedingly rich. Yet above all other people he has been righteous, good, hospitable, and strongly affectionate to the end. 1:6. Now you, archangel Michael, go from here to my friend Abraham, my beloved, and announce to him his death and assure him

Short Recension fam. E

1:1. It came to pass, when the days for Abraham to depart drew near, that the Lord spoke to Michael, saying, 1:2. "Rise and go to Abraham and say to him, 'You will indeed depart from this life, 1:3 for the days have arrived for you to put your house in order, before you are removed from the world.'"

of this: 1:7. at this time you are about to go out of this futile world, and you are about to depart from the body, and you will go to your own Master among the good."

TEXTUAL NOTES ON THE LONG RECENSION

1:1. B Q: ἐννακόσια ἐνενήκοντα πέντε (995). P V have 95, which must be a scribal error—an eye has passed from the εν in ἐννακόσια (900) to the εν in ἐνενήκοντα (90). A: ἐννακόσια ἐνενήκοντα ἐννέα (999).[1] H: 990 (πέντε omitted perhaps through *homoioteleuton*—the scribe has skipped from πέντε to πάντα). J: 905 (ἐνενήκοντα omitted by mistake?). G: 590 (πεντακόσια for ἐννακόσια and πέντε omitted; cf. H). I has ἑκατὸν ἑβδομήκοντα πέντε (175) in accord with Gen 25:7. Positing the reading of B Q (995) as original explains the most variants.[2] // H abbreviates by dropping "and all ... life." 1:2. J skips from πάντας to ἄρχοντας, omitting "welcomed" and "rich ... rulers." This is probably due not to *homoioteleuton* but deliberate abbreviation: πάντας ἀναπήρους ... ὑπεδέχετο makes perfect sense. 1:3. B J Q drop "common and" and substitute μυστήριον for ποτήριον. 1:4. B J Q omit "so that ... in order." 1:5. J abbreviates: "He has, etc." becomes simply: "He is exceedingly rich." // For εὐπορίᾳ (so B Q; G adds πολλῇ), A reads ἐμπορίᾳ (so too I H, with πολλῇ). 1:6. J drops "and announce ... death." 1:7. J omits: "and you are about to depart ... good." // G H lack "and you are about to depart ... body."

COMMENTARY

Chap. 1 contains two sections that together set *TA*'s stage. The first section is a sort of preface that summarily characterizes Abraham's virtues (vv. 1–2). Such summaries are common at the beginning of many of Plutarch's *Lives* and are a staple of other biographical and hagiographical literature; cf. Ps.-Callisthenes, *Hist. Alex. Magn. rec.* β 1; Gregory of Nyssa, *In laudem Basilii fratris* 1, ed. Stein, pp. 2, 4; Pontius of Carthage, *Vit. Cypriani* 1; John the Monk, *Artemii pass.* 1; Gerontius of Jerusalem, *Vit. Melaniae*, ed. Gorce, prologue; *Vit. John the Almsgiver* 1; *Vit. Thomas of*

---

[1] Cf. perhaps the number of souls that die every day in the Arabic and the Ethiopic respectively—99,999 and 90,999.

[2] The Ethiopic has Abraham live to be 195, the Arabic and the long Romanian 175, the Coptic 170.

Lesbos 1 = *Acta Sanctorum* Nov. 4 (1925), 234; *Vit. Pistenius* in the Ethiopic *Synaxarium*; Constantine Akropolites, *Vit. Zotici*, ed. Miller, p. 346 (stressing Zotikos' philanthropy); etc. These parallels are partial justification for James's judgment that much of chap. 1 belongs to a "mediaeval redactor."[3] No events from Abraham's life merit mention. The focus is instead upon his character. What matters is not his role in salvation-history but purported virtues, which make his later opposition to God so unexpected and comical. The second section, a record of the first of several conversations between God and Michael, explains the archangel's mission, which will be frustrated: he is to descend and tell Abraham to prepare for death (vv. 3–7).

TA 1 echoes LXX Genesis in several particulars:

1:1	ἔζησεν Ἀβραάμ ... τῆς ζωῆς αὐτοῦ
LXX Gen 25:7	ζωῆς Ἀβραάμ ὅσα ἔζησεν
1:1	δικαιοσύνη
LXX Gen 15:6	δικαιοσύνην
1:2	τῆς δρυὸς τῆς Μαβρῆς
LXX Gen 13:18	τὴν δρῦν Μαμβρή (cf. 14:13; 18:1)
1:5	ηὐλόγησα αὐτόν
LXX Gen 14:19	ηὐλόγησεν τὸν Ἀβράμ (cf. 12:2)
1:5	ὡς τὰ ἄστρα τοῦ οὐρανοῦ καὶ ὡς τὴν ἄμμον τὴν παρὰ τὸ χεῖλος τῆς θαλάσσης
LXX Gen 22:17	ὡς τοὺς ἀστέρας τοῦ οὐρανοῦ καὶ ὡς τὴν ἄμμον τὴν παρὰ τὸ χεῖλος τῆς θαλάσσης

Beyond these links, the emphasis upon Abraham's hospitality (vv. 1, 2, 5) sends one to the famous Gen 18:1–15—a text so well represented in ancient Jewish and Christian art[4]—where Abraham welcomes three strangers. The subject of his death takes the scripturally literate to Gen 25:7–11, where the Bible finishes his story. From the outset, then, *TA* encourages readers to recall Scripture. Although it rewrites and even contradicts the Bible, *TA* inevitably functions as a sort of supplement to it, and readers cannot but relate the two texts to each other.

RecShrt. 1 is, compared with RecLng. 1, very brief. It offers no extended characterization of Abraham, and nothing is said about his hospitality. Also missing is his age at death and the clear scriptural echoes (see above), although fam. B F G's ἐπληρώθησαν αἱ ἡμέραι τῆς προσκαίρου ζωῆς σου is

---

[3] James, *Testament*, 120.
[4] See von Erffa, *Ikonologie*, 2:91–102. Eusebius, *Dem. ev.* 5.9, already refers to a picture of this scene.

reminiscent of LXX Gen 25:7–8 (ἡμερῶν ζωῆς ... πλήρης ἡμερῶν); and B F G's characterization of Abraham as παντευλογήτου may be an echo of Gen 22:17 (or of RecLng.'s quotation of that verse, 1:5). RecShrt.'s brevity also appears from the way fam. E introduces Michael, who remains nothing but a name.

The distance in vocabulary between RecLng. and RecShrt. fam. E is striking. They say the same things in different ways. Ἀβραάμ, Μιχαήλ, λέγω, βίος, ἐκ(έρχομαι), and κόσμος are the only common words. Because the narratives are so different in additional ways, one can hardly here entertain the possibility of translation variants of the same Semitic original. More plausible is the guess that the author of something close to RecShrt. had heard or read something close to RecLng. and later freely reproduced an abbreviated version of what he remembered without the text in front of him. One could equally urge the opposite, that the author of RecLng. had heard or read something close to RecShrt. and, instead of reproducing the text closely, creatively expanded what he remembered.

1:1. **Abraham is 995 years of age.**[5] This disagrees with LXX Gen 25:7, which like the MT, the targums, and the rabbinic sources, says that Abraham lived to be 175 (cf. *Jub.* 21:2; 22:7; 23:8). *TA* may nonetheless be under the influence of the LXX at this point: both 1:1 and LXX Gen 25:7 name Abraham, use ζωῆς and ἔζησεν, and end by stating the number of years, ἔτη. One may in any case observe that opening the story of a life with (καὶ) ἔζησεν is a feature of the short biographies in Genesis 5 and 11 (the latter introduces Abraham's saga).

By increasing Abraham's lifespan to an incredible 995, *TA* makes him live longer than anyone else. Methuselah lived to be 969 (Gen 5:27). So Abraham belongs in the company of the antediluvians who lived such long lives (see esp. Genesis 5) and surpasses them all. Within the broader context, the incredible age, spectacularly overdone like the 7,000 servants of 17:18, not only adds to his greatness (cf. *Jub.* 23:8–13; Josephus, *Ant.* 1.104–108) but makes it all the more absurd when he refuses to obey Michael: having outlived everybody, he wants even more time. The exaggeration is in any case typical of midrashic hyperbole; cf. *T. Job* 9:2, which gives Job 130,000 sheep instead of the 7,000 of Job 1:3.

The *Testaments of the Twelve Patriarchs* give the ages of the twelve sons of Israel sometimes at the beginning (so for Reuben, Simeon, Zebulon, Dan, Naphtali, Gad, Asher), sometimes at the end (Levi, Jacob, Issachar,

---

[5] RecShrt. 2:1 fam. E speaks of Abraham as "very advanced in years" but leaves the age unspecified.

Joseph, Benjamin). Other Testaments fail to remark on the age of their heroes at death: *Testament of Job, Testament of Solomon, Testament of Moses, Testament of Isaac, Testament of Jacob.* For τὸ μέτρον τῆς ζωῆς αὐτοῦ see 15:1; Gk. *L.A.E.* 13:6; Cyril of Alexandria, *Ador.* PG 68.1117C; Epiphanius, *De mensuris et ponderibus*, ed. Moutsoulas, p. 713; Proclus, *Plat. Tim. comm.* 1.192; Michael Psellus, *Chronog.* 3.16.

Abraham has four virtues; cf. the list in Ambrose, *Abr.* 5.32: piety, faith, wisdom, righteousness, love, chastity, hospitality. The first virtue is ἡσυχία, quietness (cf. 17:7, of Death coming for saints, and Slav. P T 6:6: Michael's voice is "tranquil"). This trait characterized the Pythagoreans and later became an important Christian word signifying, among other things, stillness of soul and separation from the world (Lampe, s.v.; cf. the Hesychasts of Eastern Orthodoxy). It appears often in Christian biographical and hagiographical literature: Gregory of Nyssa, *Vit. Macrinae* 26; Theodoret of Cyrrhus, *Hist. rel.* 1.2; 2.13; Ps.-Palladius, *Hist. mon.* prol. 2; etc. In the LXX the word is most often used as a synonym of social peace (1 Chr 4:40; 2 Macc 12:3; Ecclus 28:16; cf. *Sib. Or.* 3:703). But already in Prov 11:12 we read that "a sensible person keeps quiet," ἡσυχίαν; cf. *Ps. Sol.* 12:5; Philo, *Abr.* 201; *Vit. cont.* 31, 75, 80; 1 Tim 2:11–12; *T. Ash.* 6:6. Perhaps Jewish tradition associated this characteristic with Abraham, for Philo typifies Abraham as "quiet": he sought to end quarrels "quietly" (ἡσυχῇ, *Abr.* 210, cf. 216), and he mourned for Sarah with moderation of feeling and "in quiet" (again ἡσυχῇ, *Abr.* 257). In *TA*, in 3:4 and 12, Abraham keeps quiet about miracles he has witnessed (for which RecShrt. 3:4 fam. E uses ἡσυχάζω). But in other ways he hardly seems quiet. He speaks exactly what he feels, to Michael, God, and Death, and can even be rude (7:12; 17:1–2); he is anything but pliant. So one can interpret the remark that Abraham has ἡσυχία as either ineptitude on the part of a later redactor or as part of the comic setup: the patriarch will not act as expected.

Abraham is also "meek" (πραότητι; πραότης*), an attribute paired with ἡσυχία in Plutarch, *Comp. Eum. Sert.* 2.1; *Mor.* 823F; Chrysostom, *Hom. Gen.* PG 53.313; 54.486; *Exp. Ps.* PG 55.631; Theodoret of Cyrrhus, *Hist. rel.* 11.2; Ps.-Palladius, *Hist. mon.* 4.1–2. The Bible associates this virtue above all with Moses (Num 12:3), who became Judaism's exemplar in meekness: Ecclus 45:3–5; Philo, *Mos.* 1.26; 2.79; *b. Ned.* 38a; etc. Given that *TA* models Abraham upon the law-giver, one might reckon the virtue as part of a wider Moses typology; see pp. 24–26 and cf. *Petirat Moshe* (*BHM* 1:120). But the rabbis stress Abraham's humility,[6] and mildness or

---

[6]   Samuel Sandmel, "Philo's Place in Judaism: A Study of Conceptions of Abraham in Jewish Literature," *HUCA* 26 (1955), 203–204.

meekness—especially needful for kings (cf. Isocrates, *Nic.* 23; Plutarch, *Mor.* 781A)—was widely praised in both the Greek and Jewish worlds: Plato, *Crit.* 120E; *Resp.* 375C; Lucian, *Somn.* 10; *Let. Arist.* 257, 263; *Jos. Asen.* 23:10; Josephus, *Ant.* 19.330; *2 En.* 50:2; *m. Soṭah* 9:15; *ARN* A 7; *b. Soṭah* 40a, 49b; etc.[7] It really ill suits *TA*'s Abraham, who so strenuously refuses to co-operate with Michael and shows no mercy to sinners (10:13). Is there not great irony here?

"Righteousness" (δικαιοσύνη; cf. 12:12, 18; 13:9, 10, 13; 14:2, 4; 17:7), often paired with πραότης in patristic literature under the influence of LXX Ps 44:5 (πραΰτητος καὶ δικαιοσύνης), is the quality of being "law-abiding," as in Matt 5:20 (cf. Luke 1:6). For its association with "meekness" outside of patristic sources see *T. Jud.* 24:1 and Matt 5:5–6; and for its pairing with ἡσυχία note Philo, *Abr.* 27; *Praem.* 157. Jews believed that, even before Moses received the law, the pious obeyed Torah, and Ecclus 44:19 says that Abraham "kept the law of the Most High"; cf. *Jub.* 6:17–19; *m. Qidd.* 4:14; *Gen. Rab.* 64:4. The Scripture itself attributes "righteousness" to him, most notably in Gen 15:6; cf. 18:19; 20:5; 21:23; 24:27; Josephus, *Ant.* 1.158 (ἦν δίκαιος ἀνήρ); Rom 4:3, 9; Gal 3:6; Jas 2:23; *Memar Marqah* 4:12 (Abraham is "first of the righteous"). Again, however, Abraham, who fails to hearken to God's declared will as Michael speaks it, will not live up to his billing.

The last item on the opening list of virtues is Abraham's hospitable nature, which chaps. 2ff. illustrate vividly. Here there is no irony or inflation: Abraham acts in accord with the narrator's characterization—at least until Death shows up in chap. 16. For φιλόξενος (LXX: 0) see vv. 2, 5; ms. J title; RecShrt. fam. B F G title (cf. 17:7 and 10:15, both with φιλοξενία). Because of the story in Genesis 18, the patriarch was renowned for this attribute: Philo, *Abr.* 107–114; *Quaest. Gen.* 4.8, 10; Josephus, *Ant.* 1.196 (νομίσας εἶναι ξένους), 200; *1 Clem.* 10:7; *T. Jac.* 7:22; Clement of Alexandria, *Paed.* 3.10; Ambrose, *Abr.* 1.32; *La Chaîne sur la Genèse* 1050 *ad* Gen 18:1; 1056 *ad* Gen 18:2; Ps.-Athanasius, *Quaest. Ev.* PG 28.708D (φιλόξενος ἦν ὁ Ἀβραάμ); Chrysostom, *Laz.* PG 48.988 (φιλόξενος ἦν ὁ Ἀβραάμ); Timothy of Alexandria, *Discourse on Abbaton*, ed. Budge, fol. 4b; *Vit. Elizabeth the Wonderworker* 2 = *Analecta Bollandiana* 91 (1973), 252; Gregory the Pagurite, *Encom. Pancratius*, ed. Stallman-Pacitti, p. 361; Peter the Monk, *Vit. John* 72 = *Acta Sanctorum* Nov. 2.1 (1894), 435; *ARN* A 7; *b. Soṭah* 10a; *b. B. Meṣiʿa* 86b; Tg. Ps.-Jn. Gen 21:33; *Gen. Rab.* 43:7; 47:10; *Deut. Rab.* 11:3; *Pesiq. Rab.* 42:3; etc. (In contrast to

---

[7]   See further Deirdre J. Good, *Jesus the Meek King* (Harrisburg, Pa.: Trinity Press Intl., 1999).

rabbinic tradition, *TA* does not link Abraham's hospitality to his making proselytes.) Arabic tradition calls Abraham "the father of hosts," and the main theme of Chrysostom's sermon on Genesis 18 is hospitality: *Hom. Gen.* PG 53.374–85 (again and again in this Abraham is ὁ δίκαιος). See further on v. 2. Heb 13:2 enjoins hospitality with Abraham clearly in mind (so already Chrysostom, ibid. PG 53.378), and he is presumably a host in Matt 8:11–12 = Luke 13:28–29. Like "righteousness," then, both Old and New Testament attest to Abraham's hospitality.

Ancient literature often extols φιλοξενία: Lev 19:33–34; Job 31:32; Tob 4:16; Ps.-Aristotle, *Virt. vit.* 1250b–1251b; Ovid, *Metam.* 8.618–724; Aphthonius, *Progymnasmata* 4; Philo, *Virt.* 105–106; Arrian, *Epict. diss.* 1.28.23; Dio Chrysostom, *Dei cogn.* 76; Luke 14:12–14; Rom 12:13; Tit 1:8; 1 Pet 4:9; Josephus, *Ant.* 1.250–252; *T. Zeb.* 6:5; *Did.* 4:7; Herm. *Mand.* 8.10; Herm. *Sim.* 9.27.2; *Vis. Paul* 27; *m. 'Abot* 1:15; Johnson, *Anatolia* 4.15; etc.; and there are famous stories about hospitality outside of Judaism that cultured Jews or Greco-Roman readers might recall—Homer, *Od.* 17.485–487, for example, and Ovid, *Metam.* 8.613–715. *b. Šabb.* 127a says that "hospitality to wayfarers is greater than welcoming the presence of the Shekinah."[8] Given that *TA* compares Abraham to Job (15:15), one should keep in mind that the theme also plays a central role in the traditions about Job: Job 29:12–16; 31:16–23, 32; *T. Job* 9–13; *ARN* A 7; etc.

1:2. πηγνύμι* + σκηνή (cf. 5:11; 6:4; 20:14) occurs over a dozen times in the LXX, most often for נטה + אהל = "pitch a tent" (Gen 26:25; Exod 33:7; etc.), although never in the story of Abraham; and the idiom is otherwise common: *Vit. Proph. Habakkuk* 12; Philo, *Gig.* 54; etc. Genesis, however, refers often to Abraham's "tent" (σκηνή; Gen 12:8; 13:3–4; 18:1, 2, 6, 9, 10), and it, with Sarah inside, appears regularly in Jewish and Christian art depicting the visit of the three angels in Genesis 18 (e.g. at Dura Europos). The LXX, moreover, twice speaks of Abraham "making" his tent (Gen 12:8; 13:4 A; cf. *Jub.* 16:21). Whereas in the Bible Abraham presumably lives in his tent, in *TA* it is not his home (cf. 3:1) but rather a sort of way station for travelers.

The patriarch's tent is by τῆς δρυὸς τῆς Μαβρῆς (cf. 2:1; 6:4; 20:11), as in Gen 18:1 (MT: בְּאֵלֹנֵי מַמְרֵא LXX: τῇ δρυὶ τῇ Μαμβρῇ); cf. 13:18; 14:13; *Jub.* 14:10; Gk. fr. *Jub.* 16:10 (Μαβρῆ δρυός); 1QapGen 21:19; 22:29–32; 4QAgesCreat frags. 2–4 2:4; Josephus, *Ant.* 1.196; Justin, *Dial.* 56, 86,

---

[8]   Additional rabbinic texts in Strack-Billerbeck 4:565–69. For an overview of hospitality among Greeks, Romans, Jews, and Christians see G. Stählin, *TDNT* 5 (1967), 17–25.

126.[9] The singular "Oak" in *TA* corresponds to the LXX, not to the plural of the MT.[10] Genesis refers to the "oak(s) of Mamre" three times. 13:18 says that Abraham settled and built an altar there, 14:13 that he lived there, 18:1 that the Lord appeared to him there. According to Gen 23:17, Mamre was near the burial place of the patriarchs, the cave of Machpelah (cf. 25:9; 35:27; 49:30; 50:13), and *TA* has Abraham buried "in the promised land by the Oak of Mamre" (20:11, q.v.). This makes for a nice *inclusio*: the book ends where it begins. By the first century CE a huge oak or terebinth near Hebron was identified as the famous tree of Genesis (Josephus, *Bell.* 4.533; *Ant.* 1.186; cf. 1.196 and *Bell.* 4.533), and the remains suggest that it was a place of worship.[11] Sozomen, *Hist. eccl.* 2.4, reports on an annual festival there. Jerome, *Ep.* 108.11, mentions a traveler who had seen what was left of Abraham's oak; cf. Eusebius, *Onom.*, ed. Klostermann, p. 76.1 (ἔτι νῦν δεικνυμένη τερέβινθος) and Adomnan, *De locis sanctis* 2.11. Eusebius, *Vit. Const.* 3.51–53, recounts the building of a church there to commemorate the event in Genesis 18, and archaeologists have found the gap in the pavement where the famous terebinth stood.[12]

Abraham is at a crossroads, τετράοδος* (the word is rare and unattested before Pausanias). So people come from the four points of the compass. Similarly in *T. Job* 8:6–7, they come from all regions, "and the four doors of my house were open"; cf. Job 31:32 and *ARN* A 7, which speaks of welcoming guests from the four directions, cites Job as an exemplar, and presents Abraham as surpassing Job: the patriarch went looking for wayfarers. Mamre was very near to or a part of Hebron/Kiriath-Arba (= "City of the Four"), and Hebron was a crossroads.[13]

The image of Abraham regularly receiving travelers recurs in *Gen. Rab.* 54:6. This fancifully construes Gen 21:33 to mean that Abraham built an inn, and that he welcomed passersby and gave them food and drink. *Gen. Rab.* 48:9, moreover, understands Gen 18:1–3 to be, in one important respect, typical, not exceptional: Abraham constantly wanted to serve

---

[9] The LXX manuscripts show several spellings: Μαμβρή, Μαμβρί, Μαβρῆ, Μαυρί, Μαυρῆ.

[10] The targums on Genesis consistently omit the oaks; they substitute "plain" or "vision." *Jub.* 13:1–2 has Abraham by "a tall oak," but this is not the Oak of Mamre.

[11] Cristiano Grottanelli, "The Ogygian Oak at Mamre and the Holy Town of Hebron," *Vicino Oriente* 2 (1979), 39–63, and Y. Magen, "Elonei Mamre: Herodian Cult Site," *Qadmoniot* 24 (1991), 46–55.

[12] See further Mader, *Mambre*, 2:237–97, 307–39. According to Philo, *Migr.* 165, "Mamre … in our language is 'from seeing,'" but this etymology plays no role in *TA*.

[13] Paul Wayne Ferris, Jr., "Hebron (Place)," *ABD* 3 (1992), 107.

travelers. Turner commented: "There appears to be some important connection between this part of TA and the rabbinic commentary on Gen. at
some stage in its transmission."[14] The connection is not literary. Rather,
TA and *Genesis Rabbah* presuppose an old tradition that Abraham dedicated himself to receiving strangers.

Five pairs of people represent those Abraham welcomes, ὑποδέχομαι*;
cf. RecShrt. 4:10 fam. E: ξένους ὑποδεχόμενος; the LXX never uses the word
in connection with Abraham. Taken together, these pairs show him to be
hospitable to all without exception; cf. *CIJ* 118: πάντων φίλος; *CIJ* 210:
anima bona omniorum. *ARN* A 7 similarly states that he had food for "any
who came by." The first, fourth, and fifth pairs are opposites whereas the
second and third sets are synonyms:

	dissimilar	*similar*
1	rich and poor	
2		kings and rulers
3		crippled and the helpless
4	friends and strangers	
5	neighbors and travelers	

For a similar list see 19:7. One may contrast those texts that, when
enumerating deeds of mercy, mention only the unfortunate and marginal:
Job 22:6–7; Isa 58:6–7; Isa 61:1; Matt 25:31–46; *T. Jac.* 2:23; *2 En.* 9:1;
42:8–9; Justin, *1 Apol.* 67; *b. Sotah* 14a; etc. The reason our list by contrast
includes the rich and kings is that the guests in Genesis 18 are divine. In
other words, Genesis depicts Abraham receiving the most honorable guests
imaginable, and later imagination expanded his hospitality so that it embraced also the unfortunate.

πλουσίους (cf. 1:5; 2:11; 19:7) καὶ πένητας (cf. 19:7) is a common
couple; see LXX 2 Βασ 12:1; Ps 48:3; Prov 14:20; Ecclus 13:18; etc. V. 5,
like Gen 13:2, calls Abraham himself rich (LXX: πλούσιος); cf. 1QapGen
20:31–34. For the synonymous βασιλεῖς τε καὶ ἄρχοντας, which belong
among the πλουσίους, see 4:3; LXX Ps 2:2; Isa 32:1; *Ps. Sol.* 5:11; Acts
4:26; etc. ἀναπήρους (ἀνάπηρος*; cf. Tob 14:2; 2 Macc 8:24; Acts 14:8) καὶ
ἀδυνάτους (ἀδύνατος*; often in LXX Job; cf. Tob 2:10; *3 Macc.* 4:18; *T.
Job* 9:2; Luke 14:13, 21), which belongs with the πένητας already mentioned, is not a conventional pairing. The last two pairs offer near synonymous parallelism: most "friends" are "neighbors," most "strangers" are
"travelers." With φίλους τε καὶ ξένους (cf. 3:9) cf. Plutarch, *Sol.* 5.3; Brutus,
Ep. 57.7; Porphyry, *Vit. Pyth.* 7; Constantine VII, *De legationibus* 295.

---

14   Turner, "Testament," 109.

There is no close parallel to γείτονας (γείτων*; cf. LXX Job 19:15 [for גּוּר];
Philo, *Conf.* 52; *Sib. Or.* 3:240, 459; 5:324; Luke 15:6; John 9:8; Josephus,
Ant. 5.50) τε καὶ παροδίτας (παροδίτης*; cf. Aq. 2 Βασ 12:4; *Acts John* 51,
95; *Sib. Or.* 14:33; Ps.-Athanasius, *Quaest. Ev.* PG 28.708D).

That Abraham is "righteous" (δίκαιος) and "hospitable" (φιλόξενος)
reiterates part of v. 1: δικαιοσύνη ... φιλόξενος. V. 2 adds two more virtues.
First, the patriarch is "pious." ὅσιος (cf. 9:2; 11:6; 12:15) most often
translates חסד[י]ד in the LXX. The word, which appears often in Jewish but
not Christian epitaphs—see e.g. *CIJ* 93, 158, 298[15]—is paired with δίκαιος
or a relative in Plato, *Gorg.* 507B; *1 En.* 25:5; 104:12; *Let. Arist.* 306; *Ps.
Sol.* 9:3; 10:5; Josephus, *Ant.* 9.35; *T. Gad* 5:4; *T. Benj.* 3:1; *CIJ* 321, 363,
482. Second, Abraham is "all holy." πανίερος (LXX: 0; NT: 0; Josephus:
0), which recurs in 18:1, becomes common only in Christian texts; see
Lampe, s.v., and Sophocles, *Lex.*, s.v.; one suspects a Byzantine hand.
Philo, however, does use it, even if not of people—e.g. *Virt.* 74 (the
heavenly hosts); *Her.* 75 (the mental sanctuary); *Vit. cont.* 36 (the Sabbath); *Legat.* 191 (houses of prayer).

Abraham serves God and neighbor; that is, he fulfils the two tables of
the Decalogue, the first of which summarize the demand for piety toward
the deity, the second of which require love of neighbor; cf. *T. Iss.* 5:2; 7:6;
T. Dan 5:3; Philo, *Virt.* 51, 95; *Spec. leg.* 2.63; *Decal.* 50–51, 106, 108–
110, 121; Justin, *Dial.* 44; Irenaeus, *Haer.* 4.16.3. Abraham displays, in
Philo's formulation, "holiness (ὁσιότης) to God and justice (δικαιοσύνη) to
people" (*Abr.* 208).

1:3. "Cup" (ποτήριον = כוס) most often appears figuratively in texts about
suffering, especially the suffering of God's wrath or judgment: Ps 11:6;
Lam 4:21; *Ps. Sol.* 8:14–15; Rev 16:19; *Asc. Isa.* 5:13; etc. This seems to
be the background for the use of "cup" in Gethsemane (Mark 14:36 par.;
cf. 10:38–39). But "the cup of death" (cf. 16:11, 12; RecShrt. does not use
the expression) has no such connotations in *TA*. This cup that comes upon
(ἔφθασε; cf. 5:8) Abraham is humanity's universal fate, "common" (κοινόν)
and "inexorable" (ἀπαραίτητον; ἀπαραίτητος*; cf. *Sib. Or.* 3:51; Wis
16:4, 16); cf. "the cup of Adam" = "the fate of death" in *Petirat Moshe*
(*BHM* 1:116). κοινός* frequently describes death on Greek epitaphs
(*EG* 35a.4; 67; 256.9; 266.1; 372.38; *IG* 2.3385.1; etc.) and in Byzantine literature (e.g. Vaticanus Gr. 207, f. 372r: ποτήριον νόμιζε κοινοῦ

---

[15] See further Leonard Victor Rutgers, *The Jews in Late Ancient Rome: Evidence of
Cultural Interaction in the Roman Empire* (RGRW 126; Leiden/New York/Co-
logne: Brill, 1995), 193–94.

θανάτου).[16] In 16:11 Death calls himself "the bitter cup of death," and he is the personification of the end that inevitably comes to all human beings (cf. 8:9). Cf. the targumim, which use the poetic expression, "taste the cup of death," without the connotation of wrath: Frg. Tg. Gen 40:23; Tg. Neof. 1 Gen 40:23; Tg. Neof. 1 Deut 32:1.[17] For Christian examples of τὸ ποτήριον τοῦ θανάτου (the antithesis of the Eucharist, τὸ ποτήριον τῆς ἀθανασίας) see Ps.-Callisthenes, *Hist. Alex. Magn.* rec. F 127.9; Ps.-Chrysostom, *Hom. Matt. 26:39 (In illud: Pater, si possibile est)* PG 61.753, 754, 756; George Monachus, *Chron. breve* PG 110.848A; etc. Later Byzantine art sometimes depicts Death administering a cup to the dying.[18]

The cup of death is πικρόν, a recurring word: 11:11; 13:12; 16:4 (of Death), 11 (of Death), 12 (of Death); 20:6, 7; cf. RecShrt. fam. E 13:15 (of Death); LXX 1 Βασ 15:32 (πικρὸς ὁ θάνατος for מר־המות); Eccles 7:26; *T. Job* 1:6; Josephus, *Ant.* 6.155; *Acts John* 113; Ephraem, *Metrical Hymns* 15, trans. Burgess, p. 42; Ps.-Ephraem, *Sermo de secundo aduentu et iudicio*, ed. Phrantzoles, p. 224.9 (πικρὸν καὶ δεινὸν τὸ ποτήριον; cf. *Sermo in eos, qui in Christo obdormierunt*, ed. Phrantzoles, p. 98.13); *Vit. Basil the Younger*, ed. Vilinskij 1.14 (Death makes Theodora drink a ποτήριον that is πικρόν); the inscription for the miniature in the Munich Psalter f. 1v (τὸ ποτήριον ποτίζει με τοῦ πικροῦ θανάτου).[19] If or how we should associate the cup's bitter taste with the myth that the Angel of Death's sword is tipped with gall, which he drops into the mouth of the sick that they might die (see *b. 'Abod. Zar.* 20b), is unclear. "Bitter" in any event prepares for Abraham's subsequent refusal to co-operate with Michael: no one likes what is "bitter." τὸ ἄδηλον τοῦ βίου πέρας (as also in 4:11) likewise anticipates the story to come: Abraham is not expecting death. In death, if not in life, Abraham is like everyone else. For πέρας of death see Demosthenes, *Cor.* 97; Aristotle, *Eth. nic.* 1115A; 2 Macc 5:8; etc.

---

16 G. Moravcsik, "Il Caronte Bizantino," *Rivista di studi bizantini e neoellenici* 3 (1931), 60.

17 R. Le Déaut, "Goûter le calice de la mort," *Bib* 43 (1962), 82–86; S. Speier, "Das Kosten des Todeskelches im Targum," *VT* 13 (1963), 344–45. Cf. the idiom, "to taste death," as in *Sib. Or.* 1:82; Mark 9:1; *Hist. Jos. Carp.* 22; *Gen. Rab.* 9:5; 21:5; etc. The long Romanian, ed. Roddy, p. 24, corresponding to RecLng. 1:3, has *gustări din paharul morţii*, "to taste from the cup of death."

18 Stichel, Vergänglichkeitsdarstellungen, 17–48 + plates 1–3. Does this image ultimately go back to Ancient Near Eastern depictions of deities on funerary stela holding what has been called "the cup of fate"? See James B. Pritchard, *The Ancient Near East in Pictures: Relating to the Old Testament* (2nd ed.; Princeton: Princeton University Press, 1969), plates 630, 632, 635, 636.

19 For this last see Stichel, Vergänglichkeitsdarstellungen, 25.

1:4. The text moves from earth to heaven, where we encounter God, here the "Master," ὁ δεσπότης θεός; cf. v. 7; 4:5; 8:2–3; 9:6; 11:4; 13:7; 15:9; 16:2–3; 20:12; LXX Job 5:8; Dan 9:15; Jonah 4:3; Wis 6:7; Ecclus 36:1 (δέσποτα ὁ θεός); Luke 2:29; Josephus, *Ant.* 1.20 (δεσπότης ὁ θεός); *3 Macc.* 5:28; Josephus, *Bell.* 3.373 (δεσπότην … τὸν θεόν); Rev 6:10; *Prot. Jas.* 17:2; Gk. *L.A.E.* 42:5; *CIJ* 358; Justin, *1 Apol.* 12.3; *Gk. Apoc. Ezra* 5:1, 6; *Apoc. Sedr.* 5:7; etc. Despite its early attestation, δεσπότης ὁ θεός is most common in patristic and Byzantine writers (Athanasius, Basil the Great, Chrysostom, Theodoret of Cyrrhus, Justinian, John of Damascus, George the Monk, etc.). δεσπότης is particularly appropriate here because only twice does the LXX Pentateuch use δεσπότης of God—both times in the story of Abraham (Gen 15:2, 8).

Although an angel announcing Abraham's death comes from the traditions about Moses (see p. 24), the motif shows up elsewhere, especially in later Christian hagiography; see e.g. *Hist. Jos. Carp.* 12; *Dorm. BMV* 3; *Acta graeca SS. Davidis, Symeonis et Georgii* 33, 36 in *Analecta Bollandiana* 18 (1899), 255, 257.

The second word of v. 4 is the inferential particle, τοίνυν, which reappears in 2:2. Of its 22 LXX instances, fully 10 are in *4 Maccabees*, a second temple book perhaps written in Alexandria (1:13, 15, 16, 17, 30, 31; 7:16; 13:1, 23; 16:1). Philo is also fond of the particle, which he uses almost 150 times.

God speaks to Μιχαήλ (= מיכאל, "Who is like God?"; cf. Exod 15:11; Deut 33:26), his "archangel," ἀρχάγγελον (LXX: 0; Josephus: 0); cf. Gk. *1 En.* 9:1 Sync.; Gk. *Jub.* 10:7; *L.A.E.* 25:2; 29:1; 45:1; Gk. *L.A.E.* 13:2; 37:6; Jude 9; Gk. *3 Bar.* 11:8; *4 Bar.* 9:5; *Gk. Apoc. Ezra* 1:3; *Apoc. Sedr.* 14:1; *PGM* 4.2357–2358; Theodoret of Cyrrhus, *Comm. Dan.* PG 81.1533.43; etc.[20] *1 En.* 24:6 calls him "chief of the angels"; cf. Heb. *T. Naph.* 8:4; *b.*

---

20   Lit. on Michael: Charles A. Gieschen, *Angelomorphic Christology: Antecedents and Early Evidence* (Leiden: Brill, 1998), 126–31; Hannah, *Michael*; Günter Lanczkowski, "Thot und Michael," *Mitteilungen des Deutschen Archaeologischen Instituts* 14 (1956), 117–12; Erik W. Larson, "Michael," in *Encyclopedia of the Dead Sea Scrolls* (ed. Lawrence H. Schiffman and James C. VanderKam; New York: Oxford University Press, 2000), 1:546–48; W. Lueken, *Michael: Eine Darstellung und Vergleichung der jüdischen und der morgenländisch-christlichen Tradition vom Erzengel Michael* (Göttingen: Vandenhoeck & Ruprecht, 1898); Michael Mach, "Michael," in *DDD*, 1299–1300; Cyril Mango, "St. Michael and Attis," *Deltion tēs Christianikēs Archaiologikēs Hetaireias* 12 (1984–86), 39–62; J. Michl, "Engel VII (Michael)," in *RAC* 5 (1962), 243–51; Müller, *Engellehre*, 8–35; Rohland, *Michael*; Victor Saxer, "Jalons pour servir à l'histoire du culte de l'archange saint Michel en orient jusqu'à l'iconoclasme," in *Noscere Sancta: Miscellanea in Memoria di Agostino Amore* (ed. Isaac Vázquez Janeiro; Rome: Pontificum Athenaeum Antonianum, 1985), 357–426. "Archangel" is his usual title in Greek iconographic tradition.

Yoma 37a. Older tradition tends to have four or seven archangels; Michael is always a member: *1 En.* 9–10; 20; 40:9; 87:2; 1QM 9:14–16; *Sib. Or.* 2:214–215; *Ep. Apos.* 13; *3 En.* 17:1 (Schäfer, *Synopse* 21 = 857); etc.; cf. *Ap. John* (NHC II,1) 17:29–32; Ps.-Bartholomew, *Book of the Resurrection of Jesus Christ*, ed. Budge, fol. 12b. The Old Testament names Michael three times—Dan 10:13, which introduces him as "one of the chief princes" (LXX Theod.: εἷς τῶν ἀρχόντων τῶν πρώτων), 21; and 12:1, which calls him "the great prince" (LXX: ὁ ἄγγελος ὁ μέγας; Theod.: ὁ ἄρχων ὁ μέγας) in charge of God's people; cf. *b. Ḥag.* 12b; *b. Menaḥ.* 110a. He is then in Jewish lore Israel's angelic patron; so also *1 En.* 20:5; *T. Mos.* 10:2 [?]; *b. Yoma* 77a; Tg. Ps.-Jn. Deut 32:9; Tg. Cant 8:9; cf. *Ps.-Clem. Rec.* 2:42. But some seemingly disputed this: *Jub.* 15:32; Ecclus 17:17. He fights on behalf of Israel, and later texts reiterate his status as a warrior; see e.g. 1QM 9:15 (his name is written on a tower shield); 17:6–8 (here Michael is seemingly "the prince of light");[21] 4Q285 fr. 6; *1 En.* 90:14; Rev 12:7; *b. Sanh.* 26a–b; Tg. Ps.-Jn. Gen 38:25–26 and Deut 34:3. This explains his other title, ἀρχιστράτηγος, "commander-in-chief" (cf. שר־(ה)צבא), which occurs over sixty times in RecLng.—"the author seems intent upon employing this denomination with numbing repetitiveness"[22]—in RecShrt. only in 1:1 mss. C D H I and 14:6 mss. A D; see also *Jos. Asen.* 14:7 v.l.; *2 En.* 22:6 J; 33:10; Gk. *3 Bar.* 11:4, 6, 7, 8; 13:3; *Gk. Apoc. Ezra* 4:24; *T. Isaac* 14:7; *Apoc. BMV* 23; *Gos. Bart.* 4:29; *PGM* 13.930; Theodosius of Alexandria, *Encom. on Michael*, ed. Budge, pp. 21.15, 22.26, 23.3, 47.26; Eustathius of Trake, *Encom. on Michael*, ed. Budge, p. 94.17.[23] Its origin probably lies in the identification of Michael with the ἀρχιστράτηγος δυνάμεως κυρίου who wields a sword in Josh 5:13–15 (cf. Origen, *Sel. Jes. Nav.* PG 12.821D;[24] Aphraates, *Fast.* 14; Ps.-Caesar of Nazianzus, *Dial.* 1.44); and it is consistent with the conception of angels as militaristic. Cf. the arrangement of angels into military units in 1QM. Other relevant texts include 2 Kgs 6:15–17; *4 Macc.* 4:10; *L.A.B.* 27:10; 61:8; Matt 26:53; *2 Bar.* 63:5–11; *3 En.* 22:6 (Schäfer, *Synopse* 33 = 869). ἀρχιστράτηγος remains a common title for Michael in Byzantine texts: Ps.-John of Damascus, *Ep. Theophilum* PG 95.377C; Constantine VII, *De insidiis*, ed. de Boor, p. 169.23; Anna Comnena, *Alex.* 4.6.6; etc.[25] Tradi-

---

21   See Maxwell T. Davidson, *Angels at Qumran: A Comparative Study of 1 Enoch 1–36, 72–108 and Sectarian Writings from Qumran* (Sheffield: Sheffield Academic Press, 1992), 148–49.
22   Gruen, *Diaspora*, 187–88.
23   See also Müller, *Engellehre*, 19. Gk. *Apoc. Ezra* 1:4 applies the title to Raphael.
24   On this text and its influence see Rohland, *Michael*, 50–59.
25   See further Rohland, ibid., 114–37.

tional Christian iconography depicts him with a sword in his right hand. *TA* nowhere hints at the popular Christian understanding of Michael as a healer, which perhaps grew partly out of Jewish magical invocations of his name.[26]

In *1 En.* 40:2–9 and 71, Michael is one of the angels around the throne (cf. *Exod. Rab.* 18:5), and often he is depicted as an intercessor and/or heavenly high priest: 14:6, 14; *1 En.* 9; 20:5; *4 Ezra* 7:106; *Apoc. Abr.* 10:17 (here Michael blesses Abraham); *Asc. Isa.* 9:22–23 v.l.; *2 En.* 33:10; *3 Baruch* 11–16; *Vis. Paul* 42; *Apoc. Sedr.* 14:1; Severus of Antioch, *Encom. on Michael*, ed. Budge, p. 65; Eustathius of Trake, *Encom. on Michael*, ed. Budge, pp. 97, 100; *b. Ḥag.* 12b; *b. Menaḥ.* 110a; *Exod. Rab.* 18:5 (this credits Michael with composing the intercessory Psalm 85).[27] *1 En.* 40:9 calls him "merciful and forbearing." His task in *TA*, which is to take Abraham's soul to God, has parallels in other literature, where he is psychopompos—e.g. *1 Enoch* 71; Gk. *L.A.E.* 37:4–6; Jude 9; *2 Enoch* 72 J; *4 Bar.* 9:5; *Vis. Paul* 25; *T. Isaac* 2:1; *T. Jac.* 1:6; 5:13; *Hist. Jos. Carp.* 13, 23; Severus of Antioch, *Encom. on Michael*, ed. Budge, p. 80; Eustathius of Trake, *Encom. on Michael*, ed. Budge, p. 107; Serapion, *Life of John*, trans. Mingana, p. 447; *Deut. Rab.* 11:10; cf. *3 Bar.* 11:2, where he holds the keys to the kingdom of heaven. *TA* 6:5–6 ("These are the feet of one of the three men I washed then") assumes that Michael was one of the three angels Abraham entertained in Genesis, an opinion also found in *Acts Andr. Mth.* 30; Vaticanus Copt. 58 fol. 26v (ed. Simon, *Orientalia* 3 [1934], 230); *b. B. Meṣiʿa* 86b; *b. Yoma* 37a; *Gen. Rab.* 48:10, 14; 50:2; *Pirqe R. El.* 73. But there is nothing in *TA* to indicate the further identification of Michael with Melchizedek, which the Dead Sea Scrolls seemingly attest.[28] So perhaps our text presupposes only one previous meeting between the angel and Abraham, even if some legend brings Michael into Abraham's life on multiple occasions (see on 2:2).

TA introduces Michael as though readers already know him.[29] He is a messenger, like Hermes. But he is much more than a messenger. A central character throughout chaps. 1–15, he shows up again at the end, 20:10. He is not a stock figure without personality, a colorless extension of the deity,

---

[26] See Naveh and Shaked, *Aramaic Spells*, 57 (amulet 18), 106 (amulet 31), 130 (bowl 22), 142 (bowl 27).

[27] Michael may also be the intercessor in *T. Levi* 5:5 and *T. Dan* 6:1, although he is not there named. *b. ʿAbod. Zar.* 42b, which rejects offerings to him, assumes his role as intercessor; cf. *y. Ber.* 13a.

[28] Hannah, *Michael*, 70–74.

[29] On Michael in *TA* see Colafemmina, *Testamento*, 29–33; Delcor, *Testament*, 52–57; Ludlow, *Abraham*, 73–94; Schmidt, "Testament," 79–92; Turner, "Testament," 150–55.

as angels so often are in the biblical tradition. He is rather a distinct character in his own right, whose physical appearance is detailed (chap. 2). In many ways he seems less than angelic, and his behavior hardly matches what one might expect of the general of heaven's army. He cries when Abraham and Isaac cry (3:9–10; 5:10, 14). He pretends a need to urinate (4:5). He cannot bring himself to hurt Abraham's feelings and otherwise has difficulty carrying out God's will (4:6; 8:1–3; 15:14–15). On one occasion he co-operates with Abraham when the patriarch is doing what he should not do (chap. 10, where Michael guides the chariot while Abraham slays sinners). He also needs God's help with eating in 4:9–11— which is particularly odd given that, having eaten with Abraham before (Genesis 18), he should know how to handle the same situation now. He rests on a couch (5:2). He says his prayers (5:2; 14:6, 13). And he is an engaging conversationalist (5:3). In the end, he fails in his mission (chaps. 15–16). On the whole, Michael is anything but what his title indicates, that is, "Commander-in-chief." He is instead a "mild-mannered"[30] and sympathetic figure, a bit inept, who in many ways seems much more human than angelic. The juxtaposition of his military title, appearance, and authority with his inability to get anything much done is striking, and his resultant confusion about what to do with Abraham is humorous.

Michael's presence in *TA* has its ultimate explanation in the text's use of Jewish traditions about Moses's death, in which God asks Michael to take Moses' soul, which he refuses to do; see pp. 24–26.

God calls Abraham his φίλος, and the patriarch was popularly known as such: 2 Chr 20:7; Isa 41:8; LXX 51:2; LXX Dan 3:35; *Jub.* 19:9; 30:20; CD 3:2; 4QGenPesher[a] 2:8; Philo, *Abr.* 89, 273; Jas 2:3; *TA* RecLng. 2:3, 6; 4:7; 8:2, 4; 9:7; 15:12–14; 16:5, 9; 20:14; RecShrt. 4:10; 8:2; 14:6; *4 Ezra* 3:14; Jas 2:23; *1 Clem.* 10:1; 17:2; *Apoc. Abr.* 10:5; Irenaeus, *Haer.* 4.16.2; *Ps.-Clem. Rec.* 1:32; Acacius of Caesarea in *La Chaîne sur la Genèse* 1064 *ad* Gen 18:4; Didymus of Alexandria, *Comm. Job* ad 4:17–18; Ps.-Bartholomew, *Book of the Resurrection of Jesus Christ*, ed. Budge, fol. 13a; *Tanḥ. B* Wayyera 36, Bo 7; Tg. Neof. 1 to Gen 18:17; *Koran* 4:125; etc. The present name of Hebron is el-Khalil (er Rahman) = "the friend (of the Merciful One)."[31] Moses is also sometimes called God's "friend": Exod 33:11; Philo, *Mos.* 1.156; *Sib. Or.* 2:245; etc., so this parallel might belong to a Moses typology; see pp. 24–26. The expression appears throughout *TA*. God uses

---

[30] Gruen, *Diaspora*, 184.

[31] Gen 18:17, where God asks, "Shall I hide from Abraham what I am about to do?," might be the origin of the notion of the patriarch as God's special friend. Both Philo, *Sobr.* 56, and Tg. Neof. 1 Gen 18:17 add "friend" to this text.

it: 1:4, 6; 2:3; 4:7; 8:4; 15:13; 16:5; 20:14; cf. RecShrt. 8:2; 12:5 v.l. So does Michael: 2:3, 6; 8:2; 9:7; 15:12, 14; cf. RecShrt. 4:10. Even Death uses it once: 16:9. Abraham, however, does not call himself such.

Abraham should put his affairs in order, διατάξεται περὶ τῶν πραγμάτων αὐτοῦ. Cf. *Eccl. Rab.* 8:4, which says that, when the Angel of Death arrives, one cannot say, "Wait for me until I put my affairs in order, and then I will come" (so also *Deut. Rab.* 9:3). For διατάσσω* + πράγματα (cf. v. 5; 10:10) see Josephus, *Ant.* 9.6; Ps.-Callisthenes, *Hist. Alex. Magn.* rec. α 3.32 (διάθηται περὶ τῶν πραγμάτων); John Philoponus, *Contra Proclum*, ed. Rabe, p. 330.10. LSJ, s.v. διατάσσω, II, cites examples of the verb in the middle meaning "make testamentary dispositions." The point, repeated in 4:11 (q.v.); 8:10; 15:1; and 15:7, is that it is time for Abraham to distribute his belongings to his family since he himself will no longer need them; cf. Gen 15:2–6; 21:10; 25:5–6; 2 Sam 17:23; 2 Kgs 20:1; Isa 38:1; *Jub.* 20:11–12; Ecclus 33:23; *T. Job* 1:2; 45–47; *4 Ezra* 14:13; *T. Isaac* 2:15; *T. Jac.* 1:6. There may also be a moral or spiritual dimension to getting ready. But whether or not that is so, Abraham never prepares in any way. He resists dying until the very end and so never puts things in order.

1:5. That Abraham is blessed as the stars of heaven and as the sand by the shore of the sea, that is, that he is blessed beyond reckoning, is from Gen 22:17:

TA   ηὐλόγησα αὐτὸν
                   ὡς τὰ ἄστρα τοῦ οὐρανοῦ
                         καὶ ὡς τὴν ἄμμον τὴν παρὰ τὸ χεῖλος τῆς θαλάσσης
LXX Gen 22:17   εὐλογῶν εὐλογήσω σε ...
                   ὡς τοὺς ἀστέρας τοῦ οὐρανοῦ
                         καὶ ὡς τὴν ἄμμον τὴν παρὰ τὸ χεῖλος τῆς θαλάσσης

The line is a sort of refrain in the Bible and later tradition: Gen 32:12; Isa 10:22; 48:19; Hos 1:10; LXX Dan 3:36 (with τὰ ἄστρα); *Jub.* 13:20; 14:4; 18:15; *L.A.B.* 14:2; 18:5; Rom 9:27; Heb 11:12; *1 Clem.* 32:2; *Gk. Apoc. Ezra* 3:10 (with τὰ ἄστρα); Eusebius, *Dem. ev.* 2.3 (with τὰ ἄστρα); *Gen. Rab.* 38:6; etc. In *TA*, however, where the words are also a refrain, the stars and sand refer not to the number of Abraham's descendants, that is, to the multitude that is Israel, but rather to his own physical possessions and wealth, which are beyond counting (cf. 4:11; 8:5). So in its present context, reference to the number of stars and sand by the sea indicates that Abraham has vast wealth to distribute. This elaborates upon Gen 25:5–6, which relates that Abraham gave "all that he had" to Isaac, but that he also had gifts for the sons of his concubines. It also lines up with 13:2 ("Abraham was very rich") and 24:1, which is a retrospective upon Abraham's life (the

Lord "blessed Abraham in all things"). For other references to Abraham's great wealth see 1QapGen 21:3; 22:29–32; Josephus, *Ant.* 1.165; *Sefer Ha-Yashar* 3:7–9.

The text emphasizes Abraham's wealth through repetition. He is prosperous: ἐν εὐπορίᾳ βίου; cf. 2:11; Plato, *Prot.* 321E; Isocrates, *Archid.* 73.6; Heliodorus, *Aeth.* 8.11; Michael Psellus, *Chronog.* 6.183. He has many things, πραγμάτων πολλῶν (πρᾶγμα recurs in v. 4 and 10:10). And he is exceedingly rich, ὑπάρχει πλούσιος πάνυ (ὑπάρχω is an editorial favorite: 1:1; 4:3, 4, 9, 11; 5:11; 7:8; 8:9, 11; 20:2). One is reminded especially of the beginning of the *Testament of Job*, which parades Job's extravagant wealth; cf. Chrysostom, *Hom. Ps. 48:17* PG 55.505, which cites Job and Abraham as proof that the rich can be saved (note also *Hom. Matt.* 21.2). Nowhere does *TA* hint that wealth might be a snare or problem; contrast Plato, *Leg.* 5.742E; *Resp.* 485E; CD 4:17; 6:15; *T. Jud.* 19:1–2; Mark 10:25; 1 Tim 6:10; *Ps.-Clem. Hom.* 15:9; etc. Instead *TA* presupposes the old idea that wealth is a sign of God's blessing: Prov 10:15; *T. Job* 44:5; *b. Ned.* 38a. Thus it is that Abraham can be exceedingly rich and yet at the same time exceedingly virtuous—δίκαιος (cf. v. 2 and see on v. 1) and ἀγαθός (see on v. 7), also φιλόξενος (see on v. 2) and φιλόστοργος* (LXX: 4 *Macc.* 15:13; cf. Philo, *Abr.* 168, 198 [of Abraham's feelings for Isaac in both cases]; Rom 12:10; *Jos. Asen.* 12:8; Josephus, *Ant.* 7.252). The last word adds to the recurrent use of the φιλο-root in chap. 1.[32]

1:6. Michael's mission is to tell Abraham of his impending death (ἀνάγγειλον αὐτὸν περὶ τοῦ θανάτου; cf. 7:11: ἀναγγείλω σοι τὴν μνήμην τοῦ θανάτου); the angel is to assure the patriarch of what is happening, πληροφόρησον αὐτόν. πληροφορέω* (LXX Eccles 8:11; cf. Rom 4:21; 14:5; Col 4:12; *T. Gad* 2:4; *P. Oxy.* 509.10) is popular in patristic texts (Lampe, s.v.), and the weakened sense, "inform," seems unattested before the fifth century CE (cf. Sophocles, *Lex.*, s.v.). God's speech partly anticipates his speech to Death in 16:5, after Michael has failed:

1:6   ἄπελθε πρὸς τὸν φίλον μου τὸν Ἀβραάμ ... καί
16:5   κάτελθε πρὸς τὸν φίλον μου τὸν Ἀβραάμ   καί

Readers of 16:5 will have *déjà vu*.

God's φίλος (cf. v. 4) is here "my beloved," τὸν ἠγαπημένον μοι. Although ἀγαπάω recurs in 3:3; 5:3; 8:11; 15:6, these verses do not refer to Abraham, nor is the related ἀγαπητός ever used of him: 4:1; 7:1; 20:15. The patriarch is nowhere God's "beloved" in Genesis. Isaac is, however,

---

[32] On φιλόστοργος see C. Spicq, "ΦΙΛΟΣΤΟΡΓΟΣ (A propos de Rom., XII, 10)," *RB* 62 (1955), 497–510.

Abraham's "beloved son" in Gen 22:2. Further, LXX Isa 41:8 translates אהבי with ὃν ἠγάπησα ("Abraham whom I have loved") while 2 Chr 20:7 renders אהבך with τῷ ἠγαπημένῳ. Similarly, LXX Theod Dan 3:35 refers to Abraham as τὸν ἠγαπημένον ὑπὸ σοῦ (God; cf. *4 Ezra* 3:14; *Apoc. Abr.* 9:6; *ARN* B 43; Deut 4:37 speaks more generally of God's love for "your ancestors"). Perhaps implicit in *TA*, which reiterates Isaac's status as Abraham's "beloved son" (4:1; 7:1; 8:11; 15:6), is an analogy: God loves Abraham as Abraham loves Isaac. In any case, for others "beloved" of God see Mark 1:11 par.; 9:7 par. (Jesus); *T. Benj.* 11:2 (the Messiah); *2 En.* 24:2 J (Enoch); *T. Isaac* 6:23 (the saints); *Gk. Apoc. Ezra* 5:12; 6:3 (Ezra); *m. 'Abot* 3:15 (Israel); *Vis. Paul* 20, 41, 44, 46, 50 (Paul); *EG* 569.9; 650.2.

1:7. "At this time" (ἐν τῷ καιρῷ τούτῳ; cf. 7:9), Abraham is about to go out of "this futile world," τοῦ ματαίου κόσμου τούτου; cf. the refrain in Ecclesiastes, "Vanity of vanities … all is vanity" (LXX: ματαιότης ματαιοτήτων … ματαιότης); Rom 8:20 ("For the creation has been subjected to futility," ματαιότητι); Clement of Alexandria, *Quis div.* 29 (τῆς ματαιότητος τοῦ κόσμου); Ps.-Athanasius, *Vit. Syncleticae* PG 28.1509B (τοῦ ματαίου κόσμου); Ps.-Ephraem, *Sermones paraenetici ad monachos Aegypti* 39.36 (ἐξήλθομεν ἐκ τοῦ ματαίου κόσμου); Ps.-John of Damascus, *B.J.* 21.184 (τῇ τοῦ κόσμου ματαιότητι). The language is clearly Christian. That this world is "futile"—a lesson Abraham does not yet know—relativizes the patriarch's wealth: it cannot much matter because he cannot take it with him. What counts is the more real world where the soul can be forever with the divine Master (δεσπότην; see on v. 4) as well as with "the good." Whether ἐν ἀγαθοῖς means "among good things" (cf. Eustathius of Trake, *Encom. on Michael*, ed. Budge, p. 116: "inherited ⲚⲒⲀⲄⲀⲐⲞⲚ of the kingdom of heaven") or "among good beings" or "people" (cf. the use of μετὰ τῶν δικαιῶν and related expressions on Jewish epitaphs: *CIJ* 55, 110, 118, 210, 281, 526, 632) is not said (cf. the ambiguity of *dormitio tua in bonis* in *CIJ* 212, 228, 250). But it is clear that Abraham, being himself good (so v. 5), belongs there. In this better place there is, as 20:14 puts it, "no suffering or grief or groaning" but "peace and fervent joy and life without end." The present world, by implication, is full of suffering and grief and groaning. Unlike *T. Job*, however, *TA* does not explicitly stress the contrast between the transience of this world and the permanence of the world to come (see esp. *T. Job* 33–34; cf. 1 Cor 7:31; 1 John 2:17).

     "To depart from the body" (ἐκδημεῖν ἐκ τοῦ σώματος; cf. 7:9; 15:7) followed by "go to your own Master" reminds one of 2 Cor 5:1–10, where Paul says that, although he does not want to be found naked, he prefers to depart from the body (v. 8: ἐκδημῆσαι ἐκ τοῦ σώματος) and be home with the Lord. It is unclear that *TA* 1:7 reflects Paul's language. Philo could speak of bodily life as an exile (ἀποδημία, *Her*. 82), and Plato thought of death as a departure (ἀποδήμα), a going to the gods, a change of habitation from here to some other place (*Phaed*. 63B, 67B; *Apol*. 40E–41A: ἀποδημῆσαί ἐστιν ὁ θάνατος ἐνθένδε εἰς ἄλλον τόπον; cf. *Phaed*. 118A; Iamblichus in Stobaeus, *Ecl*. 1). There is, in any case, a parallel with Genesis 12, where God calls Abraham to leave his home and to go to a place unknown to him.

Chapter 2:
Michael and Abraham meet Each Other

Bibliography: Delcor, "De l'origine de quelques traditions." Schmidt, "Testament," 1:84–86; 2:124–25.

Long Recension

2:1. The Commander-in-chief, going out from before the Lord God, went down to Abraham, to the Oak of Mamre. And he found Abraham in the field near a yoke of oxen for ploughing, sitting in front with the sons of Masek and other servants, twelve in number. And behold, the Commander-in-chief came toward him. 2:2. When Abraham saw the Commander-in-chief Michael coming from afar, looking like a most handsome soldier, then the most holy Abraham rose and met him in accord with his custom of greeting and welcoming strangers. 2:3. The Commander-in-chief greeted the righteous Abraham and said: "Greetings, most honorable father, righteous soul, elect one, true friend of the heavenly God." 2:4. Abraham said to the Commander-in-chief: "Greetings, most honorable soldier, resembling the sun and most handsome above all the sons of men. It is well you have come! 2:5 Wherefore I request of your presence, Whence has come your youth? Inform me, your supplicant, from whence (you have come) and from what army, and teach me from what road your beauty has come." 2:6. The Commander-in-chief said: "Righteous man, I come from

Short Recension fam. E

2:1. Then Michael went away, and he came to Abraham. He encountered him sitting near cattle used for plowing, and he was very advanced in age. 2:2. Abraham greeted Michael, unaware of his identity. 2:3. And he said to him, "From whence, o man, are you come, traveler on the road?" 2:4. And Michael answered him, "You are a benevolent man." 2:5. Abraham said to him, "Come, draw near to me, and sit for a while. And I will arrange that an animal be brought to us, so that we might depart and (you might) pass this time with me in our house, because it is near evening. 2:6. And in the morning you can rise and go wherever you want— lest an evil beast meet you (tonight) and trouble you." 2:7. Michael asked Abraham, saying, "Tell me what is your name before I enter into your house and become a burden to you." 2:8. Abraham answered and said, "My parents named me 'Abram,' and the Lord called me, saying, 'Rise and go from your father's house and from your land and your family, and enter into the land which I will show to you.' 2:9. I heard him, and I went into the land which the Lord spoke to me. And he changed my name

the great city; I have been sent by the great king to carry out the succession of his true friend, because the king calls him to himself." 2:7. And Abraham said: "Come, my lord, go with me into the field." The Commander-in-chief said, "I come." 2:8. Going away they sat down in the plowed field in order to converse. 2:9. Abraham said to his servants, to the sons of Masek: "Go to the herd of horses and bring two agreeable and broken horses that have been tamed, so that this stranger and I might sit on them." 2:10. The Commander-in-chief said: "No, my lord Abraham, do not bring horses, for I refuse to sit on any four-footed animal. 2:11. For is not my king rich in much merchandise, having authority over people and every kind of beast? But I refuse to sit on any four-footed animal. 2:12. Righteous soul, let us go walking on foot to your house as our minds soar." And Abraham said: "Amen, so be it, lord."

saying, 'You will no longer be called Abram. But your name will be Abraham.'" 2:10. Michael answered and said to him, "Sir, forgive me, because I am a stranger, o father of those you care for, I have heard that you went out forty stadia and brought a calf and slaughtered it for the angels who were visiting in your house, that they might rejoice." 2:11. And they arose and went, 2:12. and Abraham called Damskon, the son of Eleazar, one of his servants, saying, "Bring a beast so that the stranger might sit upon it, because he is weary from the road." 2:13. Michael answered and said, "Do not trouble the young servant. But let us walk in good spirits until we arrive at your house."

TEXTUAL NOTES ON THE LONG RECENSION

2:1. G J omit "Abraham ... found," probably through *homoioteleuton* ("Abraham ... Abraham"). // A: προεδρεύοντα. B G Q: παρεδρεύοντα. H: παρεδρεύοντος. J: παραδευόντων. I omits. Favoring the originality of A ("sitting in front") is RecShrt. 2:1 (καθιζόμενου/ν) and v. 2, which speaks of Abraham getting up, ἀναστάς. There is also the dependence upon Gen 18:1, where Abraham is sitting (cf. 19:1) and the parallelism with chapter 16; see below. // I has "son of Masek," which accords with Gen 15:2, τοῦ υἱοῦ Μασέκ.[1] Yet the plural also appears in v. 9 in most RecLng. witnesses. // G omits "And behold ... him." 2:2. G Q abbreviate by removing "the most holy Abraham." // I also abbreviates, omitting "in accord ... strangers." 2:3. G skips "true friend ... God." 2:4. After "well" A I J have ἔοικας, BQ ἧκας, G ἐλήλυθας. Did ἔοικας (cf. ἔοικεν in v. 5) or ἧκας arise as an error

---

[1] James, *Testament*, 120, and Box, *Testament*, 3, thought the singular original, but one might expect a pedantic scribe to assimilate to Genesis.

of hearing? 2:5. G drops "Inform … (you have come)." // B J Q omit "and from what army?" // J reduces the end of the sentence to: "and from what road?," G to: "and teach me from what road?" 2:6. J passes over the opening words and rewrites so as to get: "I come having been sent by the king." // I drops "because … to himself." 2:7. J omits "go with me." 2:7–8: A passes from "field" in v. 7 to "field" in v. 8. // G lacks "The Commander-in-chief … come." 2:8. I leaves out "they sat … converse." // 2:9. J omits "agreeable … tamed" as unnecessary. // I drops "so that … on them." 2:10. I omits. 2:11. G I omit. // J drops "in much merchandise … animal." // B Q abbreviate, ending with: "But I refuse this." 2:12. J abridges: "Let us go, our minds soaring."

COMMENTARY

Like stories of Greek gods who temporarily transform themselves into human beings[2] and like other Jewish and Christian tales of angels carrying out their divine missions unrecognized (cf. Tobit and Heb 13:2), *TA* 2 recounts the arrival of a heavenly being who is not perceived as such. But as chap. 1 has informed readers of Michael's mission, they know what Abraham does not and so will not understand Michael's appearance and words as he does. The situation is analogous to Genesis 18, where readers but not Abraham know that the three strangers are "the Lord," or Job, wherein the introductory scene in heaven tells the audience what is really going on while the main character remains in the dark.

Abraham's ignorance generates the irony of double entendre. When he remarks that the stranger's beauty is "above all the sons of man" (v. 4), he cannot know how true this is, and that his guest is so different because he is in fact not one of "the sons of men." Again, when Michael refers to the "great city" of "the great king" (v. 6), Abraham must think of an earthly city and king, but readers know that this is a riddle with a hidden meaning: Michael refers to the heavenly Jerusalem and God.

The chapter effectively links itself both to a past narrative in another book and to a future scene in a later chapter, for it resembles both the visit of the three angels to Abraham in Genesis 18 (upon which it, like Judg 6:11–27, is based) and likewise foreshadows the coming of Death to Abraham in *TA* 16:

---

[2]   Recall esp. Homer, *Od.* 17.485–487: "The gods in the guise of strangers from afar put on all manner of shapes, and visit the cities, beholding the violence and the righteousness of people." Philo, *Quaest. Gen.* 4.2, cites this text when discussing Genesis 18, as do some modern commentators on Genesis. Cf. *Somn.* 1.233.

Genesis 18

The Lord appears at the Oak of Mamre

Abraham is sitting and runs to meet (συνάντησιν) the three men—one being Michael according to *TA* 6:4–6

Abraham eagerly offers, through a fulsome, wordy invitation, hospitality

He serves the strangers a calf from his herd

Abraham addresses his visitors as κύριε

Abraham and the men walk off together

TA 2

The setting is the Oak of Mamre

Abraham is sitting; Michael the archangel appears and Abraham rises to meet (ὑπηντήθη) him

Abraham eagerly offers, through a fulsome, wordy invitation, hospitality

Cattle are nearby

Abraham addresses Michael as κύριε

Abraham and Michael walk off together

TA 2

The Commander-in-chief goes out (ἐξελθών) from before (ἐκ προσώπου) God and descends (κατῆλθε) to meet Abraham

Abraham is near the oak of Mamre and sitting

Abraham, seeing (ἰδών) Michael, observes that he is handsome (εὐπρεπεστάτου) and bright like the sun (ἡλιόρατε)

The patriarch rises to meet (ἀναστάς ... ὑπηντήθη) him

The archangel hails Abraham with, "Hail, most honorable ... righteous soul ... true friend of the heavenly God" (χαῖρε, τιμιώτατε ... δικαία ψυχή ... φίλε γνήσιε τοῦ θεοῦ)

Abraham speaks (εἶπεν δὲ Ἀβραὰμ πρὸς τόν) and greets Michael (χαίροις)

Abraham observes that his guest is most beautiful above all the sons of men (ὑπὲρ πάντας τοὺς υἱοὺς τῶν ἀνθρώπων) and asks him from whence (πόθεν) he has come

TA 16

God tells Death to descend (κάτελθε); Death then goes out from before (ἐξῆλθεν ἀπὸ προσώπου) God to meet Abraham

The patriarch is sitting under the trees of Mamre

Abraham, seeing (ἰδών) Death, observes that he is handsome (ὡραιότητι in v. 8; cf. εὐπρεπής in v. 6, εὐπρέπεια in v. 12) and bright like the sun (ἡλιόρατε; cf. ἡλιόμορφον in v. 6)

He rises to meet him (ἀναστάς ὑπήντησεν)

Death hails Abraham, God's true friend (φίλος γνήσιος), with, "Greetings, honorable ... righteous soul ... friend of God" (χαίροις τίμιε ... δικαία ψυχή, φίλε τοῦ θεοῦ)

Abraham speaks (εἶπεν δὲ Ἀβραὰμ πρὸς τόν) and greets Death (χαίροις)

Abraham asks Death from whence comes (πόθεν) his glory, which is above all the sons of men (ὑπὲρ πάντας τοὺς υἱοὺς τῶν ἀνθρώπων)

The first set of parallels magnifies the irony of Abraham's ignorance. He fails to see that what is happening now has happened before, that his new visitor is an old visitor; cf. 6:4–5 and see on 1:4. As for the foreshadowing of chap. 16, the parallels naturally arise because Death's mission is the same as Michael's: the latter does what the former fails to do. The correlations, however, do not include hospitality. While philanthropy is central in chap. 2, it is absent from 16ff., where Abraham, so far from being hospitable, offers his guest nothing and shuns his company.

Some of the words or phrases in chap. 2 occur more often in patristic texts than anywhere else: προσυπαντάω, v. 2; τιμιώτατε πάτερ, v. 3; πανευπρεπής, v. 4; τὸ νέον τῆς ἡλικίας, v. 5; πόθεν καὶ ἐκ ποίας, v. 5. None of these are in RecShrt. Also striking are the superlatives: εὐπρεπεστάτος (vv. 2, 4), ἱερώτατος (v. 3), τιμιώτατε (vv. 3–4). One recalls the effusive superlatives in patristic hagiographies, Christian epitaphs, and the old liturgies, such as those in the refrain from the Liturgy of Chrysostom: "Calling to remembrance our all holy (παναγίας), pure, most blessed (ὑπερευλογημένης), and glorified Lady Theotokos and Ever-Virgin Mary … ."[3]

While *TA*'s superlatives may be nothing but later medieval embellishment, there is also a possible Jewish background. Superlatives are common on ancient epitaphs, including Jewish epitaphs.[4] Not only do we often find words such as μακαριστότατος (*CPJ* 1530a; *BS* 2.183), πανάριστος (*CIJ* 1512), πασίφιλος (*CIJ* 1466), and γλυκυτάτη (*MAMA* 6.335a), but extravagant appellations can come in quick succession, as in *CIJ* 1490 ("most honorable … friend of all and without reproach, excellent one") and 1514 ("excellent woman, friend of all, who caused no pain and was friend of all"). So given that Abraham and Michael exchange greetings and that χαῖρε is so typical for epitaphs, and further that *TA* is all about death, maybe the introductory superlatives and greetings come from the graveyard. Maybe the atmosphere of the epitaph hangs over our book from the beginning.

RecShrt. 2 is similar to RecLng. 2 in outline, but the details are quite different:

---

[3]   See Lampe, s.v. πανάγιος 6 (of Mary), 7 (of saints), and s.v., πανόσιος. For examples of Christian epitaphs with superlatives see Johnson, *Anatolia* 2.7; 3.1; Gregg and Urman, *Golan* 11, 68.

[4]   See Marcus N. Tod, "Laudatory Epithets in Greek Epitaphs," in *Annual of the British School of Athens* 46 (1951), 182–90. Tod observes that, especially in the Imperial period, superlatives are particularly common in Egypt.

In RecLng. but not RecShrt.

- The Oak of Mamre, v. 1
- The field near the Oak, vv. 1, 7
- The sons of Masek and twelve servants, v. 1
- Description of Michael, his status as a soldier, and his title, "Commander-in-chief," vv. 2, 4–5
- Effusive exchange of honorifics, vv. 3, 4, 6, 12
- Questions about Michael's appearance, army, and route; cryptic answer about the great city and the great king, vv. 5–6

In RecShrt. but not RecLng.

- Abraham is old (γηραλέος; cf. LXX Gen 15:15; 21:2, 7) in appearance, v. 1
- He holds Isaac in his arms, v. 1 in fam. B F G[5]
- According to the narrator, Abraham does not know Michael's identity, v. 2
- It is near evening, v. 6 (contrast Gen 18:1)
- Abraham wants to protect Michael from any wild beast that might happen upon him, v. 6[6]
- Michael asks Abraham who he is, v. 7
- Michael worries about burdening Abraham, v. 7
- Abraham responds by telling the story behind LXX Gen 12:1 and 17:5, vv. 8–9
- Michael knows of the incident in Genesis 18, when Abraham hosted angels, v. 10
- Damskon, son of Eleazar, receives orders, v. 12

No simple explanation of the differences suggests itself. RecShrt.'s less flowery language could be more primitive.[7] But if RecShrt. deliberately abbreviates elsewhere, then its being more concise here is only expected. In line with this, RecShrt.'s failure to explain why Michael and Abraham walk instead of ride does seem in need of RecLng.'s generalization in 2:11 (Michael does not ride beasts on principle). At the same time, RecShrt. 2 is not simply an abbreviation of RecLng. 2. For one thing, the former is not significantly shorter than the latter. In Schmidt's edition, RecLng. 2 contains 33 lines, RecShrt. 2 fam. E 27 lines, RecShrt. 2 fam. B F G 30 lines. For another, and as already observed, RecShrt. contains quite a few details not in A. Were RecShrt. altogether secondary, one would have to regard these details as expansions.

Unlike chap. 1, chap. 2 confirms that a common Greek *Vorlage* lies somewhere behind RecLng. and RecShrt. Both share words that make

---

5   The remark is odd given that Isaac should be 75 at the time of Abraham's death (Gen 21:5; 25:7). But Isaac appears to be quite young in *TA*; see further on 3:7.

6   RecShrt. fam. B F G refers instead to a phantom of the night.

7   But RecShrt. 2:10 fam. B F G does have Michael address Abraham as ὑπερεπαινούμενε.

them unlikely to be independent translations of a Semitic original: ἐπιξενός— ἐπιξενόομαι (the former in RecLng. 2:2, 9; the latter in RecShrt. 2:10 fam. E), ζῷον (RecLng. 2:10–11; RecShrt. 2:5), κτῆνος (RecLng. 2:11; RecShrt. 2:12), μετεωρίζω (RecLng. 2:12; RecShrt. 2:13).

2:1. Michael obediently leaves heaven and descends to Abraham, ἐξελθών … κατῆλθε. For κατέρχομαι of heavenly descent see also 1:4; 4:10; 5:1; 7:3; 9:1; 10:1, 11; 16:5. "From before" is lit. "from (the) face of," ἐκ προσώπου; cf. 15:11, 14 and ἀπὸ προσώπου in 9:5; 16:6. In the LXX, ἐκ προσώπου translates מִלִּפְנֵי, קֳדָם מִן פָּנִים מֵעַל and related expressions about 50 times; and in 1 Βασ 21:7; Jonah 1:3 (bis), and 10, ἐκ προσώπου κυρίου renders מִלִּפְנֵי יהוה although neither ἐκ προσώπου κυρίου θεοῦ (so TA) nor ἐκ προσώπου θεοῦ occurs.[8] πρόσωπον κυρίου θεοῦ appears once: Dan 9:13. On the parallel with Job 1:12 see on 15:14. Although κυρίου θεοῦ without the definite article before θεοῦ is common in the LXX (ca. 175), the definite article appears much more often than not (ca. 900), it is the rule in Philo and the New Testament, and TA itself elsewhere includes the article after "Lord" and before "God" (8:7; 14:13; 15:14; 18:9).

"The Oak of Mamre" (see on 1:2) is the setting for Michael's appearance here because it is the setting for the theophany in Gen 18:1–2. History is replaying itself, as it will again; see above.

Abraham is sitting (προεδρεύοντα) in a field, just as in Genesis 18,[9] and just as Manoah is when the angel of the Lord appears to her in Judg 13:9, and just as Moses is when Sammael comes for his soul in *Deut. Rab.* 11:10 and *Petirat Moshe* (*BHM* 6:75). According to LSJ, s.v., προεδρεύω* (LXX: 0; Philo: 0; NT: 0; Josephus: 0), the verb can mean "to act as president" or "to sit in the front row" (as in a theatre). But Lampe, s.v., cites patristic texts with the meaning "serve, wait upon" and "attend upon, be assiduous at." So maybe, given our context, the verb connotes here eager service rather than privilege or honor.

The patriarch has oxen for ploughing, ζεύγη βοῶν ἀροτριασμοῦ (ζεῦγος*; βοῦς*; ἀροτριασμός: cf. v. 8; RecShrt. 2:1; *T. Job* 10:5; LXX: 0; Philo: 0; NT: 0; Josephus: 0). Given the parallels between Abraham and Job elsewhere, this may augment them. Cf. LXX Job 1:14 (τὰ ζεύγη τῶν βοῶν ἠροτρία) and recall that *T. Job* 10:5 gives Job 3500 yoke of oxen, 500

---

[8] Philo, however, uses this last a dozen times: *Plant.* 63.6; *Conf.* 168; *Mos.* 2.188; etc. Cf. ἀπὸ προσώπου κυρίου in *Ps. Sol.* 12:6; 15:5; *Jos. Asen.* 26:3 (Burchard).

[9] Jewish tradition paid more attention than did Christian tradition to Abraham's seated posture at Mamre; see Heinz Schreckenberg and Kurt Schubert, *Jewish Historiography and Iconography in Early and Medieval Christianity* (CRINT III/ 1,2; Assen/Maastricht/Minneapolis: Van Gorcum/Fortress, 1992), 200.

of which are for others to plough with (cf. Aristeas in Eusebius, *Praep. ev.* 9.25.2). The field is presumably the one Abraham buys from Ephron the Hittite in Genesis 23. For Abraham's oxen see Gen 12:16; 20:14; 21:27; *Jub.* 13:14. Our text presupposes that Abraham was a farmer, and it may further presuppose the legend that he invented ploughing. According to Gen 21:33—a text behind RecLng. 3:3 and 4:2—"Abraham planted a tamarisk tree (אשל) in Beer-sheba."[10] The LXX has him planting a "field" (ἄρουραν), Symmachus a "plantation" (or "plant," φυτείαν), Aquila a "thicket" (δενδρῶνα). Moreover, Tgs. Ps.-Jn., Neof. 1, and Frg. Tg. on Gen 21:33 say that he planted an orchard or garden (פרדיסא = παράδεισος); cf. *TA* 4:2; *b. Soṭah* 10a; *Gen. Rab.* 54:6.[11] While these sources tell us no more than that Abraham engaged in agriculture, *Jub.* 11:23–24 recounts that Abram taught people how to sow and till.

Abraham is with "the sons of Masek" (Μασέκ, cf. v. 9). The Bible names Masek only once, in LXX Gen 15:2: "And Abram said, 'Master Lord, What will you give to me? I am leaving childless, except for Δαμασκὸς Ἐλιέζερ,[12] the son of Μασέκ, my homebred (slave).'" The MT is problematic. The versions render it variously, and the modern commentaries regard the relevant words as corrupt: בֶּן־מֶשֶׁק בֵּיתִי הוּא דַמֶּשֶׂק אֱלִיעֶזֶר Neither Eleazar nor Damascus (assuming that this latter is not the city, although it may be) is elsewhere Abraham's heir, and מֶשֶׁק is a *hapax*. However one explains the Hebrew, the LXX, like *Jub.* 14:2 eth., has turned מֶשֶׁק into a proper name, "Masek" (cf. Philo, *Her.* 2, 40, 61), and *TA* has assumed that the one son of Masek must have had brothers. *TA* has also, without any support from Genesis, created the number twelve, which is either the number of "the other servants" (ἑτέροις παισίν) or of "the sons of Masek"

---

10   Rabbinic texts use this as a proof text for Abraham's hospitality by associating אשל with שאל ("ask"): Abraham generously gave people what they asked for; see *ARN* A 7; *b. Soṭah* 10a; *Tanḥ.* B Genesis Noah 20; *Gen. Rab.* 54:6. See further on 3:3.

11   A marginal gloss in Neofiti associates the site with Abraham's hospitality: he set within his garden "food and drink for the passers-by and for the neighbors and when, having eaten and drunk, they sought to give him the price of what they had eaten and drunk our father Abraham answered, saying to them: 'Pray before your Father who (is) in the heavens, because of his food you have eaten and of his water you have drunk.' And they did not move from there because he converted them to the name of the Word of the Lord, God of the world." Cf. the Frg. Tg. ad loc.

12   RecShrt. 2:12 fam. E^pt speaks of Δαμασκὸν Ἐλεέζερ, which presumably means "Damskon Eleazar." דמשק is a personal name in Aquila and Vulgate^pt but a place name in the Syriac and Tg. Onq. The LXX's Δαμασκὸς Ἐλιέζερ would seem to mean "Damascus Eleazar," but *La Chaîne sur la Genèse* 945 construes Δαμασκός as ὁ ἀπὸ Δαμασκοῦ.

plus "the other servants."[13] In either case, given the other parallels in our book between Abraham and Moses, perhaps this detail adds to them, for the Pentateuch closely associates the law-giver with a group of twelve, the so-called phylarchs. For Abraham's many servants see Gen 12:16; 14:14–15; 20:14; 26:15; *Jub.* 13:14; Philo, *Quaest. Gen.* 4.10. 7000 is their number in *TA* 17:18, and they reappear in 15:5 and 20:7. "And behold" (καὶ ἰδοῦ; cf. 12:16; 14:8; 16:8) is the equivalent of the Hebrew והנה (as in Gen 1:31) and the Aramaic והא (as in 1QapGen 20:30). It is a Septuagintism, one occurring a full 30 times in Genesis alone, including 18:2, which is being rewritten here.

2:2. Abraham, upon seeing another "from afar" (ἀπὸ μηκόθεν; see below), gets up to greet him: ἀναστὰς ... ὑπηντήθη; cf. 16:8, ἀναστὰς ὑπήντησεν—of Abraham meeting Death, Michael's replacement. Josephus, *Ant.* 1.196, also adds ἀναστάς to his rewriting of Gen 18:1–2. The patriarch acts according to his custom, καθότι ἔθος. The only other occurrences of καθότι ἔθος that I have found are in Scholia on Homer, *Il.* 1.465B, and Scholia on Euclid, *Elem.* 5.22. Cf. κατὰ τὸ ἔθος (used in 5:2; also Theod. Bel 15; Josephus, *Ant.* 2.313; Luke 1:9; 2:42; 22:39); καθὼς ἔθος (so G H J; *Let. Arist.* 311; Josephus, *Ant.* 14.245; 20.28; John 19:40); and καθάπερ ἔθος (Philo, *Abr.* 31). καθότι (cf. 11:9; 20:3) appears ca. 70 times in the LXX (in Philo only once: *Somn.* 2.175; NT: Acts 2:45; 4:35; 17:31; Josephus: *Ant.* 15.393; 18.90; cf. *Jos. Asen.* 2:1; 4:10; 15:8), but never directly before ἔθος.

Abraham, in accord with 1:2 (q.v.) and 5, embodies hospitality. "As is his custom" has a parallel in Tg. Neof. 1 Gen 18:2: Abraham "saluted them after the custom of the land," כנימוס ארעא cf. Ps.-Jn. on 18:8 (the MT instead has: "bowed himself down to the earth"). This may not be a coincidence as there are a few other links between *TA* and targumic tradition in Genesis 18. *TA* 2:6 says that Michael has been "sent" (ἀπεστάλην) whereas שלח repeatedly appears in Tgs. Neof. 1 on Gen 18:1–2 and Ps.-Jn. on 18:2. In *TA* 5:1, Isaac "serves" Michael while Tgs. Onq. and Ps.-Jn. on Gen 18:8 turn "he stood by them" into "he served them." Further, that Michael only appears to eat (*TA* 4:10, q.v.) is paralleled in Tgs. Neof. 1 and Ps.-Jn. on Gen 18:8, in which the angels, without consuming food, give the impression of eating.

ἀπὸ μηκόθεν ("from afar"; Philo: 0; NT: 0; Josephus: 0) does not appear in the LXX, which rather uses ἀπὸ μακρόθεν (so mss. G I H J here; cf. Matt 27:55; Mark 5:6; 11:13; 15:40; Luke 16:23, each with a verb of seeing.).

---

[13] The long Romanian, ed. Roddy, p. 24, has: "Abraham ... with his men and ten other servants."

LSJ, s.v., offers only two entries for μηκόθεν—Aesop, *Fab*. 243, and Paulus Aegineta 5.2 (μηκόθεν βλέπειν), the latter from the seventh century. To these one may add, from earlier times, *Jos. Asen*. 28:14 (Burchard) and *Vit. Proph. Isaiah* 7. But ἀπὸ μηκόθεν is another story. Although it appears in the fragment of *Apocryphon of Ezekiel* in Epiphanius, *Pan*. 64.70, and in Alexander of Aphrodisias, *Comm. Metaph*., ed. Hayduck, p. 433.1, it is characteristic of later Greek. Lampe, s.v., μηκόθεν, cites Epiphanius, *Exp. fidei* 23, and *Apophth. Patrum* PG 65.125B (Achilles 5), to which one may add the instances of ἀπὸ μηκόθεν in Epiphanius, *Pan*. 26.19; 69.41; Ps.-Mauricius, *Strat*. 11.2.15; and John Cameniates, *Expug. Thess*. 26.6.

Michael appears "like" (δίκην; cf. 20:5; the only LXX example of adverbial δίκην is Wis 12:24; cf. Josephus, *Ant*. 13.412) a handsome (εὐπρεπεστάτου; cf. 16:12, of Death) soldier (στρατιώτου); cf. v. 4 and his title, "Commander-in-chief"; also Severus of Antioch, *Encom. on Michael*, ed. Budge, p. 78, where Michael takes the form of a Greek general. He is greeted by Abraham, who is "most holy" (ἱερώτατος; cf. 15:2)—a description Philo gives again and again to Moses: *Det*. 135; *Deus immut*. 140; *Congr*. 89; *Spec. leg*. 1.15, 59; *Virt*. 175; etc. We have here the motif of encountering an angel of revelation unawares; cf. Genesis 18; Judg 6:11–24; 14:16; Tob 5:4–5; Heb 13:2. In *TA* the lack of recognition carries additional irony because Abraham has met Michael before and yet does not know him; cf. the New Testament encounters with the risen Jesus: Luke 24:16, 31, 37; John 20:14; 21:4. Perhaps indeed Abraham has met Michael more than once, for some identified Michael with Melchizedek (see on 1:4), others with the angel that saved him from a fiery furnace (*Gen. Rab*. 44:13; cf. *Exod. Rab*. 18:5), others with the angel who informed Abraham about the destruction of Sodom and Gomorrah (Theodosius of Alexandria, *Encom. on Michael*, ed. Budge, p. 14; *Pirqe R. El*. 27), still others with the angel who stopped him from bringing the knife down upon Isaac (Theodosius of Alexandria, *Encom. on Michael*, ed. Budge, p. 14; *Pesiq. Rab*. 40:6); and *Heb. T. Naph*. 9:1–5 records a conversation between Michael and Abraham.

V. 2 ends with "meeting and welcoming strangers," τοῖς ἐπιξένοις προσυπαντᾶν καὶ ἐπιδεχόμενος (ἐπιδέχομαι*). While the words are redundant given chap. 1 (which is why I omits them), they underline once more Abraham's generous hospitality. ἐπίξενος (LXX: 0; Philo: 0; NT: 0; Josephus: 0) is a relatively rare noun that recurs in v. 9 and 3:7; cf. Nicias, *Epigr*. 6.127; *P. Oxy*. 480.11; Clement of Alexandria, *Strom*. 2.9.41. *TA* also likes ἐπιξενίζω—4:1, 3; 5:13; 6:4. LSJ, s.v., προσυπαντάω*, cites *PSI* 4.292.10 (3rd CE). Lampe, s.v., cites Asterius Amasenus (d. 410), *Hom. in filium prodigum*, ed. Bretz, p. 113. Other examples include Aesop, *Fab*.

283; Polyaenus, *Exc.* 4.1; Gregory of Nazianzus, *Or. 38* PG 36.332B; Ps.-Chrysostom, *Eleem. 1–4* PG 62.770; Romanos the Melodist, *Cant.* 27.15.

2:3. Michael knows Abraham's name without being told,[14] just as the three men in Gen 18:9 know Sarah's name without being told. προχαιρετίσας ("greeting") continues the string of words with prefixes: ὑπηντήθη, ἐπιξένοις, προσυπαντᾶν, ἐπιδεχόμενος. LSJ contains no entry for προχαιρετίζω*. Lampe, s.v., cites only *TA* 2:3, and I have not found it elsewhere. Michael addresses the "righteous" (δίκαιον; see on 1:1–2) Abraham as τιμιώτατε πάτερ (LXX: 0; Philo: 0; NT: 0; Josephus: 0); cf. 2:4 (where Abraham returns the compliment to Michael: τιμιώτατε); 7:9 (again Michael of Abraham). For τίμιος see also v. 4; 3:6, 11; 6:7; 7:9; 16:9; 20:10, 12, and with τιμιώτατε πάτερ cf. *P. Lond.* 6r.5, 19, 27; *SB* 12.6; Basil the Great, *Ep.* 66; 70; Cyril of Scythopolis, *Vit. Euthymii*, ed. Schwartz, pp. 5.22, 52.10; Theodore the Studite, *Ep.*, ed. Fatouros 8.71; Anna Comnena, *Alex.* 15.8.4. RecShrt. 2:4 fam. B F G has καλὲ πάτερ. For χαίροις as a greeting (LXX: 0; Philo: 0; NT: 0; Josephus: 0) see v. 4; 16:9, 10; *Jos. Asen.* 8:2; Gk. *3 Bar.* 11:6–7; Ps.-Callisthenes, *Hist. Alex. Magn.* rec. α 1.4, 16, 17–18; *P. Lond.* 2.1; and cf. the rabbinic כירי. One may also compare the use of χαῖρε with τιμιώτατε in Eusebius, *Hist. eccl.* 10.5.15 (χαῖρε, Ἀνυλῖνε τιμιώτατε ἡμῖν; cf. 10.5.17; 10.7.1), and Basil the Great, *Ep.* 344 (χαῖρε τοίνυν τιμιώτατε). Note further *TA* 16:9, where Death says to Abraham: χαίροις τίμιε.

"Father" designates instructors in the wisdom tradition, and Paul could regard himself as the "father" of his converts (1 Cor 4:15); cf. *L.A.B.* 53:3 (Samuel to Eli); *4 Macc.* 7:9 (Eleazar addressed as "you, father" in a panegyric); *4 Bar.* 2:2, 4, 8 (Baruch to Jeremiah); *Acts John* 81 (Drusiana to John); *P. Lond.* 1914.57 (of a priest). The titular use of "father" remains rare, however, in rabbinic literature, which typically reserves the honorific for early scholars (e.g. "Abba Saul") and, above all, for the patriarchs; cf. *b. Ber.* 16b: "Our rabbis taught: The term אבות is applied only to three" (the patriarchs). אברהם אבינו is the usual rabbinic designation for Abraham. "Father" is more common in patristic and especially monastic literature (Lampe, s.v., πατήρ, A), and the precise expression, τιμιώτατε πάτερ, appears in several Christian texts (see above). Because descent from Abraham is the basis for membership in the people of God, Abraham is especially "father" in both Jewish and Christian sources: Gen 17:4–5; Exod 3:6; Josh 24:3; Isa 51:2; *L.A.B.* 32:1; Philo, *Gig.* 64; Josephus, *Ant.* 1.158; Luke 1:55; John 8:39; Jas 2:23; *T. Jac.* 7:22 ("father of fathers"); *b. Ned.* 32a; etc. Hence the correlative term, "son of Abraham": *4 Macc.*

---

14 Contrast RecShrt. 2:7, where Michael asks Abraham his name.

6:17, 22; Matt 3:9; Gal 3:7; *m. B. Qam.* 8:6; etc. *TA*, however, nowhere focuses on Abraham's status as father of the Jewish people.

Abraham is a "righteous soul," δικαία ψυχή; cf. v. 12; 7:8; 16:9, 15. The expression occurs also in Gk. *L.A.E.* 43:3, there too on the lips of Michael the archangel; cf. further Plato, *Resp.* 353E; Philo, *Spec. leg.* 1.316; Clement of Alexandria, *Strom.* 7.5.29; Eusebius, *Comm. Isa.* 2.57; etc. In 20:9–12, as in Gk. *L.A.E.* 43:3, the ψυχή is the immaterial self. But here in 2:3 ψυχή = נפש, body and soul together.¹⁵ Abraham is further the "elect one" (ἐκλεκτέ; ἐκλεκτή*). Already Neh 9:7 says that God "chose" (MT: בחרת; 2 Esd 19:7: ἐξελέξω) Abraham, and *L.A.B.* 32:1 repeats this (*elegit eum prae omnibus fratribus suis*); cf. 2 Macc 1:25 (τοὺς πατέρας ἐκλεκτούς); 4 *Ezra* 3:13 (*elegisti ... cui nomen erat Abraham*); *Apoc. Abr.* 14:2. Philo especially likes to call Abraham "elect"; see *Cher.* 7; *Gig.* 64; *Mut.* 66–71; *Abr.* 82–83. Philo's etymology of "Abraham" is in fact "elect father of sound." *TA* has already called Abraham God's "friend" (see on 1:4); here the expression becomes "true friend" (φίλε γνήσιε), as also in 2:6 and 16:5 (where Death addresses Abraham); cf. *Let. Arist.* 41 (φίλῳ γνησίῳ χαίρειν); Phocylides, *Sent.* fr. 17; *Epigr.* 10.117 (γνήσιός εἰμι φίλος).

God is "heavenly," ἐπουρανίου (ἐπουράνιος: 2:3; 4:9; 6:4; 17:11; LXX: 7, 5 in 2–4 Maccabees). The sense is local: God is in the heavens, which is where Abraham will go to meet him; cf. 1:7; 20:12–14; Plato, *Phaedr.* 256D; 2 Macc 3:39; and the Christian art that depicts departing souls and their angelic escorts going up (see on 20:12). The expression, "the heavenly God," which reappears in 17:11, is known from the LXX: 3 *Macc.* 6:28; 7:6; cf. LXX Ps 67:15 ("the heavenly"); *Sib. Or.* 1:216; 4:51, 135; Matt 18:35; 1 *Clem.* 61:2; Gk. *3 Bar.* 11:9; *Corp. herm.* fr. 12 (ed. Festugière 3:61); 3 *Bar.* 11:9; Eusebius, *Comm. Ps.* PG 23.328B; 632A; *Chron. Pasch.*, ed. Dindorf, p. 521.10. Homer uses ἐπουρανίος of the Greek gods in *Il.* 6.129; *Od.* 17.484.

2:4. Abraham, by-passing how the stranger knows so much about him, exchanges compliments and directs his questions elsewhere. As in Gen 18:3–5, he is verbose. His response parallels the angel's opening remark:

v. 3: subject (archangel) + δέ + προ- + indirect object (Abraham) + εἶπεν
    + χαίροις + τιμιώτατε + description of indirect object (Abraham)
v. 4: εἶπεν δέ + subject (Abraham) + προ- + indirect object (archangel)¹⁶
    + χαίροις + τιμιώτατε + description of indirect object (archangel)

---

¹⁵ See further Turner, "Testament," 74.
¹⁶ Cf. 3:7; 4:1, 10; 14:3 v.l., 5, 10; 18:3, 5; 20:4; also LXX Gen 17:18.

Michael, who is, like his host, "most honored" (see on v. 3), looks like a soldier (see on 1:4 and cf. 2:2) to one who is himself an accomplished soldier (Gen 14:13–16; 1QapGen 22; Tg. Ps.-Jn. Gen 14:14; Nicolas of Damascus in Josephus, *Ant.* 1.159, assigns to Abraham an "army," στρατῷ). But Michael is no ordinary soldier, for he shines like the sun (ἡλιόρατε), as do the enthroned Abel in 12:5 and Death disguised in 16:10. LSJ has no entry for ἡλιόρατος. Lampe, s.v., refers only to *TA*. The related ἡλιόμορφος describes Michael again in 7:4, the archangel Dokiel in 13:1, 10, and Death in 16:6; 17:12. Dean-Otting suggests that in these places *TA* "reveals the sun-dominated landscape of Egypt."[17] In any case the notion that angels are bright or white is a commonplace; see Dan 10:6; 4Q547 fr. 1:5; *L.A.E.* 9:1; Mark 16:5; *Vit. Proph. Elijah* 2; *Gos. Pet.* 9:36; *Pap. Chester Beatty* XVI 25a v.; *Hyp. Arch.* 93:13–15; Cyprian, *Mort.* 19; Gregory the Great, *Dial.* 4.13, 37; *Sefer Ha-Razim* 2nd Firmament 93; etc. Thus having a face like an angel, as in Acts 6:15; *Acts Paul Thec.* 3; and Ps.-Palladius, *Hist. mon.* 2, refers to radiance; cf. Add Esth 15:13; Strack-Billerbeck 2:665–66. In line with all these texts, the comparison of heavenly figures with the sun is also widespread: *1 En.* 14:18, 20 (God); *Jos. Asen.* 14:9 (an angel, probably Michael); Matt 13:43 (glorified saints); Rev 1:16 (the risen Jesus); 10:1 (an angel); *2 En.* 1:5 (two angels); 19:1; *Apoc. Zeph.* 6:11 (an angel); *Vis. Paul* 12 (angels). Michael himself was probably known as "the angel of light" (see on 1:4) while *Herm. Sim.* 8.3.3 describes him as "glorious" (ἔνδοξος), and *Gen. Rab.* 2:5 says that, wherever Michael appeared, there was the glory of the Shekinah. Eustathius of Trake, *Encom. on Michael*, ed. Budge, p. 102, has Michael "shining like the sun." Evidently, even though Michael is incognito, his metamorphosis cannot completely hide his splendor.

The Commander-in-chief is "most beautiful," πανευπρεπέστατε (cf. v. 2: εὐπρεπεστάτου), and that "above all the sons of men," πάντας τοὺς υἱοὺς τῶν ἀνθρώπων (= כל־בני(ה)אדם, as in Ps 33:13 and 89:48); cf. 4:3 (again of Michael); 16:6 (εὐπρεπὴς ὡραῖος ὑπὲρ τοὺς υἱοὺς τῶν ἀνθρώπων— of Death). LSJ, s.v., πανευπρεπής*, lists only Dio Chrysostom, *Troj.* 15 v.l., and Joannes Tzetzes, *Hist.* 8.518 (the latter with the superlative). One may add Ps.-Gregory of Nazianzus, *Christus patiens* 1287, 2057; Michael Psellus, *Poem.* 67.217; John Cameniates, *Expug. Thess.* 4.6; 22.3 (πανευ-πρεπέστατον).

"The sons of men" is a Semitism meaning "all people"; cf. LXX Prov 8:31; Isa 52:14; Jer 32:19; Dan 5:21; Joel 1:12; Gk. *1 En.* 10:7; etc. There is irony here, for even though Abraham recognizes that his guest is unlike all other human beings, he does not yet realize that he an angel and so a

---

17 Dean-Otting, *Heavenly Journeys*, 181.

"son of God."[18] To my knowledge, Michael is not elsewhere in the literature "handsome" or "beautiful." But other angels are; see 2 Macc 3:26; Josephus, *Ant.* 5.277; and *Lad. Jac.* 3:3. Further, Philo, *Quaest. Gen.* 4.5, says that Abraham's three guests had "a most excellent and divine countenance"; and in *TA*, Michael's beautiful appearance—so emphasized (2:2, 4, 5)—is part of the set up: his beauty stands in contrast with the ugliness of Death, whose appearance is so horrible that it slays people (17:6–19).

2:5. The language is formal, as though Abraham is addressing a king: "Wherefore (τούτου χάριν; see on 13:4) I request of your presence (τῆς σῆς παρουσίας; cf. 13:4, 6, with eschatological sense) … . Inform me (δίδαξόν με; see on 19:5), your supplicant (τὸν σὸν ἱκέτην) … ." Cf. 9:3 (ἱκέτην σου); LXX Ps 73:23 (τῶν ἱκετῶν σου); Ecclus 36:16 (τῶν ἱκετῶν σου); Josephus, *Ant.* 20.56 (τὸν σὸν ἱκέτην); Gregory of Nazianzus, *Ep.* 103 (τὸν σὸν ἱκέτην); etc. "Your presence" has royal connotations, for not only is the chief meaning of παρουσία "visit of a ruler," but one often addressed emperors with an abstract noun + "your" (cf. "your majesty" and "your grace").[19] In the LXX (where the word occurs only in books first written in Greek), however, παρουσία carries the purely secular sense of "arrival" or "presence": Jdt 10:18; 2 Macc 8:12; *3 Macc.* 3:17. "From whence has come (ὅθεν ἔοικεν; ὅθεν: cf. 7:4; LXX: 44, over a third in 1, 2, 3, 4 Maccabees) your youth" (τὸ νέον τῆς ἡλικίας σου) seems to reflect Abraham's puzzlement that while Michael is obviously of high rank, he is nonetheless youthful. One expects a figure of achievement and authority to be older. Our text may assume that angels, even though created near the beginning of creation (*Jub.* 2:2; *2 En.* 29:3; Tg. Ps.-Jn. Gen 1:26; etc.), appear young (as always on icons): 2 Macc 3:26, 33; Mark 16:5; Acts 1:10; Josephus, *Ant.* 5.277; *Gos. Pet.* 13:55; Cyprian, *Mort.* 19; etc. Yet given that "many things which had been said about Michael in earlier aggadic sources were transferred by the Merkabah mystics to Metatron,"[20] and given that Metatron was known as "the youth" (נער), as in *3 En.* 2:2; 3:2; 4:1, 10 (Schäfer, *Synopse* 3–6 = 884–87) and *b. Yebam.* 16b,[21] perhaps Michael was also known as "the youth."

---

[18] For angels as "sons of God" see Gen 6:2, 4; Job 1:6; 2:1; 38:7; Ps 29:1; 89:7; 4QDeut^j LXX Deut 32:8; 11QMelch. 2:14; *1 En.* 13:8; 106:5; *Pr. Jos.* fr. A in Origen, *Comm. Jo.* 2.31; etc.

[19] J. Svennung, *Anredeformen: Vergleichende Forschungen* (Uppsala: Almqvist & Wiksell, 1958), 68–69. Cf. the similar formulations in 2:5 (τὸ σὸν κάλλος); 4:6 (τὸ σὸν κράτος); and 16:10 (ἡ σὴ ἐνδοξότης).

[20] Gershom G. Scholem, *Jewish Gnosticism, Merkabah Mysticism, and Talmudic Tradition* (New York: Jewish Theological Seminary of America, 1960), 46.

[21] See further Fossum, *Name of God*, 312–13.

"From whence (you have come) and from what (πόθεν καὶ ἐκ ποίας) army (στρατιᾶς; for στρατιά* of the heavenly host or army see Gk. *L.A.E.* 38:3 v.l.; *Jos. Asen.* 14:7 [probably in connection with Michael]; *Gk. Apoc. Ezra* 6:16, 17; Vatican Gr. 1982, ed. Wenger, p. 214) and teach me (again δίδαξόν με; see above) from what road your beauty (κάλλος; cf. 16:12; 17:12) has come" underlines the two motifs of Michael as soldier and of his handsome appearance (see on v. 4). Already the LXX uses στρατιά of the heavenly host (צבא): 2 Βασ 22:19; Neh 9:6; Hos 13:4. On the parallel with the traditions about Moses see p. 24.

πόθεν καὶ ἐκ ποίας appears to be precisely paralleled otherwise only in Proclus, *Euc. elem. comm.* 728, and patristic texts: Athanasius, *Ep. Jov.* 4 PG 26.820B; Chrysostom, *Hom. Matt.* 87.1 PG 58.769; *Hom. Jo.* PG 59.89; *Laud. Paul.* 4.17; John Philoponus, *In Aristotelis physicorum libros comm.*, ed. Vitelli, p. 89.

2:6. Michael, again calling Abraham δίκαιε (cf. v. 3), does not answer the questions put to him about his youth, army, and route. He instead announces that he comes from "the great city" (ἐκ τῆς μεγάλης πόλεως) and that "the great king" (τοῦ μεγάλου βασιλέως) has "sent" (ἀπεστάλην) him. For ἀποστέλλω with angels as the object see LXX Gen 24:7; Exod 23:20; 2 Macc 11:6; 15:22–23; Tob 4:17; 12:14, 20; Matt 13:41; 24:31; Mark 13:17; Gk. *L.A.E.* 6:2; 9:3; 13:1–2 (of Michael); Justin, *1 Apol.* 63.5; etc. *TA* again uses the verb with God as subject in 4:10 (a devouring spirit); 7:8 (Michael), 11–12 (Michael); 8:10–11 (Michael); 18:3–4 (Death), 11 (a life-giving spirit).

Both city and king go unnamed, but scripturally literate readers will think of Ps 48:3, where Jerusalem is "the city of the great king" (LXX 47:3: ἡ πόλις τοῦ βασιλέως τοῦ μεγάλου). Patristic literature often quotes or alludes to this verse: Ps.-Athanasius, *Serm. major de fide* 93.7; Romanos the Melodist, *Cant.* 39.12; etc. For God as "the great King" see also Mal 1:14; *Sib. Or.* 3:56, 499; Herm. *Vis.* 3.9.8; Epiphanius, *Pan.* 19.3; etc. For other "great" cities in Jewish literature see Jonah 1:2; 3:2; *Sib. Or.* 4:82. For "the great king" of earthly kings see Eccles 9:14; Isa 36:13; Jdt 2:5; *Sib. Or.* 4:119; Isocrates, *Archid.* 6.84.2; etc.[22] Perhaps we are to assume that Abraham himself would think of Jerusalem and Melchizedek, for in Jewish tradition Melchizedek, who is well known to Abraham (Gen 14:17–24), is king of Jerusalem (= Salem in 1QapGen 22:13, the targums, and elsewhere). However that may be, the language is implicitly transferred—for

[22] Against Dean-Otting, *Journeys*, 182, there is no special connection with the ruler of Persia.

readers, not for Abraham—to the heavenly Jerusalem, a well-known conception; see *1 En.* 90:28–29; Gal 4:26; Heb 11:10; Rev 3:12; *4 Ezra* 7:26; *2 Bar.* 4:2–7; *T. Dan* 5:12–13; *4 Bar.* 5:35; *Apoc. El. (C)* 1:10; Origen, *Cels.* 7.29; *SB* 5719.5; *b. Ta'an.* 5a; *b. Ḥag.* 12b; etc.[23] According to *2 Bar.* 4:4, God gave Abraham a vision of this unearthly city. If our text presupposes this, then the irony is all the greater, for not only has Abraham already met Michael, but he knows the place from whence he comes.

Michael's mission to God's "true friend" (φίλου αὐτοῦ γνησίου; see on v. 3) is unclear, because διαδοχήν ... ἀποκομίζομαι is not a known idiom. The long Romanian, ed. Roddy, p. 25, has: *ša ša gătaescă,* "to get ready," which is ambiguous, and neither RecShrt. nor the rest of the versions help because they have nothing corresponding to 2:6. διαδοχή* means "succession"—patristic texts use it of succession of office, including the episcopal office (Lampe, s.v.)—and ἀποκομίζω* means "carry away, escort" (LSJ, s.v.; cf. LXX Prov 26:16; 2 Macc 2:15; Gk. *3 Bar.* 11:9). The two words do not seem to go together. Perhaps the text is corrupt. Given that Eusebius, *Vit. Const.* 2.35, uses διαδοχή for the inheritance of property, maybe Michael's purpose is to help Abraham set his inheritance in order.[24] This accords with the prominence of this theme in *TA*: 1:4; 4:10; 8:10; 15:1, 7. Such a reading does justice to διαδοχή but not ἀποκομίζω. So given that Michael's mission is to take Abraham to heaven, and further that ἀποκομίζω in Hippolytus, *Comm. Dan.* 4.51, and Basil the Great, *Hom.* 6.3, means "carry away (in death)," perhaps the sense is that the archangel has come to remove the patriarch from earth. This interpretation does justice to ἀποκομίζω but not διαδοχή.

The verse ends with Michael cryptically remarking that the king is calling his true friend to himself: πρὸς αὐτὸν προσκαλεῖται. The verb also appears in 1:4, where God calls Michael to himself. More importantly, it foreshadows 3:3, where the tree speaks of God calling to himself those who love him. Although God is sometimes the subject of this verb in both the LXX (Exod 3:18; Amos 5:8) and New Testament (Acts 2:39; 16:10), in itself the word has no theological connotations. Gregory of Nazianzus, *Or.* 8 PG 35.797C does, however, use it of being called away by death.

2:7. Michael, addressed as κύριέ μου (cf. MT Gen 18:3: אדני), here obeys Abraham (as also in 14:5, again with δεῦρο, a favorite word: 2:7; 7:1; 14:5,

---

[23] See further Hans Bietenhard, *Die himmlische Welt im Urchristentum und Spätjudentum* (WUNT 2; Tübingen: Mohr-Siebeck, 1951), 192–204.

[24] So the translations of Sanders and Schmidt. Craigie, Box, and Stone: "to take the place of." Delcor: "porteur d'une invitation." Janssen: "... sorgen sollte um die Ablösung eines treuen Freundes von ihm."

12 [bis]; 16:2, 4; 18:9; 20:8). But Abraham, in due course, will not obey Michael. Michael is also addressed with the respectful "lord" in v. 12; 11:8; 13:1; 14:1 (cf. 7:6), and maybe in chapter 10 (see on 10:6). This is one point at which the parallelism between Michael and Death breaks down: Abraham never calls Death "lord."

2:8. "In order to converse" = πρὸς ὁμιλίαν. ὁμιλία can mean "company" (LXX Exod 21:10; Wis 8:18; Philo, *Decal.* 109; 1 Cor 15:33), and Sanders translates our words with "beside the company" (cf. v. 1). But ὁμιλία probably here means "speech," as it does in 5:3 and 6:1 (cf. LXX Prov 7:21 and Lampe, s.v., ὁμιλία). πρός then states the goal (= "for the purpose of," as in 8:11). *Let. Arist.* 122 (πρὸς τὰς ὁμιλίας); Josephus, *Ant.* 5.191 (πρὸς ὁμιλίαν); Michael Psellus, *Chronog.* 6.4 (βραδυτέρα δὲ τὴν γλῶτταν πρὸς ὁμιλίαν); and *Theol.* 74.68 (πρὸς ὁμιλίαν τὰς γλώττας κινεῖν) supply parallels. For Abraham's posture see on v. 1.

2:9. Abraham, having presumably conversed some time with Michael, now instructs his servants, the sons of Masek (see on v. 1), to fetch horses (ἵππων; cf. v. 10) from the herd (ἀγέλην; ἀγέλη*: LXX: 11, never of horses) for the "stranger" (ἐπίξενος; see on v. 2). Abraham wants to conduct his visitor home (cf. v. 12). The beasts are, presumably out of consideration for the guest, to be "tamed" or "subdued" (δεδαμασμένους; δαμάζω*; cf. LXX Dan 2:40; *Sib. Or.* 3:501; Mark 5:4; Jas 3:7–8; Josephus, *Ant.* 3.86; etc.). The point is emphasized: "agreeable and broken," εὐμενεῖς δὲ καὶ ἡμέρους (εὐμενής*; ἡμερους*)—a regular pair: Philo, *Fug.* 99; *Legat.* 243; Basil the Great, *Ep.* 26; *Adv. Eunomium* 2 PG 29.585C; etc. MT Genesis does not assign horses to Abraham, but LXX Genesis 14 has him capturing the horses of Sodom, if only to return them.

2:10. Michael now addresses Abraham by name and calls him what the patriarch has called him, "lord," κύριέ μου; cf. 5:12; Gen 23:6, 11; 24:42; 1QapGen 22:18. Sarah calls Abraham "lord" in 5:12; 6:2, 4, 5, 8, and Isaac does the same in 7:2. So too Death in 17:7 and 18:4, which adds to the parallels between Michael and his successor. The archangel politely asks Abraham not to bring an animal. He mysteriously explains that his refusal is not an exception arising out of this situation but his rule: he refuses on principle (ἀνέχομαι τούτου; ἀνέχομαι*) to sit on a four-footed animal, ζῴου τετραπόδου—a standard expression: Aristotle, *Gen. an.* 753A; Galen, *De differentia pulsuum* 8.573; Aesop, *Fab.* 120; Origen, *Princ.* 4.2.1; etc. Both τετράπους and ζῷον occur in the LXX, but never together.[25]

---

[25]   τετράπους appears in RecShrt. 13:10 fam. E, in an otherwise unrelated verse.

2:11. Michael clarifies that his king (= God; cf. v. 6) is rich (πλούσιος ἐν ἐμπορίᾳ; cf. 1:5) and has authority (ἐξουσίαν; cf. 9:8; 13:11) over both people and every kind of beast, κτήνεσιν παντοίοις (κτῆνος*: cf. RecShrt. 2:12; παντοῖος*); cf. Nicephorus Gregoras, *Hist. Rom.* 2.623 (παντοίων ἄλλων ἀγέλας κτηνῶν) and the πάς + κτῆνος in LXX Gen 8:1; 36:6; Deut 20:14. The angel then repeats his comment from v. 10, that he refuses to sit on any four-footed animal. The thought seems to be that, if Michael wished to ride an animal, he would have an animal because his king has plenty of them. So if he is on foot, it is because he wants to be on foot. Abraham will understand this in a mundane way. But readers—who know that angels often appear on heavenly horses (e.g. 2 Kgs 6:17; Zech 1:8–11; 6:1–8; 2 Macc 3:25; 10:29–31; Rev 6:1–8; 19:14)—will wonder whether the angel refuses to ride for some mysterious reason linked to his other-worldly nature. Would his fiery nature,[26] to be inferred from his brightness, harm or even burn up an earthly animal?[27] Maybe *b. Ḥag.* 14b is relevant: R. Johanan b. Zakkai asks, "Is it proper that while you are expounding 'the work of the Chariot' and the divine presence is with us and the ministering angels accompany us that I should ride on the ass!" Schmidt, calling attention to *Acts Thom.* 40, where Thomas at first hesitates to ride a speaking ass, argues that immaterial beings do not ride on material animals: the two do not mix.[28] We in any case learn in chap. 4 that there are other facets of life, such as eating, that Michael cannot participate in.

2:12. Michael, again addressing Abraham as "righteous soul" (see on v. 3), proposes that they go to Abraham's house by foot and suggests that their spirits will soar (μετεωριζόμενοι). Throughout the LXX, μετεωρίζω* typically refers to being lifted up in arrogance: 2 Macc 5:17; 7:34; etc. But according to the dictionaries the word can also bear the figurative sense of "to soar" (of the mind or spirit), as sometimes in Philo (*Her.* 241; *Mos.* 2.139; *Spec. leg.* 1.44), and that is probably is its meaning here (so Slav.

---

26 Cf. 12:1; 4Q405 20–21–22 ii 10; *1 En.* 14:11; *2 Bar.* 21:6; *Apoc. Abr.* 19:6; *2 En.* 29:1–3; 39:5; Tertullian, *Marc.* 3.9; Evagrius of Pontus, *Gnosticus* 1.11. The rabbis, on the basis of Ps 104:4 and their equation with stars, thought angels to be made of fire; cf. *b. Ḥag.* 13b–14a; *Gen. Rab.* 78:1; *Deut. Rab.* 11:4; *Pirqe R. El.* 22; *Rev. Mos.* A 3. שׂרף means both "seraph" and "burning." Tg. Job 25:2 says plainly that Michael is "of fire." So too Michael Psellus, *Or. hagiographicae*, ed. Fisher, pp. 238–39. According to Eustathius of Trake, *Encom. on Michael*, ed. Budge, p. 132, Michael is "a minister of flaming fire."

27 This was the guess of James, *Testament*, 120.

28 Schmidt, "Testament," 1:85.

fam. 1).[29] Turner prefers "amuse oneself" and cites Socrates, s.v., with examples from the fifth century and later.

ἀμήν prefaces Abraham's final comment. Introductory "amen" also occurs in 8:7; 18:10; 20:2 (ἀμήν, ἀμήν); and in a seventh-century BCE potsherd in Hebrew.[30] With the exception of the Jesus tradition and maybe Rev 7:12 and 22:20, "amen" is otherwise used responsively, as in 20:15; RecShrt. 14:7; LXX Deut 27:15; Neh 8:6; Ps 106:48; etc.[31] It follows that *TA* is in this particular probably under Christian influence. K. Berger has instead argued that *TA* is the proof that the synoptic usage is Jewish.[32] But *TA* itself cannot establish his case, for too much of its language is later and Christian.[33] After "amen" Abraham adds: "So be it, lord," γένοιτο κύριε; cf. 14:5; 18:10; LXX Isa 25:1; Jer 3:19; 11:5; *Ps. Sol.* 4:16, 29. As Justin Martyr, *1 Apol.* 65.4, observes, γένοιτο is the equivalent of אמן, and the one translates the other in LXX Num 27:15; Deut 27:17–23; Ps 88:53; etc. So if one were to posit a Semitic ancestor for *TA* RecLng., it would presumably have at the end of 2:12 prefatory אמן אמן which recurs not only in 20:2 but also is typical of John's Gospel: 1:51; 5:19; etc. Christians, however, used both γένοιτο ἀμήν and ἀμὴν γένοιτο, and this may well suffice to explain *TA* 2:12; see *Prot. Jas.* 13; Ps.-Athanasius, *Haer.* PG 28.524C; Gregory of Nazianzus, *Carm. mor.* PG 37.813A; Chrysostom, *In Ps. 118* PG 55.700; *P. Oxy.* 925; *Sibyllla Tiburtina*, ed. Alexander, p. 22.18; Ps.-John of Damascus, *Trin.* PG 95.12A.

---

[29] So the translation of Sanders. But Craigie translates "lightly," Box "gently."

[30] John Strugnell, "'Amen, I Say Unto You' in the Sayings of Jesus and in the Early Christian Literature," *HTR* 67 (1974), 177–82.

[31] Alfred Stuiber, "Amen," *RAC* Supplement-Lieferung 1/2 (1985), 310–23. But S. Talmon, "Amen as an Introductory Oath Formula," *Textus* 7 (1969), 124–29, finds prepositive "amen" in Jer 28:6 and the Hebrew text behind LXX 3 Βασ 18:39 and Jer 15:11.

[32] Klaus Berger, *Die Amen-Worte Jesu: Eine Untersuchung zum Problem der Legitimation in apokalyptischer Rede* (BZNW 39; Berlin: de Gruyter, 1970), 4–6.

[33] So rightly Joachim Jeremias, "Zum nicht-responsorischen Amen," *ZNW* 64 (1973), 122–23.

Chapter 3: Signs and Wonders

Bibliography: Allison, "Abraham's Oracular Tree". Albert Henrichs, "'Thou Shalt not kill a Tree': Greek, Manichaean and Indian Tales," *Bulletin of the American Society of Papyrologists* 16 (1979), 85–108. James, *Testament*, 59–64. Kuhn, *Offenbarungsstimmen*, 110–14. A. Marmorstein, "Legendenmotive in der rabbinischen Literatur," *Archiv für Religionswissenschaft* 17 (1914), 132–33. Schmidt, "Testament," 2:125–27. Turner, "Testament," 110–11. Visotzky, "Conversation."

Long Recension

3:1. They went away from the field to his house. 3:2. Alongside that road stood a cypress tree. 3:3. According to the commandment of God the tree cried with a human voice and said: "Holy holy holy is the Lord, who calls those who love him." 3:4. Abraham hid the mystery, supposing that the Commander-in-chief had not heard the voice of the tree. 3:5. Coming near to the house, they sat down in the courtyard. And Isaac, seeing the appearance of the angel, said to Sarah his mother: "My lady mother, behold, the man sitting with my father is not a son of the people who dwell on the earth." 3:6. And Isaac ran and bowed down and fell at the feet of the incorporeal one. And the Commander-in-chief blessed Isaac and said: "The Lord God will grant to you his promise which he promised to your father Abraham; he will grant to you the precious oath (made to) your father and your mother." 3:7. Abraham said to Isaac his son: "Child Isaac, draw water from the well and bring it to me here in the vessel, so that we might wash the feet of this stranger, for he is weary

Short Recension fam. E

3:1. They both went, 3:2. and when they came near the city, about two stadia away, they found, in a very large road, a great tree with three hundred branches, resembling a tamarisk. 3:3. And they heard a voice from the branches which said, "Holy (are you), the one who brings the news." 3:4. And Abraham heard the voice, and he kept quiet before him; and he hid the mystery in his heart, saying, "What then is this mystery?" 3:5. When he arrived at the house, Abraham said to his servants, "Rise and go out to the herd and bring cattle. Quickly slaughter them and prepare them so that we might eat and drink, because today is a day of rejoicing. 3:6. And the servants brought (them) as Abraham had commanded. He called his son Isaac and said to him, "My beloved son Isaac, stand up, fill up the vessel with water, and bring it so that we may wash the feet of the stranger to whom we are giving our hospitality. 3:7. For I say in my soul that this will be for me the last time that I fill the basin to wash the feet of a man receiving our hospitality." 3:8. When Isaac heard his

from his long journey to us." 3:8. And running to the well, Isaac drew water in the vessel and brought it to him. 3:9. Then Abraham came and washed the feet of Michael, the Commander-in-chief. Abraham was deeply moved and he wept over the stranger. 3:10. And Isaac, seeing him weep, also wept himself. And the Commander-in-chief, seeing them both weeping, also himself shed tears with them. 3:11. Now the Commander-in-chief's tears fell into the vessel, and they became precious stones. 3:12. Abraham, when he saw what had happened, was dumbfounded; and he furtively took the stones and hid the mystery, keeping it in his heart alone.

father say this, he cried and brought the vessel and said, 3:9. "Oh father, what is this that you said, 'This is for me the last time of washing the feet of a man who is receiving hospitality in our house'?" 3:10. And Abraham, when he saw Isaac crying, himself cried greatly. And Michael, seeing them cry, cried with them. 3:11. And Michael's tears fell into the vessel and became a stone.

TEXTUAL NOTES ON THE LONG RECENSION

3:1. J lacks "from ... house." 3:2. I omits "Alongside ... road." // G abbreviates by dropping "stood ... tree." 3:3. G drops "According ... God." // After "the Lord" G adds σαβαώθ (assimilation to Isa 6:3), J ὁ θεός (which results in κύριος ὁ θεός, which occurs over 560 times in the LXX; cf. also Rev 4:8). B Q also have κύριος ὁ θεός, but after the verb. // I omits "those ... him." 3:5. J drops "with my father ... son," which is either deliberate abbreviation or homoioteleuton (καθεζόμενος ... υἱός). // A ends with κατοικούντων τὴν γῆν. This accords with LXX usage, which usually renders ישב + הארץ with κατοικέω + τὴν γῆν (Gen 34:30; Josh 24:18; etc.; cf. 1 Clem. 60:4). All the other manuscripts have a preposition. B: ἐπὶ τὴν γῆν (cf. LXX Ezek 39:26). G: ἐν τῇ γῇ (cf. Num 33:52; Josh 1:14; Jer 50:5). I Q: ἐπὶ τῆς γῆς (cf. LXX Lam 4:21; Rev 8:13; 11:10; 13:8, 10, 14; 17:2, 8). J: ἐπὶ γῆν (cf. LXX Job 38:26; Ezek 19:12; Wis 11:22). 3:6. B H Q assimilate to the LXX and New Testament by adding καὶ τῷ σπέρματι αὐτοῦ; cf. Gen 17:9; 24:7; Luke 1:55; Acts 7:5; Gal 3:16. // I lacks "his promise ... to you." 3:7. I shortens, dropping "and bring ... vessel." 3:7–4:1. G H omit "for he is ... us" and 3:8–4:1. The result is coherent. 3:7–9. J omits "for he is ... Commander-in-chief."

COMMENTARY

Chap. 3 contains three short scenes. Vv. 1–4 tell the tale of the magical tree that praises God. Vv. 5–6 relate Isaac's recognition that Michael is something other than a human being and then Michael's scripturally informed blessing of Isaac. And vv. 7–12, which return to the theme of Abraham's hospitality, focus on the washing of Michael's feet, which leads to mutual weeping and a second miracle. All three scenes send one to Scripture. The first quotes Isa 6:3 (v. 3). The second refers to God's promise to Abraham (v. 6). The third inevitably recalls the foot washing of Gen 18:4, which it imitates.

The first and third scenes mirror each other. Each relates a memorable nature miracle with a fairy-tale quality. And in each case Abraham naively tries to hide "the mystery" (vv. 4, 12). Sandwiched between the two miracles are two verses that momentarily shift attention from Abraham and introduce Isaac and Sarah. In v. 5 Isaac recognizes Michael's identity, and in v. 6 Michael blesses Isaac. Visually:

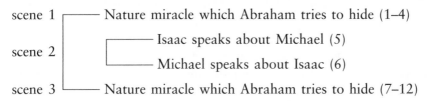

scene 1 ⎡—— Nature miracle which Abraham tries to hide (1–4)

scene 2 ⎢ ⎡—— Isaac speaks about Michael (5)
        ⎢ ⎣—— Michael speaks about Isaac (6)

scene 3 ⎣—— Nature miracle which Abraham tries to hide (7–12)

Like *TA* 2, chap. 3 is also modeled upon Genesis 18, where Abraham washes the feet of his three angelic visitors. *TA* 3, however, shows much more than just a knowledge of a famous old story. It clearly presupposes the LXX wording of the entire saga of Abraham, as appears from the following list of parallels:

v. 1, Abraham owns an ἀγρόν as he does in Gen 23:1–16

vv. 2–4, there is a miraculous δένδρον; cf. LXX Gen 18:4 and 8, both with δένδρον

v. 5, Abraham sits (ἐκαθέσθησαν, καθεζόμενος) as he does in LXX Gen 18:1 (καθημένου)

v. 5, Sarah is addressed as κυρία; cf. LXX Gen 16:4, 8, 9

v. 5, υἱός ... ἀπὸ τοῦ γένους appears also in LXX Gen 19:38

vv. 6, 8, Isaac runs (ἔδραμεν); cf. LXX Gen 18:2, where Abraham runs (προσέδραμεν)

v. 6, Isaac bows down (προσεκύνησεν); cf. LXX Gen 18:2: Abraham bows down (προσεκύνησεν)

v. 6, ηὐλόγησεν + object + καὶ εἶπε as in LXX Gen 14:19

v. 6, Michael refers to promises to Abraham and Sarah; cf. Gen 15:5; 17:5; 26:3

v. 7, εἶπεν δὲ Ἀβραὰμ πρός; cf. LXX Gen 17:18: εἶπεν δὲ Ἀβραὰμ πρός

v. 7, Abraham addresses Isaac as τέκνον as he does in LXX Gen 22:7, 8

vv. 7–8, ἀντλῆσαι ὕδωρ; cf. LXX Gen 24:13, ἀντλῆσαι ὕδωρ

vv. 7–8, Abraham has a well (φρέαρ) as also in LXX Gen 21:25–33; 22:19

v. 7, ὕδωρ ... νίψωμεν ... τοὺς πόδας; cf. LXX Gen 18:4: ὕδωρ ... νιψάτωσαν τοὺς πόδος

v. 7, Abraham speaks of Michael's ὁδός; cf. LXX Gen 18:5, τὴν ὁδὸν ὑμῶν

The influence of scriptural language recedes with v. 9 and the notice of Abraham's deep emotions; for the next few verses, the story has no Old Testament parallels.

The biblical language activates informed memories, and readers understand that *TA* 3 replays the past. Without such memories one would not only lose the enjoyable sense of *déjà vu* but also find some things puzzling. Isaac and Sarah, for instance, walk on without introductions, and v. 6 means nothing unless one knows about God's promise to Abraham. So *TA* presupposes a knowledge of Genesis.

RecShrt. 3 is very different from RecLng. 3. In the episode of the singing tree, the former has Abraham and Michael go to "the city" (which remains unspecified), not "his house" (although this is mentioned later); the tree—which no longer speaks at "God's command" and is no longer a cypress but, in E A H, ὅμοιον ἐρεικίνου (= "like a tamarisk"?)[1]—has three hundred branches; and its words, which now come from those branches, are neither addressed to God nor do they echo Isa 6:3. Rather is Michael blessed as Abraham overhears: "Holy (are you), the one who brings the news."[2] After this, RecShrt. has nothing corresponding to Isaac's recognition of Michael and Michael's blessing of Isaac but rather an account, inspired by LXX Gen 18:7–8, of Abraham directing his servants to prepare animals for a meal. Furthermore, when Abraham announces his intention to wash Michael's feet, an act RecShrt. never recounts, he already knows that he will never again perform this service for a stranger. Finally, when Michael's tears become "a stone" or "stones" (the witnesses differ), there is no remark that Abraham kept "the mystery" in his heart.

RecShrt. resembles Scripture in ways RecLng. does not when it uses πορευόμαι in v. 1 (cf. LXX Gen 18:16: συνεπορεύετο), λέγει Ἀβραὰμ τοῖς παισὶν αὐτοῦ in v. 5 (cf. LXX Gen 22:5: εἶπεν Ἀβραὰμ τοῖς παισὶν αὐτοῦ), and ἀγαπητέ in v. 6 (cf. LXX Gen 22:2, 12, 16). It is also closer to Scripture when Abraham's servants slaughter animals for a meal (cf. Gen 18:7–8) and it may, under the influence of Gen 18:1; 21:33, identify the

---

[1] See Lampe, s.v., ἐρ(ε)ικίνη. But the manuscripts show confusion here: D: ῥικίνου, C τρεκίνου, I: ἐκοίνου.

[2] But H I have "Holy holy holy," and there are additional variants.

tree as a tamarisk (see above). But RecLng. is nearer to Scripture when it borrows from Isa 6:3, refers to God's foundational promise to Abraham (v. 6; cf. Gen 15:5; 17:5; 26:3), and echoes Genesis in ways RecShrt. does not: Abraham sits, Sarah is addressed as κυρία, υἱός ... ἀπὸ τοῦ γένους appears, Isaac runs, he prostrates himself before the visitor, ηὐλόγησεν + object + καὶ εἶπε and εἶπεν δὲ ᾽Αβραὰμ πρός are used, Abraham addresses Isaac as τέκνον, Isaac draws water from Abraham's φρέαρ, and reference is made to Michael's ὁδός; see above.

How does one explain these differences, great and small? Delcor supports the priority of RecShrt., at least for the episode of the speaking tree: (i) it contains more details; (ii) "like a tamarisk" correlates with Gen 21:33; and (iii) "tamarisk" in Hebrew is אשל, which numerically is 331, and in RecShrt. the tree has three hundred branches.[3] Against all this, details can be added as well as subtracted,[4] and there is no rule that assimilation to Scripture must be primary as opposed to secondary. Students of the Synoptics may recall that, on the theory of Markan priority, Matthew often adds scriptural citations and allusions to received material. Aside from this, RecShrt. 3 fails to borrow from Isa 6:3 and is otherwise not consistently closer to Scripture than RecLng. 3; see above. Finally, 331 ≠ 300, which is why Delcor conjectures that 300 became 331 (with no support from the textual witnesses).

Kuhn argues for the priority of RecLng.[5] The cypress is, he thinks, the *lectio difficilior* because it is not from the biblical story of Abraham. This is a weak argument, for surely a scribe, knowing the Bible, could have changed a cypress into a tamarisk-like tree. Kuhn's other argument is not so easily dismissed. In RecLng., the tree sings, "Holy holy holy," in RecShrt. "Holy" alone. The refrain from Isa 6:3 also appears in the Coptic, Arabic, and Ethiopic versions, even though they are typically allies of RecShrt. So "Holy, holy, holy" at least seems original. In accord with this, *homoioteleuton* readily explains RecShrt.: an eye could easily have moved from the first ἅγιος to the third ἅγιος.

What of the rest of the chapter? RecLng. exhibits a nice structural balance (see above) which RecShrt. lacks. RecLng. also, as will become clear, is full of irony, surprise, and even some levity—all because Abraham does not yet know who Michael is until a later chapter (see on 6:6). This

---

3   Delcor, *Testament*, 97. Cf. Kohler, "Apocalypse," 583; Ginzberg, "Testament," 94; Box, *Testament*, 4, n. 1; Turner, "Testament," 111. The Bohairic has three branches while Slavonic S1 has 320. RecShrt. C D, like RecLng., offer no numbers.

4   Sanders, *Tendencies*.

5   Kuhn, *Offenbarungsstimmen*, 110–14.

delay in recognition, with its parallel in Genesis 18[6] as well as in Greco-Roman tales of visiting gods,[7] keeps the narrative on two levels. Readers know what Abraham does not, or only yet suspects, so some things have more than one meaning. RecShrt., by contrast, rapidly collapses the distance between readers and Abraham, for the patriarch already knows by the end of chap. 3 that he is about to die. And to this fact he seems resigned, so he does not resist death. The powerful and memorable picture of the perfectly obedient Abraham disobeying God is accordingly lost. RecShrt., not unlike many later accounts of Job, presents us with a predictable and orthodox hero, whose perfection exorcizes all the dramatic tension. He no longer represents the universal human condition and its fear of death but becomes an unimaginative cipher of ideal piety. This obedient Abraham also leaves the advent of Death later in the story without motivation. If the patriarch has not resisted Michael, why must another come? So even if both RecLng. and RecShrt. contain original elements, it appears that, on the whole, either RecLng. is an artistic improvement upon a tradition more faithfully represented by RecShrt., or, which is more likely, that the latter is largely a secondary narrative that suffers from brevity and a devotion afraid to play too much with a biblical hero.

3:1–2. Michael and Abraham leave "the field," ἀπέρχονται ἀπὸ τοῦ ἀγροῦ (ἀγρός*). This must be the field of Ephron son of Zohar, with the cave of Machpelah, the burial place of Sarah and Abraham; see Genesis 23; 25:9. As the angel and the patriarch travel the road towards Abraham's house (cf. 2:12), they pass a cypress tree. κυπάρισσος* appears a dozen times in the LXX, almost always for either אֹרֶן (e.g. Job 40:12) or בְּרוֹשׁ (e.g. 4 Βασ 19:23). LXX Isa 60:13; Ezek 31:3; Ecclus 24:13; and 50:10 emphasize the tree's height and majesty; cf. Josephus, *Ant.* 8.54; 9.197–198. The diction-

---

6   Gen 18:1 says that YHWH appeared to Abraham, but many if not most readers have assumed that the patriarch does not yet know where the three men are from; see William John Lyons, *Canon and Exegesis: Canonical Praxis and the Sodom Narrative* (JSOTSup 352; Sheffield: Sheffield Academic Press, 2002), 157–61 (who argues that the consensus is here wrong). On this reading, his actions are more appropriate than he knows when he bows down before them and addresses them as "lord" (the MT pointing is usually set aside by modern commentators; cf. the Samaritan Pentateuch and Targum; note also *b. Šeb.* 35b). For ancient readers who stress the delay in Abraham and Sarah's recognition of what is going on see Philo, *Abr.* 113; *Quaest. Gen.* 4.6 (here Abraham seems to be of two minds); Gregory of Nazianzus, *Or. 28* PG 36.49A; Chrysostom, *Hom. Gen.* PG 53.378–80, 383; Theodoret of Cyrrhus, *Comm. Dan.* PG 81.1500C–D; Augustine, *Quaest. Gen.* 41.
7   See Daniela Flückiger-Guggenheim, *Göttliche Gäste: Die Einkehr von Göttern und Heroen in der griechischen Mythologie* (Bern: Peter Lang, 1984).

aries state that cypress trees are often cultivated in cemeteries, which might be relevant here as the tree prophesies death. But this seems to be a contemporary observation, and I am unaware of ancient evidence of the practice. Some Greeks did, however, believe there to be a cypress in Hades; see *Orphicorum fragmenta*, ed. Kern 32a.

3:3. Just as a miracle—Sarah's conception of Isaac in her old age—occurs when the three strangers visit Abraham in Genesis, so too here: the cypress speaks at God's command, πρόσταξιν θεοῦ; cf. 9:5 (σῇ προστάξει); Gk. fr. *Jub.* 10:9; 48:5; Philo, *Vit. cont.* 86. Trees are prominent in Abraham's story in the Bible. In Gen 12:6 he travels to "the oak of Moreh."[8] In 13:18 he settles by "the oak(s) of Mamre" (cf. 14:13); see on 1:2. In 18:1–8 he serves his three visitors under one of those oaks. And in 21:33, which is undoubtedly the Scripture that lies behind the tamarisk-like tree in *TA* RecShrt. 3:3, he plants "a tamarisk tree in Beersheba" (see further below).

Although the LXX nowhere associates Abraham with a cypress, artistic evidence associates the cypress with him. The depictions of the sacrifice of Isaac at Dura-Europos and Sepphoris turn the "thicket" of Gen 22:13 into a tree (cf. Pontificio commissione di archeologia sacra Cal E29); and the tree at Dura-Europos has been plausibly identified as a cypress.[9] That this is the correct judgment seems likely because there are Christian representations of Genesis 22, presumably based upon Jewish prototypes, that feature a cypress, such as a Coptic-style, sixth-century miniature from the Etschmiadzin Evangeliary and a fifth-century lamp from Jerusalem.[10] One art historian has posited a Syro-Palestinian derivation for this cypress in the *Akedah*.[11] We are still left, whatever the provenance, with explaining the genesis of the tradition. But that there was such a tradition makes the appearance of a cypress in *TA* less unexpected than it otherwise would be

The cypress speaks or chants, and old Jewish texts, like world-wide folklore, can depict plants, animals, and objects we would regard as inorganic speaking or singing; see e.g. Homer, *Il.* 19.405–417 (a horse); Num 22:22–30 (Balaam's ass); Rev 9:13–14 (the heavenly altar); *4 Bar.* 9:30 (an

---

[8] This oak was long a cult site; cf. Gen 35:4; Deut 11:30; Josh 24:26; Judg 9:37. See further below.

[9] Rachel Hachlili, *Ancient Jewish Art and Archaeology in the Diaspora* (HO; Leiden/ Boston/Köln: Brill, 1998), 243.

[10] A. de Waal, "Das Opfer Abrahams auf einer orientalischen Lampe," *Römische Quartalschrift für christliche Altertumskunde und Kirchengeschichte* 1904, pp. 21– 34, and Alison Moore Smith, "The Iconography of the Sacrifice of Isaac in Christian Art," *American Journal of Archaeology* 26 (1922), 167.

[11] Smith, ibid.

eagle); Rúmí, *Mathnawí* 3:4268–81 (mountains); cf. Hippolytus, *Haer.* 9.25: Jews think "nothing inanimate."[12] For trees in particular see Ovid, *Metam.* 8.771–773 (a nymph inside or identical with a tree prophesies punishment to its slayer); Pliny the Elder, *Nat.* 17.243 (included in the "Notes" of a certain "Gaius Epicius" are "cases of trees that talked"); Apollonius of Rhodes, *Argon.* 4.603–605 (lamenting women are turned into or encased inside trees); *Gos. Pet.* 10:42 (Jesus' cross speaks); Philostratus, *Vit. Apoll.* 6.10 (a tree salutes Apollonius "in accents articulate and like those of a woman"); Ps.-Callisthenes, *Hist. Alex. Magn.* rec. α 3.29 (trees foretell Alexander's death; see below, p. 109); *CMC* 6.1–8.12; 9.1–10.15; 98.9–99.9 (date-palms protest being cut and having their fruit eaten). In Exodus 3, God speaks to Moses from a סנה or "bush," and *b. Šabb.* 67a classifies this as a "tree" (אילן).[13] *y. Ḥag.* 77a and *b. Ḥag.* 14b report that trees sang when R. Johanan b. Zakkai expounded the *Merkabah*, and the latter has them quoting parts of Ps 148:7, 8, 14. *Apoc. Abr.* 13:3 has a bird talk to Abraham, and in later legend the Oak of Mamre gives shade to the righteous but withdraws its cover from the unrighteous (*Zohar* 1.102b). There are also texts in which meadows and trees, like the rest of creation, praise God, although how this is conceived remains unclear: 1 Chr 16:33; Ps 65:13; 96:12; 148:9; Isa 35:1–2; 44:23; 55:12; 11QPs^a 28:6; *b. ʿAbod. Zar.* 24b; *b. Ḥag.* 14b; *b. Roš Haš.* 8a; etc.[14] Sometimes, moreover, we read of those who still understand the language of animals (*b. Giṭ.* 45a) or trees (*b. Sukkah* 28a; *b. B. Bat.* 184a; *Soferim* 16:9). Given that LXX Ezek 31:8 puts the cypress in "the garden of God," it may be relevant that the trees of paradise sometimes sing or talk: *Gen. Rab.* 13:2; Ps.-John of Damascus, *B.J.* 30.280; *Mart. Perp.* 11.[15] Similarly,

---

12 On the ubiquity of the belief in tree-spirits see J. G. Frazer, *The Golden Bough: A Study in Comparative Religion*, vol. 1 (London: Macmillan, 1890), 56–108. On the religious associations of trees in the Hebrew Bible see Carol L. Meyers, *The Tabernacle Menorah: A Synthetic Study of a Symbol from the Biblical Cult* (Missoula, Mont.: Scholars Press, 1976), 133–56.

13 Further, later superstition held that the terebinth of Mamre would sometimes appear to be on fire and yet not be burnt, just like the bush on Sinai; see W. Robertson Smith, *The Religion of the Semites: The Fundamental Institutions* (New York: Shocken, 1972), 193.

14 Note also 2 Sam 5:24, where a noise in the tree tops evidently signals God's presence to fight. Judg 9:7–15; 2 Kgs 14:8–9; and 1QapGen 19:16—this last is in a dream of Abraham—are parables or fables, not really stories of talking trees; cf. Syr. Ahiqar 8:35; *Gen. Rab.* 16:3; 83:5; Tg. Sheni Est 7:9; *Midr. Ps.* 2:14.

15 Ed. Robinson, pp. 78–80: *altitudo arborum erat in modum cypressi, quarum folia canebant sine cessatione.* See further James, *Testament*, 59–64.

in *ARN* A 1 the tree of life verbally rebukes the serpent by quoting Ps 36.[16] Is Abraham's cypress, like Michael, a denizen of paradise come to earth on a mission? And is it coincidence that the tree sings an angelic song (cf. 20:12, where the angels sing the τρισάγιον) while 4:2 calls Abraham's garden a παράδεισος, the same word LXX Genesis 2–3 uses for Eden and which our book later uses of the heavenly paradise (11:10; 14:8; 20:14)?[17]

In *TA* 3:3, the cypress prophesies death in "a human voice" (ἐβόησεν τὸ δένδρον ἀνθρωπίνη φωνή; βοάω*; ἀνθρώπινος*), which must mean in a human language; cf. Herodotus, *Hist.* 2.55–57 (φωνῇ ἀνθρωπηίη recurs three times in connection with a dove supposedly speaking); Gk. fr. *Jub.* 3:28 (ἀνθρωπίνη φωνῇ, of the speech of animals before the fall); *4 Bar.* 7:2–21 (an eagle speaks ἀνθρωπίνη φωνῇ); CMC 10.8–11 (cut trees ἔκραζον δὲ καὶ ἀνθρωπείᾳ φωνῇ). The closest parallel appears to be Ps.-Callisthenes, *Hist. Alex. Magn.*, which may come from Egypt (3rd cent. C.E.?). According to this, when Alexander was in India, two large cypress-like trees, speaking ἀνθρωπίνῳ στόματι, prophesied his death, one in the Indian language, one in the Greek language (rec. α 3.17).[18] In view of this parallel, to which James first called attention, Kuhn infers that *TA* 3 incorporates "ein ursprünglich griechisches oder hellenistisch-orientalisches Motiv."[19] There is only a distant

---

[16]   But "the tree of life" was thought of as a palm tree or olive tree, not a cypress; see Ginzberg, *Legends*, 5:98, 119. Note the absence of the cypress from the list of trees in paradise in *3 Bar.* 4:8.

[17]   Cf. Ps.-Palladius, *Hist. mon.* 21.5, where Jannes and Jambres plant a "paradise" in imitation of Eden. Sometimes commentators on Genesis 18, upon which our text is based, see it as Edenic: "The scene round Abraham's tent has a touch of a restored Eden; the simplicity of the divine visit and the homely conversation with Abraham and Sarah remind one of the intimate way in which Yahweh walked in the garden in the cool of the day, and talked with Adam; we are in the atmosphere of Paradise Regained." So S. H. Hooke, "Genesis," in *Peake's Commentary on the Bible* (ed. Matthew Black and H. H. Rowley; rev. ed.; Sunbury-on-Thames Middlesex: Nelson, 1962), 191. Cf. Bede, *Gen.* 4 on 18:14.

[18]   The story occurs in a long letter of Alexander to Aristotle, a letter which also circulated as a separate work. The legend itself was probably extant during Alexander's lifetime or shortly thereafter; see Reinhold Merkelbach, *Die Quellen des Griechischen Alexanderromans* (2nd rev. ed.; Zetemata 9; Munich: C. H. Beck, 1977), 57–62.

[19]   Kuhn, *Offenbarungsstimmen*, 113. Cf. James, *Testament*, 60–61. Islam later takes up the legend in its stories of the Waq-Waq islands, where the trees have human fruits. For an old Chinese legend in which a tree prophesies death see *The Mythology of All Races*, vol. VIII: *Chinese*, by John C. Ferguson (Boston: Marshall Jones, 1928), 101. Delcor, *Testament*, 98–101, attempts to find a specifically Orphic background. The legend of a piece of oak from Dodona on the Argonauts' ship,

parallel in Jewish tradition, in *Petirat Moshe* (*BHM* 1:128 and 6:76–77), where a supernatural voice predicts Moses' death.

What we know about the giant oak at the ancient and famous oracle of Dodona in Epirus supports Kuhn's claim. Later Dodona's priests and priestesses used several methods of divination, including interpreting the noise of rustling leaves and the sounds of the spring that flowed out of its roots (Ovid, *Metam.* 7.614–630; Suidas, s.v. Δωδώνη). Our earliest source for Dodona, however, is Homer, who speaks of Odysseus going there "to hear the will of Zeus from the high-crested oak of the god" (*Od.* 14.327–328; cf. 19.296–297). The words imply "that the will of Zeus was audible from the oak tree itself. There is nothing to indicate that the oracle was originally conveyed by the tree through other sounds such as the creaking of its trunk or the rustling of its leaves."[20] It accords with this that retellings of the tale of the Argonauts repeatedly have Athena outfitting their ship's keel with a piece of wood from the oak at Dodona, and that this timber more than once speaks directly to them to give guidance: Sophocles, *Trach.* 171–172; *Orphica, Argon.* 263, 1160; Apollodorus, *Bibl.* 1.9.16, 19; Valerius Flaccus, *Argon.* 5.65. Philo knows this legend (*Prob.* 143, quoting Aeschylus), and still others refer more generally to the oak of Dodona as itself an oracle: Aeschylus, *Prom.* 832–833 ("the oaks that speak aloud to people"); Philostratus, *Imag.* 2.33 ("it produces prophecies like the tripod at Delphi"); Virgil, *Georg.* 2.6 ("the oaks that Greeks regarded as oracles"); Scholia on Homer, *Od.* 14.327 ("when the oak tree first uttered a voice").

That the author of *TA* knew about this oak is guaranteed by the knowledge he elsewhere shows of Homer, who refers to Dodona more than once. It is likely that ancient Jews in the Hellenistic world would have associated Abraham's tree, at least that in RecLng., with the renowned oak of Dodona simply because the latter was the most famous oracular tree in Greco-Roman mythology.[21] Given, moreover, that Abraham's tree crypti-

---

already mentioned by James, appears in an Orphic source (*Orphica, Argon.* 1160). Moreover, if a tree sings when the archangel Michael walks by, Orpheus could hold creatures spellbound with his music. The stories about Dodona are, however, hardly confined to Orphic sources, and Michael neither plays music nor causes the tree to sing. Furthermore, Orpheus is a musician who charms the animals; he does not hear trees speak.

[20] H. W. Parke, *The Oracles of Zeus: Dodona, Olympia, Ammon* (Oxford: Blackwell, 1967), 13.

[21] See on 6:6. On knowledge of Homer in the Greco-Roman world see Ronald F. Hock, "Homer in Greco-Roman Education," in *Mimesis and Intertextuality in Antiquity and Christianity* (SAC; ed. Dennis R. MacDonald; Harrisburg, Pa.: Trinity Press Intl., 2001), 565–77. For knowledge of Homer among Jews see n. 23 on p. 169.

cally foretells his impending death, it is relevant that Seneca, *Herc. Ot.* 1472–1478, reports that the oak at Dodona prophesied the death of Heracles: "Very well, it is fulfilled. My fate becomes clear; this is my last day. The oracular oak and the grove that shook the temples of Cirrha with a rumbling that came from Parnassus once predicted this destiny to me: 'Heracles! You, the conqueror, will fall some day by the hand of a man you have killed. This is the end destined to you after you have traveled all over the earth, the seas, and through the realm of the shades'" (cf. Sophocles, *Trach.* 155–177, 1157–1178). In Strabo, *Geogr.* 6.1.5 and Livy 8.24.1, Dodona foretells yet another death, this time that of Alexander the Great.[22] So despite the use of Isa 6:3, the prophesying tree of *TA* 3 is closely related to pagan legend.

Despite the pagan parallels, the origin of Abraham's oracular tree probably lies in exegesis of the Hebrew Bible. According to Gen 21:33 (which has clearly influenced RecShrt. 3:3), "Abraham planted a tamarisk tree (אשל) in Beer-sheba." *Gen. Rab.* 54:6 comments: "R. Judah said, 'The word for tamarisk (אשל) means orchard, which signifies [because it supplies the letters for שאל, "ask"] ask for whatever you wish—figs, grapes, or pomegranates.' R. Nehemiah said, 'The word for tamarisk (אשל) means inn, which signifies [because it supplies the letters for שאל] ask for whatever you wish—meat, wine, or eggs." *ARN* A 7 similarly moves from the אשל of Gen 21:33 to the verb "to ask" (שאל): "And whatever one might ask for was to be found in Abraham's house, as it is said, 'And Abraham planted a tamarisk tree in Beer-sheba'" (cf. *Tanḥ.* Genesis Noah 14).

The rabbinic texts show us that at least some, when reflecting upon Gen 21:33—a text given so many different meanings in antiquity[23]—thought of people asking questions. Some connected the asking with the fruits of Abraham's orchard,[24] others with the prepared meals served at his inn for strangers.[25] But it would have been even easier to associate the asking with the tree itself—especially if one knew about the oak of Dodona. And this is, one suspects, exactly what happened. A contributor or *TA* associated Abraham's אשל with שאל and so imagined the patriarch planting a tree that responds to questions, that is, an oracle. שאל is used of consulting an oracle

---

[22] Did this tradition inspire the legend in Pseudo-Callisthenes?

[23] Barr, "Wood," and Robert Hayward, "Abraham as Proselytizer at Beer-Sheba in the Targums of the Pentateuch," *JJS* 49 (1998), 24–37. See further on 2:1.

[24] For the tradition that Abraham planted a פרדיסא = παράδεισος see *b. Soṭah* 10a; Tgs. Ps.-Jn., Neof. 1, Frg. Tg. on Gen 21:33.

[25] For the tradition that Abraham built an inn see *ARN* A 7; *b. Soṭah* 10a; *Midr. Ps.* 110:1.

in Ezek 21:21(26), and indeed of a tree or wood oracle in Hos 4:12. It is certainly easy to envisage the well-known technique of אַל תִּקְרִי[26] being applied to Gen 21:33 this way: "Do not read, 'Abraham planted a tamarisk' (אשל) but rather read, 'Abraham planted a request' (שאלה), that is, a tree that answers requests."

Such a reading may have been encouraged by a knowledge of or reflection upon Gen 12:6–7, where the Lord appears to Abraham near אלון מורה. Whether or not אלון means "terebinth" or "oak," מורה literally means "teacher." Modern commentators regularly observe that this was almost certainly "a place where divine oracles could be obtained."[27] Gunkel—who recalled Dodona when writing on Gen 12:6—rendered אלון מורה as "oracle terebinth,"[28] Moffatt (in his translation) as "the oracular oak." While Jewish tradition, including the LXX, shied away from this interpretation (see below), the Hebrew clearly suggests it. Further, Judg 9:37 speaks of people coming from the direction of אלון מעוננים which means "the diviner's oak"; and the singular, within a canonical context, suggests a reference back to Gen 12:6–7, as many commentators observe (cf. Deut 11:30; Josh 24:26; Judg 9:6). So the Hebrew Bible itself puts Abraham near an oracular tree.

Although the fact has been missed, *TA* is probably not the only ancient text to associate Abraham with a plant of praise. In the dense and obscure fr. 1 of Philo the Epic poet (2nd cent. BCE?), preserved in Eusebius, *Praep. ev.* 9.20.1, Abraham's departure to sacrifice Isaac includes these words: λιπόντι γὰρ ἀγλαὸν ἕρκος αἰνοφύτων. Holladay translates this as "For this one who left the splendid enclosure of the awesome race … ."[29] This takes αἰνοφύτα, a *hapax legomenon* in Gk. literature, to be from αἰνός (= "dread") + φυτόν (= "offspring"). Holladay sees a reference to Abraham leaving Ur, the home of Nimrod and the builders of Babel (Gen 12:1–4). Yet the context is clearly the sacrifice of Isaac, so one instead thinks of the departure for Mount Moriah, that is, of Abraham leaving the home he shares with Isaac (Gen 22:2–3). LSJ, s.v., prefers to derive the word from

---

[26] See Rimon Kasher, "The Interpretation of Scripture in Rabbinic Literature," in *Mikra: Text, Translation, Reading and Interpretation of the Hebrew Bible in Ancient Judaism and Early Christianity* (ed. M. J. Mulder; CRINT 2/1; Assen/Maastricht/Minneapolis: Van Gorcum/Fortress, 1988), 572–73.

[27] Gordon J. Wenham, *Genesis 1–15* (WBC 1; Waco, Tex.: Word, 1987), 279.

[28] Hermann Gunkel, *Genesis* (6th ed.; Göttingen: Vandenhoeck & Ruprecht, 1964), 166.

[29] Carl R. Holladay, *Fragments from Hellenistic Jewish Authors*, Vol. 2, *Poets: The Epic Poets Theodotus and Philo and Ezekiel the Tragedian* (TTPS 30/12; Atlanta: Scholars Press, 1989), 235, 254–56.

αἶνος/αἰνέω (= "praise") + φυτόν (= "plant"), in which case Philo's line means this: "For this one who left the beautiful courtyard of plants of praise ... ." It is surely not coincidence that *TA* 3 gives Abraham a courtyard (v. 5) and tells of a tree that sings praises to God (v. 3). It may also not be coincidence that Philo the Epic Poet probably hailed from Alexandria,[30] the likely provenance of *TA*. Perhaps we are dealing here with a legend of Egyptian Jewry.

One understands why rabbinic literature does not know this tradition. Despite the apparent veneration of sacred trees by such biblical worthies as Jacob, Joshua, and Deborah (Gen 35:4; Josh 24:26; Judg 4:5), Hos 4:12 forthrightly condemns those who seek answers from "a piece of wood" (עץ). Whether or not this refers to a living tree or something made from a tree (such as a cultic pole), the Hebrew Bible is full of condemnations of אשרות (Deut 16:21; Judg 6:25–26; etc.), and the rabbis, like the LXX translators and a few modern scholars, understood these to be living trees (e.g. *m. ʿOr.* 1:7–8; *m. ʿAbod. Zar.* 3:7, 9–10; the LXX translates with ἄλσος/η, "grove/s," and, in Isa 17:8; 27:9, δένδρα; cf. the Vulgate, which most often has *lucus*, "grove"). Many would have been unhappy with Abraham living near and/or listening to an oracular tree. Josephus thought it a point of boasting that the temple in Jerusalem had "no trace of a plant, in the form of a sacred grove or the like" (*C. Ap.* 1.199, quoting Ps.-Hecataeus). It is telling that the MT's "oak of teaching" in Gen 12:6 (see above) becomes "lofty oak" in the LXX and *Jub.* 13:2, "the plains of Moreh" in Targum Onqelos, "the plain that had been pointed out" in Targum Pseudo-Jonathan, and "the plain of the vision" in Targum Neofiti 1. All of these renderings diminish or eliminate the possibility of associating Abraham with an oracular oak. Barr has argued, moreover, regarding the MT's אשל ("tamarisk") in Gen 21:33, that the various renderings (see n. 23) arose from anxiety about associating Abraham with this particular אשל;[31] and de Vaux documented an analogous tendency to "ostracize" Mamre and its sacred tree.[32]

"Holy holy holy is the Lord, who calls those who love him" takes up two traditional phrases, "Holy holy holy" and "those who love him," and

---

[30] See Holladay, ibid., p. 208, citing others in agreement.

[31] Barr, "Wood."

[32] Roland de Vaux, *Ancient Israel* (2 vols.; New York/Toronto: McGraw-Hill, 1965), 2:292–93. He argues, among other things, that the plural of the MT ("the oaks of Mamre," cf. 1QapGen 21:19) represents an attempt "to water down the superstitious veneration of a particular tree," and that the singular of the versions ("the Oak of Mamre") is the older reading.

unites them with "who calls" (ὁ προσκαλούμενος; cf. 2:6).[33] "Holy holy holy" is from Isa 6:1–5, the record of Isaiah's vision that includes the words the Seraphim's call to one another: "Holy holy holy Lord Sabaoth (LXX: ἅγιος ἅγιος ἅγιος κύριος σαβαώθ); the whole earth is full of his glory" (v. 3). Variations of these words entered Jewish liturgy as the *Qedussah* and Christian liturgies as the *Trisagion* and the *Ter Sanctus*,[34] and they also occur elsewhere, including *merkabah* texts.[35] Almost all of the relevant texts remember "Holy holy holy" as belonging to an angelic hymn; cf. Tertullian, *Or.* 3: Christians can utter the *sanctus* because they are like angels. Despite this, and even though the line was scriptural and liturgical, Isa 6:3 was freely reworked, as even in the targum: "Holy in the heavens of the height, his sanctuary, holy upon the earth, the work of his might, holy in eternity is the Lord of hosts; the whole earth is filled with the brilliance of his glory." The closest parallel to *TA*'s variation is Rev 4:8, which opens with ἅγιος ἅγιος ἅγιος κύριος, follows with ὁ, and then continues with a characterization. The construction appears to be rare, but it does occur also in Ps.-Ephraem, *Sermo in pretiosam et vivificam crucem*, ed. Phrantzoles, p. 141.10 (ἅγιος ἅγιος ἅγιος ὁ ὢν καὶ ὁ ἦν καὶ ὁ ἐρχόμενος); Oecumenius, *Comm. Apoc.*, ed. Hoskier, p. 72.16 (ἅγιος ἅγιος ἅγιος κύριος ὁ θεὸς ὁ παντοκράτωρ ὁ ὢν καὶ ὁ ἦν καὶ ὁ ἐρχόμενος); and John of Damascus, *Trisag.* 14.25 (ἅγιος ἅγιος ἅγιος ὁ σταυρωθεὶς δι᾽ ἡμᾶς).[36]

"To those who love him" (τοῖς ἀγαπῶσιν αὐτόν) appears also in 1 Cor 2:9; but Paul is here evidently quoting from a lost *Apocalypse of Elijah*,[37] which in turn seems to have rewritten Isa 64:4 ("to those who wait for him" became "to those who love him"). The same phrase also appears in

[33] Box, *Testament*, 4, and Sanders, "Testament," 883, translate: "Summoning him to (be with) those that love him." But τοῖς ἀγαπῶσιν αὐτόν is unlikely to refer to the citizens of heaven (see below).

[34] Bryan D. Spinks, *The Sanctus in the Eucharist Prayer* (Cambridge: Cambridge University Press, 1991).

[35] *1 En.* 39:12; Rev 4:8; *1 Clem.* 34:6; Gk. *L.A.E.* 43:4 v.l.; *4 Bar.* 9:3; *1 Apoc. John*, ed. Tischendorf, 17; *2 En.* 21:1 J; *Mart. Perp.* 12; Ps.-Hippolytus, *De consummatione mundi* 39; Tertullian, *Or.* 3; *Apos. Con.* 7:35:3; 8:12:27; *Lad. Jac.* 2:18; *t. Ber.* 1:9; *b. Ḥul.* 91b; *3 En.* 40:2 (Schäfer, *Synopse* 58 = 924); *T. Isaac* 6:6, 24; *T. Adam* 1:4; 4:8; *Ques. Ezra* A 29; *Syr. Apoc. Dan.* 36; *Sefer Ha-Razim* 7th firmament 17; *Ma'ase Merkava*, ed. Schäfer, *Synopse* 551, 569, 593.

[36] Given these parallels, Spinks, *Sanctus*, 30, appears to be wrong in his confidence that the reading in RecLng. is not from a Christian hand.

[37] So Origen, *Comm. Matt.* 23.37; Jerome, *Comm. Isa.* 17 on 64:6; Photius, *Quaest. Amphil.* 151; see Michael E. Stone and John Strugnell, *The Books of Elijah Parts 1–2* (Missoula, Mont.: Scholars Press, 1979), 42–73.

Asc. Isa. 11:34 v.l.; *Arm. 4 Ezra* 5:40; *Acts Thom.* 36; and *Apos. Con.* 7:32:5, all of which are either dependent upon Paul or the lost *Apocalypse*. On the other hand, the phrase may have a more general background. Love of God is enshrined in the Shema (Deut 6:6), and τοῖς ἀγαπῶσιν + τὸν θεόν or αὐτόν occurs in texts unrelated to Paul or the *Apocalypse of Elijah* (e.g., LXX: Deut 7:9; Neh 1:5; Ecclus 1:10; Jas 1:12; 2:5; *Diogn.* 12:1).

The tree's words, which neither name Abraham nor say anything directly about his death, must be completely opaque to the patriarch. This interests because Greek oracles (unlike Jewish prophecies) were notoriously equivocal. They "were expressed in dark and ambiguous words and their interpretation was the crucial point."[38] Delphi's famous answer to Croesus, that he would destroy a great empire if he attacked Persia (Herodotus, *Hist.* 1.51), is typical. The Greek oracles were riddles to be solved. The Athenians had to debate what the Pythia meant by prophesying, before the battle of Salamis, that a "wooden wall" would save them (Herodotus, *Hist.* 1.140–143). Heraclitus said that Delphi does not make clear statements but rather gives signs (in Plutarch, *Pyth. orac.* 21.404D; Diels 93 = Kahn 33). This is the mysterious world to which our tree's words belong. Their ambiguity and indirectness, which constitute a μυστήριον (3:4), are characteristic of the Greek oracular style.

3:4. Abraham, supposing (νομίσας; cf. 14:14; 15:4; 16:8) that maybe Michael has not heard what he himself has heard, apparently hides the mystery by not saying anything. ἔκρυψεν ... τὸ μυστήριον recurs in v. 12, where Abraham hides the mystery of the tears that have become precious stones. The closest parallel outside *TA* is *CMC* 6.1–8.12, in which a date palm utters a warning to the man climbing it, who then says to Mani: "I did not know that this secret mystery is with you ... . Guard this mystery" (φύλαξον τὸ μυστήριον). In Henrichs' judgment, "The thematic and stylistic similarities between these two texts are too close to be accidental, and raise tantalizing questions. Was the author of the Manichaean miracle story familiar with a Syriac version of the *Testament of Abraham*? Or was the talking tree as an aretalogical motif more common in Jewish Haggadah than the evidence would suggest?"[39]

Whatever the answers to these questions, Abraham was known as one who could keep a secret. Both Philo, *Abr.*170, and Josephus, *Ant.* 1.225, stress how he kept from his family God's command to sacrifice Isaac. In

[38] Martin P. Nilsson, *Cults, Myths, Oracles, and Politics in Ancient Greece* (Lund: C. W. K. Gleerup, 1951), 124.
[39] Henrichs, "Tree," 106.

TA, his naive action generates irony, for the truth, evident from chap. 1, is that Michael knows full well what is going on. It is Abraham who is in the dark. μυστήριον (cf. רז, סוד) is here used in its secular sense of a secret to be kept from others.[40] In the LXX, μυστήριον appears in the later, Hellenistic writings (Daniel, Tobit, Judith, Wisdom, Ecclesiasticus, 2 Maccabees) and on several occasions also carries secular sense: Tob 12:7 (μυστήριον … κρύψαι), 11 (μυστήριον … κρύψαι); Jdt 2:2; Ecclus 22:22; 27:16–17, 21; 2 Macc 13:21.

The theme of secrecy is part of Gen 18:1ff., upon which *TA* 3 is built. In 18:17 God asks, "Shall I hide (LXX: κρύψω) from Abraham what I am about to do?" Tgs. Ps.-Jn., Neof. 1, and Onq. on v. 14 transform "Is anything too wonderful for the Lord" into "Is it possible for anything to be hidden from the Lord?" And the LXX's ἐγκρυφίας in v. 6 was the opportunity for commentators to remark upon keeping various sorts of secrets: Philo, *Sacr.* 59–60; Origen, *Hom. Gen.* 1; Ambrose, *Abr.* 1.33; *La Chaîne sur la Genèse* 1082 *ad* Gen 18:13; etc.

3:5. Coming "near" (πλησίον* also means "near" in RecShrt. 14:7 fam. E; cf. Jdt 7:13; 2 Macc 6:11; *4 Macc.* 8:14) Abraham's house (cf. 2:12), the patriarch and the angel sit (ἐκαθέσθησαν; cf. LXX Gen 18:1 and see on 2:1, 8) in the courtyard, αὐλῇ. αὐλή* does not appear in LXX Genesis, but for Abraham's courtyard in Philo the Epic Poet see above, on 3:3. Josephus, *Ant.* 1.196, also gives him a courtyard. Any reader who knew the layout of the church of Mamre that Constantine built would have thought of its courtyard. Given that Abraham's residence also has a *triclinium* (see on 4:1), maybe we should think of something like a Herodian palace. *Gen. Rab.* 42:8 mentions "the palace at Mamre." Later Christian art sometimes replaces Abraham's tent with a fancy permanent dwelling. For instance, in Parisinus Graecus 923, a ninth-century illustrated version of John of Damascus' *Sacra Parallela*, the miniature for Genesis 18 has "a rather elaborate building, whose dome rests on three double columns."[41]

At this point Isaac appears without introduction and beholds the stranger's face, τὴν πρόσοψιν τοῦ ἀγγελοῦ; see below. The son is, unlike his father, immediately able to see through Michael's disguise, which must be rather thin. Isaac communicates his realization not to his father but to his mother, styled κυρία, as is in LXX Gen 16:4, 8, 9. Sarah's presence is

---

[40]   See G. Bornkamm, *TDNT* 4 (1967), 810–11. Cf. P. W. van der Horst, *The Sentences of Pseudo-Phocylides: With Introduction and Commentary* (SVTP 4; Leiden: Brill, 1978), 260–61.

[41]   Kurt Weitzmann, *The Miniatures of the Sacra Parallela: Parisinus Graecus 923* (Princeton: Princeton University Press, 1979), 40. See plate VIII:27.

surprising because in Scripture she dies long before her husband dies (Gen 23:1–2; 25:7–11). So here our book goes against Torah. Given *TA*'s thorough acquaintance with Genesis, the change must be a deliberate fiction. The contradiction reminds one of 1:1, where Abraham lives to be almost 1000, even though Genesis has him die at 175. Perhaps the dissonance is intended. Is *TA* openly declaring itself a fable, not history, and that it should be interpreted accordingly?

Isaac swiftly sees that Michael is not "a son of the people (υἱός ... ἀπὸ τοῦ γένους; cf. LXX Gen 19:38; Josephus, *Ant.* 13.26; Acts 13:26) who dwell on the earth" (κατοικούντων τὴν γῆν; see p. 102 and cf. RecShrt. 6:6 fam. E), that is, a human being. So the son is more insightful than the father. Soon we shall see that Sarah also identifies Michael before Abraham does (6:3–5). Abraham may be pious and large-hearted, but he is either dim with age or in denial. We think something similar about him in chap. 10, where his righteous feelings rather than good sense lead him to strike people dead, an error God must halt.

With "the appearance of the angel" (τὴν πρόσοψιν τοῦ ἀγγελοῦ) compare Acts 6:15 (πρόσωπον ἀγγέλου); *Acts Paul* 3 (ἀγγέλου προσώπον); Ps.-Palladius, *Hist. mon.* 6.1 (προσώπον ἀγγέλου). Because angels were thought of as beings of light and because Michael has already been described as like the sun (see on 2:4), the reader thinks of a shining countenance. For the brightness of angelic faces see Dan 10:6; Rev 10:1; 2 *En.* 1:5; J 19:1; etc. On the other hand, *Num. Rab.* 10:5 says that angels are characterized by the awe-inspiring appearance of their eyes.

3:6. The text neglects Sarah's response to Isaac's astounding assertion. It stays with Isaac, who runs (ἔδραμεν; cf. v. 8; also δρομαίως in 5:7 and δρομαῖος in 5:11). He then bows down (προσεκύνησεν; cf. 6:8 [Sarah before Abraham]; 16:9 [Death before Abraham]) before Michael, falling at his feet, προσέπεσεν τοῖς ποσίν, a conventional expression: LXX Exod 4:25; Est 8:3; Jud 14:7; Mk 7:25; etc.; cf. 9:2, also there followed by τοῦ ἀσωμάτου. In many texts human beings fall at the feet of angels; see, e.g., Gen 19:1; Josh 5:14 (Joshua bowing before an angelic "Commander-in-chief," often identified in Jewish and Christian tradition with Michael); Dan 8:17; 10:9; Tob 12:16; Luke 24:5; Rev 19:10; 22:8–9; *Jos. Asen.* 14:3, 10; *Asc. Isa.* 7:21–22; 2 *En.* 1:7; *Apoc. Zeph.* 6:14; 3 *En.* 1:7 (Schäfer, *Synopse* 2 = 884); etc.[42] Despite these parallels, *TA* 3:6 is undoubtedly based upon Gen 18:2. In this, Abraham, upon seeing the three angelic men, runs to them. The LXX uses προστρέχω, and Gen 18:1–8 is, like *TA* 3:6–

---

[42] In many of these an angel rejects prostration, but there is no such admonition in *TA*.

8, suffused with a sense of haste, something the commentators have not missed; cf. Philo, *Sacr.* 59; *Quaest. Gen.* 4.3, 8; Origen, *Hom. Gen.* 1; Chrysostom, *Hom. Gen.* PG 53.382; Ps.-Chrysostom, *Contra theatra* 3; Ambrose, *Abr.* 1.33; Ps.-Ephraem, *Comm. Gen.* 15.1; *La Chaîne sur la Genèse* 1068 *ad* Gen 18:6–7; *t. Soṭah* 4:1. Abraham's haste is clearly depicted in a Mosaic at Santa Maria Maggiore, Rome: he appears to be running.[43] Origen commented on Genesis 18: Abraham "makes haste in all things. All things are done urgently. Nothing is done leisurely.... . He himself runs, his wife hastens, the servants makes haste. No one is slow in the house of a wise one" (*Hom. Gen.* 1).

When, in Genesis 18, he reaches the three strangers, Abraham bows down (προσεκύνησεν) before them. So Isaac in our story acts as his father did before—with this one difference, that the son knows that the visitor is an "incorporeal." ἀσώματος (LXX: 0; NT: 0; Josephus: 0), which recurs in 4:9; 9:2; 11:9; 14:4; 15:4, and 6—an attribute of God or the gods in Graeco-Roman writers (Xenophanes, *fr.* 23, in Clement of Alexandria, *Strom.* 5.109; Iamblichus, *Myst.* 1.16, 17, 17; Albinus, *Epit.* 10.7)—commonly describes angels and demons: Philo, *Conf.* 174; Ign. *Smyrn.* 3:2; *Apoc. Abr.* 19:6; *T. Sol.* 2:5 v.l.; *2 En.* 20:1; Lampe, s.v., D. Philo, *Abr.* 118, and *Quaest. Gen.* 4.8, uses it of the three angels visiting Abraham; so too Theodoret of Cyrrhus, *Quaest. Gen.* 69; Acacius of Caesarea in *La Chaîne sur la Genèse* 1069, 1073 *ad* Gen 18:8; Ephraem in ibid. 1071 *ad* Gen 18:8; cf. Macarius Magnes, *Apocrit.* 4.27. Theodosius of Alexandria, *Encom. on Michael*, ed. Budge, p. 4.11, uses the word of Michael.[44] The archangel is what Jewish texts otherwise call a רוח, a "spirit" (*1 En.* 15:4, 6, 7; 1QS 3:25; CD 12:2–3; etc.). That he has solid feet (v. 9) implies that, although incorporeal, he can temporarily transform himself into flesh; cf. Tertullian, *Carn. Chr.* 3.6; 6.3–5; *Res.* 62.1, who argues from the foot washing in Gen 18 that the angels were solid creatures. Certainly it is unlikely that ἀσώματος is meant absolutely. Even the early church fathers, so influenced by Hellenistic dualism, generally allow that angels have bodies of a sort: Justin Martyr, *Dial.* 57.2; Tatian, *Or.* 15; Lactantius, *Inst.* 7.20, 21; Augustine, *Serm.* 12 9.9; etc.[45]

---

[43]   See Goodenough, *Jewish Symbols*, 3:plate 1.

[44]   For its application to Michael in Coptic texts see Müller, *Engellehre*, 17.

[45]   See F. Andres, *Die Engellehre der griechischen Apologeten des zweiten Jahrhunderts und ihr Verhältnis zur griechisch-römischen Dämonologie* (Paderborn: F. Schöningh, 1914). Pseudo-Dionysius did not believe angels to have matter and form, but it would be wrong to read his sophistication into earlier writers, who tended to think of the soul as quasi-material. For later Byzantine ideas see Glen Peers, *Subtle Bodies: Representing Angels in Byzantium* (Berkeley: University of California Press, 2001).

The Commander-in-chief blesses Isaac through a pronouncement, ηὐλόγησεν τὸν Ἰσαὰκ καὶ εἶπε. ηὐλόγησεν + object + καὶ εἶπε appears only four times in the LXX, all in Genesis; and in its first occurrence it introduces God's blessing of Abraham: Gen 14:19; 27:23, 27; 48:15. In Genesis God blesses both Abraham (12:2–3; 14:19; 22:17; 24:1, 35) and Isaac (25:11; 26:3, 12, 24, 29; in all cases the verb is εὐλογέω, as here). Sanders translates Michael's words as "The Lord God will bestow (χαρίσεται; χαρίζω; cf. 8:6; LXX: 12, 9 in 2, 3, 4 Maccabees) upon you his promise which he gave to your father Abraham and to his seed, and he will also bestow upon you the precious (τιμίαν; see on 2:3) prayer (εὐχήν) of your father and your mother." He then comments: "Gen mentions no relevant *euchē*, but cf. Jub 22:6–9, where Abraham prays for his descendants."[46] On this reading, the first half of the benediction refers to Genesis (15:5; 17:5), the second half to an extracanonical legend. That εὐχή elsewhere in *TA* RecLng. means "prayer" (5:2; 14:5, 6, 8; the meaning in 5:5, however, is uncertain) favors Sanders's proposal. One can nonetheless equally take Michael's words as an instance of Semitic-like parallelism. In this case, the two halves are roughly synonymous, only the second half enlarges itself to include Sarah, and Gen 26:3 can be the intertext. In this, God speaks to Isaac: "I will be with you and will bless you; for to you and to your descendants I will give all these lands, and I will fulfill the oath (LXX: ὅρκον) that I swore to your father Abraham." Given the widespread confusion between the "oath" (ὅρκος = (ה)שבע) and the "vow" (εὐχή = נדר) in antiquity,[47] it is natural to link *TA* 3:6 to Gen 26:3. In both places the promise to parents is confirmed to their son. τοῦ πατρός σου καὶ τῆς μητρός σου is then an objective genitive: "the oath (made to) your father and mother"; cf. ἐπαγγελίας τῶν πατέρων in Rom 15:8 and *T. Jos.* 20:1. With τὴν ἐπαγγελίαν … ἣν ἐπηγγείλατο cf. Plato, *Prot.* 319A (τὸ ἐπάγγελμα ὃ ἐπαγγέλλομαι); LXX Est 4:7; 1 John 2:25; and *Prot. Jas.* 7:1. For ἐπαγγελία of God's blessing of Abraham see Rom 4:12; Gal 3:14–18, 29; 4:28; Josephus, *Ant.* 1.236 (cf. 2 *Bar.* 57:2). For ἐπαγγέλλομαι (LXX: 10, 6 in 1, 2, 3 Maccabees) of that blessing see Acts 7:5; Gal 3:19; Heb 6:13.

3:7. Abraham addresses (εἶπεν δὲ Ἀβραὰμ πρός, as also in LXX Gen 17:18) Isaac as τέκνον, as he will again in 4:2 and 5:4 (cf. LXX Gen 22:7, 8). This term of endearment, the use of παῖς in 7:8, the absence of Rebekah from our book, and Isaac's constant nearness to his parents contribute to the impression that he is quite young. RecShrt. 2:1 fam. E indeed pictures Isaac

[46] Sanders, "Testament," 883.
[47] S. Lieberman, *Greek in Jewish Palestine* (New York: Jewish Theological Seminary of America, 1942), 115–43.

in his father's arms, which, if not an original part of our book, at least shows how someone read it. Once more, then, *TA*, despite its constant dependence upon Scripture, has no problem going its own very different way for the sake of the story. In Genesis, Abraham is 100 when Isaac is born (21:5), so Isaac is 75 when Abraham dies at the age of 175 (25:7). Were *TA* in harmony with Genesis, Isaac would be 75.

Isaac is to draw water from the well, ἄντλησον ὕδωρ ἐκ τοῦ φρέατος (ἀντλέω: cf. v. 8; φρέαρ: cf. v. 8). Is the well in the courtyard (cf. 2 Sam 17:18)? Christian readers familiar with the church at Mamre would think of the famous well that was there. Both ἄντλησον ὕδωρ (cf. LXX Isa 12:3; John 4:7; *4 Bar.* 2:5) and ὕδωρ ἐκ τοῦ φρέατος (cf. LXX Num 21:22) are particularly appropriate. For ἀντλῆσαι ὕδωρ occurs in the story of Isaac meeting Rebekah (LXX Gen 24:13), ὕδωρ is brought when the three visitors show up in Gen 18:4, and the patriarchs are repeatedly associated with wells (Gen 16:14; 21:14, 19, 25, 30–33; 22:19; 24:11, 20, 62; 25:11; 26:15, 18–25, 32–33; 28:10, etc.). Moreover, Gk. fr. *Jub.* 10:17 locates "the well of the oath" (LXX Gen 21:31) near the Oak of Mamre.

Isaac is to fetch water "in the vessel," ἐπὶ τῆς λεκάνης (λεκάνη: 3:7, 8, 11; 6:6). Although the LXX uses λεκάνη in Judg 5:25 and 6:38 (for ספל; cf. *Jos. Asen.* 18:9), the word does not appear in the story of Abraham. With the water, father and son are to "wash the feet of this stranger," ἵνα νίψωμεν τοῦ ἀνθρώπου τούτου τοῦ ἐπιξένου τοὺς πόδας (νίπτω: 3:7, 9; 6:6; ἐπίξενος: see on 2:2). Cf. 4:1: ἀνθρώπου τούτου τοῦ ἐπιξενισθέντος ἡμῖν. As Michael is not a man but an angel, the superfluous ἀνθρώπου (which perhaps echoes LXX Gen 18:2: ἄνδρες) is ironic. The words depend upon LXX Gen 18:4 (καὶ νιψάτωσαν τοὺς πόδας ὑμῶν), which immediately follows a request for water and precedes a meal, as here. While the MT seems to imply that the three angels in Genesis 18 wash their own feet, the LXX implies that others will do this, presumably Abraham's servants ("let them wash your feet"; cf. Tg. Neof. 1 marg. on Gen 22:4). In *TA* 3, however, Abraham, exemplar of hospitality (see on 1:1), personally performs the task. One may compare Jerome, *Ep.* 66.11: Abraham himself washed the angelic feet. So too the Vulgate and Augustine, *Serm.* 277 9. For foot washing as an act of hospitality see Gen 19:2; 24:32; 43:24; *Jos. Asen.* 7:1; 1 Tim 5:10; Homer, *Od.* 19.308–319; Pachomius, *Rules* 51–52; etc.[48] Abraham, despite his wealth and status, is an exemplar of humble

---

[48] On foot washing in general see B. Kötting, "Fußwaschung," in *RAC* 8 (1972), 743–77; John Christopher Thomas, *Footwashing in John 13 and the Johannine Community* (JSNTSup 61; Sheffield: Sheffield Academic Press, 1991), 26–60 (pp. 37–38 on *TA* 3).

servanthood, like Jesus in John 13; cf. also 1 Sam 25:41; *Jos. Asen.* 13:15; 20:1-5; Herodotus, *Hist.* 6.19. Ancient sources typically reckon foot washing to be a menial task suited for women and slaves: Herodotus, *Hist.* 2.172; Cattalus, 64.155-163; Plutarch, *Pomp.* 73.6-7; *Mek.* on Exod 21:2; *b. Menaḥ.* 85b; *b. Ketub.* 4b, 61a.

Abraham comments that the stranger is "weary" (ἐκοπίασεν; κοπιάω*) because he has made a "long journey," ἀπὸ μακρᾶς ὁδοῦ; cf. Philo, *Mos.* 1.194 (μακρᾶς ... ὁδοῦ); Josephus, *Ant.* 8.228 (μακράν ... ὁδόν); etc. The words are doubly ironic. First, they are truer than the speaker knows. Michael has indeed come on a long journey—all the way from heaven to earth. Second, despite the journey, no angel would be tired or in need of rest.

3:8. With the exception of "running" (δραμών), which is taken from 3:6 (q.v.), the nouns and verbs of this verse correspond to Abraham's order in v. 7:

8: Ἰσαακ εἰς τὸ φρέαρ ἀντλήσας ὕδωρ ἐπὶ τῆς λεκάνης ἀνήνεγκεν πρὸς αὐτόν
7: Ἰσαακ, ἀντλήσον ὕδωρ ἐκ τοῦ φρέατος καὶ ἔνεγκε μοι ὧδε ἐπὶ τῆς λεκάνης

In this way Isaac's actions perfectly mirror Abraham's command (cf. the correlation between Jesus' command in Mark 11:2-3 and the disciples' action in 11:4-6). He is thus—unlike his father—a model of obedience.

3:9. As Abraham washes (ἔνιπτεν; see on v. 7) Michael's feet, he becomes deeply moved: ἐκινήθησαν δὲ τὰ σπλάγχνα; cf. 5:14: τὰ σπλάγχνα κινηθέντες. Readers only learn the reason for this response in 6:6 (q.v.). The σπλάγχνα (cf. רחמים) are the upper internal organs, the heart, liver, and lungs, which were thought to be the seat of emotions; cf. LXX Prov 12:10; Ecclus 30:7; *T. Levi* 4:4; *T. Zeb.* 7:3; 8:2; Luke 1:78; etc.[49] So σπλάγχνα can be a synonym for "heart." For its combination with κινέω—not found in the LXX, Philo, New Testament, or Josephus—see Gregory of Nazianzus, *Or.* 27 2.14; Ps.-Chrysostom, *Contra theatra* 3 PG 56.547; *De beato Abraham* PG 50.741; Ps.-Ephraem, *Sermo in pulcherrimum Ioseph*, ed. Phrantzoles, p. 298.2; John of Damascus, *Or. in Sabbatum sanctum* PG 96.640C; Theodore the Studite, *Ep.*, ed. Fatouros 56.4.

Abraham weeps (with ἐδάκρυσεν ἐπί cf. LXX Mic 2:6; δακρύω*) while washing the feet of the ξένος. Philo, *Quaest. Gen.* 4.2; Chrysostom, *Hom. Act.* 45.3-4; and Acacius of Caesarea in *La Chaîne sur la Genèse* 1064 *ad* Gen 18:4 all use ξένοι (cf. 1:2) of the visitors in Genesis 18 (see further on 1:1). Christian readers might recall Luke 7:36-38, where a woman washes Jesus' feet with her tears. But signs of literary dependence either way are lacking, and there is a much close parallel in the *Odyssey*; see on 6:6.

---

[49] Helmut Koester, *TDNT* 7 (1971), 548-59; also Turner, "Testament," 90-91.

3:10. The near mechanical parallelism of this verse (cf. the parallelism in vv. 7–8) makes Isaac and Michael kindred spirits:

Isaac, v. 10a   ἰδών ... κλαίοντα   ἔκλαυσεν καὶ αὐτός
Michael, v. 10b   ἰδών ... κλαίοντας συνεδάκρυσεν καὶ αὐτός

Isaac's emotion is only expected. Not so expected perhaps is Michael's sympathetic weeping (συνδακρύω*; LXX: 0; Philo: 0; NT: 0; Josephus: *Ant.* 16.104); cf. Gregory of Nazianzus, *Contra Julianum 1* PG 35.652A, quoting Rom 12:15 with κλαίουσι συνδακρύειν instead of κλαίειν μετὰ κλαιόντων. This is part of *TA*'s humanization of Michael; cf. 4:6 and especially 5:10, where Michael again cries. That angels praise God (Isa 6:3; 11QŠirŠabb.; *b. Hag.* 14a; etc.) seemingly reveals their emotional nature, and their mourning or weeping is elsewhere attested: 4Q225 2 ii 5 (see below); *L.A.B.* 19:16; Origen, *Cels.* 5.52, 55; *b. Hag.* 5b. Indeed, Isa 33:7 speaks of מלאכים (LXX: ἄγγελοι) weeping bitterly, and *b. Hag.* 5b; *Gen. Rab.* 56:5; 65:10; *Lam. Rab.* 1:23; and *Zohar* 1.120a all take the verse to refer to angels. For God's tears see *b. Ber.* 59a and *b. Hag.* 5b (cf. *Midr. Ps.* 20:1; *Lam. Rab.* 1:1).[50]

Abraham cries, then Isaac, then Michael. Similarly, in chap. 5, Isaac cries, then Abraham, then Michael, then Sarah. The contagion of weeping unites the figures in the same experience and impresses upon the reader just how much heaven feels sympathy with those on earth. Like Jesus in Heb 4:15, Michael can "sympathize with our weaknesses." This is part of *TA*'s religious optimism.

LXX Gen 23:2 says that Abraham lamented and mourned for Sarah upon her death (κόψασθαι ... καὶ πενθῆσαι), the MT that he mourned and "wept," בכה; cf. Tgs. Onq., Ps.-Jn. Furthermore, 1QapGen goes on and on about the patriarch's tears when Sarah went to Pharaoh (20:10–12, 16; cf. 22:5); and later legend emphasizes that he shed tears when offering up Isaac: *Pesiq. Rab.* 40; *Zohar* 1.120a (applying Isa 33:7 to Genesis 22). In *Gen. Rab.* 56:5–8 (citing Isa 33:7), not only does Abraham cry, but his tears melt his knife and also fall into Isaac's eyes, and the angels that look on cry too, while in 65:10 the tears of the ministering angels fall into Abraham's eyes (cf. *Lam. Rab.* 1:23). 4Q225 2 ii 5, which says that, when Abraham offered Isaac, "the angels of holiness were standing weeping above," suggests that the image of Abraham crying with Isaac and the

---

[50] On divine and angelic mourning see further Peter Kuhn, *Gottes Trauer und Klage in der rabbinischen Überlieferung (Talmud und Midrasch)* (AGJU 13; Leiden: Brill, 1978).

angels was known already at the turn of the era. Have legends surrounding Genesis 22 inspired the scene in *TA* 3?

3:11. As Michael's tears (δάκρυα: cf. 6:7; 9:2; 14:12) fall into the vessel (λεκάνης: see on v. 7), they became precious stones, λίθοι τίμιοι (= אבנים יקרת; cf. RecShrt. A C I—πολύτιμος—3 Βασ 6:1; 7:46; 2 Chr 3:6; *Jos. Asen.* 18:6; 1 Cor 3:12; etc.). The magical transformation of one thing into another is common enough in ancient texts: Gen 19:26 (Lot's wife); Exod 7:8–13 (rods into snakes), 14–25 (water into blood); John 2:1–11 (water into wine); Homer, *Od.* 24.611–612 (people into stones); Ovid, *Metam.* 3.101–130; 7.121–130 (dragon's teeth into people); 8.699–722 (a hut into a stone temple); Antonius the Hagiographer, *Vit. Symeonis Stylitis* 18 (a worm into a pearl); etc. Moreover, the *Epic of Gilgamesh* already speaks of a tree in paradise that bears precious gems (tablet 9), and tears becoming prized stones or pearls is a motif from world-wide folklore.[51] Yet the nearest Jewish parallel to *TA* 6:7 that I have been able to discover is a medieval legend that the oil from the anointing of David became diamonds and pearls.[52] Apart from the very late date, this is not about tears.

While Jewish tradition here fails, Hellenistic mythology makes up the lack. The ancient scientific treatises that discuss pearls regularly explain that oysters come up from the sea in the early morning and open up to receive the dew of heaven which they, upon returning to the deeps, incubate and turn into pearls.[53] Given the popular identification of dew with the tears of the gods (as in the myths about Eos mourning Memnon),[54] the idea that pearls might be the tears of heavenly beings was, for folklore, very near to hand. More importantly, there are Greek stories in which tears become costly stones. Apollonius of Rhodes reports a story identifying beads of amber with "the tears of Leto's son, Apollo ... the countless tears that he shed before when he came to the sacred race of the Hyperboreans and left shining heaven at the chiding of his father ..." (*Argon.* 4.611–618). This tale may or may not have been well known, but another very much like it certainly was. According to a myth oft told, when Phaethon, son of Helios, endangered the earth by his erratic driving of the sun-chariot, Zeus

---

51 John Arnott, *The Mythology of All Races*, vol. 2: *Eddic*, by John Arnott (Boston: Marshall Jones, 1930), p. 126. The Ningyo, the Japanese mermaid, cries tears of pearls.

52 See Ginzberg, *Legends*, 4:84; 6:249.

53 E.g. Pliny the Elder, *Nat.* 9.107; *Physiologus* 44; Ammianus Marcellinus 23.6.85–86. Cf. Origen, *Comm. Matt.* 10.7.

54 E.g. Ovid, *Metam.* 13.621–622; Statius, *Silvae* 5.1,34; Servius on Virgil, *Aen.* 1.489.

Chapter 3

had to strike him dead with a thunderbolt. As his sisters, the Heliades, bemoaned his fate, "from their eyes they shed on the ground bright drops of amber."[55] This is very close to what we find in *TA*.

3:12. Abraham sees what has happened, ἰδών ... τὸ γεγονός; cf. Acts 13:12; *Acts Phil.* 44. He is dumbfounded, ἐκπλαγείς; cf. 2 Macc 7:12; *4 Macc.* 8:4; 17:16. The New Testament uses ἐκπλήσσω* most often of amazement at Jesus' teaching, but in Mark 7:37 and Luke 9:43 it expresses surprise at miracles, as also in Artapanus in Eusebius, *Praep. ev.* 9.27.24: ἐκπλαγέντα ἐπὶ τῷ γεγονότι. Amazement is a stock motif of miracle stories.[56] So too is keeping what has happened a secret.[57] Evidently Isaac has missed the metamorphosis, for Abraham picks up the stones furtively (κρυφαίως*; cf. LXX Jer 44:17; 47:15; Josephus, *Ant.* 2.219; *T. Zeb.* 7:1) and hides them.

Vv. 11–12 mirror vv. 3–4 and so create an *inclusio*. In vv. 3–4 Abraham hears a miracle. In vv. 11–12 he sees a miracle. In each case the event is a "mystery" (μυστήριον; see on v. 4), and in both Abraham tries to hide it, ἔκρυψεν; see on v. 4. But vv. 11–12 go beyond vv. 3–4 in adding that Abraham kept the matter in his heart alone: μόνον ἔχων ἐν τῇ καρδίᾳ αὐτοῦ. This might remind one of Luke 2:19, where Mary lays up in her heart all that has happened. But there is no clear sign of literary dependence, and there are other parallels (e.g., Gen 37:11; LXX Dan 4:28; 7:28; *T. Levi* 6:2), as well as additional texts in which the heart is a hiding place: LXX Ps 43:22; 1 Cor 14:25; 1 Pet 3:4; *T. Reub.* 1:4 (ἔχω ἐν τῇ καρδίᾳ μου κρυπτά); *La Chaîne sur la Genèse* 1082 on Gen 18:13.

---

[55] Apollonius of Rhodes, *Argon.* 4.605–606. Cf. Ovid, *Metam.* 2.364–366; Pliny the Elder, *Nat.* 37.31; Lucian, *Dial. deor.* 24(25); Hyginus, *Fab.* 154; Quintus Smyrnaeus 5.625–629; Nonnus, *Dion.* 38.432–434; etc. The myth of the Heliades also includes talking trees, a motif that reappears in *TA* 3; see above.

[56] Theissen, *Miracle Stories*, 69–71.

[57] Theissen, ibid., 68–69.

Chapter 4: God commissions Michael again

Bibliography: Allison, "Job in the Testament of Abraham". David Goodman, "Do Angels Eat?," *JJS* 37 (1986), 160–75. Allen Kerkeslager, "Evidence for the Early History of the Amidah in 1 Cor 15:51–52," in Wright, *Multiform Heritage*, 65–78. Turner, "Testament," 112–14.

Long Recension

4:1. Abraham said to Isaac, his son: "My beloved son, go to the dining chamber and make it beautiful. And set up for us there two couches, one for me and one for this man we are entertaining today. 4:2. Make ready for us there a place to sit and a lampstand and a table with an abundance of every good thing. Make the chamber beautiful, son, and lay down fine linens and purple and silk; burn every precious and fine incense, and bring sweet-smelling plants from the garden and fill the house with them. 4:3. Light seven lamps with olive oil so that we might rejoice, because this man we are entertaining today is more glorious than kings and rulers, for his appearance indeed excels all the sons of men." 4:4. Isaac prepared everything well; and Abraham took Michael, and he went into the dining chamber, and they both sat on the couches. Between them was a table with an abundance of good things. 4:5. Then Michael rose and went outside, pretending that he needed to urinate; and he went up into the heavens in the twinkling of an eye and he stood before God, and he said to the Master: 4:6. "Lord, Lord, may your sovereignty know that I am unable to

Short Recension fam. E

4:1. Sarah, who was in her tent, heard their crying. And coming out she said to Abraham, "Why do you weep so?" 4:2. And Abraham answered her, "Nothing is wrong. Return to your tent, and busy yourself with your own things, lest you become a burden to this stranger." 4:3. Sarah withdrew as she was just about to prepare the meal. 4:4. The sun was near to setting. And Michael went out, and he was taken up into the heavens in order to worship before God. 4:5. For with the setting of the sun all the angels worship God. And Michael is the first among them, and he worships God first. 4:6. And (afterwards) all the angels returned to their own places. 4:7. But Michael answered before God and said, "Lord, bid me to ask a question before your great glory." 4:8. And the Lord said, "Speak, Michael." 4:9. And he said, "Lord, you sent me to Abraham your servant to speak to him about his withdrawal from this world and to depart from his body. 4:10. And I, Lord, did not dare to disclose a thing to him because he is your friend and a just man who welcomes strangers. 4:11. I beg of you, Lord, command to send the mention of Abraham's death into his heart, proclaim the notice of death to that just man. For I have not seen a man like him on the earth—merciful and hospitable, just, truthful, God-fearing, abstaining from every evil deed. And now know, Lord, that I am unable to proclaim the notice of death." 4:7. The Lord said, "Go, Michael Commander-in-chief, to my friend Abraham, and whatever he says to you, this indeed do, and whatever he eats, you indeed eat along with him. 4:8. But I will put the holy spirit upon his son Isaac, and I will cast the notice of death into Isaac's heart as in a vision so that in a dream he will see the death of his father, and Isaac will announce the vision, and then you can interpret it. And he will know his end." 4:9. And the Commander-in-chief said: "Lord, all the heavenly spirits are incorporeal, and they neither eat nor drink; and he has set a table with an abundance of good things that are earthly and corruptible. And now, Lord, what shall I do? How shall I remain undiscovered while sitting with him at one table with these things?" 4:10. The Lord said: "Go down to him, and do not worry about this; for while you are sitting with him I shall send upon you an all-devouring spirit, and it will consume from your hands and through your mouth all that is on the table, and you may freely rejoice together with him. 4:11. Just make sure that you interpret rightly the contents of the dream so that Abraham might know (that) the sickle of death and the uncertain end of life (have come), and that he might put all of his belongings in order, because I have blessed him as the stars of heaven and as the sand beside the seashore."

so that Abraham might know for himself, 4:12. and I will not (need to) speak to him. For this word is an extraordinary edict, that you must not go forth in the body. 4:13. Beyond that, you, Lord, from the beginning have had mercy upon our souls." 4:14. Then the Lord said to Michael, "My dear Michael, rise and go to Abraham. 4:15. And if you see him eat anything, you also eat some of it. And wherever he sleeps, you also sleep with him. 4:16. But cast the notice of Abraham's death into the heart of his son Isaac in a dream."

TEXTUAL NOTES ON THE LONG RECENSION

4:1. A passes from the αὐτοῦ that ends 3:12 to the αὐτοῦ that ends the first clause in 4:1. 4:2. G H shorten by dropping "for us there a place to sit and a lampstand and." // 4:2–3. G H also abbreviate by removing "with an abundance" and the rest of v. 2 plus the beginning of 4:3 ("Light ... oil"). 4:2–4. I omits "Make the chamber beautiful," the rest of v. 2, and all of vv. 3–4 because of *homoioteleuton*: τράπεζα(ν) ἐν ἀφθονίᾳ παντὸς ἀγαθοῦ occurs in v. 2 and at the end of v. 4. 4:3–11. H drops all that follows "we might rejoice" up through the end of the chapter. 4:3–10. G similarly omits everything after "we might rejoice" up through "rejoice also you" in v. 10. 4:5. J omits "pretending ... urinate," either out of embarrassment or because an eye jumped from the end of ἐξῆλθεν to the end of ἀνῆλθεν. The long Romanian, ed. Roddy, p. 28, replaces with: "as if to take a walk." 4:6. I substitutes "him" for "that just man." // A B I J Q omit "For I have not seen ... just man." A careless eye moved from the end of the first ἀναγγεῖλαι οὐ δύναμαι to the second. 4:7. I omits "and whatever ... do," again through *homoioteleuton* (καὶ ὅτι ... καὶ ὅτι). 4:8. B I J Q have "my holy spirit," which Rosso Ubigli, "Testamento," 74, takes to be original. // I omits "and I will cast ... in a dream." // I J drop "and Isaac will announce the vision." 4:9. B omits the second question. 4:10. J omits as unnecessary "for while you are sitting with him." 4:11. G drops "So that Abraham might know ... seashore." B I Q rewrite the scriptural line: ὑπὲρ ἄμμον θαλάσσης καὶ ὡς τοὺς ἀστέρας τοῦ οὐρανοῦ. J: ὡς τὰ ἄστρα τοῦ οὐρανοῦ καὶ ὑπὲρ ψάμμον θαλάσσης. A agrees with the LXX Gen 22:17 and is closest to the likely reading of 1:5: ὡς τοὺς ἀστέρας τοῦ οὐρανοῦ καὶ ὡς τὴν ἄμμον τὴν παρὰ τὸ χεῖλος τῆς θαλάσσης.

COMMENTARY

Chap. 4 displays the story-teller's delight in the marvelous. We travel from earth to heaven in the twinkling of an eye (v. 5) and meet a spirit who secretly devours food (v. 10). The author's fondness for description is also on display as he takes four full verses to describe Abraham's dining-chamber (vv. 1–4). The miracles and the details are not, however, the central point, which is instead how God will communicate death to an extraordinarily just man. Faced with Abraham's virtues and his extravagant hospitality, Michael cannot bring himself to discharge his divine mission. So the angel, it turns out, is a bit like the patriarch, who will also, later on, not do God's bidding. Both angel and human rather presume upon the compassionate deity, who happily enough shows great patience with each. In this way *TA* offers the edifying lesson that God, in the words of Ps 103:8, "is merciful and gracious, slow to anger and abounding in steadfast love."

Chap. 4 falls into two parts. In the first, Abraham gives Isaac detailed orders on how to prepare for Michael (vv. 1–3), after which we learn that Isaac did as he was told and that the patriarch and angel subsequently reclined together in the dining chamber (v. 4). In the second part, the scene abruptly closes as soon as it opens when Michael, on the pretense that he needs to urinate, exits and ascends to heaven (v. 5). What follows resembles commissioning narratives in the Hebrew Bible:[1]

Introduction, including report on what has already happened, v. 6
(Re)commissioning/sending of Michael: "Go ... do," v. 7–8
Michael's protest/question: "How shall I remain undiscovered?," v. 9
Reassurance and elaboration: "Do not worry ... Just make sure you interpret," vv. 10–11

Like chap. 3, chap. 4 depends heavily upon the LXX version of Abraham's story. It begins with words and phrases found in Gen 17:18; 22:2–3, 9, 12, 16; and 15:11 (see on v. 1), and it ends with a quotation from Gen 22:17. In between, the story of Abraham entertaining an angel is inspired by Genesis 18, and the problem of how an angel can appear to eat when not really eating draws upon exegetical traditions surrounding Gen 15:8 (see on v. 9). Furthermore, the image of the obedient Isaac, Abraham's beloved son, whom Abraham affectionately calls τέκνον (cf. LXX Gen 22:7, 8), goes back to Genesis 22; and that Abraham has a παράδεισος (v. 2) presupposes an extra-biblical tradition associated with Gen 21:33 (see on 2:1). Lastly, Isaac's vision in a dream, in which he learns about Abraham's death, is the counterpart of Abraham's vision in a dream, in which he learns about Isaac's birth (Genesis 15). From beginning to end, then, *TA* 4 draws upon and sends thoughts back to Genesis.

The story of Abraham is not the only scriptural subtext. *TA* 4 builds also upon Job 1–2. V. 6, as we shall see, rewrites LXX Job 1:1, 8; and 2:3. Recognition of the tacit quotation leads to the discovery that the common words appear at similar junctures in the two stories, and that in fact the structure and plot of *TA* 1–4 imitate much of Job 1–2:

---

[1] See the survey in Benjamin J. Hubbard, *The Matthean Redaction of a Primitive Apostolic Commissioning: An Exegesis of Matthew 28:16–20* (SBLDS 19; Missoula, Mont.: Scholars Press, 1974), 25–67.

TA 1–4	LXX Job 1–2
Praise of a righteous man and remarks on his good deeds and great wealth, 1:1–3, 5	Praise of a righteous man and remarks on his good deeds and great wealth, 1:1–3
Initial conversation in heaven regarding that man, 1:4–7	Initial conversation in heaven regarding that man, 1:6–12
His prosperity due to God's blessing (ηὐλόγησα), 1:5	His prosperity due to God's blessing (εὐλόγησας), 1:10
Instructions to Michael regarding hero; death is at hand, 1:4–7	Permission for Satan to work his will; disaster is at hand, 1:12
Michael goes out from before the Lord, 2:1	Satan goes out from before the Lord, 1:12
Angel speaks with Abraham, 2:1ff.	ἄγγελοι speak with Job, 1:14–18
Failure of angelic mission, 4:5–6	Satan's failure to get Job to sin, 1:13–22
Return to heaven, 4:5	Return to heaven, 2:1
Michael stands before God, 4:5	Satan stands before God, 2:1
Hero remains unaware of what is really going on, 2:1–4:5	Hero remains unaware of what is really going on, 1:6–2:13
Second conversation between Michael and God regarding Abraham, a conversation in which Abraham's unsurpassed virtues are mentioned, 4:6–11 (quoting Job 1:1, 8; 2:3)	Second conversation between Satan and God regarding Job, a conversation in which Job's unsurpassed virtues are mentioned, 2:1–6

If *TA* 1–4 recapitulates much of Job 1–2, later on, in 15:15, the *synkrisis* of Job and Abraham will become explicit: "And there is not a man like him on the earth, not even Job the marvelous man."

Given this explicit comparison, the obvious structural correlations, and the clear verbal links to Job (see on v. 6 and 15:15), it may well be that other phrases in *TA* 1–4 and later depend upon and/or are intended to echo Job. ζεύγη βοῶν ἀροτριασμοῦ in 2:1 is close to τὰ ζεύγη τῶν βοῶν ἠροτρία in LXX Job 1:14. ἔστη ἐνώπιον τοῦ θεοῦ in 4:5 (q.v.) might, when its context is taken into account, recall παραστῆναι ἐνώπιον τοῦ κυρίου in LXX Job 1:6 (cf. 2:1). In 7:2, ὑπολαβὼν δὲ Ἰσαὰκ ἤρξατο λέγειν might be a Jobian echo, for ὑπολαβών + δέ + subject + a form of λέγω is a refrain in LXX Job, where it occurs 23 times at the beginning of speeches (for ויען ... ויאמר).[2] There is the additional parallel of a common philan-

---

2   Elsewhere in the LXX only in Dan 3:95 and *4 Macc.* 8:13. The expression, which also appears in *T. Job* 36:4; 37:5; 38:5–6; 40:1, is not characteristic of patristic texts.

thropy and hospitality, for Job, like Abraham, was renowned for both of
these.[3]

TA aligns itself with rabbinic traditions that compare Job and Abraham,
often unfavorably for Job (see on 15:15). In fact, *b. B. Bat.* 15b, just like
TA 4:6, transfers the language of Job 1:8 and 2:3 to Abraham: "Now there
was a day when the sons of God came to present themselves before the
Lord, and Satan came also among them. And the Lord said unto Satan,
whence come you? And Satan answered, etc. He addressed the Holy One,
blessed be He, thus: Sovereign of the Universe, I have traversed the whole
world and found one so faithful as your servant Abraham."[4] Furthermore,
b. Sanh. 89b likewise transplants elements from Job into the story of
Abraham, and rabbinic tradition names Abraham and Job as among the
few known as "God-fearers"[5] whereas *TA* 4:6 describes Abraham as
θεοσεβής by borrowing precisely from Job 1:1, 8; and 2:3. Because there is
no real evidence that *TA* influenced the rabbis, it follows that, in using Job
1 to describe Abraham, *TA* makes a traditional haggadic move.

Abraham resembles Job in *TA* because both are unaware of what is
really going on. Job does not understand the cause of his unmerited
suffering. He is wholly ignorant of its genesis in a conversation between
God and the accuser in heaven. This is partly what gives the book its
profound poignancy. Readers have been behind the scenes. Job has not. It
is the same in *TA*. When the book opens, Abraham is in the dark. Unlike
readers, he is not privy to God's conversation with Michael in heaven, so
he does not know that his time to die has come, and he does not understand
the events that subsequently unfold around him. Saint though he is,
Abraham, in his mortality, is human like the rest of us. No more than
anyone else does he know what his future holds, nor does he understand
why certain things are happening. Abraham is, like Job, upon the earth,
and so unaware of what has been decided in heaven.

RecLng. 4 shares with RecShrt. 4 four items: Michael's exit to heaven,
his confession that he cannot fulfill his mission, God's decision to notify
Abraham of death via a dream to Isaac, and the command for Michael to

---

[3]   For Abraham's wealth and philanthropy see on 1:1 and 5. For Job's wealth see Job
      29:12–16; 31:16–23, 32; *T. Job* 9–13; *ARN* A 7; etc., and for his philanthropy, Job
      29:12–16; 31:16–23, 32; Aristeas the Exegete in Eusebius, *Praep. ev.* 9.25.1–4; *T.
      Job* 9–13; *ARN* A 7; *b. B. Bat.* 15b; *b. Meg.* 28a; *Gen. Rab.* 30:5; John Cassian,
      Conlationes 6.10.5; etc.

[4]   This is followed by a quotation of Job 1:1 used to argue precisely the opposite, that
      Job was greater than Abraham.

[5]   See *Tanḥ. B* Leviticus Wayyikra 15, and Ginzberg, *Legends*, 5:361, n. 332.

eat whatever is set before him. For the rest there are vast differences. RecShrt. fails to narrate Isaac's preparation of the dining chamber. In its place is a short scene with Sarah, who prepares dinner, as in Genesis 18 (cf. Homer, *Od.* 4.55–56; 15.92–94). RecShrt., instead of having Michael make the excuse that he needs to urinate, recounts, in accord with Jewish and Christian lore, that he has to join the praise of the heavenly host at sunset.[6] Further missing from RecShrt. are Michael's ascension "in the twinkling of an eye," his anxiety about eating human food, and the all-devouring spirit who will consume food out of the angel's mouth and hands.

The picturesque details of Abraham's dining-chamber, the angelic marvels, and the humor of Michael excusing himself to urinate make RecLng. 4 much more memorable than RecShrt. 4. The absence of Michael's delicate request could, moreover, be due to pious motives. Many Christians could not have abided either the bathroom humor or a lying angel. Further, RecShrt. now offers more than one reason for the angel's ascension—he needs to be there to praise God at the right time, and he has to tell God that he cannot carry out his mission. The inconcinnity seems secondary. Turner wrote: "in substituting an alternative excuse the redactor has not realised that this is not an excuse, but a real motive, of which he now has two, with consequent inconsistency."[7] One should also note that the Coptic, which usually sides with RecShrt., here betrays knowledge of something like RecLng., for it says that Michael exited "on a pretense" (ϨⲈⲚ ⲞⲨϨⲰⲂ).

In having Sarah prepare the meal and in speaking of Abraham's "tent" (σκηνή) rather than "house," RecShrt. 4 is closer to Genesis and could in these particulars be older than RecLng. (which mentions a tent in 5:11). If so, most of RecLng. 4:1–4 is secondary.[8] Otherwise RecShrt. 4 is a poor substitute for RecLng. It is less entertaining. It lacks most of the allusions to LXX Genesis. And RecLng.'s implicit comparison between Abraham and Job (see above), a comparison that adds meaning to the narrative and appreciation for its structure, is absent. Beyond that, in RecShrt. 4, Michael

---

[6]   *b. Sanh.* 39b; *b. Ḥag.* 12a; *Vis. Paul* 7. Gk. *L.A.E.* 7:2 and 17:1 speak, without specification, of the time when the angels ascend to worship in heaven. Cf. the exegetical tradition surrounding Gen 32:26–27: the angel that wrestled with Jacob had to finish before dawn in order to join the heavenly hosts at their appointed time of praise: Tg. Ps.-Jn. and Neof. 1 on Gen 32:26–27; *b. Ḥul.* 91b; *Gen. Rab.* 78:2; etc. Is it just coincidence that, in *b. Ber.* 27a, the notice of time in Gen 15:1 becomes an opportunity to discuss the times of prayer?

[7]   Turner, "Testament," 113.

[8]   Yet it is also possible that RecShrt. is here assimilating to Scripture, as it does elsewhere.

worries about communicating what Abraham already knows (cf. 4:7 with 3:10), which is awkward; and God's concluding word to Michael, that he should eat whatever is set before him, neither answers a question nor explicates what follows. It just hangs in the air. Is it not a remnant of something like RecLng. 4's narrative? In Schmidt's critical edition, RecLng. 4 runs to 41 lines of Greek text while RecShrt. 4 E and B F G occupy 26 lines and 28 lines respectively. The possibility of deliberate abbreviation suggests itself. It accords with this that the textual tradition of RecLng. 4 offers numerous examples of either careless or intentional omission, some quite lengthy. In other words, RecLng. 4 itself betrays movement towards a shorter text.

4:1. The chapter begins with phrases from LXX Genesis:

| *TA* 4:1 | εἶπεν δὲ Ἀβραὰμ πρός |
| LXX Gen 17:18 | εἶπεν δὲ Ἀβραὰμ πρός |

TA 4:1	Ἰσαὰκ τὸν υἱὸν αὐτοῦ
LXX Gen 22:3	Ἰσαὰκ τὸν υἱὸν αὐτοῦ
LXX Gen 22:9	Ἰσαὰκ τὸν υἱὸν αὐτοῦ
LXX Gen 25:11	Ἰσαὰκ τὸν υἱὸν αὐτοῦ

TA 4:1	υἱέ μου ἀγαπητέ
LXX Gen 22:2	υἱόν σου τὸν ἀγαπητόν
LXX Gen 22:12	υἱοῦ σου τοῦ ἀγαπητοῦ
LXX Gen 22:16	υἱοῦ σου τοῦ ἀγαπητοῦ

For Isaac as "beloved son," a status that encouraged Christians to construct parallels between Jesus and Isaac, see also *Jub.* 18:2 and Irenaeus, *Haer.* 4.5.4. Abraham directs his son to go to the chamber, εἰς τὸ ταμεῖον (ταμεῖον*; cf. LXX Isa 26:20; *Let. Arist.* 319; *Jos. Asen.* 16:5, 8; *T. Jos.* 3:3; Matt 6:6). This is the "dining chamber," the τρικλίνου. A τρίκλινος (4:1, 4; 5:3, 4, 5, 7; 7:1; 15:3; 16:7; 17:1; RecShrt.: 0; LXX: 0; NT: 0) is literally a place with three couches, like the Latin *triclinium*; cf. *Let. Arist.* 319; Philo, *Vit. cont.* 49; Josephus, *Ant.* 20.192; *Acts Pet.* 31. The first meaning of the Latin word is an arrangement of couches on three sides of a table for dining. The second sense is "dining-room,"[9] and this fits the Greek of *TA*, which refers to only two couches; cf. Ps.-Callisthenes, *Hist. Alex. Magn.* rec. α 1.10. The first meaning of the comparable rabbinic טר(י)קלין is "dining couch" (Jastrow, s.v.).

---

9   See Katherine Dunbabin, "Ut Graeco More Biberetur: Greeks and Romans on the Dining Couch," in *Meals in a Social Context: Aspects of the Communal Meal in the Hellenistic and Roman World* (ed. Inge Nielsen and Hanne Sigismund Nielsen; Aarhus: Aarhus University Press, 1998), 81–101.

Isaac is to set up two couches (κλινάρια; cf. v. 4; Acts 5:15) and, as befits Michael's beauty (cf. 2:5), make the place beautiful, καλλώπισον (καλλω-πίζω: 4:1, 2; LXX Gen 38:14; Judg 10:4; NT: 0; cf. Gk. *1 En.* 8:1; Josephus, *Ant.* 1.121; *Apoc. Sedr.* 11:7, 13; etc.). The two words with the κλιν-root may be inspired by LXX Gen 18:5 (ἐξεκλίνατε). They in any case correspond to the circumstance that the three angels at Mamre must have reclined as they relaxed under the tree, had their feet washed, then ate; see on v. 4. With "this man we are entertaining today" (τοῦ ἀνθρώπου τούτου τοῦ ἐπιξενισθέντος ἡμῖν σήμερον) cf. v. 3 (ὁ ἄνθρωπος οὗτος ὁ ἐπιξενισθεὶς ἡμῖν σήμερον) and 3:7 (τοῦ ἀνθρώπου τούτου τοῦ ἐπιξένου). ἐπιξενίζω (4:1, 3; 5:13; 6:4) has no entry in LSJ. Lampe, s.v., cites only *TA*. The LXX knows only ἐπιξενόομαι (cf. RecShrt. 2:10; 3:6; 6:10 E).

4:2. Isaac is to prepare things: ἑτοίμασον δὲ ἡμῖν ἐκεῖ; cf. LXX Num 23:29, also with ἑτοίμασον + dative pronoun + adverb of place. This means setting up a seat, a lampstand, and a table: δίφρον καὶ λυχνίαν καὶ τράπεζαν (δίφρος*; λυχνος*; τράπεζαν: 4:2, 4, 9, 10; 5:1; 6:4; 12:6, 7, 9, 13). Cf. 4 Βασ 4:10: ἐκεῖ κλίνην καὶ τράπεζαν καὶ δίφρον καὶ λυχνίαν. There is to be "an abundance (ἀφθονία) of every good thing," παντὸς ἀγαθοῦ (cf. vv. 4, 9 v.l.; 16:12; LXX Job 30:4; Ps 33:11; Philem 6; Clement of Alexandria, *Strom.* 7.3.18; etc.). ἀφθονία (cf. vv. 4, 9) appears in the LXX only in Hellenistic books: Wis 7:13; *3 Macc.* 5:2; *4 Macc.* 3:10. Yet Delcor regards ἐν ἀφθονίᾳ as a Semitism and compares the Hebrew ב of accompaniment.[10] The reference is to food; cf. v. 9 and *Gen. Rab.* 9:10: "a dish filled with all good things before them."

Abraham the host requests that the chamber (οἴκημα; cf. v. 4; LXX Ezek 16:24; Tob 2:4; Wis 13:15) be beautiful (καλλώπισον; see on v. 1). In giving his order, he twice calls Isaac τέκνον (cf. 3:7; 5:4), just as he does in LXX Gen 22:7, 8. The beautification involves covering the floor, as though the visitor were royalty; cf. 2 Kgs 9:13; Mark 11:8; Josephus, *Ant.* 9.111; *Acts Pil.* 1:2.[11] In line with this, angels can be called "princes," wear crowns or golden wreaths, and dress in royal garments: Dan 10:13, 20–21; 12:1 [of Michael]; 1QS 3:20; *1 En.* 6:3; *Jos. Asen.* 14:8–9; Rev 14:14; *T. Sim.* 2:7; *T. Jud.* 19:4; *Apoc. Zeph.* in Clement of Alexandria, *Strom.* 5.11.77; *3 En.* 17:8; 18:25; 21:4 (Schäfer, *Synopse* 22 = 858, 29 = 865, 32 = 868); etc.

Perhaps the imperative, ὑφάπλωσον, did not belong to a Jewish version of *TA*. For the active of ὑφαπλόω* (LXX: 0; Philo: 0; NT: 0; Josephus: 0) LSJ, s.v., cites only Himerius and Themistius from the 4th cent. CE and

---

[10] Delcor, *Testament*, 103.
[11] Later Christian iconography depicts the scene in Gen 18:1ff., *TA*'s subtext, as one of enthronement.

Paulus Aegineta from the 7th cent. CE. Additional examples are all Christian and/or late: Ps.-Hippolytus, *De consummatione mundi* 4.2; *Acts John* 14; Gregory of Nyssa, *Cant.*, ed. Langerbeck, p. 81.15; Ps.-John of Damascus, *B.J.* 30.275; etc.

Isaac is to lay down "fine linens," σινδόνας. σινδών (= סדין) appears again in 20:10, where Abraham's dead body receives a linen shroud. The covering also includes purple cloth, πορφύρα.* Purple cloth was expensive and associated with royalty: Judg 8:26; Est 8:15; Lam 4:5; 2 Macc 4:38; *T. Job* 39:7; *Jos. Asen.* 2:8–9; Luke 16:19; Josephus, *Ant.* 11.256; Xenophon, *Cyr.* 8.3.13; Virgil, *Georg.* 2.495; Plutarch, *Demetr. Ant.* 41.4; Crates, *Ep.* 18; 23; Ephraem, *Ep. Publium*, ed. Brock, p. 289; Tg. Onq. on Gen 49:11.[12] That Abraham has it in his house signals his great wealth (1:5), and maybe his royal status: some remembered him as a king (LXX Gen 23:6; Philo, *Abr.* 261; *Virt.* 216; Nicolaus of Damascus in Josephus, *Ant.* 1.159; Pompeius Trogus in Justinus, *Hist. Phil.* 36.2.1; *Gen. Rab.* 43:5). That Isaac lays down purple, presumably upon the floor,[13] so that Michael may walk on it, recalls the famous scene in Aeschylus, *Ag.* 855–957, where Clytemnestra talks Agamemnon into walking on purple. Tg. Sheni Est 8:15 supplies a Jewish parallel: king Mordecai walks on strewn purple as he is proclaimed king. βύσσος (= בוץ; cf. also 12:6) is "silk" or "Indian cotton." Its also being on the floor is yet another sign of wealth: LXX Gen 41:42; 1 Chr 15:27; Isa 3:23; Ezek 16:10; *Jos. Asen.* 2:8; 5:5; *T. Job* 25:7; Rev 18:12. BAGD, s.v. βύσσος, documents its regular connection with "purple." In LXX Dan 10:5 and 12:6 it is the clothing of an angel, which perhaps adds to its appropriateness here.

In addition to the fancy furniture and cloth, Isaac is to perfume the air. Every precious (πᾶν τίμιον; cf. 2:3, 4) and fine (καλόν; καλ- appears five times in *TA* 4) incense should be burned, θυμίασον ... θυμίαμα (θυμίαζω*; θυμίαμα*); cf. LXX Exod 30:7; 40:27; 1 Βασ 2:28; 1 Chr 6:49; 2 Chr 2:4; 13:11. For Delcor, the presence of aromatics and incense in a house at Mamre may reflect the circumstance that, when *TA* was written, the place was a stop on the trade route from Arabia, which was the chief source of incense.[14] One should perhaps also note that the Piacenza Pilgrim, *Itin.* 30, was particularly struck by the incense used in the Basilica at the Oak of Mamre ("they use much incense ... they offer much incense").

---

[12] See L. B. Jensen, "Royal Purple of Tyre," *JNES* 22 (1963), 104–18, and M. Reinhold, *History of Purple as a Status Symbol in Antiquity* (Latomus 116; Brussels: Colonel Chaltin, 1970).

[13] But in Ovid, *Metam.* 8.655–658, the couches are draped for guests.

[14] Delcor, *Testament*, 104.

Isaac is further to bring in "sweet-smelling plants," βοτάνας εὐόσμου. βοτάνη* (cf. LXX Gen 1:11, 12) + εὔοσμη* (LXX: 0; Philo: 0; NT: 0; Josephus: 0) occurs in Scholia on Aristophanes, *Pax* 168b; Ps.-Zonaras, *Lex.*, ed. Tittmann 1636 (13th cent.); and *Lexica Segueriana, Coll. verborum utilium e differentibus rhetoribus et sapientibus multis*, ed. Bachmann, p. 302. The phrase also appears much earlier in *Apos. Con.* 8:12:15, in a section that may well preserve part of a Jewish liturgy. The plants are from Abraham's "garden," his παράδεισος (cf. 11:10; 14:8; 20:14, all of heaven).[15] For other references to Abraham's garden see Tgs. Ps.-Jn., Neof. 1, Frg. Tg. on Gen 21:33; b. Soṭah 10a; *Gen. Rab.* 54:6. Maybe there are Edenic connotations; see further on 3:1–3. If so, is it relevant that *Pirqe R. El.* 36 associates the visit of the three angels in Genesis 18 with Abraham's discovery of the bodies of Adam and Eve in the cave of Machpelah?

4:3. Isaac should light (ἄναψον; ἀνάπτω*; cf. LXX 2 Chr 13:11: οἱ λύχνοι ... ἀνάψαι) seven lamps (λύχνους ἑπτά; λύχνος*) with olive oil (ἐλαίου; ἐλαίον*). Their light will be a sign of rejoicing (εὐφρανθῶμεν; εὐφραίνω*; cf. RecShrt. 2:10; 5:1 E; 5:1 B F G, and εὐφροσύνη in RecLng. 11:7, 8, 10). One thinks of biblical texts that associate light with joy: Est 8:16; Ps 89:16; Prov 13:9; Bar 5:9; John 5:35. Interestingly, Severus of Antioch, *Encom. on Michael*, ed. Budge, p. 66, indicates that preparing a church for the joyous festival honoring Michael involved crowning it with lanterns and draping it with cloths. A Christian reader familiar with such activities might find Abraham's actions similar, or might instead be reminded of the lamps that lighted Mamre in later times (Sozomen, *Hist. eccl.* 2.4).

The "seven lamps," which presumably stand upon the λυχνίαν of v. 2, move one to envisage a menorah, an outstanding symbol of Judaism and a famous cult object (Exod 25:31–40; Num 8:2; Zech 4:2; Eupolemus in Eusebius, *Praep. ev.* 9.34.8; Philo, *Her.* 218–220; *Mos.* 2.102–103; Rev 1:12; Josephus, *Ant.* 3.144–146; etc.; recall its presence on the arch of triumph of Titus).[16] This interests because Abraham's room also features incense, which was associated with the priesthood and was a prominent feature of the temple: Exodus 30; 31:8, 11; 1 Kgs 7:49–50; Philo, *Her.* 196–200; Josephus, *Ant.* 3.103, 220; *T. Levi* 8:10; etc. The patriarch, moreover, has σινδών, πορφύρα, and βύσσος, all of which were in the temple: Exod 25:4; 26:1, 31, 36; 27:16; 36:9–35; Philo, *Mos.* 2.111; Josephus, *Ant.* 3.103–131; *Prot. Jas.* 10:2. That temple also featured a

---

[15] On the term παράδεισος and its history see Jan N. Bremmer, *The Rise and Fall of the Afterlife* (London/New York: Routledge, 2002), 109–27.

[16] See further Goodenough, *Jewish Symbols*, 4:71–98; 12:79–83.

special τράπεζα: cf. Exod 25:23; 25:27–28; Josephus, *Ant.* 3.139–147.[17] Indeed, "the Menorah as well as the Table are the most important Temple vessels, representing the sanctity of the Temple."[18] So when Isaac perfumes his father's house with sweet-smelling plants, brings out fine linen, purple, and silk, fills the air with incense, and sets up both a table and a seven-branched candlestick, does the result not mirror the Jerusalem temple and/ or the heavenly paradise and temple where Michael lives and serves (see on 1:4)?[19] Has the Commander-in-chief left one paradise for another, exited the heavenly holy of holies for a similarly adorned chamber on the earth? Perhaps it is relevant that Philo depicts Abraham as a priest in *de Abrahamo* and that rabbinic sources sometimes trace the priesthood through Abraham (*b. Ned.* 32b; *Lev. Rab.* 25:6; etc.).

While Abraham may be hospitable to all strangers (1:1–3), he clearly treats Michael in a special way, for "this man we are entertaining today is more glorious than kings and rulers, for his appearance indeed excels all the sons of men." The words echo clauses already used:

4:3	ὁ ἄνθρωπος οὗτος ὁ ἐπιξενισθεὶς	ἡμῖν σήμερον
4:1 (q.v.)	τοῦ ἀνθρώπου τούτου τοῦ ἐπιξενισθέντος	ἡμῖν σήμερον
4:3	βασιλέων καὶ ἀρχόντων	
1:2 (q.v.)	βασιλεῖς τε καὶ ἄρχοντες	
4:3	ἡ ὅρασις αὐτοῦ ὑπερφέρει πάντας	τοὺς υἱοὺς τῶν ἀνθρώπων
2:4 (q.v.)	εὐπρεπὴς ὡραῖος ὑπὲρ	τοὺς υἱοὺς τῶν ἀνθρώπων

Only ὅρασις* (= "appearance," as in LXX 1 Βασ 16:12; Ezek 1:5; Rev 4:3) and ὑπερφέρω* (cf. LXX Dan 7:7, 20 [πρόσοψις αὐτοῦ ὑπερέφερε]; Theod. 7:24) are new.

Although Abraham rejoices, the truth is that Michael has come as the harbinger of death, and that Abraham does not want to die. So once more there is irony: the patriarch is rejoicing over an occasion that he will not, when he understands it, welcome.

4:4. The correlation between Abraham's command and Isaac's perform-ance again underlines the son's obedience and supplies a foil for Abraham's subsequent disobedience. Like v. 3, v. 4 borrows from earlier lines. "Isaac"

---

[17] For depictions of tables next to menorahs see Rachel Hachlili, *Ancient Jewish Art and Archaeology in the Land of Israel* (HO; Leiden/New York/Copenhagen/ Cologne: Brill, 1988), plates 53, 59b.

[18] So Hachlili, ibid., 251.

[19] For incense in Paradise see Gk. *L.A.E.* 29:4–5. *TA* either does not know or disregards the rabbinic prohibition of making a house in the image of the temple: *b. Menaḥ.* 28b; *b. ʿAbod. Zar.* 43a; *b. Roš Haš.* 24a–b.

is from v. 1, "prepare" (ἡτοίμασεν) from v. 2 (q.v.), "well" (καλῶς) continues the string of καλ- words (v. 1: καλλώπισον; v. 2: καλλώπισον, καλόν), "chamber" (οἰκήματι) is from v. 2 (q.v.), "dining chamber" (τρικλίνου) is from vv. 1–2 (q.v.), "they both sat" (ἐκαθέσθησαν ἀμφότεροι; ἀμφότερος*) recalls the picture of 2:8 (q.v.), "the couches" (κλινάρια) are from v. 1 (q.v.), "the table" (τράπεζα) has already been mentioned in vv. 2–3 (q.v.), and "with an abundance of every good thing" (ἐν ἀφθονίᾳ παντὸς ἀγαθοῦ) is from v. 2 (q.v.).

That Michael reclines is another motif from Genesis 18, for while the biblical text does not say explicitly that the three men sit or lay down, this is surely implicit. There are, moreover, ancient Jewish and Christian artistic representations of this scene in which they recline—the floor mosaic uncovered at the Sepphoris synagogue in 1993,[20] for example, and one of the mosaic walls in San Marco. A table is part of this artistic tradition. But one recalls also Ovid, *Fast.* 5.493–544, where Jupiter and Mercury dissemble their divinity and, as guests of the old man Hyrieus, recline on mattresses covered with linen.

4:5. Michael rises, ἐγερθείς (a form of ἐγείρω* unattested in the LXX, Philo, or Josephus but common in Matthew; cf. *T. Job* 36:1; *4 Bar.* 5:3, 7, 9). He goes outside, ἐξῆλθεν ἔξω; the expression appears four times in LXX Genesis: 39:12, 13, 15, 18. His exit is on a pretense, δῆθεν (LXX: 0; Philo: 0; NT: 0; Josephus, however, uses the word a dozen times: *Bell.* 1.272; 4.59; etc.). The angel is still hiding his identity, so Abraham, despite what he will say in 6:6, has yet to figure out what is going on.

Michael has indicated that he needs to urinate: γαστρὸς χρείᾳ ὕδατος χύσιν ποιήσας; cf. the rabbinic מים הַמֵּטִיל as in *m. Yoma* 3.2; *b. Yebam.* 76a, 80a–b. For ὕδωρ = urine see LXX 4 Βασ 18:31; Isa 36:16. It goes without saying that, if angels do not eat (see on v. 10), they also do not urinate; cf. Valentinus in Clement of Alexandria, *Strom.* 3.59.3: Jesus "ate and drank in a special way, without excreting his solids." But our text at least creates the image of Michael urinating, if only to erase it. This is part of the irreverent humor that runs throughout *TA* RecLng.—especially as χρείᾳ ("in need"; χρεία*) and χύσιν (χύσις* ὕδατος = "flood" or "spring of water"; cf. Apollonius of Rhodes, *Argon.* 4.1416; Aratus, *Phaen.* 393) stress Michael's urgency.

---

20   Zeev Weiss and Ehud Netzer, "The Sepphoris Synagogue: A New Look at Synagogue Art and Architecture in the Byzantine Period," in *Galilee Through the Centuries* (ed. Eric M. Meyers; Duke Judaic Studies Series 1; Winona Lake, Ind.: Eisenbrauns, 1999), 213–14.

Michael ascends to heaven. For ἀνέρχομαι + εἰς τοὺς οὐρανούς see also 7:4; 8:1; 15:11; 20:12; Justin, *1 Apol.* 21.3; 31.7; Gk. *L.A.E.* 43:4 v.l.; *Apoc. Sedr.* 2:3, 4; *Acts Phil.* 21:1; etc. The angel goes up in an instant, which has its parallel in *b. Ber.* 4b, which stresses Michael's speed and makes him out to be faster than Gabriel and the Angel of Death. ἐν ῥιπῇ ὀφθαλμοῦ is a Semitism.[21] It occurs also in 1 Cor 15:52, in writers who have read Paul (Origen, *Cels.* 5.17; Ps.-Hippolytus, *De consummatione mundi* 35, 37; Eusebius, *Comm. Ps.* PG 23.976B; etc.), and in the medieval Jewish *Hygromanteia of Solomon* 252v.[22] One might guess that, since Christian hands transmitted *TA*, the phrase reflects Paul's influence. But this is far from certain. Rabbinic texts know the similarly-sounding expressions, הרף עין and הַרִיפַת עין and these designate an instantaneous action (Strack-Billerbeck 2:156; Jastrow, s.v. הרף). According to Kerkeslager, moreover, "the most common use of this phrase is in rabbinic descriptions of the supernatural speed of an action by God or an angel, especially in traversing a great distance."[23] When one adds that כהרף עין at some point entered Jewish liturgy,[24] *TA* 4:5 need not be Christian. But whether Christian or not, "in the twinkling of an eye" adds to the fairy-tale quality of the narrative (cf. the story of St. Brigida in *Acta Sanctorum* Feb., 1.246 col. 1). Here again is another wonder—instantaneous travel from earth to heaven.

Michael goes to the "Master" (δεσπότην; see on 1:4) and stands before him, ἔστη ἐνώπιον τοῦ θεοῦ. The phrase, reminiscent of 1 Kgs 22:21 = 2 Chr 18:20, where a heavenly spirit stands before the Lord (LXX: ἔστη ἐνώπιον κυρίου), recurs in 8:1 (q.v.); 9:7; and 15:11. Cf. further *ARN* A 12, where Michael stands before God. The refrain helps mark the structural seams of the book; see pp. 46–47 and cf. also 7:4 and 20:12. For the parallel with LXX Job 1:14 see above, p. 129.

4:6. Michael uses the common double vocative, κύριε, κύριε, which the LXX has often: Deut 9:26; Judg 6:22; Est 4:17; etc.; cf. Philo, *Conf.* 173; Matt 7:21–22; 25:11; *b. Mak.* 24a; *b. Ḥul.* 139b. For other double vocatives see on 14:14. The repetition adds urgency. Despite such urgency, Michael

---

[21] For what follows see esp. Kerkeslager, "Evidence"; also David Daube, *The Sudden in the Scriptures* (Leiden: Brill, 1964), 75–79.

[22] For this last see Günter Zuntz, *The Text of the Epistles: A Disquisition upon the Corpus Paulinum* (London and Oxford: Oxford University Press, 1953), 39.

[23] Kerkeslager, "Evidence," 70–71. He cites, among other texts, *Mek.* on Exod 12:37, 41, 42; *Gen. Rab.* 59:11; 77:2; *Midr. Ps.* 90:13.

[24] See Kerkeslager, "Evidence," citing the version of the Amidah from the Cairo Genizah and arguing plausibly that 1 Cor 15:51–52 depends upon a Jewish liturgical source.

remains formal. He addresses God with a circumlocution, "your sovereignty," τὸ σὸν κράτος (cf. the formality in 2:5, q.v.). Perhaps we should compare the use of "the Power" (הגבורה/ἡ δύναμις) as a divine name or title in Matt 26:64 par.; *Sifre* Deut. 319; *Mek.* on Exod 14:2; 18:19; *ARN* A 37; *b. Meg.* 31b; *b. ʿErub.* 54b; *b. Yebam.* 105b; Tg. Job 5:8; etc. RecShrt. 4:7 also uses a circumlocution—either "your great glory" (fam. E) or "your holy glory" (fam. B F G). The language is that of the royal courts, and Lampe, s.v. κράτος B2, cites patristic examples of κράτος σου in addressing royalty.

Michael is unable to announce to "that just (δίκαιον; see on 1:1) man" his "notice of death." The Greek is τὴν μνήμην τοῦ θανάτου, as also in v. 8; 5:6; 7:11. The idiom may well be Christian, occurring as it does in Origen, *Fr. Ps.* 72:3; *Sel. Ps.* PG 12.1525C; Ps.-Athanasius, *De communi essentia patris et filii et spiritus sancti* PG 28.72C; Chrysostom, *Hom. Matt.* 57.2; Ps.-Ephraem, *De recordatione mortis et de uirtute ac de diuitiis*, ed. Phrantzoles, p. 250.13; *Apophth. Patrum* (systematic collection) 1:16; John of Damascus, *Encom. Joannis Chrysostomi* PG 96.773C; Ps.-John of Damascus, *B.J.* 12.107; etc. In these the sense is usually "the memory of death," that is, remembering that one must die—a monastic theme (*Apophth. Patrum* Evagrius 1, 4; Cassian, *Inst. mon.* 5.41; John Climacus, *Scala paradisi* 6 [the whole section is entitled, Περὶ μνήμης θανάτου]; Isaac of Nineveh, *First* 44, 453, 458, 464, trans. Wensinck, pp. 31, 304, 307, 311; etc.). But one may also note Ecclus 41:1: ὦ θάνατε ... σου τὸ μνημόσυνον. The reason for Michael's failure to perform his mission is that he has not seen Abraham's like on the earth, οὐκ εἶδον ἐπὶ τῆς γῆς; cf. 3:5 and especially 15:15: οὐκ ἔστιν ἄνθρωπος ὅμοιος αὐτοῦ ἐπὶ τῆς γῆς. Angelic disobedience is unexpected, but perhaps it foreshadows Abraham's defiance. Michael in any event seems to know that God is merciful and will understand (cf. 10:14).

As an explanation of Michael's failure, we get yet another list of Abraham's virtues, reminiscent of 1:1–2, 5; and 2:3, but longer. That Abraham is "hospitable" (φιλόξενον) and "just" (δίκαιον) we have learned already; see on 1:1. Here Michael adds that he is merciful, ἐλεήμονα (ἐλεέω: 4:6, 13; most often of God in the LXX but of people in Proverbs: 11:17; 19:11; 20:6; 28:22)—a characterization contradicted in chap. 10, where Abraham shows no mercy to others. Abraham is also truthful (ἀληθινόν; the word often appears in lists of virtues: LXX Exod 34:6; Ps 85:15; Tob 3:2 [with ἐλεημοσύναι and δικαίαν]; *T. Job* 4:11) and God-fearing (θεοσεβῆ; θεοσεβής* is also on such lists: Philo, *Mut.* 197; *Spec. leg.* 4.134, 170; *Jos. Asen.* 4:9; *T. Levi* 16:2; 1 Tim 2:10; *Ep. Clem. Jac.* 2:3; etc.). Philo, *Abr.* 114, says that Abraham's φιλόξενος came from his θεοσέβεια, which is probably an echo of Homer, *Od.* 6.121; 9.176. Abraham himself speaks of θεοσέβεια in LXX Gen 20:11, where the issue is treatment of strangers. Finally, he abstains from every evil, ἀπεχόμενον ἀπὸ παντὸς πονηροῦ; cf. Gk. fr. *1 En.* 104:6 (ἀπέχεσθε ἀπὸ πάντων τῶν ἀδικημάτων); 1 Thess 5:22 (ἀπὸ παντὸς εἴδους πονηροῦ ἀπέχεσθε); *Cyranides* 1:13 (ἀπέχεσθαι ἀπὸ παντὸς πονηροῦ); Ps.-Athanasius, *De virginitate* 7.23 (ὁ ἀπεχόμενος ἀπὸ παντὸς πονηροῦ). The expression comes from Job; see below.

That Michael should recite a person's virtues before God is altogether expected. Not only is he, in Jewish and Christian lore, an intercessor for the just (see on 1:4), but *3 Bar.* 11:9 has him bringing before the enthroned deity "the virtues of the righteous and the good works which they do."

Michael's words take up the summary characteristics of Job in LXX Job 1 and 2. "That just man," "not ... a person on the earth," "just, trustworthy, God-fearing," and "abstaining from every evil" are all from Job 1:1, 8; and 2:3—the latter two being the very same verses behind *TA* 15:15 (q.v.):

TA 4:6	τὸν δίκαιον ἄνδρα	ἐκεῖνον
Job 1:1	ὁ ἄνθρωπος ἐκεῖνος ... δίκαιος	

TA 4:6	οὐκ εἶδον ἐπὶ τῆς γῆς ἄνθρωπον ὅμοιον αὐτοῦ
LXX Job 1:8 A	οὐκ ἔστιν ἄνθρωπος ὅμοιος αὐτῷ τῶν ἐπὶ τῆς γῆς
LXX Job 2:3 A	οὐκ ἔστιν ... ἐπὶ τῆς γῆς, ἄνθρωπος ὅμοιος αὐτῷ

TA 4:6	ἀληθινός,	θεοσεβῆ
Job 1:1	ἀληθινός ...	θεοσεβής
Job 1:8	ἀληθινός,	θεοσεβής
Job 2:3	ἀληθινός ...	θεοσεβής

TA 4:6	ἀπεχόμενος ἀπὸ παντὸς πονηροῦ πράγματος
Job 1:1	ἀπεχόμενος ἀπὸ παντὸς πονηροῦ πράγματος
Job 1:8	ἀπεχόμενος ἀπὸ παντὸς πονηροῦ πράγματος
Job 2:3	ἀπεχόμενος ἀπὸ παντὸς κακοῦ

The lines from Job were well known. 1:1 opens the book, 1:8 and 2:3 repeat its content, and the three verses are quoted elsewhere as summary descriptions of Job; see *1 Clem.* 17:3; Clement of Alexandria, *Strom.* 4.17; 7.12; Origen, *Fr. Luc.*, ed. Klostermann 222, on 16:19; Cyprian, *Mort.* 10; Eusebius, *Praep. ev.* 7.8; *Dem. ev.* 1.5.7; Gregory of Nyssa, *Laudatio Meletii episcopi*, ed. Spira, p. 445.20; Chrysostom, *Adv. Jud.* PG 48.936; *Vit. Elizabeth the Wonderworker* 2 = *Analecta Bollandiana* 91 (1973), 252; *m. Soṭah* 5:5; *ARN* A 2; *b. B. Bat.* 15b; *Tanḥ. B* Wayyeshev 5; *Exod. Rab.* 21:7; *Num. Rab.* 22:1; cf. also the reapplication in Gregory of Nyssa, *Or. dom.* 5, ed. Oehler, p. 254.29. On how the parallels bear on interpretation see above, p. 130.

Why do Abraham's virtues disincline Michael from carrying out his divine commissioning? Is it because death in general is always a grievous thing, and Michael does not want to distress a good man? Does Michael anticipate Abraham's refusal to cooperate and not wish to abet his disobedience?

4:7. The Lord speaks for a second time and sounds like he did at the initial commissioning:

1:4   κάτελθε, Μιχαὴλ ἀρχιστράτηγε, πρὸς τὸν φίλον μου τὸν Ἀβραάμ
4:7   ἄπελθε, Μιχαὴλ ἀρχιστράτηγε, πρὸς τὸν φίλον μου τὸν Ἀβραάμ[25]

But here his instructions to Michael are to eat with Abraham and to do whatever he says: ὅτι ἂν λέγῃ σοι τοῦτο καὶ ποίει (cf. LXX Gen 31:16: ὅσα εἴρηκέν σοι ... ποίει). Is there an echo of the Lord's word in Gen 15:5— οὕτως ποίησον, καθὼς εἴρηκας? One recalls the rabbinic use of Genesis 18 to teach, in effect, "When in Rome do as the Romans do" (b. B. Meṣiʿa 86b; Gen. Rab. 48:14; Exod. Rab. 47:5; Num. Rab. 10:6). In 15:12, Michael will claim to have discharged this command: "I have hearkened to your friend Abraham, to all that he said to you, and I have fulfilled his requests."

4:8. God now explains how he will help Michael and make his task easier. God will send to Isaac τῷ πνεύματι τῷ ἁγίῳ. Perhaps the expression is from a Christian copyist and so Trinitarian, as is τῷ ἁγίῳ πνεύματι in the Christian doxology at the end (20:15). But the phrase (cf. רוח קדש) appears in the LXX and other Jewish documents: Isa 63:10; Wis 9:17; Ecclus 48:12; 1QS 8:16; CD 2:12; 5:11; 7:4; 1QH 15:7; Ps. Sol. 17:37; Apoc. Zeph. fr. in Clement of Alexandria, Strom. 5.11.77; Asc. Isa. 5:14; 6:10. It could then belong to a Jewish original, in which the spirit was equated with divine power and energy (as in Judg 13:25; 14:6, 19) or understood as the vehicle of revelation or prophecy (as in 1QH 20:12; Wis 9:17; m. Soṭah 13:2; Gen. Rab. 75:8; etc.).

"The notice of death," τὴν μνήμην τοῦ θανάτου (see on v. 6), will come first through Isaac, and that indirectly, through a dream needing interpreting (διακρινεῖς; cf. v. 11; LXX Exod 18:16; Est 8:12; Ps. Sol. 17:43; T. Job 30:4; Michael is the subject of διακρίνω in Jude 9). Interestingly enough, in the second half of the Apocalypse of Abraham, which rewrites the vision of Genesis 15, an angelic interpreter also assists Abraham. God will "cast" (ῥίψω; cf. 5:6) that notice. The closet parallel to this is in the 7th cent. work of George Pisida, In Heraclium ex Africa redeuntem, ed. Pertusi, p. 80: τὴν

---

[25]   B J Q have κάτελθε in 4:7, so that the parallelism is perfect.

μνήμην ἀεὶ ἄνω τε ῥίψας πρὸς θεόν. But there are parallels with παραρρίπτω in the 12ᵗʰ cent. Eustathius of Thessalonica, *Comm. Hom. Il.* 2.451 (παρέρριψε μνήμην τοῦ Ἀχιλλέως); 3.211 (Ὅμηρος μνήμην τῆς ἡρωΐδος Ἑλένης παραρριπτεῖ); 4.54 (παρραρρίψας καὶ μνήμην συνήθως τοῦ Ἀχιλλέως); 4.263 (παραρριπτεῖ ... Ὅμηρος μνήμην). Michael's job now becomes that of interpreter, a normal task for his kind: Dan 8:15–26; 9:20–27; Zech 1:7–6:15; *1 Enoch* 21–32; Revelation 17; *4 Ezra* passim; *2 Baruch* 55–76; *3 Bar.* 11:7; etc.

"In a vision" (ἐν ὁράματι; ὅραμα: 4:4:8, 11) is a common phrase: LXX Gen 46:2; Ecclus 43:1; Dan 2:19; Philo, *Leg. all.* 3.103; *T. Levi* 9:3; *T. Jud.* 3:10; Acts 9:10; etc. Next to ἐν ὀνείρῳ (cf. Homer, *Il.* 22.1994; *4 Macc.* 6:5) it reminds one of Num 12:6 (God speaks to prophets "in visions" and "in dreams") and Job 33:15 (see below). Yet Gen 15:1 is the likely inspiration. Here God, "in a vision" (LXX: ἐν ὁράματι; cf. 1QapGen 22:27: בחזוא), speaks to Abraham about his offspring, and a revelatory dream in the night follows (LXX Gen 15:12: ἔκστασις; MT: תרדמה; cf. *Jub.* 14:1). *TA* 4 reverses the situation: the offspring has a dream about the parent. In the first case the dream promises birth, in the second case it foretells τέλος, a word that also means "death" in 1:5 and 15:1 (but never in the LXX); cf. Herodotus, *Hist.* 1.31; Xenophon, *Cyr.* 7.3.11; Arrian, *Anab.* 3.22.2; and the meaning of קץ in Ps 39:5 and *b. Ned.* 41a.

Dreams are often vehicles of revelation in the Bible, especially in Genesis and Daniel, and they remain so in later literature.[26] Many believed, in the words of Job 33:15–17, that "in a dream, in a vision of the night ... [God] opens the ears of people, and terrifies them with warnings ..." (cf. Philo, *Migr.* 190; Josephus, *Bell.* 3.350–354; *b. Ber.* 55a–b). Dreams were also of great importance in Graeco-Roman literature (cf. Origen, *Cels.* 1.66).[27] In that literature, however, narratives usually give the contents of a dream as the dreamer sleeps. *TA* follows the usual biblical pattern of relating that an individual dreamed and then recounting the contents only after the dreamer awakes. The association of the patriarchs in particular with dreams is probably relevant for our book.[28]

---

[26] Gen 20:3, 6–7; 31:10–16, 24; 37:5–11; Num 12:6; Daniel 2; 4; 7:1; *1 En.* 14:2; 83:7; 85:1; 1QapGen 19; Ezek. Trag. in Eusebius, *Praep. ev.* 9.29.4–5; *Sib. Or.* 3:293; Philo, *Migr.* 190; *Gk. Apoc. Mos.* 2:2; *4 Ezra* 10:59; *T. Naph.* 5:1–7:1; *T. Levi* 19:1; Matt 1:20–21; 2:12–13, 19, 22; 27:19; Josephus, *Ant.* 2.13–16, 63–73, 216–219; *Ladder of Jacob*; ARN A 40; *b. Ḥag.* 14b; etc.

[27] J. S. Hanson, "Dreams and Visions in the Graeco-Roman World and Early Christianity," *ANRW* 23.2 (1980), 1395–1427.

[28] Cf. Delcor, *Testament*, 108–109.

4:9. Michael protests: he cannot carry out his task. Being one of the ἐπουράνια πνεύματα, he is incorporeal, ἀσώματα; see on 3:6. Although Jewish texts often call angels "spirits" (e.g., 1QS 3:18–19; 1QH 3:21–23; 1QM 13:2; *1 En.* 15:7), ἐπουράνια πνεύματα seems attested only in Christian texts: Clement of Alexandria, *Exc.* 1.15; Origen, *Or.* 16.2; Eusebius, *Fr. Lc.* PG 24.596C; Ps.-Chrysostom, *Annunt.* PG 60.757; etc.; and Christian sources otherwise use ἐπουράνιος in connection with angels (e.g., Ign. *Smyrn.* 6:1; *Trall.* 5:2; Pol. *Phil.* 2:1; cf. Lampe, s.v., 5b–c). (πνεύματα οὐρανοῦ does, however, appear in Gk. fr. *1 En.* 15:10.) Often, as here, ἐπουράνιος (see on 2:3) stands in contrast to "earthly" (ἐπίγειος*; LXX: 0); cf. Philo, *Plant.* 17; 1 Cor 15:40; Rev 17:20; Ign. *Trall.* 9:1; Clement of Alexandria, *Paed.* 2.1.6; Chrysostom, *Laz.* PG 48.1041; etc. It also elsewhere characterizes celestial bodies: 1 Cor 15:40; Clement of Alexandria, *Exc.* 11; Origen, *Cels.* 4.60; etc.

That angels neither eat nor drink—at least earthly food[29]—appears to have been a commonplace: Judg 13:15–16; Tob 12:19; Ecclus 16:27; *Apoc. Abr.* 13:4; Tg. Ps.-Jn. on Gen 19:3; *Num. Rab.* 10:5; 21:16; *Deut. Rab.* 11:4; *Pesiq. Rab. Kah.* 6:1; *Pesiq. Rab.* 16:2; *Pirqe R. El.* 46.[30] The Greeks thought the same about their immortals: the blessed divinities "eat no food nor drink of the shining wine" (Homer, *Il.* 5.341; Philo, *Quaest. Gen.* 4.9, seems to allude to this line when discussing Abraham and the angels). This is why Jewish and Christian expositions of Genesis 18 often state, against the plain sense of the text, that Abraham's three visitors did not partake of his food or drink: Philo, *Abr.* 110, 117–118; *Quaest. Gen.* 4.9; Josephus, *Ant.* 1.197; Justin Martyr, *Dial.* 57; Ps.-Athanasius, *Confutatio quarundam propositionum* PG 28.1377A–1380B; Theodoret of Cyrrhus, *Quaest. Gen.* 69; Macarius Magnes, *Apocrit.* 4.27; *La Chaîne sur la Genèse* 1070 and 1074 *ad* Gen 18:8; Tgs. Neof. 1 and Ps.-Jn. on Gen 18:8; *b. B. Meṣiʿa* 86b; *Gen. Rab.* 48:11, 14.[31] This exegetical tradition clearly stands behind our text. History is repeating itself.

---

[29] Manna was the food of angels (Ps 78:25; 2 Esd 1:19; *b. Yoma* 75b; etc.), and in some rabbinic texts angels feed upon the divine glory (e.g. *Gen. Rab.* 2:2). See further Goodman, "Do Angels Eat?" Cf. the nectar and ambrosia of the Greeks.

[30] One also recalls Luke 24:36–43, where Jesus proves he is *not* a spirit by eating. *Ps.-Clem. Hom.* 9:10 says that demons cannot eat, unless they enter human bodies.

[31] Significantly, *Jubilees* 16 omits the entire episode. For the contrary opinion, that the angels did eat, see *Num. Rab.* 10:5; *Pesiq. Rab.* 25:3; Ps.-Ephraem, *Comm. Gen.* 15.2. One may compare the opinion that the divine Jesus, although he did not need to eat, did so anyway: *Acts Pet.* 20; Clement of Alexandria, *Strom.* 6.9; Hilary of Poitiers, *Trin.* 10.24.

Abraham has set a table "with an abundance of good things" (cf. vv. 2, 4)—things "earthly" (ἐπιγείων; see above) and "corruptible," φθαρτῶν (cf. LXX Isa 54:17; 2 Macc 7:16; Wis 9:15; 14:8; Gk. fr. *1 En.* 2:2; *T. Benj.* 6:2). For ἐπίγειος with φθάρω* see Hippolytus, *Comm. Dan.* 4.60. Whether the meaning is that Michael never eats anything at all, or just that he cannot eat earthly and corruptible food (as opposed to manna; cf. Justin, *Dial.* 57), his concern is how, while eating with Abraham, his identity can remain undiscovered (διαλάθω; διαλανθάνω*: cf. 2 Βασ 4:6; Josephus, *Bell.* 4.62; NT: 0). That the angel must eat or appear to eat is taken for granted: to decline the man's food would be to reject his hospitality.

4:10. The Lord repeats his order for Michael to go down to Abraham (κάτελθε πρὸς αὐτόν; cf. v. 7; 1:4) and tells him not to worry: περὶ τούτου μὴ σὺ μελετῶ; cf. 1 Cor 7:21 (μή σοι μελέτω); Athenaeus, *Deipn.* 2.2.112 (μή σοι μελέτω); Chrysostom, *Eutrop.* PG 52.406 (μή σοι μελέτω). I have not found μὴ σὺ μελετῶ elsewhere, and mss. I (μή σε) and Q (μή σοι) prefer something else. The reason the angel need not worry is that, just as the holy spirit will come upon Isaac, so an "all-devouring spirit" (πνεῦμα παμφάγον; παμφάγος: 4:10; 12:10; cf. Philo, *Somn.* 2.21; LXX: 0; NT: 0; Josephus: 0) will come upon Michael.[32] This spirit will "consume" (ἀναλίσκει; for this meaning of ἀναλίσκω* see LXX Gen 41:30) the food and drink from his hands and mouth. So Michael will appear to be eating whereas the spirit is really consuming everything. Cf. *Asc. Isa.* 11:17, where the infant Jesus only appears to suckle. With this problem out of the way, Michael should be able to rejoice with Abraham, συνευφράνθητι ... μετ' αὐτοῦ (συνευφραίνομαι*; cf. LXX Prov 5:18; Philo, *Conf.* 6; *Barn.* 2:3).

In both Judg 6:21–22 and 13:15–16, where angels are offered food, they do not eat it, but the food is consumed anyway. In the former case the angel of the Lord kindles a fire that "eats" (MT: תאכל; LXX: κατέφαγεν), and other texts know the expression, "consuming fire" (אש אכלה: Exod 24:17; Deut 4:24; 9:3; 2 Sam 22:9; Philo, *Agr.* 36; Heb 12:29). All this brings us close to *TA* 4:10, where a παμφάγον spirit consumes the food that the angel does not eat. Justin Martyr, *Dial.* 57, may well connect Gen 18:7 and the text in Judg 6:21 when he comments on the former that it "bears the same meaning as when we would say about fire that it has devoured all things" (πυρός ... πάντα κατέφαγεν). The same connection may lie behind *TA* 4:10, especially as παμφάγος is often linked to fire, as in *TA* 12:10; cf. Euripides, *Medea* 1187; Philo, *Agr.* 36; *Somn.* 2.12; Clement of Alexandria, *Paed.* 2.1.3; etc. See further on 6:5.

---

[32] The Old Romanian, ed. Roddy, p. 29, has the plural, "devouring spirits."

4:11. V. 11, like most of vv. 3–4, is largely constructed out of previous clauses:

4:11   τὰ τοῦ ὁράματος   διακρινεῖς καλῶς
v. 8 (q.v.)   τὸ   ὅραμα, σὺ δὲ διακρινεῖς

4:11   τὸ τοῦ βίου ἄδηλον πέρας
1:3 (q.v.)   τὸ ἄδηλον τοῦ βίου πέρας

4:11   ἵνα ποιήσῃ διάταξιν   περὶ πάντων τῶν ὑπαρχόντων αὐτοῦ
v. 4 (q.v.)   ἵνα   διατάξεται περὶ   τῶν πραγμάτων αὐτοῦ

4:11   ηὐλόγησα αὐτὸν ὡς τοὺς ἀστέρας τοῦ οὐρανοῦ καὶ ὡς τὴν ἄμμον τὴν παρὰ
              τὸ χεῖλος τῆς θαλάσσης
1:5 (q.v.)   ηὐλόγησα αὐτὸν ὡς τὰ   ἄστρα τοῦ οὐρανοῦ καὶ ὡς τὴν ἄμμον τὴν παρὰ
              τὸ χεῖλος τῆς θαλάσσης

Whereas 1:3 associates "the uncertain end of life" with "the bitter cup of death," here there is another metaphor: "the sickle of death," τὴν τοῦ θανάτου δρεπάνην; cf. 8:9 and 10 (τῇ τοῦ θανάτου δρεπάνῃ; RecShrt.: 0). In LXX Zech 5:1–4, the seer beholds the memorable image of a flying "sickle" (δρέπανον). The angelic interpreter identifies this sickle as the curse that goes over the whole earth and that brings death (θάνατος). *Vit. Proph. Ezekiel* 5 and Rev 14:16 allude to this passage, and it lies behind those Jewish and Christian epitaphs that invoke "the sickle of the curse" (e.g. *CIJ* 768, 769; *MAMA* 6.316). But the precise phrase, "the sickle of death," appears elsewhere only in *Hist. Alex. Magn.* rec. F 127.10 and rec. K, ed. Mitsakis, p. 85.28, both Christian editions, and Ps.-Cyril of Alexandria, *Hom. diversae* 14 PG 77.1088A. Further, *Vit. Basil the Younger*, ed. Vilinskij 1.14, depicts death as carrying both a sword and a sickle (δρεπάνας), which he uses to separate the soul from the body, and Death can carry a sickle in medieval Christian art.[33] Indeed, "Der Ausdruck 'Schwert' bedeutet in der christlichen Literatur häufig das Sterben, den Tod oder den Teufel."[34] Maybe "the sickle of Death" in *TA* is due to a Byzantine redactor. Perhaps it has replaced an original "sword" (see below) or "bitter cup of death" (cf. 1:3).

Delcor compares the representations of Charon, the ferryman of Styx, with his double hammer and suggests Graeco-Roman influence upon our text.[35] He could also have cited Euripides, *Alc.* 74–76, where Death—who

---

[33] Examples in Stichel, *Vergänglichkeitsdarstellungen*, plates 1–6. For the devil with a sickle see *Apophth. Patrum* PG 65.268B (Macarius 11). Cf. Romanos the Melodist, *Cant. dubia* 77.23: θανάτου ῥομφαία.

[34] So Stichel, ibid., 37.

[35] Delcor, *Testament*, 109.

is sometimes armed in Greek art[36]—speaks of his "sword" (ξίφει), or the deadly sickle with which Kronos wounded the sky, Zeus slew Typhon, and Perseus beheaded the Gorgon, a sickle which ended up in Saturn's hands and later became the instrument of the Grim Reaper and of Father Time (cf. the Celtic Sucellos, the harvester of souls, with his scythe).[37] Also relevant are Horace, *Ep.* 2.2.178 (*metit Orcus*—Death reaps); Claudian of Alexandria, *In Eutropium.* 2.144–146 ("why do you delay, Bellona, to sound the trumpet of hell and to arm yourself with the scythe wherewith you mow people to the ground?"); and Macrobius, *Saturnalia* 5.19. But Jewish tradition knows equally of the חרב ("sword") that Sammael, the Angel of Death, wields; see, e.g., *b. ʿAbod. Zar.* 20b; *b. Ber.* 51a; *Gen. Rab.* 58:5–6; *Rev. R. Joshua b. Levi* A 4–5, trans. Gaster, p. 592; cf. also 1 Chr 21:15–16, 30; *b. Sanh.* 95b (where Gabriel slaughters the Assyrians with his sickle, מגל); and *b. B. Qam.* 60b (which speaks of the Angel of Death's "instrument," כלי). Jewish and Christian art turn the destroyer of Exod 12:23 into the Angel of Death and give him a sword.[38] In *b. Ketub.* 77b, he has a knife (סכין). Perhaps most importantly, in some versions of the legend of Moses' death, the Angel of Death puts on his sword when he comes to Moses: *Deut. Rab.* 11:10; *Petirat Moshe* (*BHM* 1:127, 128; 6:75).

Michael is told to interpret the dream "well" (καλῶς). Is the word designed to set Michael beside Isaac, who in v. 4 does his job "well" (καλῶς)? There are other parallels between angel and son. If Isaac is there to do Abraham's bidding, Michael is there to do God's bidding; and if Michael is to notify Abraham of his death, Isaac shares this task when he has his dream in chap. 5. Both figures, moreover, love the patriarch, do not welcome his death, and weep when he weeps (3:10).

---

[36] H. A. Shapiro, *Personifications in Greek Art: The Representation of Abstract Concepts 600 – 400 B.C.* (Zurich: Akanthus, 1993), 134.

[37] For images of this sickle in Graeco-Roman and Christian art see the plates at the end of Raymond Klibansky, Erwin Panofsky, and Fritz Saxl, *Saturn and Melancholy: Studies in the History of Natural Philosophy, Religion, and Art* (New York: Basic Books, 1964).

[38] Joseph Gutmann, "The Haggadic Motif in Jewish Iconography," *Eretz-Israel* 6 (60), 21.

Chapter 5: Isaac's Dream

Long Recension

5:1. Then the Commander-in-Chief Michael went down to Abraham's house and sat with him at table. Isaac served them. 5:2. After they finished the feast, Abraham made the prayer according to custom, and Michael with him. And each reclined upon his couch. 5:3. Isaac said to his father: "Father, I want to be near you, to lie down with you in this dining chamber. For I love to listen to the distinctive conversation of this all virtuous man." 5:4. But Abraham said, "No, son, but go into your chamber and rest, so that we do not become a burden to this man." 5:5. Then Isaac, receiving the blessing from them, went to his own chamber and laid down on his couch. 5:6. And about the third hour of the night God cast the notice of death into Isaac's heart as in a dream. 5:7. Waking up, Isaac rose up on his couch and came running to the dining chamber where his father was sleeping with the archangel. 5:8. Then Isaac, arriving at the door, cried out saying, "Father, father, rise now and open to me quickly, so that I might enter and hang on to your neck and say farewell to you before they take you from me." 5:9. Then Abraham, arising, opened to him; and Isaac entered, hung on his neck, and began to cry with a loud voice. 5:10. Abraham, being deeply moved, also himself cried loudly. And the Commander-in-chief, seeing them weeping,

Short Recension fam. E

5:1. Then Michael entered Abraham's house. And he found him preparing the meal. And they ate and drank and rejoiced. 5:2. Abraham said to Isaac his son, "Rise up, prepare the man's couch. For he hastens to rest. And light the lamp in the house." 5:3. And Isaac did as his father commanded him. And Abraham answered and said to his son, "Do as I told you." 5:4. Isaac answered and said to his father, "Father, allow me to come and to sleep near you." 5:5. Abraham answered and said, "We should not become a burden to this visitor who has come to us. But you go into your room and rest." 5:6. And Isaac went away to his room and he slept. And he disobeyed neither the voice nor the command of his father. 6:1. It came to pass, about the seventh hour of the night, that Isaac woke up and came to the door of his father saying, "Father, open to me so that I might enjoy your company before they take you from me." 6:2. Abraham rose and opened (the door), and Isaac came in and threw himself up on his father's neck, crying and kissing him. 6:3. Abraham wept with his son. Michael saw them and he wept with them. 6:4. In her tent, Sarah heard and rose and went to the door of the chamber where Abraham slept, and she cried out saying, 6:5 "My lord Abraham, why are you crying so late in the day? And have you brought to my lord

likewise cried with them himself. 5:11. Now Sarah was in her tent and heard his weeping and came running to them, and she found them embracing and crying. 5:12. And Sarah wept and said, "My lord Abraham, why do you cry? Tell me. 5:13. My lord, has this brother we are entertaining today brought news concerning your kinsman Lot, who dwells in Sodom, that he has died, and is it for this reason that you mourn thus?" 5:14. The Commander-in-chief replied and said to Sarah, "Sister Sarah, it is not as you say, but rather, it seems to me, your son Isaac had a dream, and he came to us crying, and when we saw him we were deeply moved and cried."

Abraham just now some news of my brother Lot, that he has died, or has something else come upon us?" 6:6. Michael answered and said, "No Sarah, servant of the righteous, I have not brought news concerning Lot."

TEXTUAL NOTES ON THE LONG RECENSION

5:1. J omits "Isaac ... them." 5:3. G has Ἰσαὰκ πρὸς Ἀβραὰμ τὸν πατέρα αὐτοῦ, which lines up exactly with LXX Gen 22:7. // A has ἐναρέτον (used of Abraham in 20:15; cf. 4 Macc. 11:5) instead of παναρέτου (so B G H J Q). I omits. 5:4. J Q omit "so that ... man." 5:6. H omits "the notice of death." 5:8. H omits "and say farewell to you." 5:9. H omits "hung ... and." This must be intentional shortening. // At the end J adds: "saying, 'Father, father, we are being separated from one another.'" 5:10. Q omits "loudly ... himself." Is this deliberate or due to *homoioteleuton* (αὐτός ... αὐτός)? 5:12–13. B drops "Abraham ... not." This looks like conscious contraction: "Abraham," "Why do you cry?," "Tell me," and "my lord" are strictly unnecessary. 5:13. A abbreviates by omitting "who dwells ... died" and "is it for this reason." // G omits "and is it ... thus?" 5:14. H drops "it seems to me."

COMMENTARY

TA 5 introduces Isaac's dream, which the next chapter will interpret. But perhaps the chapter's major function is to display the emotional bonds between four characters. Isaac wants to be near his father, and he loves Michael's words (v. 3). Abraham does not wish to burden Michael in the least way (v. 4). Both father and angel bless Isaac (v. 5). Isaac runs to his father when he fears that he might be taken from him (v. 7), and he hangs upon Abraham's neck and cries with a loud voice (vv. 8–9). Isaac's tears move both Abraham and Michael to weep (v. 10; cf. v. 14). And Sarah affectionately refers to the stranger as "brother," while he refers to her as "sister" (vv. 13–14).

These expressions of emotion do more than make readers feel sympathy for the main characters. They also set the tone for the whole book and help one to feel its subject matter. For death destroys the sort of emotional bonds paraded by our text, and it brings weeping in its wake. Death takes away the objects of our affection, and this is why we mourn.

TA 5, like previous chapters, borrows heavily from LXX Genesis, especially from the story of Abraham, and especially from chaps. 18 and 22:

5:1, Abraham sits; cf. Gen 18:1, where Abraham likewise sits

5:1, Isaac serves the angel; cf. Gen 18:8, where Abraham serves the angels

5:1–2, the angel eats or appears to; cf. Gen 18:8, where the angels eat

5:2, the angel rests; cf. Gen 18:4, where the angels rest

5:3, εἶπε δὲ Ἰσαὰκ πρὸς τὸν πατέρα αὐτοῦ, πάτερ; cf. LXX Gen 22:7: εἶπεν δὲ Ἰσαὰκ πρὸς Ἀβραὰμ τὸν πατέρα αὐτοῦ εἶπας, πάτερ

5:4, Abraham addresses Isaac as τέκνον; cf. Gen 22:7–8

5:5, father and angel bless son; cf. Gen 9:26–27; 27:1–40; 28:1–4; 32:22–32; 48:8–49:28.

5:7, 11, Isaac and Sarah run; cf. Gen 18:2, 7, where Abraham runs

5:8, πάτερ, πάτερ; cf. Gen 22:7 and the double vocative of 22:11

5:9, ἀναστὰς οὖν Ἀβραάμ; cf. LXX Gen 22:3: ἀναστὰς δὲ Ἀβραάμ

5:9, ἐκρεμάσθη ἐπὶ τὸν τράχηλον αὐτοῦ καί ... κλαίειν φωνὴν μεγάλην; cf. LXX Gen 46:29: ἐπέπεσεν ἐπὶ τὸν τράχηλον αὐτοῦ καὶ ἔκλαυσεν κλαυθμῷ πλείονι

5:10, Sarah is in her tent; cf. Gen 18:6, 9, where Sarah is in her tent

5:12–13, Abraham is addressed as κύριέ μου; cf. Gen 18:12; 23:6, 11 (note also 24:42)

5:13, Λὼτ τοῦ ἀδελφοῦ σου τοῦ οἰκοῦντος ἐν Σοδόμοις; cf. LXX Gen 14:12: Λὼτ υἱὸν τοῦ ἀδελφοῦ Ἀβράμ ... ἦν γὰρ κατοικῶν ἐν Σοδόμοις

Taken as a whole, informed readers cannot but feel that *TA* 5 partly reruns sacred history. The central event, Isaac's dream, adds to the *déjà vu*, for the patriarchal narratives are full of dreams.

RecLng. 5 and RecShrt. 5:1–6:6 tell much the same story, albeit with mostly different words. The following differences may be noted. (i) RecShrt. fam. E has Abraham prepare the dinner. RecShrt. fam. B F G is ambiguous: "Michael found them (αὐτούς) preparing the dinner." RecLng. says only, "Isaac served them." (ii) In RecShrt. but not RecLng., Isaac prepares the couches and lights the chamber (cf. RecLng. 4:1–4). (iii) RecShrt. fam. E remarks upon Isaac's obedience: "he disobeyed neither the voice nor command of his father." RecShrt. fam. B F G makes the same point with different words. Isaac's obedience to his father was a traditional topos; cf. Josephus, *Ant.* 1.232, and rabbinic treatments of the Aqedah. (iv) Isaac wakes up at the third hour in RecLng., at the seventh hour in RecShrt. (v) RecShrt. fam. E has Sarah stop at the door before she enters. RecLng. reveals this circumstance only later (cf. 7:1). (vi) In RecShrt. fam. E, Michael addresses Sarah as "servant of the righteous" (ἡ τοῖς δικαίοις ὑπηρετοῦσα). (vii) Only in RecLng. does Michael inform Sarah that Isaac has apparently had an upsetting dream. (viii) RecLng. is closer to Scripture in several respects: (a) Abraham does not sit in RecShrt.; (b) RecLng. 5:3 is nearer to the Greek of LXX Gen 22:7 than its RecShrt. counterparts; (c) only in RecLng. does Abraham address Isaac as τέκνον; (d) the blessing of father and angel in RecLng. has no parallel in RecShrt.; (e) Isaac and Sarah run only in RecLng.; (f) there is no double vocative, "Father, father," in RecShrt.; (g) RecShrt. fam. B F G does not mention Sarah's tent (although RecShrt. 4:1 does mention it); (h) only RecLng. echoes LXX Gen 14:12 with the phrase, Λὼτ τοῦ ἀδελφοῦ σου τοῦ οἰκοῦντος ἐν Σοδόμοις (see above). (ix) RecLng. 5 runs to just over 33 lines in Schmidt's critical edition. Its counterpart in RecShrt. fam. E is just under 25 lines long. RecShrt. fam. B F G has only 22 lines.

Two facts suggest that RecShrt. is an abbreviation of something like RecLng. For one thing, RecLng.'s borrowing from Genesis does not seem to be secondary. In no instance are the allusions or borrowing intrusive or artificial, as we might expect them to be were they later additions. For another, the textual tradition of RecLng. 5 displays a striking tendency to abbreviate, so the variations within RecLng. itself reveal a way from that family to RecShrt.

Given the great differences in vocabulary, one could entertain the possibility that RecLng. and RecShrt. go back to different translations of a Semitic original. Yet several shared expressions seem hardly to be independent translations of Hebrew or Aramaic:

RecLng. 5:3	τὴν διαφορὰν τῆς ὁμιλίας αὐτοῦ (cf. 6:1)
RecShrt. 6:6 fam. E	τὴν διαφορὰν τῆς ὁμιλίας αὐτοῦ
RecLng. 5:4	μὴ γενώμεθα ἐπιβαρεῖς τοῦ ἀνθρώπου τούτου
RecShrt. 4:2 fam. E	μὴ ἐπιβαρὴ γένῃ τῷ ξένῳ τούτῳ ἀνθρώπῳ
RecLng. 5:6	ἔρριψε τὴν μνήμην τοῦ θανάτου (cf. 4:8)
RecShrt. 4:16	ῥίψον δὲ τὴν μνήμην τοῦ θανάτου

Such common phrases imply a common Greek exemplar.

One way of explaining the striking verbal similarities and common story line amidst the many verbal differences is to posit that someone who had heard our story later wrote it down from memory, without a written text before him. He recalled the basic story and certain expressions but did not reproduce his source verbatim.

5:1. Michael returns to Abraham's house. The language again comes from earlier lines:

ὁ ἀρχιστράτηγος Μιχαήλ; cf. 1:4; 2:1–4, 6–7, 10; 3:4, 6, 9–11; 4:5, 7, 9
κατῆλθεν; cf. 1:4; 2:1; 4:10
τὸν οἶκον τοῦ Ἀβραάμ; cf. 2:12; 3:1, 5; 4:2
ἐκαθέσθη μετ' αὐτοῦ; cf. 2:8, 9; 3:5; 4:4, 10
τραπέζῃ; cf. 4:2, 4, 9, 10

Only "then" (τότε) and "served" (ὑπηρέτει; ὑπηρετέω*: LXX: Wis 16:21, 24, 25; Ecclus 39:4) are new.

"Isaac served them" is a transformation of Gen 18:8: "Then he (Abraham) took curds and milk and the calf that he had prepared, and set it before them; and he stood by them under the tree while they ate." In *TA*, Isaac replaces Abraham. Notably, both Tgs. Onq. and Ps.-Jn. on Gen 18:8 turn "he stood by them" into "he served them" (עליהון משמיש הוא and והוא משמש קדמיהון respectively), and Abraham is the subject of שמש in *Mek.* on Exod 18:12 and *b. Qidd.* 32b, both of which quote Gen 18:8.

5:2. The meal itself is not narrated (contrast RecShrt. 5:1). Readers assume that all has gone according to 4:10: the devouring spirit has eaten Michael's food. We learn only what happened "after they finished (τελεσθέντος; τελέω*) the feast" (δείπνου; δεῖπνον*); cf. RecShrt. 5:1 and *Prot. Jas.* 6:3 (τελεσθέντος τοῦ δείπνου). Abraham, "according to custom" (κατὰ τὸ ἔθος; see on 2:2), makes the after-dinner prayer: ἐποίησεν … εὐχήν (cf. 14:5, 6). ποιέω + εὐχή (see on 3:6) often refers to making a vow, as in LXX Judg 11:39; 1 Esd 4:46; Philo, *Spec. leg.* 1.249. Here, however, the idiom refers to prayer, as in Diodorus Siculus 20.50.6: εὐχάς … ἐποιοῦντο καθάπερ ἦν ἔθος. For grace after meals see *b. Ber.* 48b and Strack-Billerbeck 4/2:627– 39. Michael and Abraham next recline (ἀνεπαύσαντο) upon their couches, ἐν τῇ κλίνῃ; for this phrase with ἀναπαύω see 17:2; 19:2; 20:4; Cassius Dio, *Hist.* 67.15.3; Oribasius, *Coll. med.* 7.26.153; *Synopsis* 1.17.30. One may compare Gen 18:4, where the three angels clearly recline (see on 4:4); but there is a contrast with 18:8 ("he stood by them under the tree while they ate"), upon which Ps.-Ephraem commented: "Abraham did not dare recline with them, but like a servant stood apart from them" (*Comm. Gen.* 15.2). In *TA*, in contrast with Genesis and with rabbinic traditions that emphasize his service (see above), Abraham relaxes and lets others do most of the work.

5:3. The opening words echo LXX Gen 22:7, a verse which conveys the loving bond of trust between Abraham and Isaac:

TA 5:3   εἶπε δὲ Ἰσαὰκ πρὸς   τὸν πατέρα αὐτοῦ,   πάτερ
LXX Gen 22:7 εἶπεν δὲ Ἰσαὰκ πρὸς Ἀβραὰμ τὸν πατέρα αὐτοῦ εἶπας, πάτερ

The parallelism is even greater if one accepts the reading of G J, which have Ἀβραάμ. Isaac wants to rest near Abraham and Michael in the dining chamber (τρικλίνῳ; see on 4:1), for he loves the "distinctive conversation" (τὴν διαφορὰν τῆς ὁμιλίας; cf. 6:1; RecShrt. 6:6 fam. E; the idiom is otherwise unattested) of the man who is "all virtuous" (παναρέτου). πανάρετος* (LXX: 0; NT: 0; Josephus: 0) appears in Philo, *Migr.* 95; and *1 Clem.* 1:2; 2:8; 45:7; 57:3; 60:4; and it is a favorite of Eusebius. Ps.-Chrysostom, *Contra theatra* 3 PG 56.545, uses it of Abraham.

5:4. Abraham addresses his son as τέκνον, as he does in LXX Gen 22:7 and 8; see further on 3:7. So v. 4 strengthens the scriptural echo of v. 3. Isaac is not to stay but to go to his own "chamber" (τρικλίνῳ; see on 4:1) and "rest," ἀνάπαυσαι (ἀναπαύω: v. 2 v.l., 5 v.l.; 17:2; 19:2; 20:4). Abraham wishes to place upon his guest no "burden," μὴ γενώμεθα ἐπιβαρεῖς τοῦ ἀνθρώπου τούτου; cf. MT 2 Sam 15:33 (וְהָיִת עָלַי לְמַשָּׂא For ἐπιβαρής* (RecShrt. 2:7; 4:2; 5:5; LXX: 0; Philo: 0; NT: 0; Josephus: 0), LSJ, s.v., lists only Heron Mechanicus, *Belopoeica* 102.9, while Lampe, s.v., cites only TA. But Paul uses the related verb, ἐπιβαρέω, in a similar construction: 1 Thess 2:9 (μὴ ἐπιβαρῆσαί τινα ὑμῶν; so too 2 Thess 3:8). Even closer are Basil the Great, *Asceticon magnum* PG 31.1025B (μὴ ἄλλοις ἐπιβαρῆ γίνεσθαι); Ps.-Macarius, *Serm.* 64 17.2 (οὐκ ἤθελον ἐπιβαρεῖς γενέσθαι); *Hom. 1–50* 17.8 (οὐκ ἤθελον ἐπιβαρεῖς ἄλλοις γίνεσθαι); and Theodore the Studite, *Ep.*, ed. Fatouros 480.24 (τὸ μὴ ἐπιβαρὴς εἶναι). Abraham, the kind host, is concerned for his guest.

5:5. Isaac, as before, does what Abraham wishes; he returns to his own chamber (τρικλίνῳ; see on 4:1) to lie down on his own couch (κλίνης; cf. vv. 2, 7). His absence is also part of the dramatic set-up. When he has his frightening dream, he will be separated from his father and so will have to run to him.

The relation with v. 4 underlines the son's obedience. Isaac departs only after λαβὼν τὴν εὐχὴν παρ᾽ αὐτῶν. Elsewhere in *TA*, εὐχή means either "prayer" (5:2; 14:5, 6, 8; cf. *T. Jud.* 19:2; *4 Bar.* 9:3; etc.) or "oath/vow" (see on 3:6). "Prayer" in the sense of a "blessing" works here; and LXX Genesis, *TA*'s chief intertext, contains several stories in which a father blesses a son, and one in which an angel blesses a man; see Gen 9:26–27; 27:1–40; 28:1–4; 32:22–32; 48:8–49:28. Later Judaism also knows about paternal benedictions (Ecclus 3:9).[1] Lampe, s.v., however, suggests that εὐχή here might mean "permission," and he cites as support John Climacus, *Scala paradisi* 15 ("by εὐχῆς of the father").

5:6. "God cast the notice of death into Isaac's heart as in a dream" is from 4:8, with minor changes. The correlation means that God's word to Michael is now fulfilled precisely. But "about the third hour of the night" (περὶ ὥραν τρίτην τῆς νυκτός), which presumably means midnight, "the time of divine favor" in *b. Ber.* 3b, is a new detail.

5:7. The frightful dream wakes Isaac up, διϋπνισθείς (διυπνίζω*; LXX: 0; Philo: 0; NT: 0; Josephus: 0; cf. RecShrt. 6:1 E; *T. Sim.* 4:9; *Acts John* 21, 61; *Acts Pet.* 40; *Gos. Bart.* 4:57, 58; Epiphanius, *Anc.* 83.3). Seeking to reassure himself that his dream is not reality, he comes to Abraham's chamber (τρικλίνου; see on 4:1) running, ἦλθε δρομαίως (δρομαίως*); cf. *Gos. Bart.* 4:17 (δρομαίως ἐπελθών); Romanos the Melodist, *Cant. dubia* 70.6.1 (ἦλθε δρομαίως); Suidas, s.v. (δρομαίως: δρομαῖος δὲ ἦλθεν ὁ ἀνήρ). On the haste in Genesis 18 see on 3:6, where Isaac also runs.

5:8. Isaac arrives (φθάσας; cf. 1:3) at the door (πρὸς τὴν θύραν). He then cries out saying (ἔκραξε λέγων; cf. Matt 14:30; Mark 1:23; John 7:37; *4 Bar.* 2:2; 5:32; 7:15), πάτερ, πάτερ. Cf. LXX Gen 22:7 and the double vocative in the traditions about Abraham; see on 14:14. The son asks the father to "rise now and open to me (ἄνοιξόν μοι, as in 12:17; RecShrt. 6:1; LXX Cant 5:2) quickly" (ταχέως*). He wants to enter and "hang on to" his father's "neck," κρεμασθῶ ἐπὶ τοῦ τραχήλου σου; cf. v. 9; RecShrt. 6:2. This is a biblical idiom; cf. Gen 45:14 (ἔκλαυσεν ἐπὶ τῷ τραχήλῳ αὐτοῦ); 46:29 (ἐπέπεσεν ἐπὶ τὸν τράχηλον αὐτοῦ); *3 Macc.* 5:49 (ἐπὶ τοὺς τραχήλους ἐπιπίπτοντες); *Jos. Asen.* 22:5 (ἐκρεμάσθη Ἀσενὲθ ἐπὶ τὸν τράχηλον τοῦ πατρὸς αὐτοῦ); *Prot. Jas.* 9:12 (ἔδραμεν καὶ ἐκρέμασεν ἑαυτὴν εἰς τὸν τράχηλον αὐτοῦ). Before "they" take Abraham from him—the third person plural refers to angels (cf. 20:10)—Isaac wishes to say farewell, ἀσπάσωμαι. For ἀσπάζομαι (5:8; 6:8; 20:8, 9) with this sense see BAGD, s.v., 1a. Clearly Isaac intuits, even before Michael's interpretation, the purport of the dream.

5:9. Abraham rises, ἀναστὰς οὖν Ἀβραάμ; cf. 2:2; 5:8; 9:2; 17:1; 18:10; LXX Gen 22:3 (ἀναστὰς δὲ Ἀβραάμ); 23:7. That Abraham arises and opens the door corresponds to Isaac's request in v. 8, so here father obeys son. The correlation with v. 8 continues with the remark that Isaac, upon entering, hangs upon Abraham's neck, ἐκρεμάσθη ἐπὶ τὸν τράχηλον αὐτοῦ;

---

[1] See further David Philipson, "Blessing of Children," *JE* 3 (1902), 242–43.

see on v. 8. But here the narrator adds that Isaac cries "with a loud voice," κλαίειν φωνὴν μεγάλην; cf. 2 Βασ 15:23; 2 Esd 3:12; *4 Bar.* 9:8. One is reminded of Gen 46:29: Joseph "fell upon his neck, and wept with much weeping" (LXX: ἐπέπεσεν ἐπὶ τὸν τράχηλον αὐτοῦ καὶ ἔκλαυσεν κλαυθμῷ πλείονι). Here too it is a son crying over his father.

5:10. This replays the contagious weeping of 3:9–10 (q.v.; for ἔκλαυσεν ... μεγάλως cf. 7:6).

5:10	συγκινηθεὶς τὰ σπλάγχνα ὁ ᾽Αβραὰμ καὶ ἔκλαυσεν
3:9	ἐκινήθησαν δὲ τὰ σπλάγχνα τοῦ ᾽Αβραὰμ καὶ ἐδάκρυσεν

5:10	ἰδὼν δὲ ὁ ἀρχιστράτηγος αὐτοὺς κλαίοντας, ἔκλαυσε καὶ αὐτός
3:10	καὶ ἰδὼν αὐτὸν ᾽Ισαὰκ κλαίοντα ἔκλαυσεν καὶ αὐτός

There Abraham cries, then Isaac, then Michael. Here Isaac cries, then Abraham cries, then Michael cries.

The major difference is that only in 3:9–10 do we hear of Michael's tears becoming precious stones.

Isaac's tears are the grief that the thought of death and its separation brings. Abraham's tears express a father's sympathy for his son. Michael's tears communicate that sadness on earth is felt in heaven.

5:11. Sarah (already introduced in 3:5, q.v.) sleeps not in "the house" of 3:1 but "in her tent," ἐν τῇ σκηνῇ αὐτῆς. Evidently her living quarters are separated from those of the men. σκηνή (see on 1:2) recalls the several passages in Genesis in which Abraham and Sarah have a tent, including 18:1–2, where Abraham sees the three angels while he is sitting in front of his tent, and especially 18:6 ("Abraham hastened into the tent to Sarah"), 9 ("They said to him, 'Where is your wife Sarah?' And he said, 'There, in the tent'"), and 10 ("Sarah was listening at the tent entrance"); see also 12:8; 13:3, 18. The tent belongs to the stylized depictions of Genesis 18 in both Jewish and Christian art.[2] Sarah comes running (ἦλθε δρομαία), as Isaac did earlier (ἦλθε δρομαίως, v. 7, q.v.)—and just as Abraham does in

---

[2] See e.g. the depiction of the sacrifice of Isaac at Dura-Europos. Goodenough, *Jewish Symbols*, 9:71–73, identified the figure in front of the tent with Sarah. For a Christian example see Charles Rufus Morey, *Early Christian Art: An Outline of the Evolution of Style and Iconography in Sculpture and Painting from Antiquity to the Eighth Century* (Princeton: Princeton University Press, 1942), plate 178; also plates 214, 216, 217, and 218 in Kurt Weitzmann and Herbert L. Kessler, *The Cotton Genesis: British Library Codex Cotton Otho B. VI* (Princeton: Princeton University Press, 1986). In both Genesis and *TA*, Sarah's presence in the tent may be a patriarchal way of conveying her modesty; cf. Ps.-Ephraem, *Comm. Gen.* 15.2; Ambrose, *Abr.* 5.37.

Gen 18:2: "he ran from his tent" (προσέδραμεν ... ἀπὸ τῆς θύρας τῆς σκηνῆς). So this is one more element from the episode at Mamre. Sarah hears "his weeping", ἤκουσε τοῦ κλαυθμοῦ. This is presumably the weeping of the last individual mentioned, Michael. Sarah discovers Abraham, Isaac, and Michael not only crying but also embracing, περιπλακομένους. περιπλέκω = "embrace" (cf. 3 Macc. 5:49; Josephus, Ant. 8.7; Herm. Sim. 9.11.4) recurs in 15:4 (Sarah embraces Michael's feet), 5 (Isaac embraces Michael's feet); 20:6 (Sarah embraces Abraham's feet);

5:12. Sarah, without yet knowing why the others weep, now speaks with tears: εἶπε μετὰ κλαυθμοῦ; cf. LXX Dan 6:21; Jud 14:16; Gk. L.A.E. 27:3, T. Job 24:1. Their sadness is her sadness. She addresses Abraham as κύριέ μου; cf. v. 13; 2:10; LXX Gen 18:12; 23:6, 11; 24:42 (τοῦ κυρίου μου Ἀβραάμ). She wants an explanation, ἀνάγγειλόν μοι; cf. 7:1; 8:8; 17:6; 20:1; Gk. L.A.E. 6:2; 31:2; Jos. Asen. 14:7; 15:12; 19:4; 4 Bar. 2:4.

5:13. "My lord" comes from v. 12 (q.v.), "this brother we are entertaining today" from 4:1–3 (q.v.). "Your kinsman Lot, who dwells in Sodom" (Λὼτ τοῦ ἀδελφοῦ σου τοῦ οἰκοῦντος ἐν Σοδόμοις) rewrites LXX Gen 14:12: Λὼτ υἱὸν τοῦ ἀδελφοῦ Ἀβραάμ ... ἦν γὰρ κατοικῶν ἐν Σοδόμοις; cf. LXX Gen 13:12–13. The one significant difference is that, in Gen 14:12, Lot is Abraham's nephew, the son of his brother, whereas in TA, Lot is Abraham's ἀδελφός. But ἀδελφός can be used of male relatives of different degrees (Bauer-Danker, s.v.); and in Gen 13:8, Abraham says to Lot, "we are kinsmen" (MT: אחים; LXX: ἀδελφοί; cf. also LXX Gen 13:11). Sarah wonders if, perchance, Michael has brought news (φάσιν λόγου ἤνεγκε; cf. RecShrt. 3:3; 6:5–6; 4 Bar. 7:9, 10; φάσις*) concerning Lot's death. The text assumes, in accord with Genesis, that whereas Abraham and Lot originally stayed together, later the two lived in different places. Genesis does not say how or when Lot died, and there are likewise no early extracanonical legends on the subject. So given that Lot is Abraham's nephew, it is natural to suppose the former was alive when the latter died. Neither Lot nor Sodom play any more role in our book.

5:14. The Commander-in-chief replies (ὑπολαβών; see p. 29 and cf. 7:2; T. Job 36:4; 37:5; 38:5–6; 40:1) and addresses Sarah as "sister" (ἀδελφή*). This corresponds to her calling him "brother" in v. 13.[3] Sarah is not ever so addressed in Genesis, but Abraham does pass her off as his "sister" in Gen 12:10–20 and 20:1–18. Michael, who has of course known of Isaac's

---

[3]   Cf. Delcor, Testament, 111, who cites Jos. Asen. 7:8 and here dismisses the meaning "co-religionist."

dream ahead of time, dispels Sarah's fear about Lot. Hiding his knowledge, he unassumingly suggests that something else has gone wrong, ὡς ἐμοὶ δοκεῖ (the phrase occurs often in Plato; Xenophon and Chrysostom also favor it). Michael's guess is that Isaac has seen a dream, ὄνειρον ἐθεάσατο; cf. 4:8, ὀνείρῳ θεάσῃ. The rest of the verse just recapitulates for Sarah what readers already know, and with the same words: "he came to us crying, and when we saw him we were deeply moved and cried."

5:14	ἦλθεν
5:7, 8, 9	ἦλθε, εἰσέλθω, εἰσελθών
5:14	κλαίων
5:9	κλαίειν
5:14	ἰδόντες
5:10	ἰδών
5:14	τὰ σπλάγχνα κινηθέντες
5:10	συγκινηθεὶς οὖν τὰ σπλάγχνα
5:14	ἐκλαύσαμεν
5:10	ἔκλαυσεν ... κλαίοντας, ἔκλαυσε

Chapter 6: Recognition of Michael's Identity

Bibliography: David Flusser, "*Palaea Historica*: An Unknown Source of Biblical Legends," in *Scripta Hierosolymitana, Vol. XXII: Studies in Aggadah and Folk-Literature* (ed. Joseph Heinemann and Dov Noy; Jerusalem: Magnes, 1971), 59–60. Schmidt, "Testament," 1:84, 86; 2:128–29. Turner, "Testament," 117–18.

Long Recension

6:1. When she heard the Commander-in-chief's distinctive conversation, Sarah knew immediately that the speaker was an angel of the Lord. 6:2. Then Sarah made signs to Abraham to come to the door, and she said to him, "My lord Abraham, do you not know who this man is?" 6:3. Abraham said, "I do not know." 6:4. Sarah said, "You must know, my Lord, the three heavenly men who were entertained in our tent beside the oak of Mamre, when we slaughtered the calf and readied a table for them? 6:5. After the prepared meat had been eaten, the calf rose again and suckled its mother joyfully. Do you not know, my lord Abraham, that by promise they gave to us Isaac, the fruit of (my) womb? For this man is one of those three." 6:6. Abraham said, "Oh Sarah, you have spoken this truly. Glory (to you) and peace from God. For indeed late in the evening, when I washed his feet in the basin, I said in my heart: These are the feet of (one of) the three men I washed then. 6:7. Indeed,

Short Recension fam. E

6:6b. And when Sarah heard Michael speaking, she knew, from his distinctive conversation, that he surpassed everyone living on the earth, because his voice was glorious. 6:7. And Sarah said to Abraham, "How is it that you dare to cry when this man has come to us, (to be) in our house? 6:8. Or how is it that your eyes cry when the light of the tribunal[1] has risen in our house? For today is a day of rejoicing." 6:9. Abraham said, "How do you know that this is a man of God?" 6:10. Sarah answered and said, "Can it be that I am deceived when I say that this is one of the three men we entertained under the trees of Mamre, when you were away in the plain and you brought a calf and slaughtered it? 6:11. And you gave it to me, saying, 'Rise, make ready, so that we might eat with these men in our house.'" 6:12. And Abraham answered her, "Mistress Sarah, you understand well. 6:13. Because also I, when I washed his feet, knew in my heart that they were

---

[1] τῶν βημάτων (E). The sense of this is unclear. Schmidt, "Testament," 1:84, suggests a reference to the liturgical dais. He cites *Midr. Ps.* 17:5, where a reader in the synagogue is likened to an angel. C: τῶν ζευμάτων. H I: τολμημάτων.

when his tears afterwards fell into the washing-vessel, they became precious stones." And he brought them forth from the fold in his garment and gave them to Sarah saying, "If you doubt me, look at these." 6:8. Taking them, Sarah bowed down and embraced them with joy and said, "Glory to God who shows us wonders. And know, my Lord Abraham, that (all) this means for us the revelation of some important matter, whether for good or for ill."

the feet I washed under the trees of Mamre, which went to save brother Lot from Sodom. Then I knew the mystery."

TEXTUAL NOTES ON THE LONG RECENSION

6:1. Throughout *TA*, A prefers εὐθέως; most of the other manuscripts usually have εὐθύς; see 8:1; 10:12; 11:6; 13:12; 14:13; 15:11; 18:2; 20:9, 10. But some manuscripts alternate between the two forms. 6:2–4. H abbreviates by omitting "not ... must know." 6:3–4. G shortens by dropping "Abraham said ... Sarah said," words not strictly necessary. 6:4. B G I Q lack "my lord" and "in our tent." This diminishes the intertextuality. // For "slaughtered" A uses θύσαντες; cf. RecShrt. (ἔθυσας) and LXX Gen 22:9. B G H I Q have ἔσφαξας; cf. LXX Gen 22:10, which uses σφάζω of the sacrifice of Isaac. // After τὸν μόσχον, B G I Q add τὸν ἄμωμον, which has sacrificial connotations (cf. Lev 1:3, 10, etc.) // I omits "and readied a table." // H at the end: "and prepared for them the fatted (σιτευτόν) calf"; cf. LXX Judg 6:25, 28; Jer 26:21; Luke 15:23, 27, 30. 6:6. G has ἀπὸ (instead of παρὰ) θεοῦ, which may be Christian assimilation to a Pauline formula, and πατρός in A I seems obviously such; cf. Phil 1:2; Col 1:2; 2 Thess 1:2; Titus 1:4; Phlm 3.[2] // G shortens by dropping "late ... when." // A: τοῦ νιπτῆρος after ἐν τῇ λεκάνῃ; cf. v. 7; *T. Job* 25:6; John 13:5. Given the rarity of the word, A may here stand under Johannine influence. 6:7. G condenses the opening: "When the tears fell, they ... ." But then it adds "from his eyes" after "fell." // G omits "saying, 'If ... these.'" 6:8. H drops "Taking them, Sarah."

---

[2]   Contrast Strotmann, *"Mein Vater"*, 209–211, who holds A's reading to be original and Jewish.

COMMENTARY

TA 6 is firstly a dialogue between Sarah and Abraham, the upshot of which is that their visitor is from their own past, and that his presence betokens a divine revelation.

2	Sarah speaks	initial question
3	Abraham speaks	assertion of ignorance
4–5	Sarah speaks	recollection of Genesis 18
6–7	Abraham speaks	recollection of *TA* 3
8	Sarah speaks	concluding acclamation and interpretation

Sarah initiates the dialogue and concludes it, and Abraham's sentences—one of which is nothing more than "I don't know"—are sandwiched between hers. Although she calls him "my lord" (vv. 3, 5, 8), her insight surpasses his. Abraham gains full conviction about Michael's identity only after Sarah does, and it is left to her to offer the summarizing interpretation in v. 8.

Sarah identifies Michael as one of three visitors from a memorable episode in her past, when a calf was slaughtered and resurrected, and when Isaac's birth was promised (Genesis 18). Abraham then makes the same identification: the feet that he washed this evening are the same that he washed long ago (Gen 18:4). So Abraham finally catches up with readers, who earlier came to his conclusion by recognizing *TA*'s intertextuality, with its numerous parallels between past and present.

Chap. 6 not only makes the correspondence between Genesis and *TA* explicit but further adds to the implicit links:

	TA 6	Genesis
Sarah listens at the door	1–2	cf. 18:10
"angel of the Lord"	1	cf. 16:7–11; 22:11, 15
Sarah calls Abraham "my lord"	2, 5, 8	cf. 18:12
"by the oak of Mamre"	4	cf. 18:1
"the calf prepared for them"	4	cf. 18:7–8
"three men"	4, 6	cf. 18:2

The correlation is even greater than appears from this chart, for TA, which in chap. 3 tells of Michael's tears becoming precious stones, adds the miracle of the resurrected calf to the episode in Genesis 18, so both visitations are accompanied by a tangible wonder: Michael's first visit witnesses a resurrection, the second a metamorphosis.

RecLng. 6 occupies 22 lines in Schmidt's critical edition. RecShrt. 6:6b–13 fam. E runs to 17 lines, fam. B F G to 11. The latter unfolds this way:

Sarah hears Michael and asks Abraham how he can cry when a "man of God" has come, 6:7–8
Abraham asks Sarah how she knows the visitor is a "man of God," 6:9
Sarah knows that the visitor is one of the 3 angels in Genesis, 6:10–11
Michael accepts Sarah's equation and refers to saving Lot, 6:12–13[3]

Despite its relative brevity and the omission of several elements that are part of RecLng.'s intertextuality—Sarah listening at the door, "angel of the Lord," "my lord," the promise of Isaac, the washing of the feet (see above)—fam. B F G otherwise augments the parallels with Genesis 18, for it refers to Abraham's words to Sarah in Gen 18:6 as well as to Lot's deliverance from Sodom, and it uses both ποίησον (cf. LXX Gen 18:6) and φάγωμεν (cf. LXX Gen 18:5 and 8).

RecShrt. fam. E has yet a third arrangement:

Sarah recognizes Michael from his distinctive voice, 6:6
Sarah asks Abraham how he can cry when a "man of God" has come, 6:7–8
Abraham asks Sarah how she knows the visitor is a "man of God," 6:9
Sarah recognizes the visitor as one of the 3 angels in Genesis 18, 6:10–11
Abraham agrees; he fathomed this when washing Michael's feet, 6:12–13

Here Abraham, as opposed to Michael (so fam. B F G) and Sarah (so RecLng.), has the last word. As with fam. B F G, some of the links with Genesis are missing. Sarah is not listening "at the door," neither "angel of the Lord" nor "my lord" appears, and the promise of Isaac is not mentioned. On the other hand, and in agreement with fam. B F G, reference is made to Lot being saved, and both ποίησον and φάγωμεν appear. Both members of RecShrt. also concur in not mentioning the tears that became jewels, a central item in RecLng. 6; nor do they recount that the slaughtered calf returned to life. Fam. E, however, agrees with RecLng. and against fam. B F G in that the washing of the feet is a moment of revelation.

What conclusions do the textual variations suggest? First, in fam. B F G, Michael finishes with: "We saved Lot from Sodom, because we knew the mystery," which makes no sense. This seems to be a distortion of RecShrt. fam. E, where Abraham concludes with, "Then I knew for myself the mystery." This then is likely evidence of carelessness in one line of the tradition. Second, the legend of the resurrected calf, only in RecLng., depends, as we shall see, upon the Hebrew text of Genesis, which is

---

[3]   Cf. Vaticanus Copt. 58, ed. Simon in *Orientalia* 3 (1934), 217–42; 4 (1935), 222–34. Contrast *Gen. Rab.* 50:2: of the three angels Abraham entertained, two went to overturn Sodom and save Lot; these were Gabriel and Raphael. But Michael went his own way.

consistent with RecLng. originating when TA was not yet an exclusively Christian text. One must admit, however, that a Christian contributor could have inserted an originally Jewish legend. Third, Sarah is more prominent in RecLng., where she initiates the discussion, rightly interprets what has happened, and has the final word. Her status as Abraham's teacher well fits TA's tendency to turn things upside down. This is especially so if Abraham's words in vv. 6–7 are almost comedic, an attempt to save face, to assert that he did after all really figure things out before his wife did (see further below). Does RecShrt. then represent an attempt to rehabilitate Abraham for the sake of a sober piety? RecLng. alone, moreover, has Abraham confess ignorance: "I do not know" (6:3). This not only makes the wife know more than the husband, but also is in conflict with vv. 6–7, where Abraham says that he does know. Omission would be understandable, especially by a scribe in the Augustinian tradition, which prohibited lying under all circumstances.

6:1–3. When Sarah hears "the Commander-in-chief's distinctive conversation" (τὴν διαφορὰν τῆς ὁμιλίας; see on 5:3), she immediately knows that the voice belongs to "an angel of the Lord," ἄγγελος κυρίου—an expression appearing in Genesis only in the story of Abraham (16:7–11; 22:11, 15). As the following verses make plain, she remembers Michael from the encounter in Genesis 18, in which she listens to the three angels while standing at the tent's door (v. 10: Σάρρα δὲ ἤκουσεν πρὸς τῇ θύρᾳ). Much of *TA* models itself upon this scene, which is also the record of a conversation. Once again Sarah hears (ἀκούσασα δὲ Σάρρα) the voice of an angel, once again she is at the door (πρὸς τὴν θύραν), and once again she calls Abraham "my lord"—κύριέ μου in *TA* 6:2–8, ὁ κύριός μου in LXX Gen 18:12. This time, however, she does not laugh in disbelief but rather understands what is happening. From Michael's voice, Sarah infers precisely what her son earlier gathered from the stranger's appearance, namely, that he must be an angel (cf. 3:5). Abraham alone comes to the truth slowly. When Sarah makes signs (νεύει; νεύω*: cf. LXX Prov 21:1; Ezek. Trag. in Eusebius, *Praep. ev.* 9.29.5; John 13:24; Acts 24:10; Josephus, *Bell.* 1.629; *Ant.* 7.175) for her husband to come to her, and then asks if he knows who the visitor is, the patriarch confesses that he does not.

What in Michael's speech gives him away? Is it the tone, the accent, or something else? Do Judg 12:5–6, where the Ephraimites are betrayed by the way they say "shibboleth," and Matt 26:73, where Peter's Galilean accent betrays his identity, supply parallels? RecShrt. fam. E makes his voice ἔνδοξος; the Slavonic adds that it had "quietness." Schmidt conjectures that Michael speaks Hebrew, the language of creation and angels, which *Jub.* 12:25–27 claims died out after Babel and revived with Abraham.[4]

In v. 3 Abraham says that he does not know who Michael is. In vv. 6–7 he instead claims that he grasped the angel's identity when he washed his feet. Which statement is true? Perhaps the denial in v. 3 is a white lie, designed to keep Michael's identity from others for as long as possible, just as he keeps the words of the singing tree to himself (3:2–4; cf. 3:12). This is consistent with taking him at his word in vv. 6–7. Yet it seems better to take v. 3 as the self-effacing truth, vv. 6–7 as something less. In this case Abraham remains unsure about what to think until Sarah gives him her opinion, and in vv. 6–7 he is simplifying the process by which his conviction solidified. As he washed the stranger's feet, maybe he recollected the angels whose feet he had washed long ago, and yet doubts remained. This surmise fits with Michael's behavior in chapter 4, which follows the foot washing. For there the angel still hides his identity, evidently assuming that Abraham remains in the dark. Such a reading harmonizes also with Manoah's ignorance of his angelic visitor's identity in Judges 13 as well as with Philo's take on Genesis 18, according to which Abraham was of two minds about his visitors (*Quaest. Gen.* 4.6; cf. Heb 13:2, alluding to Abraham: "some have entertained angels unawares"). Erich Gruen has it right: "Abraham, as popular psychological parlance has it, was 'in denial.' If he did not acknowledge the talking tree or the metamorphosis of tears into jewels, perhaps they would have no effect. The dissimulation here was more like self-deception. But the image of the august patriarch bustling to suppress divine evidence leaves a decidedly comic impression."[5]

6:4. The intertextuality finally becomes explicit: the present stranger is a past stranger. Surely, Sarah supposes, Abraham must recall the three "heavenly" (ἐπουρανίους; see on 2:3) men they once entertained (ἐπιξενισθέντας; see on 4:1) beside the oak of Mamre (see on 1:2), when they slaughtered (θύσαντες; see under Textual Notes) a calf (μόσχον; cf. v. 5; RecShrt. 2:10; 6:10) and readied a table for them (παρέθηκας αὐτοῖς τράπεζαν; cf. *Jos. Asen.* 7:1; 15:14; and Acts 16:34, which Epiphanius, *Pan.* 74.6, reproduces as παρέθηκεν αὐτοῖς τράπεζαν). (There is no trace of the rabbinic tradition that three calves were slaughtered; see *ARN* A 13; *b. B. Meṣiʿa* 86b.) Sarah's question uses the language of LXX Genesis 18:

---

4   Schmidt, "Testament," 1:84.
5   Gruen, *Diaspora*, 188.

| *TA* 6:4 | κύριέ μου |
| *LXX* Gen 18:12 | κύριός μου |

| *TA* 6:4 | τρεῖς ἄνδρας |
| *LXX* Gen 18:2 | τρεῖς ἄνδρες |

| *TA* 6:4 | ἐν τῇ σκηνῇ |
| *LXX* Gen 18:9 (cf. vv. 6, 10) | ἐν τῇ σκηνῇ |

| *TA* 6:4 | παρὰ τὴν δρῦν τὴν Μαβρῆ |
| *LXX* Gen 18:1 | πρὸς τῇ δρυὶ τῇ Μαμβρῇ |

| *TA* 6:4 | τὸν μόσχον   παρέθηκας αὐτοῖς |
| *LXX* Gen 18:8 | τὸ μοσχάριον … παρέθηκεν αὐτοῖς |

Genesis 18 does not mention a table, but one appears often in Christian art (e.g. the mosaic of the Philoxenia at S. Vitale, Ravenna, 6th cent.).[6]

6:5. Sarah goes on to describe an event Genesis does not record. A miracle took place "after the prepared meat (τῶν κρεών; κρέας*; cf. LXX Gen 9:4; *Jos. Asen.* 10:14; *T. Jud.* 15:4; Rom 14:21; Josephus, *Ant.* 10.261) had been consumed," δαπανηθέντων. δαπανάω* is often used of fire, as in 2 Macc 1:23; 2:10; Josephus, *Ant.* 4.192; *Mart. Pol.* 11:2; so one may, with 4:10 in mind, think of the πνεῦμα παμφάγον sent by God as a sort of consuming fire. According to LSJ, s.v., κρέας can mean either "meat" or "dressed meat." In view of Gen 18:7–8, the latter is here meant. The calf (μόσχος; cf. v. 4), Sarah adds, rose again (ἠγέρθη πάλιν) and suckled (ἐθήλαζεν; θηλάζω*: cf. LXX Gen 21:7 [of Sarah]; 32:15 [of animals]; Luke 11:27; *Gk. Apoc. Ezra* 5:2 [of animals]) its mother joyfully, ἐν ἀγαλλιάσει; cf. Gk. *1 En.* 5:9; *Ps. Sol.* 5:1; *T. Jud.* 25:5; the phrase occurs often in LXX Psalms: 99:2; 104:43, etc.

This legend has attracted little attention. Delcor cites no parallel.[7] Kohler says that the story is "known in Mohammedan folklore, was known also in Essene circles, and is alluded to in the *Zohar*, Chaye Sarah, p. 127b, cf. Yalkut Reubeni Vayera, the calf showing Abraham the road to the cave of Machpelah, where the patriarchs led their immortal life."[8] He documents neither the reference to "Mohammedan folklore"[9] nor his

---

[6] The exceptions are those works that, presumably in dependence upon a Jewish prototype, depict the initial encounter, when Abraham and the three men are approaching each other.

[7] Delcor, *Testament*, 112–13.

[8] Kohler, "Apocalypse," 584, n. 1.

[9] Was Kohler vaguely recalling *Koran* 2:260, where birds cut up by Abraham (cf. Gen 15:7–11) come back to life? Very late Jewish sources also know this legend; see Ginzberg, *Legends*, 1:236; 5:229.

assertion about Essenes. Regarding the *Zohar* and *Yalkut Reubeni*, the latter, from the seventeenth century, is not likely to be independent of the former, in circulation since at least the thirteenth century; and the *Zohar* itself is ambiguous. 2.127b may presuppose the legend: "R. Eleazar said: 'Abraham came to enter the cave in this way. He was running after that calf of which we read, "and Abraham ran unto the herd, and fetched a calf"'" (cf. Gen 17:7). If this account, which rewrites Genesis 23, is placed after the episode in Genesis 18, then clearly the calf has come back to life. Unfortunately, this is not necessarily implied, for the *Zohar* says that Abraham had known about the cave long before he bought it. The language may be retrospective.

There is a parallel in the *Palaea Historica*, a Byzantine expansion of and commentary upon the biblical story from Genesis to Daniel.[10] Its retelling of Genesis 18 includes the tale that, after Abraham's guests had dined, the mother of the eaten calf appeared, seeking her own, and that when all rose from the table, the calf likewise rose to go after its mother.[11] One cannot eliminate the possibility that this episode transmits an old tradition, even though it is preserved only in a Byzantine Greek text (and its Slavonic parallel[12]) from the later Middle Ages (as well as in occasional art work presumably dependent upon that text).[13] According to Flusser, "it is most unlikely that our author took the incident from the Testament of Abraham, where it functions only as a flashback."[14] And yet we can hardly be confident that the *Palaea Historica*—which is bound next to *TA* in RecLng. ms. I—is an independent witness. Why the story being a flashback militates against dependence upon *TA* remains unclarified. Furthermore, *TA* circulated among Byzantine Greeks, and indeed in more than one recension, and

---

[10] See Vassiliev, *Anecdota*.

[11] Cf. Flusser, "*Palaea Historica*," 60. The Greek text printed in Vassiliev, *Anecdota*, 215, reads as follows: ἐγένετο δὲ μετὰ τὸ ἀριστῆσαι αὐτοὺς ἠβούλοντο ἐξελθεῖν ἀπὸ τῆς τραπέζης καὶ ἰδοὺ ἡ μήτηρ τοῦ μόσχου ἦλθεν βοῶν καὶ ζητοῦσα τὸν ἴδιον μόσχον. ἀναστάντων δὲ τούτων τῆς τραπέζης συνανέστη καὶ ὁ τεθυμένος μόσχος καὶ ἠκολούθησεν τῇ μητρὶ αὐτοῦ.

[12] For an English translation of the relevant lines of the Slavonic *Historical Paleya* see Kugel, *Traditions*, 344, which is based upon the edition of A. Popov, *Kniga Bytia Nebesi I Zemli (Paleya Istoricheskaya)* (Moscow: Imperial Society of Russian History and Antiquities of Moscow University, 1881), 43.

[13] Von Erffa, *Ikonologie*, 2:95, cites a Serbian Psalter in Munich, Cod. Slav. 4, fol. 229r, and a late Byzantine fresco in Platsa.

[14] Flusser, "*Palaea Historica*," 60. Cf. Kugel, *Traditions*, 920: It is clear that behind the *Istoricheskaya Paleya* "stand earlier Greek texts and arguably, in many instances, texts or traditions first formulated in Hebrew or Aramaic."

it was also popular among Slavic Christians. It would be incautious, then, to conclude that the *Palaea Historica*'s story is independent of *TA*.

Although the hunt for parallels to 6:5 seems to lead nowhere, it is otherwise with the search for the origin of the legend. MT Gen 18:8 reads as follows:

ויקח חמאה וחלב ובן־הבקראשר עשה ויתן לפניהם
והוא־עמד עליהם תחת העץ ויאכלו

The NRSV translates: "Then he took the curds and milk and the calf that he had prepared, and set it before them; and he stood by them under the tree while they ate." This is without question the meaning of the Hebrew. But one could, if sufficiently motivated, tendentiously avoid the plain sense of the text and identify the subject of והוא־עמד ("and he stood up") as בן־הבקר ("the calf," lit. "son of cattle"), in which case the slaughtered animal rises up: "Then he (Abraham) took the curds and milk and the calf that he had prepared, and set it before them; and it (the calf) rose up by them under the tree." Anyone familiar with the creativity of rabbinic hermeneutics will have no trouble imagining someone construing the text like this, nor envisaging a Jewish exegete making בן־הבקר one of the subjects of ויאכלו, so that the calf eats as do the others. It can be no coincidence that, according to *TA* 6:5, the risen calf "suckled its mother joyfully." Not only the resurrection of Abraham's calf but also its suckling can be discovered in the Hebrew text of Gen 18:8. As LXX Gen 18:8 does not offer the same possibilities for interpretation, either a contributor to *TA* knew a Hebrew text or, despite the failure of this miracle to turn up anywhere else in antiquity, the book adopts a legend already known and ultimately based upon a reading of the Hebrew.

Why would anyone read the Hebrew so that the calf comes back to life and suckles its mother? Kugel suggests that the legend originated from the notion that the calf was not really eaten, that the meal was an elaborate illusion.[15] That angels neither eat nor drink was a commonplace (see on 4:9). So either the animal stands up because it has not died in the first place, that is, the butchering is illusory or—perhaps this is what Kugel intimates—the calf rises from the dead because, although slaughtered, it has not been eaten and so is still in one piece, and a resurrection is possible. This does not explain the calf's suckling, and the text plainly says that the animal was in fact both killed and eaten (vv. 4–5). In chap. 4, moreover, an all-devouring spirit consumes what is set before Michael. In view of the

---

[15] *Traditions*, 344. Cf. Delcor, *Testament*, 113: "Le récit merveilleux de la recension A a pour but d'éviter l'anthropomorphisme pour des anges qui se nourrissent réellement à la manière des hommes."

far-reaching correlations between the *TA* and Genesis, so that sacred history is constantly replaying itself, the explanation of the apparent eating of the angel in the chap. 4 can be no different than the explanation of what happened in Genesis 18.

A better explanation lies in Greco-Roman mythology, which offers more than one example of a slaughtered animal or meal coming back to life. In the saga of the Argonauts, the witch Medea, deceitfully promising to make Pelias young again, illustrates her magical powers by cutting up an old ram and throwing it into a cauldron, whereupon it leaps out as a young lamb. The episode was famous. It appears in many texts and is depicted on Greek vases and marble reliefs.[16] The version in Ovid, *Metam.* 7.297–349, has the restored lamb run away "to find some udder to give him milk." This is quite close to *TA* 6:5: "the calf rose again and suckled its mother joyfully."

Another parallel is the well-known myth about Tantalus and his young son, Pelops. As an odious trick to test the knowledge of the gods, the father cuts up his son, boils him in a cauldron, and serves the flesh to the gods at a great banquet. Being undeceived, the immortals do not partake—all save Demeter, who unknowingly eats his arm. The gods then bring Pelops back to life, give him an ivory shoulder, and indignantly punish Tantalus in Hades.[17] Here again the cooking pot gives back the dead—as it does also in Hyginus' version of the story of Jupiter come down to earth after the flood to visit Lycaon (an episode that parallels the Lord God coming down to visit Sodom and Gomorrah in Genesis; see Hyginus, *Poet. Astr.* 2.4). The god is served soup with the remains of Jove's son, Arcas, in it. Jupiter, knowing the truth, punishes Lycaon by turning him into a wolf and then reassembles and reanimates Arcas.

The entertaining story of a slain animal or prepared meal returning to life was at home in the Hellenistic world. It appears, then, that a Jew, educated in or familiar with Hellenistic culture, realized, when reading the Hebrew of Gen 18:8, that the verse could be read in such a way as to make

---

[16] See e.g. Apollodorus, *Bibl.* 1.9.27; Diodorus Siculus 4.52; Pausanias, *Descr.* 8.11.2–3; Cicero, *Sen.* 23.83; Hyginus, *Fab.* 24; Nonnus, *Dion.* 18.25–30; J. E. Harrison and D. S. MacColl, *Greek Vase Paintings: A Selection of Examples* (London: T. F. Unwin, 1894), plate ii; and the marble relief in Martin Robertson, *A History of Greek Art 2* (Cambridge: Cambridge University Press, 1975), plate 122c. Related is the episode in Homer, *Od.* 12.340–396, where the slaughtered cattle of Helios bellow despite having been slaughtered.

[17] See Pindar, *Ol.* 1.26; Ovid, *Metam.* 6.401–411; Hyginus, *Fab.* 83; Servius on Virgil, *Aen.* 6.603.

the story of Abraham include a stunning event strongly analogous to something otherwise famously featured in Greco-Roman mythology. More particularly, the tale of Medea and Pelias, in a version close to Ovid's, was probably the proximate inspiration. This suggestion accords not only with what we know in general about the interpenetration of Hellenism and Judaism, especially in Alexandria, where *TA* may have been composed, but is also supported by the allusion to Homer later in the chapter; see on v. 6.

Some Christian readers might have understood the resurrection of Abraham's calf to intimate the resurrection of Jesus. Already Origen, *Hom. Gen.* 2, calls the calf of Genesis 18 a "mystery" and understands it this way: "The calf itself is not tough, but good and tender. And what is so tender, what so good as that one who humbled himself for us to death and laid down his life for his friends? He is the fatted calf which the father slaughtered to receive his repentant son." To anyone familiar with this exegesis, which appears in other writers,[18] the typological meaning of the slaughtered and resurrected calf would be transparent. This probably explains the sacrificial language in the textual variants; see Textual Notes.

Passing from her memory of the meal in Gen 18:1–8, Sarah goes on to ask a question that recalls the sequel in Gen 18:9–15 and Isaac's subsequent birth: "Do you not know, my lord Abraham (see on v. 2), that by promise (ἐξ ἐπαγγελίας) they gave (ἐδωρήσατο; δωρέω*: cf. LXX Gen 30:20; *Let. Arist.* 290; *Gk. Apoc. Ezra* 2:16) to us Isaac, the fruit of (my) womb?" The reference is to Gen 18:10, where Sarah, at the tent door, hears the three men say to Abraham, "I will surely return to you [Abraham] in due season, and your wife Sarah shall have a son" (cf. v. 14). Even though the language of promise (ἐπαγγ-) does not appear in this verse, the angelic asseveration is in fact a promise, and ἐπαγγ- is otherwise connected with God's words to Abraham; see on 3:6. The relevant sources are mostly Christian, however, and ἐξ ἐπαγγελίας seems otherwise present only in Christian sources: Gal 3:18; Clement of Alexandria, *Strom.* 1.11.53; Origen, *Hom. Jer.* 1.5; Eusebius, *Comm. Isa.* 2.5; etc. "Fruit of (the/my) womb," a Hebraism (καρπὸν κοιλίας = פְּרִי־בֶטֶן; cf. 8:6; RecShrt. 10:5), is also not part of Abraham's story in LXX Genesis, but it does occur in LXX Gen 30:2 (of Rachel) and Lam 2:20. Christian texts associate the phrase not with Abraham but rather with David (because of Ps 131:11) and with Jesus (because of Luke 1:42).

6:6. Abraham, the last in his family to see the obvious, now denies his own ignorance (contrast v. 3). He tells Sarah that he too has divined the truth,

---

[18] Von Erffa, *Ikonologie*, 2:95.

and that she has spoken rightly, ἀληθὲς εἴρηκας; cf. Plato, *Leg.* 641A; John 4:18. He further prefaces his confession with, δόξα καὶ εἰρήνη παρὰ θεοῦ (cf. Rev 5:13). This could be an echo from Paul's letters (Phil 1:2; Col 1:2; 2 Thess 1:2; Titus 1:4; Philemon 3), and the textual tradition shows assimilation to Paul; see Textual Notes. But παρά rather than ἀπό (cf. 2 John 3) would then be unexpected.

Abraham now confides what happened "late in the evening," τῇ ὀψὲ βραδύ; cf. Heliodorus, *Aeth.* 2.29: ὀψὲ καὶ βραδὺ τῆς ἡλικίας. He washed the stranger's feet in the vessel: ἔνιπτον τοὺς πόδας αὐτοῦ ἐν τῇ λεκάνῃ; see on 3:7–8 and cf. LXX Gen 18:4 (νιψάτωσαν τοὺς πόδας ὑμῶν) and *Jos. Asen.* 18:7. When he did so, Abraham said in his heart (εἶπον ἐν τῇ καρδίᾳ μου; cf. LXX Deut 8:17; 1 Βασ 27:1; Ps 9:27; Jer 13:22; Jdt 13:4; Luke 12:45; etc.), "These are the feet of (one of) the three men I washed then."[19] That Michael was one of the three men who visited Abraham in Genesis 18 also appears in rabbinic texts; see on 1:4. Given Abraham's denial in v. 3 and Michael's behavior in chapter 4, Abraham is probably stretching the truth here (see on v. 3). Washing Michael's feet evidently set him to thinking, but certainty eluded him until Sarah gave him her evaluation.

This scene has a background in Homer.[20] Anyone familiar with the *Odyssey* would immediately be put in mind of the famous footwashing scene in book 19, a scene so often depicted in ancient art[21] and the subject of more than one play.[22] There too an elderly person (in Homer it is Odysseus' old nurse, Eurycleia) washes the feet of a stranger who has been away for many years (in Homer it is Odysseus). In both cases recognition of the stranger's identity comes during the act of washing. In both texts the one washing the stranger's feet begins to cry. And in both the stranger's identity is nonetheless concealed from others until later. One can

---

[19] On the construction, οὗτοι οἱ πόδες ἐκ τῶν τριῶν ἀνδρῶν εἰσὶν οὕς ..., see Turner, "Testament," 79.

[20] Cf. Loewenstamm, "Death of Moses," 225, n. 4.

[21] See B. Kötting, "Fußwaschung," in *RAC* 8 (1972), 746–47; Odette Touchefeu-Meynier, *Thèmes Odysséens dans L'Art Antique* (Paris: E. de Boccard, 1968), 248–56; and the list of vases and reliefs in Odette Touchefeu, in *Lexicon iconographicum mythologiae classicae* (8 vols.; Zurich: Artemis, 1981–1999), 4/1:101–102, s.v. "Eurykleia." Cf. also the allusion in Petronius, *Sat.* 105: readers, it is assumed, know this story.

[22] Both Sophocles and Pacuvius wrote plays entitled "Niptra." See Cicero, *Tusc.* 2.49; Photius, *Lex.*, s.v. παρουσία. For allusions to and imitations of the scene see Dennis R. MacDonald, *The Homeric Epics and the Gospel of Mark* (New Haven/London: Yale University Press, 2000), 114–19.

hardly doubt that here *TA* moves a motif from Homer to the story of Abraham.[23]

6:7. Abraham continues by telling Sarah what readers already know from 3:9–12: when Michael's tears fell into the washing vessel, they became precious stones—καὶ γὰρ τὰ δάκρυα αὐτοῦ ὀψὲ ἐν τῷ νιπτῆρι πίπτοντα ἐγένοντο λίθοι τίμιοι. The last three words as well as τὰ δάκρυα and the verb are from 3:11 (q.v.), but ἐν τῷ νιπτῆρι (cf. *T. Job* 25:6) takes up the language of the previous verse (ἔνιπτον, νιπτῆρος). As if what he says may be too hard to believe, the patriarch brings forth the stones from the fold in his garment (in early Christian art, Abraham often wears flowing white draperies): ἐκβαλὼν ἐκ τοῦ κόλπου αὐτοῦ; cf. LXX Exod 4:6, 7; 3 Βασ 17:19; Ps.-Chrysostom, *Ascetam facetiis uti non debere* PG 48.1057 (ἔκβαλε ... ἐκ τοῦ κόλπου σου); BAGD, s.v. κόλπος, 2. Abraham then says, "If you doubt me (εἰ ἀπιστεῖς μοι, as in Chrysostom, *Hom. Matt.* 4.3; Ps.-Chrysostom, *Annunt.* PG 60.760), look at these." Like the stories in which the risen Jesus eats and lets himself be touched (Luke 24:36–43; John 20:24–29), so here too: eyes and hands should confirm that something supernatural has happened.

---

[23] Cf. the reworking of Eurycleia's recognition of Odysseus in Gregory of Nyssa's *De vita Macrinae* as analyzed by Gregory Frank, "Macrina's Scar: Homeric Allusion and Heroic Identity," *JECS* 8 (2000), 511–30. For Jewish knowledge of Homer see Gerard J. M. Bartelink, in *RAC* 16 (1991), 124–26, s.v. "Homer," and Saul Lieberman, *Hellenism in Jewish Palestine: Studies in the Literary Transmission, Beliefs, and Manners of Palestine in the I Century B.C.E. – IV Century C.E.* (New York: Jewish Theological Seminary of America, 1950), 108–14. Recall especially the Homeric images on the mosaic floor in Bet Shean donated by Leontis; see Lucille Roussin, "The Beit Leontis Mosaic: An Eschatological Interpretation," *Journal of Jewish Art* 8 (1981), pp. 6–19. Homer was known even in Palestine, and *y. Sanh.* 10:8 permits reading him on the Sabbath. See further Martin Hengel, *Judaism and Hellenism: Studies in their Encounter in Palestine during the Early Hellenistic Period*, vol. 1 (Philadelphia: Fortress, 1974), 75; idem, *Achilleus in Jerusalem: Eine spätantike Messingkanne mit Achilleus-Darstellungen aus Jerusalem* (SHAW Philosophisch-historische Klasse 1982/1; Heidelberg: C. Winter, 1982), 49–52. To Hengel's evidence one may add the Homeric character of *BS* 127 and 183; see Moshe Schwabe and Baruch Lifshitz, *Beth She'arim*, vol. II: *The Greek Inscriptions* (New Brunswick, N.J.: Rutgers University Press, 1974), 97–107, 157–67. Likewise relevant is the argument of Dennis R. MacDonald, "Tobit and the Odyssey," in *Mimesis and Intertextuality in Antiquity and Christianity* (ed. Dennis R. MacDonald; Studies in Antiquity and Christianity; Harrisburg, Pa.: Trinity Press Intl., 2001), 11–40, that the author of Tobit, writing in Hebrew, borrowed extensively from Homer.

6:8. Sarah bows down (προσεκύνησεν; see on 3:6) and embraces the stones joyfully, ἠσπάζετο ταῦτα. For ἀσπάζομαι = "embrace" see Josephus, *Ant.* 1.236. She then says, δόξα τῷ θεῷ (cf. 18:11; LXX 2 Chr 30:8; Ps 67:35; *Jos. Asen.* 20:7; Acts 12:32; Rev 11:13; etc.) τῷ δεικνύοντι ἡμῖν θαυμάσια; cf. Deut 6:22; Pausanias, *Descr.* 9.9.5 (δείκνυται ... θαῦμα); Eusebius, *Comm. Ps.* PG 23.1064A (θεὸς δεικνύναι ... θαυμάσια); Ps.-Athanasius, *Imag. Beryt.* PG 28.797B (δεικνύων τὰ θαυμάσια); Ps.-Chrysostom, *Sac.* PG 48.1069 (ἐκεῖ [on Mount Moriah] αὐτῷ [Abraham] δείκνυσιν ὁ θεὸς θαῦμα μέγα); *In parabolam de ficu* PG 59.586 (δεικνύειν τὰ θαύματα); *m. Ber.* 9:1 (ברוך שעשה נסים‎ Acclamations commonly end miracle stories and often include the δοξ-root: Matt 9:8; 15:31; Mark 2:12; Luke 5:25–26; 7:16; 13:13; 17:15; 18:43; *4 Bar.* 7:17; cf. 4QprNab.[24] Sarah's tone is equivocal. She knows that there has been a revelation, ἀποκάλυψις*; cf. the title in RecShrt. ms. E. That revelation is, however, incomplete without interpretation, and so she does not know whether it is for ill or good, κἄν τε ἀγαθὸν κἄν τε πονηρόν; cf. 8:2 for κἄν ... κἄν and 10:3 for ἀγαθὸν ... πονηρόν; also Ps.-Chrysostom, *Poenit.* PG 60.694: κἄν τε ἀγαθὴ κἄν τε φαύλη. κἄν τε ... κἄν τε is attested in *T. Sol.* 4:8 E and secular sources but is most common in patristic texts; cf. Ps.-Athanasius, *Vit. Syncleticae* PG 28.1521B; John of Damascus, *Sacr. par.* PG 95.1197A; Theodore the Studite, *Ep.*, ed. Fatouros 6.63; etc.[25] In the event, Sarah's caution is prescient. The angel has come this time not to give her a son but to remove a husband, not to give life but to take it.

[24] See further Theissen, *Miracle Stories*, 71–72, 152–73.
[25] Turner, "Testament," 97–98, discusses κἄν ... κἄν, but he ignores the patristic evidence.

Chapter 7: Isaac's Dream, Michael's Interpretation, Abraham's Refusal

Bibliography: Schmidt, "Testament," 1:46–62; 2:129. Turner, "Testament," 114–19.

Long Recension

7:1. Leaving Sarah, Abraham went into the dining-chamber and said to Isaac, "Come now, my beloved son, tell me the truth. What did you see and what happened to you that you came running to us as you did?" 7:2. Isaac replied and said: "Behold, my lord, I saw in this night the sun and the moon above my head, and their rays encircling me and illuminating the way for me. 7:3. And while I was thus seeing these things and rejoicing, I saw the heaven opened, and I saw a glorious man coming down out of heaven, shining more than the sun. 7:4. And that sun-like man came and took the sun from my head; and he went up into the heavens from whence he had come. And I grieved greatly that he had taken the sun from me. 7:5. After a moment, as I was still grieving and anxious, I saw that glorious man coming out of heaven a second time; and he also took from me, from my head, the moon. 7:6. I wept greatly and implored that glorious man and said, 'No, lord, do not take my glory from me. Have mercy upon me and hearken to me. If you must take the sun from me, at least leave the moon over me.' 7:7. But he said: 'Let me take them up into the upper kingdom, because he

Short Recension fam. E

7:1. Then Abraham said to Michael, "Disclose to me who you are." 7:2. Michael answered and said, "I am Michael." And Abraham said to him, "Explain why you have come." 7:3. Michael said to him, "You son Isaac will reveal that to you." 7:4. Abraham said to his son Isaac, "My beloved son, tell what you saw today in a dream." 7:5. Isaac answered his father, "In a dream I saw myself as the sun and moon. And there was a crown on my head. 7:6. And behold, (there was) a gigantic man, shining exceedingly from heaven as a light, called the father of lights. 7:7. And he took the sun from my head. And he left the rays with me. 7:8. I cried and said, 'I beg you, lord, do not remove the glory of my head and the light of my house and all my glory.' 7:9. The sun also and the woman and the stars lamented, saying, 'Do not remove the glory of our power.' 7:10. And the man of light answered and said to me, 'Do not cry because I have taken the light of your house. For it was taken up from toil to rest. They raise it from lowliness to a high position. 7:11. They raise him from a narrow place to a wide place. They raise him from the darkness to the light.' 7:12. And I answered and said to him,

wants them there.' And he took them from me; but he allowed their rays (to stay) upon me." 7:8. The Commander-in-chief said: "Hear, righteous Abraham. The sun which the boy saw is you, his father; likewise the moon is his mother, Sarah. And the glorious man coming down from heaven is the one sent by God, who is about to take your righteous soul from you. 7:9. And now know, most honorable Abraham, that you are about at this time to leave behind the world and life and journey to God." 7:10. Abraham said to the Commander-in-chief: "Oh latest wonder of wonders! And for the rest, is it you who are about to take my soul from me?" 7:11. And the Commander-in-chief said: "I am Michael, the Commander-in-chief, who stands before God. And I was sent to you so that I might proclaim the notice of death to you; and only then shall I return to him just as I was commanded." 7:12. But Abraham said: "Now I know that you are the angel of the Lord, and that you were sent to take my soul. Yet I will not follow you. Now just what you command—you do it!"

'I beg you, lord, take the rays with him.' 7:13. He said to me, 'All the rays do not shine on me in this hour, they are completed only in the twelve hours of the day, so that they might take all the rays.'[1] 7:14. And as the man of light was saying this these things, I indeed saw the sun of my house rising in the heavens. 7:15. And I saw the sun becoming like my father.' 7:16. And Michael answered and said, "In truth, this has truly happened. The sun, Isaac, is your father. Abraham has been taken up into heaven. 7:17. But his body remains on the earth, until 7,000 years are fulfilled. Then all flesh will be raised. 7:18. Now then Abraham, make arrangements concerning your sons. Your stewardship is at an end."

TEXTUAL NOTES ON THE LONG RECENSION

7:1. A has "coming" instead of "running" and adds at the end: κλαίων οὕτως ἐν ὀλιγωρίᾳ πολλῇ. 7:2. Instead of αὐτῶν, A B have αὐτοῦ, which refers to the sun alone. 7:2–3. I omits "and illuminating the way for me.

---

[1] The point seems to be that time has to run its course—the time of the world just like the time of the day. For Michael's association with the sun's daily schedule see *The Mysteries of St. John the Apostle and Holy Virgin*, ed. Budge, fol. 17a: "'Does the sun know when the twelve hours have come to an end, so that he may depart to the place where he sets or rises?' And the Cherubim said unto me, 'When the angels who blow the trumpets have finished, Michael knows that the twelfth hymn is finished, and he speaks to the Angel of the Sun, who goes and brings his course to an end.'"

And these things." Is this deliberate abbreviation, or has an eye passed from κυκλοῦντα in v. 2 to ταῦτα in v. 3? 7:3. A: διαλογιζομένου (cf. Gen 37:11?). B: ἀγαλλόμενος. G H Q: ἀγαλλομένου. I: ἀγαλλιωμένου. J: ἀγαλλιώμενος. // For ἄνδρα (which Schmidt prints) A has ἄστρον, which may presuppose the common equation of angels and stars. // G Q: "seven suns." Does this reflect the influence of Isa 30:26: "the light of the sun will be sevenfold"? Or was the simile traditional? Cf. the quotation from the *Apocalypse of Zephaniah* in Clement of Alexandria, *Strom.* 5.11.77: angelic thrones "sevenfold brighter than the light of the rising sun." 7:4–6. I rewrites the Greek. The sense is similar, but now the man addresses Isaac directly before he takes the moon: "I wish to take also the moon from you." 7:4–5. B Q omit "and he went up ... my head." Is this *homoioteleuton* (τῆς κεφαλῆς μου ... τῆς κεφαλῆς μου) or deliberate abbreviation? 7:5. J shortens by dropping the temporal indicators at the beginning: "after a moment, as I was still." // G drops "from my head." 7:6. B J Q omit the liturgical phrase, "Have mercy upon me and hearken to me." 7:7. After "Let me" A adds ἀρτίως (cf. 2 Βασ 15:34; Philo, *Legat.* 351; Josephus, *Bell.* 4.239). // A omits "into the heavenly kingdom ... took them." An eye probably skipped from the first αὐτούς to the third αὐτούς. Similarly, another scribal eye passed from the first αὐτούς to the second αὐτούς, which explains the omission of "into the heavenly kingdom ... them" in B J Q. // I has "the upper kingdom" (βασιλείαν), G "the upper king" (βασιλέα), H "the king" (βασιλέα). A B J Q do not help because they omit this phrase through *homoioteleuton* (see above). // B G H I J Q end with the shorter: "And he took them from me, even their rays." This changes the meaning of the sentence completely. All consolation is gone. A's reading, "but he allowed their rays (to stay) upon me," has the support of RecShrt. 7:7 ("he left the rays with me"). 7:8. J replaces "The Commander-in-chief ... Abraham" with: "'This is the dream which I saw.' And Abraham said again to the Commander-in-chief: 'Sun-like man, are you able to unravel the things seen by Isaac?' And the Commander-in-chief Michael said: 'Yes, my lord Abraham, I will unravel what Isaac saw. I am the one unraveling them.'" 7:9. A: κοσμικὸν βίον. 7:10. I carelessly drops "and ... to take." 7:11. H skips over the self-identification formula: "I am Michael ... God." I J omit "Michael the Commander-in-chief." B Q omit "Michael." A G lack "who stands before God," which is perhaps an addition from Luke 1:19; but see below. // A: ἐκέλευσέ μοι. B I Q: ἐκελεύσθημεν. G: ἐκελεύσθην σοι. H: κέλευσόν με. J: ἐκελεύσθημεν παρὰ θεοῦ.

COMMENTARY

Chap. 7 recounts a conversation with three participants (Sarah remains outside the room):

7:1	Abraham asks Isaac to explain his behavior
7:2–7	Isaac recounts his dream
7:8–9	Michael interprets the dream
7:10	Abraham asks if Michael has come for his soul
7:11	Michael identifies himself and his mission
7:12	Abraham refuses to follow Michael

The final verse, where Abraham rebuffs the angel, is the unexpected climax of all that has preceded. *TA*'s language has underlined Abraham's exceptional piety (see esp. chaps. 1–2), and the repeated description of him as "righteous" (1:1, 2, 5; 2:3, 6; 4:6; 7:8) and the intertextual links to Genesis, especially to the Akedah, have kept his famed obedience to the fore. Michael's words, however, are met with an adversative particle, ἀλλά: "Yet I will not follow you." The biblical paradigm of obedience flouts God's will. *TA* confronts death with humor.

Surely someone as pious as Abraham should acknowledge that God determines when a person's life has come to a close (cf. the concept of κῆρ = "the fate of death" in the *Iliad*). Further, the patriarch should not mind dying; it could only be a boon to leave this "futile world" to dwell among "the good" (1:7); and Abraham's own biography should encourage him to go along with Michael, for God has already lead him out of one home into an unknown land of blessing. So the patriarch's response, his adamant rebuff of Michael, for which *TA* offers no explanation, makes no sense. Readers naturally infer that, however pious Abraham may be, he, a bit like Johanan b. Zakkai in rabbinic tradition (see *b. Ber.* 28b; *ARN* A 25), nonetheless shares the normal fear of death. He simply does not wish to exit the earth. At this point, then, Abraham ceases to be saint and becomes instead common humanity. He falls under the censure of Cyprian, *Mort.* 18: "How preposterous and absurd it is, that while we ask for the will of God to be done, yet when God calls and summons us from this world, we do not at once obey the command of his will."

The intertextuality of chap. 7 is not as dense as that of the immediately preceding chapters, but several scriptural subtexts are nonetheless clearly present. Vv. 1–2, which include the phrase, "beloved son," borrow from Genesis 22 (see on v. 1). Isaac's dream, in which sun and moon stand for his father and mother, recalls Gen 37:9–10, where another patriarch (Jacob) hears another beloved son (Joseph; cf. Gen 37:3–4) dream about sun and moon, which again represent father and mother (see on v. 2). V. 6 quotes

LXX Ps 26:7, "Have mercy upon me and hearken to me." There may also be an allusion to Tobit 12:13–15: "I am Michael the Commander-in-chief, etc." sounds very much like a line from the angel Gabriel in Tobit (see on 7:11). Finally, a definite biblical aura falls upon a chapter that features a symbolic prophetic dream (so common in Genesis and Daniel; cf. also Judg 7:13–14),[2] an angelic interpreter (cf. Daniel 7–12; Zechariah 1–6), and the identification formula, "you are" (σὺ εἶ; see on 7:8). As all three of these items appear more than once in Daniel, perhaps *TA* 7 has a specifically Danielic aura.

Beyond recalling scriptural texts, *TA* 7 would probably have moved informed hearers to recall certain traditions about Moses. The Introduction collects the parallels between legends about the end of Moses and the end of Abraham in *TA* (pp. 24–27). *Sifre* Deut. 305, for example, records the following: "The Holy One, blessed be He, said to the Angel of Death, 'Go, bring me the soul of Moses.' He went and stood before him and said to him, 'Moses, give me your soul.' He said to him, 'In a place in which I am session, you have no right to stand, and yet you say to me, "Give me your soul"?' He growled at him, and the other went forth in a huff. The Angel of Death went and brought the tale back to the Omnipotent." What matters here is Loewenstamm's demonstration that *TA* is parasitic upon this legend.[3] So Abraham's refusal to follow Michael is analogous to the tale of Moses refusing to co-operate with the Angel of Death.

RecShrt. 7:1–18 (fam. E: 29 lines in Schmidt; fam. B F G: 18 lines) is almost as long as RecLng. 7 (36 lines), and the former goes beyond the latter in several ways. (i) When Abraham quizzes Michael about his identity (fam. E) and/or about his mission (both fams. E and B F G), the angel refers to Isaac: "Your son Isaac will show you" (v. 3). (ii) Abraham knows that Michael's mission has something to do with a dream of Isaac (7:4) although only readers should know this (contrast RecLng. 5:14). (iii) Isaac's dream includes a crown: "and there was a crown upon my head" (v. 5; cf. the crown in RecLng. 17:7). (iv) The man from heaven shines like the πατὴρ τοῦ φωτός, v. 6. (v) In 7:9, the sun, moon, and stars (cf. Gen 37:9) protest the removal of the sun. As Dean-Otting observes, "It is curious that in recension B Abraham is the sun in Isaac's dream but the sun also cries out with the moon and stars, 'Do not take the glory of our

---

[2] According to Dean-Otting, *Heavenly Journeys*, 189, since Jacob and Joseph have prophetic dreams in the Pentateuch, "the gift of dreams seems to be inherited," and so "it is no surprise that the gift of dreams ascribed to both Jacob and Joseph is assigned as well to the grandfather."

[3] Loewenstamm, "Testament," 219–25; cf. his "Death of Moses."

power.'"[4] (In RecLng. the moon, who represents Sarah, is also removed, even though she dies only in RecShrt.). (v) Vv. 10–11 offer a pious and poetic explication of Abraham's death:

fam. E	Do not cry because I took the light of your house
fam. B F G	Do not cry because I already took the light of your house
fam. E	for it was taken up from toil to rest
fam. B F G	for it was taken up from toil to enjoyment
fam. E	they raise it from lowliness to a high position
fam. B F G	and from lowliness to a high position
fam. E	they raise him from a narrow place to a wide place[5]
fam. B F G	
fam. E	they raise him from the darkness to the light
fam. B F G	they raise him from darkness to light[6]

(vii) After Isaac hears this, he asks that the rays of the sun, which have been left, might also be taken away (v. 12). (viii) Michael equates the rays with Abraham's body and declares that it must remain until the end of the age, 7,000 (ms. E: 6,000; Slavonic: 8,000) years after the creation, when the dead will be raised (vv. 16–17, ἐγερθήσεται πᾶσα σάρξ; the world also endures 7,000 years in RecLng. 19:7, q.v.).

Much of RecShrt. 7:1–18 strikes one as secondary, as reflecting the interests of Christian piety.[7] The allegorical equation of rays with bodies awaiting resurrection is not connected with the rest of the narrative and serves no purpose other than to state a doctrine. Turner, who in general favors the originality of RecShrt., here concedes that to "a Christian reader it might have seemed a pity that the cardinal doctrine of his faith did not once occur, and such a reader might have tried to explain the significance of the 'rays' in this way, thus adding to the text the information that Abraham's body would remain on the earth … . If there are to be Christian additions at all, apart from the obvious ones, this passage ought to be considered."[8] The

---

[4] Dean-Otting, *Heavenly Journeys*, 193.

[5] Cf. *4 Ezra* 7:12–13: "The entrances of this world were made narrow and sorrowful and toilsome … . But the entrances of the greater world are broad and safe … ."

[6] Despite the parallels in Acts 28:16; 1 Pet 2:9; and *1 Clem.* 59:2, the phrase need not be Christian; cf. Philo, *Virt.* 179; *Jos. Asen.* 8:9; *Sib. Or.* fr. 1, 27; *m. Pesah.* 10:5; and the *Passover Haggadah*, section *Běkol-dōr*: "from slavery to freedom, from sorrow to joy, from mourning to holiday, from darkness to great light, and from bondage to redemption."

[7] Contrast Schmidt, "Testament," 50–55b, who stresses an Iranian background to RecShrt. 7 and its nearness to Essene thought.

[8] Turner, "Testament," 116.

expression, "father of light," may also be Christian, for the nearest parallels are Jas 1:17 ("father of lights"), texts quoting Jas 1:17 (which entered the liturgy; cf. Basil the Great, *Liturg.* PG 31.1656A), and variant readings in Gk. *L.A.E.* 36:3 (DSN) and 38:1 (NIK).[9] The change from Isaac first weeping when the sun is taken away to then wanting, after Michael has explained death, for even the remaining rays to be removed, is clumsy, and it appears to be someone's attempt to make Isaac piously welcome the death of a saint. But this subverts the entire tone of *TA*, whose RecLng. does such a fine job of showing us the reluctance of the dying and the lamentation of the living. In line with this, RecShrt. 7:1–18 lacks the most striking feature of RecLng. 7, which is Abraham's refusal to follow Michael. Surely this is a deliberate omission for the sake of theological correctness. Somebody was unedified by the spectacle of the righteous Abraham resisting both death and God. This explains the Coptic, where Abraham piously declares: "If this is the will of God or he has determined this for me, I will not speak in opposition." How could the patriarch, whose obedience was renowned, have been less courageous than the Christian martyrs, the Maccabean martyrs, or even the pagan Socrates? The parallels with Moses and his refusal to die confirm this, for these are integral to the book, not secondary accretions; see pp. 24–27.

7:1. Abraham leaves Sarah (καταλιπών; cf. v. 9; 20:3) and re-enters the dining chamber (τρικλίνῳ; see on 4:1). Clearly she has remained at the door (cf. 6:2 and RecShrt. fam. E 6:4). The circumstance not only accords with traditional patriarchal propriety but corresponds to Genesis 18, where Sarah remains at the door of the tent during the visit of the three angels. Abraham then speaks to Isaac and says, "Come (δεῦρο; see on 2:7), my beloved son" (υἱέ μου ἀγαπητέ). Given that "my beloved son" so strongly recalls Genesis 22 (see on 4:1), it is doubtless not coincidence that *TA* uses εἶπε πρός + object in a question, to which the answer is, ἰδοῦ ἐγώ:

TA 7:1, Abraham to Isaac	εἶπε πρὸς Ἰσαάκ
LXX Gen 22:1, God to Abraham	εἶπεν πρὸς αὐτόν
TA 7:1, Abraham of Isaac	υἱέ μου ἀγαπητέ
LXX Gen 22:2, God of Isaac	τὸν υἱόν σου τὸν ἀγαπητόν
TA 7:2, Isaac's answer	ἰδοῦ ἐγώ
LXX Gen 22:1, Abraham's answer (cf. v. 11)	ἰδοῦ ἐγώ

---

[9] The phrase does not appear in the versions and seems likely due to a Christian hand. Craig Keener, in a private communication, has observed that "Father of the luminaries/stars" may have appeared in the Ugaritic text UT 76 I:4; see plates xv–xvi in Andrée Herdner, *Corpus des tablettes en cunéiformes alphabétiques découvertes à Ras Shamra-Ugarit de 1929 à 1939* (Paris: P. Geuthner, 1963), and the transcription in fig. 33. The text, however, is fragmentary.

Abraham exhorts Isaac to speak the truth: ἀνάγγειλόν μοι τὴν ἀλήθειαν; see on 5:12 and cf. Basil the Great, *In Gordium martyrem* PG 31.504C: ἀναγγεῖλαι τὴν ἀλήθειαν. The father, who clearly suspects some connection between Michael's presence and Isaac's dream (cf. 5:14), wants to know what his son saw (τί τὰ ὁραθέντα σοι) and what happened to him, τί πέπονθας (πάσχω*).

7:2. Isaac replies: ὑπολαβὼν δὲ Ἰσαὰκ ἤρξατο λέγειν. ὑπολαβών + δέ + subject + a form of λέγω is a refrain in LXX Job, where it occurs 23 times at the beginning of speeches for ויאמר ... ויען; cf. also LXX Dan 3:95; *4 Macc.* 8:13; *T. Job* 36:4; 38:6; the expression is not characteristic of patristic texts. ἤρξατο is superfluous and so probably a Semitism; cf. התחיל in e.g. *y. Ber.* 4:1; *y. Pesaḥ.* 6:1; also Tob 8:5; Josephus, *Ant.* 11.131, 200; Luke 11:29; Acts 1:1; *Gk. Apoc. Ezra* 7:5.[10] Isaac responds with ἰδοῦ ἐγὼ (see above) κύριέ μου (see on 2:10) and goes on to describe his dream, which features the sun and the moon above his head. According to v. 8, the sun stands for Isaac's father, the moon for his mother; cf. 1QapGen 19, where Abraham dreams about a cedar and a date-palm that represent himself and his wife respectively. The inspiration is Genesis 39, where Joseph dreams that the sun, the moon, and eleven stars bow down before him. When Joseph recounts his dream to his father and his brothers, his father asks, "What kind of dream is this that you have had? Shall we indeed come, I and your mother and your brothers, and bow to the ground before you?" (v. 10). Here likewise a beloved son of his father's old age (Gen 37:3–4) dreams about sun and moon (Gen 37:9), and the two lights represent his parents (Gen 37:10; cf. Philo, *Jos.* 9; Josephus, *Ant.* 2.16). And here too the son tells his dream to his father (Gen 37:9). But whereas in Genesis the sun and moon are at Joseph's feet, in *TA* they are over Isaac's head, ὑπεράνω τῆς κεφαλῆς μου; cf. 14:4 and LXX Jonah 4:6, ὑπεράνω τῆς κεφαλῆς αὐτοῦ (for על־ראשו).

Isaac's dream concerns his mother as well as with his father. RecLng., however, never records Sarah's death, who remains alive until the end; see 20:6; contrast RecShrt. 12:15–16. So her presence here is due not to events within *TA* but rather to the intertext, Genesis 37, where both sun and moon represent parents.

Isaac adds that the sun's rays (ἀκτῖνας; cf. Wis 2:4; 16:27; Ecclus 43:4; *T. Naph.* 5:4–5—the last is a dream about sun and moon, perhaps also inspired by Gen 37:9) encircle (κυκλοῦντα; κυκλόω*: cf. RecShrt. 12:12;

---

[10] See further J. Hunkin, "'Pleonastic' ἄρχομαι in the New Testament," *JTS* 25 (1924), 390–402.

LXX Ps 31:10; *4 Bar.* 8:6, 7; *1 Clem.* 22:8) him and light the way for him, φωταγωγοῦντά με. These are words of dependence and affection. Isaac's parents protect him and guide him in such a way that, without them, he would be in darkness. φωταγωγέω* appears in patristic texts (Lampe, s.v.), but 7:2 is most closely related to the one LXX appearance of the word. In *4 Macc.* 17:5 the verb is used in connection with the moon as a symbol of a mother lighting the way for her sons, just as Sarah, represented by the moon, illumines Isaac in our book: "Not so majestic stands the moon in heaven as you stand, lighting the way (φωταγωγήσασα) to piety for your seven starlike sons ... ." Is there direct dependence here? Was 4 Maccabees in a collection of Greek scriptures known to a contributor to *TA*? Delcor, citing Clement of Alexandria and Ammonius of Alexandria, thinks that the common verb belongs to "mystical language."[11] But while the verb occurs five times in Clement, only in *Protr.* 12.120 is there a clear mystical sense, and the notion of a guiding light is as old as the exodus (Exod 13:21) and has no mystical overtones in Matthew 2 (the magi's "star"). The same seems true of *4 Bar.* 5:35, which uses φωτατγωγέω: "May God guide you with light (φωταγωγήσει) to the city above, Jerusalem."

7:3. Isaac recounts that, as he was seeing "these things" (ταῦτα οὕτως ἐμοῦ θεωροῦντος) and "rejoicing" (ἀγαλλομένου; see Textual Notes), the heaven opened, τὸν οὐρανὸν ἀνεῳγότα. The expression is conventional; see LXX Gen 7:11; Isa 24:18; *T. Levi* 2:6; Gk. fr. *1 En.* 104:2; 18:6; Herm. *Vis.* 1.1.4. For it introducing a vision see Ezek 1:1; Acts 7:56; 10:11; *2 Bar.* 22:1. For it introducing an angelic descent see *3 Macc.* 6:18. In John 1:51 and Rev 19:11, as in *TA* 7, both vision and descent are present; cf. also Matt 3:16; Luke 3:21; and *T. Jud.* 24:2, where the Spirit descends. For non-Jewish parallels see Ovid, *Fast.* 3.370–374; Virgil, *Aen.* 9.20; Cicero, *Div.* 1.43.97. The text presupposes the mythopoeic cosmology common to the Ancient Near East: the sky is a solid firmament beyond which the heavenly beings dwell. From that world a glorious (φωτοφόρον) man comes down, ἄνδρα ... ἐκ τοῦ οὐρανοῦ κατελθόντα. For φωτοφόρος (cf. vv. 5, 8; 12:9; 14:8; 16:10; LXX: 0; Philo: 0; NT: 0; Josephus: 0), LSJ, s.v., cites only Suidas and the *Etymologicum Magnum*. Lampe, s.v., however, contains several entries, showing this to be a popular patristic word, beginning in the fourth and fifth centuries (Cyril of Alexandria, Eudocia, Isidore of Pelusium); cf. Sophocles, *Lex.*, s.v. The man shines (ἀστράπτοντα; ἀστράπτω*: cf. *Jos. Asen.* 23:15; the verb translates ברק in LXX 2 Βασ 22:15; Ps 143:6; cf. Wis 11:18) more than the sun, a conventional simile:

---

[11] Delcor, *Testament*, 115.

Ecclus 17:31; 23:19; Acts 26:13; Epiphanius, *Pan.* 48.10; Gregory of Nyssa, *An. res.* PG 46.68C; *Vis. Dorotheus*, ed. Kessels and van der Horst 297; etc.

Although the sun and moon are almost purely symbolic, the man is less so. For Michael looks like a man, he literally comes down from heaven, and, according to 2:4, his appearance is sunlike.

There is a very close parallel in *Jos. Asen.* 14:2ff., where Aseneth sees the heaven torn apart, after which an indescribable light appears. The light then descends and becomes a man (ἄνθρωπος ἐκ τοῦ οὐρανοῦ) who declares himself to be (in some witnesses) ἀρχιστράτηγος, which is Michael's constant appellation in *TA*. The correlation is all the more striking because *TA* 7 draws upon the story of Joseph (see above) whereas *Jos. Asen.* 14:6 draws upon the language of the story of Abraham. Thus the angel in the latter uses the double vocative, "Aseneth, Aseneth," and she responds, ἰδοὺ ἐγώ (cf. LXX Gen 22:11, which *TA* 7 also echoes). In addition, the angel calls a second time (14:6: ἐκάλεσεν ... δευτέρου), just as in Gen 22:15 (LXX: 22:15: ἐκάλεσεν ... δευτέρον; cf. also the ἐκ δευτέρου of *TA* 7:5). One may further observe that the angel first appears as a star (ἀστήρ) in *Jos. Asen.* 14:1, and that RecLng. A 7:3 has ἄστρον for ἄνδρα, and that in both texts the visionary addresses the angel with ἀνάγγειλόν μοι (*TA* 7:1, 11; *Jos. Asen.* 14:6). Is all this coincidence? Has one text influenced the other? Do both depend upon a common source or story unknown to us?

7:4. The ἄνδρα φωτοφόρον of v. 3 is here ὁ ἀνὴρ ὁ ἡλιόμορφος ἐκεῖνος. He now comes and takes the sun from Isaac's head, so that he greatly grieves, ἐλυπήθην μεγάλως; cf. Galen, *De symptomatum causis libri iii*, ed. Kühn, p. 181 (λυπεῖσθαι ... μεγάλως); Ps.-Callisthenes, *Hist. Alex. Magn.* rec. α 2.2 (μεγάλως ἐλυπούμεθα) His lamentation is the lamentation of death. ἡλιόμορφος, which recurs in 13:1, 10 (of another angel); 16:6; 17:12 (of Death, who looks like Michael); and 17:12, makes for a word-play: the sun-like man removes the sun. LSJ, s.v., cites only Castoria fr. 1, Lampe, s.v., only *TA* and Ps.-Ephraem (ed. Assemani) 3.511F (= *Prec. e sacris scripturis*, ed. Phrantzoles, p. 319.3). The word never appears in the LXX, the New Testament, Philo, or Josephus. In Athenaeus, *Deipn.* 12.542E, it refers to a beauty like the sun (cf. Eustathius of Thessalonica, *Comm. Hom. Od.*, ed. Stallbaum, 1:247), and in Ps.-Callisthenes, *Hist. Alex. Magn.* rec. λ, ed. van Thiel, p. 47, it denotes a royal appearance (cf. rec. Byz. poet. 5274).

7:5. Isaac adds that, after a moment (μετ᾽ ὀλίγον; cf. LXX Jdt 13:9; 2 Macc 11:1; Wis 15:8; *3 Bar.* 9:3; Josephus often uses this phrase), he was still grieving and anxious, λυπουμένου (λυπέω; cf. v. 4; 8:11) καὶ ἀδημονοῦντος (ἀδημονέω*); cf. Matt 26:37, λυπεῖσθαι καὶ ἀδημονεῖν. The two verbs are also coordinated, and in this order, in Athanasius, Basil, Chrysostom, and John of Damascus. Is this a Christian touch? In his sad state, Isaac saw "that glorious man" (ἐκεῖνον τὸν φωτοφόρον; cf. vv. 3–4) coming out of heaven a second time, ἐκ δευτέρου; see on v. 3 and cf. LXX Jonah 3:1; Jer 1:13; 1 Macc 9:1; *Jos. Asen.* 14:6; Mark 14:72; Heb 9:28; etc. Now he will take the moon.

7:6. Isaac weeps greatly (ἔκλαυσα δὲ ἐγὼ μεγάλως; cf. 5:10). He then implores (παρεκάλεσα; cf. 9:3; 14:10, 12, 13) "that man" (cf. vv. 4, 5), begging him not to take away sun and moon, which are his δόξαν; cf. 11:8–9, which speak of Adam's "glory." "Have mercy upon me and hearken to me" (ἐλέησόν με καὶ εἰσάκουσόν μου) comes without alteration from the liturgy, from LXX Ps 26:7.[12] Isaac hopes that, even if the sun must be removed, maybe at least the moon might be left (ἔασον).[13] But it is not to be. Death makes no exceptions (cf. 8:9).

7:7. The sun and the moon should be taken up, ἀναληφθῆναι. 15:4; 4 Βασ 2:10–11; 1 Macc 2:58; Ecclus 48:9; 49:14 (both times for נלקח); Mark 16:19; Acts 1:2, 11, 22; 2 Tim 3:16; and *T. Job* 39:12 all use this verb of bodily assumption into heaven, *4 Bar.* 9:3 and *1 Clem.* 5:7 of the soul's ascension at death; cf. the use of ἀνάλημψις in *Ps. Sol.* 4:18. The destination here is "the upper kingdom," τὴν ἄνω βασιλείαν. Patristic texts use this expression: Ps.-Basil the Great, *Constitutiones asceticae* PG 31.1372C; Gregory of Nyssa, *Or. funebris de Pulcheria,* ed. Spira, p. 465.11; Chrysostom, *Hom. Matt.* 65.3; cf. Gal 4:26 (ἡ ἄνω Ἰερουσαλήμ) and *4 Bar.* 5:35 (ἡ ἄνω πόλιν Ἰερουσαλήμ). As elsewhere in *TA,* the language is literal.

Sun and moon are removed because God wants them in the upper realm. Nothing further need be said: God's will trumps all else. So death cannot be avoided (cf. 8:9). And yet, even in death, heaven shows mercy, for the man from heaven allows the rays (cf. v. 2) of sun and moon to remain upon Isaac. Readers might think of the sun going behind a cloud, or of sundown, when the sun has disappeared and yet still shines above the horizon, or of the mythological idea that the sun and its crown of rays can be separated.[14] The circumstance in any case coheres with *TA*'s message

---

[12] That the Psalms were part of the Jewish liturgy in Egypt seems likely; see Jutta Leonhardt, *Jewish Worship in Philo of Alexandria* (TSAJ 84; Tübingen: Mohr-Siebeck, 2001), 142–74.

[13] On the sense of ἐάω here see Turner, "Testament," 80.

[14] Note *2 Enoch* 14 and Gk. *3 Bar.* 7:4; 8:1–5 and see Schmidt, "Testament," 1:49–50.

that death is not annihilation but removal to another sphere of the cosmos.[15] Moreover, that the light still comes upon Isaac implies that his parents' succor continues beyond death. The text does not, however, indicate what form their continuing guidance will take. Should we think of their intercession before God? Do they become guardian angels? Whatever the answer, death does not utterly sever the bond between child and parents.

7:8. Michael, addressing father instead of son, who now exits the story until 15:5, enjoins Abraham the "righteous" (cf. 2:3 and see on 1:1) to "hear" (ἄκουσον); cf. Tob 6:13, where another angel utters this imperative. ἄκουσον δίκαιε Ἀβραάμ recurs in 14:2; 15:6; 19:7. Michael then interprets the dream, making it out to be a simple allegory. The sun is Abraham. With ὁ ἥλιος … σὺ εἶ cf. Theod. Dan 4:20–22: τὸ δένδρον … σὺ εἶ; also 2:38. The equation is thoroughly appropriate: (i) the sun is the brightest light in the sky while Abraham is the most important person in Isaac's life; (ii) Abraham's brightness corresponds to Michael's and so makes him angelic; both are citizens of the upper world;[16] (iii) the comparison of saints to sun is a *topos*: 4 Ezra 7:97; Matt 13:43; 2 En. 22:10; etc. The moon, a lesser light, represents Sarah, and the glorious man coming down from heaven is "the one sent by God" (ἀποσταλείς; see on v. 11 and 2:6)—but the speaker does not yet identify himself with that figure. That sent one is soon to take Abraham's soul, τὴν δικαίαν σου ψυχήν (see on 2:3). Note that Isaac is here called παῖς, which is consistent with his being far younger than Genesis would lead one to expect (see on 3:7).

7:9. Michael gets Abraham's attention: νῦν γίνωσκε; cf. Gk. *1 En.* 91:10; Ps.-Callisthenes, *Hist. Alex. Magn.* rec. β 3.22. Eschewing all ambiguity, the angel indicates that "most honorable (τιμιώτατε; see on 2:3) Abraham" is about (μέλλεις) to "leave behind" (καταλιπεῖν; cf. v. 1; 20:3) "at this time" (ἐν τῷ καιρῷ τούτῳ = ההוא or בפעם הזאת) "the world" (τὸν κόσμον) and "life" (τὸν βίον; see on 1:3); cf. *Dorm. BMV* 3 (καταλιποῦσα τὸν κόσμον); Ps.-Ephraem, *Sermo in pretiosam et vivificam crucem*, ed. Phrantzoles, p. 148.4 (καταλιπόντες τὸν κόσμον). He is "to journey" (ἐκδημεῖν; see on 1:7) "to (πρός) God"; cf. πρὸς τὸ θεῖον in Josephus, *Ant.*

---

[15] Against Turner, "Testament," 114–15, there is little reason to think that the equation of rays with Abraham's body, found in RecShrt, is the proper interpretation of RecLng.

[16] Cf. *Deut. Rab.* 11:10: "the radiance of his [Moses'] appearance was like that of the sun, and he was like that of an angel of the Lord of hosts."

1.85 (of Enoch), and *Ant.* 3.96; 8.326 (both of Moses). The line recalls God's commissioning of Michael in 1:7 (q.v.): "at this time (ἐν τῷ καιρῷ τούτῳ) you are about (μέλλεις) to go out (καταλιπεῖν) of this futile world (κόσμου) and you are about to depart (ἐκδημεῖν) from the body, and you will go to (πρός) your own Master among the good." Ms. H enhances the resemblance by adding "futile" (μάταιον) to 7:9. Michael is finally fulfilling his mission. For καταλείπω of leaving behind things at death see LXX Deut 28:54; Luke 20:31; Josephus, *Ant.* 12.235.

7:10. Abraham reacts with incredulity—"Oh latest wonder of wonders!," ὦ θαῦμα θαυμάτων; cf. Hippolytus, *Haer.* 5.18.18 (θαῦμα θαυμάτων); Romanos the Melodist, *Cant.* 27.1 (θαῦμα θαυμάτων); Theophrastus the Alchemist, ed. Goldschmidt 132 (θαῦμα θαυμάτων). The only other examples of ὦ θαῦμα θαυμάτων I have found are in Archelaus the Alchemist, ed. Goldschmidt 60—from the 8th cent.—and Thomas Magister, *Ecl. nominum et verborum Atticorum*, ed. Ritschl, p. 409.1—from the 13th–14th cents. "Latest" (καινότερον; cf. Philo, *Ebr.* 159; Acts 17:21; Josephus, *Bell.* 7.259; καινός*) harks back to earlier miracles—to a tree singing and to tears becoming precious stones. Given his acerbity in v. 12, one is unsure of the tone. Is Abraham more sardonic than enthusiastic? He anyway asks a question to which he must know the answer—whether, "for the rest" (λοιπόν; cf. 13:7–8; 1 Cor 1:16; *Jos. Asen.* 24:10; 28:6, 14), that is, concerning the remaining item in the dream not yet identified, the stranger is indeed the man from heaven come to take his soul.

7:11. The visitor responds with a statement of self-revelation: ἐγώ εἰμι Μιχαὴλ ὁ ἀρχιστράτηγος ὁ παρεστηκὼς ἐνώπιον τοῦ θεοῦ. For παρεστηκὼς ἐνώπιον see LXX Judg 20:28; Jdt 4:14; Mark 15:39; etc. Just as courtiers in a human court stand, so angels stand before God in 1:4 (q.v.); Job 1:6 (παραστῆναι ἐνώπιον τοῦ κυρίου); 2:1 (παραστῆναι ἔναντι κυρίου ... παραστῆναι ἐναντίον τοῦ κυρίου); Dan 7:16; *1 En.* 40:1–2 (angels "who stand before the glory of the Lord of the spirits"); Tob 12:15; Rev 8:2; Eustathius of Trake, *Encom. on Michael*, ed. Budge, p. 132 (Michael always stands before God's throne); etc. See on 1:4 for Michael's status as a heavenly high priest. ἐγώ εἰμι appears six times in *TA*, always of a heavenly figure: Michael (7:11), God (8:7), Death (16:11, 12 [bis]; 17:5). "To stand" before someone can mean to be that someone's servant or attendant (cf. 1 Kgs 17:1; 2 Kgs 3:14; Jer 15:19; etc.). But here a more literal meaning is intended, and the emphasis is upon Michael's closeness to the deity—he dwells in the presence of God. *b. Ḥag.* 15a says that "on high there is no sitting" (contrast Rev 4:4), and 4Q405 ii–21–22 2 = 11QŠirŠabb 3–4 3 says that the celestial debirim "do not sit." Cf. the idea, based upon Ezek 1:7 ("their legs were straight"), that angels lack joints; see *y. Ber.* 1:1; *Gen. Rab.* 65:21.

Michael's statement (cf. *Acts Paul* 43 P: Michael says: "Ego sum qui consisto in conspectu dei") is remarkably similar to the self-revelatory declaration of Gabriel in Luke 1:19. There is also a close parallel in Tob ℵ 12:13–15:

Luke 1:19	ἐγώ εἰμι Γαβριὴλ
	ὁ παρεστηκὼς ἐνώπιον τοῦ θεοῦ
	καὶ ἀπεστάλην λαλῆσαι πρὸς σὲ καὶ εὐαγγελίσασθαί σοι ταῦτα
TA 7:11	ἐγώ εἰμι Μιχαὴλ ὁ ἀρχιστράτηγος
	ὁ παρεστηκὼς ἐνώπιον τοῦ θεοῦ
	καὶ ἀπεστάλην πρὸς σὲ οὕτως ἀναγγείλω σοι
Tob ℵ 12:15	ἐγώ εἰμι Ῥαφαήλ ...
	οἳ παρεστήκασιν ... ἐνώπιον τῆς δόξης κυρίου
Tob ℵ 12:13	ἀπέσταλμαι ἐπὶ σέ
Tob ℵ 12:14	ἀπέσταλκέν με ὁ θεός

TA 7:1 may stand under the influence of Luke 1:19, but this is uncertain. (i) The ἐγώ εἰμι Ῥαφαήλ of Tob 12:15 (in A B as well as ℵ) belongs to a pre-Christian text. (ii) The phrase under consideration is not in itself Christian, and there is certainly nothing unusual about παρεστηκὼς ἐνώπιον. (iii) Nor is the notion of angels standing before God uncommon (see above). (iii) Theod. Dan 12:1 has Μιχαὴλ ὁ ἄρχων ὁ μέγας ὁ ἐστηκώς. (iv) *T. Levi* 5:6 uses the formula, ἐγώ εἰμι ὁ ἄγγελος ὁ + participle. (v) *b. Ḥag.* 12b and *b. Menaḥ.* 110a introduce Michael as מיכאל (השׂר הגדול עומד). Clearly, then, we are dealing here with traditional language not confined to Christian circles. So maybe *TA* 7:10 resembles Luke 1:19 because both draw upon a traditional Jewish characterization of an angel of the Presence.

Michael finishes with a statement of his divine commissioning—"I was sent (ἀπεστάλην; see on 2:6) to you so that I might proclaim the notice of death to you" (ἀναγγείλω σοι τὴν μνήμην τοῦ θανάτου; see on 1:6)—and the assertion that he will indeed complete his task: "And only then (καὶ εἶθ' οὕτως;[17] cf. 15:1; *3 Bar.* 13:1; *4 Bar.* 9:29; *Vit. Proph. Jeremiah* 6; *Ps.-Clem. Hom.* 1:14; etc.) shall I return to him just as I was commanded," that is, Michael will take Abraham along with him. Immediately, however, this confident, exalted self-description will meet disrespect.

---

[17] For the sense of εἶθ' οὕτως here see Pieter W. van der Horst, "'Only then will all Israel be Saved': A Short Note on the Meaning of καὶ οὕτως in Romans 11:26," *JBL* 119 (2000), 521–39.

7:12. Although he acknowledges (νῦν ἔγνωκα κἀγὼ ὅτι; cf. 14:12; 18:8) that the man before him is indeed ἄγγελος κυρίου (see on 6:1) who has come from God to take his soul, Abraham resists: οὐ μὴ σε ἀκολουθήσω. The words become a refrain: 8:2, 12; 15:10; 16:6; 19:4. The refusal must be intended to surprise. In the biblical tradition, Abraham is famed for "his complete obedience" (Chrysostom, *Hom. Gen.* PG 53.378). He does not even scruple when told to sacrifice his only son (cf. Genesis 22:18; 26:5; *Jub.* 18:16). Here, however, and for no stated reason, he disobeys God's order through the Commander-in-chief Michael. He plays not the saint but the ordinary person, for whom death is the enemy, or the frightened sinner who fears the judgment (cf. Gregory the Great, *Dial.* 4.40). In other words, he embodies typical human fear. One would think that he could trust an angel attended by miracles, especially one who had blessed him in the past (Genesis 18). Should not Abraham, of all people, have "the hope to die" (Dante)? Should not "God's friend" (cf. 1:4, 6; 2:3; 4:7; 8:2; etc.) be perfectly delighted to go to God? Indeed, should he not "be incited to a yearning" for death "because of the splendor of the prospect of blessedness and a celestial abode" (Macrobius, *Somnium Scipionis* 8.2)? But Abraham resists. He does not—like Moses in some legends (see p. 24) and like the synoptic Jesus (see on 20:5)—want to die.

The chapter closes with Abraham telling Michael in effect to get lost: "Now just what you command—you do it!" (κελεύεις ποίησον). Sanders instead translates, "But you do whatever he commands" (cf. Turner in Sparks). Delcor similarly renders, "cependant fais ce qu'il ordonne." He justifies this by referring to James's text, which prints κελεύει[ς]; he then comments that "ce qu'il ordonne" seems to accord better with the context: "Il révèle l'esprit d'obéissance d'Abraham à l'égard de Dieu."[18] But this is to misread our book, which generates interest and entertains by highlighting precisely Abraham's disobedience. It also neglects the close parallel in the legend about Moses rebuking the Angel of Death (see above, p. 24). Furthermore, Schmidt's critical edition reveals no justification for James's bracket, and the second person singular indicative followed by the imperative gives good sense. Abraham is telling the angel to carry out the mission without him, that is, to go back to heaven empty-handed. Michael can obey his own words and return to God just as ordered (cf. v. 11); but Abraham will not go with him (contrast *Apoc. Abr.* 14:14, where Abraham says: "And I did what the angel had commanded me").

---

18 Delcor, *Testament*, 119.

Chapter 8: God's Speech

8:1. When he heard this word, the Commander-in-chief immediately became invisible. And he went up into the heavens, and he stood before God, and he related everything that he had seen in Abraham's house. 8:2. The Commander-in-chief also said this to the Master: "Your friend Abraham even says this: 'I will not follow you, but what you command—you do it!' 8:3. Now, Master Almighty, just what do your glory and immortal royal power command?" 8:4. God said to the archangel Michael: "Go to my friend Abraham yet once more and speak thus to him: 8:5. 'Thus says the Lord your God: "What? Have I forsaken you upon the earth? I am your God, who brought you into the land of promise. I blessed you above the sand of the sea and as the stars of heaven. 8:6. I put an end to Sarah's barrenness, and I bestowed upon you in old age the fruit of the womb, (your) son Isaac. 8:7. Amen I say to you, I will truly bless you, and I will truly multiply you seed, and I will give to you whatever you ask from me. Because I am the Lord your God, and beside me there is no other. 8:8. Tell me, why have you resisted me, and why are you grieved? And why have you resisted my messenger? 8:9. Do you not know that all from Adam and Eve have died? Not even kings are immortal. Not one of the forefathers has escaped the treasury of death. All have died, all have been taken down to Hades, and all have been gathered by the sickle of death. 8:10. But to you I did not send death. I did not allow a fatal disease to come upon you. I did not permit you to be encountered by the sickle of death. I did not allow the nets of Hades to entwine you. I did not want any evil to befall you. 8:11. For good consolation I sent my Commander-in-chief Michael to you so that you might know (your) departure from the world and that you might make arrangements concerning your house and concerning all of your possessions, and that you might bless your beloved Isaac. And now know that I do not want to cause you grief by doing these things. 8:12. Why did you say to my Commander-in-chief, 'I will not follow you?' Why have you said this? Do you not know that if I allow Death to come to you then I would see whether or not you would come (to me)?""""

TEXTUAL NOTES

8:2. G saves space by omitting "The Commander-in-chief ... Master." // I has κελεύει, which is James's conjecture for 7:12. See the discussion there. 8:2–3. H skips from the last ὅτι in v. 2 to the ὅτι in v. 3. 8:3. G drops "Now, Master Almighty" and "your glory and." 8:5. G omits "What? Have I ...

earth?" // B H omit this and "I am your God." 8:6–7. G lacks "fruit … . Amen I say to you" through *homoioteleuton* (σοι … σοι). 8:7. I omits "Amen … from me." Perhaps this is deliberate abbreviation. // H drops "and I will truly multiply you seed and." // A: εἰμὶ ἐγώ. B G H I J Q have the more biblical ἐγὼ εἰμί. 8:8. I omits "Tell me" and "And why … grieved?" // A G H lack the last question. 8:9. A leaves out "and Eve." Does this reflect Paul, where the focus is on Adam to the exclusion of Eve? // G again shortens; it lacks "Not even kings … down to Hades." // B omits: "Not one … treasury of death." // J omits: "the treasury … to Hades." // B omits "No one … treasury of death." // A: τὸ τοῦ θανάτου κειμήλιον. C: τὸ τοῦ θανάτου μυστήριον. H: τῆς τοῦ θανάτου πείρας τὸ κειμήλιον (cf. the title). I: θανάτου. I and C may be revisions prompted by the otherwise unattested τὸ τοῦ θανάτου κειμήλιον. 8:10. J conflates the first two sentences: "But to you I did not send a fatal disease to come." // H similarly conflates the second and third sentences: "I did not allow a fatal disease to encounter you with the sickle of death." // Instead of "fatal disease," G has θανατηφόρον ἄγγελον, which recalls LXX Job 33:23. // B J Q omit "I did not permit … entwine you." // G again conflates, this time the third and fourth clauses: "I did not permit the nets of Hades … ." // H drops the last two sentences. // B G J Q have "the nets of death" instead of "the nets of Hades." // G I omit the last line. 8:11. I abbreviates the last line: "And now know that I have done these things." 8:12. J omits "Why … 'follow you'?" // I omits "Do you not know … come?" // H drops "whether or not … (to me)."

COMMENTARY

Chap. 8 opens with Michael ascending to heaven (v. 1), reporting Abraham's behavior (v. 2), and asking for God's guidance (v. 3). The remainder of the chapter records the divine response, a speech that Michael should in turn deliver to Abraham (vv. 4–12).

The speech opens with two questions (v. 5) and ends with three questions (v. 12), and three questions stand in the middle (vv. 8–9). Coming from God, the questions are of course rhetorical. But the interrogatory mode gives Abraham an opportunity to respond. God is not commanding but seeking to persuade. He does not want to act against Abraham's will but with his consent.

The argument advances in three steps. First, God recounts blessings given to Abraham—the land, prosperity, Isaac, multitudinous descendants (vv. 5–7). Clearly Abraham owes much to God and has every reason to trust him. Second, God declares that death is universal, that no one escapes it (v. 9). It follows that Abraham cannot be immortal—a point he will concede in 9:5. Third, despite death's ubiquity, God has nonetheless kindly chosen to send Michael rather than Death, so that the transition to the upper world might be as painless as possible, and that Abraham might be fully prepared (vv. 10–11).

Although chap. 8, unlike the previous chapters, does not replay or revise particular biblical episodes, the scriptural intertextuality and echoes are still significant, as one can see at a glance—

8:2,4: Abraham is God's "friend"; cf. 2 Chr 20:7; Isa 41:8; LXX 51:2; LXX Dan 3:35

8:5: τάδε λέγει κύριος ὁ θεός is a biblicism, appearing 35 times in the LXX

8:5: ὑπὲρ ἄμμον θαλάσσης καὶ ὡς τοὺς ἀστέρας τοῦ οὐρανοῦ depends upon LXX Gen 22:17

8:6: "I put an end to Sarah's barrenness, and I bestowed upon you in old age the fruit of the womb, (your) son Isaac" summarizes the first part of Genesis 18

8:7: εὐλογῶν εὐλογήσω σε καὶ πληθύνων πληθυνῶ τὸ σπέρμα σου reproduces LXX Gen 22:17

8:7: ἐγώ εἰμι κύριος ὁ θεός σου appears in the LXX Decalogue: Exod 20:2; Deut 5:9

8:7: καὶ πλὴν ἐμοῦ οὐκ ἔστιν ἄλλος; cf. LXX Exod 8:6; 2 Βασ 7:22; Isa 44:6; etc.

8:9: "Do you not know that all from Adam and Eve have died?" recalls Genesis 2–3

8:11: "your beloved Isaac" derives from Gen 22:2, 12, 16

Half of these borrowings are general biblicisms tied to no text in particular; they do little more than give the text a scriptural aura. But vv. 5, 6, 7, and 9 make clear use Genesis 18 and 22, which accords with the prominence of those texts in previous chapters.

RecShrt. contains no parallel to RecLng. 8. Lacking as it does the account of Abraham's refusal to follow Michael in RecLng. 7, it has no occasion for the speech in RecLng. 8.

8:1. The Commander-in-chief immediately becomes invisible upon hearing "this word," ἀκούσας … τὸ ῥῆμα τοῦτο; cf. LXX Exod 33:4, where ἀκούσας ὁ λαὸς τὸ ῥῆμα τὸ πονηρὸν τοῦτο translates וישמע העם את־דבר הרע הזה also *Jos. Asen.* 4:9; 5:2; 8:8; 9:1; 15:2; 23:6; 24:19. The ῥῆμα (cf. 13:8; 15:5; 19:4) is Abraham's refusal (see 7:12). Invisibility (ἀφανὴς ἐγένετο; cf. *Apoc. Sedr.* 11:13, ἀφανὲς γίνεται) is regularly associated with assumptions or ascents to heaven; cf. Philo, *Quaest. Gen.* 1.86; Josephus, *Ant.* 9.28; 4.326, 323; Plutarch, *Num.* 2.2–3.[1]

---

[1]   See further Gerhard Lohfink, *Die Himmelfahrt Jesu: Untersuchungen zu den Himmel-fahrts- und Erhöhungstexten bei Lukas* (SANT 26; Munich: Kösel, 1971), 41, and esp. Arthur Stanley Pease, "Some Aspects of Invisibility," *HSCP* 53 (1942), 1–36.

Upon becoming invisible, Michael goes up into the heavens (ἀνῆλθεν εἰς τοὺς οὐρανούς; see on 4:5) and, in accord with his earlier self-declaration, stands before God, ἔστη ἐνώπιον τοῦ θεου; see on 7:11. This line and the next closely resemble both 4:5 and 15:11–12, two other places that recount ascensions of Michael:

4:5	ὁ ἀχιστράτηγος	ἐξῆλθεν ἔξω
8:1	ὁ δὲ ἀρχιστράτηγος ἀκούσας τὸ ῥῆμα τοῦτο εὐθέως	
15:11	ἀκούσας δὲ ὁ ἀρχιστράτηγος ... τοὺς λόγους τούτους εὐθέως ἐξῆλθεν ἐκ	

4:5	καὶ ἀνῆλθεν εἰς τοὺς οὐρανούς ...	καὶ ἔστη ἐνώπιον τοῦ θεοῦ
8:1	καὶ ἀνῆλθεν εἰς τοὺς οὐρανούς	καὶ ἔστη ἐνώπιον τοῦ θεοῦ
15:11	καὶ ἀνῆλθεν εἰς τοὺς οὐρανούς	καὶ ἔστη ἐνώπιον τοῦ θεοῦ

4:5	καὶ εἶπεν ... πρὸς τὸν δεσπότην, κύριε, κύριε	
8:2–3	εἶπεν ... πρὸς τὸν δεσπότην ...	παντοκράτορ
15:12	καὶ εἶπεν	κύριε παντοκράτορ

The repetition adds to the unity of the book, and the shifting of scenes reminds one of Revelation, where the imagination moves back and forth between heaven and earth; cf. also Job 1–2; Gen 17:22 ("And when he had finished talking with him, God went up from Abraham"); *Sifre* Deut. 305 and the other Jewish texts where the Angel of Death, upon being rebuffed by Moses, returns to God and relates what has happened; see p. 24.

8:2. When Michael speaks to the Master (δεσπότην; see on 1:4), he stresses that Abraham is "your friend," φίλος; see on 1:4. The expression seems to shift responsibility from Michael to God, as if the angel is saying, "He's your friend, not mine. Don't blame me." The angel then quotes the rebuke that concludes chap. 7. The repetition (close but not exact) underlies the force of the refusal, which will recur again in 15:10; 16:6; and 19:4.

8:3. After Abraham's rebuff, Michael is nonplussed, for apparently he cannot take Abraham's soul against his will. So he questions the "Master Almighty," δέσποτα παντοκράτορ. παντοκράτορ (LXX: 126) appears again in 15:12, there with κύριος. Its combination with δεσπότης—unattested in the LXX, Philo, and Josephus—may be Christian; cf. *Did.* 10:3; Athanasius, *Apol. Const.* 7.25.3; *Liturg. Greg. Naz.* PG 36.700D; Basil the Great, *Liturg.* PG 31.1644D, 1653B; Theodoret of Cyrrhus, *Hist. eccl.*, ed. Ettlinger, p. 219.10—all, as here, in direct address to God. As these sources indicate, the address belonged to the Christian liturgy (but some of the relevant verses in the *Apostolic Constitutions* belong to sections often thought to be Jewish).

As elsewhere in *TA*, the address to God is periphrastic—"What do your glory and immortal royal power command?" (κελεύει; cf. 7:12). With ἡ σὴ δόξα καὶ βασιλεία ἡ ἀθάνατος cf. *Gos. Bart.* 4:17 v.l. (ἀθανάτου σου βασιλείας); Matt 6:13 syᶜ ("yours is the kingdom and glory forever"); Ps.-Macarius, *Serm. 64* 26.1 (ἀθανάτου βασιλείας); 27.2 (ἀθανάτῳ βασιλείᾳ); Ps.-John of Damascus, *B.J.* 8.61 (ἀθανάτου βσιλείας). The related "immortal king" appears in RecLng. 15:15; 16:2; *Sib. Or.* 1:122. Delcor rightly observes how common circumlocutions for God—including יקרא = "glory" or "honor"—are in the targumim, e.g. Tg. Onq. Gen 17:22 and Exod 20:20.[2] "Royal rule," that is, (א)מלכות, is also attested as a circumlocution for the deity: Tg. Isa 31:4; 52:7; Tg. Mic 4:7; Tg. Zech 14:9; etc.[3]

8:4. God responds with a second commissioning of his messenger. Affirming that Abraham remains his "friend" (cf. v. 2 and see on 1:4), he tells Michael to go to him (ἄπελθε πρὸς ... τὸν Ἀβραάμ; cf. 1:4; 4:7; 16:5) "yet once more," ἔτι ἅπαξ; cf. 9:3; 15:7.

8:5. The word from on high begins with the authoritative τάδε λέγει κύριος ὁ θεός σου (= נאם מה־אמר יהוה אלחיך). Although the LXX never uses this precise expression, κύριος ὁ θεός σου appears 176 times, the majority in Deuteronomy; and τάδε λέγει κύριος ὁ θεός [without σου] appears 35 times: Exod 5:1; Josh 7:13; Amos 3:11; Isa 38:5; Jer 7:3; etc.[4] The formulation of self-identification prefaces two questions: "What (τί)? Have I forsaken you (σε ἐγκατέλειπα; ἐγκαταλείπω*; cf. LXX Josh 1:5; Ps 21:2; *T. Jos.* 2:4; Heb 13:5; *1 Clem.* 11:1—all with God as subject) upon the earth?" Our book's anthropomorphic God is incredulous yet patient and will answer his own rhetorical question.

God now recounts what he has done for Abraham. First, he brought him into the land of promise. The line echoes the liturgy:

TA 8:5	ἐγώ	εἰμι κύριος ὁ θεός σου
		ὁ ἀναγαγών σε εἰς τὴν γῆν τῆς ἐπαγγελίας
LXX Ps 80:11	ἐγὼ γάρ εἰμι κύριος ὁ θεός σου	
		ὁ ἀναγαγών σε ἐκ γῆς Αἰγύπτου[5]

The traditional nature of the language is also underlined by the parallel with Heb 11:9: Abraham "stayed for a time in the land he had been

---

[2] Delcor, *Testament*, 120–21.

[3] See further B. Chilton, "Regnum Dei Deus Est," *SJT* 31 (1978), 261–70.

[4] The biblical parallels render implausible the attempt of Dean-Otting, *Heavenly Journeys*, 194–95, to find a background for τάδε λέγει—which Abraham himself uses in 9:4—in royal Persian decrees; cf. Herodotus 1.69; Ps.-Callisthenes, *Hist. Alex. Magn.* rec α 1.40.

[5] Cf. LXX Lev 11:45: ἐγώ εἰμι κύριος ὁ θεός ὁ ἀναγαγών ὑμᾶς ἐκ γῆς Αἰγύπτου. κύριος + ὁ ἀναγαγών also appears in LXX 1 Βασ 12:6; Jer 2:6; 16:14.

promised," εἰς γῆν τῆς ἐπαγγελίας; cf. also 20:11 (τῇ γῇ τῆς ἐπαγγελίας); *T. Jos.* 20:1 v.l. (γῆν ἐπαγγελίας τῶν πατέρων ὑμῶν). One could, however, urge the influence of Hebrews upon a Christian scribe of *TA*. Other parallels include Origen, *Sel. Num.* PG 12.576C (εἰς τὴν γῆν τῆς ἐπαγγελίας), and Methodius of Olympus, *Symp.* 9.5 (τὴν γῆν τῆς ἐπαγγελίας). Chrysostom several times uses a compound of ἄγω + εἰς τὴν γῆν τῆς ἐπαγγελίας or something close to it: *Fr. Jer.* PG 64.789; *Int. Dan.* PG 56.236, 240; etc. The LXX has rather γὴν ἣν ὤμοσα + "to your forefathers" or "to Abraham, Isaac, and Jacob": Gen 50:24; Exod 13:5; Num 32:11; Deut 1:35; Josh 5:6; etc. Cf. the common Hebrew phrase, הארץ אשר נשבע. On the ἐπαγγελ-root and Abraham see further on 3:6 and cf. 6:5. Informed readers recall the entirety of Abraham's story in Genesis, which is about God leading the patriarch to the land of promise and giving him descendants to occupy it.

In addition to bringing him to the land of promise, God has blessed Abraham ὑπὲρ ἄμμον θαλάσσης καὶ ὡς τοὺς ἀστέρας τοῦ οὐρανοῦ. This is a revision of Gen 22:17 (where the stars come before the sand); see further on 1:5. V. 7 picks up the same verse. In *TA* the line describes Abraham's great prosperity. So here again is another sign of God's goodness. The implication seems to be both that Abraham is indebted to God and that he should, in the light of past benefits, be prepared to trust God fully now.

8:6. God continues to recount his mercies: "I put an end to Sarah's barrenness." With διαλύσας μήτραν Σάρρας τῆς στειρώσεως cf. Ps.-Callisthenes, *Hist. Alex. Magn.* rec. γ 4.26: διαλῦσαι δέσμα ἀτέκνου μήτρας. The words echo Gen 11:30: ἦν Σάρα στεῖρα (cf. the remarks about Rebekah and Rachel in 25:21 and 29:31 respectively). As for "I bestowed (χαρισάμενος; see on 3:6) upon you in old age the fruit of the womb (καρπὸν κοιλίας; see on 6:5), (your) son Isaac," this moves memories to Genesis 18, where Isaac is both promised and born. ἐν γήρει (cf. *T. Iss.* 7:9; *T. Benj.* 12:2; *Jos. Asen.* 22:6) appears three times in the LXX story of Abraham: 15:15; 21:7; 25:8.

8:7. God reverts to LXX Gen 22:17 (cf. 26:24; *Jub.* 19:15; Philo, *Leg. all.* 3.203–210; Heb 6:14; *Gk. Apoc. Ezra* 3:10), another part of which is rewritten in v. 5:

TA 8:7   ἀμήν ...
                        εὐλογῶν εὐλογήσω σε
                        καὶ πληθύνων πληθυνῶ τὸ σπέρμα σου

LXX Gen 22:17   ἦ μὴν
                        εὐλογῶν εὐλογήσω σε
                        καὶ πληθύνων πληθυνῶ τὸ σπέρμα σου

For the addition of a cognate participle to a finite verb representing the Hebrew infinitive absolute see BDF § 422. On "Amen I say to you" see on 2:12. Here ἀμήν seems to be the equivalent of the LXX's ἦ μήν = "now verily" (cf. LSJ, s.v., μήν). God's implicit argument continues to be from the past to the present: Abraham should trust for the future the God who has blessed him in the past.

To this is added "and I will give to you whatever you ask from me"— the truth of which Abraham acknowledges in 9:4. Although these words do not allude to any particular text in the story of Abraham, that story gives them substance. In Gen 15:2, Abraham prays, "O Lord God, what will you give me, for I continue childless ...?" God eventually answers by giving Sarah a son, Isaac. In Gen 18:22–33, Abraham repeatedly pleads for Sodom, finally asking God to spare the place if only ten righteous are found in it. In the event, God destroys Sodom, but only because ten righteous are not there. God's willingness to heed Abraham is clear: "For the sake of ten I will not destroy it." And in 20:17, Abraham prays for Abimelech and his household, and God heals them. So Genesis leaves one with the distinct impression that whatever Abraham asked of God, God gave him. Tgs. Ps.-Jn. and Neof. 1, where the promise of Gen 22:17 (see above) is an answer to a prayer of Abraham, reinforce this impression.

The formulation, δώσω σοι ὅσα ἂν αἰτήσῃς παρ' ἐμοῦ (cf. 20:3: ὅσα ἂν ᾐτήσω), reminds one of some early Christian texts: Matt 7:7 = Luke 11:9 (αἰτεῖτε καὶ δοθήσεται ὑμῖν); Matt 14:7 (αὐτῇ δοῦναι ὃ ἐὰν αἰτήσηται; cf. Mark 6:23); 21:22 (ὅσα ἂν αἰτήσητε); John 11:22 (ὅσα ἂν αἰτήσῃ τὸν θεὸν δώσει σοι); 15:7, 16; 16:23; Jas 1:5; *Gk. Apoc. Ezra* 7:13; cf. Ps.-Chrysostom, *Laz.* PG 62.775: ὅσα ἂν αἰτήσῃς τὸν θεὸν δώῃ σοι (rewriting John 11:22). There are, however, also Jewish parallels that weaken the case for Christian composition: LXX 1 Βασ 1:17 (ὁ θεὸς Ἰσραὴλ δώῃ σοι ... ὃ ᾐτήσω παρ' αὐτοῦ), 27; 2 Esd 6:9; Ps 2:8 (αἴτησαι παρ' ἐμοῦ καὶ δώσω σοι); 20:5.

Having asserted his goodness, God next declares his authority and sovereignty: "I am (see on 7:11) the Lord your God, and beside me there is no other." This combines two scriptural sentiments:

TA 8:7	ἐγώ εἰμι κύριος ὁ θεός σου καὶ πλὴν ἐμοῦ οὐκ ἔστιν ἄλλος
LXX Exod 20:2	ἐγώ εἰμι κύριος ὁ θεός σου
LXX Deut 5:9	ἐγώ εἰμι κύριος ὁ θεός σου[6]
LXX Exod 8:6	οὐκ ἔστιν ἄλλος πλὴν κυρίου
LXX 2 Βασ 7:22	οὐκ ἔστιν θεὸς πλὴν σοῦ
LXX Isa 44:6	πλὴν ἐμοῦ οὐκ ἔστιν θεός

---

[6] The LXX also has ἐγώ εἰμι κύριος ὁ θεὸς ὑμῶν on sixteen occasions, all of them in Leviticus.

In Exod 20:2–3, "I am the Lord your God" prefaces "you shall have no other gods before me" (LXX: ἐγώ εἰμι κύριος ὁ θεός σου ... οὐκ ἔσονται σοι θεοὶ ἕτεροι πλὴν ἐμοῦ; cf. Deut 5:6–7), and this probably explains why the two declarations are joined elsewhere in statements about God's identity:

LXX Deut 4:35   κύριος ὁ θεός σου, οὗτος θεός ἐστιν
                            καὶ οὐκ ἔστιν ἔτι πλὴν αὐτοῦ
LXX Deut 4:39   κύριος ὁ θεός σου, οὗτος θεός ...
                            καὶ οὐκ ἔστιν ἔτι πλὴν αὐτοῦ
LXX Deut 32:39   ἐγώ εἰμι
                            καὶ οὐκ ἔστιν θεὸς πλὴν ἐμοῦ
LXX Isa 45:5   ἐγὼ κύριος ὁ θεὸς
                            καὶ οὐκ ἔστιν ἔτι πλὴν ἐμοῦ θεός
LXX Isa 45:6   ἐγὼ κύριος ὁ θεὸς
                            καὶ οὐκ ἔστιν ἔτι
LXX Isa 45:21   ἐγὼ ὁ θεὸς
                            καὶ οὐκ ἔστιν ἄλλος πλὴν ἐμοῦ
LXX Isa 45:22   ἐγώ εἰμι ὁ θεός
                            καὶ οὐκ ἔστιν ἄλλος πλὴν ἐμοῦ
LXX Isa 46:9   ἐγώ εἰμι ὁ θεός
                            καὶ ἔστιν ἔτι πλὴν ἐμοῦ
LXX Joel 2:27   ἐγώ εἰμι καὶ ἐγὼ κύριος ὁ θεὸς ὑμῶν
                            καὶ οὐκ ἔστιν ἔτι πλὴν ἐμοῦ

Clearly the last part of *TA* 8:7 is not designed to recall any particular text. It is rather a biblical *topos* (cf. also 2 *En.* 36:1). In its present context, the line functions to underline the distance between God and Abraham. Who is the latter not to obey the former?

8:8. God now asks three brief questions. "Why have you resisted (ἀνθέστη-κας; cf. 9:5; LXX Job 41:1–2; Jer 27:44; 29:19) me?" reflects the circumstance that Abraham, when refusing to follow Michael, offered no explanation. So too "Why have you resisted my messenger?" (ἄγγελον; cf. Dan 10:13, where another angel is resisted). "And why are you grieved?" (λύπη; cf. 20:14 and λυπῆσαι in v. 11) reiterates the oddness of Abraham's behavior. Surely the friend of God cannot mourn at the prospect of going to God, of going to paradise where there is no grief (20:14).

8:9. The opening question and the following five assertions fall into two balanced, poetic triads:

(A) Do you not know that all from Adam and Eve have died?
(B) Not even kings are immortal.
(C) Not one of the forefathers has escaped the treasury of death.
(D) All have died,
(E) all have been taken down to Hades,
(F) all have been gathered by the sickle of death.

(A), (B), and (C) are unified by the concrete references—Adam and Eve, kings, the forefathers. (D), (E), and (F) are united by the general, repeated πάντες as well as by the increasing length of the lines. The first members of both units correspond—both (A) and (D) have πάντες ἀπέθανον—and the last members also correspond: (C) and (F) employ related metaphors: "treasury of death," "sickle of death." In the Moses traditions, upon which our book is largely based, Moses is told that all must die: *Sifre* Deut. 339; *Deut. Rab.* 10:8; the Falasha *Death of Moses*, trans. Leslau, p. 109.

God's question about Adam (who will reappear in chap. 11) and Eve belongs to a tradition that associates death with Genesis 3: Ecclus 25:24; Philo, *Quaest. Gen.* 1.45; Wis 2:23–24; Gk. *L.A.E.* 14:2; Rom 5:12; *L.A.B.* 13:8 v.l.; *4 Ezra* 3:7; *2 Bar.* 17:3; 23:4; 54:15; 56:6. For rabbinic materials see Strack-Billerbeck 3:227–29. The majority view among the rabbis was that death is not inevitable but comes only in consequence of each individual's sin: *b. Šabb.* 55a–56b; *b. ʿArak.* 17a (cf. Justin, *Dial.* 95; *Ps.-Clem. Rec.* 1:52).[7] *TA* may presuppose that its hearers see things otherwise.

"Not even kings are immortal" (cf. 19:7; ἀθάνατος: 8:3, 9; 9:5; 15:15; 16:2; 17:4) recalls ancient epitaphs that console by referring to the deaths of those who might be expected to escape death but did not: "No human was ever immortal; Theseus and the Aeacidae are proof" (*EG* 567.1–2); "Even children of the blessed gods have gone underground" (*EG* 298.7–8); cf. Homer, *Il.* 18.117: "Not even mighty Heracles escaped death." There are in fact epitaphs which point out that kings are not the exception; see e.g. W. Peek, "Korkyraische und kretische Epigramme," *Philologus* 88 (1933), 139–43: "A person shall fulfill the fate that has been allotted; kings also do so."[8] The democracy of the dead also appears in Jewish sources: Job 3:11–19; Ps.-Phoc. 112–113 ("Hades is … a common place for all, poor and kings"); *Jan. Jam.* 22jᵛ; *CIJ* 314, 335, 380, 401, 450, 544 (all with variations of οὐδεὶς ἀθάνατος); *BS* 2.193; *Deut. Rab.* 9:3 ("The Angel of Death does not say, 'Seeing that this one is king we will grant him one or two days more.' On that day there is no respecting of persons"). One may further compare Horace, *Carm.* 1.4.13–14: "Pale Death with foot impartial knocks at the poor person's cottage and at princes' palaces."

This democracy includes the "forefathers," προπατόρων (προπάτωρ*; cf. Philo, *Mos.* 2.291; Josephus, *Ant.* 4.26; *T. Levi* 9:1; Justin, *1 Apol.*

---

7 See further Ginzberg, *Legends*, 5:129–30.
8 Cf. Lattimore, *Themes*, 254–55, citing also G. Kaibel, "Supplementum Epigram- matum Graecorum ex lapidibus conlectorum," *Rheinisches Museum* 34 (1879), 215a.9: "Rulers also."

32.3, 14; Eusebius, *Dem. ev.* 5.15). Abraham is a προπατήρ in Philo, *Quaest. Gen.* 4.153; Rom 4:1; Josephus, *Bell.* 5.380; and *Apos. Con.* 7:33. (In the only LXX occurrence, *3 Macc.* 2:21, the singular is used of God.) From death none of these has escaped (ἐξέφυγεν; ἐκφύγω*); cf. Sophocles, *Ant.* 361 (Ἅιδα μόνον φεῦξιν οὐκ ἐπάξεται); Eusebius, *Dem. ev.* 9.18.2 (ἐκφεύγοντα τὸν θάνατου); Ps.-Chrysostom, *Pasch.* PG 59.733 (ἐκφεύγει τὴν τοῦ θάνατου πληγήν). While this assertion is a variant of the first two, the biblically informed will at this point think of Methuselah and those who, before Abraham, lived to such old ages: even they eventually died. Given that Enoch lived before Abraham and so must be included in this statement, perhaps our text assumes that Enoch was not translated to heaven but rather died.[9]

"The treasury of death," τὸ τοῦ θάνατοῦ κειμήλιον, appears to be without precise parallel; cf. the unparalleled "bowl of Hades" in *Gk. Apoc. Ezra* 6:26, and the גיהנם אש אוצרות in *Ozar Midrashim* Konan 7, ed. Eisenstein, p. 256. ὁ θησαυρός τοῦ θάνατοῦ is also unattested. Although κειμήλιον is absent from the LXX, it is common in Homer, Philo, and Josephus; cf. also *Sib. Or.* 14:64; *Gk. Apoc. Ezra* 1:20. Has someone formulated "the treasury of death" in antithesis to "the treasury of life," an expression Christian and later rabbinic sources know (Ps.-Gregory of Nyssa, *Annunt.*, ed. Montagna, 129; Chrysostom, *Ingressum jej. 1* PG 62.728; Ps.-Macarius, *Serm. 64* 27.1; etc.)? Or is it a variant of "the treasury of souls" (cf. *2 Bar.* 21:23; 30:1–2; this term is itself a variant of "the chamber of souls," as in *4 Ezra* 4:41; 7:32)?

"All have died" (πάντες ἀπέθανον) commences the second triad with a statement of universal experience, and one commonly expressed on ancient Greek epitaphs: οὐδεὶς ἀθάνατος.[10] This standard formula is also common on Jewish epitaphs; see e.g. *CIJ* 314, 355, 380, 401, 450, 544; *BS* 2.127.[11] One may also compare Euripides, *Alc.* 782 ("From all humanity the debt of death is due"); Ps 89:49 ("What person can live and never see death? Who can deliver his soul from the power of Sheol?"); Eccles 8:8 ("No one has authority to retain the spirit, or authority over the day of death"); Ecclus 14:17 ("All living beings become old like a garment, for the decree from of old is, 'You must surely die'"); Rom 5:12 ("death came to all

---

[9] So Tg. Onq. on Gen 5:24; *Gen. Rab.* 25:1; cf. Ginzberg, *Legends*, 5:156–57.

[10] See Lattimore, *Themes*, 253.

[11] See Joseph S. Park, *Conceptions of Afterlife in Jewish Inscriptions, with Special Reference to Pauline Literature* (WUNT 2/121; Tübingen: Mohr-Siebeck, 2000), 47–63, and van der Horst, *Epitaphs*, 120–22. Christians also adopted the standard formula; see e.g. Gregg and Urman, *Golan*, 230–31.

people"); 1 Cor 15:22 ("all died in Adam"); *Hist. Jos. Carp.* 1 ("none will escape death"; cf. 18, 28; chap. 31 explains that even Enoch and Elijah will die in the latter days); Johnson, *Anatolia* 4.12 ("There is one Hades and (the) end (of all) is the same"). The thought entered Christian liturgies at some point.[12] Particularly interesting given *TA*'s dependence upon the legends of Moses' death is *Sifre* Deut. 339, where God says, in regard to Moses protesting death, "It (death) is a decree of mine that applies to every mortal"; cf. *Deut. Rab.* 10:8; *Petirat Moshe (BHM* 1:118).

"All have been taken down to Hades" (ἐν τῷ ᾅδῃ καθείλοντο; καθαιρέω*) is just a poetic way of saying once more that all die: the same point is being emphasized again and again. ᾅδης (cf. v. 10; 19:7) translates שאול in the LXX, and its first meaning there is "netherworld," the place where all the dead reside; cf. 2 Macc 6:23; Josephus, *Ant.* 18.14; *Bell.* 2.163; Acts 2:27, 31; *4 Ezra* 4:42. By the first century CE, "Hades" had merged in some minds with "Gehenna," the place of damnation and punishment for the wicked: *Ps. Sol.* 14:9; 15:10; *3 Bar.* 4:3–5; *Apoc. Zeph.* 10:1–14; etc. In *TA*, however, "Hades" lacks its mythological associations and is not the same as "hell"; it is rather just a synonym for physical death; cf. the alternation between "death" and "Hades" in manuscripts of Acts 2:24; also *BS* 2.127: "And having gone to Hades, I , Justus, lie here, with many of my own kindred." In chaps. 11–14, souls do not, upon death, descend to Hades, the realm of the dead, but are rather immediately judged, after which the righteous go to paradise and the wicked suffer eternal destruction.

"All have been gathered by the sickle of death" (τῇ τοῦ θανάτου δρεπάνῃ συλλέγονται) returns to a metaphor first used in 4:11 (q.v.; cf. 8:10). συλλέγω* is used in connection with δρεπάνη in LXX Deut 23:25, but the sense is agricultural.

8:10. Having in v. 9 made six parallel statements about death in general, God now makes five denials regarding Abraham in particular, the upshot of which is that his case is unique. Again there is repetition and parallelism for the sake of emphasis:

1	οὐκ		θάνατος		
2	οὐκ		θανατηφόρον		
3	οὐ	συνεχώρησα	θανάτου	συναντῆσαί	σοι
4	οὐ	παρεχώρησα		-αι	σοι
5	οὐκ			συναντῆσαί	σοι

---

[12] See the *Service Book of the Holy Orthodox-Catholic Apostolic Church*, ed. Isabel Florence Hapgood (Englewood, N.J.: Antiochian Orthodox Christian Archdiocese of New York and all North America, 1975), 390 (this translates Old Church Slavonic liturgical texts).

God begins by declaring that he did not send θάνατος to Abraham. Because God is in fact telling Abraham that it is time to die, θάνατος must here be Death personified, as elsewhere in the book. So the statement simply reflects the narrative to this point: God has sent Michael instead of Death.

God next denies that he sent to Abraham a fatal disease, νόσον θανατηφόρον (νόσος: 8:10; 17:17; θανατηφόρος: 8:10; 17:17; LXX Num 18:22; Job 33:23; 4 Macc. 8:18, 26; 15:26; Jas 3:8; Sib. Or. fr. 3,33). Cf. 17:17; Plutarch, Sull. 13.2 (νόσημα θανατηφόρον); Hephaestio the Astrologer, Apotelesmatica, ed. Pingree, p. 63.15; 177.18 (νόσους θανατηφόρους); Ducas, Hist. Turco-Byzantina 32.1 (θανατηφόρος ... νόσος). He has also not allowed the patriarch to be encountered "by the sickle of death" (τοῦ θανατοῦ δρεπάνη; see on 4:11). While the latter metaphor comes from v. 9, the next assertion introduces a new expression: God has not allowed τὰ τοῦ ᾅδου δίκτυα to "entwine" (συμπλέξαι; συμπλέκω*: LXX: 13) him; cf. Theophilus Protospatharius, De corporis humani fabrica 4.7: συμπλεκόμενα πρὸς ἄλληλα ὥσπερ δίκτυον. "The nets of Hades" also appears in a line of Cassandra in Aeschylus, Ag. 1115: δικτύον ... Ἅιδου. The Jewish parallels—some of the Psalms associate "net(s)" with "pit" (e.g. 9:15; 35:7–8); 2 Sam 22:6 refers to "the cords (חבלי) of Sheol,"[13] CD A 4:15 speaks of "the nets of Belial" (מצודות בליעל; m. 'Abot 3:15 = ARN A 39 declares that "the net (מצודה) is spread over all the living"—are not so close. Maybe then TA reflects a knowledge of Aeschylus, just as there may be a knowledge of Euripides (see on 16:1). Additional links between Ag. 1115 and TA, however, seem to be missing.

If "I did not allow a fatal disease to come upon you" and "I did not permit you to be encountered by the sickle of death" and "I did not allow the nets of Hades to entwine you" are all poetic ways of saying the same thing, v. 10 ends with a slightly new point: "I did not want any evil (κακῷ/ κακός*; cf. RecShrt. 4:2) to befall you." This not only makes clear how much God cares for his "friend," but shows that passing out of this world cannot in itself be evil. For the one who has told Abraham that it is time to die is also the one who has not brought anything evil upon him.

8:11. God, moving from the negative to the positive, from what he has not done to what he has done, asserts that all has happened for Abraham's benefit, even if the patriarch has not understood this. God has sought to comfort Abraham, not to grieve him, μὴ λυπῆσαι σε; cf. v. 8 and Ecclus 30:9: λυπήσει σε. Indeed, he has acted "for good consolation," παράκλησιν ἀγαθήν; cf. 2 Macc 15:11 (ἐν τοῖς ἀγαθοῖς λόγοις παράκλησιν); Basil the

---

[13] But 1QH 11(3):9 seems to take this to mean "pangs of Sheol."

Great, *Ep.* 302.1 (παράκλησιν τοῦ ἀγαθοῦ). Thus God sent Michael so that Abraham would know ahead of time about his "departure from the world," τοῦ κόσμου μετάστασιν; cf.: Euripides, fr. 554 (τοῦ κόσμου μεταστάσεις); Polybius, *Hist.* 30.2.5 (τοῦ βίου μετάστασιν). μετάστασις by itself can mean death: Josephus, *Ant.* 18.89, 209; Chrysostom, *Hom. Jo.* 72.3 PG 59.393; *Hom. princ. Act.* PG 51.69. For rabbinic parallels see Strack-Billerbeck 2:138–39. God intended such advance knowledge to move Abraham to bless his "beloved" (see on 4:1) and to make arrangements concerning his house (cf. 2 Kgs 20:1) and all of his possessions—a theme repeated throughout *TA*:

8:11	ποιήσῃς διάταξιν	περὶ τοῦ οἴκου σου	καὶ περὶ	πάντων τῶν ὑπαρχόντων	σοι
1:4 (q.v.)		διατάξεται περὶ		πάντων	πραγμάτων αὐτοῦ
4:11	ποιήσῃς διάταξιν	περὶ		πάντων τῶν ὑπαρχόντων αὐτοῦ	
15:1	ποιήσῃς διάταξιν	περὶ τοῦ οἴκου αὐτοῦ καὶ		τὰ ὑπάρχοντα αὐτοῦ	
15:7	ποίησον διάταξιν	περὶ πάντων			

That the book ends without Abraham settling his affairs underlines his stubborn resistance: he never accepts his death.

8:12. God finishes his speech with three questions, the first two of which are parallel:

ἵνα τί ... εἶπας
ἵνα τί ... εἴρηκας

When God asks, "Why did you say to my Commander-in-chief, 'I will not follow you?,'" he is quoting Michael's words in v. 2, which replicate Abraham's words in 7:12. The repetition makes this section end as it began and so creates a sort of *inclusio*; it further keeps to the fore the major surprise of our story, namely, Abraham's disobedience. The chapter closes with God making the point that if Death were to come to Abraham, the patriarch would have no say in the matter at all: τότε ἂν εἶχον ἰδεῖν κἂν ἔρχῃ κἂν οὐκ ἔρχῃ; cf. the κἂν ... κἂν of 6:8 (q.v.).[14]

---

[14] On τότε ἂν εἶχον ἰδεῖν = "then I will see" see Turner, "Testament," 243–44.

Chapter 9: Abraham strikes a Bargain

Bibliography: Strotmann, *"Mein Vater"*, 219–23.

Long Recension

9:1. Having received the address of the Most High, the Commander-in-chief went down to Abraham. And the just man, upon seeing him, fell on his face to the ground of the earth as though dead. 9:2. The Commander-in-chief told him all that he had heard from the Most High. Now then the pious and just Abraham arose with many tears and fell at the feet of the incorporeal one and supplicated him saying: 9:3. "I beg you, Commander-in-chief of the upper powers, since you did not deem it altogether unworthy to come daily to me, sinner and your unworthy supplicant, I plead with you again now, Commander-in-chief, to serve me yet once before the Most High, and to speak to him as follows: 9:4 'Thus says Abraham, "Lord, lord, every task and word which I have asked of you, you have done, and you have given to me according to my heart and have fulfilled all my will. 9:5 And now Lord, I do not resist your might, for I know that I will not be immortal but mortal. Since then at your command all things submit and shudder and tremble before your power, I too am afraid. One more request I nonetheless request of you. 9:6. And now, Master Lord, hear my prayer. While I am yet in this body I wish to see all the inhabited earth and all the things made, which

Short Recension fam. E

7:19. And Abraham answered and said to Michael, "I beg you, Lord, if I am to go out of the body, I would like to be lifted up so that, before I am carried away, I might see all the creation which the Lord created in heaven and on earth." 7:20. And Michael answered and said, "This is not mine to do. But I will go and make a report about this to my Father, and if he gives me the order, then I will show all this to you." 8:1. And Michael went away into the heavens. And he spoke before God concerning Abraham. 8:2. And the Lord answered and said to Michael, "Return and take Abraham up bodily, and show him everything. And if he asks anything of you, do it for him, because he is my friend."

you established through one word, Master; and after I have seen these things, then I shall not grieve when I depart from (this) life."'" 9:7. Again the Commander-in-chief went up and stood before the invisible Father. And he recounted to him everything, saying: "Thus says your friend Abraham, 'I want to see all the inhabited earth while I am still alive.'" 9:8. Upon hearing these things, the Most High commanded the Commander-in-chief Michael and said to him: "Take a cloud of light and the angels who are in charge of the chariots, and go down and take righteous Abraham on the cherubic chariot and raise him high into the upper air of heaven that he might see all the inhabited world."

TEXTUAL NOTES ON THE LONG RECENSION

9:1–2. B I: "Receiving (this) the Commander-in-chief said to him ... ." An eye presumably passed from the first "Commander-in-chief" to the second. // H omits "And the just man ... . The Commander-in-chief." 9:1. A: εἰς τὸ ἔδαφος τῆς γῆς ὡς νεκρός. G J Q: εἰς/πρὸς τοὺς πόδας τοῦ ἀγγέλου/ ἀρχιστρατήγου (cf. 3:6; 9:2 ms. A). 9:2–4. I lacks "then ... . Thus." // 9:2. A alone has "and fell ... and." B G H J Q abbreviate in order not to duplicate v. 1. 9:3. H omits "and your unworthy servant." // A: ἱκέτην (cf. v. 2: ἱκέτευεν). B G J Q: δοῦλον. // G lacks "with you ... Commander-in-chief." 9:4–5. I carelessly omits "Thus says ... and yields." 9:4. B skips from σου to μου, omitting "you have done ... my heart." 9:5. J omits "because ... mortal," which is strictly unnecessary. // J omits "I too ... of you" through homoioteleuton (κἀγώ ... κἀγώ). 9:6. G abbreviates, omitting "And now ... Lord." // H drops "my prayer ... Master." // J drops "which you ... Master." 9:8. G abbreviates by omitting "command ... Michael and." // A has κατάλαβε, which may be an accidental contraction of κατελθὼν λαβέ (B H J Q) or κάτελθε λαβέ (G). I: κάτελθε Μιχαὴλ λαβών. // H drops "and raise ... heaven." // Through homoioteleuton, A omits "that he might see ... world" and the first part of 10:1 (οὐρανοῦ ... οὐρανοῦ).

COMMENTARY

Chap. 9 contains two little scenes, the first on earth, the second in heaven. Each scene is an exchange of words, and each involves Michael as the intermediary between Abraham and God:

Scene I: Michael descends

| 1–2 | Michael speaks to Abraham, summarizing God's speech |
| 3–6 | Abraham speaks to Michael, with a message for God |

Scene II: Michael ascends

| 7 | Michael speaks to God, summarizing Abraham's speech |
| 8 | God speaks to Michael, with a message for Abraham |

In his response in vv. 3–6, Abraham seems appropriately modest. He calls himself a "sinner" and an "unworthy supplicant" (v. 3). Moreover, he takes full account of God's prior speech:

8:7	God says he has blessed Abraham and given him all he has asked for
9:4	Abraham acknowledges that God has given to him all his will
8:7	God declares his lordship
9:4–6	Abraham repeatedly calls God "Lord"
8:8	God asks why Abraham has "resisted" him and his messenger
9:5	Abraham says that he does not "resist" God's might
8:8	God asks why Abraham is "grieved"
9:6	Abraham promises that he will not "grieve" if he sees all the world
8:9	God declares that none are "immortal"
9:5	Abraham confesses that he is not "immortal"

Despite the several concessions, Abraham disagrees with God: he denies that he is resisting him. The patriarch's humility and recognition of God's lordship do not, moreover, prevent him from presuming to ask for what he wants. The truth is, Abraham, afraid of death, is here "a master manipulator, exploiting his advantages with the divine."[1] His request is nothing but a delaying tactic.

God decides to give Abraham exactly what he has requested. If the patriarch wants to see all the inhabited world before he dies, then he will see it. Such a response communicates that Abraham is indeed God's "friend" (v. 7), and readers may further take away the general lesson that the gracious deity is flexible. He heeds requests.

Chap. 9 contains less intertextuality than previous chapters. There are, for example, only a few faint echoes of Genesis:

---

[1]   Gruen, *Diaspora*, 187.

– ὁ ὕψιστος as a divine title, vv. 2, 3 (on Abraham's lips), 8; cf. Gen 14:14,
  18, 19, 22 (on Abraham's lips)
– Abraham falls down (ἔπεσεν ἐπὶ πρόσωπον), v. 1; he rises and falls
  down again in v. 2 (Ἀβραὰμ ἀναστὰς προσέπεσεν); cf. Gen 17:3 (ἔπεσεν
  ἐπὶ πρόσωπον), 17 (ἔπεσεν ἐπὶ πρόσωπον); 22:7 (ἀναστὰς δὲ Ἀβραὰμ
  προσεκύνησεν)
– Abraham addresses God as δέσποτα κύριε in both v. 6 and Gen 15:8

On the other hand, the patriarch's prayer in vv. 4–6, like Jonah 2:2–9 and
so many other Jewish prayers,[2] is built largely out of traditional phrases
(marked by italics): "*Lord, lord* (this address appears often in LXX
prayers[3]), every task and word which I have asked of you, you have done,
and *you have given to me according to my heart and have fulfilled all my
will* (so LXX Ps 19:5, with the second person instead of the first). And now
Lord, I do not resist your might, for I know that I will not be immortal but
mortal. Since then at your command *all things* submit and *shudder and
tremble before your power* (this is from *Pr. Man.* 4), I too am afraid. *One
more request I* nonetheless *request of you* (these words appear in 3 Βασ
2:16, 20). *And now, Master Lord* (so LXX Jdt 5:20; Jonah 4:3; Dan 9:15),
hear my prayer" (from LXX Ps 27:2; 60:2). With the exception of 3 Βασ
2:16 and 2:20, all of the texts just cited belong to LXX prayers; and 3 Βασ
2:16 and 2:20 record a request made of a king.

In RecLng. 9:1–2, Michael summarizes God's speech in chap. 8. Because RecShrt. lacks that speech, it also naturally lacks any summary of it.
For the rest, however, RecShrt. 7:19–8:2 (both families) is not far from
RecLng. 9. Both recensions contain Abraham's request, Michael's delivery
of that request to God, and God's acquiescence. But there are differences:
(a) Abraham's speech is much longer in RecLng. because it responds to
God's speech in chap. 8. (b) RecShrt. 7:19 fam. E alone speaks of the κτῆμα
ὅλον ἔκτισεν ὁ κύριος, with which one may compare Mark 13:19: ἀρχῆς
κτίσεως ἣν ἔκτισεν ὁ θεός. (c) Only in RecShrt. does Michael respond to
Abraham. He confess that he has no say in the matter and can only report
to God: "This is not for me to do" (7:20 fam. E) or "Of myself I am not
able to do this" (fam. B F G). (d) RecShrt. says nothing about the "cloud
of light" (although note RecShrt. 12:1), an angelic escort, or "the cherubic
chariot." (e) The same things are referred to in different words; for exam-

---

[2]   Judith H. Newman, *Praying by the Book: The Scripturalization of Prayer in Second
      Temple Judaism* (SBLEJL 14; Atlanta: Scholars Press, 1999).
[3]   LXX Deut 3:24; 9:26; Judg A 6:22, 28; 3 Βασ 8:53; 1 Chr 17:24; Est 4:17b; 2 Macc
      1:24; *3 Macc.* 2:2; Ps 68:7; 108:21; 129:3; 139:8; 140:8; Amos 7:2, 5; Jer 28:62;
      Ezek 21:5.

ple, RecLng. speaks of "the Commander-in-chief," RecShrt. of "Michael," and only the former speaks of Abraham seeing τὴν οἰκουμένην (RecShrt. E 7:19 has κτῆμα).

9:1. Michael comes to Abraham for the third time. As in 2:1, a participle (λαβών) + "the Commander-in-chief" + κατῆλθε + πρὸς τὸν Ἀβραάμ describes the angel's descent. Similar language also appears in 1:4; 4:10; 5:1; and 16:5 and helps unify the narrative. παραινέσεις (LXX: Wis 8:9) = "address" is apt given that the speech in chap. 8 is full of gnomic wisdom (cf. Aristotle, *Rhet.* 2.21). The narrator refers to God with the superlative, "the Most High" (τοῦ ὑψίστου), an appellation that recurs in vv. 2, 3, 8; 14:9; 15:11, 13; 16:1, 6, 9. The title was used of pagan deities, and there was a far-flung cult of the Most High God.[4] In the LXX, ὁ ὕψιστος often translates עֶלְיוֹן, and ὁ ὕψιστος becomes popular in Greek Jewish texts; see Gk. fr. *1 En.* 9:3; 10:1; *Sib. Or.* 3:574, 580; Philo, *Legat.* 278; *T. Sim.* 2:5; 6:7; *T. Levi* 5:1; *Jos. Asen.* 9:1; Josephus, *Ant.* 16.163; etc. And it appears on Jewish inscriptions and epitaphs: *CIJ* 690, 1433, 1443; *JIGRE* 9, 22 105.[5] ὁ θεὸς ὁ ὕψιστος (cf. 14:9; 15:11; 16:9) occurs four times in the LXX version of the encounter between Abraham and Melchizedek, once on Abraham's lips (Gen 14:14, 18, 19, 22), which makes it fitting here. "The Most High" is less characteristic of Christian texts, although the New Testament has it nine times (seven in Luke-Acts). On Abraham as δίκαιος see on 1:1. The narrator's use of "just" (cf. v. 2) here is striking given the patriarch's rebuff of Michael. Readers may infer that Abraham's fear of death does not make him unrighteous.

When Abraham falls upon his face (ἔπεσεν ἐπὶ πρόσωπον), as he will again in v. 2 and 18:10 (with ἐπὶ τὴν γῆν), one is reminded of 3:6, where Isaac bows before Michael; of Gen 17:3 and 17, where, as here, Abraham falls down twice and ἔπεσεν ἐπὶ πρόσωπον is used; of Gen 18:2, where Abraham prostrates himself before three visiting angels; of *Apoc. Abr.* 10:2, which recounts that Abraham "fell face down upon the earth"; and

---

4   See Irina Levinskaya, *The Book of Acts in its First Century Setting*, vol. 5: *Diaspora Setting* (Grand Rapids: Eerdmans, 1996), 83–95 (arguing that its prevalence has been much exaggerated) and esp. Stephen Mitchell, "The Cult of Theos Hypsistos between Pagans, Jews, and Christians," in *Pagan Monotheism in Late Antiquity* (ed. Polymnia Athanassiadi and Michael Frede; Oxford: Clarendon, 1999), 81–148 (arguing for the difficulty of distinguishing between Jewish and pagan inscriptions with Theos Hypsistos).

5   In addition to Levinskaya, *Acts*, 95–97, and Mitchell, "Theos Hypsistos" (Egyptian examples on p. 146), see Paul Trebilco, *Jewish Communities in Asia Minor* (SNTSMS 69; Cambridge: Cambridge University Press, 1991), 127–45.

of the many other ancient texts in which people fall down before angels (see on 3:6). "The ground of the earth" (τὸ ἔδαφος τῆς γῆς, contrast τὸν αἰθέρα τοῦ οὐρανοῦ in v. 8) occurs in LXX Jer 38:35 (= MT 31:37 for מוסדי־ארץ) and elsewhere (cf. Diodorus Siculus 34/35.4 [ῥίψαντες ἑαυτοὺς εἰς ἔδαφος τήν τε γῆν]; Ps.-Callisthenes, *Hist. Alex. Magn.* rec. F 66.28 [ἐπροσκύνησεν τὸν ἕως ἐδάφους τῆς γῆς]; John Malalas, *Chron.*, ed. Dindorf, pp. 409.5; 419.11); and πίπτω + (εἰς) τὸ ἔδαφος is a widespread idiom: *4 Macc.* 6:7; Acts 22:7; Josephus, *Ant.* 10.126; Ps.-Callisthenes, *Hist. Alex. Magn.* rec. α 2.10; 3.1; *Acts John* 24; Procopius of Caesarea, *Bell.* 1.13.38; John Malalas, *Chron.*, ed. Dindorf, 230.20 (πεσόντες εἰς τὸ ἔδαφος τῆς γῆς). "As though dead" (ὡς νεκρός) is stereotypical language for an angelology (cf. Matt 28:4; Rev 1:17 ["I fell at his feet ὡς νεκρός"]; *4 Ezra* 10:30; note also *T. Job* 30:2). The expression underlines Abraham's sincerity: he really is, despite all his boldness, afraid. It also signals the potential danger of communicating with the Deity (Exod 20:19; Deut 5:24–27; *Exod. Rab.* 29:4).

9:2. The Commander-in-chief communicates to Abraham all that he has heard from "the Most High" (see on v. 1). The verse borrows words from v. 1 and repeats them in the same order:

v. 1	ὁ ἀρχιστράτηγος	τοῦ ὑψίστου	δίκαιος	ἔπεσεν
v. 2	ὁ ἀρχιστράτηγος	τοῦ ὑψίστου	δίκαιος	προσέπεσεν

The narrator chooses to summarize—πάντα ὅσα ἤκουσεν—rather than repeat (cf. v. 7). Abraham is called "just" (δίκαιος; see on v. 1) again as well as "pious" (ὅσιος; see on 1:2). His disobedience has not changed his status before God.

Abraham, who has fallen down and become as though dead (v. 1), now rises up (ἀναστάς; cf. 18:10; the LXX uses the word of Abraham in Gen 13:17; 21:14; 22:3; 23:3, 7), only to fall down again, this time at the feet of "the incorporeal," προσέπεσεν τοῖς ποσὶν τοῦ ἀσωμάτου; see on 3:6, where the same phrase occurs. The sequence, which moves Abraham toward Michael and shows us that the former, despite his disobedience, knows his place, reappears in 18:10, with similar vocabulary, only there the patriarch falls at the feet of Death:

9:2		οὖν ...	Ἀβραὰμ ἀναστὰς	προσέπεσεν
18:10	ἀναστὰς οὖν		Ἀβραὰμ	ἔπεσεν

Also similar is LXX Gen 23:7: ἀναστὰς δὲ Ἀβραὰμ προσεκύνησεν.

When Abraham prostrates himself at the angel's feet (cf. *Jos. Asen.* 14:10; Rev 1:17; 19:10; 22:8), he shows his emotion "with many tears," μετὰ πολλῶν δακρύων, a common phrase: 14:12; Plato, *Apol.* 34C; Plutarch, *Demetr. Ant.* 38.7; Josephus, *Ant.* 7.203; Ps.-Callisthenes, *Hist. Alex.*

Magn. rec. α 1.46; etc. Readers may recall 3:9, where Abraham weeps as he washes Michael's feet. Despite his fear and humility, the weeping Abraham does not surrender his will. He instead begins to make supplication, ἱκέτευεν αὐτόν; cf. v. 3 (ἱκέτην); 15:4 (τοῖς ποσὶν τοῦ ἀσωμάτου ἱκετεύουσα—of Sarah); LXX Ps 36:7 (ἱκέτευσον αὐτόν); 2 Macc 11:6; Philo, *Cher.* 47; Josephus, *Ant.* 3.6; *T. Sol.* 13:7; *1 Clem.* 7:7. Of 10 LXX occurrences of ἱκετεύω, half are in 2, 3, 4 Maccabees.

9:3. Abraham petitions (δέομαί σου, as in 14:10; 17:6, 9; 18:1, 9; 20:1; LXX Num 12:32; *T. Job* 3:6; *T. Jos.* 13:2; *3 Bar.* 2:4; etc.) Michael, here styled "the Commander-in-chief of the upper powers," τῶν ἄνω δυνάμεων (LXX: 0; NT: 0; Josephus: 0); cf. 14:12; Philo, *Sacr.* 59 (in Genesis 18 Abraham entertains God and two τῶν ἀνωτάτων δυνάμεων); *Gos. Bart.* 4.29 (Μιχαὴλ τὸν ἀρχιστράτηγον τῶν ἄνω δυνάμεων); Chrysostom, *Int. Dan.* PG 56.243 (Michael is τῶν ἄνω δυνάμεων); *Apoc. BMV* 22 (Μιχαὴλ ὁ μέγας ἀρχιστράτηγος τῶν ἄνω δυνάμεων); Nicephorus Bryennius, *Hist.* 4.3.23 (τοῦ ταξιάρχου τῶν ἄνω δυνάμεων Μιχαήλ); George Acropolites, *Ann.* 22.13; 88.5 (τοῦ ἀρχιστρατήγου τῶν ἄνω δυνάμεων ἐγκαθίδρυται Μιχαήλ). These powers are the angels in heaven; cf. *1 En.* 18:4; 61:1; *T. Jud.* 25:2; *Mart. Pol.* 14:1; Justin, *Dial.* 85.6; *Acts John* 104; Antonius the Hagiographer, *Vit. Symeonis Stylitis* 13; Lampe, s.v., ἄνω, B3. Already the LXX regularly translates "Lord of Hosts" (יהוה צבאות)—which came to be understood as "Lord of heavenly beings"—with κύριος τῶν δυνάμεων. Rabbis later spoke of "the upper hosts," צבא של מעלה as in *Cant. Rab.* 2:7.

Michael, according to Abraham, has not deemed it altogether unworthy (ἀπηξίωσας; ἀπαξιόω*: cf. Philo, *Spec. leg.* 1.308; Josephus, *Ant.* 15.193) to come to him "daily," καθεκάστην. LSJ, s.v., has no entry for καθέκαστον* (LXX: 0; Philo: 0; NT: 0; Josephus: 0). Although the word appears in Alexander of Aphrodisias, Ἠθικὰ προβλήματα, ed. Bruns, p. 128.20, it is known from patristic texts (Lampe, s.v.) and is common in Byzantine literature: Theodore the Studite, *Ep.*, ed. Fatouros 32.44; Michael Psellus, *Or. paneg.*, ed. Dennis 3.34; Constantine VII, *Cer.*, ed. Reiske, p. 632.17; etc. The patriarch recognizes that before Michael he is unworthy, ἀνάξιον (ἀνάξιος*; cf. LXX Est 8:13; Jer 15:19; Ecclus 25:8), a "supplicant" (ἱκέτην; cf. v. 2 [ἱκέτευεν]; 2:5) who is a "sinner" (ἁμαρτωλόν); cf. Gk. *L.A.E.* 42:6: ἀναξίαν καὶ ἁμαρτωλήν. ἁμαρτωλός (cf. *TA* 10:13–15; 11:11; 12:10; 13:3, 9, 12; 14:11; 17:8) in the LXX most often renders רשע. Whether Abraham denigrates himself generally or refers particularly to his recent disobedience of Michael is unclear. In either case it is tradition for the righteous humbly to confess their unworthiness and sinfulness; cf. 1QH 12(4):29–35; Luke

3:16; 1 Cor 15:9–10; 1 Tim 1:15. Yet Abraham's conventional confession seems to be countered by the divine voice in 10:13–14, which emphatically declares that he "has not sinned" (contrast the conviction that all human beings have sinned—1 Kgs 8:46; Ecclus 8:5; Rom 3:9–18; *4 Ezra* 8:35; etc.).

Abraham implores (παρακαλῶ; see on 7:6) the Commander-in-chief to serve him (διακονῆσαι; διακονέω*) "yet once more" (ἔτι ἅπαξ; see on 8:4; Abraham uses the expression in LXX Gen 18:32, at the end of his pleading for Sodom) before "the Most High," τὸν ὕψιστον (see on v. 1).

9:4. Abraham enjoins Michael to address God with τάδε λέγει ὁ Ἀβραάμ. The words, which show that the humble speaker (cf. v. 3) is also bold with God, recall 8:5 (q.v. for the idiom). There indeed seems to be a deliberate correlation:

8:4–5   God to Michael for Abraham
                    πρός ... ἔτι ἅπαξ
                         καὶ εἰπὲ αὐτόν
                              τάδε λέγει ὁ θεός σου

9:3–4   Abraham to Michael for God
                    ἔτι ἅπαξ ... πρός
                         καὶ ἐρεῖς αὐτῷ
                              τάδε λέγει ὁ Ἀβραάμ

Abraham addresses the Most High as "Lord, Lord" (see on 4:6), and his prayer emphasizes his submission to God by using "Lord" and "Master"— 4: κύριε κύριε; 5: κύριε; 6a: δέσποτα κύριε; 6b: δέσποτα.

Abraham concedes, in response to 8:5–7, that God has heretofore granted all his wishes. The concession is expressed in three different ways. First, Abraham allows that "every task (ἐν παντὶ ἔργῳ; cf. LXX Exod 31:3; Deut 2:7; Ecclus 32:23; etc.) and word (ἐν παντὶ ἔργῳ καὶ λόγῳ; cf. Plato, *Resp.* 382E; Ecclus 3:8; Luke 24:19; 2 Thess 2:17; *T. Gad* 6:1; Ps.-Ignatius, *Mar.* 5) which I have asked of you (ὃ ᾐτησάμην παρὰ σοῦ; cf. 8:7: ὅσα ἂν αἰτήσῃς παρ᾽ ἐμοῦ; LXX Prov 30:7: αἰτοῦμαι παρὰ σοῦ), you have done." Second, he allows that God has "given to me (ἔδωκάς μοι; cf. 8:7: δώσω σοι) according to my heart"—words that have a scriptural ring:

TA 9:4   ἔδωκάς μοι   κατὰ τῆς καρδίας μου
Judg 1:15   ἔδωκεν αὐτῇ ... κατὰ τὴν καρδίαν αὐτῆς
LXX Ps 19:5   δῴη   σοι   κατὰ τὴν καρδίαν σου
Jer 3:15   δώσω ὑμῖν ... κατὰ τὴν καρδίαν μου

Finally, Abraham says that God has "fulfilled all my will" (see below). The verbal links with 8:7 make it clear that the patriarch has listened to God's address through Michael and is responding accordingly.

"And fulfilled all my will" (cf. 15:12; 20:3) is very close to the second line of Psalm 20:4, just as "you have given to me according to my heart" is very close the first line of Psalm 20:4:

TA 9:4   ἔδωκάς μοι κατὰ τῆς καρδίας μου
             καὶ πᾶσαν τὴν βουλήν μου ἐπλήρωσας
LXX Ps 19:5 δῴη   σοι κατὰ τὴν καρδίαν σου
             καὶ πᾶσαν τὴν βουλήν σου πληρῶσαι

So Abraham, in addressing God, rewrites a line from a Psalm that is true to his experience.

9:5. Abraham continues his prayer with καὶ νῦν κύριε, a formula occurring 20 times in the LXX, most often in Kings: 3 Βασ 3:7; 8:25, 26; 4 Βασ 19:19; etc. That he does not "resist" (ἀνθίσταμαι) God's "might" (τὸ σὸν κράτος, as in 3 Macc. 6:5) is also traditional language; cf. Wis 11:21 ("Who can withstand [ἀντιστήσεται] the might [κράτει] of your arm?") and 1 Clem. 27:5 ("Who will resist [ἀντιστήσεται] the might [κράτει] of his strength?"; does this allude to Wis 11:21?). In its present context, Abraham's assertion that he does not resist refers back to 8:8, where ἀνθίστημι appears twice— "Why have you resisted me?" and "Why have you resisted my messenger?" Again Abraham is telling God that he has heard him—although here he disagrees with God's assessment of the situation. But this disagreement is followed immediately by concession. With reference to God's words in 8:9, Abraham allows (κἀγὼ γινώσκω, as in John 10:15, 27; the formulation is rare outside of patristic quotations of John) that he is indeed mortal, not immortal (ἀθάνατος, an appellation properly reserved for God: 8:3; 15:15; 16:2; 17:4).

Abraham's mortality puts him on the side of the rest of creation, which at God's command (τῇ σῇ προστάξει; cf. 3:3; Job 39:27; 4 Ezra 8:22; Athanasius, Apol. Const. 24.26) submits, ὑπείκεται (ὑπείκω*: cf. 4 Macc. 6:35; Philo, Mos. 1.156 [ταῖς προστάξεσιν ὑπεῖκον]; Heb 13:17; T. Sol. 12:1 C). Further, everything shudders, φρίττει; cf. 16:3; Theod. Dan 7:5; Jas 2:19; Sib. Or. 3:679; Justin, Dial. 49.8 ("before whom [Christ] the demons and all the principalities and authorities of the earth shudder," φρίσσει); Clement of Alexandria, Strom. 5.125.1 (citing an Orphic fragment). Everything also, at God's power (ἀπὸ προσώπου δυνάμεως; cf. LXX Jer 42:11; Gos. Bart. fr. 1:19; Eusebius, Comm. Ps. PG 23.684), trembles, τρέμει. For τρέμω with φρίσσω see 16:3; Ezek. Trag. in Eusebius, Praep. ev. 9.29; T. Sol. 2:1; Acts Phil. 1:32 ("God, before whom all the aeons shudder [φρίττουσιν] ... principalities and powers of the heavenly places tremble [τρέμουσιν] before you"). The thought is parallel to Nah 1:5: "the mountains quake before him, and the hills melt; the earth heaves before him, the world and all who live in it." But the language is even closer to *Pr. Man.* 4, which appears to be quoted here as well as in *Gk. Apoc. Ezra* 7:7; *Apos. Con.* 8:7:5; and Ps.-Chrysostom, *Prec.* PG 64.1065:

Pr. Man. 4	ὃν πάντα φρίττει καὶ τρέμει
	ἀπὸ προσώπου δυνάμεώς σου
TA 9:5	πάντα ... φρίττει καὶ τρέμει
	ἀπὸ προσώπου δυνάμεώς σου
Gk. Apoc. Ezra 7:7	ὃν πάντα φρίττει καὶ τρέμει
	ἀπὸ προσώπου δυνάμεώς σου
Apos. Con. 8:7:5	ὃν φρίττει καὶ τρέμει πάντα
	ἀπὸ προσώπου δυνάμεώς σου
Ps.-Chrysostom, *Prec.* PG 64.1065	ὃν πάντα φρίττει καὶ τρέμει
	ἀπὸ προσώπου δυνάμεώς σου

Didymus of Alexandria, *Trin.* PG 39.908B, attributes the line to "a holy man."

Before God, Abraham is, like the rest of creation, afraid: κἀγὼ δέδοικα (δείδω*); cf. *Jos. Asen.* 26:1 and Ps.-Socrates, *Ep.* 6 10 (κἀγὼ δέδοικα). Notwithstanding this, he is bold enough to make another request, μίαν αἴτησιν αἰτοῦμαι παρὰ σοῦ; so too *Apoc. BMV* 25, the context being Mary making a request of Michael on her tour of hell and heaven. Both αἰτέω + αἴτησις (cf. LXX Deut 10:12; 2 Βασ 3:13; Prov 30:7) and αἰτέω + παρὰ σοῦ (LXX Judg 8:24; 3 Βασ 3:5; 12:24; Theod. Dan 6:8) are biblical. Once again, however, Abraham borrows from a particular LXX text, this time 3 Βασ 2:16 and 20, where Adonijah asks of Solomon through Bathsheba to have Abishag for his wife:

T. Abr. 9:5	καὶ νῦν ... μίαν αἴτησιν	αἰτοῦμαι παρὰ σοῦ
3 Βασ 2:16	καὶ νῦν	αἴτησιν μίαν ἐγὼ αἰτοῦμαι παρὰ σοῦ
3 Βασ 2:20		αἴτησιν μίαν ἐγὼ αἰτοῦμαι παρὰ σοῦ

Perhaps the line from Kings suggested itself because there too a request is made through an intermediary.

9:6. Abraham prefaces his request with καὶ νῦν (as in v. 5, q.v.) + δέσποτα κύριε (see on 1:4 for δεσπότης). In the LXX, καὶ νῦν appears immediately before δέσποτα κύριε in prayers to God in LXX Jdt 5:20; Jonah 4:3; and Dan 9:15, so their combination has a biblical ring. Cf. also Cyril of Scythopolis, *Vit. Joannis Hesychastae*, ed. Schwartz, p. 208.6. One should also note that Abraham addresses God as δέσποτα κύριε in Gen 15:8 (for אֲדֹנָי יהוה, and the double title also appears in LXX Jdt 11:10; Isa 1:24; 3:1; 10:33; Jer 1:6; 4:10; Josephus, *Ant.* 20.90; *Gk. Apoc. Ezra* 5:6, 16, 26 and very often in the Christian liturgies: *Apos. Con.* 7:34:7; Epiphanius, *Liturg. praesanctificatorum* 2.29, 69; *Liturg. Greg. Naz.* PG 36.700B;

701A–B; 725A; 729A; Basil the Great, *Liturg.* PG 31.1636B; 1644D; etc. "Hear my prayer" (εἰσάκουσον τῆς δεήσεώς μου; cf. 14:10) is likewise biblical and liturgical; see LXX Est 4:17 (ἐπάκουσον τῆς δεήσεώς μου); Ps 27:2 (εἰσάκουσον ... τῆς δεήσεώς μου); 60:2 (εἰσάκουσον ... τῆς δεήσεώς μου); Jdt 9:12 (εἰσάκουσον τῆς δεήσεώς μου); cf. also Ps.-Callisthenes, *Hist. Alex. Magn.* recs. E F 107.3; *Prot. Jas.* 5:12 (δεσπότην ... ἐπάκουσον τῆς δεήσεώς μου); *Liturg. Greg. Naz.* PG 36.700D (δέσποτα ... κύριε, ἐπάκουσον τῆς δεήσεώς μου).

While yet in his body (ἔτι ἐν τούτῳ τῷ σώματι ὤν; cf. Philo, *Somn.* 1.232 [ἔτι ἐν σώματι]; 2 Cor 5:6; 12:3), Abraham wants to see "all the inhabited earth," πᾶσαν τὴν οἰκουμένην; cf. vv. 7, 8; 10:1, 12; Philo, *Deus immut.* 175; Luke 2:1; 4:5 (the devil shows Jesus "all the kingdoms τῆς οἰκουμένης"); Josephus, *Bell.* 7.43; *Acts Paul* 9:5. ὅλη is more usual with οἰκουμένη* (LXX: 0) in the New Testament but not Philo. "All the inhabited earth" is in this context roughly synonymous with "all the things made," τὰ ποιήματα πάντα; cf. Athanasius, *C. Ar.* PG 26.452C; Didymus of Alexandria, *Comm. Eccl.* 25.10. Because the latter phrase is redundant it is not repeated in vv. 7, 8; 10:1, 12.

Abraham's request to see "all the world" is ultimately based upon traditions about Moses, which Jewish hearers would probably have here recalled. For legend took the old story that Moses, at the end of his life, went to the top of Pisgah, looked in all directions, and saw the land he would not enter (Num 27:12–14; Deut 3:27; 32:48–52; 34:1–4), and much expanded it, making it a vision of most or all of creation: *L.A.B.* 19:10; *Sifre* Deut. 357; *Mek.* on Exod 17:14 (which compares Abraham's vision in Genesis 13 with Moses' vision on Nebo); etc. The dependence of *TA* upon this legend is established not only by the reliance of our book's plot upon legends about Moses' death (see the Introduction, pp. 24–27) but also by the *Apocalypse of Abraham.* Its chap. 12 opens by moving Sinai motifs to the life of Abraham (e.g., he fasts forty days and nights on Horeb), and it closes with an event recollective of Moses' experience on Nebo, as recounted by later legend: Abraham's angelic guide and interpreter promises the patriarch a universal vision: "I will ascend on the wings of the birds to show you what is in the heavens, on the earth and in the sea, in the abyss, and in the lower depths, in the garden of Eden and in its rivers, in the fullness of the universe" (cf. 21:1). Just as the *Apocalypse of Abraham* moves the motif of a worldwide vision from the life of Moses to that of Abraham, so too *TA.* Q 4:4 and Matt 4:8–9 do the same thing for Jesus, and 2 *Baruch* 76 does it for Baruch.[6]

6 See Allison, *New Moses*, 65–68, 170–71.

According to *L.A.B.* 18:5, God lifted Abraham "above the firmament and showed him the arrangements of all the stars." Other sources relate that Abraham beheld both the future and Gehenna during the covenant ceremony in Genesis 15: *L.A.B.* 23:6; *4 Ezra* 3:13–15; *Apoc. Abr.* 9:10; Tgs. Neof. 1 and Ps.-Jn. on Gen 15:17; *Midr. Ps.* 16:7; cf. *2 Bar.* 4:4. Moreover, *Apoc. Abr.* 15:1–5 turns the experience of Genesis 15 into a heavenly ascent; cf. *Gen. Rab.* 44:12. Already 1QapGen 21:8–14 puts it on a mountain. So *L.A.B.* 18:5 probably has Genesis 15 and traditions surrounding it in mind. Perhaps the same is true of *Gen. Rab.* 62:2, which includes Abraham among the righteous who see the world to come before they go there. In any case, *TA* did not invent the idea of a heavenly ascent and vision of Abraham, which may have been exegetically grounded in Gen 15:5 ("He brought him outside and said, 'Look at the stars,'" cited in *Gen. Rab.* 44:12, which takes "Look at" to mean "Look down" and infers that God raised Abraham above the firmament) and 18:17 ("Shall I hide from Abraham what I am about to do?," which *L.A.B.* 18:5 cites). Under the inspiration of traditions about Moses, *TA* has moved Abraham's universal vision from the middle of his life to the end.

The idea that one might see all of the world from a lofty location appears often in old sources; cf. the tale about Etana, a king of Kish carried to heaven by an eagle;[7] Plato, *Phaedr.* 247C ("Immortals stand on the outer surface of heaven and gaze on the eternal scene"); *1 En.* 87:3–4; Ovid, *Metam.* 12.39–42 ("There is a place in the middle of the world, between land and sea and sky, the meeting point of the three-fold universe. From this place, whatever is, however far away, is seen"); Dio Chrysostom, *2 Fort.* 14 ("If someone should raise me aloft and transport me through the sky, either, as it were, on the back of some Pegasus or in some winged car [ἁρμάτων] of Pelops, offering me the whole earth and its cities ..."); Lucian, *Icar.* (Menippus soars aloft on wings to see creation); *Acts Paul* 13 ("from heaven I looked down upon earth, and I saw the whole world"); *Gen. Rab.* 19:3 (God shows the newly-created Adam the whole world); Ps.-Callisthenes, *Hist. Alex. Magn.* rec. β 2.41 (the legend of Alexander the Great's celestial journey; *y. 'Abod. Zar.* 3:1 knows this legend).[8]

"All the things made" have been "established through one word," διὰ λόγου ἑνὸς συνεστήσας. For συνίστημι* of God creating see Gk. fr. *1 En.* 101:6; Philo, *Leg. all.* 3.10; Josephus, *Ant.* 12.22 (with ἅπαντα as object);

---

7   Stephen Langdon, *The Legend of Etana and the Eagle* (Paris: P. Geuthner, 1932).
8   On Alexander's ascent see Gabriel Millet, "L'Ascension d'Alexandre," *Syria* 4 (1923) 85–133; Ian Michael, *Alexander's Flying Machine: The History of a Legend* (Southampton: University of South Hampton, 1975).

and *1 Clem.* 27:4 (ἐν λόγῳ συνεστήσατο τὰ πάντα). The idea of creation through one word is conventional. That God spoke things into being already appears in Genesis (1:3, 6, 9, etc.); cf. Ps 33:6 (LXX 32:6: τῷ λόγῳ τοῦ κυρίου οἱ οὐρανοὶ ἐστερεώθησαν); Wis 9:1 (ὁ ποιήσας τὰ πάντα ἐν λόγῳ σου); *Jub.* 12:4. Later texts sometimes reduce the divine speech to one word, e.g., *Sib. Or.* 3:20 (ὃς λόγῳ ἔκτισε πάντα) and Philo, *Fug.* 95 (ὁ ποιῶν λόγῳ τὸν κόσμον); cf. *4 Ezra* 6:43; *Apoc. Abr.* 22:2; *Poimandres* 31; *3 En.* 40:4 (Schäfer, *Synopse* 58 = 924: creation of angels "with one word"); Timothy of Alexandria, *Discourse on Abbaton*, ed. Budge, fol. 9a. Despite *m.* '*Abot* 5:1, which says that God made the world with ten words, other rabbinic texts know of creation through a single word. Some adopt this idea to stress how effortless the creative task was (e.g. *Gen. Rab.* 12:10). Others make it clear that the single word must have been יהוה or one of its letters (*y. Ḥag.* 2:1; *b. Menaḥ.* 29b); cf. *Jub.* 36:7.

Abraham's bargain is that, once he has seen everything, he will leave life, μετέλθω τοῦ βίου (μετέρχομαι*: LXX: Wis 14:30; 1 Macc 15:4; *4 Macc.* 10:21; 18:22; cf. Demetrius the Chronographer in Eusebius, *Praep. ev.* 9.21.16, of Abraham migrating to Canaan). The patriarch will depart, he claims, untroubled, ἄλυπος* (LXX: 0; Philo, *Cher.* 86; Phil 2:28; Justin, *Dial.* 117.3; *Acts John* 106; Ps.-Callisthenes, *Hist. Alex. Magn.* rec. α 1.33; *BGU* 246.17). The word is common on Jewish epitaphs with the meaning, "who caused pain to none": *CIJ* 1494, 1514, etc.; cf. Lampe, s.v., 3. Just possibly that is the meaning here: Abraham will cause Michael or God no more grief.

9:7. The Commander-in-chief, doing Abraham's bidding, leaves him again and stands "before" (ἔστη ἐνώπιον; see on 4:5) τοῦ ἀοράτου πατρός. "The invisible Father" reappears in 16:3 and 4 (cf. ἀφανής in 8:1, of Michael becoming invisible). In 16:3 the title immediately follows ἔστη ἐνώπιον, as here, although there Death is the subject. The correlation adds to the extensive parallelism between the encounters of Abraham and Michael on the one hand and the encounters of Abraham and Death on the other. "The invisible Father" is a variant of the well-known "the invisible God." Neither appears in the LXX, although ἀόρατος occurs in Gen 1:2; Isa 45:3; 2 Macc 9:5. For "the invisible God" see 16:3–4; Diodorus Siculus 2.21.7; Philo, *Cher.* 101; *Quaest. Exod.* 2.37; Col 1:15; 1 Tim 1:17; Gk. *L.A.E.* 35:3; *2 Clem.* 20:5; Clement of Alexandria, *Strom.* 4.25.155; Ps.-Clem. *Hom.* 3:36; Eusebius, *Praep. ev.* 3.13.22; *PGM* 5.123; etc. The "invisible Father" recurs in *Acts Thom.* 39; Athanasius, *Inc.* 54; *Ep. Serap.* 4 PG 26.640D; Ps.-Athanasius, *Contra Sabellianos* PG 28.100B; Epiphanius, *Anc.* 32.3.3; Ps.-Gregory of Nyssa, *Contra Arium et Sabellium*, ed. Mueller,

p. 73.21; *Apoc. BMV* 26 (3x), 28 (2x); etc. Philo, *Abr.* 75 ("The primal God and Father of all, who is invisible," ἀειδής) and John 1:18 ("No one has seen God at any time") summarize much Jewish tradition; cf. Exod 33:18; Deut 4:12; *1 En.* 14:21; Orphica in Ps.-Justin, *Mon.* 2; Philo, *Mos.* 2.65; Josephus, *Bell.* 7.346; Clement of Alexandria, *Protr.* 6.68.3; *Apos. Con.* 7:35:9; 8:5:1; 8:15:8; *Lev. Rab.* 4:8; the targums on Gen 28:12; etc.; contrast Isa 6:5; Matt 18:10. Genesis says on more than one occasion that God "appeared" (LXX: ὤφθη) to Abraham (12:7; 17:1; 18:1). Some Jews would have understood this literally, others would not have so understood it. For God as "father" in Jewish texts see Deut 32:6; 2 Sam 7:14; Ps 68:6; *Jub.* 1:24, 28; 19:29; Tob 13:4; Wis 2:16; 11:10; 14:3; Ecclus 51:10; 4Q372 1 16; 4Q460 5 6; *3 Macc.* 5:7; 6:3; 7:6; *T. Job* 33:3, 9; 52:12 v.l.; *T. Jud.* 24:2; *T. Levi* 18:6; *m. Ber.* 5:1; *b. Ta'an.* 23b; etc. Yet the title is here from a Christian hand, for ἀόρατος πατήρ seems confined to Christian texts, and everywhere else in RecLng.—6:6 v.l.; 16:3 v.l.; 20:12, 13, 15— "Father" of God is Christian.[9]

When Michael relates Abraham's message to God, he inserts ὁ φίλος σου (see on 1:4 and 8:2) into v. 4's τάδε λέγει (see on 8:5) ὁ Ἀβραάμ, and the remainder of Michael's sentence fails to reproduce Abraham's words precisely. ἤθελον θεάσασθαι replaces θέλω ἰδεῖν, and ἐν τῇ ζωῇ μου πρὸ τοῦ ἀποθανεῖν (cf. 5:13; 9:7) με (cf. *T. Jud.* 1:1: πρὸ τοῦ ἀποθανεῖν αὐτόν) substitutes for ἔτι ἐν τούτῳ τῷ σώματι ὤν. For the rest, most of Abraham's words in vv. 4–6 are not quoted. Hearers may assume that the narrator is simply summarizing what Michael said (cf. v. 2), or perhaps that God, knowing all, need not be informed anyway. In either case, the language recalls 8:1–2:

8:1–2   ὁ δὲ ἀρχιστράτηγος ... ἀνῆλθεν ...
        καὶ ἔστη ἐνώπιον τοῦ θεοῦ
        καὶ ἀνήγγειλεν πάντα
        λέγει ὁ φίλος σου Ἀβραὰμ ὅτι

9:7   ἀπῆλθεν ὁ ἀρχιστράτηγος ...
        καὶ ἔστη ἐνώπιον τοῦ ... πατρός
        καὶ ἀνήγγειλεν ... πάντα
        λέγει ὁ φίλος σου Ἀβραὰμ ὅτι

9:8. "The Most High" (ὁ ὕψιστος; see on v. 1), upon hearing Michael, commands him to take "a cloud of light" (νεφέλην φωτός) along with the angels that are in charge of the chariots, ἐπὶ τῶν ἁρμάτων τὴν ἐξουσίαν

---

[9]   For another opinion see Strotmann, *"Mein Vater"*, 209–24, who thinks most of these are Jewish.

ἔχοντας. 10:1 will inform us that the number of these angels is sixty. For God's many chariots see 2 Kgs 6:17; Ps 68:18; Isa 66:15; Hab 3:8; Zech 6:1–8; 4Q403 1 ii 15; 4Q405 20–21–22 ii 3–5, 11; 11QŠirŠabb 2–1–9 6; *3 Enoch* 24; 37:1; etc.; and for flying chariots that transport people to heaven see 2 Kgs 2:11–12 (the ascension of Elijah, to which there is no clear allusion here); *1 En.* 57:1–2; *Sib. Or.* 2:187; *Jos. Asen.* 17:7; *L.A.E.* 25:2–3; Gk. *L.A.E.* 33:2 (ἄρμα φωτός); *T. Job* 52:6, 10; *Vit. Proph. Elijah* 15; *Gk. Apoc. Ezra* 7:6; *3 En.* 6:1 (Schäfer, *Synopse* 9 = 890); Ovid, *Metam.* 8.816–828; *T. Isaac* 7:1. The "cloud of light" has parallels in Ezek 1:4 ("a great cloud with brightness round about it and fire flashing forth continually"); Matt 17:5 (νεφέλη φωτεινή); *Vit. Proph. Jeremiah* 14 ("a cloud as of fire"); *Apoc. Adam* 71.9–10 ("the cloud of great light"); 75.19–20 ("great clouds of light"); *Acts Pet. Andr.*, ed. Tischendorf, p. 162 (νεφέλη φωτεινή); *Syr. Apoc. Dan.* 28; Theodore the Studite, *Nativ. BMV* PG 96.681A (νεφέλη φωτός); cf. also the rabbinic עַמּוּדָא דְנוּרָא as in *b. Qidd.* 81a; *b. Ketub.* 17a; etc. Behind these texts is the image of the Shekinah, the bright or fiery cloud of glory which first appears in Exod 24:15–17; cf. 40:34–38; Ezek 10:4; 2 Macc 2:8; *ARN* A 1, 2. *TA* merges this image with the cloud as a means of transport, examples of which appear in RecShrt. 10:2; *1 En.* 14:8; Dan 7:13; Mark 14:62 par.; Acts 1:9; Rev 11:12; 14:14; *Ep. Apos.* 51 (a "bright cloud"); Ps.-Chrysostom, *De legislatore* PG 56.407; *Acts Andr. Mth.* 21; *Transitus Mariae* B 17; Vatican Gr. 1982, ed. Wenger, p. 240; *Adam, Eve and the Incarnation* 48 v.l.; Ps.-Bartholomew, *Book of the Resurrection of Jesus Christ*, ed. Budge, fol. 20b; Serapion, *Life of John*, trans. Mingana, p. 447; *Syr. Apoc. Dan.* 30; *b. Sanh.* 98a; *b. Yoma* 4a (Moses ascending to heaven on a cloud, as also in *Pesiq. Rab.* 20:4); and the liturgical and iconographic tradition that the apostles were miraculously brought on clouds to gather for the Dormition; cf. John of Thessalonica, *Dorm. BVM* A 7–8, ed. Jugie, pp. 386, 388–89, and esp. *Transitus Mariae*, StSin 11, ed. Lewis, p. 49, where the apostles travel on "chariots and clouds of light" (מרכבתא ועננא דנוהרא cf. pp. 50–54, 97, 102, 105).[10] Clouds are already linked with chariots in 2 Sam 22:11 = Ps 18:11 ("He rode on a cherub ... his canopy thick clouds") and 104:3 ("You make the clouds your chariot").

Michael is to descend and take Abraham the righteous (δίκαιον; see on 1:1) on "the cherubic chariot." τὸ ἄρμα τὸ χερουβικόν recalls 1 Chr 28:18 (LXX: τοῦ ἄρματος τῶν χερουβιν; MT: הַמֶּרְכָּבָה הַכְּרֻבִים) and Ecclus 49:8 (ἄρματος χερουβιν; the Hebrew is simply מרכבה); cf. also Ps 18:11 (quoted

---

[10] Clouds as means of transport continue to appear in Christian legends of the saints; see e.g. *Acta Sanctorum* Jan., 2.605 col. 2 (Cadocus); Mar., 3.215 col. 1 (Ambrose).

above); 4Q403 1 ii 15 ("chariots ... and their cherubim"); 4Q405 20–21–22 ii 3; Gk. *L.A.E.* 22:3 (ἅρματος χερουβίμ/ικοῦ); *3 En.* 22:11; 24:1; 37:1 (Schäfer, *Synopse* 34 = 869, 37 = 903, 55 = 921); *Orig. World* 105:1–4 ("a great throne on a four-faced chariot called 'Cherubim'"); Antonius the Hagiographer, *Vit. Symeonis Stylitis* 14 ("charioteer [ἡνίοχος] of the Cherubim"); *Coptic Apoc. Paul*, ed. Budge, 51; Ps.-Bartholomew, *Book of the Resurrection of Jesus Christ*, ed. Budge, fol. 3a (ⲍⲁⲣⲙⲁ ⲛ ⲡⲉⲭⲉⲣⲟⲩⲃⲉⲓⲛ); *Dorm. BMV* 38 (Χριστὸς καθήμενος ἐπὶ θρόνου χερουβίμ); *Apoc. BMV* 26 (τὸ ἅρμα τὸ χερουβικόν); Vatican Gr. 1982, ed. Wenger, p. 224 (τὸ ἅρμα τῶν χερουβίμ). Note also *Gk. Apoc. Ezra* 7:6: God, who "drives the Cherubim ... took Elijah to the heavens on a fiery chariot." This refers to the story in 2 Kings, which does not mention Cherubim. One may think of the cherubim either flanking or preceding the chariot (cf. *T. Isaac* 7:1) or of them supporting or drawing it (cf. Ezekiel 1). Michael is in either case to raise Abraham on high (ὕψωσον αὐτόν; cf. 10:1: ὕψωσεν αὐτόν), into the air of heaven, εἰς τὸν αἰθέρα τοῦ οὐρανοῦ, as in 10:1; cf. Maximus of Tyre, *Dialexeis* 39.4, and Porphyry, *Quaest. hom. Odd.* 15.13. See on 10:1 for the concept of αἰθήρ (cf. Philo, *Conf.* 156; Josephus, *Bell.* 6.47; LXX: 0; NT: 0). The purpose of the elevation is so that he "might see all the inhabited world." These last words correspond to the patriarch's request as recorded in vv. 6 and 7:

v. 6   ἰδεῖν   πᾶσαν τὴν οἰκουμένην
v. 7   θεάσασθαι πᾶσαν τὴν οἰκουμένην
v. 8   ἴδῃ   πᾶσαν τὴν οἰκουμένην

In this way it is clear that God, in compassion and forbearance, is going to give to Abraham precisely what he has requested. In the event, however, Abraham will not see everything, because his own folly will cut his trip short (chap. 10).

"The cherubic chariot" is presumably the chariot upon which rests the throne of God, which has wheels (Ezekiel 1–3) and so is portable: Jer 49:38; Ezek 43:1–7; *1 En.* 25:3; Gk. *L.A.E.* 22:3 etc. There are, moreover, some Jewish texts in which human beings sit upon a throne in heaven, even God's throne: e.g. 4Q491 11 i 13; Ezek. Trag. in Eusebius, *Praep. ev.* 9.29.4–6; *1 En.* 45:3; 51:3; 55:4; 61:8; 62:2–3; Wis 9:4, 10; Col 3:1; Rev 7:17; 22:1, 3; *3 En.* 10:1 (ed. Schäfer, *Synopse* 13 = 894); *b. Ḥag.* 14a.[11] *TA*, however, says nothing about Abraham sitting on a throne, nor does it assign him a royal status (although see on 4:2).

---

[11]   See further on 12:4 and John J. Collins, *The Scepter and the Star: The Messiahs of the Dead Sea Scrolls and Other Ancient Literature* (ABRL 10; New York: Doubleday, 1995), 136–53.

The notion of a heavenly chariot was not just Jewish but at home in the wider Greco-Roman world; it in fact belongs to ancient Indo-European tradition and is already attested in the famous Bronze Age sun chariot from Denmark. Both Greeks and Romans had myths about the sun chariot (*H. Hom. Helios*; Ovid, *Metam.* 2.1–328; Hyginus, *Fab.* 183; etc.), just as Hindus had similar myths about Surya and his chariot (*Rig Veda* 10:29:2–5). Further, "throughout antiquity ... the departed traveled most frequently in a chariot, which had in the Roman period become the chariot of the Sun-god."[12] Cf. the ascensions of the dead in chariots in RecShrt. 14:6; *T. Job* 52:6–10; Gk. *L.A.E.* 33:2. Later, Christians transferred the imagery of the invincible sun driving his chariot to Jesus and even used it to represent "the triumphal entry of the Christian believer into heaven."[13] Jewish hearers of *TA* may well have identified the cherubic chariot of their tradition with that of Apollos or the sun god Helios or Sol, who in fact appears in synagogue floor mosaics at Hammath Tiberius, Huseifa, Beth 'Alpha, and Na'aran. Cf. how Ps.-Justin, *Coh.* 31, likens Jupiter's winged chariot to Ezekiel's vision of the merkabah, or how Christian art aligns Elijah's chariot ride with Greek representations of Helios aloft.[14]

---

[12] Franz Cumont, *After Life in Roman Paganism* (New Haven: Yale University Press, 1922), 156. See further Cumont, *Lux Perpetua* (Paris: P. Geuthner, 1949), 289–93. For examples from Etruscan art see Richardson, *Etruscans*, 248 with plates XLIVa and b.

[13] Sister Charles Murray, *Rebirth and Afterlife: A Study of the Transmutation of Some Pagan Imagery in Early Christian Funerary Art* (BAR Intl. Series 100; Oxford: BAR, 1981), 96.

[14] Jean Daniélou, *Primitive Christian Symbols* (Baltimore: Helicon, 1964), 83–88. Readers acquainted with Greco-Roman mythology might also have recalled the dragon chariot of Triptolemus: Apollodorus, *Bibl.* 1.5.2; Pausanias, *Descr.* 7.18.2; Hyginus, *Fab.* 147; etc.

Chapter 10: Abraham surveys the World

Bibliography: Allison, "Luke 9:52–56". Schmidt, "Le monde à l'image du bouclier d'Achille."

Long Recension

10:1. And the archangel Michael descended and took Abraham on the chariot of the Cherubim. He raised him high into the upper air of heaven and led him on the cloud, along with sixty angels. And Abraham traveled above all the inhabited world on the carriage. 10:2. Abraham saw the world as it was that day. He saw some people plowing, others driving wagons. In one place some were shepherding, in another place some were in fields dancing and playing and making music. In yet another place some were wrestling and some sitting in judgment; in another people were crying and then bringing the dead to a tomb. 10:3. He saw also newlyweds being escorted. To put it briefly, he saw everything that was happening in the world, both good and bad. 10:4. Now as Abraham continued, he saw swordsmen grasping sharp swords in their hands. And Abraham asked the Commander-in-chief, "Who are these?" 10:5. And the Commander-in-chief said: "These are thieves who want to work murder and to steal and to burn and destroy." 10:6. Abraham said, "Lord, hear my voice, and command that beasts come out from the thicket and devour them." 10:7. And as he spoke his word, beasts came forth from the thicket and devoured them.

Short Recension fam. E

12:1. And it came to pass, after Abraham saw the place of judgment, that the cloud brought him to the firmament. 12:2. And when Abraham looked down upon the earth, he saw a man committing adultery with a married woman. 12:3. And Abraham said to Michael, "Do you see this lawlessness? Speak so that fire may come down from heaven and consume them." 12:4. In that hour fire came down from heaven, and it consumed them. 12:5. For the Lord had said to Michael, "If Abraham asks anything of you, heed him because he is my friend." 12:6. And the cloud took him along. And again Abraham gazed intently, and he saw men on the earth, slanderers. 12:7. And Abraham said, "Open up the earth, that it might swallow them alive." 12:8. And immediately the earth swallowed them alive. 12:9. And again the cloud carried them along, and Abraham saw some coming to a desert place to commit murder. 12:10. And Abraham said to Michael, "Do you see their lawlessness?" He also said, "Let beasts come forth and devour them." 12:11. And in that hour beasts from the desert came and devoured them. 12:12. And the Lord spoke to Michael saying, "Return Abraham to the earth, and do not allow him to encircle all the crea-

10:8. And he looked at another place and saw a man and a woman who were committing adultery with each other. 10:9. And he said, "Lord, command that the earth might open up and that it might swallow them." And immediately the earth opened up and swallowed them. 10:10. And he saw in another place a man breaking into houses and stealing the possessions of others. 10:11. And Abraham said, "Lord, command that fire might come down from heaven and consume them." And as he spoke his word, fire came down from heaven and consumed them. 10:12. And immediately a voice came from heaven to the Commander-in-chief speaking thus: "Michael, Commander-in-chief, command the chariot to stand still, and turn Abraham back, lest he see all the inhabited world. 10:13. For if he were to see all those living in sin, he would destroy all the creation. For behold, Abraham has not sinned, and he does not have mercy upon sinners. 10:14. But I made the world, and I do not wish to destroy any of them. Rather I delay the death of a sinner until he turns and lives." 10:15. And he brought Abraham unto the first gate of heaven, that he might see there the judgment and the recompense, so that he might repent regarding the souls of the sinners he had destroyed.

tion, for otherwise he would destroy all the creation that I made. For he does not have compassion upon them, since he did not make them. 12:13. But I made them, wherefore I have compassion upon them. Perchance they will turn and repent of their sins and be saved." 12:14. In that hour Michael returned Abraham to the earth. 12:15. And it happened at that time that Sarah died. 12:16. Abraham buried her.

TEXTUAL NOTES ON THE LONG RECENSION

10:1. J opens with "And he descended and led, etc." This omits the redundant material from 9:8. // B abbreviates: "Michael took Abraham above all the inhabited world on the carriage." // Q lacks "on the chariot ... heaven," which is unnecessary." // Similarly, I drops "on the chariot ... him." // G shortens by ending with: "And he traveled through the inhabited world." 10:2. "He saw ... plowing" is not in I. // G omits "some were in fields." // H B, skipping from ἀγραυλοῦντας to κιθαρίζοντας, drops "dancing ... music." // J omits ἔπειτα καὶ τεθνεῶτας; perhaps a scribe moved from the end of κλαίοντας to the end of τεθνεῶτας. 10:2–3. B drops ἐν μνήματι ἀγομένους at the end of v. 2 and the first sentence in v. 3. 10:3. G lacks "happening in the world." 10:4. J has "swordsmen" without "grasping ... hands." // A has "And he asked, 'Who are these?'" 10:5. I drops the first few words—"And the Commander-in-chief said, 'These are the thieves.'" // G omits "who want ... steal." Is this due to *homoioteleuton* (κλέπται ... κλέψαι)? // 10:7. B abbreviates the verse and destroys the parallelism with v. 6: καὶ εὐθὺς ἐγένετο οὕτως (cf. G's reading in v. 9; LXX 4 Βασ 1:21 v.l.; RecShrt. 12:8, 11 B F G). // I weakens the allusion to 2 Kgs 2:23–25 by omitting ἐκ τοῦ δρυμοῦ. 10:8–11. I H place vv. 8–9 after 11, so that the second episode becomes the third. 10:9. The translation represents the reading of I (which Schmidt prints). A B H Q omit "And immediately ... them" by passing from "swallow them" to "swallowed them." // G abbreviates: καὶ ἐγένετο οὕτω (cf. B's reading in v. 7). 10:10. Schmidt prints διορύττοντας. Positing this as original is one way of explaining the variants: A: δύο ῥίπτοντας. B: δύο ὀρυσσομένους. E: διορύγοντας. G: διορύττοντες. H: διορυγοῦντας. I: δύο ὀρυγόντας. J: δύο ὁρῶντας. Q: δύο ὀρύσσοντας. // H omits "and stealing ... others." 10:11. B J Q read καταβῆ , which adds to the parallelism with 2 Βασ 1:10 and 12. // B G H Q drop "And as ... consumed them" (*homoioteleuton*) and J replaces with: "And it happened at the same time that the prayer of Abraham was heard and they were destroyed. God changed his mind with regard to Abraham." // I drops "And as he spoke his word" as well as "from heaven." 10:12. G abbreviates by omitting "Michael ... command," H by omitting "Michael, Commander-in-chief." 10:12–11:4. B Q lose the entirety of the text from "all the inhabited world" to the end of 11:4. 10:13. G drops "all those living in sin." 10:14. A has the plural, "sinners." // A ends with ζῆσαι, G H I J with ζῆν αὐτόν, as in LXX Ezek 18:23; 33:11. 10:15–11:1. H drops "so that ... destroyed" and all of 11:1. 10:15. G shortens by dropping "Abraham unto the first." // J omits "the judgment and." // J omits "so that ... souls." The abbreviation preserves the sense: "the recompense of the sinners he had destroyed."

COMMENTARY

Chap. 10 recounts Abraham's chariot ride, during which he views the terrestrial realm. Vv. 2–3, illustrating the variety of mortal affairs, offer four antithetical pairs:

- ploughing vs. driving wagons: working on foot vs. riding
- shepherding vs. dancing, playing, making music: working in fields vs. recreating in fields
- wrestling vs. judging: sporting contest vs. solemn contest
- crying and burying vs. newlyweds being escorted: mourning and death vs. celebrating and new life

Vv. 4–11, wherein Abraham sees and responds to several sinners, trail this general overview of human life. There are three similar encounters:

Abraham sees an activity

4a	εἶδεν	ἄνδρας
8	καὶ εἶδεν εἰς ἕτερον τόπον ἄνδρα	
10	καὶ εἶδεν εἰς ἕτερον τόπον ἀνθρώπους	

Abraham prays for judgment

6a	εἶπεν δὲ ᾿Αβραάμ,	κύριε …	κέλευσον ἵνα
9a	καὶ εἶπεν,	κύριε	κέλευσον ὅπως
11a	καὶ εἶπεν ᾿Αβραάμ,	κύριε	κέλευσον ἵνα

6b	ἐξέλθωσιν	θηρία ἐκ τοῦ δρυμοῦ	καὶ καταφάγωσιν	αὐτούς
9b	χάνῃ	ἡ γῆ	καὶ καταπίῃ	αὐτούς
11b	κατέλθῃ	πῦρ ἐκ τοῦ οὐρανοῦ	καὶ καταφάγηται	αὐτούς

Judgment falls

7a	καὶ ἅμα τῷ λόγῳ αὐτοῦ
9c	καὶ εὐθύς
11c	καὶ ἅμα τῷ λόγῳ αὐτοῦ

7a	ἐξῆλθον	θηρία ἐκ τοῦ δρυμοῦ	καὶ κατέφαγον	αὐτούς
9c	ἐδιχάσθη	ἡ γῆ	καὶ κατέπιεν	αὐτούς
11c	κατῆλθεν	πῦρ ἐκ τοῦ οὐρανοῦ	καὶ κατέφαγεν	αὐτούς

Vv. 12–15 close the chapter: a heavenly voice instructs Michael to halt the chariot ride. This voice contrasts Abraham's judgmental piety with the indulgent mercy of the Creator. Even so, God does not rebuke Abraham directly, nor does he ground the chariot. He rather orders that the patriarch be taken to where he may see souls being judged. In this way God can continue to fulfill Abraham's request to see everything and at the same time teach him a lesson in compassion.

Chap. 10 reflects interaction with three biblical texts that record violent acts. In 2 Kgs 2:23–25, Elisha summons bears that devour children. In Numbers 16, Moses commands the earth to open up and swallow the followers of Korah. And in 2 Kgs 1:9–12, Elijah calls down fire from heaven to consume two companies of soldiers. In each case a prophet's powerful word brings a dramatic and fearful judgment. The same thing happens in *TA* 10, where Abraham summons beasts to devour murderers, commands the earth to swallow adulterers, and calls down fire upon thieves. Our chapter, however, critically evaluates the patriarch's actions in the light of Ezekiel's refrain that God does not want the death of sinners but rather wishes them to turn and live; see on v. 14. *TA* 10 implicitly sets Scripture against Scripture and prefers God's declarations of mercy in Ezekiel to the stories in which the righteous slaughter sinners.

RecShrt. 12 E and RecShrt. 12 B F G are very close to each other as well as to RecLng. 10, but there are differences. (i) In RecLng., Abraham's vision of earth comes before and is the occasion for his seeing the judgment of departed souls. In RecShrt. the sequence is the other way around, and there is no thematic link between the two experiences. (ii) RecShrt. contains no parallel to RecLng.'s general review, in vv. 2–3, of what Abraham saw—people plowing, driving wagons, etc. This is the sort of thing one would expect an abbreviator to omit. A motive for its addition is perhaps less obvious.

(iii) The sins that Abraham sees and the judgments that he calls down vary slightly and appear in different orders:

	RecShrt. E and B F G	RecLng.
crime	adultery	theft and murder
punishment	fire from heaven	devouring beasts
crime	slander	adultery
punishment	devouring earth	devouring earth
crime	murder	theft
punishment	devouring beasts	fire from heaven

Did the variation arise when someone produced an edition of *TA* from memory, not a written text?

(iv) The intertextuality is, in general, more extensive in RecLng. (although see on v. 9). The allusion to 2 Kgs 2:23–25, where Elisha summons bears "from the thicket" to devour children, is muted in RecShrt. E and B F G, which have the beasts come "from the desert." The short texts also do not echo Ezekiel 18 or 33. (v) Although Sarah is still alive when Abraham dies in RecLng. 20, she passes on at the end of RecShrt. 12 E and B F G. The former chronology contradicts Genesis 23–25, where Abraham dies after Sarah. As elsewhere, RecLng. is less anxious about being in harmony with the Bible.

Although the basic story line of RecLng. 10 presumably goes back to an old Jewish text, ecclesiastical hands have contributed to the current text. At least seven phrases seem to be Christian:

νεονύμφους ὀψικευομένους; see on v. 3
οἱ κλέπται ... κλέψαι καὶ θῦσαι καὶ ἀπολέσαι; see on v. 5
ἐν ἁμαρτίᾳ διάγοντας; see on v. 13
οὐ θέλω ἀπολέσαι ἐξ αὐτῶν οὐδένα; see on v. 14
τὸν θάνατον τοῦ ἁμαρτωλοῦ ἕως οὗ ἐπιστρέψαι; see on v. 14
τὰς κρίσεις καὶ ἀνταποδόσεις; see on. v. 15
τὰς ψυχὰς τῶν ἁμαρτωλῶν; see on v. 15

RecShrt. 12, which recounts basically the same episode as RecLng. 10, contains none of the expressions just listed. This is consistent with the thesis that RecLng. 10 has grown from a Jewish original: the Christian elements are overlay.

10:1. Upon descending (κατελθών; see on 1:4), Michael takes Abraham "on the chariot of the Cherubim," which rests upon a cloud, and raises him into "the upper air of heaven." Sixty angels appear as escorts; cf. the forty angels who draw the heavenly chariot in 3 Bar. 6:2. Almost all of the language is taken from 9:8 (q.v. for discussion), so Michael's deed correlates perfectly with God's command:

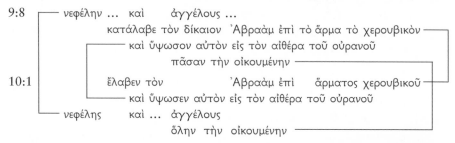

At the end of v. 1, however, ἅρμα gives way to the synonym ὄχημα* (cf. Jos. Asen. 24:19; 26:5; 27:1, 2; 28:9; Josephus, Ant. 5.284; 12.171; LXX: 0; Philo: 9; NT: 0).

In Greek thought in general, τὸν αἰθέρα τοῦ οὐρανοῦ is the rarefied air above the moon, through which the planets and stars travel.[1] For Aristotle in particular, aether is the divine fiery element of which the celestial spheres and bodies consist (Cael. 1.2–3). Others thought of it as the place of souls (IG 1.945) or of angels (P. Bod. 30 18r.23). Already in Homer, Il. 14.288, the aether is the realm above the normal air and clouds. Readers of TA are likely, then, to have thought of Abraham as moving from the celestial sphere to the divine sphere. "However, since according to the Greco-Roman understanding of the ethereal realm no earthly substance can exist

---

[1]   Christian Wildberg, John Philoponus' Criticism of Aristotle's Theory of Aether (Berlin/New York: de Gruyter, 1988), 9–12.

in this realm, this author either misunderstands this concept or is attempting to portray Abraham as so completely righteous that he, unlike anyone else, can ascend to this level and not perish."[2]

10:2–3. From his vantage point in the sky, Abraham sees all "as it was," καθὼς εἶχεν (as in Antonius the Hagiographer, *Vit. Symeonis Stylitis* 28, and John Philoponus, *In Aristotelis analytica priora comm.*, ed. Wallies, p. 216.28). He espies people ploughing (ἀροτριῶντας; ἀροτριάω*: LXX Judg 14:18; Luke 17:7; 1 Cor 9:10; Josephus, *Bell.* 2.113; etc.), an activity with which he is quite familiar from his own estate (cf. 2:1, 8). He also sees others who are not on foot but have the easier task of driving wagons, ἀμαξηγοῦντας. ἀμαξηγέω* seems otherwise unattested, but it is clearly a variant of ἀμαξεύω, which LSJ, s.v., defines as "traverse with a wagon." In another place are shepherds (ποιμαινεύοντας; ποιμαινεύω*; LSJ has no entry; Lampe, s.v., cites only *TA*) as well as other people outdoors, ἀγραυλοῦντας (ἀγραυλέω*); cf. Homer, *Il.* 18.162 (ποιμένες ἄγραυλοι); Luke 2:8 (ποιμένες ... ἀγραυλοῦντες). The latter are not working but instead dancing, playing, and making music. With ὀρχουμένους, παίζοντας, καὶ κιθαρίζοντας (ὀρχέομαι*; παίζω*) cf. Homer, *Il.* 13.731 (ἄλλῳ δ' ὀρχηστύν, ἑτέρῳ κίθαριν; Clement of Alexandria, *Strom.* 4.21, quotes this); Plato, *Euthyd.* 277E (ὀρχεῖσθον παίζοντε); LXX 2 Βασ 6:21 (παίξομαι καὶ ὀρχήσομαι); 1 Chr 15:29 (ὀρχούμενον καὶ παίζοντα). κιθαρίζω* means "play the lyre," as in LXX Isa 23:16; Josephus, *C. Ap.* 2.242; Rev 14:2; etc. In yet another place are wrestlers, παλαίοντας (παλαίω*: cf. LXX Gen 32:24, 25; Judg 20:33; Herm. *Sim.* 8.3.6). Our text does not pass a negative judgment on sport or the gymnasium, which is probably a sign of openness to Hellenistic culture.[3] There are also those sitting in judgment, δικαζομένους (δικάζω*: cf. LXX Judg 6:31; 1 Βασ 7:6; etc.). All of these are engaged in contests. The contrast lies in the greater seriousness and importance of those sitting in judgment (whose task, as readers of chaps. 12–14 will discover, has an all-important heavenly analogue).

The final pair makes for the strongest antithesis. There are those who cry and lead the dead to a tomb: κλαίοντας, ἔπειτα καὶ τεθνεῶτας ἐν μνήματι ἀγομένους (ἔπειτα*). For ἐν μνήματι see LXX 2 Chr 16:14; Luke 23:53;

---

[2] J. Edward Wright, *The Early History of Heaven* (New York/Oxford: Oxford University Press, 2000), 153.

[3] Cf. *P. Lond.* 1912, the famous letter of Claudius to Alexandrian Jews prohibiting their participation in city athletic contests. Implied is the involvement of some Jews. See further Roger R. Chambers, "Greek Athletics and the Jews: 165 B.C.–A.D. 70" (unpublished University of Miami Ph.D. dissertation, 1980), and H. A. Harris, *Trivium: Greek Athletics and the Jews* (Cardiff: University of Wales Press, 1976).

Acts 7:16; *Acts John* 72, 83, 87; Ps.-John of Damascus, *B.J.* 35.324; etc. Abraham also sees newlyweds, νεονύμφους (νεόνυμφος*). They are escorted in a procession, ὀψικευομένους; for the image see Ps 45:13–15; 1 Macc 9:37–39. LSJ offers no entry for ὀψικεύω (which recurs in 20:12); Lampe, s.v., cites only Leontius Neapolitanus, *Vit. Symeonis* 13, and Ps.-Sophronius of Jerusalem, *Liturg.* 13, neither before the 7th century. Sophocles, *Lex.*, s.v., cites further John Climacus, Theophanes, Leontius of Cyprus. The verb, like the noun, νεόνυμφος, occurs most often in the writings of Constantine VII Porphyrogenitus, an Emperor of the 10th century; and in *Cer.*, ed. Reiske, p. 6, the two, as here, appear together: ὀψικευομένων τῶν νεονύμφων.

The narrator now sums up, ἁπλῶς εἰπεῖν; the expression recurs in 17:17; 19:14; Isocrates, *Antid.* 117; *Paneg.* 154; Plutarch, *Brut.* 2.2; *Sib. Or.* prolog. 27; and often in patristic texts. The patriarch, we learn, saw "everything that was happening in the world" (πάντα τὰ τοῦ κόσμου γινόμενα; cf. Ep Jer 44: πάντα τὰ γινόμενα), both "good and evil," ἀγαθὰ καὶ πονηρά; cf. 6:8; Prov 15:3; Matt 5:45; Origen, *Comm. Jo.* 20.14; Gk. *Apoc. Paul* 7; John of Damascus, *Sacr. par.* PG 95.1113A. The following verses, however, will focus on evil.

Abraham's vision is, according to Schmidt, inspired by Homer, *Il.* 18.468–617, in which Hephaestus fashions for Achilles a great shield.[4] Upon this shield are many scenes from life—brides being lead in procession (491–93), youngsters dancing (494, 590–605), others playing music (494–95, 573–86), judges making decisions (497–508), ploughmen working (546–49), herders protecting cattle, sheep grazing in pasture (573–89). Schmidt may be right. Not only does *TA* elsewhere show a knowledge of Homer (see on 6:6), but Lucian, *Icar.* 16 (where wagon drivers and a funeral appear) rewrites this particular scene, and both Ps.-Justin, *Coh.* 28, and Clement of Alexandria, *Strom.* 5.14, interpret Hephaestus' work as analogous to God's creation of the world. Further, *Il.* 18.551 speaks of people with sharp sickles in their hands while *TA* 10:4 concerns swordsmen who grasp sharp swords in their hands. As for the meaning of the allusion, Schmidt urges that Egyptian Jews interpreted the scene to show God's care for the world, and that this divine benevolence contrasts with Abraham's destructive spirit.

10:4. Abraham continues his journey; for διερχόμενος (διέρχομαι*) δέ + subject see Plutarch, *Mor.* 215D; Eupolemus in Eusebius, *Hist. eccl.* 9.34.2; Constantine VII Porphyrogenitus, *Cer.*, ed. Reiske, p. 98; George

---

4   Schmidt, "Monde." Cf. "Testament," 2:138–39; also Colafemmina, *Testamento*, 24–25.

Monachus, *Chron. breve* PG 110.1112A. The patriarch next beholds swordsmen, ἄνδρας ξιφηφόρους. For ξιφηφόρος see 17:15; *4 Macc.* 16:20; Philo the Epic poet in Eusebius, *Praep. ev.* 9.20.1; and Basil of Seleucia, *Serm. 41* PG 109C—all of Abraham's knife. The men have in their hands "sharp swords," ξίφη ἠκονημένα (ἀκονάω*); cf. LXX Ps 44:6; 119:4 (τὰ βέλη ... ἠκονημένα). Being unsure who these people are, Abraham asks his angelic interpreter, "Who are these?" (τίνες εἰσὶν οὗτοι, as in Sus 38:3). The last part of the line closely resembles 11:8 and 12:15:

10:4	ἠρώτησεν	Ἀβραὰμ τὸν ἀρχιστράτηγον,	τίνες εἰσὶν οὗτοι;
11:8	ἠρώτησεν δὲ ὁ	Ἀβραὰμ τὸν ἀρχιστράτηγον ...	τίς ἐστιν οὗτος;
12:15	ἠρώτησεν δὲ	Ἀβραὰμ τὸν ἀρχιστράτηγον ...	τί ἐστι ταῦτα;

10:5. The Commander-in-chief identifies the swordsmen as "thieves," κλέπται (κλέπτης* always renders בנב in the LXX). These, he goes on to clarify, "want to work murder and to steal and to burn (or: slaughter) and destroy": βουλόμενοι φόνον ἐργάζεσθαι καὶ κλέψαι καὶ θῦσαι καὶ ἀπολέσαι (φόνος*; ἐργάζομαι*; κλέπτω*; θύω: cf. 6:4; ἀπόλλυμι: cf. vv. 13–15; 11:11; 14:11, 14). For φόνον + ἐργάζομαι (LXX: 0; NT: 0) see Dionysius of Halicarnassus, *Ant. rom.* 8.25.1; Philo, *Agr.* 171; Josephus, *Ant.* 5.62; 11.301; 18.49; *C. Ap.* 2.205. This seems something other than a description of ordinary thieves, who are depicted in v. 10. V. 5 appears rather to introduce soldiers, perhaps members of an invading army, who on campaign not only break two of the ten commandments by murdering and stealing (Exod 20:13, 15; Deut 5:17, 19) but in addition burn and destroy (cf. Josh 6:15–21; 8:18–29; 11:10–14).

Because of the late and Christian character of much of RecLng.'s Greek, one strongly suspects that 10:5 is an ecclesiastical reformulation, for the closest parallel appears in John 10:10 and patristic quotations of that verse:

TA 10:5	οἱ κλέπται ... κλέψαι καὶ θῦσαι καὶ ἀπολέσαι
John 10:10	ὁ κλέπτης ... κλέψῃ καὶ θύσῃ καὶ ἀπολέσῃ

10:6. Abraham cannot abide the thieves so he prays, "Lord, hear my voice." κύριε, εἰσάκουσον τῆς φωνῆς μου (cf. 9:6, with δεήσεως) appears in LXX Ps 129:2, and there are related formulas in 26:7; 27:2; 63:2; Jer 18:19. Those who hear an echo of LXX Ps 129:2 may well sense irony here. For the short Psalm is all about mercy: "If you, O Lord, should mark iniquities, who will stand? Because with you there is forgiveness ... . For with the Lord there is mercy." But with Abraham there is no mercy at all. He marks iniquities, and sinners fall.

The request is that Michael or God (see below) command (κέλευσον ἵνα) beasts (θηρία; cf. v. 7; 14:11; 17:13; 19:14) to come out (ἐξέλθωσιν) from the thicket (ἐκ τοῦ δρυμοῦ) and to devour (καταφάγωσιν; κατεσθίω: 10:6,

7, 11; 14:11) the thieves. The line mixes the language of LXX Isa 56:9 (φάγετε, πάντα τὰ θηρία τοῦ δρυμοῦ) with the episode of 2 Kgs 2:23–25, where Elisha's curse calls forth bears from the woods or thicket (LXX: ἐκ τοῦ δρυμοῦ) that maul those who have mocked the prophet (cf. *Vit. Proph. Elisha* 7 Q; Tertullian, *Marc.* 2.14). Cf. the allusion to 2 Kgs 2:23–25 in *Ps.-Clem. Hom.* 16:20 (θηρῶν ... ἀπὸ δρυμῶν) and the reference in Ps.-Adamantius, *Dial.*, ed. van de Sande Bakhuyzen, p. 32 (ἐξελθεῖν καὶ καταφαγεῖν).

When Abraham says, "Lord, hear my voice, etc.," he seems to be addressing God. It admittedly seems very odd for God, in response, to do something God does not want done (cf. v. 12), and in RecShrt. it is clear that it is Michael who does the patriarch's bidding. So one might suppose that it is the same in RecLng., that Abraham here calls Michael "lord" (cf. 2:7, 12; 11:8; 13:1; 14:1). 14:14, however, seems to exclude this possibility, for there God takes credit for destroying these people ("those you earlier thought I had destroyed").

10:7. In answer to Abraham's prayer (v. 6), beasts come forth and devour the thieves:

| 10:6 | ἐξέλθωσιν θηρία ἐκ τοῦ δρυμοῦ καὶ καταφάγωσιν αὐτούς |
| 10:7 | ἐξῆλθον θηρία ἐκ τοῦ δρυμοῦ καὶ κατέφαγον αὐτούς |

The judgment falls, as it will in vv. 9 and 12, at virtually the same moment Abraham speaks: ἅμα τῷ λόγῳ αὐτοῦ. The expression occurs most often in Plutarch, e.g. *Alex.* 38.5; cf. also Origen, *Hom. Luc.* 7.41; Eusebius, *Praep. ev.* 1.4.2; Eustathius of Thessalonica, *Comm. Hom. Il.* 1.84, 266, 637; etc.

10:8. Abraham next sees a man and woman committing adultery, εἰς ἀλλήλους πορνεύοντας—an idiom I have not found elsewhere. Like the sinners in v. 5, these also are breaking the decalogue (Exod 20:14 = Deut 5:18). One may compare *Apoc. Zeph.* 2:1–5, where the seer, raised on high by an angel, looks down upon his city and sees various daily activities, including a man and a woman upon a bed.

10:9. Abraham's response to adulterers is to pray: "Lord, command that (κέλευσον ὅπως; cf. vv. 6, 11) the earth might open up and that it might swallow them," χάνῃ ἡ γῆ καὶ καταπίῃ αὐτούς (χαίνω*; καταπίνω: 10:9; 14:11). This is a clear allusion to the dramatic and memorable punishment that came upon Korah, Dathan, and Abiram and their followers in Numbers 16. Deut 11:6; Ps 106:17; 4Q491 frags. 1–3 1–2; Ecclus 45:18–19; Philo, *Fug.* 145; *L.A.B.* 57:2; 4 *Macc.* 2:17; Jude 12; 1 *Clem.* 51:3–4; *Prot. Jas.* 9:2; Irenaeus, *Haer.* 4.26.2; and *m. Sanh.* 10:3 all refer to this incident.

Philo, *Mos.* 2.275–287; *L.A.B.* 16; and Josephus, *Ant.* 4.35–53, retell it while Josephus, *Ant.* 5.566; Rev 12:16; *Ps.-Clem. Hom.* 16:20; and *Acts Phil. Mart.* 26–27 (132–133) allude to it (see further below). There is a strong tendency in the Greek sources to use a verb + ἡ γῆ + καί + a form of καταπίνω + αὐτούς in describing or alluding to what happened:

LXX Num 16:30	ἀνοίξασα	ἡ γῆ		καταπίεται αὐτούς
LXX Num 16:32	ἠνοίχθη	ἡ γῆ	καὶ κατέπιεν	αὐτούς
LXX Deut 11:6	ἀνοίξασα	ἡ γῆ ...	κατέπιεν	αὐτούς
LXX Ps 105:17	ἠνοίχθη	ἡ γῆ	καὶ κατέπιεν	
TA RecLng. 10:9a	χάνη	ἡ γῆ	καὶ καταπίῃ	αὐτούς
TA RecLng. 10:9b	ἐδιχάσθη	ἡ γῆ	καὶ κατέπιεν	αὐτούς
TA RecShrt. 12:7 E	ἄνοιξον	τὴν γῆν	καταπίῃ	αὐτούς
TA RecShrt. 12:7 B F G	ἀνοιχθήτω	ἡ γῆ	καὶ καταπιέτω	αὐτούς
Rev 12:16	ἤνοιξεν	ἡ γῆ ...	καὶ κατέπιεν	
Prot. Jas. 9:2	ἐδιχάσθη	ἡ γῆ	καὶ κατεπόθησαν	

Furthermore, both 10:9 and the verses in Numbers are followed by fire falling from heaven (Num 16:35; *TA* 10:11), and 10:9 corresponds to Num 16:31, which recounts that judgment fell as soon as Moses spoke (LXX: ὡς δὲ ἐπαύσατο λαλῶν πάντας τοὺς λόγους τούτους; cf. Philo, *Mos.* 2.274, 282; Josephus, *Ant.* 4.51): "And immediately (καὶ εὐθύς; cf. 10:12) the earth opened up and swallowed (ἐδιχάσθη; cf. *Prot. Jas.* 9:2; διχάζω*) them." One may also note that RecShrt. 12:7 E and B F G have ἀνοίγω, in accord with the LXX sentences cited above, and further that, in RecShrt. 12:7–8 E, the wicked are swallowed ζῶντας, which comes from LXX Num 16:30, 33; cf. Philo, *Mos.* 2.281; *1 Clem.* 51:4.

10:10. Abraham sees yet a third scene. This time men are breaking through the wall of a house, διορύττοντας οἴκους (διορύσσω*: LXX Job 24:16; Ezek 12:5, 7, 12); cf. LXX Job 24:16 (διώρυξεν ... οἰκίας); Matt 24:43 = Luke 12:39 (διορυχθῆναι τὴν οἰκίαν αὐτοῦ); Himerius Sophista, *Decl.* 4.63 (διορύττῃ μὲν οἰκίας). Their goal is to steal (ἁρπάζοντας; cf. 11:6, 11; 19:11) the property (πράγματα; cf. 1:4–5) of others (ἀλλότρια). These, then, are robbers, akin to the criminals in vv. 4–7. Cf. *T. Dan* 5:7 (ἁρπάζοντες τὰ ἀλλότρια) and *Barn.* 10:4 (ἁρπάζουσιν τὰ ἀλλότρια). τὰ ἀλλότρια πράγματα occurs in Aesop, *Fab.* 170; *In Aristotelis Artem Rhetoricam Comm.* 104; and Scholia on Aristophanes, *Ran.* 563.

10:11. As before, Abraham cannot abide what he sees, so he prays: "Lord, command that (κέλευσον ἵνα, as in v. 6) fire might come down from heaven and consume them." Immediately (καὶ ἅμα τῷ λόγῳ; see on vv. 7, 9) his will is done. As with the other two punishments, this one also has a scriptural model one recalls immediately:

227

TA 10:11a	κατέλθη⁵	πῦρ ἐκ τοῦ οὐρανοῦ καὶ καταφάγηται + object
10:11b	κατῆλθεν	πῦρ ἐκ τοῦ οὐρανοῦ καὶ κατεφάγεν + object⁶
4 Βασ 1:10a	καταβήσεται	πῦρ ἐκ τοῦ οὐρανοῦ καὶ καταφάγεται + object
1:10b	κατέβη	πῦρ ἐκ τοῦ οὐρανοῦ καὶ κατεφάγεν + object
4 Βασ 1:12a	καταβήσεται	πῦρ ἐκ τοῦ οὐρανοῦ καὶ καταφάγεται + object
1:12b	κατέβη	πῦρ ἐκ τοῦ οὐρανοῦ καὶ κατεφάγεν + object⁷

Just as Elijah once called down fire from heaven, so too Abraham. For other narratives that refer or allude to 2 Kgs 1:9–12 (which Josephus, *Ant.* 9.23, retells) or are modeled upon it see Luke 9:52–56 (πῦρ καταβῆναι ἀπὸ τοῦ οὐρανοῦ καὶ ἀναλῶσαι αὐτούς); Rev 20:9 (κατέβη πῦρ ἐκ τοῦ οὐρανοῦ καὶ κατεφάγεν αὐτούς); *Vit. Proph. Elijah* 12; *Acts Phil. Mart.* 21 (127) (V: πῦρ ἐλθεῖν ἀπ᾽ οὐρανοῦ καὶ κατακαύσωμεν αὐτούς; Α: ἵνα πῦρ καταβῇ ἐκ τοῦ οὐρανοῦ καὶ καύσῃ αὐτούς). *Jos. Asen.* 25:7 should also probably be included here: if Joseph were to call upon the God of Israel, πέμψει πῦρ ἐξ/ἀπ᾽ οὐρανοῦ καὶ καταφάγεται ὑμᾶς. For accounts of fire falling from heaven that seem to be independent of 2 Kings see Gen 19:24; Lev 10:1–2; 1 Kgs 18:38; 1 Chr 21:26; Job 1:16; Ps 97:3; 2 Macc 2:10.

A form of ἐξ- or κατέρχομαι + noun + ἐκ τοῦ + noun + καὶ + a form of κατεσθίω + αὐτούς appears in both 11b and c, as already in 6b and 7a:

6b	ἐξέλθωσιν	θηρία	ἐκ τοῦ δρυμοῦ	καὶ καταφάγωσιν αὐτούς
7a	ἐξῆλθον	θηρία	ἐκ τοῦ δρυμοῦ	καὶ κατέφαγον αὐτούς
11b	κατέλθη	πῦρ	ἐκ τοῦ οὐρανοῦ	καὶ καταφάγηται αὐτούς
11c	κατῆλθεν	πῦρ	ἐκ τοῦ οὐρανοῦ	καὶ κατέφαγεν αὐτούς

The narrator's language repeats itself as Abraham's behavior repeats itself.

In 10:6–11 Abraham summons three judgments. Beasts devour murderous thieves, the earth swallows adulterers, and fire consumes robbers. These three judgments hearken back to three biblical incidents—2 Kgs 2:23–25 (Elisha and the bears); Numbers 16 (Korah's rebellion); and 2 Kgs 1:9–12 (Elijah and fire from heaven) respectively. In each case, as readers soon learn, Abraham acts inappropriately: God must show him the dire consequences of what he has done so that he might repent. Abraham should not, in other words, imitate the frightful actions of Elisha, Moses, and Elijah. One may compare *Acts Phil. Mart.* 21 (127), where Philip, in language reminiscent of 2 Kgs 2:23–25 (see above), wonders whether he

---

⁵ B J Q: καταβῇ. Is this the original reading or further assimilation to Kings?

⁶ RecShrt. 12:3 E preserves the same basic form: κατελθεῖν πῦρ ἐκ τοῦ οὐρανοῦ καὶ καταφάγη + object.

⁷ RecShrt. 12:4 E agrees exactly with 4 Βασ 1:10b and 12b.

should call down fire from heaven. A little later (26 [132]), in the face of
opposition from other apostles, he commands that the deep open up and
swallow his opponents, which in the event happens. Numbers 16 is clearly
in the background. But then Jesus appears and rebukes Philip, indeed
punishes him for being unmerciful. He further resurrects the dead who
have been swallowed (31–32 [137–138]). So here, as in *TA* 10, imitation
of the Elijah of 2 Kgs1:9–12 and of the Moses of Numbers 16 is inappro-
priate. Cf. also Luke 9:52–56. Here James and John ask Jesus if they should
command fire to come down from heaven and consume unfriendly Samari-
tans. Some texts add: "as Elijah did." Luke has Jesus respond this way:
"But he turned and rebuked them." The allusion to 2 Kings 1:9–12 is clear
enough even without the explicit remark; and again those who would act
like Elijah are condemned.

   Ps.-Clem. Hom. 16:20 holds something similar: "Openings (χάσματα;
cf. Philo, *Mos.* 2.281) of the earth did not occur (cf. Num 16:30, 32–33),
and fire was not sent down from heaven for the incineration of human
beings (cf. Gen 19:24; Num 16:35; 2 Kgs 1:9–12), and rain was not poured
out (Genesis 7–8), and a multitude of beasts was not sent from the thickets
(cf. 2 Kgs 2:23–25), and upon us the destructive wrath of God did not
begin to show itself … . For God, the creator of heaven and earth, is not
the one who in former times attacked sins, since now, being blasphemed
to the utmost, he (would) attack in the utmost. But quite the contrary, he
is long-suffering, he calls to repentance … ." Here Genesis 7–8; Numbers
16; 2 Kgs 2:23–25 and maybe 2 Kgs 1:9–12 characterize what happened
in the past, not what is happening or should happen in the present. As *TA*
10:13 contains an allusion to the flood (see on v. 13), *Ps.-Clem. Hom.*
16:20 alludes to precisely the same four texts as *TA* 10, and in order to
make a closely related point.

   There are, then, four texts that recall one or more biblical tales of
destruction and implicitly criticize them by rejecting their application to the
present:

	Genesis 7–8	Numbers 16	2 Kgs 1:9–12	2 Kgs 2:23–25
TA RecLng. 10	v. 13	v. 9	v. 11	vv. 6–7
Luke 9:52–56			v. 54	
Ps.-Clem. Hom. 16	20	20	20	20
Acts Phil. Mart.		26–27 (132–33)	21 (127)	

Given that *TA* 10 and Luke 9 are independent of each other and, further,
that *Ps.-Clem. Hom.* 16:20 and the *Acts of Philip* probably do not draw
upon *TA* 10, there appears to have been a tradition, in the spirit of Wis

11:21–12:11, of critical reflection upon several scriptural scenes of vengeance.[8]

10:12. At this point (καὶ εὐθέως; cf. v. 9) the proceedings come to a halt. God's voice comes from heaven: ἦλθεν φωνὴ ἐκ τοῦ οὐρανοῦ ... οὕτως λέγων; cf. 14:13 and LXX Gen 15:4, where καὶ εὐθύς introduces a divine voice for Abraham. One may compare any number of texts—for example, Gen 21:17; 22:11, 15 (in these a voice speaks to Abraham ἐκ τοῦ οὐρανοῦ); Exod 19:19; Deut 4:10–12; 1 Kgs 19:13; Dan 4:31 (LXX: φωνὴν ἐκ τοῦ οὐρανοῦ); Artapanus in Eusebius, Praep. ev. 9.27.21, 36; 1 En. 65:4; Sib. Or. 1:127, 267–268, 275; Matt 3:17 (φωνὴ ἐκ τῶν οὐρανῶν λέγουσα); Mark 9:7; John 12:28 (ἦλθεν ... φωνὴ ἐκ τοῦ οὐρανοῦ); Acts 7:31; 9:4; 10:13–15; 11:7–9; 2 Pet 1:18; Rev 1:10; 4:1; 10:4 (φωνὴ ἐκ τοῦ οὐρανοῦ λέγουσαν), 8; 11:12; 14:13 (φωνῆς ἐκ τοῦ οὐρανοῦ λεγούσης); 18:4 (φωνὴν ἐκ τοῦ οὐρανοῦ λέγουσαν); Josephus, Ant. 13.282; Bell. 6.300; 4 Ezra 14:1; 2 Bar. 13:1; 22:1; L.A.B. 53:3–5; 4 Bar. 9:12 (φωνὴ ἦλθε λέγουσα); Apoc. Abr. 9:1; 10:3; 19:1; Mart. Pol. 9:1; Gk. Apoc. Ezra 6:3; 7:13; Acts John 18; Acts Paul 46 (φωνὴ ἐκ τοῦ οὐρανοῦ λέγουσα); 1 Apoc. John, ed. Tischendorf, 17:2; Act Pet. (BG) 136:17–137:1; Ep. Pet. Phil. 134:13–14; 3 En. 16:4 (Schäfer, Synopse 20 = 856). For the rabbinic bat qôl see Strack-Billerbeck 1:125–34 and note esp. b. Šabb. 33b, where a heavenly voice rebukes the self-righteous Simeon b. Yohai for burning up innocent people with his eye rays. Greco-Roman parallels include Sophocles, Aj. 15–16; Theopompus, fr. 69; Dionysius of Halicarnassus, Ant. rom. 1.56.3; 5.16.2–3; 8.56.2–3; Plutarch, Mor. 355E; Is. Os. 12; Aelius Aristides, Ἡρακλῆς 36; Ps.-Callisthenes, Hist. Alex. Magn. rec. α 1.45 (ἦλθεν ... φωνή).

The voice instructs Michael to make the chariot (see on 9:8) to stand still, στῆναι τὸ ἅρμα; cf. Acts 8:38 (στῆναι τὸ ἅρμα); Gk. L.A.E. 33:3 (ἔστη τὸ ἅρμα). Perhaps he is to speak to the Cherubim who are drawing or conveying the chariot (see on 9:8). The Commander-in-chief is in any case to turn Abraham back, ἀπόστρεψον. ἀποστρέφω (cf. 15:1) appears in the LXX story of Abraham several times: 14:16; 15:16; 16:9; 18:22, 23; 22:19.

---

[8]   See Allison, "Luke 9:52–56." Although unrelated to Genesis 7–8; Numbers 16; 2 Kgs 1:9–12; and 2:10–12, the story in b. Ber. 10a is close in spirit to the texts discussed above: "There were some highwaymen in the neighborhood of R. Meier who caused him much trouble. So R. Meier prayed that they should die. His wife Beruria said to him, 'How do you make out (that such a prayer should be permitted)? Because it is written, Let hatta'im cease? Is it written, hot'im? It is written, hatta'im! Further, look at the end of the verse, "and let the wicked be no more." Since the sins will cease, there will be no more wicked people! Rather pray for them that they should repent, and there will be no more wicked.' He did pray for them, and they repented."

God does not want the patriarch to see "all the inhabited world" (see on 9:6), for as v. 13 explains, the patriarch would then destroy it. Against the tradition that Abraham is a saint to be emulated (see on 20:15), here he misbehaves. The miracles do not vindicate him but show that he has misused power. There is an analogy of sorts in *b. B. Meṣiʿa* 59b, where the multiple miracles of R. Eliezer, designed to substantiate his halakah, establish nothing. The reader laughs. Even God laughs at the end.

10:13. God prevents Abraham from seeing "all those living in sin," ἐν ἁμαρτίᾳ διάγοντας; cf. LXX Gen 42:21 (ἐν ἁμαρτίᾳ ἔσωμεν); Tit 3:3 (ἐν κακίᾳ καὶ φθόνῳ διάγοντες); Chrysostom, *Paen.* PG 49.337 (ἐν ἁμαρτίαις διέτριψα); *In Ps.* 50 PG 55.572 (ἐν ἁμαρτίᾳ διαγινόμενος); *Ecl. i–xlviii ex diversis homiliis* PG 63.589 (ἐν ἁμαρτίαις διέτριψα), 833 (ἐν ἁμαρτίᾳ διέτριψα); *Hom.* 1 *Cor.* PG 61.76 (οἱ ... ἐν ἁμαρτήμασι ζῶντες). Were he not stopped, Abraham would destroy (ἀπολέσει; cf. vv. 5, 14, 15) "all the creation," πᾶν τὸ ἀνάστημα; cf. *Sib. Or.* 8:268. ἀνάστημα* is here a variant of οἰκουμένη, which has been used repeatedly: 9:6, 7, 8; 10:1, 12. Cf. the rabbinic בריאה = "creation, formation," which is the object of God's concern (*Exod. Rab.* 9:1; etc). There is an echo of the LXX flood story, according to which God blotted out "all the creation": ἐξήλειψε πᾶν τὸ ἀνάστημα (Gen 7:23). This is the only LXX occurrence of πᾶν τὸ ἀνάστημα; cf. *Acts Andr. Mth.* 20 and Romanos the Melodist, *Cant.* 2.14, in both of which πᾶν τὸ ἀνάστημα occurs in a reference to the flood.

The explanation for Abraham's behavior is that, in contradiction to his own confession in 9:3, he has not sinned, and thus he does not "have mercy (ἐλεᾷ; cf. 7:6) upon sinners." Abraham does not understand a weakness he does not share. One may contrast Heb 4:15, where sympathy is created because Jesus shares the common human condition (despite, however, his being without sin). Perhaps readers would have found in Abraham's actions a criticism of the self-righteous and self-centered, who care only about themselves (cf. Luke 18:9–14).

That "Abraham has not sinned" (οὐχ ἥμαρτεν) was evidently a common sentiment. See *Jub.* 23:10 ("Abraham was perfect"); *Pr. Man.* 8 ("Abraham, Isaac, and Jacob ... did not sin"); Wis 10:5 (wisdom kept Abraham ἄμεμπτον).[9] This tradition has its origin in Gen 17:1, where God says to

---

[9]   Cf. *T. Mos.* 9:4 ("Never did [our] fathers nor their ancestors [the patriarchs presumably] tempt God by transgressing his commandments") and Rashi on Gen 25:7. For others without sin or "perfect" see *Jub.* 27:17 (Jacob); *Ps. Sol.* 17:41 (the messianic Son of David); Ecclus 44:17 (Noah); Heb 4:15; 7:26 (Jesus); *T. Iss.* 7:1–7 (Issachar); 2 *Bar.* 9:1 ("Jeremiah, whose heart was found to be pure from sins"); *Hist. Rech.* 11:2 (the Rechabites); *Deut. Rab.* 10:10 (Moses).

Abraham: "Walk before me and be blameless" (MT: תמים; LXX: ἄμεμπτος; cf. *Jub.* 15:3). Exegetes reasoned that if God called Abraham to be blameless, then he, who was renowned for his obedience, must have become such.[10]

10:14. God alone is the Creator: ἐγὼ δὲ ἐποίησα τὸν κόσμον; cf. Wis 9:9 (ἐποίεις τὸν κόσμον); Philo, *Opif.* 172 (πεποίηκε τὸν κόσμον); Acts 17:24 (ὁ ποιήσας τὸν κόσμον); etc. The Creator cares for the creation: "I do not wish to destroy any of them," οὐ θέλω ἀπολέσαι ἐξ αὐτῶν οὐδένα. That is, God's care is universal; no one is excluded; he is kind to all. Although the formulation appears to depend upon John 18:9 (οὐκ ἀπώλεσα ἐξ αὐτῶν οὐδένα), the sentiment is thoroughly Jewish; cf. Wis 11:23–26; *Exod. Rab.* 9:1; *Num. Rab.* 10:1; Ps 145:8–9; *Let. Arist.* 188, 207; Ecclus 18:11–13; Philo, *Sacr.* 124; Wis 11:22–12:2; *T. Zeb.* 7:2; *Mek.* on Exod 18:12; *b. Ta'an.* 7a; *b. Sanh.* 111a; *Exod. Rab.* 9:1; *Num. Rab.* 10:1. One recalls the spirit of the book of Jonah, where God cares for the pagans while the commissioned prophet does not.

The conviction of universal mercy enshrined in Jewish texts has its analogue in Greco-Roman thought. See e.g. Epicurus in Diogenes Laertius 10.139 ("A blessed and eternal being has no trouble in himself and brings no trouble upon any other being; hence he is exempt from movements of anger and partiality"); Plato, *Resp.* 380B ("To call God a cause of evil to anyone, being good himself, is a falsehood to be fought tooth and nail"); Seneca, *Ben.* 4.26 ("If you are imitating the gods, you say, 'Then bestow benefits also upon the ungrateful, for the sun rises also upon the wicked, and the sea lies open to pirates'"); Marcus Aurelius, *Meditationes* 6.1 (the reason that governs the universe "has no malice, nor does it do evil to anything"); 7.20 ("The Gods ... always put up with worthless people who are what they are and so many; nay they even care for them in all manner of ways"); 9.11 ("If you are able, convert the wrong-doer. If not, bear in mind that kindliness was given to you to meet just such a case. The Gods too are kindly to such persons and even co-operate with them for certain ends—for health, to wit, and wealth and fame, so good are they. You too can be the same"); Ps.-Libanius, *Epistolimaioi charakteres* 78 ("Do not think that God caused the terrible things that have befallen you. For God is completely free of evil. For he who orders others to flee evil would never cause evil to someone").

---

[10] Cf. how 1QapGen assumes that if, as Gen 13:17 has it, God ordered Abraham to walk through the entirety of the land, he must have done so, even if Genesis does not record such a tour.

God "delays (ἀναμένω*; for this sense, not present in the LXX, see LSJ, s.v., 2) the death of sinners," τὸν θάνατον τοῦ ἁμαρτωλοῦ; cf. LXX Ps 33:22 (θάνατος ἁμαρτωλῶν); LXX Ezek 18:23 v.l., 32 v.l.; *Ps. Sol.* 13:2 (θανάτου ἁμαρτωλῶν); and the patristic texts cited in n. 13 on p. 233. God wants the wicked to "turn and live"; cf. Plutarch, *Mor.* 551E (God "does not expedite punishment" but rather "grants time for reform"); Luke 13:6–9 (the barren fig tree receives a second chance); *Ps.-Clem. Rec.* 10:49 (the wicked should not be punished immediately as God "regards not the swiftness of vengeance but the causes of salvation, for he is not so much pleased with the death as with the conversion of a sinner"); and *Mek.* on Exod 15:5–6 (God grants an extension of time to the wicked). The divine pronouncement, which Kohler describes as "of incomparable beauty and grandeur," unlike anything "uttered by any prophet or preacher since the days of Ezekiel,"[11] reverses the situation of Genesis 18–19 (where ἀπόλλυμι is also a key word). There it is not Abraham but God who determines to destroy the wicked whereas the patriarch prays for their deliverance and God's indulgence; cf. *Gen. Rab.* 39:6; *Lev. Rab.* 10:1. *TA*'s reversal of Genesis adds to the irony of the book: the patriarch, who once upon a time pleaded for clemency, is not acting as expected.[12]

That God does not wish the death of a sinner but rather waits so that he might "turn and live" (cf. the sentiment in 2 Pet 3:9) draws upon a refrain in Ezekiel:

3:18   "If I say to the wicked, 'You shall surely die,' and you give them no warning, or speak to warn the wicked to *turn* from their wicked way, in order that they might *live*, those wicked persons shall die for their iniquity"

13:22   "You have encouraged the wicked not to *turn* from their wicked way and *live*"

18:21   "If the wicked *turn away* from all their sins that they have committed and keep all my statutes and do what is lawful and right, they shall surely *live*"

18:23   "Have I any pleasure in the death of the wicked, says the Lord God, and not rather that they should *turn* from their ways and *live*?"

18:24   "But if the righteous *turn* away from their righteousness and commit iniquity and do the same abominable things that the wicked do, shall they *live*?"

18:27   "When the wicked *turn away* from the wickedness they have committed, they shall surely *live*"

18:28:   "Because they considered and *turned away* from all the transgressions that they had committed, they shall surely *live*"

---

11   Kohler, "Apocalypse," 585.

12   *b. Šabb.* 89b does, however, depict an unmerciful Abraham who cheers for God to annihilate his sinful descendants.

18:32   "For I have no pleasure in the death of anyone, says the Lord God. *Turn,*
        then, and *live*"
33:11   "I have no pleasure in the death of the wicked, but that the wicked *turn*
        from their ways and *live*"
33:19   "And when the wicked *turn* from their wickedness and do what is lawful
        and right, they shall *live* by it"

The verbal dependence can be seen at a glance:

TA 10:14	οὐ θέλω
LXX Ezek 18:32	οὐ θέλω
LXX Ezek 18:23	μὴ θελήσει θελήσω (v.l.: μὴ θελήσει θέλω)
TA 10:14	τὸν θάνατον τοῦ ἁμαρτωλοῦ
LXX Ezek 18:32	τὸν θάνατον τοῦ ἀποθνῄσκοντος (v.l.: ἁμαρτωλοῦ)
LXX Ezek 18:23	τὸν θάνατον τοῦ ἀνόμου (v.l.: ἁμαρτωλοῦ)
TA 10:14	ἕως οὗ ἐπιστρέψαι ... καὶ ζῆν αὐτόν
LXX Ezek 3:18	ἀποστρέψαι (v.l.: ἐπι-) ζῆσαι αὐτόν
LXX Ezek 13:22	ἀποστρέψαι (v.l.: ἐπι-) καὶ ζῆσαι αὐτόν
LXX Ezek 18:21	ἀποστρέψῃ (v.l.: ἐπι-) ... ζωῇ ζήσεται
LXX Ezek 18:23	ὡς τὸ ἀποστρέψαι (v.l.: ἐπι-) καὶ ζῆν αὐτόν
LXX Ezek 18:28	ἀπέστρεψεν (v.l.: ἐπι-) ... ζωῇ ζήσεται
LXX Ezek 18:32 v.l.	ἐπιστρέψατε καὶ ζήσατε
LXX Ezek 33:11	ὡς τὸ ἀποστρέψαι (v.l.: ἐπι-) ... καὶ ζῆν αὐτόν

Ezekiel's refrain was quite popular with patristic writers, who again and
again use both τὸν θάνατον τοῦ ἁμαρτωλοῦ and ἐπιστρέψω, so perhaps *TA*
10:14 belongs to a Christian textual tradition.[13]

Some rabbinic texts connect Ezekiel's words with Abraham and the
story of Sodom. In *Tanḥ.* Wayyera 8, God is unwilling to destroy even the
wicked, and Gen 19:1; 18:23; Ezek 18:32; and 33:11 are quoted as evidence. Similarly, *Tanḥ. B* Genesis Wayyera 9 says that the righteous entreat
God for the whole world, for which the proofs are Ezek 33:11 and
Abraham's pleading for Sodom (Gen 18:20 and 25 are cited). Were Ezekiel's
words about turning and living traditionally associated with Genesis 18–
19?

---

[13]   *1 Clem.* 8:2–3; Ps.-Justin, *Quaest. et responsiones ad orthodoxos* 438C; 460A;
       Clement of Alexandria, *Strom.* 2.23; Origen, *Sel. Ps.* PG 12.1456B; Ps.-Athanasius,
       Imag. Beryt. PG 28.801A; Basil the Great, *Ep.* 44 2.16; *Asceticon magnum* PG
       31.1260A, 1284C; *Liturg.* PG 31.1649B; *Liturg. Greg. Naz.* PG 36.720C; Chryso-
       stom, *Stag.* PG 47.434; *Laz.* PG 48.1027; *Poenit. 1–9* PG 49.325; Theodoret of
       Cyrrhus, *Comm. Cant.* PG 81.76A; *XII Proph. proem.* PG 81.1740C; Ps.-John of
       Damascus, *B.J.* 24.219; 32.301; etc.

10:15. Michael is to take (ἀνάγαγε; cf. 8:5) Abraham to "the first gate of heaven," τῇ πρώτῃ πύλῃ τοῦ οὐρανοῦ; cf. 11:1. For the gate(s) of heaven—an ancient idea[14] which envisages heaven as like a walled city—see Gen 28:17; 4Q213a fr. 1 2:18; Gk. fr. *1 En.* 9:2, 10; *1 Enoch* 72–82; *3 Macc.* 6:18; *T. Levi* 5:1; *3 Bar.* 6:13; 11:2–5; 15:1 (cf. the "doors" of 2:2; 3:1; 14:1; 17:1); *2 Enoch* 13–14; *Apoc. Zeph.* 3:6, 9; *Vis. Paul* 19; *Acts Pil.* 19, 25; *Vis. Ezra* 8; Eusebius, *Mart. Pal.* 11.23; also *1 Enoch* 34–36 (multiple gates); 76; *4 Ezra* 3:19 (four gates). Many Egyptian texts envision the *ka* or soul ascending through the doors or gates of heaven (e.g. *CT* 44, 492).[15] *TA* probably presupposes a universe of several heavens or cosmic spheres, concentric shells above the earth in which there are various gates or doors (cf. Ps 78:23) through which rain and the other elements as well as angels descend and through which human souls ascend. The first gate is then the gate to the lowest sphere. (Contrast the Gnostic scheme as set forth by Origen, *Cels.* 6.31, where the lower the gate of an archon, the higher the number, which makes the first gate the entrance to the highest sphere.)

Once at the gate, Abraham will see the upshot of the deaths he has caused, which means that he will behold "the judgment" (τὰς κρίσεις), that is, "the recompense," ἀνταπόδοσεις. The sense is punitive here. Cf. 12:15 (ἡ κρίσις καὶ ἀνταπόδοσις); 13:4 (κρίσις καὶ ἀνταπόδοσις), 8; 15:12 (κρίσιν καὶ ἀνταπόδοσιν). For ἀνταπόδοσις alone see LXX Isa 61:2; Gk. fr. *1 En.* 22:11; *T. Job* 14:4; Rom 2:5. Although κρίσις and ἀνταπόδοσις are paired in *Sib. Or.* prolog. 21, this is a Christian text, and the pairing is otherwise characteristic of patristic writers: Ps.-Athanasius, *Synopsis scripturae sacrae* PG 28.352D; Gregory of Nazianzus, *Or.* 2 PG 35.444B; Theodoret of Cyrrhus, *Comm. Ps.* PG 80.1333D; etc. God knows that, when Abraham sees the fate of those he has struck down untimely and so consigned to destruction (ἀπώλεσεν), he will "repent" (μετανοήσῃ; μετανοέω*; cf. RecShrt. 12:13) of what he has done to their "souls," τὰς ψυχάς. Against Delcor, the meaning "souls" is wholly appropriate here, for the ψυχαί are disembodied spirits after death and at the judgment (cf. 20:9–12).[16] For τὰς ψυχὰς τῶν ἁμαρτωλῶν see *Gk. Apoc. Ezra* 1:11; Epiphanius, *Pan.* 66.31; Ps.-Athanasius, *Quaest. Antiochum* PG 28.612A; Ps.-Macarius, *Serm.* 64 34.3;

---

14 Edward Brovarski, "The Doors of Heaven," *Orientalia* 46 (1977), 107–15; Wolfgang Heimpel, "The Sun at Night and the Doors of Heaven in Babylonian Texts," *Journal of Cuneiform Studies* 38 (1986), 127–51. Already in the Akkadian story of *Adapa* rec. B 37–39, heaven has an entrance gate.

15 See further Zandee, *Death*, 114–25, 316–18.

16 Contrast Delcor, *Testament*, 131.

George Monachus, *Chron.*, ed. de Boor, p. 681. Here, given the dependence of v. 14 upon Ezekiel 18, the expression is probably inspired by LXX Ezek 18:4 and 20, which speak of ἡ ψυχὴ ἡ ἁμαρτάνουσα.

Chapter 11: Two Ways and Two Gates

Bibliography: Munoa, *Four Powers.* Schmidt, "Testament," 2:129–32. 139–40. Turner, "Testament," 26–29, 121–24.

Long Recension

11:1. Michael turned the chariot and took Abraham to the east, to the first gate of heaven. 11:2. And Abraham saw two ways there. One way was narrow and constricted, the other broad and spacious. 11:3. And he saw two gates there. One gate was broad, in conformity with the broad way, and one gate narrow, in conformity with the narrow way. 11:4. Outside of the two gates there, they saw a man sitting on a throne made of gold; and the appearance of that man was terrifying, like that of the Master. 11:5. And they saw many souls being driven by angels, being led through the broad way; and they saw a few other souls being carried by angels through the narrow gate. 11:6. And when the marvelous man sitting on the golden throne saw a few souls going through the narrow gate, and an immeasurable crowd being led away through the broad gate, immediately that holy, marvelous man tore out the hair of his head and the beard of his cheeks; and he threw himself from his throne to the ground, weeping and wailing. 11:7. And when he saw many souls entering through the narrow gate, then he rose from the earth and sat on his throne, rejoicing and exulting in much joy. 11:8. Abraham asked the Commander-in-chief, "My

Short Recension fam. E

8:3. Then Michael went and took upon a cloud Abraham, who was yet in his body. And the cloud carried him to the river Ocean. 8:4. And Abraham gazed intently and saw two gates, one small, the other large. 8:5. In the middle of the two gates sat a man on a throne of great glory, and a host of angels encircled him. 8:6. And he wept and laughed, and his weeping surpassed his laughter. 8:7. And Abraham said to Michael, "Who, lord, is this one who sits on the throne between these two gates in great glory, and around whom a host of angels stands, who weeps and laughs so that his weeping surpasses his laughter sevenfold?" 8:8. And Michael said to Abraham, "Do you not know him?" 8:9. And Abraham said, "No, lord." 8:10. And Michael said, "Do you see these two gates, the small and the great? 8:11. These are the two gates that lead unto glory and unto death. This first gate is the one that leads unto life, and the other gate, which stands open, is the one that leads unto destruction. 8:12. This man who sits in between them, he is Adam, the first man whom God formed. 8:13. And he brought him to this place, so that he might behold every soul that comes forth from the body, because all are from him. 8:14. If you

lord, Commander-in-chief, who is this most marvelous man who is appareled in such glory, who sometimes weeps and wails, but other times rejoices and exults with joy?" 11:9. The incorporeal one said, "This is the first-formed Adam, and he sits here in his glory, and he sees the world, as all have come from him. 11:10. And when he sees many souls entering through the narrow gate, then he rises up and sits on his throne, rejoicing and exulting in joy, for this is the narrow gate of the just that leads to life, and those who enter through it go away to paradise. And because of this the first-formed Adam rejoices, because he sees souls being saved. 11:11. But when he sees many souls entering through the broad gate, then he tears out the hair of his head and throws himself on the ground, weeping and wailing bitterly, for the broad gate is (the gate) of sinners, which leads to destruction and the chastisement of eternity. And because of this the first-formed Adam rises from his throne, weeping and mourning over the destruction of sinners, because those perishing are many, those being saved few. 11:12. For among seven thousand is scarcely to be found one soul saved and undefiled."

see him weeping, know that he sees souls being led unto destruction. 8:15. And if you see him laughing, he sees a few souls being led unto life. 8:16. See him, then, how the weeping surpasses the laughter since he sees most of the world being led through the gate of destruction. Therefore the weeping surpasses his laughter sevenfold."

TEXTUAL NOTES

11:1–2. A skips from "Abraham" in v. 1 to "Abraham" in v. 2. // J drops "to the first … heaven." // 11:3. G I J omit. // H deletes the first sentence. // James and Schmidt conjecture, without manuscript support, "One gate was broad." 11:4. G drops "like … Master." // At the end I clarifies: "of our Master, Christ." H: "the Master God." J: "our Lord Jesus Christ." 11:4–5. A has εἶδον, not the third person singular, εἶδεν. If εἶδον is a plural, it refers to Abraham and Michael. If it is singular (so the Coptic here), it anticipates the first person plural of 12:1. James accepts the first person singular as original and cites texts that switch from first person singular to third person singular: *1 Enoch*; Gk. *L.A.E.*; *Prot. Jas.* 19; *Acts Thom.* 1.[1] To this add the *Acts of the Apostles*; Ps.-Callisthenes, *History of Alexander*. // In G a single angel drives the many. 11:5–6. G omits the last word of v. 5 ("gate") through "going through" in v. 6. Did an eye skip from the final letter of πύλης to the final letter of προσερχομένας? 11:6. A omits half the verse by mistakenly skipping from the first "man" to the second "man." // J drops "an immeasurable ... gate." // B Q substitute πολλάς (cf. vv. 7, 10, 11) for ἀμετρήτους. // Only A designates Adam ὁ ὅσιος. // G omits "the hair ... cheeks." // J drops "from his throne." 11:7–11. J lacks vv. 7–10 and "But ... bitterly" in v. 11. Has a whole page been lost? 11:8–12:11. G skips from "most marvelous" to the "marvelous" of 12:11. 11:8. H drops "most marvelous man." // B H I Q omit "with joy," which diminishes the parallelism with v. 8. 11:9. A has "Commander-in-chief" instead of "incorporeal one." // B H I Q lack "and he sits here." // After "world" I adds: "and sometimes he weeps and wails and sometimes he rejoices and exults." 11:10. B H I Q lack "rises up and." // B omits as unnecessary "this is the narrow ... life, and." // A moves from the end of πύλη to the end of στενή. // A: πρωτόπλαστος Ἀδάμ; cf. *Gk. Apoc. Ezra* 2:10; *Apoc. Sedr.* 4:4; *Gos. Bart.* 1:22; Eusebius, *Eccl. theol.* 3.2. H I: Ἀδάμ ὁ πρωτόπλαστος; cf. *Ps.-Clem. Hom.* 18:13; Origen, *Fr. Eph.* 35; Epiphanius, *Pan.* 66.23, 51; Ps.-Athanasius, *Serm. major de fide* 61; *Narr. Jos.* 3:4. B Q: Ἀδάμ. Cf. the variants in v. 11. // B H Q lack "because he sees ... saved." 11:11. Through *homoioteleuton* (εἰς ... εἰς) J omits "destruction and to." // A B J Q: ὁ πρωτόπλαστος Ἀδάμ. H: ὁ Ἀδάμ ὁ πρωτόπλαστος. I: ὁ πρωτόπλαστος. Cf. the variants for v. 10. // H, with "elect" for "those being saved," echoes Matt 22:14.

COMMENTARY

The sequence of chap. 11 is reminiscent of the apocalyptic genre. Abraham sees what goes on at the first gate of heaven (vv. 2–7). He then asks for an interpretation (v. 8). Michael complies (vv. 9–12; cf. the sequences in chaps. 13 and 17–18).

The explanation in the second half recapitulates the initial report, often verbatim. The result is that readers twice see souls entering the two gates as well as Adam rejoicing and crying in response. The extended repetition, a way of underlining, amplifies the antitheses that run throughout. There

---

[1]   James, *Testament*, 123.

are two ways, two gates, two sorts of people, two fates; and Adam responds in two antithetical ways, by exulting and by wailing. The alternatives are sharp and unqualified.

One doubts that the uncompromising dualism characterized the original Jewish document. As it stands, the pessimism of chap. 11 ill fits the rest of a book that features an inordinately tolerant deity, includes recognition that some are neither just nor unjust (chaps. 13–14), allows Abraham to recall slain sinners back for a second chance (chap. 14), and teaches that suffering in this world can cancel it in the next (14:15, q.v.). Chap. 11, moreover, is not coherent. In vv. 7 and 10 "many" enter into life whereas vv. 5 and 11–12 teach that only "few" do so. And the picture of Adam alternately rejoicing and mourning surely presupposes that the damned do not outnumber the saved 7,000 to 1, or even 7 to 1. It is almost inevitable that one posit a stricter, Christian revision of a more liberal Jewish original in which the numbers of those saved and those lost were much closer to equal. The conjecture gains credence not only because so many Christians, especially after Augustine's influence (cf. *Civ.* 21), consigned the majority of humanity to damnation, but also because *TA* 11 clearly depends upon Matt 7:13–14 (cf. Luke 11:23),[2] which was a very popular text in the early church:[3]

Matt 7:13:	εἰσέλθατε διὰ τῆς στενῆς πύλης
TA 11:3	πύλη στενή
TA 11:5	διὰ τῆς στενῆς πύλης
TA 11:6	διὰ τῆς στενῆς πύλης ... προσερχομένας
TA 11:7	εἰσερχομένας διὰ τῆς στενῆς πύλης
TA 11:10	εἰσερχομένας διὰ τῆς στενῆς πύλης
TA 11:10	εἰσερχόμενοι διὰ αὐτῆς
TA 11:11	εἰσερχομένας διὰ τῆς
Matt 7:13	ὅτι πλατεῖα ἡ πύλη καὶ εὐρύχωρος ἡ ὁδός
TA 11:2	ὁδός ... πλατεῖα καὶ εὐρύχωρος
TA 11:3	πύλη πλατεῖα
TA 11:6	πλατείας πύλης
TA 11:11	πλατείας πύλης

---

[2] Although Delcor, *Testament*, 134, wonders whether Matthew and *TA* reflect a common source.

[3] See *Biblia Patristica: Index des citations et allusions bibliques dans la littérature patristique: Des origines à Clément d'Alexandrie et Tertullien* (ed. J. Allenbach et al.; Paris: Centre national de la recherche scientifique, 1975), 245; *Biblia Patristica: Index des citations et allusions bibliques dans la littérature patristique: Le troisième siècle* (ed. J. Allenbach et al.; Paris: Centre national de la recherche scientifique, 1977), 252.

Matt 7:13	ἡ ἀπάγουσα εἰς τὴν ἀπώλειαν
TA 11:11	ἡ ἀπάγουσα εἰς τὴν ἀπώλειαν
TA 11:11	ἀπωλείᾳ

Matt 7:13:	καὶ πολλοί εἰσιν οἱ εἰσερχόμενοι δι' αὐτῆς	
TA 11:5	πολλάς	
TA 11:7	πολλάς	
TA 11:10	πολλάς	
TA 11:10		εἰσερχόμενοι δι' αὐτῆς
TA 11:11	πολλάς ...	εἰσερχόμενοι διά
TA 11:11	πολλοί	

Matt 7:14	τί στενὴ ἡ πύλη καὶ τεθλιμμένη ἡ ὁδός	
TA 11:2	ὁδὸς στενὴ	καὶ τεθλιμμένη
TA 11:3	πύλη στενή ...	στενῆς ὁδοῦ
TA 11:5	στενῆς πύλης	
TA 11:6	στενῆς πύλης	
TA 11:7	στενῆς πύλης	
TA 11:10	στενῆς πύλης	
TA 11:10	πύλη ...	στενή

Matt 7:14	ἡ ἀπάγουσα εἰς τὴν ζωήν
TA 11:10	ἡ ἀπάγουσα εἰς τὴν ζωήν

Matt 7:14	καὶ ὀλίγοι εἰσὶν οἱ εὑρίσκοντες αὐτήν
TA 11:5	ὀλίγας
TA 11:6	ὀλίγας
TA 11:11	ὀλίγοι

The Christian influence throughout the chapter is so extensive that one cannot reconstruct the Jewish original beneath. Turner certainly is overly optimistic when he guesses that "in its original form the passage contained the epithets στενή and πλατεῖα, but not τεθλιμμένη ... or εὐρύχωρος (εὐρύχορος); these would be added by someone who noted a resemblance in idea, and a slight resemblance in wording, to Mt. 7.13f, and then either added the words which made it more like the New Testament, or else placed in the margin the whole passage from Mt., which a later scribe did his best to incorporate into the text. Except in this way, this instance does not really require the theory of a Christian editing or redaction of the apocalyptic part of the book."[4] So far from this being the case, it is possible that the Jewish original said nothing at all either about two ways or about two gates, for as James observed, "It is not clear why a soul whose

---

[4]   Turner, "Testament," 29.

character was sufficiently decided to allow of its being brought in by one of the two gates should then have to undergo a judgment."[5]

Throughout much of *TA*, RecShrt. appears more often than not to be a later and abbreviated version of something close to RecLng. It is otherwise in RecShrt. 8:3–16. Not only are its length and content close to RecLng. 11, but in several particulars it seems likely to be more primitive:

- its verbal overlaps with Matt 7:13–14 are less extensive[6]
- there are two gates and two ways in RecLng. 11, under the influence of Matt 7:13–14, but only two gates in RecShrt. 8
- although RecShrt. contrasts the few and the many, it is not so blatantly pessimistic as RecLng. 11:11, which hyperbolically confines salvation to one in 7,000[7]
- a few expressions in RecLng. 11 that seem late and/or Christian—e.g. ἔξωθεν τῶν πυλῶν (see on v. 4), χαίρων καὶ ἀγαλλιώμενος (see on v. 7), πανθαύμαστος (see on v. 9)—are missing from RecShrt. 8

All this is not to say that RecShrt. 8:3–16 is free of Christian influence, only that at points it commends itself as nearer any presumed Jewish original than RecLng. 11.

11:1. "The first gate of heaven" is in "the east," εἰς τὴν ἀνατολήν (ἀνατολή*).[8] That the place of judgment is a gate (so too *2 En.* 42:4 J) makes what is above like what is below, for judges sat at city gates: Deut 21:19; Isa 29:31; Amos 5:15; etc. For the heavenly paradise being in the east, the place of the rising sun, see *1 En.* 32:1–3; *T. Job* 40:3; 52:10; *2 En.* 42:3 J; *b. B. Bat.* 84a; Ephraem, *Metrical Hymns* 15, trans. Burgess, p. 32; *Dorm. BMV* 47, ed. Wenger (Vatic. Gr. 1982), p. 240 (cf. LXX Gen 2:8; Herm. *Vis.* 1.4.1; Gregory of Nyssa, *Vit. Macrinae* 23).[9] Christian texts

---

[5]   James, *Testament*, 123. Cf. Nickelsburg, "Eschatology," 41. The latter incorporates this observation in his attempt to find a traditional judgment scene behind *TA*.

[6]   στενός, πλατύς, θλίβω, and εὐρύχωρος are altogether absent from RecShrt. 8 E (although cf. 9:1, 3). στενός and εὐρύχωρος appear, however, in 8:4 B F G.

[7]   The Romanian, ed. Roddy, p. 38, makes matters even worse: only one person is saved every 7,000 years!

[8]   RecShrt. 8:3 E and B F G have Abraham go to "the river Oceanus." Cf. Josephus, *Bell.* 2.155 (virtuous souls, according to the Essenes, have "an abode beyond ὠκεανόν"); *Vis. Paul* 31 (the seer goes beyond the ocean that encircles the earth to behold the place of the godless). In Greek mythology, one has to cross the River Ocean to get to the underworld; cf. Homer, *Od.* 10.510. Ginzberg, "Testament," 94, assuming a Semitic original, speculated that the Jewish original named "the Great Sea" (cf. Gen 1:6; *2 En.* 3:3) and that this was mistranslated.

[9]   For other texts that place paradise in the north see Delcor, *Testament*, 132–33. In Greek mythology, the Isles of the Blessed are in the west. For seers in Jewish texts

characterize praying to the east—apparently also a Jewish practice: Josephus, *Bell.* 2.128; Ps.-Athanasius, *Quaest. Antiochum* 37 PG 28.620A—as longing for paradise (e.g. *Apos. Con.* 2:57:14), and the belief that Jesus Christ will return from there (cf. Matt 24:27) presupposes that he now dwells in that direction (cf. Hilary, *Tract. Ps.* 67). Some seemingly thought of the garden of Eden as being in (or having been removed to?) heaven: 2 Cor 12:2–3; *4 Ezra* 4:7–8; *2 Bar.* 4:6; *2 En.* 8:1–9:1; *Adam Story II* 7; Ps.-Bartholomew, *Book of the Resurrection of Jesus Christ*, ed. Budge, fol. 20a.[10] For its various gates see on 10:15.

11:2. Abraham sees "two ways" or "roads," δύο ὁδούς. One is "narrow and constricted, the other broad and spacious." These words, like the rest of the chapter, are clearly influenced by Matt 7:13–14; see above. Although the Jewish original cannot be reconstructed, perhaps it concerned two paths or two gates, and maybe, during Christian transmission of the text, assimilation was made to Matthew, which has both paths and gates.[11] One of the foundational texts for the two ways is Jer 21:8, which rewrites Deut 11:26 (cf. 30:15): "I set before you the way of life and the way of death." After Jeremiah, the theme of the two ways is a fixed item of Jewish moral theology and is often linked with eschatological rewards and punishments: Ps 1:6; 119:29-32; 139:24; Prov 2:13; 4:18–19; Wis 5:6-7; Ecclus 2:12; 1QS 3:13-14; *1 En.* 94:1–5; *T. Ash.* 1:3-5; Philo, *Sacr.* 2, 20–44; *4 Ezra* 7:3-9; *2 En.* 30:15 (cf. 42:10); *Mek.* on Exod 14:28–29; *Sifre* Deut. 53; *m. 'Abot* 2:9; *ARN* A 14, 18, 25; *t. Sanh.*14:4; *b. Ber.* 28b ("There are two ways before me, one leading to Paradise and the other to Gehinnom, and I dare not know by which I shall be taken"); *b. Hag.* 3b; Strack-Billerbeck 1:461-63. Christian texts include 2 Pet 2:15; *Did.* 1-6; *Barn.* 18-20; Herm. *Mand.* 6; *Ps.-Clem. Hom.* 7:7:1–3; *Apos. Con.* 1-5; *Sib. Or.* 8:399–400.

Although the motif of the two ways is Jewish, it is also Greek; the motif indeed belongs to world-wide moral tradition.[12] The *Tabula Cebetis* de-

---

journeying to the east see Dean-Otting, *Heavenly Journeys*, 199–200. In Egyptian lore, the gates to the Osirian afterlife are in the west.

[10] On the location of Eden see A. Hilhorst, "A Visit to Paradise: *Apocalypse of Paul* 45 and Its Background," in *Paradise Interpreted: Representations of Biblical Paradise in Judaism and Christianity* (ed. Gerard P. Luttikhuizen; Leiden/Boston/Cologne: Brill, 1999), 128–39.

[11] This is far from certain, however. Both *Tab. Cebetis* 15:2–3 and *Pirqe R. El.* 15 combine the imagery of road and gate or door.

[12] For literature see Hans Dieter Betz, *The Sermon on the Mount: A Commentary on the Sermon on the Mount, including the Sermon on the Plain (Matthew 5:3–7:27 and Luke 6:20–49)* (Hermeneia; Minneapolis: Fortress, 1995), 521–23. For Egyptian parallels see *CT* 1072, 1089, 1182.

scribes the path to true education thus: "Do you not also see a small door and in front of the door a way that is not much frequented; very few pass here; as it were through a trackless waste which seems both rough and rocky? ... And there seems to be a high hill, and a very narrow ascent with a deep precipice on both sides" (15:2-3). Other parallels outside the Jewish and Christian traditions include Hesiod, *Op.* 287-292; Theognis, *Elegiae* 911–914; Diogenes of Sinope, *Ep.* 30; Cicero, *Tusc.* 1.30.72; Silius Italicus, *Punica* 15:18–128; Seneca, *Lucil.* 8.3; Libanius, *Or.* 9.

In *TA* 11, the old metaphor becomes a literal description of postmortem paths (cf. Ps.-Sophocles in Clement of Alexandria, *Strom.* 5.14.121, and *Vis. Paul* 27), perhaps under the influence of non-Jewish stories that feature two ways or gates.[13] There is, for example, the story of the two lovely maidens, Vice and Virtue, who confront Heracles with two ways of life. One wishes to lead him down the easy and delightful path of pleasure so many prefer, the other down the path of toil and suffering: Xenophon, *Mem.* 2.1.21-34; Justin, *2 Apol.* 11; Clement of Alexandria, *Strom.* 2.20.107; 5.5.31; Basil the Great, *De legendis gentilium libris* 4. Even more significant are those passages in which souls, upon death, confront two ways: Plato, *Gorg.* 524A; *Resp.* 10.614C (up and right to heaven, down and left to the underworld); Virgil, *Aen.* 6.540–543 (the way forks in two directions, the right leading to Elysium, the left to Tartarus); Clement of Alexandria, *Strom.* 5.14.121 (quoting Diphilos: "two ways to Hades lead, one for the good, the other for the bad"; also quoted in Ps.-Justin, *Mon.* 3 [but there attributed to Philemon], and Eusebius, *Praep. ev.* 13.13).

One way is "narrow and constricted" (στενή καὶ τεθλιμμένη; θλίβω*), which is a Christian expression, found often in the Fathers in dependence upon Matt 7:13–14 (Clement of Alexandria, *Strom.* 5.5.31; 6.1.2; Origen, *Hom. Jer.* 14.16; etc.). There may be no Jewish or pagan examples of it. The other way is "broad and spacious," πλατεῖα καὶ εὐρύχωρος (εὐρύχωρος*). While πλατεῖα is often used of roads (BAGD, s.v.), this is not true of εὐρύχωρος. Cf., however, LXX Isa 33:21 (πλατεῖς καὶ εὐρύχωροι); Jos. Asen. 24:20 (ἡ ὁδὸς πλατεῖα καὶ εὐρύχωρος); and patristic citations of Matt 7:13–14 (Clement of Alexandria, *Strom.* 4.6.31; 5.5.31; Eusebius, *Comm. Isa.* 1.84, 93, 100; 2.6; etc.). The implied idea, in accord with Matthew, is

---

13   Tobit also narrativizes the two-way imagery; see George W. E. Nickelsburg, "Seeking the Origins of the Two-Ways Tradition in Jewish and Christian Ethical Texts," in Wright, *Multiform Heritage*, 98–99. For additional examples of "Biblical Metaphors taken Literally," see A. Hilhorst's article by that name in *Text and Testimony: Essays on New Testament and Apocryphal Literature in Honour of A. F. J. Klijn* (ed. T. Baarda et al.; Kampen: J. H. Kok, 1988), 123–31.

that vice is attractive, sin natural, whereas living virtuously is, by contrast, hard. Cf. Diogenes Laertius 4.49 ("The way which leads to Hades is easy to follow") and Tertullian, *Marc.* 2.13 ("The way of evil is broad and well supplied with travelers; would not all take its easy course if there were nothing to fear?").

11:2 inaugurates a series of stark antitheses that run throughout the chapter—

"narrow and constricted" way (11:2, 5) vs. "broad and spacious" way (11:2, 5, 11)
"broad" gate (11:3, 6, 11) vs. "narrow gate" (11:3, 6, 7, 10)
"many souls" (11:5, 6, 7, 11) vs. "few souls" (11:5, 6, 11)
Adam mourning (11:6, 11) vs. Adam rejoicing (11:7, 10)
"being saved," "life" (11:10, 11) vs. "destruction," "chastisement," "perishing" (11:11)
"the just" (11:10) vs. "sinners" (v. 11)
"seven thousand" (11:12) vs. "one" (11:12)

11:3. The two gates (δύο πύλας) correspond to the two ways. One gate is "broad," πλατεῖα; cf. Matt 7:13; *4 Ezra* 7:13; Plutarch, *Caes.* 33; πλατός does not often qualify πύλη in Greek literature. The other gate is "narrow," στενή; cf. Aeschylus, *Prom.* 729; Plutarch, *Pomp.* 14.4; *4 Ezra* 7:12.[14] It is unclear whether, in Matt 7:13–14, the gate is at the beginning of the way, on the way, or, as here in *TA*, at the end of the way. For the gate(s) to the heavenly realm(s) see on 10:15 and below on v. 7. *3 En.* 5:3 (Schäfer, *Synopse* 7 = 888) relates that, even after his expulsion from Eden, Adam dwelt at its gate. For the gate(s) to the realm of Hades, which later became the realm of the wicked dead, see Homer, *Il.* 5.646; 9.312; *Od.* 14.156; Hesiod, *Theog.* 773–774; Euripides, *Hipp.* 56–57; *Hec.* 1; Diogenes Laertius 8.34–35; Job 38:17; Ps 9:13; 24:7; 107:18; Isa 38:10; Ecclus 51:9; 1QH 6:24; *Ps. Sol.* 16:2; *Sib. Or.* 2:228–229; Wis 16:13; *3 Macc.* 5:51; Matt 7:13–14; 16:18; Rev 1:18; *2 En.* 42:1; *Odes Sol.* 17:9; 10:126; *b. Ḥag.* 15b; *b. ʿErub.* 19a; Tg. Isa 38:10. In many of these texts the expression is metaphorical, but literal gates on the way to the afterlife are a major feature of Egyptian funerary materials; see *CT* 1053, 1100–1103, 1175, 1180, and *BD* 125, 147; etc.

11:4. In front of (ἔξωθεν*) the gates, Abraham sees an unnamed man sitting on a throne fashioned of gold, κεχρυσωμένου (χρυσόω*). ἔξων (τῶν) πυλῶν is typical of earlier Greek (Plutarch, *Them.* 1.3; Xenophon, *Anab.* 1.4.5; *Acts John* 48; etc.) whereas ἔξωθεν (τῶν) πυλῶν, as here, may be confined to later sources, e.g., Ps.-Callisthenes, *Hist. Alex. Magn.* rec. Byz. poet., ed.

---

[14]   RecShrt. 8:4, 5, 10 E has instead μικρός and μεγαλή.

Reichmann 5773; George Monachus, *Chron. breve* PG 110.1041; Constantine VII, *Cer.*, ed. Reiske, p. 458.[15] For golden thrones see Homer, *Il.* 8.442; 1 Kgs 10:18; 2 Chr 9:17–18; Ps.-Orph. E T 33–34 in Eusebius, *Praep. ev.* 13.12; Aristobulus in Eusebius, *Praep. ev.* 13.13.5; *Vis. Paul* 21; *Petirat Moshe* (*BHM* 1:122); and Byzantine icons of Mary and Jesus.[16] Osiris, the judge of the dead in Egyptian myth, sits on a golden throne.

V. 9 will identify the seated man with Adam, who in *Mek.* on Exod 14:29 and *Gen. Rab.* 21:50 faces the two ways; cf. *2 En.* 30:15 J. Jewish tradition often enthrones human beings in heaven; see *TA* 12:4–13:4 (Abel's throne); 4Q215 4:9 (the Messiah's throne); Ezek. Trag. in Eusebius, *Praep. ev.* 9.29.4–6 (the throne of Moses); Ps.-Orph. E T 33–34 in Eusebius, *Praep. ev.* 13.12.5 (the throne of Moses or Abraham); *T. Job* 33:3–5 (Job's glorious throne); Matt 25:31 (the Son of man's throne); Rev 4:4; 11:16; (the thrones of the twenty-four elders); *Apoc. El. (C)* 1:8 (thrones for the righteous); *T. Isaac* 2:7 (Isaac's throne); *3 En.* 10:1 (Schäfer, *Synopse* 13 = 894; Metatron's throne of glory); note also Psalm 110, which appears to depict an enthronement alongside God, and the plural "thrones" in Dan 7:9. [17] See further on 12:4. There are texts that make Adam a king: Philo, *Opif.* 148; Wis 10:2; *4 Ezra* 6:54; *2 En.* 30:12 J; Timothy of Alexandria, *Discourse on Abbaton*, ed. Budge, fol. 13a; *Pesiq. Rab.* 48:2 (cf. Gen 1:26–28).

Moses in the *Exagoge* of Ezekiel (in Eusebius, *Praep. ev.* 9.29.4–6), the Son of man in *1 Enoch* (45:3; 51:3; 55:4; 61:8; 62:2–3), Wisdom in Wis 9:4, 10, and the lamb of God in Revelation (7:17; 22:1, 3) all sit on the divine throne (see further on 9:8). Whether Adam does so in our book is unclear.[18] Timothy of Alexandria, *Discourse on Abbaton*, ed. Budge, fol. 13a, reports that God put Adam on a great throne, gave him a crown of glory, handed him a royal scepter, and made the angels worship him. Elsewhere Adam's heavenly throne is Satan's old throne, as in *L.A.E.* 47:3: Adam "will sit on the throne of him who overcame him," that is, Satan; cf. Gk. *L.A.E.* 39:2–3.

---

[15] RecShrt. 8:5: ἀνὰ μέσον τῶν (δύο) πυλῶν.

[16] Ancient Near Eastern examples in Martin Metzger, *Königsthron und Gottesthron: Thronformen und Throndarstellungen in Ägypten und im Vorderen Orient im dritten und zweiten Jahrtausend vor Christus und deren Bedeutung für das Verständnis von Aussagen über den Thron im Alten Testament* (AOAT 15/1; Kevelaer/Neukirchen-Vluyn: Butzon & Bercker/Neukirchener, 1985), 301–302.

[17] Despite Munoa's interesting argument in *Four Powers*, 46–51, 62–81, 98–109, one remains doubtful that Adam in *TA* 11 is modeled on "the Ancient of Days" in Daniel 7.

[18] Given that Abraham sees God's throne in the *Apocalypse of Abraham*, does *TA* here draw upon some such tradition?

Late Jewish and Christian texts envisage Adam seated inside paradise or before its gates: Timothy of Alexandria, *Discourse on Abbaton*, ed. Budge, fol. 13a; *Yalqut Hadash*; and the vision of an Essex laborer preserved in Matthew Paris, *Chron. Majora*, ed. Luard, Rolls Series 2.509.[19] Similarly, in Ps.-Bartholomew, *Book of the Resurrection of Jesus Christ*, ed. Budge, fol. 13b, Adam is at the Gate of Life so that he might be the first to salute all the righteous as they enter into the heavenly "Jerusalem, the city of Christ."

Adam's appearance (ἰδέα*) is "terrifying," φοβερά; cf. esp. 13:2, of Abel; also *Apoc. Abr.* 23:5; Gk. *3 Bar.* 4:3.[20] That Adam is here like God recalls Gen 1:26 and 5:3, where he is created in God's image and likeness (the latter uses ἰδέαν). Whether there is further an allusion to LXX Ezek 1:26 (ἡ ἰδέα τοῦ ἀνθρώπου; cf. *1 En.* 46:1; *Apoc. Abr.* 10:4) is uncertain.[21] In any event, it is specifically his fearful appearance that makes Adam like τοῦ δεσπότου. The definite article points to God, and the expansion in H (τῷ δεσπότῃ θεῷ) construes the words this way (cf. the christological clarifications in I and J). For "Master" as a title for God in *TA* and elsewhere see further on 1:4. Like Death's appearance (17:14–16), God's is terrible or fearful; cf. Rev 20:11, where heaven and earth flee the face of the enthroned.

11:5. The "many (disembodied) souls" (πολλὰς ψυχάς; cf. vv. 7, 10, 11; Matt 7:13) are being "driven" (ἐλαυνομένας; cf. 12:1) through the broad way by angels, obviously against their will (12:1 gives the angels whips). In contrast to this are the "few souls," ψυχὰς ὀλίγας; cf. vv. 6, 11. They are not "driven" but rather "carried," ἐφέροντο, as in 12:16; cf. ἀναφέρω in 13:12–13; 14:8; also Matt 4:6 = Luke 4:11, quoting Ps 91:11–12. For

---

[19]   James, *Testament*, 30, conveniently prints the Latin of this last text. Cf. the depiction of an enthroned Adam in the 6th cent. CE Armenian *Concerning the Death of Adam* 16–22. For the relevant Hebrew of *Yalqut Hadash* see Johann Andreas Eisenmenger, *Entdecktes Judenthum, oder gründlicher und wahrhaffter Bericht* (Königsberg: n.p., 1711), 2:320. Cf. the position of 'Akatri'el Yah in "The Secret of Sandalon" (*Ma'aśe Merkava*, ed. Schäfer, *Synopse* 597): he "sits at the entrance to paradise." C. R. A. Morray-Jones, "Transformational Mysticism in the Apocalyptic-Merkabah Tradition," *JSJ* 43 (1992), 17, argues from this text, among others, that some mystical Jewish circles "associated or identified the primordial Adam with the divine *kabod*." If he is right, does *TA* perhaps mock that tradition by depicting Adam's contrasting emotional responses?

[20]   RecShrt. B F G instead describes Adam as παμμεγέθης, that is, "very large." Adam is also a giant in *Apoc. Abr.* 23; *b. Ḥag.* 12a; *b. Sanh.* 38b; *Gen. Rab.* 8:1; Ps.-Bartholomew, *Book of the Resurrection of Jesus Christ*, ed. Budge, fol. 11a. For other giant figures see n. 9 on p. 259.

angels as assistants and witnesses at the eschatological judgment see 12:1–8; *1 En.* 1:9; 53:3; 54:6; 55:3; 56:1–4; 62:11; 63:1; 100:4; 11QMelch. 2:9, 14; *T. Levi* 3:2–3; Matt 13:41–42, 49; 24:31; 25:31; Rev 14:15–19; *2 En.* 10:3; *Apoc. Zeph.* 4:6–7; Sahidic fragment; Strack-Billerbeck 1:672–73, 974; etc. Our text recalls others that feature two angelic groups, one good, one bad (e.g., Rev 12:7; *Pirqe R. El.* 15). Note also *T. Ash.* 6:4–6, where troubled souls are tormented by the evil spirits they served in life whereas peaceful souls meet the angel of peace and are led to eternal life; *Apoc. Zeph.* 3:1–9, where some angels weep over lost souls while others rejoice over them; *Apoc. Paul* (Nag Hammadi) 22, where four angels "with whips in their hands" are "goading the souls on to the judgment"; and Hippolytus, *Univ.* 33, where the unjust, dragged by "the angels of destruction," go unwillingly, "with force as if dragged in chains."

The contrast between the few and the many, here from Matthew, is a biblical *topos* (cf. also Asclepius 22: "There are not many pious in the world—nay, there are so few that they could easily be numbered"). From the days of Noah (Genesis 6) to the days of Moses (Exod 23:2; 32) and on to the days of the prophets (1 Kgs 19:10; Ezek 9:8-10; etc.), it is always the many who follow the wrong path. Those who do good are few. In the present text, this takes the extreme form of *massa damnata*, which became standard belief in the middle ages;[22] cf. *4 Ezra* 7:47-51; 8:1–3, 55; 9:20–22; *2 Bar.* 44:15; 48:43; *Gos. Bart.* 1:33 (three out of three thousand are saved); Chrysostom, *Hom. Act.* 24 PG 60.189; *b. Sanh.* 97b; *b. Menaḥ.* 29b; contrast Isaac of Nineveh, *Second* 40.10, ed. Brock, p. 166 ("the majority of humankind will enter the kingdom"). See further on vv. 11–12.

The association of angels with the two ways is traditional. In *Pirqe R. El.* 15, two groups of angels are near doors by the way of evil; those without are merciful, those within cruel. In 1QS 3:20–21, the Prince of light rules those walking in the ways of light and the angel of darkness rules those walking in the ways of darkness. Cf. *Barn.* 18:1: "There are two ways of teaching and power, one of light and one of darkness … . Over the one are set the light-bearing angels of God, but over the other angels of Satan."

11:6. Adam, as yet unidentified for Abraham, is characterized as "marvelous," θαυμάσιος (bis; cf. v. 8: πανθαύμαστος) and "holy," ὅσιος. The former adjective makes him resemble his son Abel (12:5, 11; 13:1) and Job

---

21 Fossum, *Name of God*, 276, thinks "there can be no doubt" of this. Cf. Munoa, *Four Powers*, 99.

22 See the texts in George Gordon Coulton, *Five Centuries of Religion*, vol. 1 (Cambridge: Cambridge University Press, 1923), 445–49.

(15:15); the latter makes him like Abraham (cf. the title; 1:2; 9:2; 12:15). When Adam sees few being saved, his response is dramatic. He tears the hair from his head and beard: ἥρπαζεν τὰς τρίχας τῆς κεφαλῆς αὐτοῦ καὶ τὰς παρειὰς τοῦ πώγωνος (παρειά also appears in 16:6). The vivid ἥρπαζεν τὰς τρίχας is not a known idiom. τὰς παρειὰς τοῦ πώγωνος, whose meaning is unclear, is also unparalleled, although Meletius of Antioch, *Ep.*, ed. Bell, p. 74, has: μετὰ τοῦ πώγωνος καὶ τῶν παρειῶν. The act of mortification, which is related to shaving the hair or beard in mourning (Job 1:20; Isa 15:2; Jer 7:29; 41:5; Mic 1:6), recalls Ezra's action in 1 Esd 8:68 (cf. Ezra 9:3): κατέτιλα τοῦ τριχώματος τῆς κεφαλῆς καὶ τοῦ πώγωνος (cf. *Agade* 2.205: "the young women did not restrain from tearing their hair"). Adam further throws himself down from his throne, going from exaltation to abasement; cf. Isa 47:1; Ezek 26:16; Jonah 3:6. Finally, he weeps and wails, κλαίων καὶ ὀδυρόμενος; cf. vv. 8 (κλαίει καὶ ὀδύρεται), 11 (κλαίων καὶ ὀδυρόμενος); 20:7 (ἔκλαιον … ὀδυρόμενοι); Homer, *Od.* 8.577; Plato, *Resp.* 388B; Gk. *L.A.E.* 27:2; Josephus, *Ant.* 6.358; *3 Bar.* 13:1; Gk. fr. *Asc. Isa.* 1:10; *Apoc. Sedr.* 11:1; etc. His mourning has an analogy in *L.A.E.* 1:1; 4:3; 8:1–2; 9:1–4, which recount the sorrow of Adam and Eve after their sin. Later literature emphasizes this theme of Adam and Eve mourning: *Adam, Eve and the Incarnation* 20, 25, 38; *History of the Forefathers* 1, 26–28; *History of Adam and his Grandsons* 4; *Adam Story I* 1, 13; etc.

11:7. Abraham now sees "many souls entering through the narrow gate." The language is from v. 6, but here those passing through the narrow gate are "many" instead of "few." "Many" are also saved in v. 10 but only a "few" in vv. 5–6, 11–12. In the Jewish original those saved and those lost were probably "many." If so, Christian redaction, under the influence of Matt 7:13–14, created the antithesis between the "many" and the "few"— an antithesis which it did not, however, consistently carry through. For the gate or entrance leading into eternal life see Ezra 7:6-8; *Sib. Or.* 2:150; Rev 22:14; Herm. *Sim.* 9.12.5; *Apoc. Zeph.* 3:9; *Ps.-Clem. Hom.* 3:18; *T. Jac.* 2:17; *Pesiq. Rab.* 179b.

If the sight of many going through the broad gate moves Adam to tear out his hair, throw himself to the ground, and weep and wail (v. 6), the sight of those entering life undoes all that. He rises from the ground and returns to his throne: ἐκαθέζετο ἐπὶ τοῦ θρόνου αὐτοῦ; cf. *CTA* 6.3.10–21 (El, who has been mourning for Baal, laughs and takes his seat when the latter returns from death); *CTA* 17.2.8–15 (Danil goes from mourning to laughing and takes a seat); *Apoc. Abr.* 6:1 (Abraham laughs and groans at once); *Prot. Jas.* 17:2 (Mary laughs and is sad alternately; cf. *Ps.-Mt.* 13). More distant parallels include: Gk. *Vis. Paul* 7 (at the time of prayer, one angel rejoices because of good deeds, another is sad because of bad deeds);

Apoc. Zeph. 3:1–9 (evil angels rejoice over three sinners while good angels weep over them); *b. Ber.* 18b (a dead man mourns because his sons are about to die and laughs because they are highly esteemed). Adam can now rejoice and exult with much joy: ἐν εὐφροσύνῃ πολλῇ χαίρων καὶ ἀγαλλιώμενος; cf. ἐν εὐφροσύνῃ μεγάλῃ in 2 Chr 20:27; 30:21.[23] The combination of the final two verbs, in this order, is common in Christian texts: Matt 5:12; Rev 19:7; *Prot. Jas.* 36; *Acts Thom.* 107; Origen, *Mart.* 4.4; Eusebius, *Hist. eccl.* 5.1; *Comm. Isa.* 2.39; Ps.-Ephraem, *De patientia*, ed. Phrantzoles, p. 308.13; etc. But *T. Job* 43:15 and *4 Bar.* 6:19 supply likely Jewish examples.

11:8. Abraham, calling Michael κύριέ μου (cf. 2:7; 13:1; 14:1; 15:4), asks him (ἠρώτησεν δὲ ὁ Ἀβραάμ, as in 15:1, without ὁ) about "this most marvelous man": τίς ἐστιν οὗτος ὁ ἀνὴρ ὁ πανθαύμαστος; cf. 13:1: τίς ἐστιν ὁ κριτὴς οὗτος ὁ πανθαύμαστος; The man is "appareled (κοσμούμενος; κοσμέω*) in glory," δόξῃ. The question incorporates a Jewish *topos*. CD 3:20 and 1QS 4:23 refer to "Adam's glory" (כבוד; cf. 4Q504 fr. 8; 2 *En.* 30:11 J; *b. Sanh.* 59b; *Deut. Rab.* 11:3). Ecclus 49:16 declares Adam's "splendor" (תפארת) to be "above every living being in creation" (cf. 2 *En.* 30:11–12). Ezek 28:13 covers the primal man in "every precious stone" and seats him on the mountain of God.[24] Other texts speak of Adam's glorious garments (*Pesiq. Rab.* 37:2; *Pesiq. Rab. Kah.* 6:5; cf. Ps 8:5), of his glorious dwellings (Gk. *L.A.E.* 20:2 v.l.; *3 Bar.* 4:16; *b. B. Bat.* 75a; Tgs. Ps.-Jn. and Onq. on Gen 3:21; *Gen. Rab.* 20:12; *Pesiq. Rab.* 14:10; *Pesiq. Rab. Kah.* 26:3), and of his glorious face (*Tanḥ.* B Genesis Bereshit 25; Leviticus 'Ahare Mot 3; *b. B. Bat.* 58a; *Gen. Rab.* 12:6; *Lev. Rab.* 20:12; cf. the "Light-Adam" in *Orig. World* 108:21). Relevant Christian parallels include Ps.-Ephraem, *Comm. Gen.* 2.4, 14; *Adam, Eve and the Incarnation* 1, 9; *Adam Story I* 5; Timothy of Alexandria, *Discourse on Abbaton*, ed. Budge, fol. 13a.[25] Unlike those Jewish texts that have Adam redeemed at the end (*L.A.E.* 47; Gk. *L.A.E.* 39) or Christian texts that have him redeemed at Christ's resurrection (*Acts Pil.* 24–27; *T. Adam* 3:4), in *TA*, which has very little to say about the culmination of history, Adam has already, during the days of Abraham, regained his Edenic glory (cf. perhaps Wis 10:1–2 and Tertullian, *Paen.* 12).

---

23 RecShrt. 8:6, 7, 15 E: γελάω.
24 On this text see esp. Daniel E. Callender, Jr., *Adam in Myth and History: Ancient Israelite Perspectives on the Primal Human* (HSS; Winona Lake, Ind.: Eisenbrauns, 2000), 87–135.
25 Munoa, *Four Powers*, 82–112, has a survey of Adam's exaltation in Jewish and Christian texts.

Adam is here πανθαύμαστος, "most marvelous." The word, which reappears in 13:1 (of Abel), is unattested in classical literature but known from later patristic texts, where it often refers to Mary: Theodore the Studite, *Nativ. BMV* 4 PG 96. 684C; Ps.-John of Damascus, *Pass. Artemii* 52 PG 96. 1300A; George Hamartolos, *Chron.*, ed. de Boor, p. 189.7; etc. Suidas, s.v. Ἀβραάμ, uses it of Joseph. On virtues with prefatory παν- see p. 86.

11:9. The "incorporeal one" (ἀσώματος; see on 3:6) tells Abraham that the man who sits in glory (see on v. 8) is "the first-formed Adam," πρωτόπλαστος Ἀδάμ; cf. vv. 10, 11; 13:2, 5.[26] Although πρωτόπλαστος is popular with Christian writers (cf. *Gos. Nic.* A 3(19); *Narr. Jos.* 3:4; Lampe, s.v.), it appears also in Jewish writings: Gk. fr. *Jub.* 3:28; *Sib. Or.* 1:285; Philo, *Quaest. Gen.* 1.32; *Quaest. Exod.* 2.46; Wis 7:1; 10:1; Gk. *L.A.E.* title; *3 Bar.* 4:9; *Gk. Apoc. Ezra* 2:10 (πρωτόπλαστον Ἀδάμ); *Apoc. Sedr.* 4:4 (πρωτόπλαστον Ἀδάμ); and according to Anastasius of Sinai, *Hex.* 12 7, there was a Jewish book entitled *The Testament of the Protoplasts*. In addition to the conventional *topoi*—Adam is glorious, he is the first-formed, all have come from him (πάντες ἐξ αὐτοῦ ἐγένοντο; cf. Philo, *Opif.* 136; *4 Ezra* 3:21; 6:54; and the association of Adam with πᾶς in Rom 5:18; 1 Cor 15:22)—we learn that Adam sees (all) the world: βλέπει τὸν κόσμον.[27] Evidently he is, like Abraham in chaps. 9 and 10, able from his high vantage point above the earth to see what transpires below. For other narratives in which raised figures behold everything see on 9:8. None of them concerns Adam. The rabbis, however, took Gen 5:1 ("This is the book of the generations of Adam") to mean that God showed Adam all the generations that would follow him: *b. ʿAbod. Zar.* 5a; *b. Sanh.* 38b; *Gen. Rab.* 24:2; *Midr. Ps.* 139:6.

11:10. When Adam sees many souls going through the narrow gate (see on v. 7), he rises up and sits on his throne, rejoicing and exulting in joy. The language is from v. 7. But here it is added that "this is the narrow gate of the just that leads to life" (ἡ ἀπάγουσα εἰς τὴν ζωήν, as in Matt 7:14), and that "those who enter through it go away to paradise," παράδεισον; see on 4:2. This is of course Adam's first dwelling, from which he was exiled after his disobedience. His righteous descendants are allowed to return; cf. *T. Levi* 18:10; Rev 2:7; *Apoc. Sedr.* 16:6. The way of life is the way to paradise (cf. the road to the tree of life in Gen 3:24). Of the texts that speak of the just entering paradise or Eden, some envisage the place as upon the

---

[26] Cf. RecShrt. 8:12: "Adam, the first man that God formed" (ἔπλασεν; C: πρωτόπλαστος).

[27] According to RecShrt. 8:13, he sees "every soul coming out of its body."

earth (*1 En.* 32:2–6; *Apoc. Abr.* 21:3–6), others (including *TA*) as being in heaven (*L.A.E.* 25:3; Gk. *L.A.E.* 37:5; Luke 24:43; 2 Cor 12:2–3; *2 En.* 8:1–9:1).

"And because of this the first-formed (πρωτόπλαστος; see on v. 9) Adam rejoices, because he sees souls being saved" (ψυχὰς σῳζομένας), is redundant. Are the redundant words secondary? For ψυχή with σῴζω see v. 12; 14:3; Diodorus Siculus 37.19; LXX Gen 19:17; 1 Βασ 19:11; Jer 31:6; Amos 2:14; *Ps. Sol.* 17:17; Josephus, *Ant.* 9.240; Mark 3:4; Jas 1:21; 5:20; *Barn.* 19:10; etc.

11:11. This verse summarizes the content of v. 6 but stands in antithetical parallelism to v. 10:

10   when he sees many souls entering through the narrow gate
11   when he sees many souls entering through the broad   gate

10   then he rises up and sits on his throne, rejoicing and exulting in joy
11   then he tears out the hair of his head and throws himself on the ground, weeping and wailing bitterly

10   this is the narrow gate of the just that leads to life and those who enter through it go away to paradise.
11   the broad gate is (the gate) of sinners, which leads to destruction and to the chastisement of eternity.

10   And because of this the first-formed Adam rejoices, because he sees souls being saved
11   And because of this the first-formed Adam rises from his throne, weeping and mourning over the destruction of sinners, because those perishing are many, those being saved few.

With "weeping and wailing bitterly" (κλαίων καὶ ὀδυρόμενος πικρῶς) cf. vv. 6, 11; 20:6–7; LXX Isa 22:4 (πικρῶς κλαύσομαι); 33:7 (πικρῶς κλαίοντες); *Jos. Asen.* 10:15 (ἔκλαυσε πικρῶς); Matt 26:75 = Luke 22:62 (ἔκλαυσεν πικρῶς); *Mart. Isa.* 1:10 (ἔκλαυσεν πικρῶς); *Prot. Jas.* 27:1 (ἔκλαυσεν πικρῶς); *Gk. Apoc. Ezra* 5:8 (ἔκλαυσα πικρῶς); Ps.-Callisthenes, *Hist. Alex. Magn.* rec. E 6.3 (ἔκλαυσαν πικρῶς); and see further on 20:6. "The broad gate is (the gate) of sinners" (ἁμαρτωλῶν; see on 9:3), and it "leads to destruction," ἡ ἀπάγουσα εἰς τὴν ἀπώλειαν (so also RecShrt. 8:11 E). For ἀπώλεια with eschatological sense see 12:2; Gk. fr. *1 En.* 22:12; 98:10; *Ps. Sol.* 2:31; 3:11; 13:11; Matt 7:13 (ἡ ἀπάγουσα εἰς τὴν ἀπώλειαν); Phil 3:19; Heb 10:39; 2 Pet 2:1; 3:7; Rev 17:8, 11; *Gk. Apoc. Pet.* 1:2; *Gk. Apoc. Ezra* 4:21. Whether this destruction is annihilation (as in Egyptian myth) or eternal chastisement is unclear. For τὴν κόλασιν τὴν αἰώνιον, a common phrase, see Matt 25:46; *T. Reub.* 5:5; *2 Clem.* 6:7; *Mart. Pol.* 2:3; Justin, *1 Apol.* 8.4; *Dial.* 117.3; etc. The line recalls not only Matt 7:13–14 and

25:46 but also *2 Bar.* 85:13: "There is the sentence of corruption, the way of fire, and the path which brings to Gehenna." "The destruction of sinners" (ἀπωλεία τῶν ἁμαρτωλῶν; cf. above and see on 12:2 for ἀπώλεια) is not a stock phrase, although there is a parallel in *Ps. Sol.* 3:11: ἡ ἀπώλεια τοῦ ἁμαρτωλοῦ.

The verse ends with "because those perishing are many, those being saved few." Given that the rest of this chapter is so influenced by Matt 7:13–14, these words may reflect another Matthean line (without synoptic parallel); cf. Textual Notes:

TA 11:11	διότι πολλοί εἰσιν οἱ ἀπολλύμενοι, ὀλίγοι δὲ οἱ σῳζόμενοι
Matt 22:14	πολλοὶ γάρ εἰσιν κλητοί, ὀλίγοι δὲ ἐκλεκτοί

Other parallels include: Plato, *Phaed.* 69C (ναρθηκοφόροι μὲν πολλοί, βάκχοι δέ τε παῦροι, in Clement of Alexandria, *Strom.* 1.19; 5.3); *4 Ezra* 8:1 (*hoc saeculum fecit altissimus propter multos, futurum autem propter paucos*), 3 (*Multi quidem creati sunt, pauci autem saluabuntur*); *Barn.* 4:14 (πολλοὶ κλητοί, ὀλίγοι δὲ ἐκλεκτοὶ εὑρεθῶμεν); Clement of Alexandria, *Strom.* 1.1 (τὸ τοῖς πολλοῖς κρυπτόν, τοῦτο τοῖς ὀλίγοις φανερὸν γενήσεται); 5.9 (πολλοὶ κακοί, ὀλίγοι δὲ ἀγαθοί).

When Adam laments the fate of many sinners, readers might infer his culpability in their fate.[28] Yet the thought is not explicit, and subsequent chapters emphasize the moral responsibility of each individual in the scales of judgment, not the devastating effects of Adam's failure.

11:12. The gloomy, hyperbolic conclusion accords with vv. 5–6, 11–12, where only a few are saved, not with vv. 7 and 10, where "many" are saved. Even from among a vast number of human beings, here specified as "seven thousand,"[29] there is "scarcely to be found" (μόλις εὑρίσκεται; μόλις*; cf. Dionysius of Halicarnassus, *Ant. rom.* 5.49.2; Philo, *Mut.* 34; Josephus, *Bell.* 4.30) one "soul saved (ψυχὴ σῳζομένη; see on v. 10) and undefiled," ἀμόλυντος*. Although ἀμόλυντος characterizes the spirit of wisdom in Wis 7:22 and an unpolluted soul in Arrian, *Epict. diss.* 4.11.8, the moral application of the word (whose basic sense is "not leaving any stain") is typical of Christian texts: *Apos. Con.* 3:7:6; 6:11:6; Gregory of Nazianzus, *Ep.* 244; etc. For the application to virginity see Lampe, s.v., and for other texts in which most human beings are lost see on v. 5.

---

28 Cf. Turner, "Testament," 122–23.
29 Contrast RecShrt. 8:7, 16 E: Adam's crying exceeds his laughter sevenfold.

Chapter 12: The Postmortem Judgment

Bibliography: S. G. F. Brandon, "The Weighing of the Soul," in *Myths and Symbols: Studies in Honor of Mircea Eliade* (ed. Joseph M. Kitagawa and Charles H. Long; Chicago/London: University of Chicago Press, 1969), 91–110. Ellul, "Testament d'Abraham". James, *Testament*, 70–72. Macurdy, "Platonic Orphism". Munoa, *Four Powers*. Nickelsburg, "Eschatology". Schmidt, "Testament," 1:71–78; 2:132, 140. Turner, "Testament," 124–29.

Long Recension

12:1. While he was saying these things to me, behold, (there appeared) two angels of fiery appearance and merciless intention, and (they were) relentless of countenance; and they drove a myriad of souls, mercilessly striking them with fiery whips. 12:2. And the angel grabbed one soul with his hand; and they drove all the souls into the broad gate to destruction. 12:3. And we followed the angels and entered within that broad gate. 12:4. And in the middle of the two gates stood a terrifying throne, in appearance like crystal, flashing forth as fire. 12:5. And a marvelous man, resembling the sun, like unto a son of God, sat upon it. 12:6. Before him stood a table with the appearance of crystal, wholly made of gold and silk. 12:7. On the table lay a book; its thickness was three cubits and its width was six cubits. 12:8. On the right and on the left stood two angels who were holding a papyrus roll and ink and a reed-pen. 12:9. In front of the table sat a glorious angel holding a scale in his hand. 12:10. On his left sat a fiery angel, altogether merciless and relentless, holding in his hand a trumpet, which contained an all-

Short Recension fam. E

9:1. And Abraham said to Michael, "Is it the case then that the one unable to enter through the narrow gate is unable to enter into life?" Michael said to him, "Yes." 9:2. Abraham cried out saying, "Woe to me! What will I do? For I am a man of broad girth. 9:3. And I will be unable to enter into the narrow gate, because only a child of about ten would be able to enter through it." 9:4. And Michael said, "You will easily enter through it, and all who are holy like you. But most of the world will enter through the gate that leads unto destruction." 9:5. And with Abraham standing and marveling in that hour, behold, there was an angel driving about six thousand souls, and he held in his hand one soul. And he conducted the thousands of souls into the gate leading unto destruction. 9:6. Abraham said, "Are these going unto destruction?" 9:7. And Michael answered and said to Abraham, "Let us go and seek among these souls; and if we find one worthy to be brought into life, we will carry it." 9:8. And Michael and Abraham went and sought, and they did not find one worthy of life, except only that one which the angel held in his

consuming fire that tests sinners. 12:11. And the marvelous man, sitting on his throne, judged and declared a verdict upon the souls. 12:12. The two angels on the right and the left were making a written register. The one on the right recorded upright deeds and the one on the left recorded sins. 12:13. And the one in front of the table, the one holding the scale, weighed the souls. 12:14. And the fiery angel, the one holding the fire, tested the souls with fire. 12:15. And Abraham asked the Commander-in-chief, "What are these things that we see?" And the Commander-in-chief said, "These things that you see, pious Abraham, are the judgment and recompense." 12:16. And behold! the angel holding the soul in its hand brought it before the judge. 12:17. And the judge said to one of the angels serving him, "Open for me this book, and find for me the sins of this soul." 12:18. And opening the book he found the balance of its sins and of its upright deeds to be equal. He neither gave it over to the torturers nor (did he set it) among the saved, but he placed it in the middle.

hand. For he had found her sins to be equal to her good deeds. And he did not leave her in difficulty or in rest, but in a place in between. 9:9. Those (other) souls he took to perdition. 9:10. And Abraham said to Michael, "Tell me, lord, the angel who drives on the thousands of souls, is he or is he not the one who carries them from the body?" 9:11. Michael answered and said, "Death brings them unto the place of judgment, so that the judge may judge them." 10:1. Abraham said to Michael, "I want you to conduct me to the place of judgment, so that I might see how he judges." 10:2. Then Michael made the cloud convey Michael and Abraham to a place, of which paradise is a part. 10:3. When he arrived at the place where the judge was, an angel came and handed over to the judge that soul which the angel held in his hand. 10:4. And he heard the soul crying out, "Have mercy upon me, Lord." 10:5. The judge said to him, "How can I show mercy to you when you did not show mercy to your daughter? But you rose up against the fruit of your womb and you murdered her. 10:6. And the soul answered and said, "I did not commit murder, but she spoke falsely against me." 10:7. The judge commanded the one who writes down the record to come. 10:8. And behold, there were Cherubim bearing two books, and with them was a man, exceedingly great, who had three crowns on his head. 10:9. And one was higher than the other crown(s). These are called "witnesses." 10:10. And the man had in his hand a golden reed. And the judge said to him, "Set forth the sin of this soul." 10:11. And the man opened up one of the two books with the Cherubim and looked up the sin of the soul. 10:12. And the man answered and said,

"O wretched soul, how can you say that you have not committed murder? 10:13. Did you not, upon the death of your husband, go forth and commit adultery with the husband of your daughter, and then kill your daughter?" 10:14. And he spoke to her in that hour of the other sins that she had committed. 10:15. Hearing these things, the soul opened her mouth and cried and said, "Alas, because all the sins that I committed while I was in the world, I had forgotten. But here they are not forgotten." 10:16. Then the servants of wrath took her and tortured her.

TEXTUAL NOTES ON THE LONG RECENSION

12:1. I omits "While ... things," perhaps due to *homoioteleuton* (ἀμόλυντος ... λαλοῦντος). // A: ἡμῖν. C: ἐμέ. E P: ἐμαυτοῦ. D L M: αὐτοῦ. H omits. James plausibly conjectured an original ἐμοί. // A has the long description of the two angels: "with fiery appearance ... drove." B H I J Q omit, and the description has no parallel in RecShrt. fam. E. The closest parallel is *Vis. Paul* Arn. 11. Although the vivid description may be secondary, RecShrt. 9:5 B F G has ἐλαύνων. // J specifies: "seven thousands." Cf. RecShrt. E: "six thousands." // James conjectured ἐν πυρίναις χαρζαναῖς, which Schmidt prints. The manuscripts are corrupt. A: ἐν πυρίνῳ χαρίζων. B Q: αὐτοὺς ἀλξάνες. D M: ἐν πυρίνῳ θεάφῃ. H: αὐτὰς πυρίναις χαρζάνες. I: ἐν πυρίναις χαρζάνοις. J: καὶ καταξαίνοντες. 12:3. B omits "and entered ... gate." Maybe this is conscious abbreviation, or maybe it is due to *homoioteleuton* (καί ... καί). 12:6. A lacks "and silk," probably through *homoioteleuton* (χρυσοῦ ... βύσσου). 12:7–9. B skips from the "table" in v. 7 to the "table" in v. 9. 12:7. J Q skips from the first "cubits" to the second: "its thickness was six cubits." // For "three" A has "thirty," E "six," P "seven," D L M "eight." // A lacks "and its width was six cubits," which Schmidt nonetheless prints. // Instead of "six" (so H I Q), D L M have "twelve," E "ten," J "sixty," P "twenty." // 12:8. H J Q omit "and ink," perhaps because an eye skipped from the end of "papyrus roll" (χάρτην) to the end of "ink" (μέλαν). 12:9–10. J skips from the "angel" in v. 9 to the "angel" in v. 10. 12:11. B skips from the first καί to the second καί, omitting "and the marvelous ... judged." 12:12. Q lacks: "The two angels ... register." Did someone note the redundancy of the angels writing what must already be in the book of v. 7? 12:13. J abbreviates by omitting "the one holding the scale." 12:13–14. I passes from "holding" in v. 13 to "holding" in v. 14. 12:14. H lacks "And ... tested." // G drops "the one holding the fire." 12:16. I abbreviates by dropping "in its hand." // G drops "brought it before the judge," skipping from the end of "his" (αὐτοῦ) to the end of "judge" (κριτοῦ). 12:17–18. B passes from the end of ψυχῆς in v. 17 to the end of αὐτῆς in v. 18. 12:18. J omits "And opening the book," perhaps because this makes one wonder what the balance might be used for. // A: αὐτὴν ζυγάδας τὰς ἁμαρτίας καὶ τὰς δικαιοσύνας ἐξ ἴσου. B: ζυγὰς τὰς ἁμαρτίας ταύτης καὶ τὰς δικαιοσύνας ἐξ ἴσου. G omits αὐτὴν ζυγάδας and ἐξ ἴσου. Cf. H: τὰς ἁμαρτίας καὶ τὰς δικαιοσύνας αὐτῆς ἴσου. I offers a count: ζυγὰς δέκα τὰς ἁμαρτίας τῆς ψυχῆς καὶ τὰς δικαιοσύνας ἕξη. Q: τὰς ἁμαρτίας τῆς ψυχῆς ζυγάδας καὶ τὰς δικαιοσύνας ἐξ ἴσου. J: δικαιοσύνας καὶ ἁμαρτίας ὅσον ἡ δικαιοσύνη ὁμοίως ἡ ἁμαρτία. J seems a later paraphrase. I's count makes no sense and must be secondary. The difficult ζυγάδας/ ζυγάς must be original, which makes G and H abridgements. Something close to A B or Q has the best chance of being pristine. // I lacks "He neither ... placed it."

COMMENTARY

Chap. 12, which happily refrains from depicting the tortures of hell, has three sections. Vv. 1–10 set the scene for postmortem judgment by introducing in rapid succession a confusing host of characters—two punishing angels (v. 1), a multitude of condemned souls (v. 1), a soul separated from that multitude (v. 2), a marvelous man on a throne (v. 5), two recording angels (v. 8), a glorious angel with a scale (v. 9), and a fiery angel with a trumpet (v. 10). These characters are associated with a series of interesting objects—fiery whips (v. 1), a terrifying throne (v. 4), a crystal-like table (v. 6), a large book (v. 7), writing materials (v. 8), a scale (v. 9), and a trumpet (v. 10). Vv. 10–15 next tell us what the various heavenly characters do, all of which Michael, in response to Abraham's question, puts under the heading, "the judgment and recompense" (v. 15). Finally, vv. 16–18 concern the plight of an individual whose bad deeds and good deeds are equal.

The chapter features dyads. A pair of angels drives souls through the broad gate (vv. 1–2). Inside and between the two gates is a wondrous man seated on a throne (vv. 4–5, 11), and he is very like the wondrous man who sits on a throne outside the gate (11:4). To the right and to the left of the table are two angels who hold writing instruments and materials (v. 8).

One records just deeds, the other sins (v. 12). In front of the table is yet another angelic pair, both seated. One holds a scale for weighing souls, the other fire to test souls (vv. 9–10, 13–14). The symmetry of the setting—which matches the arrangement of an Egyptian court[1]—mirrors the symmetry of the final verses, in which the righteous deeds and sins of an individual are perfectly balanced.

The chapter generates many questions. If souls are whipped by merciless angels through the broad gate to destruction, is their character not already known, their fate determined? What then is the point of the judgment? Or have they already been judged? Or do the saved and the condemned somehow advertise themselves clearly, so that it is only those in between who need to be judged? But if this is so, why does 13:3–5 say that Abel judges everybody? Again, if there is a book, why is there also a balance? And if there is a balance, why is there fire for testing? Or is the fire for those whose good and bad deeds balance the scale evenly? And what is the function of recording angels if sins and good deeds are already written in the book on the table (vv. 17–18)? The soul put on trial is weighed but not tested by fire. Why? Is it just that weighing alone helps a reader's imagination to see that the good deeds equals the bad? Furthermore, the next chapter will speak of two additional judgments, one by the twelve tribes of Israel at the *parousia*, and another by God—more seeming redundancy.[2]

Maybe *TA* 12 is difficult because, being mythical, it lacks any interest in consistency—like texts which describe hell as full of fire and yet dark, or as a place of destruction and yet eternal (Matt 5:22; 7:13; 8:12; 18:8). Still, it remains possible that infelicitous additions turned a more coherent scene into a less coherent one. RecShrt. 9–10, which lacks the scale[3] and the test of fire, is certainly less complex. Is it in some ways more original? Nickelsburg has urged that "what was originally a traditional Jewish judgment scene has been expanded and fleshed out with details from a comparable Egyptian piece."[4] He attributes the two angels, the book, the results of the judgment, Abel's office as judge, and the trial by fire to Jewish tradition. The glorious throne, the angelic writing materials and instruments, the placement of the book on a table, and the trial by balance are then due to secondary Egyptian influence.[5] The conflation of two tradi-

---

[1] See James Henry Breasted, *Ancient Records of Egypt: Historical Documents*, vol. 2 (Chicago: University of Chicago, 1906), 273 (# 675).
[2] For a similar redundancy in Egyptian eschatological texts see n. 7 on p. 279.
[3] But RecShrt. fam. E 9:8 does use ἰσοζυγέω; see on 12:14.
[4] Nickelsburg, "Eschatology," 39.
[5] For Egyptian parallels see below on vv. 6–7, 8, 9, 10, 12; 13:2.

tions, which Nickelsburg associates with the redactor of RecLng., produced the inconcinnities.

It is likely that *TA* 12 has a complex redactional history, for (a) v. 2a
looks like an interpolation; (b) the narrator suddenly switches to the first
person; and (c) parts of chaps. 11–13 do not fit the spirit of the rest of *TA*.
It is unclear, however, whether Nickelsburg's distinction between Jewish
and Egyptian motifs should be endorsed. Only the table is without some
sort of parallel in Jewish sources. Dan 7:9–10 features thrones, fire, angels,
judgment, and books. In *1 En.* 41:1–2, people "are weighed in the balance," humanity is divided into the company of the holy ones and sinners,
and the latter are "expelled" and "dragged off." *3 En.* 18:24–25 (Schäfer,
Synopse 28–29 = 864–65) refers to recording angels, books of the dead and
of the living, and scrolls and pens in angelic hands. Moreover, and as
Nickelsburg observes, even if Egyptian motifs seem superimposed over a
Jewish scene, one need not postulate an original edition of *TA* or coherent
source that did not have those motifs. If an Egyptian Jew first produced
RecLng., he may have mixed, without concern for their perfect coherence,
eschatological ideas or *topoi* from his Jewish tradition with motifs from his
Egyptian environment.

Notwithstanding the Egyptian and Jewish parallels, one should not
overlook the parallels in Plato.[6] Plato speaks of two entrances to the
afterlife, one to heaven, one to the underworld (*Resp.* 614C; *Gorg.* 524A);
of heavenly judges between the two entrances (*Resp.* 614C); and of disembodied spirits being carried against their will, and of some being punished
by fiery beings (*Resp.* 615E–616A; *Phaed.* 108B). He also depicts the
separation of the dead into the just, the unjust, and those in between (*Resp.*
614C; *Phaed.* 113D). Whether any Jews who heard *TA* were familiar with
Plato we cannot discover, but if there were such, *TA* 12 may well have
recalled the *Republic* to their minds.

RecShrt. 9:1–10:16 E and B F G open with Abraham asking about the
narrow gate. He is afraid that he is too big to squeeze through it (9:1–3;
in E he says he is too "broad"; in B F G he says that even a fifteen-year old
could not enter). After Michael assures him otherwise (9:4), we see an angel
(not two angels, as in RecLng.) driving "myriads" (so B F G) or "six
myriads" (so E) of souls to destruction (9:5). At this point Michael proposes that he and Abraham search among those souls for someone worthy
of life (9:7). They then espy an angel holding in his hand a soul whose sins
are the same as the rest of its deeds (9:8 E: τὰς ἁμαρτίας ἰσοζυγούσας μετὰ

---

[6]   See esp. Macurdy, "Platonic Orphism."

τῶν ἀγαθῶν ἔργων αὐτῆς; B F G uses ἴσος). After Abraham learns that the angel holding that soul is Death (9:10–11),[7] the patriarch asks to see the place of judgment (10:1). Michael leads him on a cloud to paradise (10:2; contrast RecLng., where the gates are immediately adjacent to the place of judgment). Here there is a judge (later identified as Abel, as in RecLng.) and an exceedingly large man (later identified as Enoch: 11:3) who are engaged in evaluating a soul taken from the multitude (10:3–7). The judge, in assessing the soul, asks the large man to find the record of its sins in the books of the cherubim, from which the court learns of its adulterous and murderous acts (10:8–15). It is then handed over for torment (10:16).

In at least two particulars RecShrt. might be more ancient than RecLng. The first is Abraham's anxious misapprehension about being too large to squeeze through the narrow gate. Humor, which runs throughout RecLng. as opposed to RecShrt., is presumably characteristic of the story behind both recensions. Similarly, Abraham's slowness to understand is a recurrent motif in the former recension, not the latter. So if, as appears, RecLng. is, on the whole, the more primitive text, maybe RecShrt. has here retained a scene that dropped out of the other recension. Yet this is far from certain, for the scene might be a Christian adaptation of the images in Matt 7:13–14 (the narrow gate) and 19:23 par. (the camel and the eye of a needle)—two texts exegetical history has often brought together (Clement of Alexandria, *Quis div.* 26.7; Origen, *Cels.* 6.16; etc.).

RecShrt. also might be primitive in having Enoch present at the judgment as the divine scribe, a chore RecLng. gives to two angels. His exalted status in Judaism is well-attested,[8] and his features in RecShrt. are paralleled in Jewish writings—his giant size (*3 En.* 9:2; 48C:5 [Schäfer, *Synopse* 12 = 893, 73]),[9] his being crowned (*3 En.* 12:3–5; 13:1; 48C:7 [Schäfer,

---

[7] This identification is odd, for Death's function here remains unclear, and the link with the later portions, where Death takes souls from bodies, remains undeveloped.

[8] For an overview see VanderKam, *Enoch*. Recall Enoch's later identification with Metatron: Tg. Ps.-Jn. on Gen 5:24; *3 Enoch*; *Midr. Gedullath Mosheh* 2.

[9] For other gigantic heavenly figures see Eusebius, *Praep. ev.* 9.29, quoting Ezekiel the Tragedian (Moses' vision of a giant throne, which implies a giant body); *Gos. Pet.* 40 (Jesus and two angels); Herm. *Sim.* 9.6.1 (the Son of God); Hippolytus, *Haer.* 9.13.1–3, quoting Elchasai (an angel, maybe Jesus Christ; cf. Epiphanius, *Pan.* 19.4.1–2; 30.17.6); Cyprian, *Mort.* 19 (an angel); Athanasius, *Vit. Ant.* 66.3 (the Devil is as tall as the clouds); *Rev. Mos.* A 9, 11, 17, 19, 22, 47. For texts about Adam see n. 20 on p. 246. The *Shi'ur Qomah* texts (ed. Schäfer, *Synopse* 939–78), which concern God's giant body, are also comparable, although their date and the date of whatever traditions they contain are disputed.

Synopse 15–16 = 896–97, 73]),[10] and his scribal office (*Jub.* 4:17–24; *1 En.* 12:3–4; 15:1; 4Q203; 4Q227; Tg. Ps.-Jn. on Gen 5:25; *Jub.* 4:23 says that he is now in Eden, "writing condemnation and judgment of the world"; cf. 10:17: he will "report every deed of each generation in the day of judgment"). Perhaps Enoch the scribe was replaced by two recording angels. The demotion could carry forward an impulse that VanderKam detects in RecShrt., in which Enoch is only an assistant. VanderKam views this as an implicit criticism of "devotees of Enoch who saw him as the son of man, the judge of the last days" (cf. *1 Enoch* 70–71).[11]

Apart from Abraham's misunderstanding and Enoch's presence, RecShrt. seems likely to be secondary; it is certainly confusing. One soul is singled out because its sins weigh the same as the rest of its works (how the angel knows this before the judgment is not said); see 9:5 and 8. This equivalence, however, plays no further role in the story. RecShrt. 10 in fact seems to contradict it, for here we learn that the soul murdered her daughter that she might take her daughter's husband. How can such a one have good and bad deeds in equal measure? This of course assumes that the soul of RecShrt. 10 is the same as that in 9:5 and 8. Ms. E does not make this equation (because it lacks the pertinent phrase in 10:3); but this hardly improves matters. For if there is more than one soul, then the first soul, the one 9:5 and 8 introduce, comes on the scene for no reason at all. In RecLng., however, the soul whose good and bad deeds are balanced is an integral part of the story. Its plight becomes the opportunity for Abraham to become empathetic; it gives him a chance to undo the folly of condemning sinners (chap. 11); it allows him to become once again the Abraham of Genesis 18, who pleads for mercy on behalf of others. Without this element, RecLng. cannot move forward. RecShrt., to the contrary, reads better without it.

12:1. Depending upon the original text of 11:4–5 and how it is understood, this is the first or second time *TA* uses the first person. For examples of the transition from first person to third person or *vice versa* see the Textual Notes on 11:4–5. Is the switch an attempt to make the narrative more vivid, or does our narrative incorporate a source that used the first-person singular? The Sahidic uses the first person singular regularly in its account of Abraham's heavenly tour.

The appearance of two angels interrupts the conversation between Michael and Abraham. For angelic pairs see Gen 19:1; *3 Macc.* 6:18; *L.A.B.* 64:6; Luke 24:4; John 20:12; *2 En.* 1:4; *Vis. Paul* 17; *3 En.* 18:23–

---

10   In RecShrt., Enoch has three crowns which are "witnesses" (fam. E) or "the crowns of witness" (so B F G). This accords with the three tribunals of RecLng. 13.

11   VanderKam, *Enoch*, 158.

25 (Schäfer, *Synopse* 28–29 = 864–65); *b. Ḥag.* 16a. Here the two angels are reminiscent of the "adversary angels" that accompany the wicked in *t. Sanh.* 17:3; cf. CD 2:5–6; *Deut. Rab.* 3:11; *Eccl. Rab.* 4:3. They are of "fiery appearance," πύρινοι τῇ ὄψει; cf. Plutarch, *Quaest. conv.* 648A: τῇ ὄψει πυρωπόν. πύρινος reappears in vv. 10 (of an angel), 14 (of an angel); 13:1 (of an angel), 11 (of an angel); 17:14 (of a dragon's head), 15 (of a sword); 19:8 (of the face of Death). In its three LXX occurrences, the word refers solely to heavenly phenomena (Ezek 28:14, 16; Ecclus 48:9). Gk. *1 En.* 14:11 speaks of the fiery (πύρινα) Cherubim, and in Rev 9:17 four angelic riders have fiery (πυρίνους) breastplates. Other texts linking πύρινος to angels include *3 Apoc. John*, ed. Vassiliev, p. 317 (two angels with fiery swords); *Gos. Bart.* 4:12 (the fiery chains on Beliar), 46 (angels who throw fiery stones); Gk. *T. Adam* 1:12 (the fiery ranks of angels). On the widespread idea that angels were made of fire see on 2:11. In the present context, "fiery" serves as a frightening variant of the common description of angels as "bright."

The two angels display "merciless intention" (ἀνηλεεῖς τῇ γνώμῃ; cf. v. 10; γνώμη*) and "relentless (ἀπότομοι; ἀπότομος: 12:1, 10; 13:11; 19:5; LXX: Wis 5:10; 6:5; 11:10; 12:9; 18:15) countenances" (τῷ βλέμματι; cf. 16:1; 17:8; 19:4). The description may be a later addition (see Textual Notes). ἀνηλεής (LXX: *3 Macc.* 5:10; cf. Jas 2:13; *T. Gad* 5:11) is used in *T. Job* 16:2 of Satan mercilessly destroying Job's livestock with fire, and demons exhibit ἀνελεημοσύνη in Esaias, *Capitula de exercitatione spirituali* PG 40.1209B. But the closest parallel to our text is *Vis. Paul* Arn. 11, where angels in charge of sinning souls at the judgment are without mercy (*sine misericordia*) and without pity (*nullam habentes pietatem*), have furious countenances, and shoot fire from their mouths (cf. 17). Cf. also 11Q11 3:5–6 (God sends an angel who will not show mercy) and Herm. *Sim.* 6.3.2, where "the angel of punishment" is "pitiless" and "altogether without compassion."

The two angels drive "a myriad of souls," μυριάδαν ψυχάς (μυριάς*); cf. RecShrt. 9:5, 10; Stobaeus, *Flor.* 1.49.44 (μυριάδας ψυχῶν); *Chron. Pasch.*, ed. Dindorf, p. 461.15 (ψυχῶν μυριάδας). They "mercilessly (ἀνηλεῶς; see above) strike (τύπτοντες; τύπτω*) them with fiery whips," πυρίναις χαρζαναῖς. Parallels include Plato, *Resp.* 615E–616A, where "savage" men, "fiery all through (διάπυρου) to behold," seize murderous tyrants and carry them away; they bind some and on the way to the bottomless pit flay their skins on thorn bushes; Hippolytus, *Univ.* 35, where "angels of punishment" forcefully drag the unjust as though they are unwilling prisoners; *Acts Pet.* 41, where Nero dreams of being scourged; *Apoc. Zeph.* 4:4 Akhmimic (see below); Athanasius, *Vit. Ant.* 9.8, where the saint is whipped and stung by demons; 40.5, where demons lash Anthony and each other with whips; *Vis. Dorotheus*, ed. Kessels and van der Horst 131, 143–63, where Christ has angels whip the seer Dorotheus as punishment; folio 7 verso of the *Coptic Enoch Apocryphon* catalogued as "Pierpont Morgan Library. Coptic Theological Texts 3," where the angel has a "rod" (ⲣⲁⲃⲁⲟⲥ), evidently to punish sinners; *Sifre* Deut. 357, where "the souls of the wicked" are taken by "merciless and cruel angels" who "drag their souls along"; and *b. Mo'ed Qaṭ.* 28a, where the Angel of Death has a "fiery rod." Angels are often the means of punishing the wicked: Ps 78:49; *1 En.* 53:3; 56:1; 62:11; 63:1; 66:1; CD 2:5–6; 1QS 4:12; LXX Ecclus 39:28; *L.A.B.* 15:5; Matt 13:49; Revelation 16; *T. Levi* 3:2–3; *Apoc. Zeph.* Sahidic fr.; Akhmimic 4:4; *2 En.* 10:3 ("merciless angels carrying instruments of atrocities torturing without pity"); *Apoc. Paul* (Nag Hammadi) 22; Arnobius, *Gent.* 2.15; etc. The instruments of torture are like the torturers: both are fiery (cf. Gen 3:24, which associates the cherubim with a flaming sword).[12]

LSJ has no entry for χαρζανή*. Lampe, s.v., cites only *TA* and offers, without explanation, the meaning: "chain (?)"; cf. Constantine VII, *Cer.*, ed. Reiske, pp. 623, 624, where χαρζάνιον is an ornamental chain. If this is right, one may note that, in *1 En.* 10:4, 12; 53:3; 88:1, 3; *Jub.* 5:6; and Rev 20:1–2, angels punish by binding, presumably with chains (cf. *Sib. Or.* 3:150–151 and the punishment of the Titans in Greek mythology); cf. *Rev. Mos.* A 47, trans. Gaster, p. 584: the angels of destruction hold "fiery chains." But τύπτοντες goes better with "whips," and punishing angels have whips in *Apoc. Zeph.* Sahidic fr.; Akhmimic 4:4 ("fiery scourges"— ⲫⲣⲁⲅⲉⲗⲓⲟⲛ ⲛⲕⲱϩⲧ—in the hands of the myriads and myriads of angels in charge of the ungodly at the judgment); *Apoc. Paul* (Nag Hammadi) 22 (angels "with whips in their hands" goad "the souls on to the judgment"); and *Rev. Mos.* A 44, trans. Gaster, p. 583 ("angels of destruction ... lash them with fiery whips"). Moreover, the Talmud knows the expression, פּוּלְסֵי דְנוּרָא which Jastrow, s.v., פּוּלְסָא, defines as "heated discs or rings strung on a lash"; cf. *b. Ḥag.* 15a (of the punishment of Metatron); *b. Yoma* 77a (of the punishment of Gabriel); *b. B. Meṣiʿa* 47a, 85b. *3 En.* 16:5, in a variant of the story in *b. Ḥag.* 15a, uses the similar פּוּלְסָאוֹת שֶׁל אוּר (Schäfer, *Synopse* 20 = 856)

12:2. For comparable images see Plato, *Phaed.* 108B ("the appointed spirit drags her [the earth-bound soul] away by force"); *1 En.* 41:1–2 (sinners are "expelled" and "dragged off"); 55:3 ("seized by the hands of the angels on

---

12 For Egyptian tormentors and their instruments see Zandee, *Death*, 20–24, 78–81, 200, 328–32, 340–41.

the day of tribulation and pain"). "The angel" is awkward given v. 1, which introduces two angels. Nickelsburg thinks that the verse is a secondary addition.[13] However that may be, shifting attention briefly from the mass to an individual—"While one of the angels grabbed a soul"—perhaps adds pathos. Readers might, at this point, imagine one of the condemned trying to escape and being hauled back. But vv. 16–18 will identify this soul as one whose sins and good deeds are equal, a fact anticipated by the separation at this earlier juncture.

The remark that the angels drive (διήγαγον; cf. 10:13) souls into the broad gate to "destruction" (ἀπώλειαν; see on 11:11) simply reprises 11:5 and 11. Are we to think that the identities of the righteous and the wicked are, as in Persian sources (cf. *Wizīdagīhā ī Zādspram* 35:32), already apparent, so that only those in between must be judged? Plato, *Gorg.* 523E, 524D–525A, says that souls without clothing or bodies more readily reveal their true character, and in Lucian, *Cat.* 24–28, the judge of the underworld looks for στίγματα on souls. In *TA* 13, however, judgment is not by sight.

12:3–4. Upon following the angels through the broad gate, Abraham beholds, "in the middle (cf. v. 18) of the two gates," a "terrifying (φοβερός) throne." In 11:4 and 13:2, the one seated on a throne is fearful, but here it is the throne itself, its "appearance" (εἴδει; cf. 20:5), that has this quality. Although Delcor says that φοβερὸς ἐν εἴδει is "vraisemblablement un hébraïsme" (ἐν = ב),[14] θρόνος φοβερός seems to be Christian; cf. Ps.-Hippolytus, *De consummatione mundi* 39; Ps.-Chrysostom, *De salute an.* PG 60.735; Ps.-Ephraem, *Sermo paraeneticus de secundo aduentu domini*, ed. Phrantzoles, p. 217.14; Romanos the Melodist, *Cant.* 31 pro. 3; Ps.-John of Damascus, *B.J.* 8.64; etc. The throne is "like crystal" (κρυστάλλου; κρυστάλλος*; cf. 12:6: κρυσταλλοειδής; Gk. *1 En.* 14:18; Rev 4:6; also *1 En.* 14:18: God's throne looks "like ice"), and it flashes forth "as fire," ἐξαστράπτων ὡς πῦρ; cf. 17:15 for the verb; also LXX Dan 10:6; Nah 3:3; *T. Job* 46:8. The text clearly depends upon the famous vision of God's throne in Ezek 1:4–28; cf. 4Q405 frags. 20–21–22; Daniel 7; *1 En.* 14:18; 18:8; *L.A.E.* 25:3; Rev 4:2–11; *Apocalypse of Abraham* 18; *3 Enoch* 1, 21, 25; etc.[15] The LXX has ἐν μέσῳ (1:4, 13), θρόνος (1:26, *bis*), κρύσταλλος (1:22), ὡς ... πῦρ (1:13, 27), and ἐξαστράπτω (1:4, 7). Perhaps, given the intertext, readers should infer that Abel, unlike Adam, sits upon God's

---

13 Nickelsburg, "Eschatology," 41–42.
14 Delcor, *Testament*, 138.
15 David J. Halperin, *The Faces of the Chariot: Early Jewish Responses to Ezekiel's Vision* (TSAJ 16; Tübingen: Mohr-Siebeck, 1988).

throne, as do others in a few texts; see on 9:8.[16] But this is far from certain, for Jewish sources can set multiple thrones in eschatological contexts: Dan 7:9; Matt 19:28; *b. Ḥag.* 14a; *b. Sanh.* 38b; Tg. Neof. 1 on Gen 15:17.

12:5. Abraham beholds upon the throne "a marvelous (θαυμαστός; cf. 18:6) man." He "resembles the sun"; cf. the tradition, based either upon Gen 4:1, 5–6, that Abel's brother, Cain, was "lustrous": *L.A.E.* 21:3; *Pirqe R. El.* 21. The rare ἡλιόρατος (see on 2:4) makes the man angelic because it makes him resemble Michael, so it is no surprise that he is "like unto a son of God," ὅμοιος υἱῷ θεοῦ; cf. Theod. Dan 3:92 (ὁμοία υἱῷ θεοῦ for דָּמֵה לְבַר־אֱלָהִין; *1 En.* 106:5 ("He is not like a human being, but he looks like the children of the angels of heaven to me ... . His eyes are like the rays of the sun, and his face is glorious"); Epiphanius, *Pan.* 67.7 (ὅμοιον τῷ υἱῷ τοῦ θεοῦ). "Son of God" (only here in *TA*) means an angelic being, as in Gen 6:2, 4; Deut 32:8; Job 1:6; 2:1; 38:7; Ps 29:1; 89:7; Dan 3:25; *1 En.* 13:8; *Pr. Jos.* fr. A in Origen, *Comm. Jo.* 2.31; *Did.* 16:1; etc.

12:6–7. In Egyptian depictions of Osiris judging the dead, he is often enthroned in front of a table.[17] In our text, the table before the marvelous figure is κρυσταλλοειδής* (cf. v. 4 and LXX Wis 19:21). It is wholly made of (ὅλως διά; cf. Josephus, *Ant.* 11.147) gold (cf. 11:6, of Adam's throne) and silk (βύσσου; see on 4:2). The size of the book sitting (βιβλίον κείμενον; see below) on the table is given as three cubits thick (τὸ πάχος αὐτοῦ πήχεων τριῶν; πάχος*) and six cubits wide (τὸ πλάτος αὐτοῦ πήχεων ἕξ; πλάτος*). Cf. Zech 5:1–2 (a scroll twenty cubits long and ten cubits wide; see the commentary in *b. Ἐrub.* 21a); *Rev. John* 3 (ed. Tischendorf, p. 72: "And I directed my vision, and I saw a book lying [βιβλίον κείμενον], its thickness [τὸ πάχος αὐτοῦ], as I thought, being seven mountains; and its width [μῆκος; so RecLng. 12:7 H] the mind of a human being is unable to comprehend"; this book contains, among other things, "the judgments and righteousness of all the human race"); *3 En.* 18:25 (Schäfer, *Synopse* 29 = 865: the length of an angelic scroll is "3,000 myriads of parasangs," the size of a pen "3,000 parasangs").

Jewish and Christian texts often refer to heavenly books. There is the book of life, with the names of the righteous written within: Exod 32:33; Dan 12:1; Mal 3:16; *1 En.* 104:1; *Jub.* 30:22; 36:10; CD B 20:18–19; *Jos. Asen.* 15:4; Luke 10:20; Phil 4:3; Rev 3:5; *1 Clem.* 45:8; Herm. *Vis.* 1.3.2; Herm. *Sim.* 2.9; *Apoc. Zeph.* 3:5–9; *T. Jac.* 7:27; Origen, *Comm. Jo.* 5.7;

---

[16] Cf. Christopher Rowland, *The Open Heaven: A Study of Apocalyptic in Judaism and Early Christianity* (New York: Crossroads, 1982), 108.

[17] Forman and Quirke, *Hieroglyphs*, 141.

Ps.-Bartholomew, *Book of the Resurrection of Jesus Christ*, ed. Budge, fol. 4a; *b. Roš Haš.* 16b; *Shemoneh 'Esreh* benediction 12; etc. There is also the book that names the damned: *1 En.* 81:4; 89:61–77; 90:17, 20; 98:7–8; 104:7; *Jub.* 30:22; *2 Bar.* 24:1; *Apoc. Zeph.* 3:5–9; *b. Roš Haš.* 16b; etc. There are further the heavenly tablets of destiny that tell of things before they come to pass: Jer 22:30; Dan 8:26; 12:9; 4QapocJacob fr. 1; 4QAgesCreat frags. 1, 5–6; *1 En.* 81:1–3; 93:1–15; 108:7; *Jub.* 16:9; 32:21; Rev. 5:1; *T. Levi* 5:4; *2 En.* 22:11; *Hist. Jos. Carp.* 26; etc.; and there are also, as in *TA* 12, books for the recording of human deeds: Ps 56:9; 139:16; Dan 7:10; *1 En.* 47:3; *Jub.* 5:13–16; *4 Ezra* 6:20; *2 Bar.* 24:1; Rev 20:12, 15; *Asc. Isa.* 9:22; *2 En.* 19:5; *Apoc. Zeph.* 7:1–11; *m. 'Abot* 2:1; *b. Ned.* 22a; *b. Ta'an.* 11a; etc.[18] Several of these texts associate the heavenly book(s) with a heavenly throne: Dan 7:9–10; *1 En.* 47:3; 90:20; Rev 5:1; 20:12–15. Perhaps the far-flung combination goes back to Ancient Near Eastern ritual in which the king was both enthroned and handed a heavenly book.[19]

12:8. Two angels, different from the pair in v. 1, stand (ἵσταντο; cf. vv. 4, 6) "on the right and on the left," ἐκ δεξιῶν ... ἐξ ἀριστερῶν; cf. v 12; 13:9. For angels to the right and left see 1 Kgs 22:19 = 2 Chr 18:18; Origen, *Mart.* 18. Here the angels must be to the right and to the left of the table of v. 6. They hold a papyrus roll, ink, and a reed-pen, χάρτην καὶ μέλαν καὶ κάλαμον; cf. Synesius of Cyrene, *Ep.* 157 (κάλαμον καὶ χάρτην καὶ μέλαν); Chrysostom, *Ep.* 128 PG 52.688 (κάλαμον καὶ χάρτην καὶ μέλαν); Basil the Great, *Ep.* 330.1 (καλάμῳ καὶ μέλανι καί ... χάρτῃ); Gregory of Nyssa, *Contra usurarios*, ed. Gebhardt, p. 197.16 (τὸν κάλαμον ... τὸν χάρτην ... τὸ μέλαν). Whether each angel holds all three items, or whether two items belong to one angel, the other item to the other angel, is not said: the picture remains vague. In *3 En.* 18:25 (Schäfer, *Synopse* 29 = 865), two angels each hold in one hand a scroll, in the other a pen, and Christian icons often depict an angel holding a pen and a scroll with the names of the saved and the un-

---

[18] See further Leo Koep, *Das himmlische Buch in Antike und Christentum: Eine religionsgeschichtliche Untersuchung zur altchristlichen Bildersprache* (Theophaneia 8; Bonn: P. Hanstein, 1952). For Graeco-Roman parallels see pp. 6–13. Macurdy, "Platonic Orphism," 218–19, also calls attention to some Greek parallels, such as Aeschylus, *Eum.* 275 ("Hades within the earth is a mighty accountant of mortals and notes everything in his recording mind") and Euripides, fr. 506 (ed. Nauck: "Do you believe that sins spring up on wings to heaven and that someone writes them down on the tablets of Zeus, and that Zeus inspects them and gives judgment to mortals?").

[19] See Geo Widengren, *The Ascension of the Apostle and the Heavenly Book* (UUÅ 7; Uppsala/Leipzig: Lundequistka bokhandeln, 1950).

saved.[20] χάρτης* (LXX: Isa 8:1; Jer 43:2, 6, 23) most often means "sheet of paper" (BAGD, s.v.); but here the meaning is "papyrus roll," as in 2 John 12. It is often associated with both μέλαν = "ink" (LXX: 0; cf. *4 Bar.* 6:19: χάρτην καὶ μέλανα) and κάλαμος = "reed-pen" (LXX Ps 44:2; *3 Macc.* 4:20; cf. Ps.-Chrysostom, *De turture seu de ecclesia sermo* PG 55.602; Anna Comnena, *Alex.* 1.13); and the latter two words likewise occur together (e.g., *P. Oxy.* 326; 3 John 13). The names of the two angels and the meaning of what they do is clarified in 13:9–14. For recording angels see Ezek 9:2; *1 En.* 89:61–63, 76; 90:14 (cf. 104:7); *2 En.* 19:5; 22:11; *Apoc. Zeph.* 3:5–9; *3 En.* 18:24–25 (Schäfer, *Synopse* 28–29 = 864–65); also below on 12:12. In Egyptian religion, the scribe-god Thoth writes down the verdicts of the postmortem assize, and there are texts that refer to his "writing-kit" (e.g. *BD* 94, from the papyrus of Nu) and to his "reed-pen, papyrus, and palette."[21] He often holds papyrus and pen in funerary art.[22]

12:9. Before the table is an angel who is "glorious," φωτοφόρος; see on 7:3. He holds a "scale," ζυγόν; cf. v. 13; 13:1, 10, 14. For God weighing human beings with a "scale" or "balance" see LXX Job 31:6 v.l.; Ps 62:10; Prov 16:2; 21:2; 24:12; Dan 5:27; *1 En.* 41:1; 61:8; *Ps. Sol.* 5:4; *4 Ezra* 3:34; *2 Bar.* 41:6; *2 En.* 44:5; 49:2; 52:15; *Apoc. Zeph.* 8:5; *t. Qidd.* 1:13–14; *y. Qidd.* 1:10; *Eccl. Rab.* 10:1; Jerome, *Comm. Isa.* 18 on 66:24; Chrysostom, *Ep. Theod.* 21; and the *Coptic Enoch Apocryphon* catalogued as "Pierpont Morgan Library. Coptic Theological Texts 3, fols. 1–9."[23] The motif becomes particularly prominent in medieval Christianity, with Michael in charge.[24] It also appears in the traditional funeral service of the Orthodox

---

[20] See e.g. plate 180 in Hamann-Mac Lean and Hallensleben, *Monumentalmalerei.*

[21] See e.g. "The Complaint of the Peasant" in *ANET*, pp. 409–10 (trans. J. A. Wilson). On writing materials in Egypt see A. Lucas and J. R. Harris, *Ancient Egyptian Materials and Industries* (4th ed.; London: E. Arnold, 1962), 336–38.

[22] Forman and Quirke, *Hieroglyphs and the Afterlife*, 144.

[23] Text and English translation in Pearson, "Pierpont Morgan Fragments," 275, 277. Folio 1v: " ... of the archangel. He put it upon the balances of righteousness." Folio 7v: "he takes [the g]ood deeds, and he sets them on the other side. If he sees the sins drawing down (the balances) more than the good deeds, he takes his rod which is in his right hand, and he [sets] it upon" (text breaks off).

[24] Leopold Kretzenbacher, *Die Seelenwaage: Zur religiösen Idee vom Jenseitsgericht auf der Schicksalswaage in Hochreligion, Bildkunst und Volksglaube* (Klagenfurt: Landesmuseum für Kärnten, 1958); Karl Ludwig Skutsch, "Eine Untersuchung über die Entwicklung des Wägungsgedankens von der Antike bis ins christliche Mittelalter," *Die Antike* 12 (1936), 49–64. Although the artistic tradition of Nemesis and Dike/Iustitia holding scales influences Christian depictions of Michael, *TA* shows no such influence.

Church: "Have mercy upon me, all-holy angels ... for I have no good deed to balance the burden of my evil ones."[25] Most of the older texts seem to use "scale" or "balance" as a metaphor. But as with the two ways in chap. 11, so here too: the old metaphor has become literal; there is a scale that weighs human deeds. This has probably happened under Egyptian influence.[26] The idea of a *post-mortem* weighing was well-known in Egypt from the Middle Kingdom on.[27] It appears, for example, in the *Coffin Texts*, and in vignettes illustrating the *Book of the Dead* (in the latter the heart is weighed; see e.g. 30B). But the idea was also known in Greece from an early time, as the small gold and bronze scales discovered in old graves in Knossos, Mycenae, and elsewhere seemingly attest.[28]

If the righteous are on the narrow road, and if the unrighteous are on the wide road, then what need is there of a book of deeds? And if there is a book of deeds, what is the purpose of scales? The next verse will add yet a fourth instrument—fire. Perhaps the multiple instruments of judgment are analogous to the multiple judges in chapter 12—every matter is established by more than one witness (Deut 19:15). But this is not plainly said. It may well be that the Egyptian setting has had an impact here, for Egyptian texts and illustrations can combine several methods of judgment (e.g. books, scales, and judges).[29]

12:10. To the left of the angel who is in front of the table (v. 9), a "fiery" (πύρινος; see on v. 1) angel is seated (cf. v. 5; 11:4). Unlike Adam and Abel, however, his throne is not mentioned. Our author is apparently more interested in exalting the human judges than he is in glorifying the angels, who function as assistants. Like the two angels in v. 1, this one is also "merciless (ἀνηλεής; see on v. 1) and "relentless" (ἀπότομος; see on v. 1). What distinguishes him is that he holds in his hand not a whip, as does the

---

[25]   G. Spyridakis, "Τὰ κατὰ τὴν τελευτὴν ἔθυμα ἐκ τῶν ἁγιολογικῶν πηγῶν," Ἐπετηρὶς τῆς Ἑταιρείας Βυζαντινῶν Σπουδῶν 8 (1953–1954), 97.

[26]   See esp. Schmidt, "Testament," 71–78.

[27]   Details in Brandon, "Weighing of the Soul." Ellul, "Testament," 77–78, contains illustrations.

[28]   Griffiths, *Divine Verdict*, 287–91. Cf. Zeus' weighing Achilles and Hector in Homer, *Il.* 22.208–212. According to Emily Vermeule, *Aspects of Death in Early Greek Art and Poetry* (Berkeley: University of California Press, 1979), 160, the Greek *psychostasia* "is a supernatural confirmation of the inevitable, just as in Egypt it had been the external sign of the judgment already made by the habits of a man's life." Brandon, "Weighing of Souls," also documents postmortem judgment by weighing in Zoroastrian, Islamic, and Buddhist texts.

[29]   Brandon, *Judgment*, 31–42; Griffiths, *Divine Verdict*, 239–42.

angel in v. 1, nor a papyrus roll, ink, and a reed-pen as do the angels in v.
8, but a "trumpet," σάλπιγγα; cf. the rabbinic סלפינגס.³⁰ Angels often blow
trumpets in Jewish and Christian texts: Gk. *L.A.E.* 22:1–3; 37:1; Revelation 8–9; *Apoc. Zeph.* 9:1; 10:1; 11:1, 6; 12:1; *Ques. Ezra* B 11:9. But here
the trumpet is not an instrument of sound. It rather contains an "all-
consuming fire" (πῦρ παμφάγον; see on 4:10) that tests sinners—
δοκιμαστήριον τῶν ἁμαρτωλῶν; cf. *Pirqe R. El.* 4, where God holds a
scepter of fire in his hand, and *Syr. Apoc. Dan.* 33 ("a fiery trumpet will
sound"). Does σάλπιγγα here have the sense that שופר sometimes does in
rabbinic texts, namely, a horn-shaped box (cf. Jastrow, s.v., and the commentaries on Matt 6:2)? James suggests instead that we envisage "a blow-
pipe: the flame, celestial in its nature, becomes intensified and tests the
souls (or their works) as silver is tried."³¹ Delcor thinks the text is corrupt
and proposes an original σῦριγξ = "channel" or "tube."³² δοκιμαστήριον*
is rare (LXX: 0; Philo: 0; Josephus: 0; NT: 0), and Lampe offers no entry,
but the word does appear in Basil the Great, *Hom. Ps.* PG 29.244C, and
Ps.-Macarius, *Serm. 64* 2.3; 57.1. LSJ, s.v., cites Menander, *Mon.* 537;
Arrian, *Epict. diss.* 3.6.10, to which one may add: Stobaeus, *Flor.* 1.3.56,
and Hesychius, *Lex.* K 4156. For fire as a means of testing (as opposed to
punishment) see Ps 66:10–12 (with δοκιμάζω); Jer 6:29; Zech 13:9; Mal
3:2–3; *Sib. Or.* 2:252–254; 1 Cor 3:12–15 (with δοκιμάζω); 1 Pet 1:7 (with
δοκιμάζω); Rev 3:18; *Midr. Ps.* 1:21; and further below, on v. 14. Egyptian
funerary texts often refer to fire; see e.g. *CT* 1089, 1091, 1107, 1116.

12:11. The "marvelous (θαυμάσιος; cf. v. 5) man," identified in 13:2 as
Abel, judges the souls and passes a verdict, ἀπεφήνατο (ἀποφαίνω*: LXX:
Job 27:5; 32:2; 2 Macc 6:23; 15:4; cf. *Let. Arist.* 19, 20, 53). On why Abel
should be the judge of humanity—a role he plays nowhere else in Jewish
or Christian literature—see on 13:2. Whatever the solution, the motif of a
human being judging others in the after-life or in an eschatological context
appears in more than one Jewish text. In 11QMelch 2:13, Melchizedek
"will exact the vengeance of El's judgments." In *1 Enoch* 70–71, Enoch is
identified as the Son of man, who sits on the eschatological throne of
judgment (61:8; 62:5; 69:29). In *2 Bar.* 72:2–6, God's Messiah "will
summon all the nations, and some of them he will spare, and some of them
he will slay" (cf. Isa 11:4). In Matt 25:31–46, Jesus as the Son of man sorts
the sheep from the goats. Related pictures appear in *Psalms of Solomon* 17

---

³⁰ But in the long Romanian, ed. Roddy, p. 39, he holds a book with recorded sins.
³¹ James, *Testament*, 125.
³² Delcor, *Testament*, 140.

and (probably) 4Q246 col. 2. Rev 20:4 assumes that certain followers of Jesus will sit on thrones and have judgment committed to them. 1 Cor 6:2 declares that "the saints will judge the world."[33]

12:12. Referring to the angels in v. 8, we now learn, in words that 13:9 will repeat, that they are making a written record, ἀπεγράφοντο (cf. 13:1, 9). One is reminded of Thoth, the Egyptian god who records the results of postmortem judgment. A more distant parallel appears in Aeschylus, *Eum.* 273–275, where Hades holds all to account with his "all-recording mind." For ἀπογράφω of the recording of human deeds in heaven see Gk. fr. *1 En.* 98:7–8 ("sins being written down (ἀπογράφεται) [by angels] every day in the presence of the Most High ... your injustices which you have committed unjustly are written down (ἀπογράφονται) [by angels] every day") and Gk. *Vis. Paul* 10 ("angels daily write down (ἀπογράφονται) all your deeds in heaven"). *Jub.* 4:6, without referring to written records, has angels making known good and bad deeds before God. That the angel on the right registers upright deeds (δικαιοσύνας; see on 1:1), the one on the left sins, ἁμαρτίας (cf. vv. 17–18; 10:13; 13:9–10; 14:2, 4, 14), reflects an old prejudice: the right is good, the left bad; cf. Eccles 10:2; Plutarch, *Mor.* 282E; *2 Bar.* 54:13; *b. Šabb.* 63a; 88b; *Num. Rab.* 22:9; *Koran* 90:20; the Latin *sinister*.[34] One may compare 1 Kgs 22:19, where "all the host of heaven" stands to God's right and left (cf. *L.A.E.* 25:3), and esp. *Cant. Rab.* 1:9:1, where those said to be at God's right hand incline towards acquittal, those at the left towards condemnation. The right is also the direction of salvation and left the direction of condemnation in Plato, *Resp.* 614C; Virgil, *Aen.* 6.540–543; Matt 25:31–46; and Ephraem, *Ep. Publium*, ed. Brock, pp. 282, 292. Note that righteous deeds and sins remain undefined: the text presumes that readers belong to a common moral tradition.

The function of the angelic register is unclear. According to James, the recording angels "register what is happening on earth for future insertion in the book"; cf. *Apoc. Zeph.* 3:5–9.[35] Nickelsburg, on the contrary, suggests that "the two angels copy out the record of the sins and righteous deeds and lay the two sheets in the two pans of the balance." He then adds: "A little less likely explanation is that the angels' records are entered as loose leaves into the book and are taken out and weighed at the time of judgment."[36] This last suggestion seems to harmonize with *Pesiq. Rab. Kah.* 25:2; see on 12:18.

---

[33] For Egyptian parallels see Zandee, *Death*, 38–41.
[34] Greek examples in W. Grundmann, *TDNT* 2 (1964), 38.
[35] James, *Testament*, 124.
[36] Nickelsburg, "Eschatology," 30.

12:13. "The one in front of the table, the one holding the scale," refers back to v. 9 (q.v.). The angel weighs the souls, ἐζύγιζεν τὰς ψυχάς (cf. 13:10; Prov 16:2: יהוה רוחות וְתֹכֵן) which contrasts with later Egyptian lore, in which it is the heart that is typically weighed (although ψυχή and καρδία can have the same meaning). ζυγίζω, which recurs in 13:10, is not listed in LSJ, and Lampe, s.v. ζυγιάζω, cites only TA. But the verb is likely a variant spelling of ζευγίζω. The latter is attested with the sense "yoke in pairs" (e.g. 1 Macc 1:15; Aq. Num 25:3), which could readily be transferred to setting up a balance, especially as ζυγός means "balance" as well as "yoke" (Lampe, s.v.).

12:14. This line, which refers back to v. 10 (q.v.), is parallel to the previous verse:

13   καὶ ὁ ... ὁ τὸν ζυγὸν κατέχων, ἐζύγιζεν   τὰς ψυχάς
14   καὶ ὁ ... ὁ τὸ   πῦρ   κατέχων, ἐδοκίμαζε ... τὰς ψυχάς

Unlike the angel who holds the scale, the "fiery" (πύρινος; see on v. 1) angel tests (ἐδοκίμαζε; cf. 13:1, 11, 13, 14) souls through fire (διὰ πυρός). For fire as an instrument of eschatological or (as here) postmortem judgment, which is so prominent in Iranian tradition, see Isa 66:24; Ezek 38:22; Mal 4:1; *Jub.* 9:15; *1 En.* 10:6; 54:1–2, 6; 90:24–25; 91:9; 100:9; 102:1; *Ps. Sol.* 15:4–5; 1QS 2:8, 15; 1QpHab 10:5, 13; Ecclus 21:9; *Sib. Or.* 2:303–305; 3:53–54, 672–674; 4:159–161; *4 Macc.* 9:9; 12:12; *Jos. Asen.* 12:11; Matt 3:10, 12 = Luke 3:9, 17; 2 Pet 3:10; Rev 20:10; Josephus, *Ant.* 1.20; *T. Zeb.* 10:3; *T. Jud.* 25:3; *4 Ezra* 7:36–38; 13:10–11; *2 Bar.* 44:15; 48:39; 59:2; Gk. *3 Bar.* 4:16; *Apoc. El. (C)* 5:22–24, 37; *b. Ḥag.* 15b; etc. Verbal parallels include Ps 66:10–12 ("For you, O God, have tested [LXX 65:10: ἐδοκίμασας] us ... we went through fire"); Zech 13:9 ("I will put this third into the fire [LXX: διὰ πυρός], refine them as one refines silver, and test [δοκιμῶ] them as gold is tested" [δοκιμάζεται]); Wis 3:6 ("Like gold in the furnace he tried [ἐδοκίμασεν] them"); 1 Cor 3:13 ("the work of each builder will become visible, for the Day will disclose it, because it will be revealed with fire, and the fire will test what sort of work each has done" [δοκιμάσει]); 1 Pet 1:7 (διὰ πυρὸς δὲ δοκιμαζομένου); Herm. *Vis.* 4.3.4 (those who have "fled from the world" are "tried" [δοκιμάζεται] even "as gold is tried [δοκιμάζεσθε] in the fire"); Clement of Alexandria, *Strom.* 6.11.86 (τῶν διὰ πυρὸς ... δοκιμαζομένων); Origen, *Sel. Ps.* PG 12.1664A (διὰ ... τοῦ πυρὸς δοκιμάζει τὰς ψυχὰς τῶν ἀνθρώπων); Athanasius, *Exp. Ps.* PG 27.585C (δοκιμαζομένων ὡς διὰ πυρός); *Vit. Syncleticae* PG 28.1548C (διὰ τοῦ πυρετοῦ δοκιμάζῃ); Ps.-Macarius, *Hom. 1–50* 25.9 ("Because the immaterial and divine fire is accustomed to enlighten and to test [δοκιμάζειν] souls"); Theodoret of Cyrrhus, *Comm. ep. Paul. proem.* PG 82.252A (διὰ πυρὸς δοκιμαζόμενος). Despite the many biblical parallels, and despite the association of postmortem fire with judgment in Egyptian texts (see above), the language may be Christian; see on 13:13.

12:15. To Abraham's question concerning what he has seen (τί ἐστι ταῦτα; cf. LXX Zech 1:9; 2:2; 4:4, 5, 13; 6:4), Michael first offers a generalization: "the judgment and recompense," ἡ κρίσις καὶ ἀνταπόδοσις. On this seemingly Christian expression see on 10:15. The question and answer sequence reminds one of the many apocalyptic texts in which a seer does not understand what he sees and so must ask questions of an *angelus interpres*; see also 7:8 and cf. Daniel 8–12; Ezek 40:3–4; Zech 1:7–6:8; *1 Enoch* 18, 21–27; *4 Ezra* 9–10; *Apoc. Pet.* 16; etc. On Abraham as "pious" (ὅσιε) see on 1:2.

12:16. The generalization in v. 15 now begins to be spelled out by what takes place. Following the prefatory καὶ ἰδού (see on 2:1), Abraham is directed toward "the angel holding the soul in its hand," a reference back to v. 2 (q.v.; cf. 14:2). We now learn that this angel is bringing a soul before the judge.

12:17. The judge gives an order to one of the angels "serving" (καθυπ-ουργούντων) him. καθυπουργέω* (LXX: 0; Philo: 0; NT: 0; Josephus: 0) is not common until patristic writers; see Ps.-Athanasius, *Hom. in occursum domini* PG 28.976.46; Ps.-John of Damascus, *B.J.* 18.151; Constantine VII, *Virt. vit.*, ed. Büttner-Wobst and Roos, 1:136.18; etc. The angel is to open the big book on the table and to find the sins of the soul.

12:18. The book, not the scale, indicates that the "balance" (A Q: ζυγάδας; B: ζυγάς; cf. 14:2) of "sins" (ἁμαρτίας; see on v. 12) and "good deeds" (δικαιοσύνας; see on v. 12 and 13:9) is identical, ἐξ ἴσου; cf. LXX Exod 26:24. How this works is unclear. It would seem that the book makes the scales redundant (although see on v. 12). In any event, the angel neither places the soul among "the saved" (τοῖς σῳζομένοις; cf. 11:11: οἱ σῳζόμενοι) nor hands it over to the torturers, βασανισταῖς. With βασανιστής* cf. Philo, *Spec. leg.* 4.82, and Matt 18:34. The related βασανισμός and βασανιστήριον appear in *4 Macc.* 6:1; 7:24; 8:12, 19, 25; 9:6; 11:2. The former is used of angels who torment the damned in *Mart. Pol.* 2:3 and Gk. *Apoc. Pet.* 8:3; and the related δυσβασάνιστος refers to punishment in the afterlife in *Sib. Or.* 7:128; so too the verb βασανίζω in RecShrt. 10:16 E (cf. fam. B F G: τοῖς βασανισταῖς) and *T. Ash.* 6:5. The angel places the soul "in the middle," εἰς τὸ μέσον; cf. v. 4; Gk. *1 En.* 26:1; 28:1; the expression is a favorite of Plutarch and rare in later Greek.[37] LSJ has no entry for ζυγάς;

---

[37]   Cf. RecShrt. 9:8 E: ἐν τόπῳ μεσότητος. B F G: ἐν μέσῳ τούτων.

neither does Lampe.[38] But there are late texts where ζυγάς seems to mean "measure" (e.g., Ps.-John of Damascus, *Pass. Artemii* PG 96.1285B), and in Isidore of Pelusium, *Ep.* 10 PG 78.185B; Stephen the Deacon, *Vit. Stephani Iunioris* PG 100.1076A; and *Mart. Carpus, Papylus, Agathonice* 35, it means "pair" or "couple"; and the related ζυγός can mean "balance" (LSJ, s.v.; cf. 12:9, 13; 13:1, 10, 14). The gist of our line is in any case plain: the scale is not tipped one way or the other. Cf. RecShrt. 9:8 E: "For he found that the sins evenly balanced [ἰσοζυγούσας] her good works."

Rabbinic texts envisage the possibility of a balance between good deeds and sins. *t. Sanh.* 13:3 speaks of three classes of human beings—those destined for everlasting life, those destined for shame, and those whose deeds are evenly balanced; cf. *t. Sanh.* 13:3; *b. Roš Haš.* 16b; *Ruth Rab.* 3:1. The rabbinic בינוניים = "those in the middle" in these texts resembles *TA*'s εἰς τὸ μέσον. Similarly, *Pesiq. Rab. Kah.* 25:2 teaches that "when both pans of the scale of justice balance exactly, a person's iniquitous deeds on one side and his good deeds on the other, the Holy One lifts out from the pan of iniquities one of the writs attesting the man's guilt, so that the good deeds tip the balance." The idea was probably traditional, even though its first Jewish appearance is in *TA*. Its ultimate derivation is Egyptian depictions of the postmortem scale. The famous Egyptian folktale, often thought to supply the background for Luke 16:19–31, preserved in Demotic in Papyrus DCIV of the British Museum, refers to a man whose good and bad deeds are equally balanced. There are, however, also Iranian parallels. Zoroastrian texts know of a place called *Hamēstagān*, where those whose evil deeds and good deeds are equal or balanced go for postmortem correction.[39] And from the Greek world, Plato, *Phaed.* 113D, says that when the dead come to the place of judgment, the judges divide the souls into those who have lived well and piously, those who have not so lived, and those who have lived in between (μέσως; these last are later divided into those who can be healed and those who cannot be healed). A triadic division of the dead appears early on in Greek sources: a few blessed souls, such as Achilles, are in the Elysian fields; a few terrible souls are in a region of woe with Tantalus and Sisyphus; most are in Hades. For a patristic parallel see Augustine, *Enchir.* 110: there are the very good, who do not

---

[38] Lampe, s.v. ζύγιος, cites only Gregory of Nazianzus and *TA* 12:18.

[39] See Jal Dastur Cursetji Pavry, *The Zoroastrian Doctrine of a Future Life: From Death to the Individual Judgment* (2nd ed.; New York: Columbia University Press, 1929), 50, 74, n. 90, 90–91, 113, and the texts translated in R. C. Zaehner, *Zurvan: a Zoroastrian Dilemma* (New York: Biblo and Tannen, 1972), 399–401, 414.

need our prayers after they die; there are the not-so-very-good, who can profit from intercessory prayers; and there are the very bad, who are beyond help.

Chapter 13: The Judgment Interpreted

Bibliography: Delcor, *Testament,* 59–62. Fishburne, "1 Corinthians III. 19–15". James, *Testament,* 50–55. Munoa, *Four Powers.* Nickelsburg, "Eschatology". Saul M. Olyan, *A Thousand Thousands Served Him: Exegesis and the Naming of Angels in Ancient Judaism* (TSAJ 36; Tübingen: Mohr-Siebeck, 1993), 78–79. Schmidt, "Testament," 1:63–78; 2:132, 141–43.

Long Recension

13:1. And Abraham said, "My lord Commander-in-chief, who is this most marvelous judge? And who are the recording angels? And who is the sun-like angel who holds the scale? And who is the fiery angel who holds the fire?" 13:2. The Commander in chief said, "Observe, all holy and just Abraham, the fearful man sitting on the throne. This is the son of the first-formed, the one called Abel, whom the most evil and fratricidal Cain killed. 13:3. And he sits here to judge all the creation, and he carefully examines the righteous and sinners, for God said, 'I do not judge you, but every person will be judged by a person.' 13:4. For this reason it was given to him to judge the world until his great and glorious *parousia.* And then, just Abraham, will be the perfect judgment and recompense, eternal and unalterable, which no one is able to question. 13:5. Every person has arisen from the first-formed, and because of this, each will first be judged by his son. 13:6. And in the second *parousia,* everything that breathes and every person will be judged by the twelve tribes of Israel. 13:7. But in the third place, every

Short Recension fam. E

11:1. And Abraham answered and said to Michael, "Lord, who is this judge? And who is the other one, who makes sins known?" 11:2. And Michael said to Abraham, "Do you see the judge? He is Abel, the first martyr. And he was brought unto this place in order to judge. 11:3. This (other) one, who makes (sins) known, is Enoch, your father. He is the teacher of heaven and scribe of righteousness. 11:4. And the Lord sent him here that the sins and the righteous deeds of each might be inscribed." 11:5. And Abraham said to Michael, "How is Enoch able to weigh the lot of souls, since he has not seen death? Or is he able to pass sentence upon every soul?" 11:6. And Michael said, "If the sentence were contrary to the written decision, it would not be agreed to. Yet Enoch does not pass judgment of himself. 11:7. Rather the Lord is the one who passes sentence, and Enoch is the one who records. 11:8. For Enoch prayed to the Lord saying, 'I do not wish to pass sentence upon a soul lest I become oppressive to someone.' 11:9. And the Lord said to Enoch, "I will give a signal to you, that you should

person will be judged by God, the Master of all. And then finally the end of that judgment (will be) near, and the sentence (will be) fearful, and none can undo (it). 13:8. And therefore the judgment and recompense of the world take place through three tribunals. And so a matter is not made secure by one or two witnesses, but every matter will be established by three witnesses. 13:9. The two angels, those at the right and at the left, are the ones who record all sins and righteous deeds. The angel on the right records the righteous deeds, the one on the left the sins. 13:10. The sun-like angel, the one holding the scale in his hand, he is Dokiel the archangel, the just weigher, and he weighs sins and righteous deeds in the righteousness of God. 13:11. The fiery and relentless angel, the one holding fire in his hand, he is Puriel the archangel, who has authority over the fire, and he tests the deeds of people through fire. 13:12. And if the fire burns up the work of anyone, immediately the angel of judgment takes him and carries (him) away to the place of sinners, a most bitter cup. 13:13. But if the fire tests the work of anyone and does not kindle it, he is vindicated, and the angel of righteousness takes him and carries him away to salvation in the inheritance of the just. 13:14. And so, just Abraham, all things in everybody are tested by fire and by balance."

record the sins of a soul in the book. 11:10. And if that soul receives mercy, you will find that its sins have been erased and that it will enter into life. 11:11. But if a soul does not find mercy, you will find its sins inscribed, and it will be cast into chastisement."

TEXTUAL NOTES ON THE LONG RECENSION

13:1. G abbreviates by dropping "My lord, Commander-in-chief." H reduces the address to "Lord." // Q, passing from ὁ to ὁ, omits "sun-like" and "who holds the scale? And who is." // Through *homoioteleuton* I drops the last question, moving from κετέχων to δοκιμάζων. 13:2. J abbreviates by dropping "all holy and just Abraham" while B H I Q omit only "and just," perhaps because an eye skipped from the end of πανόσιε to the end of δίκαιε. // After "son," B G I J Q specify (τοῦ) Ἀδάμ. H adds the name after "first-formed." // A: πονηρότατος. B Q: πονηρὸς καὶ ἀδελφοκτόνος. G I: πονηρότατος ἀδελφοκτόνος. H: ἀδελφὸς αὐτοῦ. J: πονηρός. One can only guess the original. 13:3. A: οὐκ ἐγὼ κρίνω τὸν κόσμον. This anticipates v. 4 and echoes the New Testament (see on v. 4). // At the end, A has "is judged" instead of "will be judged." 13:4. A has the superlative δικαιότατε (cf. 16:11; 17:10; 18:6 v.l.; 19:14; 20:3) instead of δίκαιε. 13:5. A has τοιούτου ἄνθρωπου, which refers to Adam ("judged by this man"). The origin of this variant is unclear. The revised sentence perhaps makes better sense in and of itself, but it ill suits the context. The other manuscripts have υἱοῦ, with variants. 13:6. G H I J Q, although differing in details, have the twelve tribes being judged "by the twelve apostles" (B: "the apostles"). This clearly depends upon Matt 19:28 = Luke 22:28–30. A's simple "by the twelve tribes" is usually reckoned original because of its Jewish character. Yet it remains possible that an ancestor of A had the Christian reading, κριθήσονται ὑπὸ τῶν δώδεκα ἀποστόλων αἱ δώδεκα φυλαί, and that an eye passed from the first to the second δώδεκα, after which the case of φυλαί was corrected to the genitive.[1] One could also posit that the "twelve apostles" replaced an original "twelve patriarchs" (cf. *T. Jud.* 25:1–2; *T. Benj.* 10:7) or "twelve phylarchs" (φυλάρχων could have become φυλῶν) or "twelve judges" (cf. *Shemoneh 'Esreh* benediction 18), but all this is speculation. The problem is more difficult because Christians might have understood A in light of the tradition that the church is the new Israel; see the commentary on v. 6. 3:7. B Q open with τῇ δὲ τρίτῃ, which implies a third *parousia*. // G omits "then finally" and "that judgment," which leaves: "and the end is near." // J drops "the end is near." // B J omit "And the sentence ... undo (it)." // H I omit "and none can undo (it)," and G omits this and all of v. 8. 13:8. J skips from the end of κρίσις to the end of ἀνταπόδοσις, perhaps intentionally. 13:9. J omits as otiose "those at the right ... righteous deeds." B Q similarly omit "those at the right ... left." // At the end, A B G H Q have τοὺς ἁμαρτωλούς instead of τὰς ἁμαρτίας (so I J). 13:10. J abbreviates by omitting "in his hand," G by omitting "he is Dokiel ... weigher," I by omitting "is Dokiel the archangel." // A: ὁ Δοκιήλ. B Q: Δίκαιος. // J omits all from "in his hand." 13:10–14:4. J lacks "in the righteousness of God" and all of 13:11–14:4. 13:11. H drops "and relentless ... Puriel, the archangel." An eye probably passed from "angel" to the end of "archangel." // G drops "he is Puriel the archangel" and "over the fire." // A: Πυρουήλ. I Q: Πυροήλ. 13:12. B G H I Q have ἅψεται (cf.

---

[1]   Contrast James, *Testament*, 53–54.

v. 13) as well as κατακαύσει. // H drops (in order to abbreviate?) "imme-diately ... judgment." // A: ποτήριον. B G H Q: κολαστήριον (cf. Lucian, *Ver. hist.* 2.30). Given the common -τήριον ending, one suspects a scribal slip or partial lacuna, not a conscious alteration, but the direction of the change is unclear. 13:13. I drops as unnecessary "and does not ... vindi-cated."

COMMENTARY

In 12:15, Abraham asks one general question, "What are these things that we see?" Michael then identifies the activities of various angelic figures without naming those figures. This leaves Abraham with yet more ques-tions, four of which he now asks.

13:2–4 and 9–14 address Abraham's queries about the judge and the four angels (v. 1). Vv. 5–8, by contrast, focus upon the eschatological consum-mation, which is irrelevant to the larger plot. They also mention the twelve tribes of Israel, which show up nowhere else in our book; and they puzzle by announcing three judgments, which are both redundant and without close Jewish parallel.[2] Finally, they offer a reason for Abel's exalted office (v. 5), whereas vv. 2–4 already do that. So vv. 1–4 + 9–14 may represent an older sequence which concerned postmortem judgment only; and per-haps this was later expanded under the Egyptian model of three stages of jurisdiction,[3] to make room for traditions about the final, universal judg-ment.[4] Both Jewish and Christian texts regularly combine Hellenistic post-mortem judgment with biblical historical eschatology (cf. *1 Enoch* 22; Luke; and *4 Ezra* 7); but nowhere else do we read of a first, second, and third *parousia*.

It is possible that vv. 4–8 come from a Christian who identified Abel with Jesus and the twelve tribes with the church, for those typological

---

[2]   The closest parallel is in the Apocalypse of Weeks (*1 En.* 93:1–10 and 91:12–17), which views the eschatological transition as a protracted process that ends with three weeks of judgment: in the eighth week Israel is judged, in the ninth week the nations are judged, in the tenth week the angels are judged. Revelation 19–20 also offers consecutive judgments, but there are only two, and they are historical, not postmor-tem.

[3]   Delcor, *Testament*, 61, 146–47, observes that in Roman times the Egyptian court system had three stages of jurisdiction: the strategos, the epistrategos, and the supreme court.

[4]   So too Nickelsburg, "Eschatology," 41–47. Contrast James, *Testament*, 54, who argues instead for the secondary character of vv. 9–14.

equations are well attested; see on vv. 2 and 6. Yet this may be too subtle a suggestion. It remains odd, on the hypothesis that vv. 4–8 are Christian *ab initio*, that Jesus is not named. Further, while vv. 4–8 contain some Christian language, this is true of the entirety of the chapter, for all of the following words and phrases are under suspicion of being ecclesiastical:

πανόσιε; see on 13:2

δικαίους καὶ ἁμαρτωλούς; see on 13:3

ἐνδόξου ... παρουσίας; see on 13:4

κρῖναι τὸν κόσμον; see on 13:4

κρίσις καὶ ἀνταπόδοσις; see on 13:4

δευτέρᾳ παρουσίᾳ; see on 13:6

τὸ τέλος ἐγγύς, καὶ φοβερὰ ἡ ἀπόφασις, καὶ ὁ λύων οὐδείς; see on 13:7

ἄγγελος ... ὁ ἐπὶ τὸ πῦρ ἔχων τὴν ἐξουσίαν; see on 13:11

εἴ τινος τὸ ἔργον κατακαύσει; see on 13:12

εἴ τινος δὲ τὸ ἔργον τὸ πῦρ δοκιμάσει ... σῴζεσθαι; see on 13:13

τὸν τόπον τῶν ἁμαρτωλῶν; see on 13:13

τὰ πάντα ἐν πᾶσιν; see on 13:14

No portion of chap. 13 is free of Christian redaction, so we cannot use the presence of ecclesiastical language to separate sources. We can, however, surmise that the Christian contributions come from early rather than later medieval times, for as Turner observed: "In the *Test. Abr.* an angel named Dokiel, not Michael, does the weighing. There is no Devil or Virgin Mary to incline the balances for or against the soul. Michael shows Abraham this scene, but he himself takes no part in it"—all of which distinguishes our text from later Christian themes.[5]

The various facts seem best accounted for by postulating that our chapter has gone through at least a three-stage development:

(a) Vv. 2–3 + 9–14 may depend upon a Jewish depiction of postmortem judgment in response to Abraham's question in v. 1

(b) Vv. 4–8 may represent a secondary expansion largely motivated by a desire to include the universal judgment of all

(c) Christian hands have introduced ecclesiastical language, most obviously in vv. 12–13; and B G H I J Q have even put "the (twelve) apostles" into the second judgment (see Textual Notes)

One could go a step further and speculate that RecShrt. 11, the parallel to RecLng. 13, preserves a stage before (a). For neither RecShrt. fam. E nor fam. B F G shows any sign of the secondary material in vv. 5–8; and it is quite possible, as observed on pp. 259–60, that the angels of RecLng. are secondary, that they have displaced Enoch, who is the record keeper in

---

[5]   Turner, "Biblical Greek," 221, n. 1.

RecShrt. 10–11 (both families). In line with this, the likely Christian phrases in RecLng. (see above) do not appear in RecShrt. Still, caution is in order. For one thing, RecShrt. itself contains several phrases that one must suspect are Christian:

ὁ πρῶτος μαρτυρήσας, 11:2 E; cf. Sozomen, *Hist. eccl.* 7.19.3; Michael Psellus, *Poem.* 53.361; Photius, *Bibl.*, ed. Bekker, p. 118B.3 PG 103.501B; also the common patristic and liturgical title of Stephen, ὁ πρωτομάρτυς

τὰς ἁμαρτίας καὶ τὰς δικαιοσύνας, 11:4 E; cf. John 16:8; Origen, *Comm. Rom.* 15.1; Gregory of Nyssa, *Castig.* PG 46.316C; etc.

εἰσελεύσεται εἰς τὴν ζωήν, 11:10 E; cf. *Ps.-Clem. Hom.* 3:52; Origen, *Comm. Matt.* 15.13; Ps.-Macarius, *Serm. 1–22, 24–27* 1.1; 10.3

τὰς ἁμαρτίας αὐτῆς γεγραμμένας, 11:11 E; cf. Origen, *Cels.* 7.18; *Hom. Jer.* 10.8; Theophanes Continuatus, *Chronog.*, ed. Bekker, p. 439

βληθήσεται εἰς τὴν κόλασιν, 11:11 E; cf. Didymus of Alexandria, *Man.* PG 39.1104B; Ps.-Ephraem, *Sermones paraenetici ad monachos Aegypti* 39.135

Beyond this, RecShrt. elsewhere seems as often as not an abbreviated form of RecLng.; and in the present case, perhaps the confusion and redundancy vv. 5–8 introduce were best handled through simple omission.

Whatever the relationship of RecLng. 13 to RecShrt. 11, the two are formally similar. In both cases Abraham asks about what he has seen in the previous chapter, and in both cases Michael gives the names and functions of those figures. The main difference is that, while both depict Abel as the judge, RecShrt. has no angels: all the focus is shifted to Enoch, "the scribe of righteousness" (cf. *1 En.* 12:4).[6]

13:1. The several figures that crowd the stage in chap. 12, a crowding more reminiscent of Egyptian than Jewish judgment scenes,[7] move Abraham to ask four questions. These follow the order of the narrative in chap. 12. The first question concerns the identity of the judge, called "marvelous" (θαυμαστός) in chap. 12 but here "most marvelous" (πανθαύμαστος). The

---

[6] Enoch's status as "the scribe of righteousness" may have been particularly prominent in Egypt; see Birger A. Pearson, "Enoch in Egypt," in *For a Later Generation: The Transformation of Tradition in Israel, Early Judaism, and Early Christianity* (ed. Randal A. Argall, Beverly A. Bow, and Rodney A. Werline; Harrisburg, Pa.: Trinity Press Intl., 2000), 216–31. "Enoch the scribe (of righteousness)" is even called upon on tombstones.

[7] Note e.g. *CT* 1070, 1071 and see Brandon, *Judgment*, 31–42, and Griffiths, *Divine Verdict*, 201–30. For illustrations of judgment scenes crowded with figures see the foldouts opposite pp. 330 and 344 in E. A. Wallis Budge, *Osiris and the Egyptian Resurrection* (London/New York: P. L. Warner/G. P. Putnam's Sons, 1911).

adjective makes him like the Adam of 11:8 (q.v.), which is natural enough: father is like son. The second question concerns the identity of the two "recording" (ἀπογραφόμενοι) angels in 12:8 and 12 (q.v. for ἀπογράφω)— a question that as a matter of fact goes unanswered: v. 9 only brings forward information chap. 12 already gives. The third question concerns "the sun-like (ἡλιόμορφος) angel who holds the scale." The reference is to 12:9 (q.v.; in this the angel is "glorious," φωτοφόρος) and 13. Cf. the descriptions of Michael in 7:3 and 4 (q.v. for ἡλιόμορφος): in the former he is φωτοφόρος, in the latter ἡλιόμορφος. The fourth question—"And who is the fiery angel who holds the fire?"—goes back to 12:10 and 14. In clarifying the identities of these last two angels, yet two more angels will be introduced, the angel of judgment and the angel of righteousness (vv. 12–13); but Michael will say nothing about them.

13:2. Michael answers, in the order that he asks them, the questions of the "just" one (δίκαιε); cf. vv. 4 and 14 and see on 1:1. The patriarch is "all holy," πανόσιε. πανόσιος* is a late patristic word; cf. John Climacus, *Scala paradisi* 4 PG 88.658A; Ps.-John of Damascus, *Fide dormierunt* PG 95.273B; Photius, *Bibl.*, ed. Bekker, p. 472A PG 104.113C; Sophocles, *Lex.*, s.v. Michael begins with the man sitting on the throne, who is "fearful" (φοβερόν); cf. v. 7. The adjective describes Adam in 11:4 and Abel's throne in 12:4. This man is "the son of the first-formed," πρωτο-πλάστου; see on 11:9 and cf. Gregory of Nyssa, *Contra Eunomium*, ed. Jaeger, 1.1:610. That is, he is "the one called Abel," ἐπιλεγόμενος Ἄβελ. For ἐπιλογέω* + proper name see Josephus, *Ant.* 13.120, 268; John 5:2; *Mart. Pol.* 6:2; Gk. *L.A.E.* 2:2 ("the blood of my son, ἐπιλεγομένου Ἄβελ"). This Abel was killed (ἀπέκτεινεν; cf. LXX Gen 4:8; ἀποκτείνω: 13:2; 18:3) by Cain, "the most evil" (πονηρότατος)—an adjective Josephus applies to Cain in *Ant.* 1.53; cf. Philo, *Quaest. Gen.* 1.59; 1 John 3:10–12. Cain is also "fratricidal," ἀδελφοκτόνος; cf. Herodotus, *Hist.* 3.65; Plutarch, *Mor.* 256F. This word describes Cain in *Apos. Con.* 8:12:21 and Chrysostom, *Hom. Rom.* PG 60.620. The related ἀδελφοκτονία is used of him in Gk. fr. *Jub.* 4:15; Philo, *Agr.* 21; 1 *Clem.* 4:7; Epiphanius, *Pan.* 38.5; Chrysostom, *Hom. Rom.* PG 60.505; and for ἀδελφοκτονέω of Cain see Theophilus of Antioch, *Autol.* 2.30. Ἄβελ ὃν ἀπέκτεινεν Καίν, which also appears in Gk. *L.A.E.* 4:3, is straight from Gen 4:25; cf. Gk. fr. 1 *En.* 22:7: Ἄβελ ὃν ἐφόνευσε Καίν.

No other ancient text makes Abel an eschatological judge (although Philo, *Quaest. Gen.* 1.59, speaks of his pastoral work as "preparatory to rulership and kingship"). V. 3 explains that "every man is judged by man," v. 5 that Abel's status as Adam's son qualifies him to judge everybody. The clarifications leave much unclarified. Why must the judge be the particular man Abel? There are several theories:

(i) Maybe someone took "the one like a son of man" in Dan 7:13 to be the equivalent of "the son of Adam." This is the view of Munoa, and it may be correct.[8] Certainly some Christian readers have taken the New Testament's "son of man" to mean "son of Adam."[9] But Munoa's attempt to show the dependence of TA's judgment scene upon Daniel 7 is inconclusive. Certainly the verbal parallels are scanty.[10]

(ii) One could posit that a Semitic precursor of TA, or a Semitic exegetical tradition it incorporates, referred, in dependence upon Dan 7:13, to the judge as בֶן אָדָם which a translator wrongly took to be Abel.[11] The targum on Ezekiel regularly translates the Hebrew בֶן אָדָם = "son of man" with the Aramaic בַר אָדָם that is, "son of Adam."

(iii) In Egyptian eschatology, Osiris judges the dead from his golden throne, and he is the first martyr, and that at the hands of his brother. So maybe Abel is the Jewish equivalent of Osiris.[12] TA otherwise shows a likely debt to Egyptian ideas of postmortem judgment, so this is another plausible thesis.

(iv) Perhaps Abel's role as judge developed out of his status as the first innocent to be murdered. The expectation that the righteous will judge their persecutors is attested (cf. 1 En. 38:5; 48:9; 95:3; 96:1; 98:12), and perhaps in some circles Abel became the embodiment of this idea. In line with this, 1 En. 22:5–7 has Abel's spirit bringing suit not only against Cain but also against "all his seed," and Tg. Neof. 1 on Gen 4:8 has Cain deny postmortem judgment, which Abel defends. This tradition also appears in Ps.-Jonathan and elsewhere.[13] Already James suggested that Abel, as the first martyr, was thought "entitled to act as judge of saints and sinners alike," and further that Gen 4:10 ("The voice of your brother's blood cries

---

[8] Munoa, Four Powers, 31–42. Cf. James F. McGrath, John's Apologetic Christology: Legitimation and Development in Johannine Christology (SNTSMS 111; Cambridge: Cambridge University Press, 2001), 98.

[9] Delbert Burkett, The Son of Man Debate: A History and Evaluation (SNTSMS 107; Cambridge: Cambridge University Press, 1999), 9–11, and Joel Marcus, "The Son of Man as the Son of Adam," RB 110 (2003), 38–61.

[10] Cf. Nickelsburg, "Eschatology," 36.

[11] Cf. Schmidt, "Testament," 1:64.

[12] Cf. Ellul, "Testament," 73–82. One may note that Abraham replaces Osiris in Luke 16:19–31, if indeed this rewrites the Egyptian folktale preserved in Demotic in Papyrus DCIV of the British Museum.

[13] See further Jouette M. Bassler, "Cain and Abel in the Palestinian Targum: A Brief Note on an Old Controversy," JSJ 17 (1986), 56–64.

to me from the God"; cf. Heb 12:24) was "interpreted after a too literal fashion" and "influenced our author in his selection of Abel as judge."[14]

(v) James observed that there was a tendency in some "obscure sects" to exalt Adam, Seth, and Melchizedek, and he suggested that this might explain Abel's role as judge of humanity.[15] Seth was, according to Gen 4:25, the replacement of Abel, so they might be equated.

Which one of these explanations, or which combination of them, is right, or whether the truth lies elsewhere, remains beyond recovery. Whatever the answer, many Christian texts, for obvious reasons, regard the slaughtered Abel as a Christ figure; see Heb 12:24; Irenaeus, *Haer.* 4.25.2; Melito of Sardis, *Pasch.* 428–430; Augustine, *Civ.* 15.7; Methodius of Olympus, *Symp.* Hymn 11; Symmachus, *Vit. Abel* 8; etc. Given this, one wonders whether Christian scribes or readers could have identified Abel with Jesus.

13:3. Abel sits and judges "all the creation," πᾶσαν τὴν κτίσιν; cf. v. 6; RecShrt. 12:12; Gk. fr. *1 En.* 18:1; Jdt 16:14; Tob 8:5; *3 Macc.* 2:2; *Jos. Asen.* 12:1; Mark 16:15; etc. In particular, both "the righteous and sinners" (δικαίους καὶ ἁμαρτωλούς) he "carefully examines" (ἐλέγξων); cf. *Ps. Sol.* 17:25 (ἐλέγξαι ἁμαρτωλούς); Herm. *Vis.* 1.1.5 (τὰς ἁμαρτίας ἐλέγξω). ἐλέγχω* refers to the last judgment in Gk. fr. *1 En.* 1:9; Jude 15; *T. Benj.* 10:10; etc. Although δίκαιος καὶ ἁμαρτωλός appears in *Ps. Sol.* 2:34, the combination is typical of patristic writers; see Ps.-Hippolytus, *De consummatione mundi* 37.2; Gregory of Nazianzus, *Or.* 14 PG 35.889C; Chrysostom, *Hom. Rom.* PG 60.654; etc.; and its appearance in *Gk. Apoc. Ezra* 2:9 is probably Christian.

The explanation of Abel's exalted role is difficult: "I do not judge you," God has said, "but every person will be judged by a person." This statement is otherwise unattested (although some have read John 5:27 as though it were a parallel: Jesus has authority to judge because he is a son of man).[16] Is it an interpretive paraphrase and expansion of Gen 9:6, "Whoever sheds the blood of a person, by a person shall that person's blood be shed"? Delcor observes that these words gain judicial sense in Onqelos: "The one who sheds the blood of man before witnesses, by

---

[14] James, *Testament*, 125. Cf. Delcor, *Testament*, 142–44, emphasizing the targumic traditions.

[15] James, *Testament*, 125–26. Cf. Macurdy, "Platonic Orphism," 223–24. Note also Frederick H. Bosch, *The Christian and Gnostic Son of Man* (SBT 2/14; London: SCM, 1970), 109–10. Epiphanius, *Pan.* 39.5.1, assigns to the Sethians an apocalyptic book "by the name of Abraham."

[16] E.g. F. P. Badham, "The Title 'Son of Man,'" *Theologisch Tijdschrift* 45 (1911), 44–45.

sentence of the judges will his blood be shed, for in the image of God He made man."[17] Whether or not there is a scriptural basis, the idea that God's eschatological judgment is in the hands of a human representative is common enough; see on 11:4.

13:4. "For this reason" (τούτου χάριν), that is, in view of the divine declaration in v. 3, God has appointed Abel to "judge the world" (κρῖναι τὸν κόσμον) until "his great and glorious *parousia*," τῆς μεγάλης ἐνδόξου αὐτοῦ παρουσίας. A reference to Abel's *parousia* as opposed to God's seems unlikely because the former's role is now ended. The LXX does not use κρίνω + κοσμόν, a construction that occurs in the New Testament (John 3:17; 12:47; 1 Cor 6:2; Heb 11:7); in *Gk. Apoc. Ezra* 3:3 ("that great day and the epiphany which prevails to judge the world"); and in other Christian texts (*Barn.* 4:12; *Sib. Or.* 8:219; Ps.-Athanasius, *De virginitate* 19; etc.). But *Sib. Or.* 4:184 appears to supply a Jewish example.

παρουσία (lit. "presence"; cf. v. 6; 2:5; 2 Cor 10:10) designated both the official arrival of a high-ranking person, especially king or emperor (cf. *adventus* and 3 *Macc.* 3:17), as well as the manifestation of a hidden deity.[18] In *TA* 13:4, it means God's public, eschatological "arrival" (not "return"). The word came into Judaism with reference to God's acts in salvation-history (cf. Josephus, *Ant.* 3.80, 203; 9.55), and it may, in pre-Christian times, have already been used of God's eschatological coming (cf. *T. Jud.* 22:2; 2 *Bar.* 30:1; 2 *En.* 32:1; LXX Dan 7:13 uses πάρειμι of the arrival of the one like a son of man). Sanders supposes that "the term was probably more common in Jewish literature than can now be directly demonstrated."[19] That could be; certainly the word of itself does not require a Christian hand. Still, παρουσία with eschatological sense is characteristic of Christian writings: Matt 24:1; 1 Cor 15:23; 1 Thess 2:19; 5:23; 2 Thess 2:1, 8, 9; Jas 5:7–8; 2 Pet 1:16; 1 John 2:28; *Vit. Proph. Jeremiah* 13; *Gk. Apoc. Pet.* 1; *Apoc. Sedr.* title; Ps.-Chrysostom, *Ador.* 2 PG 62.747; etc. The characterization of God's or Jesus' *parousia* as "great" (μεγάλης) is admittedly rare (cf. Ps.-Athanasius, *Annunt.* PG 28.937A). It is presumably modeled upon the well-attested qualification of "the Day (of the Lord)" as "great": Jer 30:7; Joel 2:11; Zeph 1:14; Mal 4:5; *Jub.* 23:11; 1 *En.* 10:6; 98:10; Acts 2:20; Jude 6; Rev 6:17; *Gk. Apoc. Ezra* 3:3; etc.; cf. Ps.-Macarius, *Serm.* 64 40.3: ἐν τῇ μεγάλῃ ἡμέρᾳ τῆς ἐνδόξου αὐτοῦ

---

[17] Delcor, *Testament*, 143. Cf. Piattelli, "Testamento," 117, n. 4.

[18] Lit.: P. L. Schoonheim, *Een semasiologisch Onderzoek van Parousia* (Aalten: Gebr. de Boer, 1953); Klaus Thraede, *Grundzüge griechisch-römischer Brieftopik* (Zetemata 48; Munich: C. H. Beck, 1970), 95–106.

[19] Sanders, "Testament," 890, n. 13a.

παρουσίας. What proves our phrase to be Christian is the use of ἔνδοξος with παρουσία, for although Tit 2:13 ("the glorious epiphany of the great God and our Savior Jesus Christ") is only a distant parallel, later Christian writers frequently characterize Jesus' second *parousia* as "glorious": Justin Martyr, *Dial.* 49.2; 110.2; Eusebius, *Ecl. proph.*, ed. Gaisford, p. 194 (ἐνδόξου αὐτοῦ παρουσίας); Gregory of Nazianzus, *Sanc. bapt.* PG 36.424C (τῆς ἐνδόξου αὐτοῦ παρουσίας); Didymus of Alexandria, *Fr. Ps.*, ed. Mühlenberg, 155.14 (ἐνδόξου αὐτοῦ παρουσίας); Theodoret of Cyrrhus, *Eranistes*, ed. Ettlinger, p. 166.20 (τῆς ἐνδόξου αὐτοῦ παρουσίας); Ps.-Macarius, *Serm. 64* 22.1 (ἐνδόξου αὐτοῦ παρουσίας); John of Damascus, *De immaculato corpore* PG 95.408C (τῆς ἐνδόξου αὐτοῦ παρουσίας); etc. Even though it is, in *TA* 13:4, God's *parousia*, not that of Jesus, this is no decisive objection to seeing a Christian hand here, for Christians identified Jesus with θεός and so could have identified God's *parousia* with that of the divine Jesus; cf. Tit 2:13; Ps.-Chrysostom, *Ador. 2* PG 62.747; see above. One could, nonetheless, posit a Jewish text with παρουσία, to which a Christian added the qualifying ἔνδοξος.

Michael continues the explanation by informing "just" (δίκαιε; cf. vv. 2, 4 and see on 1:1) Abraham of what comes after the *parousia*—"the perfect judgment and recompense," τελεία κρίσις καὶ ἀνταπόδοσις. For κρίσις καὶ ἀνταπόδοσις see on 10:15. τέλειος* + κρίσις is not a fixed expression, but one may note Basil the Great, *Hom. dicta tempore famis et siccitatis* PG 31.324A (ἐν τῇ τελευταίᾳ κρίσει); Gregory of Nyssa, *De virginitate* 4.5 (τὸ τέλος κατάκρισις); Athanasius, *Exp. Ps.* PG 27.85A (τὴν τελευταίαν κρίσιν). When the final judgment comes, it will be "eternal and unalterable," αἰώνια καὶ ἀμετάθετος. ἀμετάθετος*, although a good patristic word used in connection with things divine (Lampe, s.v.; cf. Heb 6:17–18), also appears with the meaning "unalterable" in secular Greek (LSJ, s.v.) as well as in the LXX (*3 Macc.* 5:1, 12) and Josephus, *C. Ap.* 2.189. The unalterable judgment will be just in the sight of all, for no one will be able "to question" (ἀνακρῖναι) it. Why this is so appears from vv. 6ff.

This verse potentially subtracts from Abel's authority. For he judges only until God's *parousia*, and if God's judgment only confirms Abel's, is not one of their judgments otiose? And if God's judgment does not confirm Abel's—a possibility our text admittedly does not envisage—then why the first judgment? Such questions, however, miss the rhetorical point, which is that the convergence of judgments will leave no place for protest. If Abel, the tribes, and God concur on something, then it must be so.

13:5. "Every person has arisen from the first-formed" reprises 11:9 (q.v.), which also uses πρωτόπλαστος. But how does this explain why "each will first (πρῶτον—note the wordplay) be judged by his son"? One might instead infer that it is Adam himself who is best fitted to judge (cf. ms. A; H makes Adam and Abel judges). Probably we should think that the son of Adam is, like everyone else, a descendant of the first man, so that if he is the judge, all are first judged by one like them. But the logic is hardly tight. Any descendent of Adam would thus be qualified.

13:6. "The second *parousia*" surprises, for while v. 4 mentions a *parousia*, it is not there presented as the first of two or more advents; it is rather the final judgment, which brings "the perfect judgment and recompense, eternal and unalterable, which no one is able to question." Does v. 6 wrongly understand v. 4? In any case, "second *parousia*" is a Christian, not a Jewish, expression; it appears again and again from the second century on: Justin Martyr, *Dial.* 14.8; 49.2; *3 Apoc. John*, ed. Vassiliev, pp. 318.2; 319.1; Eusebius, *Dem. ev.* 4.16; 5.28; Athanasius, *Exp. Ps.* PG 27.229D, 305A; John V of Jerusalem, *De sacris imaginibus contra Constantinum* PG 95.329C; Photius, *Bibl.*, ed. Bekker, p. 254A PG 103.985D; etc. The judgment is universal as it includes "every person" (πᾶς ἄνθρωπος; cf. v. 7) and indeed "everything that breathes," πᾶσα πνοή*; cf. LXX Ps 150:6; *3 Bar.* 8:7; Pol. *Phil.* 2:1; *Acts John* 8; etc. All will be judged by "the twelve tribes of Israel," τῶν δώδεκα φυλῶν τοῦ Ἰσραήλ; cf. LXX Exod 24:4; Josh 4:5; Matt 19:28; Luke 22:30; the expression is not common apart from patristic texts influenced by Matt 19:28 = Luke 22:30. The idea may be that Israel judges through its representatives, perhaps the twelve patriarchs or the twelve phylarchs or some analogous body of twelve (see Textual Notes). Christians could have thought of the church, for they have often identified the tribes of Rev 7:4–8 with followers of Jesus,[20] and they have commonly understood the church to be the new or true or restored Israel; cf. John 11:51–52; 1 Pet 1:1, 17; 2:11; 2 Esd 1:33–40; Lampe, s.v. Ἰσραήλ 4, 5. On a more literal reading, which would hold for a postulated Jewish original, we have the old idea that Israel or the saints judge the Gentiles or the lawless, as in Dan 7:22 (cf. v. 27); *Jub.* 32:19; 1QpHab 5:4; 1QH 4:23–27; Wis 3:8; *Apoc. Abr.* 29:19; cf. 1 Cor 6:2; *Sib. Or.* 3:781–782.

13:7. The introductory τὸ τρίτον seems to mean "in the third place" or "the third time" (BAGD, s.v. τρίτος, 1b). How this third judgment is related to the second is unclear. Are they near in time? Or is there a chronological progression, so that Abel judges people after death, after which the twelve tribes judge before or during the messianic kingdom, after which, at the advent of the world to come, everyone is judged by God, the

---

[20]   See David E. Aune, *Revelation 6–16* (WBC 52B; Nashville: Word, 1998), 445–47.

Master, δεσπότου θεοῦ τῶν ἁπάντων? [21] For δεσπότης see on 1:4 and cf. 20:12; Ecclus 36:1 (δέσποτα ὁ θεὸς πάντων); Athanasius, *Apol. sec.* 69.3 (δεσπότου τῶν ἁπάντων θεοῦ); Epiphanius, *Pan.* 43.2 (θεὸς ὁ πάντων δεσπότης). It is certainly not a question of different people being judged at different judgments; each judgment rather embraces all:

13:3 πᾶς ἄνθρωπος ἐξ ἀνθρώπου κρίνεται
13:6 κριθήσονται ὑπό ... πᾶσα πνοὴ καὶ πᾶσα κτίσις
13:7 ὑπό ... κριθήσονται πᾶς ἄνθρωπος

One might imagine that the first judgment, as in Zoroastrian eschatology and Plato, *Phaed.* 114A–B, is purifying, so that there is another chance for salvation at the second and third judgments, in which case a sort of purgatory might be envisioned. But the text does not develop such an idea, and v. 8 seems to exclude it. There the agreement of the three witnesses is assumed: each judgment issues the same verdict. For God as the eschatological judge see *1 En.* 1:9; 25:4; *Sib. Or.* 2:214–220; 4:40–44, 183–184; 8:242; *L.A.B.* 3:10; *2 Bar.* 82:2; 85:15; *T. Benj.* 11:8–9; *Apocalypse of Abraham* 31; *2 En.* 65:6–8; *Apoc. El. (C)* 5:30; etc.

With God's judgment, "the end" (τέλος) will be "near," ἐγγύς; cf. 15:1: ἤγγικεν τὸ τέλος. "Fearful" (φοβερά; cf. v. 2) will be its "sentence," ἀπόφασις* (LXX: 0; NT: 0); cf. RecShrt. 11:5, 6, 8 E; Philo, *Migr.* 162; Josephus, *Bell.* 1.542; *T. Levi* 6:8; *T. Gad* 4:6; *Vit. Proph. Elisha* 3. The adjective is consistent with the pessimism of chaps. 11–12, which estimate that most will not enter into life. Here matters are made worse by the statement that "none can undo (it)," ὁ λύων οὐδείς (λύω*). As in *4 Ezra* 7:45, there comes a point past which there is no mercy; see further on 14:7. Perhaps *TA*, or at least chap. 13 in its present form, is consciously anti-Origenist, for it seemingly adopts the position of Jerome, Augustine, and the Councils of Constantinople in 543 and 553: hell is unalterable and eternal. There is no hope for a temporal punishment or for the universalism of Origen, Gregory of Nyssa, Evagrius, Diodore of Tarsus, Theodore of Mopsuestia, and Isaac of Nineveh. The possibility of saints praying some souls out of hell is also seemingly excluded (contrast chap. 14 and *Apoc. Pet.* 13; *Vis. Paul* 43; *Greek Apocalypse of the Virgin*).

A sermon of uncertain date and uncertain authorship contains the following: ὁ βίος βραχύς, ἡ δὲ τέχνη μακρά, τὸ τέλος ἐγγύς, καὶ ὁ φόβος πολύς, καὶ ὁ λύων οὐδείς ("Life is short, the art is long, the end is near, and fear is great, and no one can undo it": Ps.-Chrysostom, *De patientia* PG

---

[21] So Schmidt, "Testament," 1676.

60.727).[22] This line, which reappears in George Monachus the Chronographer, *Chron.*, ed. de Boor, p. 684 = *Chron. breve* PG 110.845D–848A, is a Christian adaptation of the famous line attributed to Hippocrates (*Aph.* 1): ὁ βίος βραχύς, ἡ δὲ τέχνη μακρά, ὁ καιρὸς ὀξύς, ἡ δὲ πεῖρα σφαλερή, ἡ δὲ κρίσις χαλεπή ("Life is short, the art is long, opportunity is fleeting, the experiment is perilous, the decision is difficult"; cf. Galen, *In Hippocratis aphorismi comm. vii* 17b; Theophilus Protospatharius, *De urinis* 2.246). Hippocrates' five-fold characterization of the doctor's task became proverbial (cf. the Latin, *Ars longa, vita brevis*). Now the first two sentiments in Ps.-Chrysostom reproduce Hippocrates, but the last three, which are new, create a five-part religious statement, one strikingly paralleled in *TA* 13:7:

De patientia	τὸ τέλος ἐγγύς, καὶ ὁ φόβος πολύς,	καὶ ὁ λύων οὐδείς
TA	τὸ τέλος ἐγγύς, καὶ φοβερὰ ἡ ἀπόφασις,	καὶ ὁ λύων οὐδείς

Given that *De patientia* is clearly a rewriting of Hippocrates, not *TA*, it seems to follow either that the latter draws upon Ps.-Chrysostom or that both are reproducing a (well-known?) Christian revision of Hippocrates' first aphorism. The latter is more likely as *TA* 13:7 speaks of κρίσεως ἐκείνης, which is a possible point of contact with Hippocrates (ἡ δὲ κρίσις χαλεπή), but not Ps.-Chrysostom.

13:8. The justification for the complex procedure recounted in the previous verses is now given. "The judgment and recompense of the world" (ἡ κρίσις τοῦ κόσμου καὶ ἀνταπόδοσις; cf. v. 8; John 12:31 [κρίσις ... τοῦ κόσμου]; and see on 10:15) is made "through three tribunals," διὰ τριῶν βημάτων. βῆμα* (cf. RecShrt. 6:8 E) has the sense of "tribunal" in Rom 14:10; 2 Cor 5:10; and *Hist. Jos. Carp.* Cod. C 13:8 but never in the LXX. With only one witness or even two, no "matter" (λόγος) is "safeguarded," ἀσφαλίζεται. For ἀσφαλίζω* (LXX: 5; NT: 4; cf. *Let. Arist.* 104; *T. Job* 5:3; 6:2; 39:8; *Vit. Proph. Elisha* 17) with figurative sense see Ign. *Phld.* 5:1; Ps.-Athanasius, *Hom. de passione et cruce domini* PG 28.189A (προασφαλίζεται λόγος); Epiphanius, *Pan.* 51.21 (ἐπασφαλίζεται ... ὁ λόγος). But three witnesses guarantee truth: "every matter (ῥῆμα)[23] will be established by three witnesses." The final clause is from LXX Deut 19:15:

LXX Deut	ἐπὶ στόματος τριῶν μαρτύρων σταθήσεται πᾶν ῥῆμα
TA	ἐπὶ τριῶν μαρτύρων σταθήσεται πᾶν ῥῆμα

---

[22] Cf. the related lines in Ps.-Chrysostom, *De salute an.* PG 60.737 (ὁ χρόνος μικρός, ἡ δὲ κρίσις μακρά, καὶ τὸ τέλος ἐγγύς, καὶ ὁ φόβος πολύς, καὶ ὁ ἐλεῶν οὐδείς), and *In evangelii dictum et de virginitate* PG 64.40 (ὁ βίος βραχύς, ἡ δὲ κρίσις μακρά).

[23] On the Semitic ῥῆμα = *res* see Turner, "Testament," 89.

Deut 19:15 is a legal rule and is often quoted or alluded to as such: Num 35:30; Deut 17:6; 11QTemple 61:6–7; 64:8–9; Philo, *Spec. leg.* 4.53–54; Josephus, *Ant.* 4.219; Strack-Billerbeck 1:790–91. It becomes a principle of ecclesiastical discipline in Matt 18:16; 2 Cor 13:1; and 1 Tim 5:19. More relevant for *TA* 13:8 is Revelation 11:1–14, if Deut 19:15 is partial inspiration for the "two witnesses," who are eschatological figures. But the closest parallel is the so-called "Johannine Comma," the textual variant (from the third or fourth century) in 1 John 5:7–8. This declares that "there are three who testify in heaven: Father, Word, and Holy Spirit; and these three are one." Here the principle of three witnesses from Deut 19:15 is embodied by three heavenly figures.

Plato, *Gorg.* 523E–524A, depicts three judges on the far side of death. They do not, however, judge one after the other but are responsible for different groups of people.

13:9. This line, which again stresses the symmetry in the arrangement of the heavenly court, adds nothing new. It is, surprisingly, only a restatement of 12:12:

13:9	οἱ δὲ δύο ἄγγελοι οἱ ἐκ δεξιῶν καὶ ἐξ ἀριστερῶν
12:12	οἱ δὲ δύο ἄγγελοι οἱ ἐκ δεξιῶν καὶ ἐξ ἀριστερῶν
13:9	οὗτοί εἰσιν οἱ ἀπογράφονται τὰς ἁμαρτίας καὶ τὰς δικαιοσύνας
12:12	ἀπεγράφοντο
13:9	ὁ μὲν ἐκ δεξιῶν ἄγγελος ἀπογράφεται τὰς δικαιοσύνας
12:12	καὶ ὁ δεξιὸς ἀπεγράφετο τὰς δικαιοσύνας
13:9	ὁ δὲ ἐξ ἀριστερῶν τοὺς ἁμαρτωλούς
12:12	καὶ ὁ ἐξ ἀριστερῶν ἀπεγράφετο τὰς ἁμαρτίας

Nickelsburg has suggested that, in a source behind *TA*, the angels on the right and left were, like Adam, Dokiel, and Puriel, given names. He suspects that the angel on the right was Michael, the angel on the left Satan, and that someone thought it awkward for Satan to be in heaven and impossible for Michael to identify the other angel with himself, so the names were deleted.[24] Whether or not this conjecture is correct, it is certainly peculiar that the interpretation in v. 9 just repeats what has been said before and so is no interpretation at all, and that in this chapter only the angels of fire and balance are named.

13:10. The angel who is "sun-like" (ἡλιόμορφος; cf. v. 1 and see on 7:4) and holds the scale in his hand (κατέχων ἐν τῇ χειρὶ αὐτοῦ; cf. v. 1 and see on

---

24 Nickelsburg, "Eschatology," 44.

12:9) is the ἀρχάγγελος (see on 1:4) Δοκιήλ. Doubt hangs over the origin of the name, found in ms. A (see Textual Notes) and not clearly attested outside of *TA*.[25] The explanations are several. None is clearly correct. (i) Moïse Schwab derives the name from the Hebrew דקק = "to be fine, to crush" (cf. דק = "thin, fine"), so the meaning is something like "divine precision."[26] Similarly, Box suggested an original דוקיאל. According to Jastrow, s.v., דוק, can mean "to examine carefully."[27] (ii) Schmidt suggests that Δοκιήλ is a corruption of שדקאל = "justice of God."[28] For him this is a sign of Egyptian origin, for SATQVIEL appears on a gem with an image of Anubis, who oversees the weighing of souls in Egyptian scenes of the judgment. (iii) Saul M. Olyan finds the origin of the name in an exegesis of Isa 40:22 ("It is he who stretched out the heavens like a veil," כדק), the reason being that דק = "veil" is a *hapax legomenon* appearing in a theophanic context, a circumstance that otherwise generates angelic names.[29] (iv) Another possible biblical source is Isa 40:15: "Even the nations are like a drop from a bucket, and are accounted as dust *on the scales*; see, he lifts up the isles like dust" (MT: כדק; Tg.: כדוקא). Here we find both the root דק and scales.[30] (v) Since an angel named דלקיאל is attested,[31] one might posit (in a Semitic precursor) a corruption to ד(ו)קיאל = Δοκιήλ. (vi) *Sefer Ha-Razim* 5th Firmament 11 knows of an angel called דנהיאל. Could this have come into Greek as Δοκιήλ? (vii) Perhaps the original text read ΔΟΚΙΜΑΖΙΗΛ, an obvious play on δοκιμάζω or δοκιμασία, and a scribal eye passed from the first Ι to the second Ι, with the resultant ΔΟΚΙΗΛ.[32] With this one could compare the angel Φαμαῆλ of Gk. *3 Bar.* 2:5, which presumably derives from the Greek φάμα/φήμη + Hebrew אל.

Dokiel is "the just weigher," ὁ δίκαιος ζυγοστάτης (ζυγοστάτης*: LXX: 0; Philo: 0; NT: 0; Josephus: 0; LSJ, s.v., cites Cercidas 4.33; Artemidorus

---

[25] דוקון may be an angelic name in line 2 of amulet 57.733 of the Israel Department of Antiquities; see Naveh and Shaked, *Amulets and Magic Bowls*, 90. But the context is fragmentary.

[26] Moïse Schwab, *Vocabulaire de l'angélologie d'après les manuscrits hébreux de la Bibliothèque Nationale* (reprint ed.; Milan: Archè, 1989), 213 ("subtilité divine"). Cf. J. Michl, "Engel V (Engelnamen)," *RAC* 5 (1962), 210.

[27] Box, *Testament*, 22, n. 2. Cf. Delcor, *Testament*, 147. Neither observes the happy coincidence, on this analysis, that the Greek δοκιμάζω = "assay, test."

[28] Schmidt, "Testament," 1:75–76.

[29] Olyan, *A Thousand Thousands*, 78–79.

[30] Cf. Ginzberg, "Testament," 95.

[31] E.g. *Sefer Ha-Razim* 3rd Firmament 9, 44, and 50 and the pages of a magic book printed in Naveh and Shaked, *Amulets and Magic Bowls*, 218.

[32] James, *Testament*, 55, thought "Dokiel" to be a pun on δοκιμάζω.

Daldianus, *Onir.* 2.37; and *Cod. justin.* 10.73.2; Lampe, s.v., cites Nilus, *Ep.* 3.246 = Isidore of Pelusium, *Ep.* 1.141, and Proclus Constantino-politanus, *Or.* 2.1). Even if Δοκιήλ is derived from a Semitic root, might some Greek readers have sensed a word play with δίκαιος? In any case stress is put upon the δικ- root by the note that Dokiel weighs "sins and righteous deeds" (τὰς ἁμαρτίας καὶ τὰς δικαιοσύνας; cf. 12:18; 13:9; 14:2)— not souls, as in 12:13—"in (accord with) the righteousness of God," ἐν δικαιοσύνῃ θεοῦ; cf. 2 Pet 1:1. God, through Dokiel, guarantees that people get their just deserts. One may compare the use of δικαιοσύνη in connection with God's judgment in Isa 5:16; 10:22; *Ps. Sol.* 2:10, 15–18, 32–35; 4:24 ("the Lord our God is a great and powerful judge in righteousness"); 5:1–4 ("your righteous judgments ... an individual and his fate are on the scales before you; he cannot add any increase contrary to your judgment, O God"); 8:7–8, 23–24; 9:2–5. Despite these Jewish parallels, Pauline influ-ence (cf. esp. Rom 1:17; 3:21–22; 10:3; 2 Cor 5:21) remains a possibility given the Christian language throughout chap. 13 and the use of 1 Corinthians in vv. 12–14 (see below).

13:11. This is closely parallel to the previous verse:

13:10	The sun-like	angel, the one holding the scale in his hand,
13:11.	The fiery and relentless angel, the one holding	fire	in his hand,

13:10	he is Dokiel the archangel,
13:11	he is Puriel the archangel,

13:10	the just weigher,
13:11	who has authority over the fire,

13:10	and he weighs sins and righteous deeds	in the righteousness of God
13:11	and he tests	the deeds of people through fire

The angel who is fiery and "relentless" (ἀπότομος; cf. 12:10 and see on 12:1), who holds fire in his hand (cf. 12:14; 2 *Bar.* 6:4), is the archangel Πυρουήλ. Unlike "Dokiel," the origin of this name is clear. Πυρουήλ is from πῦρ + אל, and the name is formed on the model of Uriel, אוריאל = "fire of God" (Greek: Οὐριήλ),[33] a well-known angel, often reckoned among the four, five, or seven archangels; see *1 En.* 20:2 v.l.; 21:5–22:3; 27:2; 33:3; 72:1; 80:1; 82:7; *Sib. Or.* 2:215, 227; *L.A.E.* 48:1; *4 Ezra* passim; *T. Sol.* 2:4, 7; 8:9; 18:7; *Pr. Jos.* in Origen, *Comm. Jo.* 2.31; idem, *Philoc.* 33:19; *3 Bar.* 4:7 slav.; *Apoc. El. (C)* 5:5; *Gk. Apoc. Ezra* 6:2; *Gos. Bart.* 4:29; *Acts Phil.* 1:12; *Sefer Ha-Razim* 1st Firmament 87; etc. It is unlikely that

---

[33] *Pesiq. Rab.* 46:3 has Uriel on God's left, which matches the place of Puriel in *TA* 12:10.

a contributor to *TA* coined the name, for פוריאל is otherwise attested.[34] Puriel tests "deeds." For ἔργα (contrast the singular ἔργον in v. 13) as the objects of eschatological judgment see Gk. fr. *1 En.* 98:6; Heb 6:10; 1 Pet 1:17; Rev 22:12; etc. The testing is done "through fire" (see on 12:14), for Puriel "has authority over the fire": ὁ ἐπὶ τὸ πῦρ ἔχων τὴν ἐξουσίαν. The phrase looks like a reminiscence of Rev 14:18: ἄγγελος … ὁ ἔχων ἐξουσίαν ἐπὶ τὸ πῦρ. For angels as authorities over natural phenomena see *1 Enoch* 82 (where Uriel has power over the lights in the sky); Rev 7:1; 9:11; 16:5; and *3 Enoch* 14. Elsewhere the angel of fire is Gabriel (*3 En.* 14:4 (Schäfer, *Synopse* 18 = 899); *b. Pesaḥ.* 118a), or Nathaniel (*L.A.B.* 38:3); *Jub.* 2:2 speaks generally of "the angels of the spirit of fire." Rev 14:18 leaves its angel unnamed.[35]

13:12–13. The parallelism of vv. 12a and 13a clearly depends upon 1 Cor 3:10–15 (a proof text for purgatory in the West but not the East):[36]

13:12	εἴ τινος τὸ ἔργον κατακαύσει
13:13	εἴ τινος δὲ τὸ ἔργον
1 Cor 3:14	εἴ τινος τὸ ἔργον
1 Cor 3:15	εἴ τινος τὸ ἔργον κατακαήσεται

The link is confirmed by additional parallels of both content—Paul's subject is also different fates at the fiery eschatological judgment—and vocabulary:

13:11	ἔργα διὰ πυρός
1 Cor 3:15	τὸ ἔργον … διὰ πυρός
13:13	τὸ πῦρ δοκιμάσει
1 Cor 3:13	τὸ πῦρ δοκιμάσει
13:13	σώζεσθαι
1 Cor 3:15	σωθήσεται

If the fire of judgment "burns up" (κατακαύσει; κατακαίω*) someone's "work" (ἔργον; cf. v. 11, with the plural), immediately "the angel of judgment" (ὁ ἄγγελος τῆς κρίσεως)—evidently yet another angel, one not

---

[34] E.g. the pages of a magic book printed on p. 224 of Naveh and Shaked, *Amulets and Magic Bowls*, 225. Cf. the פרואל of *Sefer Ha-Razim* 2nd Firmament 119 and the פראל of 2 130.

[35] So too the Aramaic incantation bowl that speaks of "the head of the kingdom of fire"; see Edward M. Cook, "An Aramaic Incantation Bowl from Khafaje," *BASOR* 285 (1992), 79–81.

[36] Cf. Colafemmina, *Testamento*, 35. Contrast Fishburne, "1 Corinthians III. 10–15," who argues that Paul depends upon the *Testament*.

known by this title in other texts—carries that one away (ἀποφέρει; ἀποφέρω*; cf. RecShrt. 8:3; *Vit. Proph. Habakkuk* 12: ἀπενεχθήσονται ὑπὸ ἀγγέλων). The destination is τὸν τόπον τῶν ἁμαρτωλῶν; cf. *1 En.* 90:24; Ps.-John of Damascus, *B.J.* 30.282 (ὁ τόπος τῶν ἁμαρτωλῶν). This place is, in contrast to so many later Christian apocalypses, left undescribed. The result is in any case "a most bitter cup," πικρότατον ποτήριον. The superlative distinguishes this from "the bitter cup of death" (see on 1:3). This judgment is worse than death.

The fire does not burn up everyone's work. There are those that it tests and "does not kindle," μὴ ἄψεται. In 15:14–15 ἅπτω means "touch," but here the sense is "kindle," as in Jdt 13:13; Luke 8:16; Acts 28:2; etc. When there is no burning, the individual is "vindicated." δικαιοῦται (δικαιόω*) creates a word play with the preceding Δοκιήλ as well as with δικαιοσύνης and δικαίων, words soon to follow (13:14; 14:2, 4, 8). "The angel of righteousness" (ὁ τῆς δικαιοσύνης ἄγγελος), who presumably is not Dokiel, also appears in 14:8; *4 Bar.* 6:6 (cf. 8:9; 9:5); and John of Thessalonica, *Dorm. BVM* A 5, ed. Jugie, p. 382 (here he is the opposite of the angel of wickedness; these two come for human beings upon death). He is evidently the counterpart of "the angel of judgment" (v. 12). So there is a third pair of angels in this chapter. His job is to take the vindicated "to salvation," εἰς τὸ σῴζεσθαι; cf. 14:2, 3, 4, 8; Ps.-Plato, *Alc. maj.* 126A; LXX Gen 32:9; *1 Clem.* 37:5; Chrysostom, *Hom. Gen.* PG 54.507. For the notion of a blessed state immediately after death see *1 En.* 9:10; 20:8; 22; 60:8; 62:15; 2 Macc 7:9, 36; *4 Macc.* 7:18–19; 13:17; 16:25; 17:18–19; 18:23; Philo, *Sacr.* 5; *Spec. leg.* 1.345; *Vit. cont.* 13; *Gig.* 14; Wis 3:1–4; *T. Job* 39:12–13; 40:3; 52:8–12; *L.A.E.* 43–47; Luke 16:19–31; 23:42–43; 2 Cor 5:1–10; Phil 1:19–26; Josephus, *Ant.* 18.14; *Bell.* 1.648; 7.344; *4 Ezra* 7; *Vis. Paul* 21–30; *Hist. Rech.* 15:9–10; *b. Ber.* 28b; ARN A 25; Tg. Ps.-Jn. on 1 Sam 25:29; etc. "The inheritance of the just" (τῷ κλήρῳ τῶν δικαίων) is a phrase from LXX Ps 124:3 (for גּוֹרל הצדיקים cf. 1QH 19(11):11–12; 1Q34 fr. 3 1:2). It seems to appear thereafter only in quotations of or allusions to that line—e.g. *1 Apoc. John*, ed. Tischendorf, 23:7; Origen, *Sel. Ps.* PG 12.1301A, 1640A; Theodoret of Cyrrhus, *Comm. Ps.* PG 80.1888A; cf. κλῆρον ἐν τοῖς ἡγιασμένοις in Acts 26:18 and τοῦ κλήρου τῶν ἁγίων in Col 1:12. But whether there is here an allusion to LXX Ps 124:3 is unclear.

13:14. In his summary, Michael addresses Abraham as δίκαιε, which makes for a nice *inclusio* with the beginning of the speech (v. 2; cf. also v. 4). "All things in everybody" (τὰ πάντα ἐν πᾶσιν) is comprehensive: nothing escapes the tests of fire and balance (cf. Mark 9:49). The phrase itself is attested to my knowledge only in Christian literature, where it is inspired by 1 Cor 12:6; 15:28; and Eph 1:23; see Origen, *Comm. Jo.* 1.32, 25; Ps.-Eusebius of Emesa, *Fr. Cor.* 3.14–18; Ps.-Gregory of Nyssa, *Contra Arium et Sabellium*, ed. Mueller, 3.1.79; Epiphanius, *Pan.* 55.5; 69.77; etc.

Chapter 14: Abraham Repents and Intercedes

14:1. Abraham said to the angel, "My lord, Commander-in-chief, how is it that the soul which the angel held in his hand was sentenced to be (placed) in the middle?" 14:2. The Commander-in-chief said, "Hear, righteous Abraham, (it was) because the judge found its sins and its righteous deeds to be balanced. And he gave it over neither to judgment nor to salvation—until the judge and God of all comes." 14:3. Abraham said, "And what yet does the soul need in order to be saved?" 14:4. The Commander-in-chief said, "If it could get one righteous deed more than (the number of its) sins, it will come to salvation." 14:5. Abraham said to the Commander-in-chief, "Come, Michael, Commander-in-chief, let us pray for the soul, and let us see if God will hear us." And the Commander-in-chief said, "Amen, so be it." 14:6. And they made petition and prayer to God for the soul. And God heard their prayer; and rising from their prayer they did not see the soul standing there. 14:7. And Abraham said to the angel, "Where is the soul?" 14:8. The Commander-in-chief said, "It was saved by your righteous prayer. And behold! a glorious angel took it and carried it into paradise." 14:9. Abraham said, "I glorify the name of God Most High and his immeasurable mercy." 14:10. Abraham said to the Commander-in-chief, "I beg you, archangel, listen to my plea, and let us again call upon the Lord, and let us prostrate ourselves for his pity. 14:11. And let us entreat his mercy for the souls of the sinners whom I, once despising, destroyed, those whom, because of my words, the earth formerly swallowed, and the wild beasts rent in two, and the fire formerly consumed. 14:12. Now I know that I sinned before God. Come, Michael, Commander-in-chief of the upper powers, come let us beg God with earnestness and many tears, that he might forgive me my sin and grant them absolution." 14:13. And immediately the Commander-in-chief hearkened to him and they prayed before the Lord God. After they called upon the Lord for a long while, a voice from heaven came saying: 14:14. "Abraham, Abraham, the Lord has heard your prayer and your sins are forgiven. And those (persons) you earlier thought I had destroyed, I have recalled them and brought them unto eternal life on account of my utter goodness. 14:15. But for a time I repaid them with judgment, but those I requite while they live on the earth, I will not requite in death."

TEXTUAL NOTES

14:1. B G H I J Q: "to the Commander-in-chief." 14:2. I through
homoioteleuton moves from the first εἰς to the second εἰς. 14:3–4. H skips
from εἶπεν δὲ Ἀβραάμ at the beginning of v. 3 to εἶπεν δὲ Ἀβραάμ at the
beginning of v. 5. 14:4. A lacks "the Commander-in-chief said." 14:5. A
omits "Abraham said to the Commander-in-chief." // G omits "to the
Commander-in-chief," which is probably deliberate abbreviation. // B H I
J Q omit "Come, Michael, Commander-in-chief," which also may be
conscious contraction. // G drops the superfluous "and let us see if God will
hear us." 14:5–6. I skips from the first καί in v. 5 to the fourth καί in v. 6.
// 14:6. J moves from the first καί to the fourth καί, omitting "And they
made petition and prayer to God for the soul. And God heard their
prayer." // A omits: "And God heard ... see the soul." 14:7. A omits "to
the angel." 14:8. Q skips from the first αὐτήν to the second αὐτήν, the
result being: "And behold! he carried it into paradise." 14:8–9. J abbreviates by omitting "And behold! ... paradise" as well as all of v. 9. 14:9. B
G H I J omit the entire verse. This may be due to a desire to condense. Yet
because both vv. 9 and 10 open with εἶπεν δὲ Ἀβραάμ, *homoioteleuton* may
be the explanation. 14:10. G shortens by omitting "and let ... Lord."
14:11. G lacks "And let ... mercy." // B Q omit "his mercy." // 14:11–12.
J omits "the earth ... upper powers." As the resultant text makes sense, one
suspects conscious abridgement. 14:12. B drops "of the upper powers,
come." // G omits "come let us ... tears." // B H I J Q lack "with earnestness
... tears." // B omits μοι and J has αὐτοῖς, changes introduced out of respect
for Abraham (see further on 14:14). // I omits "and grant them absolution." 14:12–13. J omits "and grant ... hearkened to him." Either an eye
passed from one καί to another or the omission is deliberate abbreviation.
14:13. G lacks "from heaven," words which might appear awkward because Abraham is seemingly in heaven. 14:14. G H I J Q: εἰσήκουσα τῆς
φωνῆς τῆς δεήσεώς σου. This imitates the LXX Psalter: 27:2, 6; 30:23;
114:1. // J omits "and your sins are forgiven" and so again makes Abraham
look better. So too the long Romanian. // H omits "have recalled them
and," which is not strictly necessary. // B G H I J Q lack "eternal." // "On
account of my utter goodness" is missing from J, either because of
homoioteleuton (ἤγαγον ... ἀγαθότηταν) or theological caution. 14:15. A
omits "But for a time ... judgment." // G drops the end of the verse: "but
those I requite, etc." Was it theologically objectionable? // H moves from
ἐγώ to the end of ἀποδώσω, omitting δὲ οὕσπερ ἀποδώσω. // At the end
A has ἀπαιτήσομαι instead of ἀποδώσω.

COMMENTARY

The first half of this chapter, which optimistically shows God undoing death, is a dialogue between Michael and Abraham. The patriarch has, from his tour of the postmortem judgment, learned not to condemn others (cf. Matt 7:1–5; Luke 6:41–42). The initial dialogue is interrupted only by the narrator's comment in v. 6, which recounts the upshot of prayer for the soul "in the middle":

1	εἶπεν δὲ Ἀβραάμ	question	
2	εἶπεν δὲ ὁ ἀρχιστράτηγος		answer
3	εἶπεν δὲ Ἀβραάμ	question	
4	εἶπεν δὲ ὁ ἀρχιστράτηγος		answer
5a	εἶπεν δὲ Ἀβραάμ	request	
5b	καὶ εἶπεν ὁ ἀρχιστράτηγος		agreement
6	Narrator: description of outcome		
7	εἶπεν δὲ Ἀβραάμ	question	
8	εἶπεν δὲ ὁ ἀρχιστράτηγος		answer
9	εἶπεν δὲ Ἀβραάμ	doxology	

In the second half of the chapter, Abraham, encouraged by the success of his first prayer, proposes another prayer, this one for the sinners slain in chap. 10 (vv. 10–12). Michael and Abraham then jointly intercede for those sinners, after which a divine voice responds (v. 13). That climactic voice ends the chapter with a summary of what has happened and a general theological lesson (vv. 14–15). With this Abraham's heavenly journey is over (15:1).

RecLng. 14 has no RecShrt. parallel, and although it features several phrases likely to be Christian (see on vv. 2, 6, 9, 10, 12, 14), its basic content is presumably ancient. Given the Jewish and Christian debates regarding intercession for the dead (see on v. 5 and on 13:7), we can be certain that Abraham's effective prayer would have troubled some.[1] While, for example, only some Christians rejected altogether prayers for the dead (e.g. Arius in Epiphanius, *Pan.* 75.3; cf. Cyril of Jerusalem, *Catech. 1–18* 5.10, referring to "many"), many or most denied them for the unbaptized

---

[1]   So also Delcor, *Testament*, 150. For Jewish caution about relying too much upon intercession see R. Le Déaut, "Aspects de l'intercession dans le Judaïsme," *JSJ* 1 (1970), 35–57. Note *b. Sanh.* 104a: "A son can help his father, but a father cannot help his son, as it is written, 'And there is none that can deliver out of my hand.' Abraham cannot deliver Ishmael ... ." The *Koran*, interestingly enough, refers to Abraham's attempted intercession for Sodom only to speak against it (11:74–77).

dead (cf. Augustine, *Enchir*. 110; *Civ*. 21.24);[2] and those God calls back through Abraham's intercessions in *TA* 14 can hardly be baptized Christians. So omission from a text as loosely transmitted as *TA* would be natural. In contrast to RecShrt., moreover, the narrative sequence of RecLng. makes perfect sense: Abraham strikes down sinners, then he beholds what happens at the judgment of the dead, then he repents of what he has done, then he asks God to restore those he destroyed earlier, which in the event God does. In RecShrt., the sequence is simply two-fold— Abraham sees the judgment, then Abraham strikes down sinners. There is no repentance. Here Abraham's education concerning postmortem judgment is not firmly linked to anything that has gone before, and his striking down sinners does not lead to any change in his character, nor is it an integral part of the plot. It is rather an episode unto itself, unconnected with the rest of *TA*. It looks like a remnant from some fuller version of the story. Finally, RecLng. 14, with its imperfect Abraham who repents as well as its extraordinarily gracious God, accords with the spirit of the original *TA*; see Introduction, pp. 48–52.

14:1. Abraham, apparently satisfied with Michael's answers to the questions of 13:1, next asks (εἶπεν δὲ Ἀβραὰμ πρός; see on 2:4) about the soul described in 12:2, 16–18, the soul in the angel's hand, the soul sentenced (κατεδικάσθη; καταδικάζω*) to be in the middle, ἐν τῷ μέσῳ; cf. 12:4 (12:18 uses εἰς τὸ μέσον) and see pp. 272–73. For "my lord" of Michael see on 2:7.

14:2. Michael responds with ἄκουσον δίκαιε Ἀβραάμ (see on 7:8). He then explains that "the judge" (= Abel) found the soul's "sins and righteous deeds" (ἁμαρτίας ... καὶ τὰς δικαιοσύνας; see on 13:10) to be "balanced," ζυγάδας; see on 12:18. So the soul cannot enter κρίσιν = "condemnation" (cf. H: τοῖς βασάνοις). Nor can it enter "salvation," εἰς τὸ σῴζεσθαι; cf. vv. 3–4 and see on 11:10; 13:13. The upshot seems to be that it stays where it is—"until the judge and God of all comes," ἕως οὗ ἔλθῃ ὁ κριτὴς καὶ θεὸς τῶν ἁπάντων; cf. Ps.-Athanasius, *Quaest. Antiochum* PG 28.609B (ἕως οὗ ἔλθῃ ὁ κριτής). For "judge of all" see also Hippolytus, *Ben. Is. Jac.*, ed.

---

[2] In *Enchir*. 110, Augustine indicates that prayer for the dead works not for those who are very good or very bad but for those who are "not very bad," that is, those in between. For full discussion of the issue see Jeffrey A. Trumbower, *Rescue for the Dead: The Posthumous Salvation of Non-Christians in Early Christianity* (Oxford: Oxford University Press, 2001). He argues that, apart from speculation about Christ's descent into hell, hope for the unbaptized dead appears in, among others, Paul, maybe 1 Peter, the *Apocalypse of Paul*, *Sib. Or.* 2, the *Acts of Paul and Thecla*, Clement of Alexandria, Perpetua, Origen, Gregory of Nyssa, Evagrius Ponticus, the early Jerome, the two Aviti from Spain, and Vincentius Victor.

Brière, p. 76.1; Epiphanius, *Pan.* 69.7; Gregory of Nazianzus, *Ep.* 202.15; Didymus of Alexandria, *Fr. Ps.*, ed. Mühlenberg, 931, 1059; Ps.-Chrysostom, *In operarios undecimae horae*, ed. Voicu (*Augustinianum* 18 [1978], 353–56), lines 33, 148; and for "God of all" *Vis. Paul* 14; Eusebius, *Ecl. proph.*, ed. Gaisford, p. 32; Athanasius, *Exp. Ps.* PG 27.121A; Gregory of Nyssa, *Cant.*, ed. Langerbeck, p. 141.9; Didymus of Alexandria, *Fr. Ps.*, ed. Mühlenberg, 1058; Theodoret of Cyrrhus, *Comm. Ps.* PG 80.985D; Romanos the Melodist, *Cant.* 33.23. For their combination see 13:7; 20:3; Heb 12:23 (κριτῇ θεῷ πάντων); Cyril of Alexandria, *Comm. Matt.*, ed. Reuss, fr. 52.8 (τῷ κριτῇ πάντων θεῷ); and Severianus Gabalensis, *Fr. ep. 1 Cor.*, ed. Staab, p. 245.15 (ὁ θεὸς δὲ πάντων κριτής).

It is hard to imagine the soul (and others like it, if there are any) staying in the area of judgment throughout the remainder of time. Does the text assume a place of holding that goes unmentioned? It in any case seems likely that "until the judge and God of all comes," which is grammatically awkward, is secondary; this would be consistent with its having Christian parallels. Note that there is no reference to the judgment by the twelve tribes at the second *parousia* (13:6).

b. Roš Haš. 17a teaches that, according to the Hillelites, when good deeds and iniquities are balanced in the scale of judgment, God's "grace inclines towards grace." *y. Qidd.* 1:10 says that, in such an event, God removes a bad deed so that the good deeds will be greater. Cf. *y. Sanh.* 10:1: when deeds are balanced, God "tears up one bond among the transgressions, so that the honorable deeds will then outweigh the others." Similar is folio 7 verso of the *Coptic Enoch Apocryphon* in the Pierpont Morgan Library. In this, when the angel of mercy sees sins drawing down the balance, he puts his rod on the scale to tip it the other direction.[3] Although *TA* also features divine grace (v. 14) in the judgment, God does not take the initiative to save but is rather moved by human prayer; cf. perhaps *t. Sanh.* 13:3 and *b. Roš Haš.* 16b–17a, where, according to the Shammaites, those neither righteous nor wicked will go to Gehenna yet be saved after they scream out in pain.

14:3. Abraham, showing his compassion for the first time, asks what the soul is in need of (λείπεται; λείπω*) in order to be saved, again εἰς τὸ σῴζεσθαι; cf. vv. 2 and 4 and see on 11:10; 13:13. He does not ask what would damn the soul, which shows where his sympathies lie. Having learned how dreadful the afterlife can be, Abraham has a newfound compassion.

---

[3] See Pearson, "Coptic Enoch Apocryphon," 275.

14:4. If the soul gains (κέκτητο; κτάομαι: 14:4; 16:1; 20:15) only one righteous deed more (ὑπεράνω = "beyond," as often in the LXX; cf. 7:2) than its sins, the latter will be outweighed and it will come εἰς τὸ σῴζεσθαι; see above. How many such souls there might be is not said. We do not learn if this is a common case or a rare one.

14:5. Abraham bids Michael to "come" (δεῦρο; see on 2:7) and "pray for the soul": ποιήσωμεν εὐχὴν ὑπὲρ τῆς ψυχῆς; see on 5:2; cf. 14:6 and Eusebius, Vit. Const. 4.71: τὰς εὐχὰς ὑπὲρ τῆς βασιλέως ψυχῆς. The patriarch's hope is that God will "hear," ἐπακούσεται; cf. 17:9; God is often the subject of this verb: T. Iss. 2:4; Jos. Asen. 14:1; Prot. Jas. 2:4; 4:1; 20:3; etc. Michael wholeheartedly agrees: "Amen, so be it." Cf. Gk. L.A.E. 33:5, where the angels pray God to forgive the dead Adam's sins, and Apoc. Sedr. 14:1, which is modeled on our passage: "And Sedrach said to the archangel Michael, 'Hear me ... help me and intercede that God may be merciful to the world.'" For ἀμὴν γένοιτο see on 2:12.

Abraham now becomes "in character," that is, he reverts to his well-known role as intercessor. In Gen 18:16–33, he again and again asks God to spare Sodom on account of the righteous therein. He is also an intercessor in Genesis 20; see below. Because of Genesis, Abraham was sometimes thought of as an effective and paradigmatic intercessor; cf. RecShrt. 4:13 v.l. (Abraham from the beginning had mercy on all); Jub. 22:9 (Abraham prays for his descendants); 1QapGen 20; Apoc. Zeph. 11:4 (Abraham, Isaac, and Jacob intercede for those in postmortem torment); b. 'Erub. 19a (Abraham brings up Israelites from Gehenna); Gen. Rab. 35:2 ("Abraham can intercede from his time" to the time of R. Simeon b. Yohai); 39:11 ("Abraham would pray for barren women until they conceived, for the sick and they would be healed").[4] Also relevant is the rabbinic notion of the salvific זכות = "merit" of Abraham, Isaac, and Jacob, about which the rabbis had many debates: Mek. on Exod 17:12; Frg. Tg. P on Gen 29:26; Tg. Neof. 1 on Num 23:9; Gen. Rab. 44:16 ("When our children become corpses, lacking sinews and bones, your [Abraham's] merit will sustain them"); etc.[5] This idea becomes vividly connected with postmortem judgment in b. 'Erub. 19a (Abraham brings up and receives Israelites from Gehenna) and Gen. Rab. 48:8 (Abraham sits at the gate of Gehenna and

[4] Cf. Koran 19:48, where Abraham says to his father, the idol maker: "I will implore my Lord to forgive you; for to me he has been gracious ... . I will call upon my Lord and trust that my prayers will not be ignored." Contrast 9:114 and 60:4, which deny Abraham's intercessory power.
[5] See A. Marmorstein, The Doctrine of Merits in Old Rabbinical Literature (New York: Ktav, 1968).

sees to it that no circumcised Israelite, however sinful, descends there). *TA* 14 is clearly related to these rabbinic texts. Cf. also *Apoc. Zeph*. 11, where Abraham, Isaac, and Jacob pray for those in postmortem torment.

1 En. 63:8; Heb 9:27; *L.A.B*. 33:5 (this denies the efficacy of prayers of the "fathers" for the dead); *4 Ezra* 7:102–115 (this cites Genesis 18 but denies that Abraham and others will be able to intercede on judgment day; Jerome refers to this in *Vigil*. 7); 9:12; and *2 En*. 53:1 (cf. *2 Bar*. 85:12) speak against prayer for the dead—a practice that presumably grew out of memorial rituals commonly conducted at burial sites. *TA* is on the other side of this issue, as are 2 Macc 12:39–45; Bar 3:4; *Sifre* Deut. 210; *b. Soṭah* 10b; *Eccl. Rab*. 4:1; *Pirqe R. El*. 53 (David intercedes for the dead Absalom). Christian parallels include *Apoc. Pet*. 13; Tertullian, *Mon*. 10; Arnobius, *Gent*. 4.36; Eusebius, *Vit. Const*. 4.71; *Apos. Con*. 8:41:2–5 (this may take up a Jewish original); Cyril of Jerusalem, *Catech*. *19–23* 5.9; Epiphanius, *Pan*. 75.3; *Vis. Paul* 43; *Greek Apocalypse of the Virgin*. (Note also Plato, *Phaed*. 114A–B, which raises the possibility of deliverance from torment even after being sentenced.) Particularly interesting for comparison is Philo, *Praem*. 166: the dead have in their favor not only "the clemency and kindness" of God, "who ever prefers forgiveness to punishment," but "the holiness of the founders of the race, because with souls released from their bodies they show forth in that naked simplicity their devotion to their ruler and cease not to make supplication for their sons and daughters, supplications not made in vain, because the Father grants to them the privilege that their prayers should be heard." Most Christians believed in prayer for the dead, but usually not for the unbaptized dead. For rare exceptions see Ps.-John of Damascus, *Fide dormierunt* PG 261D–264A, and Anon. Monk of Whitby, *Vit. Greg*. 29, ed. Colgrave, pp. 126–28.

14:6. This verse opens by largely repeating v. 5, so that the actions of Michael and God correlate with Abraham's request:

| 5 | Abraham's request | ποιήσωμεν | | εὐχὴν | ὑπὲρ τῆς ψυχῆς |
| 6 | Michael's act | ἐποίησαν | δέησιν καὶ εὐχὴν ... | | ὑπὲρ τῆς ψυχῆς |

| 5 | Abraham's hope | ἐπακούσεται ... | ὁ θεός |
| 6 | God's response | εἰσήκουσεν | ὁ θεός |

While the LXX knows only the combination δέησις καὶ προσευχή (3 Βασ 8:45; 2 Chr 6:19, 35; Jer 11:14; cf. 1 Tim 5:5), δέησις καὶ εὐχή (as here) appears in the Fathers and late Byzantine texts: Basil the Great, *Regulae mor*. PG 31.816D; Chrysostom, *Pecc*. PG 51.363; *Exp. Ps*. PG 55.445; Ps.-Sphrantzes, *Chron. sive Maius*, ed. Grecu, p. 506.3. On Michael as intercessor (as also in v. 14) see on 1:4, and for angels in general as intercessors note Job 33:23–28 (for rescue from the Pit); Tob 12:15; *1 En*. 15:2; 40:6;

47:2; 104:1; *T. Levi* 3:5; 5:6; *T. Dan* 6:1–2; *ARN* A 3; Heb. *T. Naph.* 9:2. For warning against relying upon angelic intercession see *y. Ber.* 9:2 and *Midr. Ps.* 4:3.

14:7. Because it has disappeared, Abraham asks where the ψυχή (= disembodied self; see on 10:15) is. Given Michael's answer in v. 8, which tells of an angel carrying that soul away, one infers that Abraham's face has been on the floor, and/or that his eyes have been closed in prayer, for he has missed what has happened (cf. v. 10; 9:1).

In Egyptian depictions of postmortem judgment, where the heart is on one pan, the feather of Maat on the other, a balanced scale at the judgment saves. But in *TA*, where righteous deeds are on one side, sins on the other, a balanced scale does not save. Closer to *TA* is medieval Christian art, in which demons often appear attempting to tip a closely balanced scale of judgment. Something similar happens in our book, except that it is a question of Abraham seeking to tip the scale in the soul's favor.

14:8. The soul, Michael says, has been "saved (σέσωσται; see on 11:10) by your righteous prayer," εὐχῆς ... δικαίας; cf. Gregory of Nyssa, *Cant.*, ed. Langerbeck, p. 164.16; *Ep.* 11.5. He does not say, "our righteous prayer." The angel, who presumably interprets rightly, attributes the soul's salvation exclusively to the man's intercession (cf. v. 14).

Michael, underlining his point with καὶ ἰδοῦ (see on 2:1), clarifies: a "glorious" (φωτοφόρος; see on 7:3) angel—not Michael—took the soul to "paradise," παραδείσῳ; see on 4:2; 11:10; and 20:14. The remark illustrates 13:13: "the angel of righteousness takes him and carries him away to salvation in the inheritance of the just."

14:9. Abraham glorifies (δοξάζω; cf. 15:5: δοξάζοντες τὸν θεόν) "the name of God Most High," τὸ ὄνομα τοῦ θεοῦ τοῦ ὑψίστου; cf. 17:11 (τοῦ ὀνόματος τοῦ θεοῦ τοῦ ζῶντος); *Jos. Asen.* 9:1 (ἐν τῷ ὀνόματι τοῦ θεοῦ τοῦ ὑψίστου); *PGM* 5.45 (ἐν ὀνόματι τοῦ ὑψίστου θεοῦ). The closest LXX parallel is: τῷ ὀνόματι κυρίου τοῦ ὑψίστου (Ps 7:18; 12:6); but the LXX does often have ὁ θεὸς ὁ ὕψιστος: Gen 14:18–20; 1 Esd 6:30; Ps 77:35; Theod. Dan 5:18, 21; *3 Macc.* 7:9; etc.; cf. also RecLng. 15:11; 16:9; *T. Jud.* 24:4; Mark 5:7; Acts 16:17; etc. On God as "Most High" see on 9:1. Abraham also magnifies God's "immeasurable mercy," ἔλεος αὐτοῦ τὸ ἀμέτρητον (ἀμέτρητος: 11:6; 14:9); cf. v. 11. Although δοξάζω + τὸ ὄνομά σου as a direct address to God appears in Jewish literature (e.g., LXX Ps 85:9, 12; Dan 3:26; *Ps. Sol.* 17:5), δοξάζω + τὸ ὄνομα τοῦ θεοῦ seems confined to Christian texts: Herm. *Vis.* 3.4.3; Ps.-Ignatius, *Philad.* 10:1; Didymus of Alexandria, *Comm. Zech.* 2.297; *Fr. Ps.* 862, 929; Basil the Great, *Ep.* 222.1. Moreover, ἀμέτρητος after ἔλεος sounds patristic; cf.

Eusebius, *Hist. eccl.* 5.1.32, 42 (quoting *Ep. Lugd.*); Ps.-Ephraem, *Prec. ad dei matrem*, ed. Phrantzoles, pp. 357.11, 369.7, 374.5; Ps.-Athanasius, *Doctrina ad Antiochum ducem* 2.12; Ps.-John of Damascus, *B.J.* 11.93; etc. Given this, and given that v. 10, like v. 9, opens with "Abraham said," even though nothing has interrupted Abraham's speech, one suspects that v. 9 is secondary and from a later Christian hand.

14:10. Having had one prayer answered, Abraham is emboldened to offer another. Recalling those he formerly condemned, and now aware of how terrible the afterlife can be, he asks Michael (δέομαί σου ἀρχάγγελε; see on 1:4; 9:3) to join him in again calling upon (παρακαλέσωμεν; cf. vv. 12, 13 and see on 7:6) the Lord: προσπέσωμεν τοῖς οἰκτιρμοῖς αὐτοῦ. For προσπίπτω (see on 3:6) + οἰκτιρμοῖς (οἰκτιρμός*) + genitive pronoun (of God), which is not a common idiom, see Theodore the Studite, *Ep.*, ed. Fatouros 42.29; Ps.-Ephraem, *Prec. e sacris scripturis*, ed. Phrantzoles, pp. 296.10, 343.5. For the biblical and liturgical εἰσάκουσον τῆς δεήσεώς μου = "listen to my plea" see on 9:6.

14:11. Abraham now specifies the objects of his intercession, namely, those he once despised (κακοφρονήσας; κακοφρονέω*; cf. Aq. 2 Βασ 15:31; LXX: 0; Philo: 0; NT: 0; Josephus: 0) and destroyed (ἀπώλεσας; cf. 10:13–15). For them he wants to pray for mercy, δεηθῶμεν ... ἔλεος; cf. v. 9; *Acts John* 35; Eusebius, *Comm. Ps.* PG 23.1032A; Gregory of Nyssa, *Inscr. Ps.*, ed. McDonough, p. 45.11; Ps.-Dionysius Areopagita, *Ep.* 8.44; etc. He is speaking of those he slew by his words (cf. 10:7, 11: τῷ λόγῳ αὐτοῦ) in chap. 10—where the sequence is instead: devouring beasts, swallowing earth, falling fire. He calls them, as does God in 10:13–14, "sinners" (ἁμαρτωλῶν; see on 9:3). But this divinely endorsed characterization does not prevent Abraham from now feeling compassion for those unfortunates. He now realizes, among other things, that he himself is a sinner too (v. 12).

Although the order is different, the wording is much the same as in chap. 10: Abraham is using the earlier language of the narrator (with the exception of διαμερίζω*; cf. RecShrt. 12:10 C I):

14:11	κατέπιεν ἡ γῆ
10:9b	χάνη ἡ γῆ καὶ καταπίῃ αὐτούς
10:9c	ἐδιχάσθη ἡ γῆ καὶ κατέπιεν αὐτούς
14:11	διεμερίσαντο τὰ θηρία
10:6b	ἐξέλθωσιν θηρία ἐκ τοῦ δρυμοῦ καὶ καταφάγωσιν αὐτούς
10:7a	ἐξῆλθον θηρία ἐκ τοῦ δρυμοῦ καὶ κατέφαγον αὐτούς
14:11	κατέφαγεν τὸ πῦρ
10:11b	κατέλθῃ πῦρ ἐκ τοῦ οὐρανοῦ καὶ καταφάγηται αὐτούς
10:11c	κατῆλθεν πῦρ ἐκ τοῦ οὐρανοῦ καὶ κατέφαγεν αὐτούς

See further pp. 227–29, which discuss the dependence upon 2 Kgs 2:23–25 (Elisha and the bears); Numbers 16 (Korah's rebellion); and 2 Kgs 1:9–12 (Elijah calling fire from heaven).

14:12. Following the scriptural precedent of confessing sins while uttering intercessory prayer (cf. 1 Kings 8; Nehemiah 1; Daniel 9), Abraham now acknowledges (νῦν ἔγνωκα ἐγὼ ὅτι; cf. 7:12; 18:8; LXX Jonah 1:12) that he himself has sinned before God: ἥμαρτον ἐνώπιον τοῦ θεοῦ; cf. LXX Gen 39:9 (ἁμαρτήσομαι ἐναντίον τοῦ θεοῦ; Chrysostom, *Stag.* PG 47.470, and *Hom. 2 Cor.* PG 61.442, cites this in the form: ἁμαρτήσομαι ἐνώπιον τοῦ θεοῦ; cf. *Ingressum jej.* PG 62.763); Jdt 5:17 (ἥμαρτον ἐνώπιον τοῦ θεοῦ); *Jos. Asen.* 7:5 (οὐχ ἁμαρτήσω ἐνώπιον κυρίου τοῦ θεοῦ); Origen, *Or.* 10.1; 30.2; Ps.-Ephraem, *Sermo in pulcherrimum Ioseph*, ed. Phrantzoles, p. 280.6; etc. Viewing the postmortem judgment has revealed that, instead of punishing sinners, as he did in chap. 10, Abraham should, like God, show them mercy (10:13). How such mercy harmonizes with the terrible judgment that awaits sinners after death is not said, but then the tension between judgment and mercy runs throughout many ancient Jewish and Christian writings.[6]

Despite Michael's statement that Abraham's prayer saved the soul in the middle (v. 8), the patriarch now entreats the "Commander-in-chief of the upper powers" (see on 9:3) to join him again, as if their combined prayer might somehow be more persuasive: παρακαλέσωμεν τὸν θεόν. Precisely the same exhortation appears in Chrysostom, *De incomprehensibili dei nat.* 3.11, and *2 Redit.* PG 52.448, but παρακαλέω + τὸν θεόν is otherwise common enough and not confined to patristic texts: Josephus, *Ant.* 3.78; 6.25; Gk. *L.A.E.* 27:2; 29:12; etc. Abraham calls for prayer μετὰ σπουδῆς (cf. *T. Levi* 13:7; σπουδή*) καὶ πολλῶν δακρύων. The expression has its closest parallels in the Fathers and may well be Christian: Gaius, *fr.*, ed. Routh, p. 132 (μετὰ πολλῆς σπουδῆς καὶ δακρύων); Eusebius, *Hist. eccl.* 5.28 (μετὰ πολλῆς σπουδῆς καὶ δακρύων); Chrysostom, *Hom. Act.* 45.2 PG 60.316 (μετὰ σπουδῆς ... μετὰ δακρύων). Abraham hopes that God might forgive him his own sin (ἀφήσει μοι τὸ ἁμάρτημα; cf. v. 14; LXX Job 42:10;

---

[6]   Richard Bauckham, "The Conflict of Justice and Mercy: Attitudes to the Damned in Apocalyptic Literature," *Apocrypha* 1 (1990), 181–96 = *The Fate of the Dead: Studies on the Jewish and Christian Apocalypses* (NovTSup 93; Leiden/Boston/Cologne: Brill, 1998), 132–48. Tertullian, *Marc.* 4.23, rightly observes that both mercy and judgment belong to both Testaments. Later the rabbis often discuss the relationship between the two attributes. Although God for them exhibits both, mercy characteristically trumps judgment: *Sifre* Num. 8:8; *Tanḥ.* B Leviticus Tazri'a 11; *b. Ber.* 7a; *b. 'Abod. Zar.* 3b; etc. But contrast *y. Ber.* 5:3 and *y. Meg.* 4:10.

Jos. Asen. 11:18; *T. Job* 42:8; *4 Bar.* 2:3) and grant those he destroyed absolution, αὐτοὺς συγχωρήσει. Cf. *Apoc. Sedr.* 15:5 and see Lampe, s.v. συγχωρέω 5. The logic seems to be that, if Abraham's sin can be forgiven, its effects should likewise be undone. Not only that, but others should likewise be forgiven. For prayers for the forgiveness of the sins of the dead see Arnobius, *Gent.* 4.36; Augustine, *Conf.* 9.13; *Apos. Con.* 8:41; Theodoret of Cyrrhus, *Hist. eccl.*, ed. Ettlinger, pp. 338–39.

14:13–14. Michael immediately hearkens (εἰσήκουσεν; cf. v. 10) and, with Abraham, prays "before the Lord God": ἐποίησαν δέησιν ἐνώπιον κυρίου τοῦ θεοῦ; cf. v. 6; 3 Βασ 8:59 (δεδέημαι ἐνώπιον κυρίου τοῦ θεοῦ); *Prot. Jas.* 40:12 (ἡ δέησίς σου ἐνώπιον κυρίου τοῦ θεοῦ); Tg. Neof. 1 Gen 30:2 (נבעי קדם ייי). Their prayer lasts for quite some time, ἐπὶ πολλὴν δὲ ὥραν; cf. Josephus, *Ant.* 8.118 (ἐπὶ πολλὴν ὥραν προσκυνήσας); *Acta Justini et septem Sodalium* 4:1; Didymus of Alexandria, *Comm. Ps. 29–34*, ed. Gronewald, p. 218. The response is "a voice from heaven" (see on 10:12). The expression is so stereotyped that it occurs here even though the recipient is not on the earth. The voice calls out, "Abraham, Abraham." On the double vocative see on 4:6 and cf. Gen 46:2 (God to Jacob); Exod 3:4 (God to Moses); 1 Sam 3:10 (God to Samuel); *Jub.* 23:3 (Jacob to Abraham); Matt 23:37; Luke 8:24; 10:41; 22:31; Acts 9:4 (the risen Jesus to Saul); *T. Levi* 2:6 (an angel to Levi); *T. Job* 24:1; *2 Bar.* 22:2 (a voice from heaven to Baruch); Strack-Billerbeck 1:943; 2:258. In this particular case, readers are reminded of LXX Gen 22:11, where a voice from heaven (ἐκ τοῦ οὐρανοῦ, as here) calls out, "Abraham, Abraham"; cf. 22:1; *Jub.* 18:1, 10; Philo, *Somn.* 1.195; *Apoc. Abr.* 8:1; 9:1; 19:1; 20:1; Ps.-Athanasius, *Hist. de Melchisedech* PG 28.528D; etc.

If in chap. 10 the heavenly voice halts Abraham from destroying more sinners, here the voice informs him that those slain earlier have been brought into eternal life. Once again, "the prayer of the righteous is powerful and effective" (Jas 5:16); see further on v. 8. The divine declaration affirms Abraham by taking up his language—"the Lord has heard your prayer and forgiven your sins":

14:14, God	εἰσήκουσα κύριος τῆς δεήσεώς σου
14:10, Abraham	εἰσήκουσον τῆς δεήσεώς μου
14:14, God	ἀφίεταί σοι ἡ ἁμαρτία
14:12, Abraham	ἀφήσει μοι τὸ ἁμάρτημα

But God goes beyond what Abraham has asked. He does not just recall (ἀνεκαλεσάμην; ἀνακαλέω*; LSJ, s.v., I, gives examples of the verb meaning "call up the dead") to their previous lives the sinners who were seemingly destroyed (ἀπώλεσας; ἀπόλλυμι is a key verb in LXX Genesis 18). They get more than another chance: they are in fact brought "into eternal life," so their fate is the same as that of the soul "in the middle." εἰς ζωὴν αἰώνιον (cf. 20:15), which appears in *Ps. Sol.* 3:12 and LXX Dan 12:2 (for לְחַיֵּי עוֹלָם, became a favorite of Christians: Matt 25:46; John 4:14, 36; Acts 13:48; Rom 5:21; *Acts Thom.* 76; Eusebius, *Dem. ev.* 6; etc. But one should not make much of this given that לחיי עולם appears on Jewish epitaphs: *JIGRE* 133; Noy, *JIWE* 1.81, 82, 118, 129a, 183; cf. *BS* 2.129: εἰς τὸν [βίον] αἰώνιο[ν].

The sinners are saved not solely because of Abraham's prayer but also on account of God's "utter goodness." Because δι᾿ ἄκραν ἀγαθότηταν is used of divine goodness also in *Dorm. BMV* 5; Theodore the Studite, *Ep.*, ed. Fatouros 64.15, and Maximus the Confessor, *Capita de caritate* 3.25, again a Christian hand seems present.

Among the resurrected dead are those the earth swallowed, as in Numbers 16. *Acts Phil. Mart.* 26–27 (132–133) supplies a striking parallel. In this, Philip's passion gets the better of him, and he commands that the deep open up and swallow his enemies, which happens. Not only does the language, like that in *TA*, recall Numbers 16 (see on 10:9), but Jesus punishes Philip and undoes the apostle's wayward deed by resurrecting the dead who have been swallowed up (31–32 [137–138]). The similar events may reflect Jewish tradition. *m. Sanh.* 10 lists several groups who will suffer exclusion from the world to come. Among them are "the company of Korah," which will "not rise up again, for it is written, 'And the earth closed upon them' (Num 16:33), in this world, 'and they perished in the assembly' (Num 16:33), in the world to come. So R. Akiba" (10:3). Akiba's verdict is immediately countered by words attributed to R. Eliezer: "It says of them also, 'The Lord kills and makes alive, he brings down to Sheol and brings up'" (1 Sam 2:6). Here R. Eliezer opines that although the insurgents against Moses have gone down to Sheol, they will be graciously brought back.[7] So while we have here the arresting image of Korah and his companions in misfortune returning to the surface of the earth, in *TA* and *Acts Phil. Mart.* 31–32 (137–38) those who share their fate are likewise brought back to life. Is this just a coincidence? Is some common story or exegetical tradition in the background?

14:15. God explains that the sinners Abraham encountered have indeed been repaid (κρίσιν αὐτοὺς ἀνταπέδωκας); cf. 15:12; LXX Isa 35:4. In patristic texts, κρίσις + ἀνταποδίδωμι* most often appears in citations of

---

[7]   Cf. R. Judah b. Bathyra's opinion in *b. Sanh.* 109b and *Num. Rab.* 18:13. In *y. Sanh.* 10:5 and *ARN* A 36, R. Joshua b. Levi cites 1 Sam 2:6 to the same end. Contrast *L.A.B.* 16:3.

Isa 35:4; but cf. *Ps.-Clem. Hom.* 16:20; Cyril of Alexandria, *Comm. Isa.* PG 70.752C. This repayment lasts only "for a time," πρόσκαιρος*; cf. *4 Macc.* 15:2, 8, 23; *Jos. Asen.* 12:15. The reason is that those God requites (ἀποδώσω; ἀποδίδωμι*) while they are alive "on the earth" (ἐπὶ τῆς γῆς; cf. 3:5 v.l.; 15:15; 18:10 v.l.), he does not "requite in death": ἐν τῷ θανάτῳ οὐκ ἀποδώσω. The verb is often used of divine retribution: RecShrt. 10:3 E; *Ps. Sol.* 2:16; Matt 6:4, 6, 18; 16:27; Rom 2:6; Rev 22:12; etc. The idea, which is not, to my knowledge, expressed in patristic theology, harmonizes with the rabbinic notion that suffering and death may atone and allow entrance into the world to come; see *Mek.* on Exod 20:20 ("Precious are chastisements, for the three good gifts given to Israel which the nations of the world covet were all given only at the price of chastisements. And they are these: the Torah, the land of Israel, and the world to come"; cf. *Sifre* Deut. 32; *b. Ber.* 5a); 21:27 ("If a person can at the price of suffering obtain his release from the hands of flesh and blood, all the more should it be that he thus can obtain his pardon from heaven"); *m. Sanh.* 6:2 ("May my death be an atonement for all my sins"); and *Sifre* Deut. 324 ("After Israel's punishment ceases, it will never be reimposed").[8] A similar idea appears already in *1 En.* 22:12–13 (some sinners "were judged during their lifetime, and for that reason they need not be recompensed either immediately after death or at the great day of judgment"),[9] and probably in *2 Bar.* 78:6 ("the things you have suffered now" are "for your good so that you may not be condemned at the end and be tormented").

If those who die violently are not condemned at the judgment, then the horror of chaps. 17 and 19 is shown to be without substance. In revealing to Abraham his various faces and what they mean, Death lists in detail a host of violent deaths. Yet it seems that Death only works the salvation of his victims if those requited on earth through violent deaths are not requited in heaven. What happens to such is not said. Perhaps they enter heaven. Perhaps they are annihilated if they are sinners (as in Egyptian eschatology). They must in any event be spared the judgment depicted in chaps. 11–13.[10]

---

8   See further E. P. Sanders, *Paul and Palestinian Judaism: A Comparison of Patterns of Religion* (Philadelphia: Fortress, 1977), 168–72.

9   So George W. E. Nickelsburg, *1 Enoch 1* (Hermeneia; Minneapolis: Fortress, 2001), 308.

10 So Kolenkow, "Genre Testament," 145–46 (wrongly supposing that Abraham asks in 20:1 about "untimely" death; the term there is παράλογος, not ἄωρος). Cf. Nickelsburg, *Introduction*, 152.

Chapter 15: Abraham reneges

Bibliography: Allison, "Job in the Testament of Abraham". Schmidt, "Testament," 1:7–8, 18; 2:133, 143–44. Turner, "Testament," 146–48.

Long Recension

15:1. The voice of the Lord spoke also to the Commander-in-chief, "Michael, Michael, my minister, return Abraham to his house, for behold, his end has drawn near, and the measure of his life has come to an end, and he will set in order the affairs of his house and his possessions and all that he wants (to set in order); and then directly you will take him and bring him to me." 15:2. The Commander-in-chief, turning the cloud, brought the most holy Abraham to his house. 15:3. And going up into his dining chamber, he sat on his couch. 15:4. His wife Sarah came and embraced the feet of the incorporeal one, supplicating (him) and saying, "I thank you, my lord, that you have brought lord Abraham. For behold, I thought he had been taken up from us." 15:5. Isaac his son came, and he embraced his neck. And all his menservants and maidservants made a circle and likewise embraced Abraham, glorifying the holy God. 15:6. The incorporeal one said to Abraham, "Listen, most righteous one, behold your wife Sarah, behold also your beloved son, behold all your menservants and maidservants encircled around you. 15:7. Set in order all that you want (to set in order), because the day has drawn near in which you are

Short Recension fam. E

12:14–16. In that hour, Michael returned Abraham to the earth. 12:15. It happened at that time that Sarah died. 12:16. Abraham buried her.

about to depart the body and go to the
Lord." 15:8. Abraham said, "Did the
Lord say this, or do you speak this of
your own accord?" 15:9. The Commander-in-chief said, "Whatever the
Master commands, that I say to you."
15:10. Abraham said, "I will not follow
you." 15:11. The Commander-in-chief,
after hearing these words, immediately
departed from Abraham and went up
into heaven and stood before God the
Most High. 15:12. And he said, "Lord
Almighty, behold I have hearkened to
your friend Abraham, to all that he said
to you, and I have fulfilled his requests;
and I showed to him your power, and
all the earth under heaven, and the sea,
judgment and recompense—by means
of cloud and chariot I showed him. And
again he says, 'I will not follow you.'"
15:13. And the Most High said to the
Commander-in-chief, "Does my friend
Abraham again speak thus, 'I will not
follow you?'" 15:14. And the archangel
said in the presence of the Lord our
God, "Your friend Abraham speaks
thus. And I refrain from touching him,
because from the beginning he is your
friend, and he did all things pleasing
before you. 15:15. And there is not a
man like him on the earth, not even Job
the marvelous man. For this reason
I refrained from touching him. Command, eternal king, any word and it
will be done."

TEXTUAL NOTES ON THE LONG RECENSION

15:1. G omits "the voice of the Lord." // J lacks "the voice of the Lord"
and has only one "Michael." // H omits "Michael, Michael ... his house"
because a scribe has skipped from the end of κυρίου to the end of αὐτοῦ.
// B abbreviates by dropping "Michael, my minister." // B Q omit as
redundant "behold ... near" while J for the same reason omits "and the

measure ... end." // G lacks the "his" that qualifies "end" as well as "and the measure ... will." // J lacks the "his" that qualifies "life" and "has come ... (to set in order)." // Only B Q have καὶ τὰ ὑπάρχοντα / τῶν ὑπαρχόντων, but this accords with other lines in *TA*; see on 8:11. 15:2. G H I J open with: "Turning the chariot and the cloud." // B Q omit "the cloud, brought." // H drops "the most holy Abraham" while B G I J Q lack "most holy." 15:3. I abbreviates: "And he went up into his dining chamber." // Q passes from the first αὐτοῦ to the second. // A lacks "on his couch." 15:5. B Q omit "and he embraced his neck," passing from the αὐτοῦ in the first clause to the αὐτοῦ at the end of the second. // H drops "glorifying the holy God," which is not strictly necessary, and B G H I J Q lack "holy," which may be secondary. 15:6. B omits "your wife ... son." // J omits "maidservants ... around you." 15:8–10. G passes from "Abraham said" in v. 8 to "Abraham said" in v. 10, which may be due either to *homoioteleuton* or to a desire to abbreviate. 15:11. G assimilates to 8:1 by inserting ἀφανὴς ἐγένετο καὶ before "immediately." // J abbreviates by dropping "departed ... Abraham and." 15:11–12. H omits all from "and went up ... his requests." 15:12. J shortens by dropping "behold ... said to you, and." // G omits "to you and his requests." // J lacks "and I showed to him your power." Is the reason *homoioteleuton* (καί ... καί)? // H drops "your power and." 15:13. J, omitting "I will not follow you," again abbreviates: "Does my friend speak thus?" 15:14. A omits. // H replaces "said in the presence of the Lord our God" with simple ναί. // A lacks "Your friend Abraham ... touching him," which is partly redundant in view of v. 15. // J abbreviates by omitting "your friend Abraham." // H shortens by dropping "because from the beginning ... all." 15:15. G J omit "not even ... done" as unnecessary. H similarly omits "not even ... him" while I drops "not even ... man." Obviously some scribes were uninterested in the Job typology (so too the long Romanian, ed. Roddy, p. 45). // B Q: Ἰώβ. A: Ἰακώβ, which Turner labeled "weak and pointless."[1] G H I and J are all deficient here because they lack the relevant clause; see above. "Job" is original, Ἰακώβ perhaps an error of the ear. While some ancient sources make Abraham and Job contemporaries (see the Commentary), Jacob was, according to biblical chronology, a scant fifteen years old when Abraham died,[2] and the narratives of grandfather and grandson do not overlap,[3] so

---

[1] Turner, "Testament," 148.
[2] Abraham was 100 when Isaac was born (Gen 21:5). Abraham died at 175 (Gen 25:7). Isaac was 60 when Jacob was born (Gen 25:26).
[3] This also holds for extracanonical materials, with only a few exceptions, such as *b. B. Bat.* 16b, which has Jacob comfort Isaac upon Abraham's death.

a comparison of them would be unusual. More importantly, the language of *TA* 15:14–15 is clearly based upon the book of Job (see the Commentary), and chaps. 1–4 contain a developed Job typology. // Only A has "the marvelous," but this fits Job (the reading of B Q) better than Jacob (so A); cf. LXX Job 21:5; 42:11; *T. Job* 6:1; 24:10. Further, θαυμάσιος is characteristic of *TA*: 6:8; 11:6 (bis, cf. v. 8); 12:11 (ὁ ἀνὴρ ὁ θαυμάσιος); 16:10 (ἀνὴρ θαυμάσιε).

COMMENTARY

Chap. 15, which concludes the heavenly tour begun in chap. 9, consists of a sequence that partly replays 7:8–8:3, the story of Abraham's first refusal and what followed:

15:1	God orders Michael to return Abraham to his home	
15:2–3	Abraham arrives at home	
15:4–5	Family and servants welcome Abraham	
15:6–7	Michael tells Abraham it is time to die	cf. 7:8–9
15:8	Abraham questions Michael	cf. 7:10
15:9	Michael reaffirms his mission	cf. 7:11
15:10	Abraham refuses to die	cf. 7:12
15:11	Michael exits and ascends to heaven	cf. 8:1
15:12	Michael explains his failure to God	cf. 8:2–3
15:13	God queries Michael's report	
15:14–15	Michael explains further	

While chap. 15 inescapably recalls 7:8–8:3, it equally sends readers back to Job 1–2, chapters that also lie beneath chaps. 1–4; see pp. 128–30. Not only does v. 15 explicitly mention Job, but there are phrases that come from canonical Job; see on vv. 11, 14, 15. The contexts for the common phrases are, moreover, similar: in both stories God discusses with a heavenly being the fate of a saint upon the earth.

Most of RecLng. 15 has no parallel in RecShrt. But RecShrt. fam. E 12:14–16 does have this: "In that hour, Michael returned Abraham to the earth. It happened at that time that Sarah died.[4] Abraham buried her." Fam. B F G is very similar: "And about the ninth hour Michael returned Abraham to his own house. Earlier his wife had died. And he buried her." In both families the notice of Abraham's return and of Sarah's death is

---

[4]   C clarifies: "His wife Sarah, not having seen what had happened to Abraham, was consumed with grief and handed over her soul; and after Abraham returned he found her dead."

immediately followed (13:1ff.) by a new section introducing what happened "when" (ὅτε) the days of the death of Abraham "drew near" (ἤγγικεν). So the time between the episode in 12 and the episode in 13 is unspecified; readers may make it as short or long as they like.

RecShrt. 12:14–16, which feels so rushed, is surely deliberate abbreviation of something close to RecLng.'s storyline. RecLng., where Sarah is alive for Abraham's departure from this life, clearly contradicts Genesis, where Abraham buries Sarah in Genesis 23 then remarries and finally dies in Genesis 25. In RecShrt., however, the story breaks between chaps. 12 and 13 (see above), which allows readers to imagine some time passing between Abraham's tour of the heavens and his subsequent death. The sequence makes for a better fit with the biblical record. Not only does Sarah die before Abraham, but the former event does not clearly occur immediately before the latter.

It is also telling that RecLng. 15 is, as the verse-by-verse commentary shows, repetitious, and while this adds to the dramatic tension, the textual tradition shows a very strong tendency on the part of scribes to abbreviate. That someone might have omitted the entire section would suit the strong tendency of RecShrt. to improve Abraham's image. Just as RecShrt. omits the patriarch's original refusal to cooperate with Michael, so it eliminates all traces of his second refusal. Further, this omission leaves the introduction of Death in the following chapter without good explanation, another sign of imperfect editing of a story that remains coherent in RecLng.; see p. 14.

15:1. ἡ φωνὴ τοῦ κυρίου (cf. Gen 3:8; 15:4; Exod 15:25; Acts 7:31; etc.), which refers back to 14:13, now speaks to Michael, using the double vocative as it did when addressing Abraham; see on 14:14. The angel is a λειτουργός, which Lampe, s.v., 3, shows to be a common patristic designation for angels. But it is used of Jacob = Israel, identified as an archangel, in fr. A of the *Prayer of Joseph* in Origen, *Comm. Jo.* 2.31, presumably a Jewish source; and still other Jewish texts speak of angels as λειτουργοί: LXX Ps 102:21; 103:4 (quoted in Heb 1:7; *1 Clem.* 36:3); Philo, *Virt.* 74; *T. Sol.* 4:13 D; cf. *Jub.* 31:14; *T. Levi* 3:5 (οἱ ἄγγελοι ... λειτουργοῦντες). God commands Michael to "return" (ἀπόστρεψον; see on 10:12) Abraham to where the journey began, "to his house," εἰς τὸν οἶκον αὐτοῦ; cf. v. 2; 5:1; 17:1. The reason is that his "end has drawn near" (ἤγγικεν τὸ τέλος αὐτοῦ), that is, "the measure of his life has come to an end," τὸ μέτρον τῆς ζωῆς αὐτοῦ τελειοῦται. "The measure of his life" is from 1:1 (q.v.), but τελειόω* appears only here. Although "the end has drawn near" echoes Matt 24:14 and 1 Pet 4:7, where τέλος refers to the world's consummation, as also in *TA* 13:7 (τὸ τέλος ἐγγύς), here it designates an individual's death;

cf. 1:5; 4:8; and Ps.-John of Damascus, *B.J.* 35.322: τὸ τέλος (of Abenner) ἤγγισεν. The message that Abraham's time is up has already been communicated to readers and to Michael in chap. 1, and to Abraham himself in chap. 7. But now the declaration comes after the deal struck in chap. 9. God has done what Abraham asked, and it is past time for Abraham to keep his end of the bargain.

As earlier, the announcement of death is accompanied by the instruction to have Abraham set his affairs in order; see on 8:11. But God will permit no more delay after that: "and then directly" (καὶ εἶθ' οὕτως; see on 7:11) Michael will have to take (παράλαβε) him and bring (προσάγαγε) him to God; cf. God's instructions to death in 16:5: λαβὲ αὐτὸν καὶ ἄγαγε αὐτόν ... παράλαβε.

15:2. "Turning the cloud" (see on 9:8), Michael brings the ἱερώτατον (see on 2:2 and p. 86) Abraham to his house. The description of Michael's actions correlates with God's imperative in v. 1 and so emphasizes the angel's obedience (which Abraham will subsequently question, v. 8):

| 15:1 | ἀπόστρεψον ... | εἰς τὸν οἶκον αὐτοῦ ... προσάγαγε |
| 15:2 | διαστρέψας ... ἤγαγεν ... εἰς τὸν οἶκον αὐτοῦ | |

15:3. Abraham ceases to be a passive passenger and now directs himself, going where he wants to go. The language recalls Isaac's similar action in 5:5:

| 15:3 | ἀνελθὼν ἐν τῷ | τρικλίνῳ αὐτοῦ ἐκάθισεν ἐπὶ τῆς κλίνης |
| 5:5 | ἀπῆλθεν ἐν τῷ ἰδίῳ τρικλίνῳ καὶ | ἀνέπεσεν ἐπὶ τῆς κλίνης |

For Abraham's τρίκλινος see on 4:1. He will return to it and again sit on his couch in 17:2, after he has encountered Death. Perhaps we are to think that he is, as there, tired (cf. 19:2). Or perhaps his retirement to his room is a physical expression that he does not want to go anywhere, that he will not cooperate with Michael and God.

15:4. Sarah, who has not been part of the action since chap. 6, comes and embraces (περιεπλάκη; cf. v. 5 and see on 5:11) the feet of the incorporeal one, τοῦ ἀσωμάτου; see on 3:6 and cf. 9:2; 20:6; Ps.-Chrysostom, *Meretr.* PG 61.732 (περιπλεκομένην ... τοῖς ποσίν); Theophanes Continuatus, *Chronog.*, ed. Bekker, p. 238.6 (περιεπλάκη ποσίν). Michael has obviously followed Abraham into the house. The mention of Michael's feet recalls the story in chap. 3 (cf. 6:6–8) as well as its biblical inspiration, Gen 18:4. Sarah is said to supplicate (ἱκετεύουσα; see on 9:2) Michael, although no request follows. She opens with εὐχαριστῶ σοι, κύριε, a phrase found in Christian texts: *Acts Thom.* 15, 19; Ps.-Basil, *Constitutiones asceticae* PG 31.1329C; Ps.-Ephraem, *Capita centum* 95.8; Asterius the Sophist, *Hom. Ps.* 18.18; etc. But there are other parallels: PGM 4.1060; 11a:15; 12.173; *Vit. Aesopi* G

29. Sarah is thankful because she thought her husband "had been taken up from us," ἀναληφθέντα αὐτὸν ἀφ᾽ ἡμῶν; see on 7:7. She somehow learned that her husband had been removed to heaven, and she wrongly assumed that he would not return. For her, he has returned from the dead.

15:5. If the mother embraces Michael, the son embraces (περιεπλάκη; cf. v. 4 and see on 5:11) the father. Isaac falls not at the feet but upon the neck, just as he did in 5:8–9; cf. Theophanes Confessor, Chronog., ed. de Boor, p. 195 (περιπλακέντες ἀλλήλων τῷ τραχήλῳ); Theophanes Continuatus, Chronog., ed. Bekker, p. 477 (περιπλακέντες τῷ τραχήλῳ). Abraham's male (δοῦλοι; cf. 19:7; 20:7) and female (δουλίδες; cf. 20:7 v.l.; T. Job 27:3; παιδίσκας is used in v. 6; 17:18) servants (cf. 2:1, 9; 17:18; 18:3, 9) also show affection. They gather around their master in a circle (κύκλῳ; cf. v. 6) and likewise "embrace" (περιεπλάκησαν) him. People gathering or standing κύκλῳ around a dying saint is a common motif in Christian hagiography; see e.g. Gregory the Great, Dial. 4.40; Vit. Evaristus 42 = Analecta Bollandiana 41 (1923), 321; Vatican Gr. 1982, ed. Wenger, p. 230; John of Thessalonica, Dorm. BVM A 12, ed. Jugie, p. 395; Acta graeca SS. Davidis, Symeonis et Georgii 33 = Analecta Bollandiana 18 (1899), 255; Vit. Theodore the Ruler 12, ed. Markopoulos, p. 269; and the icons of the Dormition. So Abraham's death is here foreshadowed: the celebration will soon give way to mourning. See further on 20:6–7.

For οἱ δοῦλοι καὶ αἱ δουλίδες see Aristophanes of Byzantium, Nomina aetatum (fragmenta), ed. Miller, p. 279; Acts Phil. 5:23; 6:17 V; Theodore the Studite, Ep., ed. Fatouros 66.13; etc. Unlike Isaac, the servants give speech to their feelings by "glorifying the holy God," δοξάζοντες τὸν θεὸν τὸν ἅγιον; cf. 6:6; Judg B 9:9; Jos. Asen. 20:5; T. Job 16:7; Matt 9:8; Luke 5:25; Rom 15:9; Josephus, Ant. 8.22; T. Jos. 8:5; 3 Bar. 17:4; 4 Bar. 7:17; Acts John 19; etc.; but in each of these the object is "God," not "the holy God." For the latter (never following δοξάζω) see LXX Isa 5:16; 10:20; 14:27; 43:15; 45:11; Hab 1:2; Noy, JIWE 159; Basil the Great, Ep. 290.1; Ps.-Basil, Enarrat. Isa. 5.169; etc.

15:6. The incorporeal (ὁ ἀσώματος; cf. v. 5 and see on 3:6) tells the δικαιώτατε (for the superlative see 16:11; 17:10; 19:14; 20:3; Acts Euplius 3:3; Gregory of Nazianzus, Macc. laud. PG 35.913D) Abraham to pay attention (ἄκουσον; cf. 7:8; 14:2; 19:7 v.l., all of which have ἄκουσον δίκαιε). A series of three ἰδού's summarizes the scene already depicted in vv. 4–5. The repetition adds pathos—this man is truly loved (cf. 5:8; 20:6–7). So he is not alone in his desire to avoid death; those around him also do not want him to leave. παῖδες καὶ παιδίσκαι recurs in 17:18, where the servants are numbered at 7,000. The phrase occurs several times in the

LXX and moreover refers specifically to Abraham's servants in Gen 12:16; cf. the references to Abraham's παῖδες καὶ παιδίσκαι in Origen, *Comm. Jo.* 20.10; Chrysostom, *Hom. Gen.* PG 53.300, 301; Didymus of Alexandria, *In Gen.*, ed. Nautin and Doutreleau, p. 228.4.

15:7. This verse, in which Michael tells Abraham to set his affairs in order because his death is nigh, is mostly a concatenation of phrases used earlier; it says nothing new either to Abraham or to readers:

15:7	ποίησον διάταξιν	περὶ	πάντων ὧν ἐὰν βούλῃ	
1:4	διατάξεται	περὶ	πάντων	
4:11	ποιήσῃς διάταξιν	περὶ	πάντων	
8:11	ποιήσῃς διάταξιν	περὶ ...	πάντων	
15:1	ποιήσῃς διάταξιν	περὶ ...	πάντα ὅσα	βούλεται
15:7	ἤγγικεν ἡ ἡμέρα			
15:1	ἤγγικεν τὸ τέλος			
15:7	μέλλεις ἐκδημεῖν ἐκ τοῦ σώματος			
1:7	μέλλει ἐκδημεῖν ἐκ τοῦ σώματος			
15:7	πρὸς τὸν	θεὸν	ἔρχεσθαι	
1:7	πρὸς τὸν ἴδιον	δεσπότην ἀπελεύσει		
7:9	πρὸς τὸν	θεὸν	ἐκδημεῖν	

15:8. Abraham asks whether Michael's words are from the Lord or from himself—an accusation he will later make against Death (19:4). The question must be insincere, a lame excuse for continued disobedience. Abraham knows that Michael is more honorable than kings and rulers (4:3), that miracles accompany him (3:2, 11), that he promised the birth of Isaac (6:4–5), and that he has an expert knowledge of heavenly things (9–14). Moreover, that the patriarch trusts the angel is evident from his asking Michael to pray with him (14:5,12). He cannot possibly believe that the archangel is lying to him. Abraham is simply being contrary. The irony is profound. The saint who was willing to kill his son at God's command (Genesis 22) is now unwilling himself to die in extreme old age when it is time to pass on. On the parallel with traditions about the death of Moses see p. 24.

15:9. Michael responds by stating the obvious: he is nothing but an instrument of the Master (ὁ δεσπότης; see on 1:4), doing what has been commanded, ἐκέλευσεν; see on v. 15.

15:10. Although much has happened since Abraham initially refused to depart this life, and although Abraham's request to see all the world has been granted, the patriarch says exactly what he said earlier: οὐ μή σε ἀκολουθήσω (cf. 7:12, q.v.). He has reneged on his bargain with God—an act altogether at odds with Scripture's depiction of him as the paradigm of obedience but wholly in accord with his character throughout *TA*. Readers might imagine that the postmortem judgment has made him even more anxious about death than he was before, but the text does not say this.

15:11. Once more readers have déjà vu, as this line recounts an event that repeats the past; see on 4:5 and 8:1. With ἐξῆλθεν ἐκ προσώπου τοῦ Ἀβραάμ cf. v. 14; LXX Gen 4:16; 4 Βασ 5:27, and for God as "Most High" see on 9:1.

15:12. Michael, nonplussed, addresses God as κύριε παντοκράτορ; cf. 15:14 v.l.; *Pr. Man.* 1 in *Apos. Con.* 2:22:12; *4 Bar.* 1:5; 9:6; 8:3; *Apos. Con.* 7:35, 36; 8:11, 16, 37, 40; Eusebius, *Dem. ev.* 8.2; *Chron. Pasch.*, ed. Dindorf, p. 271; etc. The angel stresses that he has heeded and "fulfilled" (ἐπλήρωσα; cf. 9:4) whatever God's "friend" (see on 1:4; cf. vv. 13–14) has asked, πάντα ὅσα εἶπεν; cf. 4:7 ("whatever he says to you, this indeed do"); LXX Exod 19:8; 1 Esd 4:57; 1 Macc 11:53; Philo, *Conf.* 58; *T. Jud.* 17:4; patristic texts use this expression only with reference to Exod 19:8, which is not alluded to here. This general assertion is then filled out with specifics. Abraham has seen, first of all, God's δυναστείαν. The word may mean "(divine) power," as in some patristic texts (Lampe, s.v. δυναστεία 4); but "province" or "realm" (see Lampe, s.v., 3) would also be appropriate. In addition, Abraham has seen heaven and earth and the sea (although this last is not mentioned earlier) as well as "judgment and recompense," κρίσιν καὶ ἀνταπόδοσιν; see on 10:15. διὰ νεφέλης καὶ ἀρμάτων (cf. 9:8; 10:1; 15:1) is tacked onto the end and seems superfluous. Does it underline the extraordinary nature of Abraham's experience and so the special honor shown to him?

15:13. Not only has Abraham refused Michael, but now the "Most High" (cf. v. 11 and see on 9:1), who must know the truth, belabors the angel's statement, as though perhaps the latter has not spoken the truth: "Does my friend (cf. vv. 12, 14 and see on 1:4) Abraham again speak thus?" (οὕτως could mean "simply," cf. BGAD, s.v., 4; but the parallel in the next line makes this unlikely). Readers should probably hear incredulity in God's voice—"Surely it just can't be that my friend Abraham, the model of obedience, who was willing to sacrifice his only son at my word, again refuses to do he has been told."

15:14. Michael enlarges his analysis of the situation by heaping praise upon Abraham. The praise, as well as the repeated notice that Abraham is God's "friend" (cf. vv. 12–13 and see on 1:4), makes the patriarch's refusal to cooperate all the more ironic and puzzling. It also justifies Michael's hesitancy. "In the presence of the Lord our God" (ἐκ προσώπου κυρίου τοῦ θεοῦ ἡμῶν; cf. v. 2 and see on 2:1) is strictly unnecessary, but the regal language adds solemnity. More importantly, it probably echoes Job 1–2. For (a) the next verse compares Abraham with Job; (b) if vv. 14–15 say that Michael hesitates to "touch" (τοῦ ἅψασθαι) Abraham, LXX Job uses ἅπτω = "contact in order to harm" to describe the afflicting of its hero, particularly near the book's beginning (1:11, 12, 19; 2:5; 19:21); (c) *TA* 1–4 has a typological relationship with Job 1–2 (see pp. 128–30); and (d) in Job 1:12 v.l., Satan, who is the obverse of Michael, goes out ἀπὸ προσώπου κυρίου, and in 2:2 Satan *speaks* "before the Lord" (εἶπεν ὁ διάβολος ἐνώπιον τοῦ κυρίου).

In addition to being God's "friend," Abraham has "from the beginning" (ἐξ ἀρχῆς; cf. RecShrt. 4:13; ἀρχή*) done everything pleasing before God, πάντα τὰ ἀρεστὰ ἐνώπιόν σου ἐποίησεν (ἀρεστός*); cf. *3 Bar.* 8:5 (τῷ θεῷ ἀρεστά); Ps.-Ephraem, *Sermones paraenetici ad monachos Aegypti* 47.135 (τὰ ἀρεστὰ ἐνώπιον αὐτοῦ ἐποίησε); idem, *In illud: Attende tibi ipsi* 10.43 (τὰ ἀρεστὰ ἐνώπιον αὐτοῦ ποιοῦμεν); Ps.-Sphrantzes, *Chron. sive Maius*, ed. Grecu, p. 170.2 (τὰ ὅσα ἀρεστὰ τοῖς ἐπηκόοις ἐποίησε).

15:15. "There is not a man like him on the earth." The words clearly echo Job:

TA 15:15	οὐκ ἔστιν ἄνθρωπος ὅμοιος αὐτοῦ	ἐπὶ τῆς γῆς
LXX Job 1:8 A	οὐκ ἔστιν ἄνθρωπος ὅμοιος αὐτῷ τῶν ἐπὶ τῆς γῆς	
LXX Job 2:3 A	οὐκ ἔστιν κατ᾽ αὐτὸν τῶν ἐπὶ τῆς γῆς, ἄνθρωπος ὅμοιος αὐτῷ[5]	

So 15:15, which recalls two verses from Job that 4:6 (οὐκ εἶδον ἐπὶ τῆς γῆς ἄνθρωπον ὅμοιον αὐτοῦ) has already recalled, reactivates the Job typology that runs throughout chaps. 1–4; see pp. 128–30.

Abraham is exalted over "Job, the marvelous man," ὁ θαυμαστὸς ἄνθρωπος; cf. John Philoponus, *Contra Proclum*, ed. Rabe, p. 318: θαυμαστὸν ἄνθρωπον. The comparison is odd if Abraham lived before Job, but the latter was variously dated. Many identified Job with the Jobab of Gen 36:33–34 and had him marry Jacob's daughter: LXX Job 42:17b; *L.A.B.* 8:8; *T. Job* 1:1 (but *T. Job* 1:6 v.l. makes Job a brother of Nahor, who was Abraham's brother: Genesis 11); Eusebius, *Dem. ev.* 1.6; Chrysostom, *Comm. Job* preface, ed. Hagedorn, p. 1; Tg. Ps.-Jn. on Gen 36:11. Others put him in the time of Moses (e.g. R. Joshua b. Levi b. Lahma in *b. B. Bat.* 15a; cf. *b. Soṭah* 11a) or even later (see further *b. B. Bat.* 15a–b). But according to Simeon b. Lakish in Bar Kappara's name in *y. Soṭah* 5:6, Job was a contemporary of Abraham. This opinion also

---

[5] LXX Job 1:8 B S (οὐκ ἔστιν κατ᾽ αὐτὸν τῶν ἐπὶ τῆς γῆς) and 2:3 (οὐκ ἔστιν κατ᾽ αὐτὸν τῶν ἐπὶ τῆς γῆς, ἄνθρωπος) are also close.

appears in *Tanḥ. B* Numbers Shelah 27; *Gen. Rab.* 57:4; *Apos. Con.* 8:5:11–12; 8:12:63–64 (these presumably reflect a Jewish *Urtext*); and Jerome, *Quaest. hebr. Gen.* ad 22:20–22; cf. Cyprian, *Ep.* 75.3, and Ps.-Cyprian, *De duobus montibus* 5.1–2, ed. Burini, pp. 156–58. Maybe this earlier dating presupposes his identification with the Jobab of Gen 10:29, especially as Uz (cf. Job 1:1) is mentioned in the nearby 10:23. In any case, 4QpaleoJobᶜ, written in archaic paleo-Hebrew script, is evidence that someone at Qumran thought the book to be of very great antiquity.

The *synkrisis* of Abraham and Job, which does not function as polemic against the latter,[6] is altogether natural. Both men were famous converted pagans (cf. *Num. Rab.* 14:2: Abraham and Job came to their knowledge of the true God unaided; Basil the Great, *Ep.* 236.7: both Abraham and Job were taught by God).[7] Both were thought of as kings.[8] Both received new names from God (Job was once, according to legend, Jobab).[9] And both were paragons of philanthropy.[10] Further, if Job suffered terribly, Abraham was widely remembered as one who had himself undergone very difficult trials.[11] Not only had he been tested when offering Isaac, but convention eventually came to hold that "Abraham our father, may he rest in peace, was tested ten times" (*m. 'Abot* 5:3).[12] Perhaps the number ten itself owes

---

[6]   Contrast Delcor, *Testament*, 47–51.

[7]   See Irving Jacobs, "Literary Motifs in the Testament of Job," *JJS* 21 (1970), 4–5. LXX Job 42 makes Job an Edomite king. The *Testament of Job* tells of his conversion to monotheism. The majority opinion among the rabbis is that Job was a Gentile; see *b. B. Bat.* 15b. Already the Bible indicates that he is a Gentile by (a) making him hail from "the land of Uz"; (b) failing to give him a genealogy; and (c) omitting any reference in Job to Israel's history.

[8]   For Abraham see on 4:2. For Job see LXX Job 42:17; Aristeas the Exegete in Eusebius, *Praep. ev.* 9.25.3; *T. Job* 28:7; 29:3–4; 31:1.

[9]   See *T. Job* 2:1 ("Now I used to be Jobab before the Lord named me Job"); cf. LXX Job 42:17; Aristeas the Exegete in Eusebius, *Praep. ev.* 9.25.3. For this as a parallel with Abraham see Olympiodorus of Alexandria, *Comm. Job* ad 42:17b, ed. Hagedorn, p. 396, and cf. Jacobs, "Literary Motifs," 8–9; also Annette Joshiko Reed, "Job as Jobab: The Interpretation of Job in LXX Job 42:17b–e," *JBL* 120 (2001), 51.

[10] See on 1:1–2 and cf. Chrysostom, *Comm. Job* ad 1:3, ed. Hagedorn, pp. 5–6.

[11] Cf. *Tanḥ. B* Numbers Shelah 27; Didymus of Alexandria, *Comm. Job* preface, ed. Henrichs, p. 40. LXX Gen 22:1 uses πειράζειν of the sacrifice of Isaac, and while neither this verb nor πειρασμός appears in LXX Job, they are naturally used of him elsewhere; e.g., Aristeas the Exegete in Eusebius, *Praep. ev.* 9.25.3; Olympiodorus of Alexandria, *Comm. Job* Hypothesis, ad 1:7, ed. Hagedorn, pp. 4, 17.

[12] See further Jdt 8:25–27; Ecclus 44:19–21; 1 Macc 2:51–52; *Jub.* 17:17–18; 19:2–3, 8; *ARN* A 34, B 37; etc.

318   Chapter 15

something to a comparison with Job, for in Job 19:3 we read, "These ten
times you have cast reproach upon me." However that may be, the comparison of Abraham and Job was conventional, and *b. Sanh.* 89b, just like
TA, borrows from Job to fill out the story of Abraham; see *Jub.* 17:12–16
(cf. 4Q255 2 I 8); *Testament of Job* 1–4 (cf. *Jubilees* 12; *Apocalypse of
Abraham* 1–8; *Gen. Rab.* 38:13); *ARN* A 2, 7; *t. Soṭah* 6:1; *Tanḥ.* B
Leviticus Wayyikra 15; Numbers Mattot 1; *y. Ber.* 9:5; *b. B. Bat.* 15a–16b;
b. Soṭah 31a; *Gen. Rab.* 49:9; Tg. Job 30:19; *Midr. Ps.* 26:2 (cf. *Sem.* 8).
Relevant Christian texts include *1 Clem.* 17:2–4; Clement of Alexandria,
Strom. 4.17; Origen, *Hom. Gen.* 8.10; Chrysostom, *Comm. Job* ad 1:3, ed.
Hagedorn, pp. 5–6; Olympiodorus of Alexandria, *Comm. Job* ad 42:11
and 17b, ed. Hagedorn, pp. 390, 396; *Vit. Elizabeth the Wonderworker* 2
= *Analecta Bollandiana* 91 (1973), 252. These texts further reveal that
Abraham's superiority to Job was a topos (cf. *ARN* A 7; *b. B. Bat.* 15b;
Gen. Rab. 49:9; *Midr. Ps.* 26:2), and that describing Abraham in terms
drawn from Job 1–2 was conventional; see p. 130.[13]

Because of Abraham's status, Michael has refrained from touching
(φείδομαι τοῦ ἅψασθαι, as in v. 14, q.v.) him. So nothing is left but to ask
God for further direction: "Command (κέλευσον; cf. 7:11; 8:3; 9:8; 15:9—
all of God commanding Michael), eternal king (ἀθάνατε βασιλεῦ; LXX: 0;
NT: 0; Josephus: 0; cf. 16:2; *Sib. Or.* 1:173; 8:250; Philo, *Somn.* 2.100;
Clement of Alexandria, *Strom.* 2.20.121; Constantine VII Porphyrogenitus,
Cer., ed. Reiske, p. 2 [ἀθάνατε βασιλεῦ]),[14] any word and it will be done,"
τι ῥῆμα καὶ γενήσεται; cf. LXX Job 2:9; *T. Job* 25:10; 26:2 (all with εἰπόν
τι ῥῆμα).[15]

---

[13] See further Joanna Weinberg, "Job versus Abraham: The Quest for the Perfect God-
Fearer in Rabbinic Tradition," in *The Book of Job* (BETL 114; ed. W. A. M. Beuken;
Leuven: Leuven University Press/Peeters, 1994), 281–96.

[14] Oddly enough, the long Romanian, ed. Roddy, p. 44, transfers "immortal king" to
Abraham: "There is no one on earth like him and he is like some immortal king."

[15] James, *Testament*, 96, prints: τί ῥῆμα γενήσεται (cf. B I): "Command … what thing
shall be done."

Chapter 16: God sends Death to Abraham

Bibliography: Delcor, *Testament*, 57–59.   James, *Testament*, 55–58.   Ludlow, *Abraham*, 95–118.   Schmidt, "Testament," 1:93–101.   Strotmann, *"Mein Vater"*, 223–24.

Long Recension

16:1. Then the Most High said, "Summon here to me Death, the one who has a shameless face and merciless look." 16:2. And Michael the incorporeal, going away, spoke to Death, "Come, the Master of creation, the immortal King, summons you." 16:3. Upon hearing this, Death quivered and trembled, being afflicted with great cowardice. And coming with much fear he stood before the invisible Father, trembling and groaning and shaking, awaiting the command of the master. 16:4. The invisible Father then said to Death, "Come then, bitter and savage name of the world, hide your savageness and all your putrefaction, and put away all your bitterness. Put on your beauty and all your glory. 16:5. And go down to my friend Abraham and take him and bring him to me. Yet also now I say to you, that you come to this place without terrifying his soul. Rather take this one with fawning because he is my true friend." 16:6. Hearing these things, Death went out from before the Most High and put on a brightly shining robe, and he made his countenance like the sun, and his appearance became more beautiful than that of the sons of men. Having put on the form of an archangel, with his cheeks flashing like fire, he went away to Abra-

Short Recension fam. E

13:1. Now when the days of Abraham's death drew near, Death did not dare to approach him to take his soul from his body. So the Lord said to Michael, 13:2. "Go away and adorn Death with great beauty, and send him to Abraham that he might see him with his eyes." 13:3. And Michael, going away, adorned Death with great beauty and sent him to Abraham. 13:4. Abraham, seeing Death sitting near him, feared greatly. [C: And Death said to Abraham, "Greetings, holy soul. Greetings, friend of the Lord God. Greetings, comforting hospitality of travelers."] 13:5. And Abraham answered and said, "I entreat you, reveal to me who you are. (But) withdraw from me, 13:6. for ever since I saw you sitting near me, my soul has been troubled within me. 13:7. I am altogether unworthy of you. For you are an exalted spirit. I am but flesh and blood. Wherefore I am unable to endure your glory. 13:8. For I perceive that your beauty is not of this world."

ham. 16:7. The righteous Abraham went out of his dining room and sat under the trees of Mamre, holding his cheeks in his hands, and awaiting the command of the archangel. 16:8. And behold, a pleasing odor came to him, and an effulgence of light. Turning around Abraham saw Death coming to him in great glory and beauty; and rising, he greeted him, supposing him to be the archangel. 16:9. And Death, seeing him, bowed before him saying, "Greetings, honorable Abraham, righteous soul, friend of God the Most High and companion of angels." 16:10. Abraham said to Death, "Greetings, sun-like guardian of the law, supremely glorious, splendid and most marvelous man. From whence has your glory come to us, and who are you?" 16:11. Death said to him, "Abraham, most righteous father, behold, I speak to you the truth. I am the bitter cup of Death!" 16:12. Abraham said, "No! You are rather the comeliness of the world. You are the glory and loveliness of the angels and of men. You are the most pleasing of all appearances. And you say, 'I am the bitter cup of death!' Should you rather not say, 'I am the fairest of all good things'?" 16:13. Death said, "Father, I speak to you the truth. That which God named me—that I have spoken to you." 16:14. Abraham said, "Why have you come here?" 16:15. Death said, "Because of your righteous soul have I come." 16:16. Abraham said to him, "I understand what you say, yet I will not follow you." But Death was silent and did not answer.

TEXTUAL NOTES ON THE LONG RECENSION

16:1. A has κεκλημένον instead of κεκτημένον (so H I G). B J Q omit. 16:2.
A G H lack "the incorporeal." // H omits "of creation ... King." 16:3. A
omits "And coming ... awaiting." This is due to *homoioteleuton*—an eye
passed from the end of συνεχόμενος to the end of ἀπεκδεχόμενος. // G H:
"invisible God." B Q: "God and invisible Father." I: "immortal Father."
J: "invisible Father."[1] // G omits "trembling ... shaking" as redundant.
16:4. B drops "then, bitter and." // G abbreviates by omitting "name" and
"hide ... putrefaction." // Instead of σαπρίαν (so B I Q), A has the unin-
telligible παροιάς. Schmidt conjectures an original παρειάς. 16:5. G H J
abbreviate by dropping "you come to this place." 16:6. H drops "from ...
High," which is unnecessary. // A lacks "and he made ... sun." // G omits
"and his appearance ... men." // Instead of μορφήν, H has στολήν. // G
(continuing to abbreviate) and J lack "with his ... fire." 16:7. G drops
"went out ... room and" as superfluous. 16:8. J omits "and an effulgence
... coming to him." // Q abbreviates by dropping "saw Death ... rising."
16:10. A Q: θεσμοσυλλήπτωρ. Given that this word is otherwise unattested, it is no surprise to find variants. B I omit. H: θεσμοῦ ἀντιλήπτωρ—
obviously an interpretation of what A Q have. G: θερμὲ συλλήπτωρ. J:
συλλήπτωρ. 16:11. H drops "Abraham ... the truth" as unnecessary.
16:12. I shortens by dropping "Abraham said ... cup of death!" // J omits
"of the world ... the angels, and." This leaves a shorter sentence that still
makes sense. // "You are the glory" is not in H. // G H lack the last half:
"And you say, etc." // J omits "Should you rather ... good things'?" 16:13–
14. I omits vv. 13–14, but the conversation remains intelligible. 16:16. A
lacks "Abraham said to him." // H omits "I understand ... say." // B Q lack
"and did not answer."

COMMENTARY

The chapter falls into two parts. The first part recounts events in heaven:
God orders Michael to summon Death, who in turn comes to receive his
instructions: God commands Michael to summon Death (v 1); Michael
summons Death (v. 2); Death arrives (v. 3); God instructs Death (v. 4).
Unlike Michael, who converses with God, Death receives his instructions
without comment, so we do not know what he thinks; he remains a

---

[1] Strotmann, *"Mein Vater"*, 222–23, argues for the originality of "invisible God"
here.

mystery. His chief characteristic is pliability: "Death adopts a plethora of personae: the quaking subordinate, the fearsome agent, the handsome charmer, the hideous mass murderer, the professional commentator, and the crafty deceiver."[2] To which one may add that, in chap. 18, he emulates Abraham's piety and prays for the unfortunate.

The second part of chap. 16 takes place on earth, on Abraham's estate. The scene is set in such a way as to recall both chap. 2 (see below) and Genesis 18 (see on vv. 6–8). Death and Abraham exchange extravagant greetings, after which Death answers a series of three questions from Abraham:

v. 10 Abraham's question "From whence has your glory come to us, and who are you?"
v. 11   Death's answer   "I am the bitter cup of Death!"
v. 12 Abraham's question "Should you rather not say, 'I am the fairest of all good things'?"
v. 13   Death's answer   "That which God named me—that I have spoken to you"
v. 14 Abraham's question "Why have you come here?"
v. 15   Death's answer   "Because of your righteous soul have I come"

Abraham responds to all this by refusing to cooperate, which is exactly what he did earlier. But Death, unlike Michael, does not go anywhere; he cannot be driven away—a circumstance that symbolizes his character for all people.

Chap. 16 is the major hinge in the narrative. Until now, the story has been about Michael's attempt to take Abraham's soul. But Michael has failed, so God now calls another to undertake his task. Despite the disparate characters of Death and Michael, their missions are the same—to bring Abraham's life to an end. The point is underscored by manifold repetition: this chapter generates déjà vu:

Parallels with chaps. 1–2

the Master calls Michael 1:4 // 16:1–2 the Master calls Death
"Go down ... to my friend Abraham" 1:4 // 16:5 "go down to my friend Abraham"
Michael leaves the presence of God 2:1 // 16:6 Death leaves the presence of God
Michael goes to the oak of Mambre 2:1 // 16:7 Death goes to the trees of Mambre
Abraham is sitting 2:1 // 16:7 Abraham is sitting
Abraham rises and greets Michael 2:2:2–3 // 16:8 Abraham rises and greets Death
Michael's identity is hidden 1–2 // 16:4–5 Death's identity is hidden
Michael is bright as the sun 2:4 // 16:10 Death is bright as the sun
Michael greets Abraham 2:3 // 16:9 Death greets Abraham

---

[2]   Gruen, *Diaspora*, 192, rightly remarks that "the author has a congenial sense of humor."

χαίροις τιμιώτατε ... δικαία ψυχὴ φίλε ... τοῦ θεοῦ 2:3 //
16:9 χαίροις τίμη ... δικαία ψυχὴ φίλε τοῦ θεοῦ
Michael is asked where he is from 2:5 // 16:10 Death is asked where he is from
πανευπρεπέστατε ὑπὲρ πάντας τοὺς υἱοὺς τῶν ἀνθρώπων 2:4 //
16:6 εὐπρεπὴς ὡραῖος ὑπὲρ τοὺς υἱοὺς τῶν ἀνθρώπων

Other parallels

Michael stands before God 4:5; 8:1; 15:11 // 16:3 Death stands before God
"Go ... to my friend Abraham" 4:7; 8:4 // 16:5 "go down to my friend Abraham"
Michael identifies himself with ἐγώ εἰμι 7:11 //
16:11 Death identifies himself with ἐγώ εἰμι
"I will not follow you" 7:12; 15:10 // 16:16 "I will not follow you"

History replays itself for Abraham and so for readers. The intratextual repetition itself adds to the parallelism, for chapters 1–2 are themselves highly repetitious in as much as they also replay another story from Abraham's life, namely, his encounter with the three men in Genesis 18.

RecShrt. 13:1–8 seems secondary vis-à-vis RecLng. 16. As argued on p. 311, the former, by opening with "Now when the days of Abraham's death drew near," allows readers to create harmony with the chronology of Genesis, which has Abraham dying some time after Sarah's demise. RecLng., by contrast, plainly contradicts Genesis because Sarah is alive when Abraham dies. Furthermore, RecShrt. keeps its potential harmony with the Bible only at the expense of internal incoherence, for the two parts of the book (1–12 and 13–14) are no longer integrated. Michael goes to Abraham to take his soul in 1–12, but he never does so, and no explanation is given. He quits his task without a word. Then Death comes in his place in 13–14. But why Death arrives on the scene in place of Michael is never explained. By omitting Abraham's resistance to Michael, later piety has not only deprived the patriarch of his humanity but drained the text of its logic.

16:1. For "the Most High" (cf. vv. 6, 9) see on 9:1. Because Michael—who at this point ceases to be a major character—is obedient, κάλεσόν μοι is answered by καλεῖ σε in v. 2. "Death" (τὸν θάνατον), who will henceforth stick by Abraham for the rest of the book, is here personified.[3] The personification of Death—who has no authority over Abraham in later Jewish tradition[4]—is attested in the Old Testament (Ps 49:15; Isa 25:8;

---

[3] On personified "Death" see Pieter van der Horst, in *DDD*, s.v., "Thanatos," and the literature cited there; also A. P. Bender, "Beliefs, Rites, and Customs of the Jews connected with Death, Burial, and Mourning," *JQR* 6 (1894), 317–47.

[4] E.g. *b. B. Bat.* 17a. But *Gen. Rab.* 58:6 says that Abraham, upon Sarah's death, saw the Angel of Death defying him.

28:15, 18; Jer 9:21; Hos 13:14; Hab 2:15), in the Pseudepigrapha (*Ps. Sol.*
7:4; *Asc. Isa.* 9:16 [this is Christian]), in the New Testament in Revelation
(1:18; 6:8; 20:13–14; 21:4) and perhaps Paul (Rom 5:14, 17; 6:9; 1 Cor
15:26, 54–55), and in later Christian writings (e.g. *Orig. World* 106:23–
29; *Melch.* 2:5; Ps.-Bartholomew, *Book of the Resurrection of Jesus Christ*;
Timothy of Alexandria, *Discourse on Abbaton*; *History of Joseph the
Carpenter*; the Coptic *Assumption of the Virgin*).[5] In Greco-Roman mythology, death is personified as Thanatos, the brother of Sleep: Hesiod,
Theog. 211–212, 756–757; Homer, *Il.* 14.231; 16.667–675, 682; Aeschylus
fr. 141 (255); Sophocles, *Oed. col.* 1223, 1574–1577; *Aj.* 854–855; *Phil.*
797; Euripides, *Alcestis* (here Death has central role); Horace, *Carm.*
1.4.13–14; Virgil, *Aen.* 11.197; etc.[6] Pausanias, *Descr.* 3.18.1, says that
there were statues of Death and Sleep in Sparta.

Death has (κεκτημένον; cf. 14:4; 20:15) both "a shameless face"
(ἀναίσχυντον πρόσωπον) and "a merciless look," ἀνέλεον βλέμμα. His
appearance makes him resemble the two punishing angels in 12:1: ἀνηλεεῖς
τῇ γνώμῃ καὶ ἀπότομοι τῷ βλέμματι. Other parallels, all of them late,
include Ps.-John of Damascus, *De azymis* PG 95.389A (ἀναισχύντῳ
προσώπῳ); Nicephorus Confessor, *Refut.* 74.23 (ἀναιδεῖ προσώπῳ καὶ
ἀναισχύντῳ γνώμῃ); and Scholia on Demosthenes, *Or.* 19.540 (τοῦ
προσώπου τὸ ἀναίσχυντον). ἀναίσχυντος* is absent from the LXX and
New Testament but appears in Philo and Josephus as well as *T. Job* 24:7
and *Apoc. Sedr.* 9:5. ἀνέλεος* is also missing from the LXX, Philo, and
Josephus, but it appears in the New Testament in Jas 2:13. The related
ἀνίλεως (cf. Jas 2:13 v.l.) is used in *TA* 17:8 (with βλέμματι), ἀνηλεῶς in
12:1 (see above), ἀνηλεής in 12:1 and 10. To call death "merciless" was
perhaps conventional; cf. Hesiod, *Theog.* 765.

Because Death resembles the angels in 12:1, because he can look like an
archangel (v. 6), and because he dwells in heaven (see on v. 2), he is surely
some sort of angel. Hellenized Jews would certainly have been encouraged

---

5   The Egyptian origin of these narratives is consistent with a Christian provenance for
    our *Testament*; cf. James, *Testament*, 58. But the personification of death is hardly
    confined to Egyptian sources; see Winfrid Cramer, *Die Engelvorstellungen bei
    Ephräm dem Syrer* (Orientalia Christiana Analecta 173; Rome: Pontifical Institute
    of Oriental Studies, 1965), 77–79.
6   According to van der Horst, "Thanatos," 1611, "Death as an acting and speaking
    figure in *Test. Abr.* is undoubtedly due to the influence of Greek literature, especially
    the *Alcestis*." Perhaps this is so, esp. as *TA* prefers to use "Death" rather than
    "Angel of Death." The main parallel between *TA* and the *Alcestis* is lengthy
    dialogue between Death and the protagonist.

to think of Death as an angel because, in Greek art, Thanatos typically has
wings.[7] Cf. Horace, *Sat.* 2.1.58: "Death hovers round with sable wings."
Later Judaism, moreover, personified Death precisely as the Angel of
Death; see LXX Job 20:15 A (cf. 33:23);[8] Prov 16:14; *2 Bar.* 21:23; *b. Ned.*
49a; *b. 'Abod. Zar.* 5a; *b. Mo'ed Qaṭ.* 28a; *b. Ḥul.* 7b; *b. B. Qam.* 60b;
Tg. Job 18:13; Tg. Ps 89:48; 91:5; Tg. Hab 3:5; *Eccl. Rab.* 8:8; *Midr. Ps.*
9:1; etc.[9] As in *TA*, this angel acts at God's bidding: *3 En.* 48D:5 (Schäfer,
Synopse 78); *Sifre* Deut. 306 (the order to take Moses); *y. Kil.* 9:3; *b. Ber.*
62b; *b. B. Meṣi'a* 86a; *b. Ketub.* 77b; *b. B. Qam.* 60a; *b. Sukkah* 53a;
Pesiq. Rab. Kah. suppl. 1:10; etc. He is often called Sam(m)ael, which may
mean "poison of God" (סם + אל; cf. our book's "bitter cup of death" and
the tradition that the Angel of Death's sword has a drop of gall upon it
which falls into mouths and brings death; see on 1:3 and 4:11).

16:2. Michael, the incorporeal (ἀσώματος; see on 3:6), who is (in contrast
to Abraham) obedient as always, goes away and speaks to Death, who is
evidently not far away. (In *b. Ber.* 4b, the Angel of Death dwells with the
other angels, in heaven; and in *Exod. Rab.* 18:5, he stands with Michael
in the divine presence). He orders him to "come" (δεῦρο; see on 2:7), for
God "summons" (καλεῖ; cf. v. 1) him. The imperative gains force by
Michael's reference to God as both "Master" and "King." He is "the
Master of creation" (ὁ δεσπότης τῆς κτίσεως; see on 1:4) and "the immortal
King" (ὁ ἀθάνατος βασιλεύς), the latter an appellation drawn from 15:15
(q.v.). Cf. LXX *3 Macc.* 2:2 (βασιλεῦ τῶν οὐρανῶν καὶ δέσποτα πάσης
κτίσεως); *Acts John* 13 (δέσποτα πάσης κτίσεως); Athanasius, *Ep. Max.* PG
26.1088A (δεσπότης τῆς κτίσεως); Gregory of Nyssa, *Contra Eunomium*,
ed. Jaeger 1:2.123 (τοῦ δεσπότου τῆς κτίσεως); *Cant.*, ed. Langerbeck, p.
367.3 (τῷ δεσπότῃ τῆς κτίσεως); etc.

---

[7]   See the numerous illustrations in Otto Waser, "Thanatos," in *Ausführliches Lexikon
der griechischen und römischen Mythologie* 5 (1924), 481–527; also the plates in
Jean-Claude Eger, *Le Sommeil et la Mort dans la Grece Antique* (Paris: Sicard,
1966).

[8]   For the interesting argument that the picture of Death in RecShrt. may grow out of
reflection upon Job 20:15–16 and 23–25 in particular, see Schmidt, "Testament,"
1:95–96.

[9]   Biblical texts that were often understood to refer to the Angel of Death and which
accordingly contributed to his mythology include Exod 12:23 ("the destroyer"); 2
Sam 24:15–16 (a destroying angel); 2 Kgs 19:35 (the angel who kills much of the
Assyrian army); 1 Chr 21:15 (a destroying angel; the targum makes this the "Angel
of Death"). Sometimes there are several "angels of death": Job 33:22 ("those who
bring death"); MT Prov 16:14 (מלאכי־מות; cf. *Syr. Men.* 446); BHM 1:157.

16:3. Despite his power and terror, Death is, before God (4:5; 8:1; 15:11), humbled like everyone else. So in the divine presence Death quivers and trembles, ἔφριξεν καὶ ἐτρόμαξεν (τρομάζω*: cf. *Jos. Asen.* 6:1; 14:10; 23:15; 26:8); see further on 9:5 (φρίττει καὶ τρέμει). The closest verbal parallels are late: Ps.-Chrysostom, *De pseudoprophetis* PG 59.563 (φρίξατε καὶ τρομάξατε); *Etymologicum magnum*, ed. Gaisford, p. 244.19 (φρίττειν καὶ τρομαίνειν). But the content has a close parallel in *3 En.* 14:2 (Schäfer, *Synopse* 17 = 898), where Sammael (see above) fears and trembles before God, and in Ps.-Bartholomew, *Book of the Resurrection of Jesus Christ*, ed. Budge, fol. 2a, where Death is greatly afraid and trembles and shakes before the triumphant Jesus. Cf. also 4Q510 fr. 1, which prays that the ravaging angels may be frightened and terrified, and Jas 2:19, where the demons shudder (φρίσσουσιν).

Death reacts to God the way human beings react to Death: he is "afflicted with great cowardice," δειλίᾳ πολὺ συνεχόμενος (δειλία*); cf. Ps.-Chrysostom, *Hom. Ps. 75* PG 55.595: δειλίᾳ πολλῇ καὶ φόβῳ πολλῷ. So Death approaches with great fear and stands before "the invisible Father," ἐλθὼν ἔστη ἔμπροσθεν τοῦ ἀοράτου πατρός; see on 4:5 and cf. 19:1: ἐλθὼν ... ἔστη ἔμπροσθεν αὐτοῦ. On God as "invisible" (cf. v. 4) see the discussion on 9:7, which 16:3 partly duplicates. Death's fear and cowardice are outwardly expressed by "trembling and groaning and shaking" (φρίττων καὶ στένων καὶ τρέμων) as he awaits the master's command, ἀπεκδεχόμενος τὴν κέλευσιν τοῦ δεσπότου; cf. 9:5 again; also LXX Gen 4:12, 14 (στένων καὶ τρέμων); Eusebius, *Comm. Ps.* PG 23.1037D (στένειν καὶ τρέμειν); Chrysostom, *Hom. Jo.* PG 59.148 (φρίξατε, στενάξατε); Romanos the Melodist, *Cant.* 36.1.9 (φρίξῃ, στενάξῃ). The redundancy with the first part of the verse adds emphasis. The psychological effect upon readers is obvious: Death, in reality, is far less powerful than he seems. Indeed, next to God, Death is nothing. Perhaps readers will even laugh: fearful Death (cf. Heb 2:15) is himself afraid. ἀπεκδέχομαι* (LXX: 0; Philo: 0; Josephus: 0), in contrast to New Testament usage (Rom 8:19, 23, 25; 1 Cor 1:7; Phil 3:20), has purely secular sense.

16:4. "The invisible Father" (cf. v. 3 and see on 9:7) orders Death to come closer (δεῦρο), addressing him as the "bitter and savage name of the world," τὸ πικρὸν καὶ ἄγριον τοῦ κόσμου ὄνομα; cf. 17:8, 17, 18; Herm. *Mand.* 12.4.6 (πικραῖς καὶ ἀγρίαις, part of a description of "the commands of the devil"); Chrysostom, *Hom. Rom.* PG 60.660 (πικρότεροι καὶ ἀγριώτεροι); Libanius, *Ep.*, ed. Foerster, p. 386.9 (πικρά τε ἦν καὶ ἄγρια). πικρός has characterized death before (see on 1:3). ἄγριον, which often describes wild beasts in the LXX (Exod 23:11; Dan 2:38; etc.), is new, but it will henceforth be repeated over and over (17:8, 13, 14, 16; 19:12).

God asks Death to alter his appearance, which is naturally hideous. Thanatos is to hide his "savageness," ἀγριότητα; cf. above and 17:8–11, 14, 17–18; 18:1–2, 9; 2 Macc 15:21; Josephus, *Ant.* 16.363; Herm. *Mand.* 12.1.2. He must conceal all his "putrefaction," σαπρίαν; cf. 17:8–9; RecShrt. 13:14, 20; 14:1(–2). In place of these things he is to put on beauty (ὡραιότητα; cf. v. 8; 17:6, 7, 12; 18:1–2; LXX Ps 44:3; Isa 44:13; etc.) and glory (ἐνδοξότητα; cf. v. 10; LSJ, s.v., records only late uses of this word, which is most common in Justinian). V. 8 records the fulfillment of this order. The closest parallel appears to be Timothy of Alexandria, *Discourse on Abbaton*, ed. Budge, fol. 24b, where God instructs the Angel of Death concerning those written in the book of life: "You will not go to them in your terrible form but you will go to them and treat them with gentle tenderness"; also fol. 27b, where he puts on "a face like Michael's." Note also *Hist. Jos. Carp.* 13, where Joseph prays that Death may come in a pleasant and happy countenance, unaccompanied by frightful demons, and *Rev. Mos.* A 22, trans. Gaster, p. 577: Death is ugly and "full of fiery eyes," and those who looked at him fall "down in dread." Rabbinic literature does, however, attest both to the ability of Death to disguise himself (e.g., *b. Mo'ed Qaṭ.* 28a, where the Angel of Death adopts the guise of a poor man) and to the different deaths experienced by the wicked and the righteous (e.g. *Midr. Ps.* 11:6, where the Angel of Death pulls the soul of the righteous out of its body gently but, with the wicked, "it is as though he were pulling tangled rope through a narrow opening"). Given that some Jews identified Satan and Death (cf. *b. B. Bat.* 16a; Tg. Ps.-Jn. Gen 3:6; *Deut. Rab.* 11:10),[10] and that Death is here typologically related to the Satan of Job 1–2 (see pp. 128–30), it is relevant that, in some texts, Satan transforms his appearance: 2 Cor 11:14 (Satan can disguise himself as "an angel of light"; this is not an allusion to *TA*); *L.A.E.* 9:1 ("Satan transformed himself into the brightness of angels"); *T. Job* 6:4 (Satan disguises himself as a beggar); 17:2 (Satan is a king); 23:1 (he is a bread seller); Athanasius, *Vit. Ant.* 25.1; 28.9 (demons can take any shape; in 40.3 the Devil appears as a monk); Severus of Antioch, *Encom. on Michael*, ed. Budge, p. 78 (the Devil appears as a man); Eustathius of Trake, *Encom. on*

---

[10] On the identification of Death with Satan in Wisdom see Yehoshua Amir, "The Figure of Death in the 'Book of Wisdom'", *JJS* 30 (1979), 154–78. Note also that "Death and the Devil were occasionally, though inconsistently, equated in the writings of the fathers." So Jeffrey Burton Russell, *Satan: The Early Christian Tradition* (Ithaca and London: Cornell University Press, 1981), 46, n. 49. See further Ps.-Macarius, *Hom. 1–50* 11.10–11; Lampe, s.v. θάνατος, B6; and Jean Rivière, "Mort et démon chez les Pères," *RSR* 10 (1930), 577–621.

Michael, ed. Budge, pp. 101 (the Devil becomes a nun), 110 (he takes "exceedingly varied forms"), 115–21 (he disguises himself as an archangel and passes himself off as Michael), 123 (he becomes a lion).[11]

16:5. The line recalls earlier verses:

16:5   κάτελθε   πρὸς τὸν φίλον μου τὸν Ἀβραὰμ καί
1:4   κάτελθε... πρὸς τὸν φίλον μου   Ἀβραὰμ καί
4:7   ἄπελθε ... πρὸς τὸν φίλον μου τὸν Ἀβραὰμ καί
8:4   ἄπελθε   πρὸς τὸν φίλον μου τὸν Ἀβραὰμ

The parallelism is not fortuitous but thematic: Death is now taking over Michael's assignment.

Because Abraham is God's "friend" (see on 1:4), even his "true friend" (φίλος ... γνήσιος; see on 2:3), Death must be careful. He is to fawn (μετὰ κολακείας) over him and not terrify him, μὴ ἐκφοβήσῃς τὴν ψυχὴν αὐτοῦ. μετὰ κολακείας (cf. 17:7) usually means "with flattery," and it is often derogatory (cf. Cassius Dio 52.3.3); but here it must mean "fawning" in the positive sense of courting favor, as in Chrysostom, *Oppugn.* PG 47.323, where it is teamed with προσηνείας (cf. *Hom. Eph.* PG 62.148). ἐκφοβεῖν τὴν ψυχήν seems to be a patristic expression; cf. Ps.-Ephraem, *Quod non oporteat ridere et extolli*, ed. Phrantzoles, p. 205.4 (ἐκφοβοῦντες τὴν ἁμαρτωλήν μου ψυχήν); *Prec.* 10 (ἐκφοβοῦντες τῇ ταπεινῇ μου ψυχῇ); Evagrius of Pontus, *Tract. ad Eulogium* PG 79.1132C (τὴν ψυχὴν ἐκφοβούντων); Constantine VII, *Or. ad milites*, ed. Ahrweiler, line 51 (τὰς ὑμετέρας ψυχὰς ἐκφοβεῖν). With God's formal ἀλλὰ καὶ νῦν τό λέγω σοι cf. Abraham's formula in 19:5: ἀλλὰ καὶ τοῦτο λέγω σοι.

16:6. Upon receiving his orders, Death silently obeys. Without comment, he goes out "from before the Most High," ἐξῆλθεν ἀπὸ προσώπου τοῦ ὑψίστου. One is reminded not only of Michael in 2:1 but of Satan in Job; cf. esp. 1:12 v.l. (ἐξῆλθεν ... ἀπὸ προσώπου τοῦ κυρίου), which like our verse follows a divine warning about what not to do (see further on 15:14). Thanatos puts on "a brightly shining robe" (περιεβάλετο στολὴν λαμπροτάτην; contrast 17:13: περιεβάλετο στολὴν τυραννικήν); cf. *Gos. Pet.* 55 (στολὴν λαμπροτάτην, of the "young man" at Jesus' tomb); Eusebius, *Dem. ev.* 4.17 (τὴν λαμπροτάτην στολήν, the clothing of the risen Jesus); *Eccl. theol.* 3.16 (λαμπροτάταις στολαῖς, of resurrected saints); Cyril of Jerusalem, *Procatech.* 4.13 (λαμπροτάτην στολήν, of the baptismal robe); Ps.-John of Damascus, *B.J.* 32.300 (στολὴν λαμπροτάτης περιβαλὼν δόξης).

---

11   On demonic shape-shifting see A. Delatte and C. Josserand, "Contribution à l'étude de la démonologie Byzantine," *Annuaire de l'Institut de philologie et d'histoire orientales et slaves* 2 (1934), 218–19.

Thanatos makes his countenance "like the sun," ἐποίησεν ὄψιν ἡλιό-μορφον; cf. Michael's appearance in 2:4 and contrast again the antithesis with 17:13: ἐποίησεν ὄψιν ζοφεράν. His appearance is now "more beautiful than that of the sons of men," εὐπρεπὴς ὡραῖος ὑπὲρ τοὺς υἱοὺς τῶν ἀνθρώπων; cf. 2:4 (q.v., of Michael): ἡλιόρατε καὶ πανευπρεπέστατε ὑπὲρ πάντας τοὺς υἱοὺς τῶν ἀνθρώπων. All of this adds to the parallelism between Death and Michael; see above.

Putting on his robe and making his countenance sun-like means that Death has "put on the form of an archangel," ἀρχαγγέλου δὲ περικείμενος μορφήν. For περίκειμαι see also 17:12; 19:2; Ep Jer 24, 58; and cf. *Ps.-Clem. Hom.* 20:18 (ἡ περικειμένη σοι πλάνος μορφή); Basil the Great, *Adv. Eunomium 1–3* PG 29.564A (μορφὴ καὶ σχῆμα περίκειται); Didymus of Alexandria, *Fr. Ps.* 1036 (ὁ τὴν τοῦ δούλου μορφὴν περικείμενος). This makes explicit what the description implies: Death is in some sense replacing Michael. The one more detail that is added—cheeks flashing like fire (ταῖς παρειαῖς αὐτοῦ πῦρ ἀπαυγάζων [ἀπαυγάζω*]; for παρειά see on 11:6)—reinforces the point because of the earlier stress on Michael's bright-ness (2:4; 3:5, although nowhere is anything said about Michael's cheeks). V. 8 will even inform us that Abraham mistakes Death for Michael.

16:7. The "righteous" (δίκαιος; cf. vv. 9, 11, 15 and see on 1:1) Abraham goes out from his "dining room" (τρικλίνου; see on 4:1) and then sits under "the trees of Mambre," Μαβρινῶν; see on 1:2; the plural agrees with the MT—בְּאֵלֹנֵי מַמְרֵא—against the singular in 1:2 and the LXX. The book is replaying not only chap. 2 but also Genesis 18, where Abraham sits under the oak of Mamre and greets angelic visitors. Waiting for Michael, the patriarch holds his cheeks in his hands: τὴν σιαγόνα αὐτοῦ τῇ χειρὶ κατέχων (σιαγών*). Abraham is presumably downcast because, despite his resist-ance heretofore, he knows in his heart that the inevitable must be near. Cf. LXX Job 21:5, if χεῖρα θέντες ἐπὶ σιαγόνι is a call to sadness: "Look at me and marvel; put your hand upon your cheek." Abraham's posture is common in Byzantine art. Individuals who are in mourning or brooding or feeling remorse are frequently depicted with head in hand(s), often while sitting.[12] Examples include depictions of Adam and Eve after the fall, of Job on the dung heap, of the disciples in Gethsemane, of Peter after denying Jesus, of the witnesses of the crucifixion, and of the women at Jesus' tomb.[13] In all this the Byzantines were following a classical tradition, in

---

[12] See esp. Maguire, "Sorrow in Middle Byzantine Art," 132–40.

[13] See Maguire, ibid., figs. 13, 14, 17, 22, 24, 38, 39. For pagan examples see figs. 1, 2, 12, 16. Note also Hamann-Mac Lean and Hallensleben, *Monumentalmalerei*, plates 265–66.

which holding one's head could communicate deliberation or tiredness; cf. the famous statue of Hercules by Lysippus (cf. Nicetas Choniates, *De statuis ant.* PG 139.1041A–1057A) and the depiction of the aged and sad Kronos on the tomb of Cornutus in the Vatican Gardens.[14]

16:8. Death should stink (cf. 17:17; John 11:39) but here instead gives off "a pleasing odor," ὀσμὴ εὐωδίας; cf. 17:17; LXX Gen 8:21; Lev 1:13; Eph 5:2; etc. Death should also be the darkness of the tomb yet rather gives off "an effulgence of light," φωτὸς ἀπαύγασμα*; cf. Wis 7:26 (ἀπαύγασμα ... φωτός) and Basil the Great, *Ep.* 6.12 (a φωτὸς ἀπαύγασμα that is angelic; the expression is frequent in patristic writings). The disguise is complete.

Abraham turns (περιστραφείς; περιστρέφω*) and sees Death approaching "in great glory and beauty," ἐν πολλῇ δόξῃ καὶ ὡραιότητι; cf. 17:6: ἐν ... δόξῃ καὶ ὡραιότητι τοιαύτῃ. His appearance shows that he has complied with God's order in v. 4 (q.v.). It also inevitably recalls Michael's appearance; see 2:4–5; 4:3. Supposing (νομίζων; see on 3:4) Death to be Michael, the patriarch rises and greets him, ἀναστὰς ὑπήντησεν αὐτόν. Both the content and the vocabulary recall Abraham's initial encounter with Michael (2:2: ἀναστὰς ... ὑπηντήθη), which in turn is modeled upon Gen 18:2.

16:9. When Death bows before the patriarch and utters greetings, he is again replaying Abraham's initial encounter with Michael:

16:9: χαίροις τίμιε Ἀβραάμ, δικαία ψυχή, φίλε   τοῦ θεοῦ τοῦ ὑψίστου
2:3:   χαίροις τιμιώτατε πάτερ, δικαία ψυχή, φίλε γνήσιε τοῦ θεοῦ τοῦ ἐπουρανίου

See on 2:3. The parallelism is broken at the end by the addition of "companion of angels," τῶν ἀγγέλων ὁμόσκηνε (ὁμόσκηνος*); cf. Ps.-Chrysostom, *De jejunio homiliae 1–7* PG 60.713: τῶν ἀγγέλων ὁμόσκηνον. The characterization refers to Abraham's encounters in both *TA* and Genesis.[15] But one also recalls texts that associate angels with human congregations: LXX Ps 137:1; 1Q28a 2:8–9; 1QM 7:6; 1 Cor 11:10.

16:10. When Death is close enough, Abraham can see that he is not Michael. So he asks, in words that echo 2:5, "From whence has come your glory?" (πόθεν ἥκεν ἡ σὴ ἐνδοξότης), and "Who are you?" (τίς εἶ σύ;). Greetings (χαίροις) and effusive praise preface queries, as in 2:4–5, but even more so here. ἡλιόρατε comes from 2:4 (q.v.). For the content cf. the Moses traditions in which he queries the Angel of Death: Deut. Rab. 11:10; *Petirat Moshe* (*BHM* 1:127–28; 6:76); and the Falasha *Death of Moses* (trans.

---

14 For discussions with illustrations of the Greek materials see Gerhard Neumann, *Gesten und Gebärden in der griechischen Kunst* (Berlin: de Gruyter, 1965), 125–52.

15 RecShrt. 13:6 has Abraham invite Death into his house. Cf. Philo, *Abr.* 107, and see Delcor, *Testament*, 157–58.

Leslau, p. 109: "Who art thou …? What hast thou come to do?"). Both LSJ and Lampe lack entries for θεσμοσυλλήπτωρ*. Schmidt translates: "gardien des lois," and this seems the best guess (cf. H: θεσμοῦ ἀντιλήπτωρ). ἐνδοξότατε (cf. v. 10) ὑπερένδοξε (ὑπερένδοξος*), which also seems without precise parallel, means something like "most glorious above glory." Cf. the description of Michael in 4:3: "more glorious (ἐνδοξότερος) than kings and rulers." φωτοφόρος was also earlier used of the archangel; see 7:3, 5, 8. ἀνὴρ θαυμάσιε, by contrast, recalls not Michael's appearance but that of Adam and Abel; see 11:6 and 12:5, 11. That Abraham praises Death more than Michael generates comedic irony. The patriarch, now facing what he has been fleeing, greets what he does not want.

16:11. If Death's appearance may deceive, his words hide nothing. Showing due deference, he addresses Abraham as "most righteous (δικαιότατε; see on 1:1 and 15:6) father" (πάτερ; cf. v. 3 and see on 2:3). He then declares that he speaks truly (λέγω σοι τὴν ἀλήθειαν; cf. v. 13 and 18:6) and identifies himself (ἐγώ εἰμι; see on 7:11) as "the bitter cup of Death," τὸ πικρὸν τοῦ θανάτου ποτήριον; see on 1:3. When Michael first communicated to Abraham the nearness of his death, he did this indirectly, through the interpretation of a dream given to another. Death goes immediately and directly to the point.

16:12. The contradiction between Death's appearance and speech brings incredulity. Abraham sees "the comeliness of the world" (ἡ εὐπρέπεια τοῦ κόσμου; cf. v. 6) and "the glory and loveliness of the angels and of men" (ἡ δόξα καὶ τὸ κάλλος τῶν ἀγγέλων καὶ τῶν ἀνθρώπων; see on 2:5 for τὸ κάλλος); indeed, he sees "the most pleasing of all appearances," πάσης μορφῆς εὐμορφότερος; cf. the end of the verse: παντὸς ἀγαθοῦ εὐμορφότερος. For "angels and men" see 1 Cor 4:9; T. Jos. 19:8; Justin, Dial. 88.5; Tatian, Or. 7.2; Clement of Alexandria, Protr. 4.63; Strom. 4.7.51; Basil the Great, Ep. 46.2; etc.; cf. "men and angels," as in Philo, Virt. 74; 1 Cor 13:1; Justin, Dial. 141.1; etc. Abraham's praise comes in the form of three parallel statements and is bracketed by two words starting with εὐ-.

σὺ εἶ ἡ εὐπρέπεια	+ genitive (τοῦ κόσμου)
σὺ εἶ	+ genitives (τῶν ἀγγέλων καὶ τῶν ἀνθρώπων)
σὺ εἶ … εὐμορφότερος	+ genitive (παντὸς ἀγαθοῦ)

To Abraham, his visitor cannot possibly be "the bitter cup of death" (cf. v. 11 and see on 1:3). He seems rather "the fairest of all good things" (see above). As in Genesis 18, so here: the identity of the heavenly visitor(s) is concealed.

16:13. Death, again politely addressing Abraham as "father," insists (honestly) that he speaks the truth. He is repeating in part v. 11:

v. 11   πάτερ ... λέγω σοι τὴν ἀλήθειαν
v. 13   πάτερ   λέγω σοι τὴν ἀλήθειαν

He goes on to add that, in calling himself "the bitter cup of death" (v. 11), he has simply reported what God has named him (ὅπερ ὠνόμασεν; ὀνομάζω*).

16:14. Accepting Death's words, Abraham now asks, "Why have you come here?" The question is no longer whence (cf. 2:5) but why (cf. 7:10). At this point, however, readers more than suspect that Abraham knows full well what is going on. His question amounts to stalling.

16:15. Death again speaks honestly and straightforwardly. He has come "because of" (διά; cf. 18:4 and see BDAG, s.v., 5) Abraham's soul, that is, because it is time to take his soul to the other world.

16:16. Abraham fully understands, οἶδα τί λέγεις; cf. Matt 26:70. Still, he tells Death what he told Michael: οὐ μή σε ἀκολουθήσω; see on 7:12 and cf. 15:10. Death says nothing, ἐσιώπα καὶ οὐκ ἀπεκρίθη; cf. Mark 14:61: ἐσιώπα καὶ οὐκ ἀπεκρίνατο. We do not here learn whether Death does nothing because he is, as was Michael, confused, or because he is simply being patient in the knowledge that Abraham cannot hold out much longer. In either case, he does not, unlike Michael, return to heaven.

Chapter 17: Death reveals Himself

Bibliography: James, *Testament*, 55–58. Schmidt, "Testament," 1:93–114. Turner, "Testament," 132–36.

Long Recension

17:1. Abraham arose and went into his house, and Death followed him there. Abraham went up to his dining room. Death also went up. Abraham rested upon his couch. Then Death also came, and he stood at his feet. 17:2. Then Abraham said, "Go away from me, because I want to rest in my bed." 17:3. But Death said, "I will not go away until I take your spirit from you." 17:4. Abraham said to him, "By the immortal God I say to you, speak to me the truth. Are you Death?" 17:5. Death said to him, "I am the one who destroys the world." 17:6. Abraham said, "I beg you, since you are Death, tell me this, do you come like this to all, in pleasing form and in glory and with such beauty?" 17:7. Death said, "No my lord, for your righteous deeds and your boundless hospitality and the magnitude of your love for God have become a crown on my head; and in beauty and in great tranquility and with fawning I come to the righteous. 17:8. But to sinners I come in this way: in much putrefaction and savageness and with great bitterness and with savage countenance. And I come without mercy to sinners, to those who themselves did not show mercy." 17:9. But Abraham said, "I beg you, listen to me and show me your savageness and

Short Recension fam. E

13:9. And Death said to Abraham, "I say to you, in all the creation that God created, no one like you has been found. 13:10. For he [God] searched among the angels and archangels, among rulers and authorities, among thrones and in all the earth, including four-footed animals and wild beasts of the earth and all that is in the water, even unto the heaven, and none like you has been found." 13:11. And Abraham said to Death, "You dare to lie, for I see your beauty, that it is not of this world." 13:12. And Death said to Abraham, "You think that this is my beauty? And that with everyone I make myself this beautiful?" 13:13. And Abraham said, "Whose beauty then is this?" 13:14. Death said to Abraham, "No one is more putrid than me." Abraham said to him, "Reveal to me who you are." 13:15. Death said, "I am the bitter name. I am weeping. I am the fall of all." 13:16. Abraham said to him, "And who are you?" And Death said, "I am Death, the one who carries away the soul from the body." 13:17. And Abraham said to him, "Are you Death? Are you able to impel all to be brought forth from the body?" 13:18. Death said to Abraham, "Do you think that this beauty is mine? Or that I do this with all your putrefaction." 17:10. Death said, "You are unable to behold my savageness, most righteous one." 17:11. Abraham said, "Indeed will I be able to behold all of your savageness on account of the name of the living God, because the power of my heavenly God is with me." 17:12. Then Death put off all his beauty and loveliness and all his glory and his sun-like form that he had worn. 17:13. And he put on a robe of tyranny, and he made his face gloomy, more fierce than all wild beasts and more unclean than all uncleanness. 17:14. And he showed to Abraham seven fiery dragons' heads and fourteen faces—the face of a blazing fire and great fierceness, and the face of a horrible precipice, and the face of a murky darkness, and the face of a most gloomy viper, and a face more fierce than an asp, and the face of a fearful lion, and the face of a horned serpent and basilisk. 17:15. He showed him also the face of a fiery sword, and a sword-bearing face, and a face of lightning flashing fearfully, and the sound of a fearful thunder. 17:16. He showed also another face, that of a fierce, storm-tossed sea, and of a savage, boiling river, and of a fearful three-headed dragon, and cups filled with poisons. 17:17. And, to put it briefly, he showed him great savageness and intolerable bitterness and every fatal disease that brings death untimely. 17:18. So then from the stench of Death and the great bitterness and savagery seven thousand male and female servants died. 17:19. And the righteous Abraham came to the faintness of death, so that his breath failed.

all? No. 13:19. But if anyone is righteous, they [the angels?] take all his righteousness and it becomes a crown on my head, and I go to him in persuasiveness and in his own righteousness. 13:20. But if anyone is a sinner, I go to him in great putrefaction, but also they [the angels?] make all his sins into a crown on my head, and in great fear I disturb him greatly." 14:1. And Abraham said to him, "Show to me also your putrefaction." 14:2. And Death removed righteousness from himself, and he revealed to him putrefaction. This is how he revealed himself: he had two heads. 14:3. Some of his heads had the faces of dragons. Because of this some die from asps. 14:4. But other heads are like swords. Because of this some die by the sword as (well as) by the bow. 14:5. In that hour seven servants of Abraham died because of the fear of Death.

TEXTUAL NOTES ON THE LONG RECENSION

17:1. J drops "into his house ... rested." The result is: "Abraham arose and went onto his couch." // B H I Q omit: "into his house ... went up." This may be due to *homoioteleuton* (εἰς ... εἰς) or deliberate abbreviation (cf. J). // G drops "followed ... went up," which results in: "Abraham arose and went into his house. So too Death." // B I Q strike "Abraham rested ... also came." 17:2. A: "Go away, go away from me." // 17:4. G omits all but "Abraham said to him." // J drops the superfluous "speak to me the truth." // A has "us" instead of "me." 17:5. G drops "Death said to him." // 17:6. G omits "Abraham ... Death.'" // 17:7. J again abbreviates by dropping "and the magnitude ... God." This leaves: "your boundless hospitality for God," which must refer to Genesis 18, perhaps understood as Abraham serving the Trinity. // H drops "magnitude ... God." // J drops "on my head ... the righteous." // Maybe through *homoioteleuton* (καί ... καί) I omits "and in beauty." 17:8. J lacks "in much putrefaction and." // B H Q drop "and savageness," and H also omits "with great bitterness." // J shortens by omitting all from "and with great bitterness" to the end. // B G cancel "And I come ... show mercy." 17:9. H omits "I beg ... me and." // J drops "and all your putrefaction." 17:10–11. H. omits "most righteous one" and the first part of v. 11 ("Abraham ... savageness"); an eye passed from one ἀγριότητα to another. 17:11. B Q lack "Abraham said ... your savageness." // J reduces the whole sentence to: "He said, 'My God is with us.'" // G abbreviates by dropping "to behold ... savageness." 17:12. J omits "put off ... loveliness" as well as "and the sun-like form which" and changes the final verb to ἀπεβάλλετο. This leaves: "Then Death put off all his glory." // G deliberately shortens also; it drops "all his beauty and loveliness and." 17:13. J omits "and more unclean ... uncleanness." // A: καθαρσιωτέρα. B G H I Q omit. James plausibly conjectured an original ἀκαθαρσιωτέραν, which is what Schmidt prints. 17:14. A lacks "and the face ... precipice." // H lacks "and the face of a horrible ... gloomy viper" (*homoioteleuton*: καὶ πρόσωπον ... καὶ πρόσωπον). // Q omits "the face of a murky darkness," again through *homoioteleuton* (καὶ πρόσωπον ... καὶ πρόσωπον). // G's omission of "the face of a horrible precipice ... darkness" and of "the face of a gloomy viper ... basilisk" and of the first part of v. 15 ("He showed him also the face of a fiery sword") has the same explanation (καὶ πρόσωπον ... καὶ πρόσωπον). // A B I omit "and the face more fierce than an asp," again making the same mistake (καὶ πρόσωπον ... καὶ πρόσωπον). 17:15. H also omits "the face of a fiery sword," yet again probably through *homoioteleuton* (καὶ πρόσωπον ... καὶ πρόσωπον). // B J Q omit "and a face of lightning ... thunder." 17:17. J drops "And, to put it briefly." 17:17–

18. J shortens again by dropping "and every ... savagely." // H drops "brings death untimely" and the first part of v. 18, "So then from the stench of Death." 17:18. A opens with ὡς. G: ὥστε οὖν. I: ὥστε οὕτως οὖν ἐκ. Q: ὥσπερ ἐκ. The original can only be guessed. I have translated ὥστε οὖν ἐκ. // J omits "male and female servants" but adds "his wife and his son." This explains the omission of Isaac and Sarah from chap. 20 in ms. J. // A has simply ἑπτά. J prefaces this with χιλιάδες, B H I Q with different clauses that conclude with χιλιάδε(α)ς. The long Romanian, ed. Roddy, p. 47, has 7,000, and the fantastic number suits the fairy tale atmosphere of the original. A's more realistic "seven," which appears in RecShrt. but is less than the "twelve" in 2:1, may be a later rationalization.[1] Genesis leaves the impression that Abraham had many servants (see on 2:1), and Philo, *Quaest. Gen.* 4.10, says he had a multitude. 17:19–18:1. J drops "so that ... failed" and the first three words of 18:1 (καὶ ταῦτα οὕτως). Is this again deliberate abbreviation? // Q omits "his breath failed" and, like J, the first three words from 18:1.

COMMENTARY

Chap. 17 falls into two parts, the first being a dialogue between Abraham and Death, the second being a detailed account of Death's self-revelation to the patriarch:

I. Dialogue between Abraham and Death, 1–11
    A. Narrative introduction, 1
    B. Conversation, 2–11
        i.   Abraham asks Death to leave, 2   question
        ii.   Death refuses to leave, 3
        iii. Abraham asks Death if he is indeed Death, 4   question
        iv.   Death affirms his own identity, 5
        v.   Abraham asks Death if he is always beautiful, 6   question
        vi.   Death indicates his dual nature, 7–8
        vii. Abraham asks to see Death's putrefaction and savageness, 9   question
        viii. Death says Abraham is unable to do this, 10
        ix.   Abraham responds that God's name will protect him, 11

---

[1] The Coptic counts 18; but here there are also servants (unnumbered) who fall on their faces and so survive.

II. The self-revelation of Death, 12–19
   A. Death's appearance, 12–17
      i. Death puts off his beauty, 12
      ii. Death puts on his true form, 13–17
         a. Summary description, 13
         b. The seven heads and fourteen faces, 14–16
         c. Summary description, 17
   B. The results, 18–19
      i. 7,000 servants die, 18
      ii. Abraham almost dies, 19

Beginning with 17:18–19, "the tone of the story changes. Abraham, once active and strong, is now increasingly succumbing to the listlessness of death. Although no clear explanation is given at first for the change that has come over him, he apparently has come to witness more than he can bear."[2]

Like the heavenly tour in earlier chapters, *TA* 17 and its interpretation in chap. 19 are strongly reminiscent of Jewish apocalyptic literature. The dialogue between the recipient of a vision and its mediator, the symbolic nature of that vision, the presence of fantastic beasts and mythical imagery, the subsequent interpretation of those beasts and imagery by the mediator, and the reference to the several ages of world history recall *1 Enoch*, *4 Ezra*, *2 Baruch*, and other instances of the genre, apocalypse.

Apart from Abraham's declaration that God's name will protect him (v. 11), nothing in this chapter is comforting. It seems rather designed, from beginning to end, to create fear and revulsion. The words and roots that are repeated confirm this: ἄγριος: 8, 13, 14, 16, 16; ἀγριότης: 8, 9, 10, 11, 14, 17, 18 // φοβερός: 14, 15, 16; φοβερῶς: 15 // πύρινος: 14, 15; πῦρ: 14; πικρία: 8, 17, 18 // σαπρία: 8, 9. The repetition of πολύς (vv. 7, 8, 14, 17, 18) and πᾶς (vv. 9, 11, 12, 12, 13, 13, 17) magnifies the effect.

RecShrt.—whose fams. E and B F G largely agree here—differs from RecLng. in several respects. (i) It is shorter, mostly because (ii) RecLng. describes seven heads and fourteen faces at length whereas RecShrt. refers to only two heads. (iii) Death recounts Abraham's incomparable nature in RecShrt. 13:9–10, which has no counterpart in RecLng. (iv) RecLng. saves the interpretation of the heads and faces for a separate section. The interpretations in RecShrt. are, by contrast, given by the narrator along with the initial descriptions. (v) 7,000 servants die in RecLng., only seven in RecShrt.

---

2   Wills, *Novel*, 252.

The hypothesis that RecShrt. grew out of a longer recension resembling RecLng. and that it reflects a desire to abbreviate, readily accounts for differences (i), (ii), and (iv); and two more facts accord with RecShrt. being derivative. First, fam. E says that Death has two heads and then refers to "some" (τινές) heads and then to still "other" (ἄλλαι) heads.[3] Clearly this text, despite its explicit statement, εἶχεν δύο κεφαλάς, presupposes more. Fam. B F G contains a similar inconcinnity. After speaking of "three dragon faces," it refers to only two: "He had three dragon faces, and because of the face [πρόσωπον, singular], some die suddenly from asps. The other form [ἡ δὲ ἑτέρα μορφή] was like a sword ... ." One suspects that something structurally close to the Bohairic lies beneath these two problematic texts: "He had a multitude of heads, some with serpent faces, others casting forth fire ... ."[4] This in turn could easily be a summary of what we find in RecLng.

A second puzzling aspect of RecShrt. encourages one to deem it secondary. In both families, the two symbolic heads or faces represent two ways of dying—from asps and by sword. But given the many different ways people die, readers must wonder why asps and swords alone merit mention. If Death is revealing himself, one expects a much more comprehensive vision. RecLng. supplies one. So again one thinks of RecShrt. as representing an infelicitous abbreviation.[5] One sympathizes with James, who remarked that the description of Death in RecShrt. "is so disproportionately short and so jejune as at once to convey a strong suspicion that something is wanting."[6]

17:1. Abraham will not follow Death (16:16), so Death will follow him. The verse, with its close parallel in 19:1, contains six short sentences with much parallelism. The first, third, and fifth lines have Abraham as their subject. The matching second, fourth, and sixth lines have Death as their subject. Each of the three pairs tells us first what Abraham does and then how Death responds:

Abraham arose (ἀνέστη δὲ Αβραάμ) and went into his (αὐτοῦ) house
   And Death (καὶ ὁ θάνατος) followed him there

Abraham went up (ἀνέβη δὲ Ἀβραάμ) to his (αὐτοῦ) dining room (see on 4:1)
   Death also (καὶ ὁ θάνατος) went up

---

[3] RecShrt. A corrects by substituting μία for τινές and ἡ ἑτέρα for ἄλλαι and adjusting accordingly.
[4] Translation of MacRae, "Coptic Testament," 338, 340 (who emends ⲚⲈⲂⲞⲨϨⲒ to ⲚⲈϨⲂⲞⲨⲒ).
[5] Although the Coptic is usually reckoned a relative of RecShrt., the unpublished Sahidic fragments reportedly refer to faces of a panther and basilisk.
[6] James, *Testament*, 48.

Abraham rested (ἀνέπεσεν δὲ Ἀβραάμ; see on 5:4) on his (αὐτοῦ) couch (see on v. 2)
    Then Death also (καὶ ὁ θάνατος) came, and he stood at his feet

The repetition conveys Death's persistence; he is a stalker Abraham cannot get rid of.

The sequence replays Abraham's experience with Michael:

3:1: Abraham and Michael go away from the field to the house
4:4: Abraham and Michael go into the dining chamber and sit on the couches
5:2: Abraham and Michael recline upon couches.

In chap. 17, however, no invitation is issued and no arrangements are made; nor does anyone in Abraham's household greet Death or serve him. This is an unwelcome guest, an intruder. Perhaps ἀνέστη δὲ Αβραάμ is a biblical echo, for Abraham is several times the subject of ἀνίστημι in the LXX: Gen 13:17; 21:14 (ἀνέστη δὲ Αβραάμ); 22:3, 19; 23:3, 7. The repeated αὐτοῦ stresses that Abraham's property means nothing when it comes to death. The patriarch may be in his house, in his own chamber, and on his couch, but none of this matters: Thanatos goes where he wills.

17:2–3. Although Abraham is the embodiment of hospitality, welcoming rich and poor, kings and rulers, the crippled and the helpless, friends and strangers, neighbors and travelers (1:2), he is positively rude to Death. The patriarch tells him to go away, ἄπελθε ἀπ' ἐμοῦ; cf. 19:2; 20:11; LXX Exod 10:28; 2 Chr 16:3. His excuse is that he wants to rest in his bed, ἀναπαύεσθαι ἐν τῇ κλίνῃ μου; cf. v. 1 and see on 5:2. Readers may infer that the patriarch is tired after his tour of the world, which would accord both with his old age (1:1) and with his posture in 16:7. Death in any case will not be moved (cf. 19:3). Implicitly distinguishing himself from Michael, he bluntly avows that he will not go away (ἀναχωρῶ; so too 19:3) and come back later; he will stay until he has taken (λάβω) Abraham's "spirit" (πνεῦμα) from him. Cf. the use of λαμβάνω + ψυχήν in 7:8, 10, 12; also John 20:22. Here πνεῦμα = ψυχή and so is the immaterial, real self, as also in 18:8; cf. the parallelism between 17:3 and 19:3 and see further Matt 27:50; Luke 23:46; Acts 7:59; Gk. L.A.E. 32:4.

17:4. In 16:15, Abraham accepted Death's testimony about himself. Here, however, the patriarch feigns ignorance of his intruder's identity; it is as if the former conversation never happened—even though εἰπὲ ἡμῖν τὸ ἀληθές echoes what Death said earlier: 16:11 (λέγω σοι τὴν ἀλήθειαν); 16:13 (λέγω σοι τὴν ἀλήθειαν). So Abraham invites Death to take an oath: "By the immortal God I say to you, speak to me the truth. Are you Death?" For κατά in oath formulas see Thucydides 5.47.8; BGU 248.13; LXX 2 Chr 36:13 (κατὰ τοῦ θεοῦ); Isa 45:23; Jdt 1:12; Mt 26:63 (κατὰ τοῦ θεοῦ τοῦ ζῶντος); Heb 6:13, 16; Herm. Sim. 9.10.5; Herm. Vis. 3.2.3; 4 Bar. 8:10;

Justin, *Dial.* 85.3; Eusebius, *Dem. ev.* 7.3.13; *PGM* 4.3019 (κατὰ τοῦ θεοῦ τῶν Ἑβραίων), 3039; etc. Again Abraham appears to be stalling. For "the immortal God" (τοῦ θεοῦ τοῦ ἀθανάτου) see *Sib. Or.* 1:53, 56; 2:214, 260; 12.232; *Apoc. Sedr.* 5:6; Didymus of Alexandria, *Trin.* PG 39.788A, 888A, 905A; Johnson, *Anatolia* 3.18; 4.16; etc.; also the standard ἀθάνατοι θεοί of the Greeks: Homer, *Il.* 3.298; 15.44; *Od.* 9.107; 14.119; etc.

17:5. Death continues to speak with brutal honesty: "I am the one who destroys (λυμαίνων) the world." Cf. 19:7 (λυμαίνω τὸν κόσμον) and Ps.-Bartholomew, *Book of the Resurrection of Jesus Christ*, ed. Budge, fol. 2a (Death: "I who am wont to destroy everyone"). Death's self-identification (with ἐγώ εἰμι; see on 7:11), which replaces his earlier description of himself as the "bitter cup of death" (16:11, 12), could come from Zoroastrian mythology. For the parallel in *Arda Viraz Namag* 100:1 see on v. 8. But Jewish tradition does know of an envoy, angel, or satan who brings death and is called משחית; see e.g. Exod 12:23; 2 Sam 24:16; 1 Chr 21:12–15; Wis 18:25; 1 Cor 10:10; Rev 9:11; *b. Ber.* 16b; Tgs. Neof. 1 and Ps.-Jn. on Exod 4:24; and *Deut. Rab.* 3:11.[7] For demons as "destructive" (λυμαντικός) and the Devil as "destroyer" (λυμεών) in patristic texts see Lampe, s.v. The LXX, like early Greek literature, knows λυμαίνω only as a middle deponent, as in Jer 28:2: λυμανοῦνται τὴν γῆν; cf. Herm. *Vis.* 4.1.8; 4.2.4; *PGM* 13.302.

17:6. Whether it is simply because he wants more time or also because he is genuinely curious, Abraham—now conceding his interlocutor's identity (ἐπειδὴ σὺ εἶ ὁ θάνατος)—implores (δέομαί σου; cf. v. 8 and see on 9:3) Death to tell him (ἀνάγγειλόν μοι; see on 5:12) whether he comes to everyone in such "pleasing form" (ἐν εὐμορφίᾳ; cf. *Acts John* 35; Epiphanius, *Pan.* 25.2; and εὐμορφία in 16:12), with "glory" (δόξῃ) and with "such beauty" (ὡραιότητι τοιαύτῃ; cf. vv. 7, 12). The threefold description recalls the depiction of Death in 16:8 (δόξῃ καὶ ὡραιότητι) and Abraham's words in 16:12 (δόξα ... εὐμορφότερος): the patriarch is repeating himself. His query expresses dissonance between expectation and experience. While Abraham has heretofore believed Death to be horrible, Death has turned out to be beautiful. Yet the following explanation clarifies that, while Death may come to all, he does not come to all in the same way.

17:7. Death does not brush aside Abraham's question but, as before, answers truthfully, and with due deference, addressing him as κύριέ μου (see on 2:10). He responds that Abraham's "righteous deeds" (δικαιοσύναι; see

---

[7]   See further S. A. Meier, "Destroyer," in *DDD*, 456–64.

on 1:1) and his "boundless (ἄμετρον; cf. 15:1 v.l.) hospitality" (φιλοξενίας; see on 1:1) as well as the "magnitude" (μέγεθος*) of his "love (ἀγάπης) for God" are a crown (στέφανος*) on Death's own head. μέγεθος + ἀγάπης is a patristic expression: Ps.-Athanasius, *Sermo in ramos palmarum* 4.1; Didymus of Alexandria, *Comm. Ps. 29–34*, ed. Gronewald, p. 205.13; Chrysostom, *Hom. Eph.* PG 62.51; Oecumenius, *Comm. Apoc.*, ed. Hoskier, p. 66.16. But all these texts refer to God's or Christ's love, not human love for God (for this see on 3:3).

The athletic image of a victor's crown often betokens eschatological triumph in Jewish and Christian texts; see, e.g., Wis 5:15–16; 1QH 17(9):25; 1QS 4:7–8; 1 Cor 9:25; 2 Tim 4:8; Rev 2:10; 3:11; *T. Benj.* 4:1; *T. Job* 4:9–10; *2 Bar.* 15:8; *4 Ezra* 2:46; *Apoc. El. (C)* 1:8; *Asc. Isa.* 7:22; *Mart. Pol.* 17:1; *Gk. Apoc. Ezra* 6:17; *Vis. Paul* 12 v.l.; *b. Ber.* 17a; *b. Šabb.* 104a. Post-mortem crowns are also attested in the Graeco-Roman world, perhaps in part because of the secular practice of awarding crowns posthumously and because graves were sometimes decorated with wreaths, which accordingly became signs of immortality. Note Plato, *Resp.* 363C–D (the righteous in the house of Hades recline on couches and are crowned in wreaths), and Apuleius, *Metam.* 11.24 ("a beautiful garland was wound around my head, with bright palm leaves shooting out like rays of light"). It is unclear if the crown in *TA* is literal. Is στέφανος rather maybe a metaphor, as so often in the wisdom tradition—Prov 4:19; 14:24; Ecclus 1:18; 6:31; 15:6; etc.; cf. *CPJ* 3.1530a.6: "crowned in his wisdom."[8] Or do the dying righteous have a vision of a crowned Thanatos approaching? Whatever the answer, angels do often wear crowns: *Jos. Asen.* 14:9 (of Michael); Rev 14:14 (Jesus in angelic form); *2 En.* 14:2 A; *3 Bar.* 6:2; *Apoc. Zeph.* fr. in Clement of Alexandria, *Strom.* 5.11.77; *3 En.* 12:4; 16:2; 17:8; 18:23, 25; 21:4 (Schäfer, *Synopse* 15 = 896, 20 = 856, 22 = 58, 28–29 = 864–65, 32 = 868).[9] Further, divinities in the Graeco-Roman world also regularly appear with crowns; see Ep Jer 8 ("People take gold and make crowns for the heads of their gods"); Philo, *Legat.* 103; Arrian, *Epict. diss.* 4.8.30; Tertullian, *Cor.* 7 (PL 2.85A–86A: a list of examples).

In addition to the Zoroastrian parallel noted in the commentary on v. 8, there is also an interesting Jewish parallel. A number of rabbinic texts teach

---

[8] Graeco-Roman literature also can use "crown" metaphorically: Euripides, *Iph. Aul.* 194 ("Salamis's crown" = "Salamis's pride"); Aristophanes, *Nub.* 959 ("to crown" = "to adorn"); Ps.-Heraclitus, *Ep.* 4 (Heraclitus crowned himself through his virtuous behavior); *Tab. Cebetis* 22:1 ("Happiness crowns him with her power," cf. 23:3; 24:2); etc.

[9] See further Green, *Keter*, 58–68.

that the prayers of Israel ascend to heaven, where they are woven into crowns for God and/or Israel; see e.g. *Lev. Rab.* 24:8: "Each day the exalted ones [angels] wreath the blessed Holy One with three 'holies,' as it says, 'Holy, holy, holy.' What does the Holy One do? He places one upon His head and two upon the heads of Israel ... ." This and related texts[10] display "a certain supraliteralism regarding prayer's 'ascent,' as though the words themselves actually penetrated the utter gates and entered the heavens, passing into the hands of the proper angel. If they are then 'woven' or 'tied' into wreaths or crowns, the words would seem to be depicted as quasi-material 'objects' that could be linked in such a manner."[11] Obviously this turning of the prayers of the righteous into crowns in heaven is not far from turning the deeds of the righteous into crowns in heaven.

17:7 has a thematic parallel in Jas 1:12, which promises "the crown of life" for those who love God. Because the next verse resembles Jas 2:13 (see below), one wonders whether James has influenced our book. In any event, the most striking feature of 17:7 does not appear in the New Testament text. In *TA* it is not the one who loves God who wears a crown. The crown woven by Abraham's deeds is instead worn by another (see further on v. 8).

When Death approaches the righteous, he comes "in beauty and in great tranquility and with fawning." Cf. Timothy of Alexandria, *Discourse on Abbaton*, ed. Budge, fol. 24b, where Abbaton, who frightens the wicked to death, goes to the righteous "with gentle tenderness" (cf. fols. 23a, 27a–b). ἐν ὡραιότητι (cf. vv. 6, 17) and κολακεία hark back to God's directions to Death in 16:4 (cf. v. 8; 17:6) and 5 (q.v.). But ἐν ἡσυχίᾳ (cf. Philo, *Somn.* 2.263; 1 Tim 2:11–12; *T. Ash.* 7:3) takes us back to the prologue, to 1:1 (q.v.), where ἡσυχία is one of Abraham's virtues. Hence just as Death wears a crown that Abraham has woven with his deeds, so Death's tranquil demeanor reflects Abraham's tranquil character.

17:8. This verse, the obverse of Matt 5:7 ("Blessed are the merciful, for they shall obtain mercy") binds itself to v. 7 by opening with an antithetical chiasmus:

$$
\begin{array}{ll}
\text{v. 7} & \text{v. 8} \\
\text{ἐν ἡσυχίᾳ πολλῇ καὶ κολακείᾳ} & \text{τοῖς δὲ ἁμαρτωλοῖς} \\
\text{ἀπέρχομαι} & \text{ἀπέρχομαι} \\
\text{τοῖς δικαίοις} & \text{ἐν πολλῇ σαπρίᾳ καὶ ἀγριότητι}
\end{array}
$$

Death's appearance and character mirror the deeds of those he comes to (v. 7). So he comes without mercy (ἀνίλεως*; see on 16:1) to sinners

---

[10] E.g. *Exod. Rab.* 21:4; *Midr. Ps.* 19:7; 88:2.

[11] So Green, *Keter*, 41. Pp. 31–41 discuss in detail this tradition.

(ἁμαρτωλοῖς; see on 9:3), to those who have not themselves shown mercy, πράξασιν ἔλεον; cf. MT Gen 24:49 (חסד עשים; Athanasius, *Exp. Ps.* PG 27.80.26 (ἔπραξαν τὸν ἔλεον). The formulation might be inspired by Jas 2:13, especially given the rarity of ἀνίλεως:

| 17:8 | ἀνίλεως ἀπέρχομαι τοῖς ἁμαρτωλοῖς τοῖς μὴ πράξασιν ἔλεον |
| Jas 2:13 | κρίσις ἀνέλεος | τῷ μὴ ποιήσαντι ἔλεος |

Ps.-Ephraem, *Prec. e sacris scripturis*, ed. Phrantzoles, p. 346.17, paraphrases Jas 2:1 in a form closer to *TA* 17:8 than to Jas 2:1: ἡ γὰρ κρίσις ἀνίλεως ἔσται ἐκεῖ τοῖς μὴ πράξασιν ὧδε τὸν ἔλεον.

When Death appears to sinners there is "much putrefaction and savageness" (πολλῇ σαπρίᾳ καὶ ἀγριότητι; see on 16:4) as well as "great bitterness" (μεγίστη πικρίᾳ; see on 16:4) and a "savage countenance," ἀγρίῳ τῷ βλέμματι; see on 16:1. The series, like its antithesis in v. 7, harks back to 16:4:

| 17:8 | σαπρίᾳ ... ἀγριότητι ... πικρίᾳ ... ἀγρίῳ |
| 16:4 | πικρόν ... ἄγροιν ... ἀγριότητα ... σαπρίαν ... πικρίας |

Jewish literature has no close parallel to the notion that Death appears differently to saints and sinners, although in *Midr. Ps.* 11:6 the Angel of Death behaves gently to the former, forcefully to the latter (see on 16:4). Iranian literature does, however, offer parallels.[12] According to *Menog i Khrad* 2:125–26, when the righteous die, their good deeds meet them in the form of a beautiful young woman (so also *Hadhokht Nask* 2:25; cf. *Vendidad* 19:30). When the wicked die, however, they are confronted by a hideous figure: "I am no girl, but I am your own acts, O hateful one of bad thought, bad word, bad act, bad inner self" (*Menog i Khrad* 2:170–271).[13] That this is in fact part of the background to this section of *TA* gains support from four observations. (i) Zoroastrian texts indicate that the righteous soul, upon death, smells a pleasant odor, "more fragrant than any other wind" (*Hadhokht Nask* 2:220–221), and this is close to *TA* 16:8, where "a pleasing odor" is a harbinger of Death.[14] (ii) If Death in *TA* appears to Abraham as "more beautiful than the sons of men" (16:6), the

12 Cf. Schmidt, "Testament" (1992), 1684.
13 Cf. Ephraem, *Ep. Publium*, ed. Brock, p. 277: "Look at their evil thoughts, which have now [at the eschatological assize] taken on bodily form, and stand there in front of their masters accusing them."
14 On the evil smell in Zoroastrian texts see on v. 18. It is interesting that the reference to good and bad odors in Gregory the Great, *Dial.* 4.37 (cf. 4.15–17) occurs in a context clearly influenced by Zoroastrian eschatology (e.g. the walking over a bridge that spans the abyss).

Chapter 17

young girl in *Menog i Khrad* is more beautiful than any other on earth (2:125–126; cf. *Hadhokht Nask* 2:24). (iii) The righteous deeds of Abraham become, in *TA* 17:7, a crown worn by another, which he beholds. Similarly, in *Hadhokht Nask* 2 and *Menog i Khrad* 2, good deeds also somehow take a physical form and then appear before the righteous.[15] (iv) Death declares, in *TA* 17:5, "I am the destroyer of the world." With this one may compare *Arda Viraz Namag* 100:1, where the seer, on a tour of hell, says, "Then I saw the Evil Spirit, death-dealing, destroyer of the world."

17:9. Abraham implores Death (δέομαί σου; cf. v. 6 and see on 9:3) to heed him, ἐπάκουσόν μου; cf. *PGM* 4.1948–1949: δέομαι, δέσποτα Ἥλιε, ἐπάκουσόν μου. He wants to see Death without his disguise, to see his savageness and putrefaction, ἀγριότητα ... καὶ σαπρίαν; see on 16:4. Abraham does not explain his curiosity, but the conversation and anything he can get Death to do will delay the end.

17:10. Death declares that Abraham, the δικαιότατε (see on 1:1 and 15:6), is unable to see his ἀγριότητα; see on 16:4. Cf. Timothy of Alexandria, *Discourse on Abbaton*, ed. Budge, fol. 23a: when people see the face of Abbaton = Death, "their souls will be unable to abide in them, even for a moment." Death seemingly hesitates to disobey the divine order to hide his ugliness from Abraham (16:4–5). V. 8 mentions Death's putrefaction, savageness, and bitterness, v. 9 his savageness and putrefaction, v. 10 only his savageness (so too v. 11). The focus upon ferocity anticipates the revelation of vv. 12ff., which is full of faces that terrify.

17:11. Abraham contradicts Death:

Death, v. 10	οὐ μὴ δυνηθῇς θεάσασθαι		τὴν ἐμὴν ἀγριότητα
Abraham, v. 11	ναί, δυνήσομαι θεάσασθαί σου πᾶσαν τὴν		ἀγριότητα

Abraham is confident because he will be protected by "the name of the living God," τοῦ ὀνόματος τοῦ θεοῦ τοῦ ζῶντος; cf. 14:9: (τὸ ὄνομα τοῦ θεοῦ τοῦ ὑψίστου) and Moses' ability to withstand Death by using God's name; see p. 25. The boast is at home in the world of ancient magic, where amulets, Aramaic incantation bowls, and other magical texts, both Jewish and Christian, attribute prophylactic properties to the sacred name, יהוה, and its derivatives יה, יהו, etc. While God's name usually binds demons and removes illnesses and others misfortunes, here it protects against Death. "The living God" (= אֱלֹהִים חיים) is common in the Bible and biblically-

---

[15] Cf. also *Vis. Paul* 14–15, where the deeds of the good and wicked stand before them after death.

inspired literature: Deut 5:26; Josh 3:10; Ps 42:3; Isa 37:4; Philo, *Decal.* 67; *T. Job* 37:2; *Jos. Asen.* 11:10; Matt 16:16; 26:63; Acts 14:15; Rom 9:26; Heb 3:12; Rev 7:2; *P. Oxy.* 924.11; *PGM* 12.79; *t. Ber.* 7:13; *Tanḥ. B Wa'era* 2; etc.[16] "The name of the living God" sounds like an oath formula, so one might compare Matt 26:63 ("I adjure you by the living God")[17] and *T. Sol.* 1:13 ("As the Lord God of Israel lives," cf. 5:12). But the closest parallels appear in Jewish magical texts. An amulet in Aramaic in the New York Public Library contains the phrase, "By the name of the living God" (בְּשָׁמָה דְאֱלָהָא חַיָּה, and a Syriac magic bowl at the Smithsonian similarly has, "By your name, living God" (בְּשָׁמָךְ אֱלָהָא חַיָּא)[18]

Abraham elaborates, with a word-play, that his ability (δυνήσομαι; cf. v. 10) comes from God's power, δύναμις τοῦ θεοῦ; cf. 9:5; the phrase is common: 2 Macc 11:13; Matt 22:29; etc. For God giving strength see 2 Sam 22:33; Ps 138:3; Hab 3:19; Phil 4:13. The "heavenly" (ἐπουρανίου; see on 2:3) God is "with him," μετ' ἐμοῦ. In the biblical tradition God's presence "with" Israel was both an historical memory (Num 23:21; Deut 2:7) and an eschatological hope (Isa 43:5; Ezek 34:30; Joel 2:27; Zech 2:10–11; 11QTemple 29:7–10); but God (and, in Christian texts, Jesus Christ) is also especially "with" certain individuals, including the patriarchs, often to protect or empower them: Gen 26:3, 24; 28:15; 31:3; 48:21; Exod 3:11–12; Judg 2:18; 6:12; Ruth 2:4; Matt 18:20; 28:20; Luke 8:28; Acts 7:9; 18:10; 2 Tim 4:22; *m. 'Abot* 3:6; *Mek.* on Exod 20:24; etc.[19] Note above all *Apoc. Abr.* 29:21: "I [God] am with you [Abraham] forever."

17:12. Without instructions from God, Death puts off (ἀπεκδύσατο; ἀπεκδύω*; LXX: 0; cf. Philo, *Mut.* 233; Col 3:9) his "beauty and loveliness," ὡραιότητα καὶ τὸ κάλλος; cf. LXX Ps 44:4 (τῇ ὡραιότητί σου καὶ τῷ κάλλει σου); Origen, *Cels.* 6.76 (ὡραιότητα καὶ κάλλος). His glory and the sun-like form (ἡλιόμορφον μορφήν; see on 7:14) that he has worn (περιέκειτο; cf. 19:2) are now laid aside. The sentence is nicely balanced:

---

16 See further Cilliers Breytenbach, *Paulus und Barnabas in der Provinz Galatien: Studien zu Apostelgeschichte 13f.; 16,6; 18,23 und den Adressaten des Galaterbriefes* (AGAJU 38; Leiden/New York/Cologne: Brill, 1996), 60–66.

17 Cf. the amulet in Naveh and Shaked, *Amulets and Magic Bowls*, 40 (amulet 1).

18 See Naveh and Shaked, *Aramaic Spells*, 91 (amulet 27) and 139 (bowl 26) respectively.

19 See further W. C. Van Unnik, "*Dominus Vobiscum*: The Background of a Liturgical Formula," in *New Testament Essays: Studies in Memory of Thomas Walter Manson, 1893–1958* (ed. A. J. B. Higgins; Manchester: University of Manchester Press, 1959), 270–305.

ἀπεκδύσατο

    πᾶσαν τὴν ὡραιότητα καὶ τὸ κάλλος

  καὶ πᾶσαν τὴν δόξαν   καὶ τὴν ἡλιόμορφον μορφὴν

ἣν περιέκειτο

The verse recalls the descriptions of Death in chap. 16, and what God commanded there—Death must hide his normal appearance—is being undone here:

17:12 τὴν ὡραιότητα καὶ τὸ κάλλος καὶ πᾶσαν τὴν δόξαν καὶ τὴν ἡλιόμορφον μορφήν

16:4 τὴν ὡραιότητα   τήν ἐνδοξότητα

16:6 ὡραῖος   ἡλιόμορφον μορφήν

16:8 ὡραιότητι   δόξῃ

16:12   καὶ τὸ κάλλος   ἡ δόξα

17:13. καὶ περιεβάλετο (cf. 16:4, 6) στολὴν τυραννικὴν καὶ ἐποίησεν ὄψιν ζοφεράν, παντὸς θηρίου ἀγριωτέραν καὶ πάσης ἀκαθαρσίας ἀκαθαρσιωτέραν exhibits a pleasing symmetry:

καί + verb + noun + adjective

καί + verb + noun + adjective

παντός + noun + comparative adjective ending in -ιωτεραν

πάσης + noun + comparative adjective ending in -ιωτεραν

Having put off his beauty, Death adopts a totally different appearance; cf. the fearful appearance of the Angel of Death in the Moses traditions; see p. 25. He dons "a robe of tyranny." The expression, which has no precise parallel, is set up in antithesis to 16:6:

17:13 περιεβάλετο στολὴν τυραννικήν

16:6   περιεβάλετο στολὴν λαμπροτάτην

τυραννικός* does not here mean "royal" but rather "tyrannical," as in its two LXX occurrences (*3 Macc.* 3:8; *4 Macc.* 5:27) and *Jos. Asen.* 23:6. The adjective, although awkward with "robe," is appropriate for Death, who typically acts against the wishes of his subjects. One is reminded of Rom 5:14 (ἐβασίλευσεν ὁ θάνατος), and Death's status as a king or tyrant appears elsewhere, especially in patristic texts: Josephus, *Ant.* 15.70; Ps.-Epiphanius, *Hom. 1–6* PG 43.452C; Chrysostom, *Hom. Matt.* PG 36.3 57.416; Theodoret of Cyrrhus, *Comm. ep. Paul.* PG 82.128C; Timothy of Alexandria, *Discourse on Abbaton*, ed. Budge, fols. 1a, 5a, 23a, 30b; *Hist. Jos. Carp.* 18; Ps.-John of Damascus, *B.J.* 7.54; etc.

    Death changes not only his robe but his very face, making it ζοφερός*, "gloomy" (cf. ζοφοειδής in v. 14). Cyril of Jerusalem, *Catech. 1–18* 19.4, uses ζοφερός of the Devil, and the related ζόφος often refers to the nether regions of death: Homer, *Il.* 15.191; *Od.* 20.356; 2 Pet 2:4, 17; etc. The transformation is appropriate given that those Death approaches are themselves gloomy: they become what he is, and vice versa. Again there is an antithesis with 16:6:

17:13   ἐποίησεν ὄψιν ζοφεράν
16:6   ἐποίησεν ὄψιν ἡλιόμορφον

ζοφερός is naturally the antithesis of something bright (cf. Chrysippus, fr. 429.3).

Death is more fierce than all wild beasts, παντὸς θηρίου ἀγριωτέραν. He has returned to his former, natural state; see 16:4 (with ἀγριότης). A reader might also recall 10:6–7, where wild beasts devour sinners.

Death's transformation renders him "more unclean that all uncleanness," πάσης ἀκαθαρσίας ἀκαθαρσιωτέραν (ἀκαθαρσία*, ἀκαθάρσιος*; LSJ, s.v., has no entry for the latter; Lampe, s.v., cites only *TA*). The first meaning of this must be that Death is literally dirty, filthy. He embodies the stench and decay that beset lifeless bodies (cf. v. 17). A Jewish audience, however, would also think of the ceremonial uncleanness of corpses, as in Num 6:6–8; 19:11–22 (with ἀκαθαρσία); Josephus, *C. Ap.* 2.205; Matt 23:27 (πάσης ἀκαθαρσίας); *m. Kelim* 1:4; *m. 'Ohal.* 17–18; etc. πᾶς + ἀκαθαρσία (= כל טמא) appears several times in the LXX (e.g. Lev 5:3; 22:4, 5; Judg 13:7; Tob 3:14; 1 Macc 13:48) and thereafter often in Jewish and Christian literature: Gk. fr. *1 En.* 10:20, 22; *Ps. Sol.* 8:12; Philo, *Deus immut.* 132; *Acts John* 41; Clement of Alexandria, *Strom.* 3.4.28; Origen, *Adnot. Lev.* PG 17.21C; John of Damascus, *Sacr. par.* PG 96.364B; etc.

If v. 13 refers to Death's "face," vv. 14–16 inform us that Death has many faces—a notion one can find in world-wide mythology; cf. the occasional Christian depictions of Death with a Medusa-like head (e.g. Ms. Cotton Tib. VI, London, from the 11th century).[20] Greeks sometimes spoke of the "face" (πρόσωπον) or "mask" (προσωπεῖον) of death; see e.g. Plutarch, *Mor.* 1104E; Ps.-Galen, *Definitiones medicae*, ed. Kühn, 19.397.6; Chrysostom, *Hom. diversae* PG 63.474; *Pasch.* PG 52.767; Cyril of Alexandria, *Comm. Hos.-Mal.*, ed. Pusey, 1:274.16. Cf. also *Hist. Jos. Carp.* 21, which refers to the faces of Death and his army. That death has multiple "faces" is novel for an old Jewish text. The plurality likely derives from Gen 23:3: "Abraham rose up from beside his dead." Jewish interpreters did unexpected things with the Hebrew: ויקם אברהם מעל פני מתו. *Gen. Rab.* 58:6 holds that "Abraham saw the Angel of Death defying him."

---

[20]   This appears to be an ancient motif, already found in Etruscan art; see Richardson, *Etruscans*, 242. For the various faces of demons in the afterlife in Egyptian myth see Zandee, *Death*, 328–30.

Tanḥ. B Leviticus 'Aḥare Mot 9 takes מתו to mean "at his [Abraham's] death"; so too *Lev. Rab.* 20:11; cf. how *Tanḥ. B* Deuteronomy Beraka 2 and *Tanḥ.* Deuteronomy Beraka 3 turn the לפני מותו of Deut 33:1 into a story about Moses confronting the Angel of Death. Given that *TA* has the patriarch encounter personified Death at the end of his life and that Death then shows him many faces, it is unlikely coincidence that the Hebrew of Gen 23:3 can be literally read so that Abraham confronts "the faces at his death" or "the faces of his (Angel of) Death" (פני מתו. As elsewhere, *TA* seems to preserve a legend that presumably originated in imaginative reflection upon the Hebrew text (and not the LXX, which has no possible reference to "faces": καὶ ἀνέστη Ἀβραὰμ ἀπὸ τοῦ νεκροῦ αὐτοῦ).

17:14. Death now shows (ὑπέδειξε; ὑποδείκνυμι*; cf. RecShrt. fam. E 7:20; 8:2) himself to Abraham, who beholds seven "fiery dragons' heads," κεφαλὰς δρακόντων πυρίνους. For πυρίνος see on 12:1. δράκων, which in the LXX translates both לויתן ("Leviathan," e.g. Job 40:25; Isa 27:1) and תנ(ני)ן ("[sea-]serpent," e.g. Deut 32:33; Job 7:12; Lam 4:3), reappears in v. 16 and 19:5, 7. Some ancients thought that dragons lived in Egypt (*Acts Thom.* 108), as also most if not all of the other animals referred to in this chapter. Christians thought of the devil as a dragon (Lampe, s.v. δράκων), and there is in the underworld, according to *3 Bar.* 4:3–5, a dragon that eats the bodies of the unrighteous dead. Gregory the Great, *Dial.* 4.40, tells two stories in which dying individuals are assaulted by demonic-like dragons; and in this context Gregory also speaks of the terrible images of hideous spirits that can afflict the dying.

19:7 (q.v.) unfolds the symbolic significance of the seven heads: they are seven ages. One might conjecture influence from Rev 12:3: δράκων πυρρὸς μέγας, ἔχων κεφαλὰς ἑπτὰ καὶ κέρατα δέκα. Not only does this speak of the heads of seven dragons, but those heads are πυρρός ("fiery red"), and they have a symbolic significance; see Rev 17:9–14. But this parallel is probably rather an example of the common use of a traditional motif. The notion of a beast, including a δράκων, with multiple heads (cf. v. 16), is found throughout the world (e.g. the five-headed Tiamat and the world serpent of Indian lore, Cesa); and it is quite at home in Graeco-Roman mythology; see Hesiod, *Theog.* 825–826; Homer, *Il.* 11.39; Apollodorus, *Bibl.* 2.5.2; Diodorus Siculus 4.11.5; etc. One thinks especially of Typhoeus (who had 100 heads) and the Lernean Hydra (seven or nine heads) that Hercules slew. The image goes back to ancient sources (cf. *CTA*, ed. Herdner, 5.1.1–3: "the serpent tortuous, Shalyat of the seven-heads"), and it is found elsewhere in Judaism: Ps 74:14 ("the heads of Leviathan"); *T. Sol.* 12:1 (a demon who appears as a δράκων τρικέφαλος; see on v. 16); *b. Qidd.* 29b (a demon "in the guise of a seven-headed dragon," תנינא).[21] Christian examples include *Odes Sol.* 22:5 ("the dragon with seven heads," of the devil); *Ap. John* (NHC II,1) 11:30–31 (a serpent's face with seven heads); *Pistis Sophia* 2:66–71 (a basilisk with seven heads); Ps.-Epiphanius, *Hom. 1–6* PG 43.460B (τὰς κεφαλὰς τῶν δρακόντων); Timothy of Alexandria, *Discourse on Abbaton*, ed. Budge, fol. 22b (seven-headed Death, constantly changing; see p. 35). Schmidt has also called attention to an Egyptian parallel, the god Tutu.[22] This deity, popular in the Roman period, usually has the body of a sphinx, a human head, a serpent's tail, and additional animal heads emerging from its human head (often for a total of seven heads).[23]

Abraham also sees "fourteen faces," πρόσωπα δεκατέσσαρα. How these fourteen faces are related to the seven heads is unclear. One might envisage two faces on each head (cf. RecShrt. 14:3–4). One might also imagine a series of changing images and compare the tales in which gods take on one form after another, as in the story of Peleus, who held the sea nymph Thetis as she became in succession a bird, a tree, and a tiger (Ovid, *Metam.* 11.241–246), or as in the story of Menelaus, who with his three companions held Proteus as the latter changed into a lion then into a serpent (δράκων) then into a leopard then into a boar then into running water and then into a tall tree (Homer, *Od.* 4.456–459). This was the view of James: "the picture presented to us is that of a constantly changing Protean figure, turning from serpent to wild beast, and again into fire, water, sword, poison-cup, and so forth."[24] This is consistent with the use of μεταμόρφωσις in 19:5 and with Timothy of Alexandria, *Discourse on Abbaton*, ed.

---

[21] James, *Testament*, 57, cites as a parallel *Yalkut Reubeni* 116, where the demon Bedargon (cf. the Greek δράκων?) has fifty heads; but he asserts that this "is an isolated and probably very late fiction." For the Ancient Near Eastern materials see Cyrus H. Gordon, "Leviathan: Symbol of Evil," in *Biblical Motifs: Origins and Transformations* (ed. Alexander Altmann; Cambridge, Mass.: Harvard University Press, 1966), 1–9.

[22] Schmidt, "Testament," 1:105–10.

[23] See further Olaf E. Kaper, "The God Tutu in Behbeit el-Hagar and in Shenhur," in *Egyptian Religion: The Last Thousand Years: Studies Dedicated to the Memory of Jan Quaegebeur* (Orientalia Lovaniensia Analecta 84; ed. Willy Clarysse, Antoon Schoors, and Harco Willems; Leuven: Leuven University Press, 1998), 1:139–57; Jan Quaegebeur, "Tithoes," in *Lexikon der Ägyptologie*, vol. 6: *Stele-Zypresse* (ed. Wolfgang Helck and Wolfhart Westendorf; Wiesbaden: O. Harrassowitz, 1986), 602–606 (with literature).

[24] James, *Testament*, 56. One recalls in this connection the transfiguration of Krishna in the *Bhagavad-Gita*.

Budge, fol. 22b, which is probably influenced by our text: "Seven heads shall be on top of your [Death's] head, and they will [constantly] change their shapes and forms" (cf. fol. 23a). Further, given the probable Egyptian origin of *TA*, one may note that the gods of Egyptian mythology are characterized by their ability to change their appearance.[25] The point, however, is not the coherence of the vision but its symbolic meaning (cf. the ten horns and seven heads of Rev 13:1—how do they go together?).

The fourteen faces—it seems unlikely that πρόσωπον here instead means "appearance"—are divided into three sets, one of seven faces, one of three, one of four:

Group 1	face of a blazing fire and great fierceness
	face of a horrible precipice
	face of a murky darkness
	face of a most gloomy viper
	face more fierce than an asp
	face of a fearful lion
	face of a horned serpent and basilisk
Group 2	face of a fiery sword
	a sword-bearing face
	face of lightning flashing fearfully and the sound of a fearful thunder
Group 3	face of a fierce, storm-tossed sea
	face of a savage, boiling river
	face of a fearful three-headed dragon
	face of cups filled with poisons

καὶ ὑπέδειξε introduces the first group (v. 14), ἔδειξεν δὲ καί the second group (v. 15), ἔδειξεν δὲ καί the third group (v. 16). In the first set, πρόσωπον appears precisely seven times, and expanded descriptions with καί at the beginning and end mark an *inclusio*:

1. καὶ πρόσωπον πυρὸς φλογερώτερον καὶ πολλῆς ἀγριότητος
2. καὶ πρόσωπον κρημνοῦ φρικωδεστάτου
3. καὶ πρόσωπον σκοτώδους γνοφερώτερον
4. καὶ πρόσωπον ἐχίδνης ζοφοειδέστατον
5. καὶ πρόσωπον ἀσπίδος ἀγριώτερον
6. καὶ πρόσωπον λέοντος φοβεροῦ
7. καὶ πρόσωπον κεράστου καὶ βασιλίσκου

The last four faces belong to beasts.

---

[25] Claude Traunecker, *The Gods of Egypt* (Ithaca/London: Cornell University Press, 2001), 42–43. Cf. the plasticity of demonic forms in Byzantium; see n. 11 on p. 328. The Coptic version of the *Visio Pauli* interestingly enough adds a long section on the faces of powers of darkness; see Budge's edition, fols. 24a–25a.

The first face is that of "a blazing fire and great fierceness" (φλογερός*; LXX: 0; Philo: 0; NT: 0; Josephus: 0; for ἀγριότητος see on 16:4); cf. Nonnus, *Dion.* 16.378 (φλογερῷ πυρί); 31.45; Eudocia Augusta, *Mart. Cypriani* 2.183 (φλογεροῦ πυρός), 336 (πυρὸς φλογεροῦ). Saadia Gaon, *Book of Belief and Opinions* 6.7, supplies a very late parallel: the Angel of Death appears to the dying "in the form of yellowish fire filled with eyes composed of bluish fire." Also comparable are the ancient traditions about the face of the Antichrist being as a flame of fire.[26]

The second face is more concrete: "the face of a horrible precipice." κρημνός recurs in 19:5, 9; cf. LXX 2 Chr 25:12; Mark 5:13; *T. Jud.* 2:4; etc. With φρικώδης* cf. φρίσσω in 9:5; 16:3. The adjective appears in LXX Hos 6:11, several times in Philo, never in the New Testament, often in patristic texts (Lampe, s.v.). Josephus, *Vita* 275, uses the superlative; cf. Epicurus, *Ep.* 3.125: "Death is the most terrifying (φρικωδέστατον) of evils." Readers will imagine a frightful fall from a steep, jagged cliff.

The third face is that of "a murky darkness" (σκοτώδης*; LXX: 0; Philo: 0; NT: 0; Josephus: 0; cf. Plato, *Resp.* 518C; Aq. Mic 4:8; γνοφερός* [= δνοφερός; cf. *Sib. Or.* 4:13; 5:292]; LXX: 1; Philo: 0; NT: 0; Josephus: 0). Is this what one beholds from the top of a steep precipice? And is LXX Job 10:21 (σκοτεινὴν καὶ γνοφεράν) echoed, as in Ps.-Macarius, *Serm. 1–22*, 24–27 18.2 (ἐν γῇ σκοτεινῇ καὶ γνοφερᾷ); Maximus the Confessor, *Quaest. ad Thalassium*, ed. Laga and Steel, p. 64 (τὴν γῆν τὴν σκοτεινὴν ὄντως καὶ γνοφεράν); and Ps.-John of Damascus, *B.J.* 14.120 (γῆν σκοτεινὴν καὶ γνοφεράν)?

The series of four animal faces begins with that of a "most gloomy viper"; for ἔχιδνα see also 19:14–15; ζοφοειδής*; LXX: 0; Philo: 0; NT: 0; Josephus: 0. LSJ, s.v., cites only Hippocrates, *Mul.* 1.11, and Aretaeus, *Sign. acut. diut.* 2.13. Cf. Gk. *3 Bar.* 4:3, where the εἰδέα of Hades is ζοφώδης. Although "most gloomy viper" seems to be novel, ζοφοειδέστατον harks back to the ζοφερός of v. 13. While the exact species of snake ἔχιδνα denotes is unknown, it must be poisonous; cf. Herodotus, *Hist.* 3.109; Acts 28:3.

A face more fierce than an asp, another sort of poisonous snake, appears next; cf. Philo, *Somn.* 2.89: ἀσπίδων ἀγριώτεροι. Once more the descriptive adjective takes up earlier language (cf. vv. 8–11 and see on 16:4). Although BAGD, s.v., defines the ἀσπίς (cf. 19:13–14) as an "Egyptian asp" (cf. Philo, *Somn.* 2.88), this may be too specific.[27] In any case,

---

[26] See the summary in J.-M. Rosenstiehl, "Le portrait de l'Antichrist," in *Pseudépigraphes de l'Ancien Testament et manuscrits de la Mer Morte 1* (Marc Philonenko et al.; Paris: Presses Universitaires de France, 1967), 48.

[27] Isidore of Seville, *Etym.* 12.12–20, lists a variety of asps.

1QH 11(3):16–18 associates Sheol and Abaddon with an "asp" (אפעה); cf. also 4Q ʿAmramᵇ fr. 1:13; see below, p. 353. The sixth beast's face is that of a "fearful lion" (λέων recurs in 19:14; for φοβερός see on 11:4); cf. Amos 3:8 ("The lion has roared, and who will not fear?"); Cosmas Indicopleustes, *Top.* 8.10 (λέοντι φοβερῷ); John of Damascus, *Sacr. par.* PG 95.1328D (τὸν λέοντα φοβερόν). In 1 Pet 5:8, the devil is like a roaring lion on the prowl.

The series of seven faces ends with that of a "horned serpent and basilisk"; cf. Epiphanius, *Pan.* 59.13: βασιλίσκου πρόσωπον. LSJ, s.v., identifies the substantive κεράστης (cf. 19:13; LXX Prov 23:32) as a "horned serpent or asp." It similarly suggests that βασιλίσκος (cf. 19:13–14) is an "Egyptian asp" (cf. BAGD for ἀσπίς; it certainly has nothing to do with the modern basilisk, *Basiliscus plumifrons*, or "Jesus Christ lizard"). But this mundane interpretation of βασιλίσκος is unlikely to be correct. In post-classical Greek lore as well as in Roman and Christian sources, the basilisk is a mythological creature, like the unicorn (cf. the δράκων above)— although it may have its origin in rumors about Egyptian cobras. Pliny the Elder, *Nat.* 8.33, described it this way: "It is a native of the province of Cyrenaica, not more than twelve inches long, and adorned with a bright white marking on the head like a sort of diadem. It routs all snakes with its hiss, and it does not move its body forward in manifold coils like other snakes but advances with its middle raised high. It kills bushes not only by its touch but also by its breath and scorches up grass and bursts rocks. Its effect on other animals is disastrous … ." Pliny introduces this passage by remarking that the basilisk has the same power as the "catoblepas," which kills those who look into its eyes. Cf. Heliodorus, *Aeth.* 3.8 ("by only breath and glance it will shrivel and cripple whatever it happens to meet"); Aelian, *Nat. an.* 2.5 ("at the sight of it the longest snake not after an interval but on the instant, at the mere impact of its breath, shrivels"); and Isidore of Seville, *Etym.* 12.6 (the basilisk is "the king of snakes, so that those who see it flee, for it kills them by its smell, and it kills the one it looks at. Indeed, at sight of it no bird in flight passes unharmed, but however distant it is, it is devoured, burned up by its mouth …"). Christian legend, which found the basilisk in Isa 59:5, eventually gave the creature the upper body of a rooster and sometimes called it "cockatrice."

The list of animals in 17:14 has its closest biblical parallel in LXX Ps 90:13 (which Christians regularly referred to Christ's victory over Death in Hades; cf. Cyril of Jerusalem, *Catech. 1–18* 3.11): "You will tread on the ἀσπίδα and βασιλίσκον, and you will trample on the λέοντα and the δράκοντα." But our text need not allude to the Psalm. Dragons are associated with lions also in LXX Job 4:10; Ezek 32:2; Ecclus 25:16, and lions

with asps in Isa 30:6 (in an oracle concerning animals of the desert); and
vipers and asps appear side by side in Artemidorus, *Onir.* 4.56 (here also
in close connection with the dragon and basilisk); Justin, *1 Apol.* 60.2;
Gregory of Nyssa, *Contra Eunomium*, ed. Jaeger 1:1.519; Theodoret of
Cyrrhus, *De providentia* PG 83.628C; Antonius the Hagiographer, *Vit.
Symeonis Stylitis* 11. Cf. also the warning against false teachers in Ps.-
Ignatius, *Ant.* 9:6 ("Beware of ... serpents ... dragons, asps, basilisks,
scorpions"); Origen, *Cels.* 4.54 ("dragons and asps and basilisks"); and
Eusebius, *Praep. ev.* 7.16.3 (Scripture calls the devil "dragon and serpent
... an engenderer of deadly poison, a wild beast, and a lion devouring
humanity, and the basilisk among reptiles"). One should note, however,
that perhaps the closest parallel to Death having divers forms and to
Abraham's ability to endure it with God's power is Ps.-John of Damascus,
B.J. 37.341–342, which does indeed take up LXX Ps 90:13: "Sometimes
he [the devil] appeared to him [Ioasaph] in black ... sometimes with a
drawn sword he leapt upon him ... . At other times he assumed the shapes
of all manner of beasts, roaring and making a terrible din and bellowing;
or again he became a dragon, adder, or basilisk." Ioasaph, unshaken,
declared, "I shall go upon the adder and basilisk, which you are like. You,
the lion, and the dragon I will tread under my feet, for I am strengthened
with the might of Christ" (cf. *TA* 17:11).[28]

The closest extra-biblical Jewish parallel to Death's self-revelation in
TA 17 is fr. 1 of 4Q ʿAmram[b] from Qumran. In this a "watcher" appears
to Moses' father, perhaps as the latter is dying: "His appearance was
terrifying [like that of an a]sp (פ]תן)), [and] his cl[oak] was multi-colored,
and it was extremely dark ... and his face was like that of a viper (עכן)... ."
Not only does this frightful being, who is elsewhere named Melchireša' (fr.
2:3), look like both an asp and a viper, but he wears a cloak or robe, and
his face is mentioned. Furthermore, *Asc. Isa.* 1:8 also calls Sammael by the
additional name Malkira, a variant of Qumran's מלכי רשע(cf. 4Q280 2),[29]
and Sammael is sometimes identified with the Angel of Death (see on 16:1).
Maybe then *TA* 17 represents a development or outgrowth of an old
Jewish tradition about a horrible being that comes for souls at death.

17:15. The next three faces, which form a second group, are, like the first
three faces, inanimate. The first is of "a fiery sword," ῥομφαίας πύρινον

---

[28] This story may be partly inspired by Athanasius, *Vit. Ant.* 9.6, where phantasmal
    (φαντασίας) demons take the forms (μορφάς) of lions, bears, leopards, bulls, serpents,
    asps, scorpions, and wolves in order to torment Anthony.
[29] Paul J. Kobelski, *Melchizedek and Melchireša'* (CBQMS 10; Washington, D.C.:
    Catholic Biblical Association of America, 1981), 81–82.

(ῥομφαία: 17:15; 19:5, 10; for πύρινος see on 12:1); cf. *Sib. Or.* 3:673 (ῥομφαῖα πύρινοι); *Jos. Asen.* 23:15 (Burchard) (ἤστραπτον αἱ ῥομφαῖα αὐτῶν ὡς φλόγα πυρός); *Gos. Bart.* 1:24 (ῥομφαία πυρίνη); *Acts Phil.* 1:6 (ῥομφαίαν πυρός); *Syr. Apoc. Dan.* 24. Even though LXX Gen 3:24 has φλογίνην ῥομφαίαν (cf. Gk. *L.A.E.* 28:3), biblically literate readers might recall the flaming sword of the Cherubim that guards paradise, especially as other texts refer to or allude to that sword with πύρινος, not φλογινός: *Gos. Bart.* 1:24; Ps.-Chrysostom, *In sancta et magna parasceve* PG 50.816; Gregory of Nyssa, *Vit. Macrinae* 24 PG 46.984D. The next face is "sword-bearing" (ξιφηφόρον; see on 10:4). How exactly this differs from the previous face is unclear.

The third face in the second series is "lightning" (ἀστραπῆς; cf. 19:6, 13) that is "flashing fearfully," φοβερῶς ἐξαστράπτον (φοβερῶς*; cf. φοβερός in the next clause and in vv. 14, 16; for ἐξαστράπτω see on 12:4, where the verb is used with φοβερός). The sight is accompanied by "the sound of a fearful thunder": ἦχον βροντῆς φοβερᾶς (ἦχος*; βροντή: 17:15; 19:6, 13; with φοβερός cf. vv. 14, 16 and see on 11:4).

17:16. The first two faces in the final group represent the dangerous waters of the world, its oceans and rivers respectively. The first is the face of a "fierce, storm-tossed sea," θαλάσσης ἀγρίας κυματιζούσης (for ἄγριος cf. vv. 8, 13, 14 and see on 16:4; κυματίζω: 19:5, 12; LXX: 0; Philo: 0; NT: 0; Josephus: 0); cf. Euripides, *Herc. fur.* 851 (θαλάσσαν ἀγρίαν); Josephus, *Bell.* 1.410 (ἀγρίαν ... θάλασσαν); Jude 13 (κύματα ἄγρια θαλάσσης); Socrates Scholasticus, *Hist. eccl.* 2.23 (τῆς θαλάσσης ὁμοίως κύμασιν ἀγρίοις); etc. The next face is by contrast that of inland water—"a savage, boiling river," ποταμὸν ἄγριον κοχλάζοντα (ποταμός: 17:16; 19:5, 11; for ἄγριος see above; κοχλάζω recurs in 19:5, 11; cf. *Jos. Asen.* 16:13; *Acts Matt.* 3:4 [of the boiling filth of Gehenna]; *Vis. Paul* 31 [ποταμὸν κοχλάζοντα—also of a place of postmortem punishment]; Sozomen, *Hist. eccl.* 5.9; LXX: 0; Philo: 0; NT: 0; Josephus: 0). The boiling of the river is a metaphor for its violence: it is flowing swiftly and foaming (cf. 19:11).

The thirteenth face is "of a fearful three-headed dragon," δράκοντα τρικέφαλον φοβερόν. For δράκων and φοβερός see above on v. 14. This dragon, unlike that introduced in v. 14, is three-headed (τρικέφαλος*; LXX: 0; Philo: 0; NT: 0; Josephus: 0). There is a striking parallel in *T. Sol.* 12:1, where Solomon confronts a demon who appears as a three-headed dragon, δράκων τρικέφαλος; and later Christian texts speak of the devil as a three-head dragon; see Eusebius of Alexandria, *Serm. 1–12* PG 86.403–404 = *Serm. 17* PG 62.722; Romanos the Melodist, *Cant.* 43.20; perhaps this is a sort of anti-Trinity; cf. Dante's three-headed Satan). One guesses that these several references to a three-headed dragon are inspired by Cerberus, the three-headed dog of hell, for he is sometimes said to be dragon-tailed and to have other attributes of snakes or dragons: Apollodorus, *Bibl.* 2.122; Horace, *Carm.* 3.11.17–18; Ovid, *Metam.* 10.20; Virgil, *Aen.* 6.417–425. But there were also other three-headed creatures, such as Chimaira, who had "three heads, one of a glowering lion, another of a goat, and yet another of a savage dragon; her front was a lion, her back a dragon, and her middle a goat" (Hesiod, *Theog.* 321–323); Hecate, the three-faced goddess of crossroads (Artemidorus Daldianus, *Onir.* 2.37.5; Pausanias, *Descr.* 2.30.2); Geryone, whom Heracles killed during one of his labors (Hesiod, *Theog.* 287–294; Apollodorus, *Bibl.* 2.106–109); and Selene in *PGM* 4.2785–2890, who is "three-headed," "three-faced," and "three-necked" (2786, 2821–2822) and has attributes of serpents or dragons (2801, 2805, 2862–2863).

The entire series of faces concludes with "cups filled with poisons," ποτήρια μεμεστωμένα φαρμάκων (for μεστόω see 3 *Macc.* 5:1, 10; Acts 2:13); cf. 19:6 (τὰ ποτήρια τὰ δυσώδη φάρμακα καὶ μεμεστωμένα) and 16 (ποτήρια δηλητήρια φάρμακα μεμεστωμένα), which interpret the present verse. Apart from 2 Macc 10:13 (Ptolemy's suicide), the biblical saga does not feature tales of death by poison, but the broader Greek and Roman worlds had many stories of people drinking poison, including Socrates (Plato, *Phaed.* 117A–118), Alexander the Great (Ps.-Callisthenes, *Hist. Alex. Magn.* rec. α 3.31), Claudius Caesar (Suetonius, *Claud.* 44), and Theramenes (Cicero, *Tusc.* 1.40.96). Especially famous also were the attempted poisonings of Theseus by Medea (see Euripides, *Medea*; etc.) and of Odysseus by Circe (Homer, *Od.* 10). Later Christian art sometimes depicts Death handing a cup to the dying, and the literature makes reference to the ποτήριον τοῦ θανάτου (e.g. Ps.-Chrysostom, *Hom. Matt. 26:39 [In illud: Pater, si possibile est]* PG 61.754, 756; John of Damascus, *De duabus in Christo voluntatibus* 41.7; George Monachus, *Chron. breve* PG 110.848A; etc.); see further on 1:3.

17:17. The narrator now sums up (ἁπλῶς εἰπεῖν; see on 10:3) by saying that Death showed (ἔδειξεν, as in vv. 15, 16) Abraham "great savageness" and "intolerable bitterness." πολλὴν ἀγριότητα is appropriate given the repetition of ἄγριος and ἀγριότης in the previous lines (vv. 8, 9, 10, 11, 13, 14, 16); and πικρίαν ἀβάστακτον recalls v. 8 (μεγίστη πικρία, which follows πολλῇ ... ἀγριότητι). The only new word is ἀβάστακτος* (LXX: 0; Philo: 0; NT: 0; Josephus: 0), which LSJ, s.v., citing Plutarch, *Ant.* 16.2, and *IGRom.* 4.446, defines as "not to be borne or carried" (cf. *Gos. Bart.* 2:2, 4) but which Lampe, s.v., on the basis of patristic texts, says can also mean "intolerable," as it clearly does here. The word is rare outside of non-Christian sources.

The final part of the summary speaks of "every fatal disease that brings death untimely," πᾶσαν νόσον θανατηφόρον ἀώρως θνήσκοντα. For νόσον θανατηφόρον see on 8:10. The notion of an untimely (ἀώρως: 17:17; 18:9; 19:11) death appears several times in the LXX: Prov 10:6; 11:30; 13:2; Wis 4:5; 14:5; Ecclus 16:3 v.l.; Isa 65:20 (all with ἀώρος); note also Isa 38:10; 4 Ezra 10:34; 3 En. 48C:12 (Schäfer, Synopse 75). The theme is particularly prominent on Greek epitaphs, which again and again use ἀώρος to lament those taken prematurely or unexpectedly by death, especially infants and youngsters.[30] Jewish epitaphs also use ἀώρος.[31] It is consistent with the probable origin of TA in Egypt that, according to Lattimore, although ἀώρος is used in "the very earliest preserved Attic inscriptions, and likewise on pre-Roman epitaphs from the Aegean," later on it appears "almost entirely in the East, particularly in Egypt."[32] To this one may add that ἀώρος is one of the most common epithets on Jewish grave inscriptions from Egypt.[33] One should note, however, that the theme also appears frequently in Byzantine literature.[34]

---

[30] See Lattimore, Epitaphs, 184–87; van der Horst, Epitaphs, 45–48; and esp. Ewald Griessmair, Das Motiv der Mors Immatura in den griechischen metrischen Grabinschriften (Commentationes Aenipontanae 17; Innsbruck: Wagner, 1966). On the ἀώροι as a class that haunt the living see Erwin Rohde, Psyche: The Cults of Souls and Belief in Immortality among the Greeks (London/New York: K. Paul, Trench, Trubner/Harcourt, Brace, 1925), 593–95. On "The Fear of Premature Death in Ancient Egypt" see the article of that name by A. de Buck, in Pro Regno, Pro Sanctuario: Een Bundel Studies en Bijdragen van Vrienden en Vereerders (ed. W. J. Kooiman and J. M. van Veen; Uitgever/Nijkwek: G. F. Callenbach, 1950), 79–88; also Zandee, Death, 70–71. Although one is unsure how to judge such things, on p. 81 de Buck claims that "the fear of premature death seems to have been deeply rooted in the soul of the Egyptians."

[31] See van der Horst, Epitaphs, 45–48.

[32] Lattimore, Epitaphs, 185–86. It does, however, also appear in literary texts, including patristic texts from a variety of places: Euripides, Orest. 1030; Alc. 168; Ps.-Plutarch, Consolatio ad Apollonium 113D; Cassius Dio 45.46; Origen, Enarrat. Job PG 17.61A; Basil the Great, Quod deus non est auctor malorum PG 31.332B; Chrysostom, Laz. PG 48.1022; Theodoret of Cyrrhus, Comm. Isa. 14.181; etc.

[33] See CIJ 1452, 1453, 1456, 1460, 1461, 1467, 1468, 1469, 1470, 1472, 1473, 1474, 1476, 1481, 1482, 1484, 1485, 1486, 1494, 1496, 1500, 1501, 1502, 1504, 1508, 1512, 1519, 1525, 1528; JIGRE 12, 102, 103, 104, 132.

[34] Hans-Georg Beck, Die Byzantiner und ihr Jenseits: Zur Entstehungsgeschichte einer Mentalität (Munich: Bayerische Akademie, 1979), 18.

17:18. For the first time the narrator speaks of "the stench of Death," τῆς ὀσμῆς τοῦ θανάτου; cf. 2 Cor 2:16; Origen, *Comm. Jo.* 20.44 (ὀσμὴ θανάτου); Chrysostom, *Diab. 1–3* PG 49.261 (ὀσμὴ θανάτου); Ps.-Chrysostom, *Meretr. 1–3* PG 61.709 (ἡ τοῦ θανάτου ὀσμή). Given the other parallels between our chapter and Zoroastrian eschatology (see on v. 8), one should note that, according to *Hadhokht Nask* 3:17–20, the wicked, upon death, breath an odor "more foul-smelling than any other wind."[35] Sometimes in Christian sources it is the Devil who stinks; see e.g. Eustathius of Trake, *Encom. on Michael*, ed. Budge, p. 110.

"The great bitterness and savagery" (πολλῆς πικρίας καὶ ἀγριότητος) picks up the summary in the previous verse (q.v.), but we now learn the result—the death of 7,000 "male and female servants" (παῖδες καὶ παιδίσκας; cf. LXX Gen 12:16 and see on 2:1; 15:5–6). Unlike Abraham (cf. v. 19), God's name does not protect these individuals (v. 11). And as in Greek mythology, where those who see the Medusa die, and as in Jewish thought, where those who see God die (Exod 19:21; 33:20), so here too: sight kills. The impossibly spectacular number—for 7,000 as a large, round number see 1 Kgs 19:18; 20:15, 30; 1 Chr 7:5; 18:4; 19:18; Job 1:3; *T. Job* 16:3; Rev 11:13; etc.—recalls the equally overdone 995 years of 1:1, and it adds to the marvelous quality of the narrative and highlights Abraham's uniqueness: he alone, out of 7,000, can withstand the onslaught. The number may also correspond to the seven heads of v. 14: for each head, 1,000 die.

17:19. Even righteous (δίκαιος; see on 1:1) Abraham is not unaffected. He comes εἰς ὀλιγωρίαν θανάτου (ὀλιγωρία: 7:1 v.l.; 17:19; 18:8; 19:2; 20:7). The expression, ὀλιγωρίαν θανάτου, which appears again in 18:8 (where Abraham himself speaks) and 20:7, seems otherwise unattested, and the meaning is uncertain. ὀλιγωρία (LXX: 0; NT: 0) typically means "an esteeming lightly" or "neglect of duty" (LSJ, s.v.); cf. Philo, *Congr.* 151; *T. Job* 14:5; 20:1; Josephus, *Ant.* 5.179. In *Gos. Bart.* 4:44, however, ταῖς λοιπαῖς ὀλιγωρίαις ἐκ τῶν θησαυρῶν αὐτῶν appears to mean: "the rest of the things from their treasury that weaken people."[36] Given this, and given that ὀλιγωρίαν θανάτου is immediately followed (as also in 18:8) by "so that his breath failed" (ἐκλείπειν τὸ πνεῦμα αὐτοῦ; cf. LXX Ps 141:4: ἐν τῷ ἐκλείπειν ἐξ ἐμοῦ τὸ πνεῦμά μου), the expression in *TA* probably means "the

[35] For parallels in Coptic texts see Zandee, *Death*, 341.
[36] See Wilhelm Schneemelcher, "The Gospel of Bartholomew," in *New Testament Apocrypha: Gospels and Related Writings* (ed. Wilhelm Schneemelcher and R. M. Wilson; Louisville: Westminster/John Knox, 1991), 552, n. 35.

faintness of death," that is, the lack of strength preceding death.[37] This also well suits the context in 20:7. One may compare Dan 10:17 ("For I am shaking, no strength remains in me, and no breath [πνεῦμα] is left in me") and *4 Ezra* 6:37 ("For my spirit was greatly aroused, and my soul was in distress"), both of which describe responses to visions; also *Petirat Moshe* (*BHM* 6:77), where Moses' spirit is too weak or in too much difficulty to leave the body (שֶׁנַּפְשׁוֹ מתקשה לצאת cf. the Falasha *Death of Moses*, trans. Leslau, p. 110).

---

[37] Cf. Box, *Testament*, 31: "a deadly faintness," "a physical sensation of weariness, produced by the shock, is meant."

Chapter 18: The Resurrection of Abraham's Servants

Long Recension

18:1. And so seeing these things, the all-holy Abraham said to Death, "I beg you, all-ruinous Death, hide your savageness and put on the beauty and the form that you had formerly." 18:2. Immediately Death hid his savageness and put on the beauty that he had formerly. 18:3. Abraham said to Death, "Why did you do this, that you killed all my male and female servants? Or did God send you for this?" 18:4. And Death said, "No my lord, it is not as you say. I was rather sent here because of you." 18:5. Abraham said to Death, "And how is it that these have died, if the Lord did not speak it?" 18:6. And Death said to Abraham, "Believe, most righteous Abraham, that indeed this is a marvel, that you too were not snatched away with them. But I nonetheless speak to you the truth. 18:7. For if indeed the right hand of the Lord had not been with you in that hour, you also would have departed from this life." 18:8. And the righteous one said, "Now I know that I have come to the faintness of death, so that my breath failed. 18:9. But I beg you, all-ruinous Death, since the servants died untimely, come, let us pray to the Lord our God that God might hearken to us and raise those who died untimely because of your savageness." 18:10. And Death said, "Amen, let it be so." Then rising Abraham fell on his face upon the ground praying,

Short Recension fam. E

14:5b. But Abraham prayed to the Lord, and he raised them.

and Death with him. 18:11. And God
sent a spirit of life upon those who had
died and they were made to live again.
Then the righteous Abraham gave glory
to God.

TEXTUAL NOTES ON THE LONG RECENSION

18:1–3. G omits all that follows "said to Death" up through "Abraham
said to Death" in v. 3. 18:1. H J omit "and put on the beauty ... formerly."
// B Q drop "you had formerly." 18:2. I omits the entire verse, perhaps
passing from τὸ πρότερον at the end of v. 1 to τὸ πρότερον at the end of
v. 2. // H J lack "immediately." // "His savageness" is missing from B J. /
/ H strikes "and put on ... formerly." // B J Q similarly shorten by dropping
"that he had formerly." 18:3. J drops "my male and female servants? Or."
// I omits "my" and shortens the last clause to "Did (he) send you for this?"
18:4. H omits. // G abbreviates: "And Death said, 'No. But I was sent for
you.'" // J is similarly brief: "No my lord. I was rather sent for you." 18:5.
G J drop "to Death." // G turns "How is it that these have died, if the Lord
did not speak it?" into "How is it that these have died untimely if you were
sent to me?" 18:6. J drops "that indeed this is a marvel." This could be due
to *homoioteleuton* (ὅτι ... ὅτι), but given J's habit of abbreviating, one
guesses the omission is instead deliberate. 18:7. J shortens: "that hour, you
would have departed." 18:8. J omits "And the righteous one said" and
adds at the end: "and I scarcely survived." 18:9. J omits "all-ruinous ...
untimely." // At the end G abbreviates to "and raise them." 18:10 G drops
"And Death ... let it be so" as well as "and Death with him." 18:11. J omits
"upon those who had died."

COMMENTARY

Chap. 18 extends the parallelism between Abraham's meetings with Michael
and his encounter with Death (see Introduction, pp. 43–47). Earlier, in
chap. 14, the patriarch joined the archangel in prayer, once to help a
deceased soul lacking one good deed, once to resurrect sinners Abraham
had prematurely struck down. Now, in chap. 18, Abraham joins in prayer
with Death, this time for those Death's self-revelation in response to
Abraham's inquisitiveness slew untimely. In both chapters Abraham is the
cause of deaths he later regrets; in both cases he asks the heavenly being
who has come for his soul to unite with him in prayer and undo what has

been done; in both cases the heavenly being agrees; and in both cases God brings back the dead. The vocabulary common to these incidents underlines the parallelism between them; see on vv. 8–9. So too do the similar sequences:

14:1–8	*18:1–11*	*14:10–15*
Abraham asks a question, "How is it that the soul was sentenced to be placed in the middle?"	Abraham asks a question, "Why did you (Death) do this?" (kill the servants)	
Michael responds: his deeds are balanced	Death responds: he was not sent to do this	
Abraham asks a second question, "What yet remains that the soul might come to salvation?"	Abraham asks a second question, "How is it that these (servants) have died?"	
Michael responds: it needs one more righteous deed	Death responds: it is a marvel Abraham is not dead	
Abraham enjoins Michael to pray with him for the soul in the middle	Abraham enjoins Death to pray with him for the slain servants	Abraham enjoins Michael to pray with him for the slain sinners
Michael says, "Amen, let it be so"	Death says, "Amen, let it be so"	
Abraham and Michael pray for the soul	Abraham and Death pray for the slain sinners	Abraham and Death pray for the slain servants
God hears their prayer; the soul goes to paradise	God hears their prayer; the dead are resurrected	God hears their prayer; the dead are resurrected
Abraham glorifies God	Abraham glorifies God	

One implication of these parallel episodes, in two of which people die at the wrong time but then are resurrected, is that God does not wish human beings to die prematurely. When Abraham's feelings of outrage and his idle curiosity unjustly bring lives to an untimely end, and when he understands that he has behaved wrongly, God is willing, at his behest, to turn back the clock and give life to the dead.

Because RecLng. 14 has no parallel in either family of RecShrt., the latter cannot display the extensive parallelism just observed. RecShrt. does inform us that "Abraham prayed to the Lord, and he raised them" (sc. the servants). This remark, however, is made in passing, is as brief as possible, and remains undeveloped and unconnected to the wider narrative. In

RecLng.'s much longer version, Abraham's intercession for the slain servants is an integral part of the structure of the entire book. It helps unify the
whole by binding the episodes with Michael to the episodes with Death:
one section replays the other.

One cannot exclude the bare possibility that RecLng. 18 has grown out
of something close to RecLng. 14:5b. Maybe a series of scribes or editors
or perhaps a creative redactor expanded an aside and created a series of
parallels between chaps. 14 and 18 and so greatly improved the literary
balance and flow of the narrative. Yet this seems unlikely. The similarities
between Abraham and Michael praying in one section and Abraham and
Death praying in another enhance a parallelism that naturally arises out of
a tale in which the patriarch first encounters one heavenly being and then
later meets another with the same mission. RecShrt. 14:5b is probably a
curtailed statement explicable in terms of a tendency to abbreviate (mani-
fest in mss. G and J of RecLng. 18) and/or a failure to perceive, or a lack
of interest in, the numerous and subtle ways that chap. 14 prefigures chap.
18 and chap. 18 reruns chap. 14.

There are other ways in which RecShrt. 14:5b seems secondary. This
recension says nothing about the effect of Death's self-revelation upon
Abraham, nor why that revelation slays servants but not the master.
Furthermore, we do not learn, as we do in RecLng., that Death went on to
hide his ugliness and returned to his former state. The text instead just goes
on to tell us that God took Abraham's soul as in a dream. The upshot is
that the scene in which Death is revealed comes to no conclusion. Does
Death remain as he is? Does he immediately return to heaven? If so, why?
And how is it that Death can fail to carry out God's command to take
Abraham? The narrative leaves readers frustrated with unanswered questions and goes on to the next thing. Once more we feel that RecShrt. is
abbreviating, and here so much so that the narrative borders on the
incoherent.

18:1. Abraham begs (δέομαί σου; cf. v. 9 and see on 9:3) Death to hide his
savageness (ἀγριότητα; see on 16:4) and to put on the "beauty" (ὡραιότητα;
see on 16:4) and form (μορφήν; cf. 16:6) that he had formerly. The request
and Death's response conclude a series that begins in chap. 16:

From savageness to beauty
16:4   God to Death   *Hide* your *savageness* ... . *Put on* your *beauty*
16:6   Death's obedience   Death ... became more *beautiful* ... . Having *put on* the
                             form of an archangel

From beauty to savageness
17:9   Abraham to Death   Show me your *savageness*
17:12 Death's response   Death *put off* all his *beauty* ... and his sun-like *form*

From savageness to beauty

18:1   Abraham to Death   *Hide* your *savageness* and *put on* the *beauty* and the *form* that you had formerly

18:2   Death's response   Death *hid* his *savageness* and *put on* the *beauty* that he had formerly

By asking Death to return to his former state, Abraham is in effect agreeing with the wisdom of God's original order to Death:

God, 16:4   κρῦψαί σου τὴν ἀγριότητα ... περιβαλοῦ δὲ τὴν ὡραιότητα

Abraham, 18:1   κρῦψαί σου τὴν ἀγριότητα καὶ περιβαλοῦ   τὴν ὡραιότητα

Abraham's appellation, "all-holy" (πανίερος; see on 1:2), is the antithesis of Death's appellation, "all-ruinous" (πανώλεθρε; cf. v. 9). The description of Death as πανώλεθρος (LXX: 0; NT: 0; Josephus: 0) appears to be Christian, even though πανώλεθρος is attested from Herodotus on (LSJ, s.v.) and appears in Philo, *Cher.* 52; see Eusebius, *Vit. Const.* 2.27 (θάνατον πανώλεθρον); Theophylact Simocatta, *Hist.* 4.14 (πανώλεθρον ... θάνατον); Ps.-Chrysostom, *In Ps. 94:1* PG 55.617 (πανώλεθρον ... θάνατον); etc.

18:2. Death instantly obeys Abraham; the former's deed corresponds to the latter's word:

Request in v. 1   κρῦψαί σου τὴν ἀγριότητα
                 καὶ περιβαλοῦ τὴν ὡραιότητα
                     ἢν εἶχες τὸ πρότερον

Response in v. 2   ἔκρυψεν   τὴν ἀγριότητα αὐτοῦ
                 καὶ περιεβάλετο τὴν ὡραιότητα αὐτοῦ
                 ἢν εἶχεν τὸ πρότερον

18:3. Having gained relief from Death's savageness, Abraham now thinks of all his male and female servants, τοὺς παῖδας καὶ παιδίσκας; cf. 17:18 and see on 2:1 and 15:5–6. He asks why Death killed them. The irony is that they died because Death just did what Abraham wanted. But Abraham fails to see this and so wonders if perhaps God is to blame, if God sent (ἀπέστειλεν; cf. vv. 4, 11) Death for them.

18:4. Death again calls Abraham "lord"; cf. 17:7, where the phrase is, as here, οὐχὶ κύριέ μου. And once more Death speaks truly: God sent (ἀπεστάλην; cf. vv. 3, 11) him for Abraham alone (cf. 16:15). Has Death, by taking lives at Abraham's behest, been disobedient to God? With ἕως ὧδε cf. Luke 23:5 and the Aramaic עַד־כֹּה, as in Dan 7:28.

18:5. Abraham is puzzled because he assumes that, if his servants have died tragically, then God must have willed it. The patriarch seems to share the view of Isa 45:7 ("I form light and create darkness, I make weal and create woe; I the Lord do all these things") and Amos 3:6 ("Does disaster befall a city unless the Lord has done it?").

18:6. Death responds to the most righteous (δικαιότατε; cf. vv. 8, 11 and see on 1:1) Abraham's question by changing the subject slightly. He thinks it is a "marvel" (θαυμαστόν; cf. 12:5) that Abraham, unlike his servants, was not snatched away, ἀφηρπάγης (ἀφαρπάζω*; LXX: 0; Philo: 0; NT: 0; cf. Josephus, *Bell.* 5.437; *Sib. Or.* 5:519); Delcor compares Paul's use of ἁρπάζω in 2 Cor 12:2 (although Paul's transport is temporary),[1] to which one should add *TA* 19:11. Death emphasizes his point by insisting, as he did earlier, that he speaks the truth: ἀλλὰ ὅμως (cf. Wis 13:6; *4 Macc.* 13:27; 15:11) λέγω σοι τὴν ἀλήθειαν (so also 16:11, 13).

18:7. Death offers the only explanation for Abraham's survival: the Lord's "right hand" (ἡ δεξιὰ χείρ) must have been with him (μετὰ σοῦ; see on 17:11). See further on 20:8. The language recalls especially the Psalms, where God's right hand saves (Ps 17:7; 20:7; 44:4; 60:7; 108:7; 138:7; cf. Job 40:14), holds and protects people (Ps 18:36; 63:9; 73:23; 139:10; cf. Isa 41:10; Wis 5:16; *Ps. Sol.* 13:1), and is full of strength (Ps 89:14; cf. Isa 62:8; *4 Ezra* 16:13; *3 Enoch* 48A). As in 16:3, where Death cowers before the divinity, so here too: Death is no rival to God. "Departed from this life" (τοῦ βίου τούτου ἀπαλλάξαι; ἀπαλλάσσω: cf. 19:15–16) is conventional; see Euripides, *Hel.* 102 (ἀπηλλάχθη βίου); Diodorus Siculus 38/39.15 (τοῦ βίου ... ἀπαλλάξας); *P. Fay.* 19.19 (ἀπαλλάσσομαι τοῦ βίου); *Acts John* 74 (τοῦ βίου τούτου ἀπηλλάγη); Cyril of Alexandria, *Comm. Hos.-Mal.*, ed. Pusey, 2:72 (ἀπαλλάξαι ... τοῦ βίου); etc.

18:8. The righteous one (ὁ δίκαιος; cf. vv. 6, 11; 17:19 and see on 1:1) responds by recognizing (νῦν ἔγνων κἀγὼ ὅτι; cf. 7:12; 14:12) yet again that truly he is facing Death. His words repeat those of the narrator in 17:19 (q.v.):

18:8   εἰς ὀλιγωρίαν θανάτου ἦλθον ὥστε ἐκλείπειν τὸ πνεῦμά   μου
17:19   ἦλθεν εἰς ὀλιγωρίαν θανάτου   ὥστε ἐκλείπειν τὸ πνεῦμα αὐτοῦ

18:9–10. Abraham requests "all-devouring Death" (see on v. 1) to join him in a prayer to God: δεηθῶμεν κυρίῳ τῷ θεῷ; cf. Tob 8:4 and the recurrent τοῦ κυρίου δεηθῶμεν of the Byzantine liturgies. The plea for the Lord to resurrect (ἀναστήσῃ; cf. Herodotus, *Hist.* 3.62, and early Christianity's use of ἀνίστημι for Jesus' resurrection) the deceased servants (παῖδες; see on 17:18) is designed to recall Abraham's earlier requests to Michael to pray with him for the soul "in the middle" (14:5–6) and for the sinners the patriarch struck down (14:10–13):

---

[1]   Delcor, *Testament*, 165.

18:9 And the righteous one said, "But I beg you (δέομαί σου), all-ruinous Death (see on v. 1), since the servants died untimely (ἀώρως; see on 17:17), come (δεῦρο), let us pray (δεηθῶμεν) to the Lord our God (κυρίῳ τῷ θεῷ) that God might hearken (εἰσακούσῃ ἡμῖν ὁ θεός) to us and raise those who died untimely (ἐξαώρους; ἐξαώρος*) because of your savageness" (ἀγριότητος; see on 16:4). 18:10. And Death said, "Amen, let it be so" (ἀμὴν γένοιτο; see on 2:12). Then rising Abraham fell (ἔπεσεν) upon his face upon the ground praying (προσευχόμενος), and Death with him.

14:5 Abraham said to the Commander-in-chief, "Come (δεῦρο), Michael, Commander-in-chief, let us pray for the soul, and let us see if God will hear (ἐπακούσεται ἡμῖν ὁ θεός) us." And the Commander-in-chief said, "Amen, so be it" (ἀμὴν γένοιτο). 14:6. And they made petition and prayer (εὐχήν) to God for the soul.

14:10. Abraham said to the Commander-in-chief, "I beg you (δέομαί σου), archangel, listen to my plea, and let us again call upon the Lord, and let us prostrate ourselves (προσπέσωμεν) for his pity. 14:11. And let us entreat (δεηθῶμεν) his mercy for the souls of the sinners whom I, once despising, destroyed, those whom, because of my words, the earth formerly swallowed, and the wild beasts devoured, and the fire formerly consumed. 14:12. Now I know that I sinned before God. Come (δεῦρο), Michael, Commander-in-chief of the upper powers, come (δεῦρο), let us beg God with earnestness and many tears, that he might forgive me my sin and grant them absolution." 14:13. And immediately the Commander-in-chief hearkened to him and they prayed before the Lord God (κυρίου τοῦ θεοῦ).

The common vocabulary can be seen at a glance:

18:9–10	14:5–6	14:10–13
δέομαί σου		δέομαί σου
δεῦρο	δεῦρο	δεῦρο
δεηθῶμεν		δεηθῶμεν
κυρίῳ τῷ θεῷ		κυρίου τοῦ θεοῦ
εἰσακούσῃ ἡμῖν ὁ θεός	ἐπακούσεται ἡμῖν ὁ θεός	
ἀμὴν γένοιτο	ἀμὴν γένοιτο	
ἔπεσεν		προσπέσωμεν
προσευχόμενος	εὐχήν	

The parallel in content goes beyond Abraham joining with a heavenly figure in the attempt to bring the dead back to life, for although chap. 14 does not use ἀώρως, the idea is there too: in both cases Abraham is seeking to bring back to life people who died prematurely due to his uninvited intrusion into their lives.

That Abraham rises (ἀναστάς) before falling on his face may be explained in the light of 17:1–2: he is still reclining upon his couch. But it is also possible that ἀναστάς is pleonastic and so a Semitism. ἔπεσεν ἐπὶ πρόσωπον ἐπὶ τὴν γῆν is biblical Greek, occurring as it does five times in the LXX: Josh 5:14; Ruth 2:10; 1 Βασ 17:49; 2 Βασ 14:22, 33 (for נפל + ארץ +אל פנים); cf. also *Jos. Asen.* 23:14; Justin, *Dial.* 62.5; Eusebius, *Hist. eccl.* 1.2.12; etc. That Death, whose job it is to snatch souls, so readily collaborates with Abraham in a prayer to bring individuals back to life is unexpected. "If Death can restore life, we are indeed in wonderland."[2] One does not anticipate Death showing mercy. But Death's cooperation is required to maintain the parallelism with chap. 14. Beyond that, readers may infer that Abraham's favor in God's eyes is what causes Death to behave so out of character.

18:11. God sends (ἀπέστειλεν) a "spirit of life" (πνεῦμα ζωῆς) upon those who have died (τελευτήσαντας), and they are made to live again (ἀνεζωο-ποιήθησαν). πνεῦμα ζωῆς = חיים רוח is a biblical expression and refers back to the creation account in Gen 2:7 (cf. 1:30), where God breathes into Adam the "breath of life"; see Gen 6:17 (LXX: πνεῦμα ζωῆς); 7:15 (LXX: πνεῦμα ζωῆς), 22; Job 32:8; 33:4; Ezek 1:20–21 (LXX: πνεῦμα ζωῆς); 10:17 (LXX: πνεῦμα ζωῆς); 37:5 (LXX: πνεῦμα ζωῆς); Jdt 10:13 (πνεῦμα ζωῆς); 4 *Ezra* 3:5; cf. Rom 8:2; *T. Reub.* 2:4 (πνεῦμα ζωῆς); *Jos. Asen.* 19:11 (πνεῦμα ζωῆς). In LXX Ezek 37:5, the spirit of life animates dry bones, which later Jews thought of as a picture of the eschatological resurrection. One may also compare Judg 9:23, where God "sends" an evil "spirit" (ἐξαπέστειλεν ὁ θεὸς πνεῦμα). But the closest conceptual parallel appears to be Rev 11:11, where a πνεῦμα ζωῆς from God brings back slain prophets from the dead.

ἀναζωοποιέω*, according to Sanders, who cites *Jos. Asen.* 8:11(9) and 15:4(5), is "probably Egyptian Jewish."[3] The rare verb (LXX: 0; Philo: 0; NT: 0; Josephus: 0) also appears in *Jos. Asen.* 27:10 (Burchard), and Sanders may be correct. But ἀναζωοποιέω is likewise a patristic word, and Christian hands may explain its presence in both *TA* and *Joseph and*

---

2   Gruen, *Diaspora*, 190.
3   Sanders, "Testament," 894.

Aseneth; cf. Gk. *Odes Sol.* 11:12; *Acts Xanth.* 41; Ps.-Justin, *Quaest. Graecae ad Christianos* PG 6.1485B; Epiphanius, *Anc.* 85.3; Ps.-Macarius, *Serm. 64* 7.9; 53.4; etc.

Upon seeing the restoration of his servants, the righteous (δίκαιος; cf. vv. 6, 8 and see on 1:1) Abraham gives glory to God. ἔδωκεν τὴν δόξαν τῷ θεῷ (so too Acts 12:23) recalls Abraham's response in 14:9 ("I glorify [δοξάζω] the name of God Most High"), where God answers another intercessory prayer. Cf. also Gk. *L.A.E.* 4:2 (δώσωμεν δόξαν ... τῷ θεῷ); Hippolytus, *Comm. Dan.* 2.29 (διδόντες δόξαν τῷ θεῷ); Eusebius, *Comm. Ps.* PG 23.649A (διδόναι δόξαν ... τῷ θεῷ); George Monachus, *Chron. breve* PG 110.932A (ἔδωκεν δόξαν τῷ θεῷ). Although two have prayed and have had their prayer answered, only one is said to give glory to God: Death presumably cannot exult in the dead being restored to life.

Chapter 19:
The Interpretation of Death's Self-Revelation

Bibliography: Schmidt, "Testament," 1:101–14; 2:145.

19:1. And going up into his couch he rested. Death also came, and he stood before him. 19:2. Abraham said to him, "Go away from me, for I want to rest, for my spirit is enveloped by faintness." 19:3. And Death said, "I will not withdraw from you until I take your soul." 19:4. And Abraham, with stubborn look and angry face, said to Death, "Who commanded you to say this? You speak these words of yourself, bragging, and I will certainly not follow you until the Commander-in-chief Michael comes, and I will go with him. 19:5. But also this I say to you, If you want me to follow you, teach me all about your metamorphoses—the seven fiery dragon heads, and what is the face of the precipice, and what is the relentless sword, and what is the boiling river, and what is the turbid sea that savagely storms. 19:6. Teach me also about the insufferable thunder and the fearful lightning and what are the cups filled with stinking poisons. Teach me about all of this." 19:7. And Death said, "Listen, o righteous Abraham. For seven ages I destroy the world, and I lead all down to Hades, kings and rulers, rich and poor, slaves and free. And because of this I showed to you the seven dragon heads. 19:8. I showed you the face of fire because many are burned up by fire and die, and through a fiery face they see Death. 19:9. And I showed you the face of the precipice because many fall down from the height of trees (or) a cliff and, passing out of existence, they die, and they see Death in the form of a precipice. 19:10. And I showed you the face of the sword because many are carried away by the sword in wars, and they see Death in a sword. 19:11. And I showed you the face of the great, boiling river, because many are snatched away by the inbreaking of strong (flood) waters, and they are borne away by mighty rivers and they drown, and they die, and they see Death untimely. 19:12. And I showed you the face of the savage, stormy sea, because many come to grief in the sea, in a great wave, and finding themselves among the wreckage, they (sink) beneath the waves, (and) they see Death as the sea. 19:13. And I showed you (the face of) the insufferable thunder and the fearful lightning because many human beings, in the hour of wrath, encounter the coming of insufferable thunder and fearful lightning and are carried off, and thus they see Death. 19:14. And I showed you also venomous wild beasts—asps and basilisks, leopards and lions and lionesses, and bears and vipers; in a word, I showed you the face of each wild beast, most righteous one, because many human beings are carried away by wild beasts. 19:15. Others are removed by the horned serpent; yet others swell up from and are cut off by the viper, still others swell up from and are cut off by poisonous serpents and the viper. 19:16. And I showed you the cups mixed with noxious poisons because many people, being given poison to drink by others, are through deceit removed at once."

TEXTUAL NOTES

19:1. B J Q omit "And going … rested." 19:2. G omits "for I want to rest." Either an eye skipped from the first "for" (ὅτι) to the second, or G deemed the clause superfluous. // G omits "my spirit." 19:3. H drops "until I take your soul." 19:4. J omits "and angry face, said to Death," H "said to Death." // G abbreviates by omitting, "Who commanded … bragging, and." // G again abbreviates by dropping "the Commander-in-chief Michael comes, and I will go with him" and the first part of v. 5, with this result: "I will not follow you until you teach me … ." // J drops "and I will go with him." 19:5. A: ὑπερθέλεις. B H I J Q: εἰ μὲν θέλεις (which is what I have translated). Schmidt prints εἴ περ θέλεις. // J abbreviates, dropping "the seven fiery dragon heads" and all that follows up through the end of v. 6. // A has "seven evil (πονηράς) heads." // G H I drop "that savagely storms." 19:6. G omits "Teach me also." // H abbreviates by omitting all after the initial "Teach me." // I omits "and what are the cups … all of this." // B G Q drop "Teach me about all of this." 19:7. B J Q omit "rich and poor." // B G H I Q have πυθμένα/ν/ας with ᾅδου—"the depth of Hades"; cf. LXX Prov 14:12; 16:25; 1 Apoc. John, ed. Tischendorf, 20; Ps.-Gregory Thaumaturgos, In omnes sanctos PG 10.1201B; and the commentary on v. 7. 19:8. H omits the entire verse. // P V condenses the rest of the chapter after "I showed you the face of fire" to: "because of the great abundance of your glory." So similarly C E: "because of the great abundance of your command" (διατάξεως). The meaning of the related reading in D L M is unclear: διὰ τὴν διάταξιν ὅπως τῶν σῶν ἐν διαθήκῃ ποιήσεις. // B Q, moving from πυρός to πυρίνου, drop "are burned by fire and die, and through." // J similarly shortens: "many by fire see Death." 19:9. G drops "the face." // J shortens by omitting "fall down … they die, and." B Q similarly drop "fall down … existence." // G omits all after "they die" as well as all of v. 10. // I omits "and passing … precipice." 19:10. H omits the entire verse. // J drops "I showed you, because many in wars," which does not leave a clear sentence. Did an eye pass from the final ς in ῥομφαίας to the final ς in πολέμοις? 19:11. After "strong (flood) waters," I moves all the way to the closing verb of v. 14, ἀναιροῦνται. // G condenses by omitting "snatched away" and "and by mighty rivers." // B J Q omit as redundant "and they are borne … rivers." // J drops "and they die untimely." 19:12. H skips over the whole verse. // B J Q lack "I showed you," "stormy," "because many," and "in the sea, in a great wave." So too G, but retaining "stormy." // G also omits "and finding themselves among the wreckage." // B Q drop "they (sink) beneath the waves." 19:13. The text is corrupt. Schmidt prints: τῆς δὲ βροντῆς τῆς ἀνυποφόρου καὶ τῆς φοβερᾶς ἀστραπῆς ἔδειξά σοι, διότι πολλοὶ τῶν ἀνθρώπων ἐν ὥρᾳ θυμοῦ δρακόντων καὶ ἀσπίδων καὶ κεράστων καὶ βασιλίσκων καὶ τυχόντες βροντῆς ἀνυποφόρου καὶ ἀστραπῆς φοβερᾶς ἐλθούσης ἀνάρπαστοι γίνονται καὶ οὕτω τὸν θάνατον βλέπουσιν. I have translated this, omitting δρακόντων ... βασιλίσκων καί as almost certainly displaced. // B J Q drop διότι ... ἀνθρώπων. // Instead of θυμοῦ, H has θανάτου, which James thought original. // A omits everything after βασιλίσκων and all up to and including βασιλίσκους in v. 14. // G lacks βροντῆς ... ἐλθούσης. // J drops γίνονται καὶ οὕτω. 19:14. B G J Q omit "and lionesses ... vipers." // B Q and J in different ways condense 19:14–20:5 into one summary comment. 19:15–16. G omits. 19:16. H like G omits the whole verse. // Schmidt prints παρευθύς. A: παρ᾽ εὐθείς. I: ἤγουν.

COMMENTARY

The first function of chap. 19 is to interpret the vision of chap. 17. So it is appropriate that the latter chapter opens by borrowing from the former; see on vv. 1–3.

Abraham's question in vv. 5–6 harks back to chap. 17, although the correlation is inexact with regard to both order and content:

Abraham's vision in chap. 17	*Abraham's question in chap. 19*
seven fiery dragon heads	seven fiery dragon heads
the faces—	the faces—
blazing fire and great fierceness,	the precipice
a horrible precipice	the relentless sword
a murky darkness	the boiling river
a gloomy viper	the turbid sea that savagely storms
a fierce asp	the insufferable thunder and the fearful
a fearful lion	lightning
a horned serpent and basilisk	the cups filled with stinking poisons
a fiery sword	
a sword-bearing face	
lightning flashing fearfully and the	
sound of a fearful thunder	
a fierce, storm-tossed sea	
a savage, boiling river	
a fearful three-headed dragon	
cups mixed with poisons	

Likewise imperfect is the correlation between Death's lengthy explanation in vv. 7–16 and Abraham's query in vv. 5–6. In this case, however, the order of the common items is exactly the same:

Abraham's question in chap. 19	*Death's explanation in chap. 19*
dragon heads	dragon heads
	fire
precipice	precipice
sword	sword
river	river
sea	sea
thunder and fearful lightning	thunder and lightning
	venomous wild beasts
	asps
	basilisks
	leopards
	lions
	lionesses
	bears
	vipers
	horned serpent
	viper
	poisonous serpents and viper
the cups filled with stinking poisons	cups mixed with noxious poisons

The most puzzling aspect of the chapter is the failure of the vision in chap. 17 and its interpretation in chap. 19 to line up closely—although the first and last heads match (just as they do in the two lists in chap. 19). There are, moreover, things in chap. 19 that do not appear in chap. 17 and things in chap. 17 that do not appear in chap. 19 (marked with an asterisk*):

Death's interpretation in chap. 19	*Abraham's vision in chapter 17*
dragon heads	seven fiery dragon heads
	fourteen faces—
fire	blazing fire and great fierceness,
precipice	a horrible precipice
sword	a murky darkness*
river	a gloomy viper
sea	a fierce asp
thunder and lightning	a fearful lion
venomous wild beasts*	a horned serpent and basilisk
asps	a fiery sword
basilisks	a sword-bearing face*
leopards*	lightning flashing fearfully and the
lions	sound of a fearful thunder
lionesses*	

bears*	a fierce, storm-tossed sea
vipers	a savage, boiling river
horned serpent	a fearful three-headed dragon*
viper	cups mixed with poisons
poisonous serpents* and viper	
cups mixed with noxious poisons	

The imperfect correspondence may be partly due to textual corruption. Chap. 19 seems to have suffered greatly in the course of its transmission.

The chapter belongs to a sequence that has close parallels in Jewish apocalyptic literature. In Dan 7–8; Zechariah 1, 4, 6; *4 Ezra* 10–13; and *2 Baruch* 36–40, 53–74, for instance, (i) a seer sees a vision (some cases involve fantastic beasts); (ii) he then asks for an interpretation; and (iii) in response an angel enumerates and explains the vision item by item. In *TA*, however, the supernatural, angelic interpreter is not Gabriel or some other angel who encourages and comforts the seer but is instead the frightening being, Death, who interprets his own frightful appearance.

The chief structural feature of chap. 19 is its repeated variation of the following sentence pattern:

τὸ δὲ πρόσωπον + genitive +
    ἔδειξά σοι, διότι + preposition +
        τελευτῶσιν +
            βλέπουσιν/θεωροῦσιν τὸν θάνατον

Vv. 8, 9, 10, 11, 12, 14, and 16 all reflect, to one degree of another, this basic blueprint.

RecShrt. offers no parallel to RecLng. 19. The reason is that the self-revelation of Death in RecShrt. 14 is accompanied by an explanation: "14:3. Some of his heads had the faces of dragons. Because of this some die from asps. 14:4. But other heads are like swords. Because of this some die by the sword as (well as) by the bow." Here Abraham, who presumably has the narrator's knowledge, need not ask any questions. But, as argued on pp. 337–38, RecShrt. 14:3–4 is enigmatic, for there are many more than two ways to die. One guesses that the briefer version is an infelicitous abridgement, and that the fuller version plus its needed interpretation better represent an older form of our story.

19:1. In 18:10 (q.v.), Abraham left his couch; here he returns to it. He needs to rest. The reader feels the weariness of old age. See on 5:2, which is similar: ἀνεπαύσαντο ... ἐν τῇ κλίνῃ. The line recalls also 15:2–3, where Abraham, followed by Michael, goes into his dining chamber and sits on couch, and esp. 17:1, where the patriarch tries to get away from Death:

19:1   καὶ ἀνελθὼν ἐν τῇ κλίνῃ αὐτοῦ ἀνέπεσεν
         ἐλθὼν καὶ ὁ θάνατος ἔστη κατὰ πρόσωπον αὐτοῦ

17:1   ἀνέπεσεν δὲ Ἀβραὰμ ἐπὶ τῆς κλίνης αὐτοῦ
         ἦλθεν οὖν καὶ ὁ θάνατος καὶ ἔστη παρὰ τοὺς πόδας αὐτοῦ

19:2. If 19:1 replays 17:1, 19:2 now replays 17:2:

19:2   εἶπεν δὲ Ἀβραὰμ πρὸς αὐτόν
         ἔξελθε   ἀπ᾿ ἐμοῦ
           ὅτι θέλω ἀναπαύεσθαι

17:2   εἶπεν οὖν Ἀβραάμ
         ἄπελθε, ἄπελθε ἀπ᾿ ἐμοῦ
         ὅτι θέλω ἀναπαύεσθαι

But Abraham adds a clarification this time, a clarification called forth by his weakness following Death's self-revelation: "my spirit (πνεῦμα; see on 17:4) is enveloped (παρίκειται; see on 16:6) by faintness," ἐν ὀλιγωρίᾳ; cf. 18:8. See further on 17:19.

19:3. Death's stubbornness matches Abraham's. The text continues to play off of the sequence at the beginning of chap. 17:

19:3   καὶ ὁ   θάνατος εἶπεν
         οὐκ ἀναχωρῶ ἀπὸ σοῦ ἕως οὗ λάβω τὴν ψυχήν σου

17:3   ὁ δὲ θάνατος λέγει
         οὐκ ἀναχωρῶ   ἕως οὗ λάβω τὸ   πνεῦμα σου ἀπὸ σοῦ

19:4. Abraham now expresses his upset. His look becomes stubborn (στερρῷ τῷ βλέμματι; στερρός*), his face angry: ὀργίλῳ τῷ προσώπῳ (ὀργίλος*); cf. George Pisida, *In bonum patricium* 135: πρόσωπον ... ὀργίλον. Although there is no perfect parallel to στερρῷ τῷ βλέμματι,[1] the form of expression is typical of our book; cf. 12:1 (ἀπότομοι τῷ βλέμματι); 16:1 A (ἀνελεεῖ τῷ βλέμματι); 17:8 (ἀγρίῳ τῷ βλέμματι). Note also Ps.-Chrysostom, *Annunt.* PG 60.756: αὐστηρῷ τῷ προσώπῳ καὶ ὀργίλῳ τῷ βλέμματι.

When Abraham asks, "Who commanded you to say this? You speak these words of yourself," he is turning a question he earlier asked Michael (15:8) into an accusation:

19:4   τίς ὁ προστάξας (cf. 20:3) σοι τοῦτο λέγειν;
         σὺ ἀφ᾿ ἑαυτοῦ ταῦτα λέγεις τοιαῦτα ῥήματα

15:8   ὁ κύριος εἶπεν
         ἢ   ἀφ᾿ ἑαυτοῦ σὺ τοῦτο λέγεις;

---

[1]   The reading of B H I J Q, αὐστηρῷ for στερρω, has a parallel in Ps.-Chrysostom, *In natale domini et in sanctam Mariam genitricem* 30.1, ed. Leroy in *Muséon* 77 (1964), 163–73: αὐστηρῷ τῷ βλέμματι.

Abraham adds that Death is "bragging" (καυχώμενος; καυχάομαι*), with the implication that he is bragging falsely. But the ironic truth is that it is Abraham who is being false. For when he declares that he will not follow Death (οὐ μή σε ἀκολουθήσω; see on 7:12) until Michael comes, there is no reason to believe him. More than once the patriarch has refused to follow the Commander-in-chief. The saint is lying.

19:5–6. Abraham, having made one suggestion, that he will go with Death if Michael comes (v. 4), now proposes something else. He will, he avows (ἀλλὰ καὶ τοῦτο λέγω σοι; cf. 16:5: ἀλλὰ καὶ νῦν λέγω σοι), capitulate if Death instructs him about his "metamorphoses": δίδαξόν με πάσας σου τὰς μεταμορφώσεις. Cf. δίδαξόν με in 2:5 (bis) and δίδαξόν μοι in 17:9; δίδαξόν με is a refrain in the LXX Psalms: 24:4, 5; 118:12, 26, 64, 66, 68, 108, 124, 135; 142:10. μεταμόρφωσις* appears in neither the LXX nor the New Testament, but Ps 33:1 Sym. uses the related verb (μεταμορφόω) as does the New Testament: Matt 19:2; Mark 9:2 (of Jesus' transfiguration); 2 Cor 3:18; Rom 12:2 (of Christian transformation); cf. also Philo, Mos. 1.57; Legat. 95. In Gk. fr. Asc. Isa. 1:2 and many Christian texts, the noun is used of Jesus' transfiguration, and it is characteristic of Christian, not Jewish sources (Lampe, s.v.). In TA, the sense is akin to that in Ps.-Clem. Hom. 5:23, which speaks of the gods taking various forms in order to gain various ends; cf. Artemidorus, Onir. 2.12; Ps.-Callisthenes, Hist. Alex. Magn. rec. α 1.7.

Abraham asks about the "seven fiery dragon heads" (τὰς ἑπτὰ κεφαλὰς τῶν δρακόντων τὰς πυρίνους) of 17:14 (κεφαλὰς δρακόντων πυρίνους); see the commentary on that verse. In the earlier vision, the heads introduce fourteen faces. Here, however, the patriarch mentions only six faces. The order is not exactly the same in the two lists, and the six faces seem to be a representative sample of the earlier fourteen (even though not one of the animals in the first list appears here); see above, p. 370. Death's response, which interprets faces those verses do not mention, confirms the representative character of the list in vv. 5–6.

"The face of the precipice" (τὸ πρόσωπον τοῦ κρημνοῦ; cf. v. 9) refers to the "horrible precipice" (κρημνοῦ φρικωδεστάτου) in 17:14 (q.v.). "The relentless sword" (ἡ ῥομφαία ἡ ἀπότομος; cf. v. 10; for ἀπότομος see on 12:1; LSJ, s.v. 3c, cites its use in connection with gladiatorial combat) is presumably the "fiery sword" (ῥομφαίας πύρινον) of 17:15 (q.v.). "The boiling river" (ὁ ποταμὸς κοχλάζων; cf. v. 11) and "the turbid sea that savagely storms" (ἡ βεβορβορωμένη θάλασσα ἡ ἀγρίως κυματίζουσα; cf. v. 12; βορβορόω*) take readers back to 17:16 (q.v.), where the order is reversed: the face of a "fierce, storm-tossed sea" (θαλάσσης ἀγρίας κυματιζούσης) is first, the face of "a savage, boiling river" (ποταμὸν ἄγριον κοχλάζοντα) second. Cf. Athenaeus, *Deipn.* 7.66 (θάλασσα βορβορώδης); Ps.-Chrysostom, *Ador.* PG 62.752 (ἡ θάλασσα ἐβορβοροῦτο); *Etymologicum Gudianum* Add. B 267.25 (ἐν βορβόρῳ θαλάσσης).

At the beginning of 19:6, Abraham again says, δίδαξόν με (see on v. 5), and at the end he will close with δίδαξόν μοι, which creates an *inclusio*:

δίδαξόν με (v. 5)
    dragon heads
    precipice
    sword
    sea
    river
δίδαξόν με (v. 6a)
    thunder and lightning
    cups filled with stinking poisons
δίδαξόν μοι (v. 6b)

"The insufferable thunder and the fearful lightning" (τῆς βροντῆς τῆς ἀνυποφόρου καὶ τῆς φοβερᾶς ἀστραπῆς; cf. v. 13) picks up 17:15 (ἀστραπῆς φοβερῶς ἐξαστράπτον καὶ ἦχον βροντῆς φοβερᾶς); see *ad loc*. For ἀνυπόφορος (cf. v. 13; LXX: 0; Philo: 0; NT: 0; Josephus: 0), Lampe, s.v., cites only *TA*; but the word does occur in Constantinus Manasses, *Compendium chron.* 2695, and Eustathius of Thessalonica, *Comm. Hom. Il.* 4.7. "The cups filled with stinking poisons" (τὰ ποτήρια τὰ δυσώδη φάρμακα καὶ μεμεστωμένα; cf. v. 16) refers to 17:16 (ποτήρια μεμεστωμένα φαρμάκων). Here as well as there and in v. 16 below, the poisonous cups close the list to which they belong. There is probably no close connection with "the stench (ὀσμῆς) of Death" in 17:18. For δυσώδης* (LXX: 0; NT: 0; cf. Philo, *Mos.* 1.204; Josephus, *Ant.* 2.297; *Gos. Bart.* 4:13) with φάρμακον see Ps.-Aristotle, *Probl.* 865A (τὰ φάρμακα ... δυσώδη); Plutarch, *Mor.* 509E (δυσώδη φάρμακα).

19:7. Death accepts Abraham's second proposal: he will interpret his own metamorphoses. The narrator does not tell us why Death grants the patriarch's wish. But the lull in the action, which allows the interpretation, is a gift to readers who remain uncertain about the meaning of the vision in chap. 17, or at least of some of its details.

Death invites righteous (δίκαιε; see on 1:1) Abraham to "listen" (ἄκουσον); cf. Michael's introductory words in 14:2, which preface another interpretation of something Abraham has seen: ἄκουσον δίκαιε Ἀβραάμ (see also on 7:8). Death opens by declaring that he has seven dragon heads because he destroys the world for seven ages, τοὺς ἑπτὰ αἰῶνας ἐγὼ λυμαίνω τὸν κόσμον. The remark recalls 17:5 (q.v.). New, however, is the symbolic number: it stands for the seven ages of the world. For the notion, attested in several other sources, and inspired by Persian and Hellenistic schematizations of history, that the world will last for seven periods, see RecShrt. 7:16; *L.A.B.* 28:8; *Barn.* 15:4; *2 En.* 33:1–2; Irenaeus, *Haer.* 5.28.3 (cf. 5.30.4); Hippolytus, *Comm. Dan.* 4.23–24; Augustine, *Civ.* 22.30; *b. Sanh.* 97a; *Pirqe R. El.* 19.[2] Although the interpretation is altogether different, it is interesting that the seven heads of the dragon in Revelation also have allegorical meaning; see Rev 17:1–18.

During the seven ages that Death destroys the world, he leads all down to Hades, εἰς ᾅδην κατάγω (κατάγω*); cf. 1 Βασ 2:6 (κατάγει εἰς ᾅδου); *1 Clem.* 4:12 (κατήγαγεν εἰς ᾅδου); Ps.-Hippolytus, *Fr. Prov.* 14 (εἰς ᾅδου κατάγοντα); Ps.-Chrysostom, *Hom. 1–3 in Gen.* PG 56.532 (κατάγει εἰς ᾅδου πυθμένα); Ps.-John of Damascus, *Pass. Artemii* PG 96.1280A (εἰς τὸν ᾅδου πυθμένα κατάγουσι). For the meaning of "Hades" see on 8:9. "Kings and rulers, rich and poor, slaves and free" (βασιλεῖς καὶ ἄρχοντας, πλουσίους καὶ πένητας, δούλους καὶ ἐλευθέρους) is intended to be a comprehensive generalization; see the commentary on 1:2 and cf. 4:3 and 8:9; also Ps.-Ephraem, *Interrogationes et responsiones*, ed. Phrantzoles, p. 78.1 (βασιλεῖς καὶ ἄρχοντες ... πλούσιοι καὶ πένητες, δοῦλοι καὶ ἐλεύθεροι); *De locis beatis*, ed. Phrantzoles, p. 301.6 (βασιλέων, ἀρχόντων ... πλουσίων, πενήτων ... δούλων, ἐλευθέρων); *Interrogationes ac responsiones*, ed. Phrantzoles, p. 221.12 (βασιλεῖς καὶ ἄρχοντες, καὶ πλουσίους καὶ πένητες, καὶ δοῦλοι καὶ ἐλεύθεροι).

19:8. Death begins not where Abraham did, with the face of the precipice, but with the first face in chap. 17, that of fire (see on 17:14), which the patriarch ignored in his question in vv. 5–6. Death explains that many people die (τελευτῶσιν; cf. vv. 9, 11; 17:18; 18:11 and see on v. 15) by being burned up by fire, ὑπὸ πυρὸς καιόμενοι (καίω*). These unfortunates—πολλοί, as throughout the following verses—see Death through a fiery face (πυρίνου προσώπου), that is, as they are dying they see Death coming for them through the flames around them. Is τὸν θάνατον βλέπουσιν (see on v. 10) a Christian idiom? Cf. Theodoret of Cyrrhus, *Comm. ep. Paul.* PG 82.121B; Ps.-Callisthenes, *Hist. Alex. Magn.* rec. E 127.4; Eustathius of Thessalonica, *De capta Thessalonica* 100.16.

In v. 18 and its sequel, it becomes clear that Death's faces stand for various sorts of deaths. For a partial rabbinic parallel see *b. Mo'ed Qaṭ.*

---

[2]   See further D. S. Russell, *Method and Message of Jewish Apocalyptic* (OTL; London: SCM, 1964), 224–29; Jean Daniélou, *The Theology of Jewish Christianity* (London/ Chicago: Darton, Longman, & Todd/H. Regnery, 1964), 396–404.

28a, which also lists various types of deaths (sorted mostly by age). Even closer, however, is Claudius Ptolemy, *Tetr.* 4:9, which catalogues different deaths and attributes them to astrological factors. E.g., "if Saturn is in quartile to the sun from a sign of the opposite sect, or is in opposition ... he causes death by trampling in a mob, or by the noose, or by indurations," etc. Ptolemy's long list includes death from wild beasts (cf. v. 14), poisonous creatures (cf. v. 14), drowning (cf. v. 11), shipwreck (cf. v. 12), and falling from a height (cf. v.9).[3]

19:9. Death next interprets the face of the precipice (πρόσωπον τοῦ κρημνοῦ) of 17:14 and 19:5. It represents the fact that "many" (πολλοί, as throughout vv. 8–16) die (τελευτῶσαιν; see on vv. 8 and 15) by falling down (κατερχόμενοι) ἀπὸ ὕψους (ὕψος*); cf. Claudius Ptolemy, *Tetr.* 4.9: ἀπὸ ὕψους κατακρημνιζομένους. The fall is from δένδρων or a κρημνοῦ. Such people see Death in the form (τύπον; τύπος*) of a precipice. The mention of trees is unexpected, and it does not make sense that those who fall from trees would see a precipice. But perhaps consistency is not to be expected in visionary material, and the precipice presumably represents all deaths due to misadventure from heights. Those who fall are said to pass out of existence. The expression, ἀνύπαρκτοι γινόμενοι, is unusual, but for the participial construction see on v. 15. ἀνύπαρκτος* (cf. Sym. Job 24:17; Ps 95:5; Prov 19:7) is common in patristic texts, where however it usually has philosophical sense (Lampe, s.v., gives the two chief meanings as "non-existent" and "not possessing independent existence"). Box translates it here as "swoon."

19:10. The third face is that of "the sword" (τῆς ῥομφαίας), which in v. 5 also follows the precipice. Its explanation is straightforward—"many" (πολλοί, as throughout vv. 8–16) are "carried away" (ἀναιροῦνται; cf. v. 14) by the sword in wars, ἐν πολέμοις (πόλεμος*). The idiom is well attested: Rhetorica Anonyma, *Problemata rhetorica in status*, ed. Walz 8, p. 409.3 (ἐν πολέμῳ ... ἀναιρεῖσθαι); Ps.-Justin, *Coh.* 25C (ἐν πολέμῳ ἀναιρεθέντος); Athanasius, *Ep. Amun* 68.5 (ἐν πολέμοις ἀναιρεῖν); etc. "They see Death" ends the sentence, as it does in the surrounding verses:

8			θάνατον βλέπουσιν
9	θεωροῦσιν	τὸν	θάνατον
10	θεωροῦσιν ...	τὸν	θάνατον
11		τὸν	θάνατον βλέπουσιν
12			θάνατον βλέπουσιν
13		τὸν	θάνατον βλέπουσιν

---

[3]   See further Schmidt, "Testament," 1:103–104, who cites additional astrological texts.

19:11. The fourth face, again following the order of vv. 5–6, is that of a "great, boiling river" (μεγάλου ποταμοῦ τοῦ κοχλάζοντος; see on 17:16). "Many" (πολλοί, as throughout vv. 8–16) are snatched away (ἁρπαζόμενοι; see on 10:10; the Byzantine liturgies use the word to describe what Death does[4]) by the inbreaking (ὑπὸ ἐμβάσεως; the expression is otherwise unattested and so of uncertain meaning; ἔμβασις*—LXX: 0; Philo: 0; NT: 0; Josephus: 0—usually means "embarkation" or "entrance") of floods, of "many waters." ὑδάτων πολλῶν = רבים מים in the LXX in contexts where God rescues people from trouble; see e.g., LXX Ps 17:17; 28:3; 92:4; 143:7; cf. also Sib. Or. 3:319; John 3:23; Rev 1:15; 14:2; etc. Those who drown (ἀποπνίγονται; ἀποπνίγω*: cf. Gk. fr. Jub. 48:14; Luke 8:33; Claudius Ptolemy, Tetr. 4.9) are borne away (ἐπαιρόμενοι; ἐπαίρω*) by "mighty rivers," μεγίστων ποταμῶν. When they die (τελευτῶσιν; see on v. 8) they "see Death" (see on v. 10) "untimely" (ἀώρως); see on 17:17 and cf. the παρευθύς of v. 16.

19:12. The fifth face to be interpreted, still following the order of vv. 5–6, is that of "the savage, stormy sea," τῆς θαλάσσης τῆς ἀγρίας κυματιζούσης; cf. v. 5 and see on 17:16. "Many" (πολλοί, as throughout vv. 8–16) who sail the sea "come to grief," περιπεσόντες (περιπίπτω*; for the meaning see BDAG, s.v., 2b and cf. T. Dan 4:5). These are overtaken by "a great wave," κλυδωνίῳ μεγάλῳ; cf. κλύδωνος μεγάλου in 1 Macc 6:11. The expression is not common, and just maybe there is a distant Homeric echo, for in Od. 5.291ff., where Odysseus is dragged under the water (ὑπόβρυχα), μέγα κῦμα occurs several times. At first those overtaken by the sea's surge find themselves among the floating wreckage, ναυαγίοις (ναυάγιον*; LXX: 0; Philo: 0; NT: 0; cf. Josephus, Bell. 3.425). But eventually they sink beneath the waves, ὑποβρύχιοι γίνονται (ὑπόβρυχιος*; LXX: 0; NT: 0; Josephus: 0; cf. Philo, Det. 152; Claudius Ptolemy, Tetr. 4:9).

19:13. Still following the order in vv. 5–6, Death next explains the thunder and the lightning, τῆς δὲ βροντῆς τῆς ἀνυποφόρου καὶ τῆς φοβερᾶς ἀστραπῆς; see on 17:15 and cf. vv. 5–6. "Many human beings" (πολλοὶ τῶν ἀνθρώπων; cf. vv. 14, 16; 20:2) encounter these elements "in the hour of wrath," ἐν ὥρᾳ θυμοῦ (θυμός*); the cryptic expression appears to have no parallel. This wrath is presumably God's.[5] Storms express the divine anger; cf. Deut 32:41; Ps 104:4; Rev 16:17–20; Sib. Or. 8:429–436 and recall the lightning

---

[4]   Stichel, Vergänglichkeitsdarstellungen, 27. Cf. Gregory of Nyssa, Vit. Macrinae 9–10; Amphilochius of Iconium, Hom. Sabb. PG 39.89B. For Egyptian parallels see Zandee, Death, 85–87, 184–86, 335–36.

[5]   So also Delcor, Testament, 170.

bolts of Zeus. Readers will envisage people being struck by lightning and thus being "carried off," ἀνάρπαστοι γίνονται (ἀνάρπαστος*); cf. the ὑποβρύχιοι γίνονται of v. 12, and for ἀνάρπαστος + γίνομαι see Lucian, *Char.* 17.4; Gregory Thaumaturgos, *Eccl.* PG 10.1012B; Ps.-Eusebius, *Ant. mart. coll.* PG 20.1529A; etc. Implicit is the idea that natural disasters are in fact not natural but "acts of God." For the severe textual problems see Textual Notes ad loc.

19:14. Death speaks in general of "venomous wild beasts," θηρία ἰοβόλα; cf. *Sib. Or.* 1:371; 13:167; Aëtius, *Iatricorum liber 13* 11.5; Claudius Ptolemy, *Tetr.* 4.9; Epiphanius, *Pan.* 37.9. But only the first two and the last of the following seven animals are in fact venomous: asps // basilisks // leopards // lions // lionesses // bears // vipers. J understandably inserts καί after ἰοβόλα. This makes "venomous wild beasts" the first in the series, not the ill-fitting head for a list.

Asps, basilisks, lions, and vipers, although not mentioned in Abraham's question in vv. 5–6, do appear in the original vision in chap. 17, so their presence here does not surprise; see the discussion on 17:14. Unexpected, however, are leopards (παρδάλεις; πάρδαλις* = נמר in the LXX), lionesses (σκύμνους; σκύμνος* usually means "lion cub," but in the LXX it sometimes signifies a lioness, לביא, as in Gen 49:9; Num 23:24; Joel 1:6), and bears (ἄρκους; ἄρκος* = ד(ו)ב in the LXX). The latter might remind readers of 2 Kgs 2:23–24, where bears maul children, especially as *TA* 10 alludes to this story. Leopards and lionesses, to the contrary, do not seem to carry any intertextual or intratextual echoes, despite the parallel in LXX Hos 13:8–9 (with πάρδαλις, ἄρκος, σκύμνοι, and θηρία). They are simply additional examples of dangerous wild beasts.

For ἁπλῶς εἰπεῖν see on 10:3. "I showed you the face of each wild beast" (παντὸς θηρίου) may refer back to the list just given as well as to the vision in chap. 17. But it is equally possible that παντὸς θηρίου means "every wild beast," and that the lists in both chaps. 17 and 19 are representative: although Abraham sees the faces of all wild beasts that kill people, the narrator names only some of them. This option gains force from the presence in v. 14 of creatures not mentioned earlier.

19:15. As it stands, Schmidt's text contains three parallel lines:

ἄλλοι μὲν ὑπὸ κεράστου   ἀπαλλάσσονται
ἕτεροι δὲ ὑπὸ ἐχίδνης   ἀποφυσούμενοι ἐκλείπουσιν
ἄλλοι δὲ ὑπὸ ὄφεων ἰοβόλων καὶ ἐχίδνης ἀποφυσούμενοι ἐκλείπουσιν

The pattern of the sentence—subject + preposition + creature causing death (+ participle describing state of the deceased) + verb denoting death—reflects earlier lines:

8	πολλοὶ ὑπὸ πυρὸς	καιόμενοι	τελευτῶσιν
9	πολλοὶ ἀπὸ ὕψους	... ἀνύπαρκτοι γινόμενοι	τελευτῶσιν
11	πολλοὶ ὑπὸ ἐμβάσεως	... ἀποπνίγονται	τελευτῶσιν

The anticlimactic v. 15 is, like v. 13, corrupt. Not only does one expect the ἁπλῶς εἰπεῖν of v. 14 to close the series (cf. ms. G, which omits vv. 15–16; H drops v. 16), not introduce more items, but v. 14 has already mentioned vipers, and the second and third clauses both end (at least in ms. A) in ἐχίδνης ἀποφυσσούμενοι ἐκλείπουσιν, which suggests dittography. Furthermore, ms. A leaves two lines blank after the first ἐκλείπουσιν (cf. 17:19; 18:8; 20:5). The original seems beyond recovery. LSJ has no entry for ἀποφυσόω* (bis).[6] Lampe, s.v., cites only TA, and I have found no additional examples.

19:16. The list ends, like those in vv. 5–6 and chap. 17, with "the cups full of noxious poisons," ποτήρια δηλητήρια φάρμακα μεμεστωμένα; cf. v. 6 and see on 17:16. δηλητήρος* is common with φάρμακον: Athenaeus, *Deipn.* 3.28; Josephus, *Bell.* 1.272, 592; Chrysostom, *Hom. Phil.* PG 62.295; Ps.-Callisthenes, *Hist. Alex. Magn.* rec. Byz. poet. 5965 (τὸ ποτήριον δέδωκεν Ἀλεξάνδρῳ ... δηλητήριον ... φαρμάκου); etc. The sudden nature (παρευθύς*—is this original? see Textual Notes) of a death by poison—a feature common to the previous fatalities but heretofore unremarked upon—is emphasized. Also underlined is the element of deceit: παραλόγως* (cf. παράλογος in 20:1). For this word meaning (as here) "fraudulently," LSJ, s.v., 4, cites OGI 665.33 (from 1st cent. CE Egypt).

---

[6] But it does, citing Aristophanes and Aristotle, list ἀποφυσάω, with the meaning, "blow away."

Chapter 20: Abraham's Death

Bibliography: James, *Testament*, 72–75, 126–30.   Schmidt, "Testament," 2:146–47.   Strotmann, "*Mein Vater*", 215–19.   Turner, "Testament," 137–38.

Long Recension

20:1. Abraham said, "I implore you, Death, is there a death that is unlooked for? Tell me." 20:2. Death said, "Amen, amen, I say to you by the truth of God's word, that there are seventy-two deaths. And there is one death that comes to the righteous, (a death) that has its set time. Many people in one hour come to death and are handed over to the grave. 20:3. Behold, since I have explained to you all that you have asked, now I say to you, most righteous Abraham, abandon every design of yours and refrain from asking anything more and come follow me, as the judge and God of all commanded me." 20:4. Abraham said to Death, "Go away from me for a bit longer so that I might rest in my couch, because I am very fainthearted. 20:5. Ever since I saw you with my eyes, my strength indeed has failed. All the limbs of the flesh of my frame seem to me to be like a heavy lump of lead, and my spirit is most vexed. Remove yourself for a bit. For I cannot bear to see your form." For the sweat from his face came down like drops of blood. 20:6. Isaac

Short Recension fam. E

14:6. And it came to pass, when Abraham turned, that Death brought forth his soul as in a dream. Chariots of the Lord God came and took his soul to heaven, blessing the friend of the Lord. They brought him unto rest. 14:7. Isaac buried his father Abraham next to his mother, glorifying God Most High, to whom be glory unto the ages of ages. Amen.[1]

---

[1]   RecShrt. I contains a much longer ending very close to RecLng. It includes the kiss of Death's right hand, Michael, the divinely-woven shroud, burial on the third day, angelic singing, paradise, the tents of the just, the call to imitate Abraham, and a Trinitarian doxology.

his son came and fell upon his breast,
weeping. His wife Sarah also came and
embraced Abraham's feet, weeping bitterly. 20:7. And all the servants came
and wept, mourning bitterly. And Abraham entered the faintness of death. 20:8.
Death said to Abraham, "Come, kiss
my right hand, and cheerfulness and life
and strength will return to you." 20:9.
For Death had tricked Abraham. And
he kissed his hand, and immediately his
soul adhered to the hand of Death.
20:10. And immediately Michael the
archangel stood nearby with a host of
angels, and they took his precious soul
in their hands in a divinely woven linen
shroud. 20:11. And they tended the
body of the righteous Abraham with
divinely-smelling ointments and perfumes until the third day after his death.
And they buried him in the promised
land by the Oak of Mamre. 20:12. Escorting his precious soul, the angels went
up into heaven, singing the trisagion
hymn to the Master of all, God. And
they set him down so that he might
worship the God and Father. 20:13. And
after much praise and glorification (of
God), the undefiled voice of the God
and Father came speaking thus: 20:14.
"Now take my friend Abraham to paradise. The tents of my righteous ones and
the lodgings of my saints Isaac and
Jacob are there, in his bosom. No suffering or grief or groaning is there but
peace and fervent joy and life without
end." 20:15. After which, let us also,
my beloved brothers, emulate the hospitality of the patriarch Abraham, and let
us acquire his virtuous conduct, so that
we might be found worthy of eternal
life, glorifying the Father and the Son
and the Holy Spirit, now and ever and
unto ages of ages. Amen.

TEXTUAL NOTES ON THE LONG RECENSION

20:1–2. I omits "is there ... me" as well as the beginning of v. 2, "Death said, 'Amen.'" The resultant text makes no sense. 20:2. G H I omit "word." // G H I make the seventy-two (H: seventy) deaths "untimely" deaths, which ill-suits the context. The patriarch is not asking if there is an untimely death, because that is the character of those deaths he has just encountered. // H drops "And there is ... set time." // H I drop the superfluous "and are handed ... grave." 20:3. Instead of "abandon every design of yours and refrain from asking anything more" A has: τί γὰρ οὖν; followed by πᾶσαν βουλὴν κατάλιπε κ.τ.λ. // A: "God of all." G: text. H: "God." I: "Lord and judge of all." 20:5. H omits "Remove yourself for a bit." // Without "For the sweat from his face came down" (which Schmidt prints), A ends up with: "I cannot bear to see your form, (which is) like drops of blood." // G: "For from his face (προσώπου) water (ὕδωρ) came down." // Schmidt: θρόμβοι. A: θρόμβη. G: βρομβοί. H: δροβῆ. I: δρομή. // 20:6. G shortens by dropping "and fell upon his breast." So too I, save that it retains "his," which leaves the nonsensical αὐτοῦ αὐτοῦ. // A mistakenly omits "weeping. His wife Sarah ... and." // J omits "and embraced ... bitterly." 20:7. G leaves out "All the servants ... bitterly." // H ends with "wept bitterly," omitting "mourning" and "And Abraham ... death." // D L M add, in accord with many Greco-Roman stories in which masters on their death beds free slaves, that Abraham released his slaves: καὶ ἐπέταξεν ἐλευθερωθῆναι αὐτοὺς πάντας.[2] 20:8. In H Death begins by remarking upon Abraham's sluggish state: ἰδοὺ ἐν πολλῇ ῥαθυμίᾳ κατάκειτα τὸ πνεῦμα. // G drops "and cheerfulness ... to you." 20:9. G omits the opening clause: "For Death ... Abraham." // Schmidt prints ἐκολλᾶτο. A: ἐκόλλειτο. B: κεκόληκεν. G Q: κεκόλληκεν. H: κεκόλυκεν. I: παρέστη κεκόλλητας. J: κόλυκε γὰρ αὐτοῦ. // In G the remarks about the divinely woven cloth of linen and the divinely-smelling perfume (v. 10, slightly rewritten) follow immediately after "the hand of Death." 20:10. H drops "with a host of angels." // H drops "in his hands ... shroud." // After "their hands" J adds: "singing praises for three days." // J drops "in a ... shroud." // B Q lacks "divinely-woven." 20:11. H J omit the opening words: "And ... perfumes." // H abbreviates further by dropping "of the righteous man ... land." // G also shortens, dropping "until the third day ... . And." // J omits "until the third ... his death" and "him ... land." 20:12. G drops vv. 12–14 and most of

---

2 See Edward Champlin, *Final Judgments: Duty and Emotion in Roman Wills, 200 B.C.–A.D. 250* (Berkeley: University of California Press, 1991), 131–54. Abraham's servants are also freed in the Coptic, Arabic, and Ethiopic.

v. 15, ending at this point with a short doxology. // H omits "went up into heaven." // J skips from "into" (εἰς) to "so that" (εἰς)—*homoioteleuton*. // H drops "to the Master" through the opening words of v. 13: "And after ... glorification (of God)." // B Q become explicitly Christian at the end: "before the God and Father and our Lord Jesus Christ." 20:13. J omits "And after much praise and glorification (of God)" (cf. H). // B omits "the undefiled ... thus." // H I J Q lack "of the God and Father." 20:14. H J drop the needless and very awkward, "The tents ... bosom." B I Q similarly omit "my" and "and the lodgings ... bosom." // H lacks "and life ... end" and ends the book with: "to our God be glory and might." 20:15. B I Q omit "and let us acquire ... conduct." // Instead of "and let us acquire ... conduct" J has: "Always and ever let us acquire peace and love, the salt of the virtues." // J omits: "glorifying the Father ... Spirit." // There are several variants for the doxology, all involving standard liturgical phrases. // I adds: "The account of the life (βίου) of the just and hospitable Abraham, (and) of his death, has taken its end. So now may we sinners also be found worthy unto the kingdom of God, where the righteous Abraham is."

COMMENTARY

After a final question and answer sequence (vv. 1–3), chap. 20 narrates Abraham's death. His great distress (vv. 4–5) and the mourning of family and servants (vv. 6–7) set the stage. Everyone—readers, Isaac, Sarah, servants, Death, and maybe even Abraham—knows what is about to happen, yet the patriarch again orders Death to depart (v. 4). His words fall upon deaf ears. Death, who has gained Abraham's trust by heretofore honestly answering his questions, ignores his feeble plea and reverts to a trick, to which the now frail patriarch falls. In the hope that kissing Death will, as promised, bring life and strength, Abraham acts accordingly, where-upon his soul adheres to Death's hand. We then read, in short order, about the ascent of Abraham's soul (vv. 10, 12–14), which immediately comes into the custody of angels, and of the angelic burial of his body (v. 11). The book ends with a paraenetic conclusion and doxology (v. 15).

God's original intention, announced in chap. 1, to bring Abraham to paradise, comes to its realization in chap. 20 (see on v. 14). Happily, then, the end harks back to the beginning. Michael, who has been absent for several chapters, now returns to see the fulfillment of his original mission, as outlined in 1:4–7. Abraham, whose virtues are recounted (v. 15) as in chap. 1, is buried at the Oak of Mamre (20:11), which is where we first met him (1:2). God calls Abraham "my friend" (20:14), as he did in his very first utterance (1:4). The patriarch goes to dwell in the tents of the right-eous (v. 14), whereas chap. 1 speaks of his pitched tent (1:2). The "trisagion hymn" that the angels sing in v. 12 also belongs here, for it takes us back to 3:2–3, where the cypress sings, "Holy, holy, holy." The correlations between beginning and end enhance the book's unity and make for a satisfying denouement.

Sanders places v. 15 in brackets and comments: "A Christian exhorta-tion and doxology."[3] If this implies that the preceding verses are of a different character, that is, not Christian, then one must demur. Turner gets it right when he observes that "the whole" of the final section "is suspected to be Christian" because of "the number of apparently late words (θεοΰφαντος, μύρισμα, θεόπνευστος, τρισάγιος, ὀψικεύω, ἀνύμνησις, δοξολογία) in so short a passage, and the reference to 'the God and Father.'"[4] He then, however, unaccountably goes on to add that this "is not at all certain," evidently because "the Jewish element is strongly marked." But the Christian contribution is without question extensive.

First, there is the high number words and phrases that are, as the verse-by-verse commentary shows, either late or characteristic of Christian as opposed to Jewish sources, words and phrases that are hardly confined to the chapter's final lines:

v. 2, prefatory ἀμήν, ἀμήν
v. 2, ἐν ἀληθείᾳ θεοῦ λόγου
v. 3, καὶ δεῦρο ἀκολούθει μοι
v. 3, ὁ κριτὴς τῶν ἀπάντων καὶ θεός
v. 5, τὰ μέλη τῆς σαρκός
v. 5, ταλανίζω meaning "vex"
v. 5, κατῆλθε ... ὁ ἱδρὼς ... αὐτοῦ ὡσει θρόμβοι αἵματος
v. 6, ἔπεσεν ἐπὶ τὸ στῆθος αὐτοῦ κλαίων
v. 6, ὀδυρομένη πικρῶς (cf. v. 7)
v. 10, πλῆθος ἀγγέλων at the death of a saint
v. 10, θεοΰφαντος
v. 11, μύρισμα
v. 12, ὀψικεύοντες
v. 12, τρισάγιον ὕμνον
v. 12, unqualified τοῦ θεοῦ καὶ πατρός

3 Sanders, "Testament of Abraham," 895, n. Box, *Testament*, 38, and Stone, *Testa-ment*, 56, also have the last sentence in brackets. Cf. Vegas Montaner, "Testa-mento," p. 527. Colafemmina, *Testamento*, 34, labels v. 14 a Christian interpreta-tion.
4 Turner, "Testament," 137–38. In his contribution to Sparks' edition of *TA*, Turner puts 20:20 in a footnote without explanation.

v. 13, ἄχραντος of the divinity

v. 13, δοξολογία

v. 13, ἀνύμνησις

v. 14, οὐ λύπη οὐ στεναγμός following "Abraham's bosom"

v. 15, ζηλόω + πολιτεία

v. 15, ἀδελφοί μου ἀγαπητοί

v. 15, ἀξιωθῶμεν τῆς αἰωνίου ζωῆς

v. 15, δοξάζοντες τῷ πατρὶ καὶ τῷ υἱῷ κ.τ.λ.

Clearly Christian hands have been active throughout the chapter. One cannot simply cut out a phrase here or there and so recover a Jewish document. Perhaps Kohler already saw this when he wrote that "the entire end of the book ... seems to betray a Christian hand."[5] He did not, however, specify what he meant by "the entire end of the book."

Second, chap. 20 contains a bit of a Christ typology. We read, in v. 5, that the sweat from Abraham's face "came down like drops of blood." The formulation depends upon Luke 22:44, and in both places we have to do with someone who is struggling with death.[6] Immediately after this, Isaac, troubled over Abraham's impending death, comes and falls upon his father's breast. The Greek, ἔπεσεν ἐπὶ τὸ στῆθος αὐτοῦ κλαίων, borrows the language of John 13:25 and 21:20, verses that refer to the disciple who fell upon Jesus' breast when inquiring about the latter's impending fate; see on v. 6. So again Abraham's end is like the end of Jesus. One recalls how often early Christian literature borrows from Jesus' passion in telling tales of the deaths of the saints (e.g. Stephen in Acts 7 and Mary in John of Thessalonica, Dorm. BVM A 12, 14, ed. Jugie, pp. 397, 401).

Third, the stereotypical Christian nature of Abraham's death is apparent when one compares it with the account of Mary's passing in the Dormitio Mariae—a book in which Mary learns of her death through an angel, in this case Gabriel. I have used Tischendorf's edition.[7]

---

[5] Kohler, "Apocalypse," 591.

[6] Colafemmina, Testamento, 75, n. 82, and Vegas Montaner, "Testamento," p. 525, observe the parallel.

[7] Constantinus Tischendorf, Apocalypses Apocryphae (Leipzig: Herm. Mendelssohn, 1866), 95–112. This text (referred throughout this chapter as Dorm. BMV) has many relatives; see esp. the collection in Wenger, L'Assomption; also the discussion in Mary Clayton, "The Transitus Mariae: The Tradition and Its Origins," Apocrypha 10 (1999), pp. 74–98. But Tischendorf's text (catalogued as # 101 in Geerard's Clavis Apocryphorum Novi Testamenti and as # 1056 in Bibliotheca hagiographica graeca) offers the most parallels to TA. Note, however, that Vatic. Gr. 1982 refers to Mary on her κλίνης; see Wenger, 230, and cf. TA 20:4.

Motif	Dormitio Mariae	Testament of Abraham 20
host of angels	πλήθη ἀγέλλων, 38	πλήθους ἀγέλλων, 10
divine voice	φωνὴ τοῦ οὐρανοῦ, 45	φωνὴ τοῦ θεοῦ, 13
joy	ἀγαλλίασθω, 39, 43	ἀγαλλίασις, 14
τίμιος used of the dying	τίμιον σῶμα, 39, 45, 48, 49 τίμιους πόδας, 45 τίμιον λείψανον, 49	τίμια ψυχή, 10
paradise as future home	παραδείσῳ, 39, 48, 49	παράδεισον, 14
peace	εἰρήνη, 39	εἰρήνη, 14
kiss of right hand	δεξιὰν κατεφίλει, 40	δεξιὰν ἠσπάσατο, 8–9
ἄχραντος describing an aspect of the deity	ἄχραντος of Christ's right hand, 40, 44	ἄχραντος of God's voice, 13
falling at feet of saint	πρὸς τοὺς πόδες αὐτῆς, 41, 45	τοῖς ποσίν, 6
singing of angels	ὑμνῳδίας, 44, cf. 48	ψάλλοντες, 12
supernatural perfume	εὐωδίας, 45, 49 μύρον εὐωδίας, 48	μυρίσμασι θεοπνεύστοις καὶ ἀρώμασιν, 11
angels active for 3 days	ἕως τριῶν ἡμερῶν, 48	ἕως τρίτης ἡμέρας, 11
burial of body while soul is in heaven	apostles bury Mary, her soul is in heaven	angels bury Abraham, his soul is in heaven, 11–12
Abraham, Isaac, and Jacob	the apostles see Abraham, Isaac, and Jacob waiting for Mary in heaven, 49	Abraham in paradise with Isaac and Jacob, in his bosom, 14
editorial imperative that readers might be "worthy"	ἀξιωθῶμεν, 50	ἀξιωθῶμεν, 15
standard doxology	δοξάζοντες … τὸν υἱὸν ἅμα τῷ πατρὶ καὶ τῷ ἁγίῳ	δοξάζοντες τῷ πατρὶ καὶ πνεύματι νῦν κ.τ.λ.

These parallels do not prove that *TA* depends upon the *Dormitio Mariae* (a sixth century work?[8]) or *vice versa*.[9] As the commentary shows, there are parallels in other texts also, so we may have here to do with a family of motifs typical of Christian tales of the deaths of saints. Yet given that some editions of *TA* are bound with the *Dormitio* (see p. 00), readers of one text would no doubt have thought of the other.

---

[8]   Simon Claude Mimouni, *Dormition et Assomption de Marie: Histoire des traditions anciennes* (Théologie historique 98; Paris: Beauchesne, 1995), 118–27.

[9]   But *James*, 33–34, finds the *Dormitio* dependent upon *TA*.

Despite the strong Christian character of *TA* 20, a Jewish original presumably lies behind it. While that original cannot be reconstructed, one can make the good guess that it presented Abraham's end as being like Moses' end, for the entirety of our book draws upon old Jewish legends about Moses' departure, and pp. 24–27 of the Introduction draw the following parallels that involve chap. 20 specifically:

(a)   God sends (the Angel of) Death to Abraham and Moses
(b)   Both saints command (the Angel of) Death to go away
(c)   Death comes through a kiss
(d)   Michael and other angels appear as escorts
(e)   There is great mourning
(f)   The souls of Abraham and Moses ascend to heaven
(g)   Angels bury their bodies
(h)   The angels sing praises

While both Jewish and Christian sources come to associate most of these motifs with other figures, they appear to have originally been clustered around the death of Moses. One surmises that an informed Jewish audience, listening to a hypothetical Jewish *Vorlage* of *TA*, would have perceived a Moses typology: Abraham's death mirrors the death of the lawgiver.

What is the relationship between RecLng. 20 and RecShrt. 14:6–7, which feels so rushed and anticlimactic? The key observation is that items (b)–(e) and (g)–(h) appear only in RecLng., and as those items belong to the cycle of Moses legends that gave birth to our story, one infers that they were probably an original part of that story. If so, then RecShrt. represents, as so often, an abbreviation—as does ms. N of RecLng.—and RecLng. is more faithful in preserving an older form of our story. At the same time, RecLng. has recast the whole in a later ecclesiastical style and vocabulary and added many hagiographical elements.

The one item in RecShrt. that might be ancient is the presence of the chariots to take Abraham's soul. Not only has Abraham ridden on a chariot earlier in RecLng. (chaps. 9ff.), but *T. Job* 52:6–10 and Gk. *L.A.E.* 33:2 also feature chariots carrying away saintly souls at death.[10] The inference is, however, far from certain, for the motif does not belong to the legends about Moses' death while it is at home in Christian tradition: *T. Isaac* 7:1; *Dorm. BMV* 38; *Apoc. BMV* 26; *Hist. Jos. Carp.* 28; etc.

---

[10]   Given that Greek art often depicts the dead being carried to the grave in a chariot, the heavenly chariot may well be, in addition to an echo of 2 Kgs 2:1–12, an extension of common ritual.

20:1. Imploring Death (δέομαί σου; see on 9:3), Abraham—like "a depressed patient on an analyst's couch"[11]—asks (ἀνάγγειλόν μοι; see on 5:12) whether there is a death that is παράλογος* (LXX: 0; NT: 0; there is a wordplay with the παραλόγως of 19:16). The word means "unexpected" or "unlooked for" (LSJ, s.v.). Its use with θάνατος, seemingly unparalleled, probably refers, as we might put it, to a death in one's sleep (cf. v. 2) or, as the Greeks would have had it, a painless death from the gentle arrows of Apollo. Abraham has just confronted a long series of horrible images, and he wants to know if there is something less dreadful, a death that falls upon people unexpectedly, that is, which comes unheralded by sickness, violence, pain, or other tragic circumstances.[12] One may compare the story that Julius Caesar, when discussing, the night before he died, what sort of death is best, declared, "That which is unexpected" (ἀπροσδόκητος; see Plutarch, Caes. 63). Cf. also the use of ἐξαπίνης in CPJ 1511.1 ("the one who has suddenly gone") and b. Mo'ed Qaṭ. 28a: "Our rabbis taught: If one dies suddenly (פתאום), this is reckoned as being snatched away. If one is ill one day and dies, this is reckoned as being hustled away." The passage goes on to indicate that protracted deaths of three or more days are punishments.

20:2. Death, who does in fact speak the truth, prefaces his answer with a long oath formula: ἀμήν, ἀμήν, λέγω σοι ἐν ἀληθείᾳ θεοῦ λόγου. For "Amen I say to you" see on 2:12. The doubling of "amen" has good Jewish precedent; see Num 5:22 (MT: אמן אמן LXX: γένοιτο, γένοιτο); Neh 8:6 (MT: אמן אמן; 1 Esd 9:47 v.l. (ἀμήν, ἀμήν); Ps 41:13 (MT: אמן ואמן LXX 40:13: γένοιτο, γένοιτο); 72:19 (MT: אמן ואמן LXX 71:19: γένοιτο, γένοιτο); Tob 8:8 v.l. (ἀμήν, ἀμήν); 1QS 1:20; 2:10, 18; 4Q286 frags. 5, 7:8 (אמן אמן several times); m. Soṭah 2:3, 5; b. Šeb. 36a; Noy, JIWE 1.173, 187; Gregg and Urman, Golan Heights 12; etc. אמן אמן is particularly common in Jewish magical texts.[13] But the prefatory position of "amen, amen," so characteristic of John's Gospel, where it appears twenty-five times, is probably Christian in TA, as it is in Gos. Bart. 5:2 and Antonius the Hagiographer, Vit. Symeonis Stylitis 28 (triple "amen"). The prefatory formula of surety is here lengthened by the addition of "by the truth of God's word," ἐν ἀληθείᾳ θεοῦ λόγου. This too appears to be Christian; cf. Origen, Comm. Matt. 13.11 (ἐν τῇ ἀληθείᾳ τοῦ λόγου τοῦ θεοῦ); Apollinaris,

---

11 So Wills, Novel, 254.
12 Cf. Dean-Otting, Heavenly Journeys, 214, who thinks Abraham is asking about a death he desires for himself.
13 See e.g. Naveh and Shaked, Amulets and Magic Bowls, 40, 46, 56, 146, 152, etc.; also PGM 22b.21, 25; 15a.29–30 (triple "amen").

Fr. Ps. 141 (ἐν ἀληθείᾳ θεοῦ); Didymus of Alexandria, *Comm. Ps. 22–26:10*, ed. Gronewald, p. 93.17 (ἐν τῇ ἀληθείᾳ τοῦ θεοῦ); Gregory of Nyssa, *Cant.*, ed. Langerbeck, p. 287.15 (διὰ τῆς ἀληθείας τοῦ λόγου).

There are, Death announces, seventy-two different sorts of deaths. How many of these Abraham has learned about is unclear. Perhaps Death has instructed him regarding them all and the narrator has shared only part of what has transpired. Seventy two is, in any case, presumably a number of completion or fullness, as in LXX Genesis 10 (the nations of the world); *Let. Arist.* 46–50 (the LXX translators); Luke 10:1, 17 v.l. (the missionaries of Jesus); *Ps.-Clem. Rec.* 1:40 (the missionaries of Jesus); *3 En.* 17:8; 18:2–3; 30:2 (Schäfer, *Synopse* 22 = 858, 23–24 = 859–60, 47 = 913; the princes and nations of the world); *m. Neg.* 1:4 (the different sorts of leprosy; cf. *Sifre* Lev. 129:1; *Tanna d. El.* 5); *m. Yad.* 3:5; 4:2 (the seventy-two elders). The closest parallel may be Gk. *L.A.E.* 8:2 v.l., where, on account of his sin, seventy-two plagues afflict Adam.[14]

One death comes to the "righteous," δίκαιος. It has its set and fitting time, ὅρον (ὅρος*; for this sense cf. LXX Exod 9:5; Neh 2:6; and Mark 16:14 W: "the set time [ὁ ὅρος] of the years of Satan's power"). The meaning is that God has determined the time that the just depart, and to such—they are πολλοί—death comes "within one hour," παρὰ μίαν ὥραν (note the wordplay with ὅρον). In other words, they do not suffer long but rather are quickly "handed over to the grave," παραδιδόμενοι τῷ τάφῳ; cf. Origen, *Cels.* 8.30 (παραδιδόναι ... ταφῇ); Eusebius, *Hist. eccl.* 7.16.1 (ταφῇ παραδίδωσιν); Ps.-Eusebius, *Ant. mart. coll.* PG 20.1528D (ταφῇ παραδίδωσι); Theodoret of Cyrrhus, *Eranistes*, ed. Ettlinger, p. 212.20; Aesop, *Prov.* 88.4 (τάφοις παραδίδωσι); etc. Is this a Christian locution? Comparable is the old sapiential notion that the righteous generally live good, full lives whereas the wicked have bad, untimely ends; cf. Prov 10:3–4, 24, 27–29[15] and the stories of Judas' end in Matt 27:5 (he hangs himself); Acts 1:18 (he bursts open); and Papias, ed. Bihlmeyer and Schneemelcher fr. 3 (a wagon runs over him).[16] From one point of view, the

---

14   According to Ginzberg, *Legends*, 5:123, "A sentence employed in amulets reads: 'And mayest Thou, O God, protect him against the seventy-two kinds of diseases, which afflict this world.'" He does not, however, cite documentation.

15   *Midr. Mishle* 10 teaches that righteousness saves one from an "unnatural death" and comments on Prov 10:2: "When the moment comes for the downfall of an evil person, nothing can avail that one ... ." Cf. *b. Šabb.* 156b.

16   One might also cf. Cyprian, *Mort.* 15, which speaks of the good quickly being martyred. But one must distinguish our text from the notion that "Those whom the gods love, die young," an idea with its Jewish parallel in Wis 4:14: God hastened (ἔσπευσεν) to remove Enoch from his corrupt generation.

death that befalls the righteous will come to the just Abraham in this very chapter. He has hardly suffered at all when his soul departs. From another point of view, however, he has dragged things out by his disobedience to both Michael and Death so that the process has taken longer than it should.

20:3. Death becomes insistent, even though he still addresses the patriarch with respect as δικαιότατε; see on 1:1 and 15:6. Death reminds Abraham that he has answered all of his questions. So it is time for the patriarch to quit procrastinating, ἄφες πᾶσαν τὴν βουλήν σου; cf. 9:4, πᾶσαν τὴν βουλήν μου, which draws upon LXX Ps 19:5. He must cease asking questions, κατάλιπε τοῦ ἐρωτᾶν ἔτι ἅπαξ (the last two words translate אַךְ־הַפַּעַם in the LXX, as in Gen 18:32). He must now, without further delay, follow Death: καὶ δεῦρο ἀκολούθει μοι; cf. 15:12, 13; 19:5. Despite Gk. *L.A.E.* 18:5 (δεῦρο ... ἀκολούθει μοι), the imperative is probably Christian. For otherwise the precise formulation, καὶ δεῦρο ἀκολούθει μοι, appears elsewhere only in Matt 19:21 = Mark 10:21 = Luke 18:22 and in Christian quotations of that line. Death notes at the end that he is only asking, after all, for what God has ordered, προσέταξέν μοι; cf. 19:4; Demosthenes, *Epitaph.* 1.3; *Ps.-Clem. Hom.* 12:19. For "the judge and God of all" (ὁ κριτὴς τῶν ἀπάντων καὶ θεός), another likely Christian formulation, see on 14:2.

20:4. Abraham ignores Death's words. He does not follow Death but instead continues to resist God's will. Yet he implicitly concedes that his time is short, for he asks Death to go away (ἄπελθε ἀπ᾽ ἐμοῦ, as in 17:2, q.v.) for just "a bit longer," ἔτι μικρόν (μικρός*). He still wants, as he did before Death revealed himself, to rest upon his couch: ἀναπαύσωμαι ἐν τῇ κλίνῃ μου; cf. 17:2. He explains that he is "very fainthearted": ἀθυμία πολλή μοι; cf. Plutarch, *Sull.* 11 (ἀθυμίαν δὲ πολλήν); Ps.-John of Damascus, *B.J.* 22.192 (ἀθυμία πολλῇ); etc. Although Death has since hidden his ferocity (18:1–2), the patriarch has not recovered from the dreadful encounter in chap. 17. Abraham is, despite everything, starting to slip into death.

20:5. Admitting his weakness, Abraham confesses that, "ever since" he saw Death with his own eyes (ἐθεασάμην σε τοῖς ὀφθαλμοῖς—a good biblical idiom: Zech 9:8; Ecclus 16:5; Luke 2:30; 1 John 1:1; *L.A.B.* 24:4; etc.), his "strength has indeed failed," καὶ ἡ ἰσχύς μου ἐκλείπει; cf. Origen, *Hom. Jer.* 14.10 (ἰσχὺς τοῦ Ἰησοῦ ἐκλείπει), 11 (ἰσχὺς ἐκλείπουσα); Eusebius, *Comm. Ps.* PG 23.780A. The expression is from the Psalter:

LXX Ps 37:11 ἐγκατέλιπέν με ἡ ἰσχύς μου
LXX Ps 70:9 ἐν τῷ ἐκλείπειν τὴν ἰσχύν μου

Perhaps it was the association of Psalm 37 with the suffering of Jesus (cf. Luke 23:49) that encouraged the insertion, later in this verse, of words from Luke 22:44.

Further clarifying his current state, Abraham declares that the limbs of the flesh of his frame (τὰ μέλη τῆς σαρκὸς τῆς ἐμῆς ἁρμονίας; cf. LXX Ezek 37:7; Ps.-Phoc. 102; μέλος*; ἁρμονία*) seem to him (μοι φαίνονται; cf. Herodotus, *Hist.* 2.134; Plato, *Crit.* 46B; φαίνω*) to be like (δίκην; see on 2:2) "a heavy lump of lead," μολύβδου βάρος (μόλυβδος*—more often μόλιβος in the LXX, but the manuscripts vary; βάρος*); cf. RecShrt. fam. E 11:8 ms. A (ἐπίβαρυς). One recalls the English idiom, "heavy heart." τὰ μέλη τῆς σαρκός appears to be a Christian expression; see Ps.-Justin, *Res.* 592C; Gregory of Nyssa, *Hom. 1–8 in Eccl.*, ed. Alexander, p. 381.9; Epiphanius, *Pan.* 64.52; Chrysostom, *Hom. Rom.* PG 60.493; *Acts Phil. Mart.* 36; etc. With μολύβδου βάρος one may compare Appianus, *Mithridatica* 135 (μολυβδαίνας βαρυτάτας); Aelian, *Nat. an.* 1.15 (μολύβδον βάρυν); Chrysostom, *Hom. Phlm.* PG 62.707 (τὸ μολύβδου βαρύτερον); etc., as well as the common use of βάρος for emotional distress, as in Sophocles, *Oed. col.* 409; Philo, *Mos.* 1.14; Rev 2:24; *P. Oxy.* 7.1062.14; etc.

"My spirit is vexed" translates τὸ πνεῦμά μου ἐν πολλῷ ταλανίζεται. LSJ, s.v., says that ταλανίζω* (LXX: 0; Philo: 0; NT: 0; Josephus: 0) means "call" or "deem unhappy." Although Lampe, s.v., gives this as the first meaning in patristic writers (with whom this word is extremely popular, especially as an antonym of μακαρίζω), he cites *TA* and Chrysostom, *In dimissionem Chananaeae* 2 (ed. Montfaucon 3.434A), for the meaning "vex" or "torture." To this one may add *Acts Xanth.* 34: "But why do you vex (ταλανίζεις) me, O wretched soul?"

Abraham asks Death not to go away forever but only to remove himself (μετάστηθι; μεθίστημι*; cf. LXX 3 Βασ 15:13; 1 Macc 11:63; Josephus, *Ant.* 19.297; *T. Iss.* 1:12; *1 Clem.* 44:5)—if only for just a bit, ἐν ὀλίγοις (= ἐν ὀλίγῳ, which occurs in mss. G I). The patriarch's plea is that he cannot bear (οὐχ ὑποφέρω; ὑποφέρω*) to see Death's form (εἶδος; cf. 12:3). It is hard to know what this means, since Death has, according to 18:2, returned to his beautiful state. Should readers infer that, although the narrator has neglected to mention the fact, Death has once more reverted to his hideous form? But then surely those around Abraham (vv. 6–7) would be dead (cf. 17:18). Perhaps, then, we should imagine that Abraham cannot abide even Death's beauty, now that he knows his true nature.

The last line in the verse is Christian. While θρόμβοι αἵματος has secular parallels (e.g., Hippocrates, *De mulierum affectibus i–iii* 9.19), and while there is a parallel of sorts in *Jos. Asen.* 4:11 (ἱδρὼς ἐρυθρὸς πολύς pours over Aseneth's face), there can be little doubt that our narrator's words are from Luke:[17]

TA   κατῆλθε ... ὁ ἱδρὼς ... αὐτοῦ ὡσεὶ θρόμβοι αἵματος
Luke 22:44   ὁ ἱδρὼς αὐτοῦ ὡσεὶ θρόμβοι αἵματος καταβαίνοντες

Perhaps reminiscence of the suffering righteous one in the Psalter earlier in the line moved someone to think about Jesus. In any event, there is an analogy between the Abraham of TA 19 and the Jesus of Luke 22. Both are saintly figures who, facing death, wish to avoid it (Jesus: "If you will, remove this cup from me"; cf. Heb 5:7). In both cases, moreover, the hero suffers in the presence of a heavenly emissary.

20:6–7. Isaac is referred to as ὁ υἱὸς αὐτοῦ; cf. 3:7; 4:1, 8; 5:14; 15:5; LXX Gen 21:5, 8. This is not because he is being introduced, which he is not, but in order to underline that death divides the closest human bonds. For the same reason, Sarah here is ἡ γυνὴ αὐτοῦ; cf. 15:4; LXX Gen 17:19; 18:9–10; 24:36. Weeping, Isaac comes and falls upon his father's breast, στῆθος*. The Greek again recalls a line from the canonical Gospels and so continues the typology: in his death, Abraham is in some ways like Jesus or foreshadows him:

TA   ἔπεσεν   ἐπὶ τὸ στῆθος αὐτοῦ   κλαίων
John 13:25 ἀναπεσὼν (v.l.: ἐπιπεσὼν) ... ἐπὶ τὸ στῆθος τοῦ Ἰησοῦ λέγει
John 21:20 ἀνέπεσεν   ... ἐπὶ τὸ στῆθος αὐτοῦ

Apart from John 13:25 and 21:10 and later Christian versions of those lines, TA 20:6 is the only Greek text with a form of πίπτω followed by ἐπὶ τὸ στῆθος. There are additional similarities: (i) In each case ἐπὶ τὸ στῆθος is immediately followed by a genitive referring to the hero of the book— αὐτου = Abraham in the one case and αὐτοῦ = τοῦ Ἰησοῦ in the other. (ii) In TA and John 13:35, "upon his breast" introduces an action of someone worried about the hero. Isaac weeps. The beloved disciple asks a question. Both are disconcerted. (iii) Death is, in both texts, near.

Although given the nature of the evidence it can only be a conjecture, one does wonder if, before Christian hands reworked our story, the picture of Isaac weeping over Abraham was modeled, not upon John 13:25 and 21:10, but (like perhaps TA 5:9) upon LXX Gen 46:29 and 50:1:

46:29   ἐπέπεσεν ἐπὶ τὸν τράχηλον αὐτοῦ καὶ ἔκλαυσεν κλαυθμῷ πλείονι
50:1   ἐπιπεσὼν Ἰωσὴφ ἐπὶ τὸ πρόσωπον τοῦ πατρὸς αὐτοῦ ἔκλαυσεν

---

[17] Cf. Justin Martyr, Dial. 107.7–8; Raguel, Mart. Pelag. 111, ed. Rodríguez Fernández, p. 74 (as Pelagius the martyr stands, blood rather than sweat flows from his body drop by drop).

It would not have been difficult to turn something close to these lines, which unlike John's text but like *TA* 20:5 concern fathers and sons and use κλαίω, into an allusion to John's Gospel.

Sarah, joining Isaac, comes and embraces Abraham's feet, περιεπλάκη τοῖς ποσὶν τοῦ Ἀβραάμ; see on 15:4 and for περιπλέκω 5:11. In RecShrt., Sarah dies before Abraham dies, in accord with Genesis 23–25. But RecLng. contradicts the biblical chronology—not out of ignorance of it, for our book shows a profound knowledge of Genesis, but because the narrator is more interested in telling a good story than in adhering to Scripture (cf. Abraham's age in 1:1). Under the influence of Gen 49:33 (Jacob "drew up his feet into the bed"), *T. Levi* 19:4; *T. Iss.* 7:9; *T. Gad* 8:4; and *T. Jos.* 20:4 all contain a similar notice about their patriarchal heroes (cf. *Jub.* 23:1, of Abraham). Yet these texts do not depict someone embracing the feet of a dying person. As precedent or background for this gesture one thinks rather of the countless Byzantine icons of the lamentation of Jesus or the Dormition, in which people embrace the feet of the dead Mary or especially Jesus.[18] Christian readers familiar with such icons might understand Sarah's action as part of the parallelism between Abraham and Jesus.

Like Isaac, Sarah too mourns. ὀδυρομένη (for ὀδύρομαι see on 11:6) πικρῶς (cf. v. 7; 11:11) has close parallels only in Christian texts; cf. Athanasius, *Fug.* 8.4 (ὀδύρονται πικρῶς); *Acts Xanth.* 35 (πικρῶς ὀδύρῃ); Ps.-Basil of Seleucia, *Vit. Theclae* 1.13 (ὀδυρομένων πικρῶς); etc.

Abraham's servants also show up, so the whole household is present. The servants' response is akin to that of both Isaac and Sarah:

ἦλθεν   δὲ   Ἰσαὰκ ὁ υἱὸς   αὐτοῦ ...   κλαίων
ἦλθε   δὲ καὶ ἡ Σάρρα ἡ γυνὴ αὐτοῦ ...   ὀδυρομένη πικρῶς
ἦλθοσαν δὲ   πάντες οἱ δοῦλοι   καὶ ἔκλαιον   πικρῶς ὀδυρόμενοι

Abraham himself, as we are told for the third and last time, has "entered the faintness of death," εἰς ὀλιγωρίαν θανάτου; cf. 19:2 and see on 17:19.

Vv. 6–7 closely resemble two previous scenes, both of which also feature περιπλέκω and the entirety of Abraham's household. First, the verses replay part of chap. 5. There Isaac, upon waking from his prophetic dream, goes to Abraham (who is in his chamber), hangs upon his neck, and cries (vv. 7–11, with κλαίω and περιπλέκω). Sarah soon joins him. She too

18 See Maguire, "Sorrow in Middle Byzantine Art," figs. 32 (Mary), 38 (Jesus), 63 (Jesus) 72 (Jesus), 77 (Jesus), 80 (Jesus), 72. For later and western examples see Gertrud Schiller, *Iconography of Christian Art*, vol. 2: *The Passion of Jesus Christ* (Greenwich, Conn.: New York Graphic Society, 1972), plates 549, 575, 576, 579, 593–97, 602, 603, 613.

cries (vv. 11–12). Their mourning for Abraham's death begins here. It ends in chap. 20, for which there has thus been a rehearsal.

Second, chap. 15 stands as a sort of antithesis to chap. 20. In the former, Abraham, thought to be dead, is found to be alive. Sarah offers thanksgiving while Isaac and the servants—who are together with the matriarch in Abraham's chamber—embrace the patriarch and glorify God (vv. 4–5, again with περιπλέκω). So while chap. 15 shares the joy that comes from cheating death, chap. 20 communicates the profound grief that comes when death separates loved ones.

20:8. Death lies for the first time. He declares that Abraham can have "cheerfulness and life and strength," ἱλαρότης καὶ ζωὴ καὶ δύναμις (ἱλαρότης*); cf. the verbal parallel in Cyril of Alexandria, *Comm. Hos.-Mal.*, ed. Pusey, 1:79 (ζωῇ καὶ εὐφροσύνῃ καὶ ἱλαρότητι) and the parallel of content in Ps.-Palladius, *Hist. mon.* 25.3 (an angel fills Piammonas with strength by taking him by the hand). All the patriarch needs to do is come forward (δεῦρο) and kiss (ἄσπασαι) Death's "right hand," δεξιάν μου χεῖραν. For ἀσπάζομαι (see on 5:8) meaning "kiss" see LSJ, s.v., 2; Lampe, s.v., 3, and for kissing the hand see Homer, *Il.* 24.478; *Od.* 16.16; 21.225; 24.398; Arrian, *Epict. diss.* 1.19.24; Lucretius, *De rerum nat.* 1.316–318; Job 31:27; Ecclus 29:5; *b. Ber.* 8b; etc. Such a kiss can either show affection or—more relevant for our text—be a sign of submission, as when a servant kisses the hand of a master or a subject kisses the hand of a king.

Abraham's kiss of Death's right hand creates a nice contrast with 18:7, where Death declares: "if indeed the right hand of the Lord had not been with you in that hour, you also would have departed from this life." God's right hand saves whereas Death's right hand kills. There is, moreover, irony in that a kiss is typically a sign of affection, so when it becomes the instrument of deception, as also in Gen 27:26–27; Prov 27:6; and Matt 26:49 par. (the kiss of Judas), and indeed brings death, everything is upside down. For the association of death and a kiss, which is at home in the Moses traditions due to a fanciful exegesis of Deut 34:5 ("And Moses died there ... עַל־פִּי יהוה"), see *T. Job* 52:8 ("the one who sat in the great chariot got off and kissed [ἠσπάσατο] Job"); *Vis. Paul* 14 (the angels "received the soul of the body, and immediately they kissed [*salutauerunt*; ἠσπάσαντο] it"); Gk. *Hist. Rech.* 15:9 (when the soul leaves, angels ἀσπάζονται it; cf. 16:1); *ARN* A 12; *b. B. Bat.* 17a (Moses, Aaron and Miriam all died by a kiss); *b. Ber.* 8a (death by a kiss "is like drawing a hair out of milk" and is the easiest of all deaths; cf. *Midr. Ps.* 11:6); *b. Mo'ed Qaṭ.* 28a (Miriam died "by the divine kiss"); *Deut. Rab.* 11:10 (God "took his [Moses'] soul with the kiss of the mouth"); *ARN* A 12 (citing Deut 34:5: God took

Moses' soul "by means of a kiss"); Tg. Ps.-Jn. on Deut 34:5 (Moses died
"by the kiss of the Memra of the Lord"); *Petirat Moshe* (*BHM* 1:129,
citing Deut 34:5: when Moses finally agreed to die, God "kissed him and
took his soul through the kiss"; so also 6:77).[19] Perhaps the idea lives on
in the modern idiom, "the kiss of death," which now refers to anything
that dooms a person or project. In our text, however, the divine or angelic
kiss that brings death is transformed into the kiss of one dying and so in
the background is the notion, encouraged by the supposed link between
soul and breath,[20] that the soul departs with the last breath or from the
mouth; cf. Pindar, *Nem.* 1.47; *EG* 547.7–8; LXX Job 41:13 ("His breath
is as live coals, a flame goes forth from his mouth"); *Gk. Apoc. Ezra* 6:4;
Apoc. Sedr. 10:3; *Hist. Jos. Carp.* 19 (in this death is at hand when Joseph's
soul nears his throat); Gregory the Great, *Dial.* 4.40 (Death in the form of
a dragon puts his head to a dying man's mouth and steals his breath);
Armenian *Life of Moses* ("with the opening of his [Moses'] mouth, he gave
up his ghost").[21] This is the antithesis of Gen 2:7, where the breath of life
animates; here instead it departs, and death follows. Christian art can
depict the soul (under the guise of an infant) coming from the mouth of the
dying (e.g. the 10th cent. fresco of the Dormition at Ayvali Kilise,
Cappadocia and Codex Dion. 65, fol. 11v).[22] When Abraham's lips touch
Death's hand, his soul will stick (v. 9). Although the kiss should bring life
and blessing,[23] it instead empties the body of its life-force.

When Death promises that Abraham will, through a simple kiss, soon
have "cheerfulness and life and strength," he is attempting to deceive. But,
as v. 14 shows, the truth is that kissing Death's hand will bring Abraham
to where there is "peace and fervent joy and life without end." So Death

---

[19] See further Klaus Haacker and Peter Schäfer, "Nachbiblische Traditionen vom Tod
     des Mose," in *Josephus-Studien: Untersuchungen zu Josephus, dem antiken Judentum
     und dem Neuen Testament* (ed. Otto Betz, Klaus Haacker, and Martin Hengel;
     Göttingen: Vandenhoeck & Ruprecht, 1974), 166–70.

[20] Recall Gen 2:7, Anaximenes' equation of ἀήρ with ψυχή (Aëtius, *Iatricorum liber*
     13 1.2–3), and the use of πνεῦμα to mean both "soul" and "breath." Cf. Plato,
     Epigr. 5.78 ("When I kissed Agathon, I had his soul on the lips") and Franz
     Cumont, *Recherches sur le Symbolisme funéraire des Romains* (Paris: P. Geuthner,
     1942), 119–20.

[21] Michael E. Stone, *Armenian Apocrypha relating to the Patriarchs and Prophets*
     (Jerusalem: Israel Academy of Science and Humanities, 1982), 155.

[22] For this last see Stichel, *Vergänglichkeitsdarstellungen*, plate 8.

[23] Cf. Gen 2:7; 48:10; 2 Kgs 4:34; Ezek 37:9–10; *T. Benj.* 1:2; *Jos. Asen.* 19:10; John
     20:22; *Odes Sol.* 28:7; *Gos. Phil.* 59:3–4; and *Scriptores hist. Augustae* 1.25, where
     kissing king Hadrian brings healing. See further G. Stählin, *TDNT* 9 (1974), 123–
     24, on kissing images of gods for strength and health.

is (unwittingly?) speaking the truth, and although Abraham wants things to go one way, when they go another it is all for the best. The deception is, in other words, for his own good. Even Abraham's disobedience does not frustrate God's good intentions for him.

20:9. Trusting Death for the first time, and longing for the cheerfulness, life, and strength he once had, Abraham does what he is told. But Death, having gained Abraham's confidence, has lied for the first time; he has laid a trick, πεπλάνηκεν (πλανάω*). Cf. b. Šabb. 30b and Ruth Rab. 1:17: the Angel of Death must, because one cannot die while studying Torah, trick the ever-studious David into going outside the school for a bit. For additional stories of Death tricking rabbis see b. Mo'ed Qaṭ. 28a. Given the sometime identification of Death with the Devil (see on 16:4), it is relevant to observe that the latter is typically characterized as a deceiver; see on 16:4 and note T. Jud. 19:4; Rev 12:9; 20:3, 8, 10; Apos. Con. 7:32:4.

When Abraham kisses Death's hand (ἠσπάσατο τὴν χεῖρα αὐτοῦ; see on v. 8), instantly the patriarch's soul (ἡ ψυχή) adheres (ἐκολλᾶτο; for κολλάω* + ἐν see LXX Deut 28:60; 29:20; 4 Βασ 5:27) to Death's hand. Cf. esp. Ps.-Bartholomew, Book of the Resurrection of Jesus Christ, ed. Budge, fol. 18a: "Michael made a sign over my mouth ... . Then straightway my soul sprang out from my body, and alighted on the hand of Michael." Abraham never resigns himself to death. He expires still wanting to live. Note that the narrator says nothing about the pain of death itself; contrast Josephus, C. Ap. 2.203, which mentions the suffering when soul separates from body.

20:10. If Abraham's kiss brings instant death, it also instantly (εὐθέως) brings Michael and a "host" (πλήθους; πλῆθος*) of unnamed angels. For Michael as psychopompos see on 1:4. For πλῆθος ἀγγέλων see 1 Clem. 34:5; Gk. 3 Bar. 9:3; 1 Apoc. John, ed. Tischendorf, 17:12; 18:7; 26:1, 3; Eusebius, Comm. Ps. PG 23.1157C; Ps.-Athanasius, Sermo de patientia PG 26.1301C; Apophth. Patrum Moses 1; etc.; also Luke 2:13. The expression, although it may well come from Judaism, is missing from the LXX and is typically Christian; and it describes the angelic party that arrives for Mary's soul in the Dormitio; see p. 387. Often in Christian hagiography the angels that come for saints at death are a multitude; cf. Ps.-Bartholomew, Book of the Resurrection of Jesus Christ, ed. Budge, fol. 3a; Eustathius of Trake, Encom. on Michael, ed. Budge, p. 127; Gregory the Great, Dial. 4.16; Vatican Gr. 1982, ed. Wenger, p. 230; John of Thessalonica, Dorm. BVM A 12, ed. Jugie, p. 396; etc. The angels appear in order to "take" (ἦραν) Abraham's "honored soul," τὴν τιμίαν αὐτοῦ ψυχήν; cf. v. 12; 2:3, 4; 7:9; 16:9. Christian accounts of dying saints often use τίμιος; cf. Gk.

Apoc. Ezra 7:15 (Ezra's "precious and holy body"); *Dorm. BMV* 48 (Mary's "precious body"; see further p. 387 above); *Mart. Hyacinth of Amastria* 8 (= CCGS 21, p. 62: Hyacinth's "precious corpse"); Ps.-John of Damascus, *B.J.* 40.363 (Joasaph's "precious body").

That Michael and/or angels take the souls of the righteous to heaven is a commonplace in early and medieval Christianity.[24] The New Testament proof text is Luke 16:22: "The poor man died and was carried away by the angels to Abraham's bosom."[25] Relevant Jewish parallels include *1 En.* 71:5 (Michael carries off Enoch's spirit); Gk. *L.A.E.* 37:4–6 (Michael takes Adam to paradise); *T. Job* 52:5–6 ("those who come for his [Job's] soul" are in chariots); *T. Ash.* 6:5; *4 Bar.* 9:5 (Michael opens the gates of heaven and leads the righteous in—but this may be Christian); *b. Ketub.* 104a ("when a righteous man departs from the world he is welcomed by three companies of ministering angels"); Tg. Cant. on 4:12 (angels bring the souls of the righteous to Eden); *Deut. Rab.* 11:10 (Michael comes for Moses); *Petirat Moshe* (*BHM* 1:129: angels accompany Moses' soul); other rabbinic texts in Strack-Billerbeck 2:223–25.[26] The idea was a natural development of the apocalyptic *topos* of angels accompanying seers to heaven. But there was also certainly influence from the Greco-Roman

---

[24] See Herm. *Vis.* 2.2.7; Herm. *Sim.* 9.27.2; *Asc. Isa.* 7:23; Clement of Alexandria, *Quis div.* 42.16; Tertullian, *An.* 53; *Cult. fem.* 2.13; *Act. Perp. Fel.* 11; *Hist. Rech.* 14:3–4; *T. Isaac* 2:1; 7:1–2 (Michael is sent at Isaac's death, and cherubim and angels accompany his ascension); *T. Jac.* 5:13; Eusebius, *Comm. Ps.* PG 23.404C; Athanasius, *Vit. Ant.* 60 (cf. Palladius, *Hist. Laus.* 6:7; 8:5; Ps.-Palladius, *Hist. mon.* 22.9); Gregory of Nyssa, *Vit. Macrinae* 24 PG 46.984D; Jerome, *Vit. Paul.* 14; Chrysostom, *Hom. Matt.* 54.7; *Dorm. BMV* 38; *Vis. Paul* 14; Ps.-Palladius, *Hist. mon.* 11.8; 14.16; *Hist. Jos. Carp.* 13 (Joseph prays for Michael to come to him at death; cf. 22–23); Ps.-Macarius, *Vis. de sanctis Angelis* PG 34.224–29; *Digenis Akrita* G 8.196 (3560); etc. See further Jean Daniélou, *The Angels and their Mission according to the Fathers of the Church* (Westminster, Md.: Newman, 1957), 95–105. A later variant of this motif is the legend that angels carried the body of Catherine of Alexandria to Mount Sinai.

[25] Note also that, when Jesus ascends in Acts 1, two angels appear (many more show up in later Christian pictures of and homilies on this scene; so e.g. the Rabbula Gospels). Angels are also associated with his resurrection, and in *Gos. Pet.* 10:39 two angels support Jesus as he exits his tomb. For pertinent texts from western liturgy see Athanasius Recheis, *Angels: Spirits, Magnificent and Mighty* (Collegeville, Minn.: Liturgical Press, 1976), 44–47.

[26] Note also *2 En.* 36:2; 55:1; 67:2; *3 En.* 6:1 (Schäfer, *Synopse* 9 = 890); *Memar Marqah* 5:3 ("all the hosts of the heavenly angels" meet Moses as he begins his ascent). Discussion in Mach, *Entwicklungsstadien*, 148–59. 4Q 'Amram, where two angels dispute over Moses' father, may not be a deathbed scene.

world, where Hermes/Mercury (cf. the Etruscan Turms), Cerberus, and others serve as psychopompos; see Homer, *Od.* 24.1, 9; Diogenes Laertius 8.31; Hyginus, *Fab.* 251; Tertullian, *An.* 53; etc.[27] Plato, *Phaed.* 107C–108D, contains a general statement about guardian spirits leading the dead to their judgment, and Greek art is, from an early time, filled with winged creatures carrying off the dead. Particularly wide-spread were the depictions of the death of Sarpedon, with Hypnos and Thanatos carrying away the slain warrior's body while his winged *eidolon* or soul hovers above. [28] As soon as one conceives of death as the start of a journey to a new place above the earth, flying escorts naturally appear; see further on v. 12.

The angels take Abraham's soul in their hands, in "a divinely woven linen shroud," σινδόνι θεοΰφάντῳ. Cf. *2 En.* 22:6, where Michael gives the ascended Enoch glorious clothing, and *Petirat Moshe* (*BHM* 1:129), where Michael supplies a purple linen cloak for Moses' body. For σινδών (cf. Heb. סדין) see on 4:2, where fine linen and incense are in Abraham's chamber. Here the σινδών is akin to the typical linen winding sheet used for burial; cf. Herodotus, *Hist.* 2.86; Gk. *L.A.E.* 40:1–4; Matt 27:59; Mark 15:46; Luke 23:53; *Gos. Pet.* 6:24; *Gos. Heb.* fr. 7; *Acts Phil. Mart.* 37 V. (In the Mishnah people are characteristically buried in "wrappings" or "shrouds": e.g. *m. Sanh.* 6:5; *m. Ma'aś. Š.* 5:12; cf. *y. Kil.* 9:3; *b. Mo'ed Qaṭ.* 27b.) Whether or not the earlier scene in chap. 4 foreshadows this latter one, here Abraham is in the shroud, which the angels grasp and lift. This is clearly a Christian touch. For although the notion of garments made in heaven is Jewish (cf. *T. Job* 46:8; Gk. *L.A.E.* 20:1–2; *Asc. Isa.* 1:5; 3:25; 4:16–17; *b. Šabb.* 114a; Tg. Onq. Gen 3:21), it is equally Christian (Rev 3:4–5; 6:11; 7:9, 13–14; Herm. *Sim.* 8.2.3; *Asc. Isa.* 7:22; 8:14, 26; 9:2, 9, 17–18, 24–25; 11:40; *4 Ezra* 2:39); and θεοΰφαντος* with the meaning "divinely woven" is a patristic word. To the examples in Lampe, s.v., which include Ps.-John of Damascus, *B.J.* 16.136, where the word is used of the heavenly garments stored up for the saints, see also Ps.-Ephraem, *Prec. ad dei matrem*, ed. Phrantzoles, p 367.1 (θεοΰφαντος πορφύρα, of clothing in Eden); Romanos the Melodist, *Cant.* 16.2 (θεοΰφαντον στολήν, of the robe of paradise); Theodore the Studite, *Nativ.* BMV PG 96.681A

---

[27] For discussion and speculation about the influence of Greco-Roman ideas of ascent to heaven upon Jewish thought see Goodenough, *Jewish Symbols*, 8:121–66.

[28] See esp. Dietrich von Bothmer, "The Death of Sarpedon," in *The Greek Vase: Papers based on Lectures presented to a symposium held at Hudson Valley Community College at Troy, New York in April of 1979* (ed. Stephen L. Hyatt; Latham, N.Y.: Hudson Valley Community College and Hudson-Mohawk Association of Colleges and Universities, 1981), 63–80 + plates.

(θεοΰφαντου περιβολαίου, of the clouds of heaven); and Michael Psellus, *Poem*. 55.117 (τὴν θεοΰφαντον στολήν, of Adam's robe). For parallels of content see *Hist. Rech*. 14:4 (at death, angels receive the soul of a Rechabite in shining stoles); Tertullian, *Cult. fem*. 2.13 ("the stoles of martyrdom are being prepared" for saints carried away by angels); *Hist. Jos. Carp*. 23 v.l. (Michael and Gabriel wrap Joseph's body in a shining cloth); *Acts Phil. Mart*. 38 (the dying Philip prays that Jesus might clothe him "in your shining robe"); Ps.-Bartholomew, *Book of the Resurrection of Jesus Christ*, ed. Budge, fol. 18a (a certain Siophines declares that, upon death, an angel put his soul in a byssus cloth); Eustathius of Trake, *Encom. on Michael*, ed. Budge, pp. 128–29 (Michael welcomes a woman's soul in a garment of light); *Act. Perp. Fel*. 11 (angels carry off the souls of martyrs without touching them with their hands, which seemingly implies that the souls are conveyed in some sort of garment, as in depictions of the Dormition, where Mary's departing spirit, wrapped in a white garment, is carried by Christ to angels or carried by angels to Christ).[29] In Christian iconography, one should note, souls are often depicted as infants, in swaddling-like clothes.[30]

20:11. The angels take care of (ἐκήδευσαν) the "righteous" (δικαίου; see on 1:1) man's body (τὸ σῶμα). κηδεύω* (LXX: 0) typically refers to burying or (as here) taking care of a corpse; cf. Philo, *Migr*. 159; *T. Job* 39:10; Mark 6:29 v.l.; Josephus, *Ant*. 9.227. For the word immediately preceding τὸ σῶμα see Gk. *L.A.E*. 40:6; Sopater the Rhetorician, Διαίρ. ζητ., ed. Walz 8:87; Ps.-Callisthenes, *Hist. Alex. Magn*. rec. Byz. poet. 3916; etc.

The angels administer "divinely-smelling ointments" (μυρίσμασι θεοπνεύστοις) and "perfumes," ἀρώμασιν; cf. Plutarch, *Alex*. 20 (ἀρώματων καὶ μύρων); Luke 23:56 (ἀρώματα καὶ μύρα). μύρισμα*, θεόπνευστος*, and ἄρωμα* are all *hapax legomena* for *TA*, and the first two do not appear in the LXX. For ἄρωμα as fragrance or spice to counter the odor of death see LXX 2 Chr 16:14 (with μύρον); Chariton, *Chaer*. 1.8.3; Plutarch, *Sull*. 38:3; Mark 16:1; Luke 23:56; 24:1; John 19:40. Lampe, s.v., cites for μύρισμα only *TA*, and LSJ, s.v., cites only *Cat. Codicum Astrologorum* 8(1). To this one may add Ps.-Chrysostom, *De Joseph et de castitate* PG 56.587; *De Susanna* PG 56.591; John of Damascus, *Sacr. par*. PG 95.1329B; Michael Psellus, *Poem*. 2.212.

---

[29]   J. Myslivec, in *Lexikon der christlichen Ikonographie* 4 (1972), 334–35. Cf. John of Thessalonica, *Dorm. BVM* A 12, ed. Jugie, p. 396. Jerome, *Vit. Paul*. 14: Paul's soul shines as in a snow-white robe as he ascends amid angels. For a possible Egyptian background see Morenz, *Geschichte*, 69.

[30]   See e.g. plates 26, 127, 154, 162, 163, 231, 285, 333 in Hamann-Mac Lean and Hallensleben, *Monumentalmalerei*.

θεόπνευστος does not, against Lampe, s.v., C, mean "sweet-smelling." The word rather matches the θεοΰφαντος of the previous verse and carries something close to its usual sense, "divinely inspired"; cf. *Sib. Or.* 5:308, 407; Ps.-Phoc. 129 (an interpolation); 2 Tim 3:16. If Abraham's soul is wrapped in a heavenly garment, his body is enveloped in ointments made in heaven. One is reminded of the hagiographical motif of a supernatural odor attending the death or burial of a saint; cf. Antonius the Hagiographer, *Vit. Symeonis Stylitis* 28; *Dorm. BMV* 48; Vatican Gr. 1982, ed. Wenger, p. 230; Cyril of Scythopolis, *Vit. Joannis Hesychastae* 17; Gregory the Great, *Dial.* 4.15–17, 28; John of Thessalonica, *Dorm. BVM* A 12, ed. Jugie, p. 396; etc.

The angels continue in their task "until the third day" (ἕως τρίτης ἡμέρας) after Abraham's death (τελειώσεως); cf. *T. Job* 5–7 (the mourners forbid Job from being buried until "after three days"); *Apoc. Zeph.* 4:7 (angels "spend three days" escorting the ungodly in the air before they cast them into eternal punishment); *Dorm. BMV* 48 (the angelic songs after Mary's death last for three days; cf. the "Euthymiac History" in John of Damascus, *Or. secunda in dormitionem sanctae Dei genitricis Mariae* 18, ed. Kotter, p. 537); and *Acta Graeca SS. Davidis, Symeonis et Georgii* 9 in *Analecta Bollandiana* 18 (1899), 219 (the dying David says that he will depart "after the third day").[31] Perhaps these texts reflect the Greek custom of burying the departed three days after death.[32] Turner, positing an early, Palestinian *TA*, and observing that it was, for obvious reasons, the usual custom in Palestine to bury people on the day of death (cf. *b. Mo'ed Qat.* 28a), suspects that the three day motif is secondary. That no fear of defilement is expressed shows, he urges, a Christian hand, and that the body can remain unburied for three days points to somewhere "not in the East but in a more temperate climate."[33]

τελείωσις* (cf. RecShrt. 7:18) literally means "completion" or "fulfillment," as in LXX Judg 10:9; Luke 1:45. It refers to the end of history in Gk. fr. *1 En.* 2:2; 10:14; 16:1; *T. Reub.* 6:8. But in *TA* the word clearly means "death," a sense LSJ, s.v., fails to document but which is quite common in patristic texts. Lampe, s.v., supplies examples.

[31] See also James, *Testament*, 126–27, who cites excerpts from "a spurious Homily or Apocalypse of S. Macarius" which I have not been able to identify. In some respects the text is close to *Apoc. Zeph.* 4:7.
[32] On burial on the third day see Donna C. Kurtz and John Boardman, *Greek Burial Customs* (Ithaca, N.Y.: Cornell University Press, 1971), 144–46.
[33] Turner, "Testament," 137.

Sem. 8.1 records the habit of visiting graves "until the third day" in order to prevent premature burial (examples of which *Semahoth* gives). This custom is undoubtedly related to the folk belief, presupposed by John 11:17; 39; *T. Job* 53:7; and *4 Bar.* 9:12–14, that the soul of an individual remains near its body for three days after death. *Gen. Rab.* 100:7 reads: "Up the to third day the soul keeps returning to the body, thinking that it will go back in"; cf. *y. Mo'ed Qaṭ.* 3:5; *Lev. Rab.* 18:1. This was a common belief in Byzantine Christianity, and it is also attested in Zoroastrian sources (e.g. *Hadhokht Nask* 2:3–20; *Vendidad* 19:28; *Menog i Khrad* 2:114).[34] Evidently the angels, then, wait until Abraham's soul can no longer return to its body. Because, however, ἕως τρίτης ἡμέρας is not a common phrase in Greek literature, because it occurs in the Greek Bible only in Matt 27:64 in connection with Jesus' resurrection, and because Abraham's death otherwise echoes Jesus' passion, the mention of three days may, for a Christian audience, have added to the parallels with Jesus; see above, p. 386.

Abraham is buried "in the promised land," ἐν τῇ γῇ τῆς ἐπαγγελίας; see on 8:5. This accords with Gen 25:9. But Genesis has him buried in "the cave of Machpelah" (cf. *Jub.* 23:7) and not, as here, "by the Oak of Mamre," ἐν τῇ δρυΐ τῇ Μαβρῇ; see on 1:2. Cf. Gen 35:8, where Deborah is buried under an oak; 1 Sam 31:12–13, where bones are interred under a tamarisk tree; the assumption traditions that have Mary's body under the Tree of Life in paradise;[35] and *Acts Pet. Paul* 84, where Peter's body is placed under a terebinth. Has Gen 18:4 ("rest yourselves under the tree"), which *Gen. Rab.* 48:10 associates with dwelling in tents in the age to come, been of influence? The contradiction between *TA* and Genesis does not amount to much, for Gen 23:17 and 25:9 locate the cave of Machpelah "east of Mamre," and Mamre and Hebron (the traditional location of Machpelah) are quite close and even identified in Gen 23:19 and 35:27; see on 1:2. Cf. *Acts Andr. Mth.* 15, where Abraham lies buried in a cave in the

---

[34] For full discussion see Emil Freistedt, *Altchristliche Totengedächtnistage und ihre Beziehung zum Jenseits-Glauben und Totenkultus der Antike* (Liturgiegeschichtliche Quellen und Forschungen 24; Münster: Aschendorff, 1928), 53–72. Some texts, however, make the seventh day after death the decisive one; see Box, *Testament*, 36, n. 4, and cf. *b. Šabb.* 152a. The liminality of the soul between death and Hades, which involves its delay in moving on, is also part of Greek tradition; see Jan Bremmer, *The Early Greek Concept of the Soul* (Princeton: Princeton University Press, 1983), 93–94, and Robert Garland, *The Greek Way of Death* (Ithaca, N.Y.: Cornell University Press, 1985), 38–41. Cf. Macrobius, *Somnium Scipionis* 13.10: "ejected souls for a long time hover about their bodies."

[35] See Wenger, *L'Assomption*, 240.

field of Mamre. On the literary level, "by the Oak of Mamre" works well because it creates an *inclusio*. Our book opens by saying that Abraham "pitched his tent at the crossroads by the Oak of Mamre" (1:2), and when we, along with Michael, first meet the patriarch, he is by that oak (2:1). So the story ends where it began (cf. p. 384).

That the angels themselves bury Abraham has its parallels in *L.A.E.* 48:1–3 (Michael and Uriel bury Adam); Gk. *L.A.E.* 40:1–7 (Michael and others bury Adam and Abel); 43:1 (the angels bury Eve while Michael stands by; contrast *L.A.E.* 51:1); *Hist. Rech.* 15:7 (angels make sepulchers for the Rechabites); 23:2 (angels bury Zozimus); *Hist. Jos. Carp.* 25 (two angels wrap Joseph's body in their shining garments); Serapion, *Life of John*, trans. Mingana, p. 447 (Michael and Gabriel bury Zechariah). In our book this motif is probably indebted to the Moses traditions given how much *TA* otherwise draws upon them. Although many Jews took Deut 34:4–5 (אתו יקבר) to mean that God buried Moses, others held that Michael or the angels buried his body; see Philo, *Mos.* 2.291; Jude 9; Origen, *Princ.* 3.2.1; Tg. Ps.-Jn. on Deut 34:6; *Deut. Rab.* 11:10; Ps.-Oecumenius, *Jude*, ed. Hentenius, p. 629B; *Palaea Historica*, ed. Vassiliev, pp. 257–58; *Slavonic Life of Moses* 16; the Falasha *Death of Moses*, trans. Leslau, p. 111; etc.[36]

20:12. The angels escort (ὀψικεύοντες; see on 10:3; the verb is Christian) Abraham's "precious soul," τιμίαν αὐτοῦ ψυχήν; see on v. 10. In accord with the notion that heaven is above, the angels ascend, ἀνήρχοντο εἰς τὸν οὐρανόν; see on 4:5. The text suggests flight of some sort, and Jewish, Greek, Roman, and Christian sources all give wings to the dead and their escorts; see e.g. *EG* 175.3–4 ("the soul has flown into the air"); 243.5 ("Your soul has flown away"); *IGRom* 4.1579 ("fluttering souls"); *CIJ* 1510 ("my soul has flown to the holy ones"); *Hist. Rech.* 15:10 syr. (souls fly spiritually); Athanasius, *Vit. Ant.* 66 (souls ascend as if with wings). Icons of Mary's ascension typically have angels with wings, and sometime around the turn of the era Jews, like so many others, had generally come to believe that "omnis spiritus ales est" (Tertullian, *Apol.* 22.8).[37]

As the angels ascend, they sing "the trisagion hymn to the master of all, God": ψάλλοντες τὸν τρισάγιον ὕμνον τῷ δεσπότῃ τῶν ὅλων θεῷ (ψάλλω*,

---

[36] On this tradition see esp. Richard J. Bauckham, *Jude, 2 Peter* (WBC 50; Waco, Tex.: Word, 1983), 67–76; also Joannes Tromp, *The Assumption of Moses: A Critical Edition with Commentary* (SVTP 10; Leiden/New York/Cologne: Brill, 1993), 275–81.

[37] Discussion in Mach, *Entwicklungsstadien*, 185–91, with references to the secondary literature.

τρισάγιος*, ὕμνος*). For "the master of all" see on 1:4 and cf. 13:7; Philo, *Plant.* 91; *Spec. leg.* 4.153; Josephus, *Ant.* 1.72; Justin, *Dial.* 140.4; *Ps.-Clem. Hom.* 3:72; Eusebius, *Vit. Const.* 2.55; etc. While this title is known to Jewish sources, and while τρισάγιος has its equivalent in the rabbinic קדושות ג' in *Lev. Rab.* 24:8 and elsewhere, the expression, τρισάγιον ὕμνον, appears otherwise exclusively in Christian sources, and these no earlier than the fourth century; cf. Chrysostom, *Mart.* PG 50.710 (τρισάγιον ὕμνον ψάλλοντες); Romanos the Melodist, *Cant.* 56.1; John of Damascus, *De hymno trisagio ad Jordanem* passim; Ps.-Mauricius, *Strat.* 12.8.22 (ψάλλειν τὸν τρισάγιον ὕμνον); etc. Earlier, in 3:2–3 (q.v.), a cypress sings the trisagion, so again the end of the book sends us back to the beginning (cf. p. 384). For angels singing at the death of a saint see *Hist. Rech.* 16:1; Gk. *L.A.E.* 43:4; *Dorm. BMV* 48; Ps.-Palladius, *Hist. mon.* 11.8; 14.7; John of Thessalonica, *Dorm. BVM* A 5, ed. Jugie, p. 382; Eustathius of Trake, *Encom. on Michael*, ed. Budge, p. 129; *Pass. ant. SS. Sergii et Bacchi* 12; Paphnutius, *Life of Apa Onnophrios the Anchorite*, ed. Budge, fol. 56b; Gregory the Great, *Dial.* 4.15, 16; Cyril of Scythopolis, *Vit. Sabae* 43; *Vit. Joannis Hesychastae.* In several manuscripts of Gk. *L.A.E.* 43:4, the angels sing specifically the trisagion at Eve's death.

The angels set Abraham down (ἔστησαν αὐτόν) that he might worship (εἰς προσκύνησιν; προσκύνησις*; LXX: Ecclus 50:21; *3 Macc.* 3:7; cf. *Gk. Apoc. Ezra* 7:16) "the God and Father," τοῦ θεοῦ καὶ πατρός. On God as "Father" (cf. vv. 13, 15) see on 9:7. Parallels include *4 Ezra* 4:78 (when spirits leave the body they return to God and "adore the glory of the Most High"); Gk. *L.A.E.* 35:2 (the dead Adam is soon prostrate before God in heaven); *Hist. Rech.* 16:1a (angels escort a soul until it comes to where it "worships the Lord"), 2 (the Son of God brings a soul forward "so that it may worship his Father"); *Vis. Paul* 14, 25–26; *Vit. Evaristus* 42 = *Analecta Bollandiana* 41 (1923), 321 (angels set Evaristus before God's throne); and *Acta Graeca SS. Davidis, Symeonis et Georgii* 37 = *Analecta Bollandiana* 18 (1899), 258 (when George of Lesbos dies he goes to do obeisance before God). "The God and Father" would be odd for LXX or New Testament Greek; one expects a possessive genitive (cf. *3 Macc.* 5:7; Gal 1:4; 1 Thess 3:3; 3:13) or other qualifier. But the unqualified name appears in the Corpus Hermeticum (*Poim.* 21:5; Κλείς. 2:3; 14:4) and is common in patristic texts: Justin, *2 Apol.* 6.5; *Apos. Con.* 8:5:11; Didymus of Alexandria, *Trin.* PG 39.792A; Procopius of Gaza, *Comm. Isa.* PG 87/2.1945.38, 2005.24; John of Damascus, *Sacr. par.* PG 95.1256C; etc.

20:13. On the φωνὴ τοῦ θεοῦ, which here speaks to those in heaven, see on 10:12. The LXX always has φωνὴ κυρίου τοῦ θεοῦ, but Christian texts know the simpler φωνὴ τοῦ θεοῦ—Justin, *Dial.* 119.6; Origen, *Cels.* 6.62;

Eusebius, *Comm. Isa.* 1.98; etc. The voice is "undefiled." Although ἄχραντος* (LXX: 0; NT: 0; cf. Symm. Lam 4:7; Philo, *Sacr.* 139; Josephus, *Bell.* 5.219; Gk. *Apoc. Ezra* 2:11; *Apoc. Sedr.* 4:3) is well attested in classical Greek (LSJ, s.v.), its application to the divinity is characteristic of patristic texts (Lampe, s.v.). For it describing a voice see Severianus Gabalensis, *Job* PG 56.572, and Photius, *Bibl.*, ed. Bekker, p. 263B PG 103.1016C. It also appears in accounts of the deaths of saints in Gk. *Hist. Rech.* 16:2 ("the undefiled Father") and the *Dormitio Mariae* (see p. 387).

The divine voice sounds forth only after much "praise and glorification," ἀνυμνήσεως καὶ δοξολογίας, a combination seemingly otherwise unattested. Unlike the well-known verb ἀνυμνέω, the noun ἀνύμνησις* is rare. LSJ has no entry, and Lampe, s.v., which gives the meaning as "praise," cites only Sophronius of Jerusalem, *Or.* 8 PG 87.3664A (7th cent.). Earlier than this is Romanos the Melodist, *Cant.* 32 pro. 1 (6th cent.). Later examples include Photius, *Bibl.*, ed. Bekker, p. 262A PG 103.1012B (9th cent.), and Michael Attaliates, *Hist.*, ed. Bekker, p. 237.17 (11th cent.). δοξολογία* is attested much earlier, and not just in Christian sources: *Prot. Jas.* 13:1; Eusebius, *Hist. eccl.* 10.4; Gk. *Hist. Rech.* 16:4 (angels sing the "doxology" of praise); Iamblichus, *Myst.* 2.10; etc. Yet its non-Christian use is rare. See further the long entry in Lampe, s.v. As in *TA*, the word is used in connection with the Trisagion also in Basil, *Hist. mystagogica* 59; Chrysostom, *Hom. Isa. 6:1 (In illud: Vidi dominum)* 1:1; and Photius, *Bibl.*, ed. Bekker, p. 245A PG 103.957B. Indeed, Byzantine Christians referred to the trisagion as a "doxology"; cf. Cyril of Scythopolis, *Vit. Euthymii*, ed. Schwartz, p. 45.14; John of Damascus, *Trisag.* 28.6.

20:14. The next to last sentence takes one back to the very beginning, to chap. 1. There God commanded the archangel Michael; here he commands a host of angels. There God spoke of τὸν φίλον μου Ἀβραάμ (1:4, q.v.). Here he likewise speaks of τὸν φίλον μου τὸν Ἀβραάμ. There God spoke about Abraham's dying and joining God in heaven. Here his words come to completion: Abraham has died and entered "paradise," παράδεισον; see on 4:2 and 11:10. Our book has come to its proper end.

This happy conclusion is, however, marred by a striking inconcinnity. Abraham, God says, has come to "the tents of my righteous ones and the lodgings of my saints Isaac and Jacob," αἱ σκηναὶ τῶν δικαίων μου καὶ μοναὶ τῶν ἁγίων μου Ἰσαὰκ καὶ Ἰακώβ (Ἰακώβ*; cf. 15:15 v.l.).[38] The sentence implies what cannot be, namely, that Isaac and Jacob have already died

---

[38] Although it depends upon RecLng., the old Romanian omits and so avoids the clumsy phrase.

and gone to paradise. For σκῆνος of a heavenly dwelling see Luke 16:9; Heb 8:2; 9:11–12; Rev 15:5 (cf. *4 Ezra* 7:80; *2 En.* 41:2); and for Abraham's earthly tent see on 1:2. Here the tents and lodges are in Abraham's "bosom," κόλπῳ; cf. 6:7. So not only does Abraham join his living son and grandson, but the patriarch is in his own "bosom." One doubts that the book originally ended on such a jarring note. As Turner puts it, "the absurdity of Abraham being uplifted into his own bosom is so patent that one must conclude this passage to be a later addition."[39] If one postulates a Jewish original, one must surely attribute the awkwardness to a Christian hand. B H I J Q all lack the offending words (see Textual Notes). Is A here secondary?

αἱ σκηναὶ τῶν δικαίων, a phrase linked to "the bosom of Abraham, Isaac, and Jacob" in *IG* 5.660 and *BE* 1.67.671, is from LXX Ps 117:15 (for אהלי צדיקים. The biblical context seems significant. Not only do vv. 14–18 refer to "song" and to "the voice of exultation," but the psalmist says that he will not die but live, and he further declares that God "has not given me over τῷ θανάτῳ." Whether or not Psalm 118 had an eschato-logical or messianic interpretation in pre-Christian Judaism (a disputed question), later interpreters naturally read Ps 118:14–18 as having to do with post-mortem salvation after death; see e.g. Didymus of Alexandria, *Fr. Ps.* 1076.1; Chrysostom, *Exp. Ps.* PG 55.333;[40] Romanos the Melodist, *Cant.* 48.14; *Midr. Ps.* 118:17. *TA* probably assumes a similar reading of this part of the Psalm.

μοναὶ τῶν ἁγίων (μονή*) is not from the Old Testament. Perhaps John 14:2 lies in the background: "in my Father's house are many μοναί." In any case, μοναὶ τῶν ἁγίων are the abode of the saints in heaven in Ps.-Athanasius, *Quaest. in scripturam sacram* PG 28.749C, and Ps.(?)-Cyril of Alexandria, *Hom. diversae* 14 PG 77.1080D. The singular occurs in Ps.-Macarius, *Serm.* 64 3.2, and μονὴν ἐν τῇ βασιλείᾳ σου is a liturgical phrase by the fourth century.[41] The modern commentaries on John 14:2 raise the ques-tion of whether μονή represents Aramaic אונא/אינא, which means "night-lodging" (cf. Origen, *Princ.* 2.11.6). However that may be, *TA* uses the word as do the patristic texts listed in Lampe, s.v., 1c, to which add Symeon Metaphrastes, *Vit. Matronae prima* 49 = *Acta Sanctorum* Nov. 3 (1910) 811F. Cf. also *1 En.* 39:4 ("dwelling places of the holy ones and

---

[39] Turner, "Testament," 137.

[40] Chrysostom says here that the Psalm projects an image of the resurrection even before the New Testament, and he links the mentions of "tents" with Abraham.

[41] H. B. Swete, "Prayer for the Departed in the First Four Centuries," *JTS* 8 (1907), 507.

their resting places," cf. v. 5); 45:3 ("resting places"); 48:1; Philo, *Somn.* 1.256 ("your Father's house"); *4 Ezra* 2:11 ("everlasting habitations"); 6:35, 41; *2 En.* 61:2 ("many shelters have been prepared" in heaven), 3–4; Irenaeus, *Haer.* 1.14.3 ("the upper rooms"); Athanasius, *Vit. Ant.* 45 (ἐν οὐρανῷ μονάς); *Hist. Jos. Carp.* 1 ("the house of my [Jesus'] Father"; cf. 30); *Tanḥ. B* Leviticus Emor 9 ("every righteous person has a מדור in Eden"); *b. B. Bat.* 75b (palaces and mansions in the world to come); *Hekalot Rabbati*, ed. Schäfer, *Synopse* 277 (בְּמחנות קודשים.

"In his bosom" (or "lap"; cf. BDAG, s.v., κόλπος, 1), which suggests proximity to and fellowship with the patriarch (cf. John 1:18; 13:28), recalls the formulation in Luke 16:22 (τὸν κόλπον Ἀβραάμ) and esp. 23:

TA 20:14 Ἀβραάμ ... ἐν τῷ κόλπῳ αὐτοῦ
Luke 16:23 Ἀβραάμ ... ἐν τοῖς κόλποις αὐτοῦ

Given the Christian character of the surrounding text, and indeed the use of Luke 22:34 in v. 5, one suspects Lukan influence here; but see below.

In *4 Macc.* 13:17, Abraham, Isaac, and Jacob receive martyrs (v.l.: εἰς τοὺς κόλπους), and late Jewish texts know the expression, חיקא/חיק אברם (Strack-Billerbeck 2:225–27).[42] Despite the sparse attestation, Luke 16:22–23, which speaks of Abraham's "bosom" without explanation, is probably sufficient to show that some pre-Christian Jews had interpreted the notion of being with the ancestors after death (cf. 1 Kgs 1:21; 11:21) to mean being near the patriarch Abraham in particular. Presumably the expression, "the bosom of Abraham," was modeled on the common remark, found on epitaphs, that the buried lie in the "bosom" of the earth (as in *IG* 7.2534, 2538; *EG* 422; *CIJ* 1510; *CIL* 1.10; 6.20370).[43] *TA* 20:14 should not, however, be cited as evidence for the antiquity of the phrase in Judaism, for the verse, as noted, belongs to a context thoroughly rewritten by Christian hands, and "the bosom of Abraham (and Isaac and Jacob)"—which Eastsern icons sometimes represent by placing either miniature people in the laps of the patriarchs or little torsos inside the opening in Abraham's tunic[44]—was quite popular among followers of Jesus: *Ps.-Clem. Hom.* 8:4:1; *Apos. Con.* 8:41:2; Epiphanius, *Pan.* 42.11; Romanos the Melodist, *Cant.* 30.1; *SEG* 6.295.5–6; *CIG* 9116, 9117; *IG* 14, 189; Johnson, *Anatolia* 4.16; etc. It appears to have been particularly prevalent

---

42 See further Rudolf Meyer, *TDNT* 3 (1966), 824–26.

43 But Delcor, *Testament*, 175, suggests a connection with Num 11:12.

44 For the former see e.g. the recently restored window at Deir al-Surian in the Sketis (reproduced at http://syrcom.cua.edu/Hugoye/Vol1No2/HV1N2Innemee.html); for the latter see e.g. the west bays of naos in the Serbian Church of the Pantokrator at the Monastery of Deèani.

as an epitaph among Egyptian Christians,[45] and it is part of the Coptic Liturgy ("O Lord, repose all their souls in the bosom of our holy fathers Abraham, Isaac, and Jacob").[46]

Paradise—here identified with Abraham's bosom, as in *P. Oxy.* 16.1874r15–16 and *IGA* 5.541; other texts may distinguish the two[47]—is the elimination of human ills, a place where there is no suffering or grief or groaning, πόνος οὐ λύπη οὐ στεναγμός (πόνος*; λύπη: cf. 8:8; στεναγμός*). One may compare LXX Isa 35:10 ("sorrow and grief [λύπη] and groaning [στεναγμός] have fled away"; cf. 51:11; the targum gives these verses eschatological sense); *1 En.* 25:6 v.l. ("sorrow, pain, toil, and blows"[48] will not enter paradise); Rev 21:4 ("mourning and crying and suffering [πόνος] will be no more" in the new heaven and new earth);[49] Coptic Asclepius, Nag Hammadi 6:8:78 (the places of demons are filled with "weeping, mourning, and groaning"); *1 Apoc. John*, ed. Tischendorf, 27 (in the future world οὐκ ἔστιν πόνος, οὐκ ἔστιν λύπη, οὐκ ἔστιν στεναγμός); Ps.-Chrysostom, *Poenit.* PG 60.703 (in paradise οὐκ ἔστι πόνος, λύπη, καὶ στεναγμός). Clearly this is a *topos*. The combination, οὐ λύπη οὐ στεναγμός, might nonetheless take hearers back to LXX Genesis 3, where λύπη and στεναγμός enter the world after the sin of Adam and Eve (see especially the curse of Eve in 3:16). If so, the theme of paradise regained is emphasized.

If suffering, grief, and groaning are absent, present are "peace and fervent joy and life without end," εἰρήνη καὶ ἀγαλλίασις καὶ ζωὴ ἀτελεύτητος (εἰρήνη: cf. 6:6; ἀγαλλίασις: cf. 6:5; ἀτελεύτητος*). Cf. Ps.-Macarius, *Serm.* 64 49.2 (ἀγαλλίασιν καὶ τρυφὴν καὶ ζωὴν αἰώνιον); *Hom. 1–50* 5.415 (ἀγαλλίασις ... εἰρήνη ... ζωὴ αἰώνιος), and Cyprian, *Mort.* 2 (the kingdom

---

[45] So Lattimore, *Themes*, 303. He also cites Latin cases of *in gremio Abraham*: CE 684.10; 749.5. Note further the cemetery inscription in Gustave Lefèbvre, *Recueil des inscriptions grecques chrétiennes d'Égypte* (Cairo: Institut français d'archéologie orientale, 1907), no. 48: Michael conducts the worthy to the bosom of the holy fathers Abraham, Isaac, and Jacob. For the Latin liturgies see James, *Testament*, 128–29. On pp. 73–74 James refers to Christian art, and on this see E. Lucchesi Palli, in *Lexikon der christlichen Ikonographie* 1 (1968), 30. Also relevant are texts in which Abraham and others welcome saints into heaven or appear in accounts of the world to come—Matt 8:11–12 = Luke 13:28; *Vis. Paul* 27, 47; *Dorm. BMV* 49; *Acts Andr. Mth.* 17; etc.

[46] *The Coptic Liturgy of St. Basil* (Cairo: Coptic Orthodox Church, 1993), 16.

[47] Iiro Kajanto, "The Hereafter in Ancient Christian Epigraphy and Poetry," *Arctos* 12 (1978), 27–53.

[48] The Greek is: βάσανοι καὶ πληγαὶ καὶ μάστιγες οὐκ ἅψανται αὐτῶν.

[49] Delcor, *Testament*, 175, supposes that the "final redactor" of the Testament would have been put in mind of this verse from Revelation.

is "praemium uitae et gaudium salutis aeternae et perpetua laetitia"). Particularly close to our text is Gregory of Nyssa, *Or. dom.* 5, ed. Oehler, p. 258.33, which takes up LXX Isa 35:10:

LXX Isa 35:10	αἴνεσις καὶ ἀγαλλίαμα, καὶ εὐφροσύνη ...
	ἀπέδρα ὀδύνη καὶ λύπη καὶ στεναγμός
Gregory of Nyssa, *Or. dom.*	ἀπέδρα ὀδύνη καὶ λύπη καὶ στεναγμός
	ἀντεισέρχεται δὲ ζωὴ καὶ εἰρήνη καὶ ἀγαλλίαμα
TA 20:14	οὐκ ἔστιν πόνος οὐ λύπη οὐ στεναγμός
	ἀλλ᾽ εἰρήνη καὶ ἀγαλλίασις καὶ ζωὴ ἀτελεύτητος

There is no need to posit that *TA* depends upon Gregory or *vice versa*. Other texts are close to these: Ps.-Ephraem, *De virtute, ad novitium monachum* 4.103; *Sermo in secundum adventum domini nostri Iesu Christi*, ed. Phrantzoles, p. 43.7; see also above. Isa 35:10 lent itself to antithetical expansion. There are, furthermore, many examples of ἀπέδρα ὀδύνη καὶ λύπη καὶ στεναγμός directly following mention of "the bosom of Abraham"; see e.g. Ps.-Dionysius Areopagita, *Eccl. Hierarchia* 125; Ps.-John of Damascus, *Fide dormierunt* PG 95.252A; *IGA* 5.564, 657, 664, 665; *SEG* 8.871, 873. The combination was well known from Christian epitaphs. It was also liturgical, as appears from *Apos. Con.* 8:41:4;[50] *IGA* 5.647 (a Byzantine epitaph with liturgical excerpts); and the *Sarum Manual* (in sinum patriarcharum tuorum, Abrahae scilicet amici tui, et Isaac electi tui, atque Iacob dilecti tui, quo aufugit dolor et tristitia atque suspirium, fidelium quoque animae felici iocunditate laetantur).[51] *TA* 20:14, then, presents a slight variation of a liturgical phrase commonly found on grave markers.[52]

20:15. The book ends with a moral exhortation, which the long Romanian expands.[53] The exhortation cannot be original, for it misses the central concerns of the story. *TA* does not, despite chap. 1, focus on Abraham's "hospitality" (φιλοξενίαν; cf. 17:7 and see on 1:1) or his "virtuous con-

---

[50] Although some have thought this to preserve a Jewish liturgical text, their reasons are insufficient; see David A. Fiensy, *Prayers Alleged to be Jewish: An Examination of the Constitutiones Apostolorum* (BJS 65; Chico, Calif.: Scholars Press,1985), 149–50.

[51] James, *Testament*, 128, cites the *Sarum Manual* but fails to remark upon the link with Isa 35:19.

[52] Against Delcor, *Testament*, 175, there is no influence from Isa 25:8ff.

[53] Ed. Roddy, p. 52: "Likewise should we, my beloved brothers, receive travelers, strangers, the poor, and everyone, that we may give them rest and hospitality in our houses; that we, too, might be found worthy of the gift of eternal life ... ."

duct" (ἐνάρετον ... πολιτείαν; ἐνάρετος*: see Textual Notes on 5:3; πολιτεία*
= "conduct" also in Gk. *L.A.E.* prologue; *1 Clem.* 2:8; *Diogn.* 5:4; *Mart.
Pol.* 13:2); cf. Ps.-Palladius, *Hist. mon.* prol. 1: the Egyptian monks are a
model of ἐναρέτου πολιτείας.[54] So the call to emulate (ζηλώσωμεν) the
patriarch's hospitality and to acquire (κτησώμεθα; see on 14:14) his way of
virtue are out of place. These imperatives do, however, reflect the fact that
the manuscripts of *TA* typically belong to collections of hagiography.
There are close parallels in Chrysostom, *Hom. Gen.* 41 PG 53.379
(ζηλώσωμεν τοῦ δικαίου [sc. Abraham] τὴν ἀρετήν), and *Vit. Elizabeth the
Wonderworker* 2 = *Analecta Bollandiana* 91 (1973), 252: τὸ τοῦ πατρι-
άρχου Ἀβραὰμ σφόδρα ζηλοῦντες φιλόξενον. Earlier texts in which Abraham
is clearly a moral model include *Jub.* 17:17–18; 19:3–4, 8–9; Ecclus 44:19–
22; 1 Macc 2:51–52; *4 Macc.* 15:28–30; 16:18–23; Gal 3:6–9; Heb 11:8–
9, 17–19; Jas 2:21–24; *1 Clem.* 17:1–2. ζηλόω* (in both LSJ, s.v., and
Lampe, s.v., the first sense is "emulate," a sense not found in the LXX,
Philo, the New Testament, or Josephus) + πολιτεία is common in patristic
texts: Origen, *Fr. Luc.*, ed. Klostermann 57; Basil the Great, *Sermones de
moribus a Symeone Metaphrasta coll.* PG 32.1345B (see below); Chrysostom, *Hom. Ps.* PG 55.664; etc. Note also the μιμησάμενον αὐτῶν τὴν
πολιτείαν in Ps.-Palladius, *Hist. mon.* prol. 2, which sets forth the purpose
of the narrative, and the similar τὸν βίον ζηλώσασα that introduces the
story of Domnina in Theodoret of Cyrrhus, *Hist. rel.* 30.1.

The closing concern of the narrator is that he and his brothers—for
ἀδελφοί μου ἀγαπητοί see 1 Cor 15:58; Phil 4:1; Jas 1:16, 19; 2:5;
Chrysostom, *Hom. Act.* 11.3 PG 60.98; the expression is most common in
Ps.-Ephraem—should draw the right moral conclusion from the book, and
that they accordingly "might be found worthy" (ἀξιωθῶμεν; ἀξιόω*) of
eternal life, τῆς αἰωνίου ζωῆς (only here in *TA*; cf. *4 Macc.* 15:3; *Ps. Sol.*
3:12; John 17:3; and the עולם ייח on some Jewish epitaphs, e.g., *CIJ* 1526;
Noy, *JIWE* 1.81, 82, 118). This is standard fare for Christian hagiography.
Indeed, the closing sentence of *TA* displays a well-attested pattern: (a) moral
exhortation to emulate hero (often with direct address; cf. also Gk. *3 Bar.*
17:4), (b) promise of eternal reward, and (c) standard doxology (cf. the
liturgical versions of the Lord's Prayer):

Mart. Pol. 22: "We pray that you are well, brothers ... and may it be granted to
us to come into the kingdom of Jesus Christ following his [Polycarp's] footsteps ...
that the Lord Jesus Christ might gather me [Pionius, the copier] together with his

---

[54] Note also the use of πολιτεία at the beginning of *Vit. Evaristus* title (*Analecta
Bollandiana* 41 [1923], 295).

elect into his heavenly kingdom, to whom be glory with the Father and the Holy Spirit unto ages of ages. Amen."

Basil the Great, *Sermones de moribus a Symeone Metaphrasta coll.* PG 32.1345B: "Let us flee the evil of the former, but the conduct (πολιτείαν) of the latter let us emulate (ἐκζηλώσωμεν), so that we might also share in the coming good, in Christ Jesus our Lord, to whom be glory and might, now and ever and unto ages of ages. Amen" (cf. PG 32.1168A, 1360B).

Chrysostom, *In sanctum Stephanum* PG 63.932: "Let us emulate (ζηλώσωμεν) the longing of this one, and let us imitate his virtue (ἀρετήν), so that we might enjoy the crowns laid up, through the grace of the only-begotten Son of God, to whom be glory along with the Father and the Holy Spirit, now and ever, and unto the ages. Amen."

Prayer of St. Athanasius, ed. Budge, fol. 67a–b: "And as for us, O my beloved, let us follow the teachings of our father Athanasius ... . And even if we are not able to attain to the measure of our fathers, nevertheless let us be very diligent in the matter ... if you do what is good, he will ... cause you to meet him face to face ... through Jesus Christ, our Lord, to whom be all glory and honor as is meet for him, and to his good Father, and to the vivifying and consubstantial Holy Spirit, now and ever and always and forever."

Vit. Daniel the Stylite 102 = *Analecta Bollandiana* 32 (1913), 229: "Let us do our utmost to follow in his [Daniel's] steps ... that we may find mercy and grace in the day of judgment from the Father, the Son, and the Holy Spirit, now and ever and to all eternity. Amen."

Vit. John the Almsgiver 46 = *Analecta Bollandiana* 45 (1927), 74: "So let us also strive to imitate the achievements which I have described of this our saintly father John, and as we are strangers and pilgrims in this life let us lay up treasures in the life to come ... . May it be granted to us all to obtain these things by the grace and loving-kindness of our Lord Jesus Christ to whom, together with the Father and the Holy Spirit, be glory, honor, and power now and always and unto the ages of ages. Amen."

Vit. Marinos, ed. Richard, p. 12: "Let us, then, beloved, zealously emulate the blessed Mary and her patient endurance, so that on the day of judgment we may find mercy from our Lord Jesus Christ, to whom belongs glory and dominion to the ages of ages. Amen."

In addition to these examples, there are countless patristic and Byzantine books that conclude with ἀξιωθῶμεν followed by a reference to obtaining heaven: Ps.-Basil, *Constitutiones asceticae* PG 31.1337C; Ps.-Epiphanius, *Hom. in assumptionem Christi* PG 43.485C; Chrysostom, *Stat.* 9 PG 49.111 (and many other places in Chrysostom); Theodoret of Cyrrhus, *Comm. Ezek.* PG 81.904B–C; *Dorm. BMV* 50; Ps.-Macarius, *Hom. 1–50* 49.5; 50.4; *Vit. Athanasia of Aegina* 20, ed. Halkin, p.195; *Vit. Theodora of Arta* PG 127.908D; Symeon Metaphrastes, *Vit. Matronae prima* 49 = *Acta Sanctorum* Nov. 3 (1910) 811D; cf. *Syr. Apдд·Ðan.* 40. Because there is such a strong tendency in later Byzantine hagiography to conclude by asking for the intercession of the saint whose story has been told, our ending, which makes no such appeal to Abraham, is likely to belong to the earlier Byzantine period.

Index of References

1. Bible

2. Old Testament Pseudepigrapha

3. Dead Sea Scrolls and Related Texts

4. Apostolic Fathers

5. Nag Hammadi Codices

7. Rabbinic Literature

7.3 Babylonian Talmud

8. Classical and Ancient Christian Writers and Works

Pseudo-Sophocles
in Clement of Alexandria,
Strom. 5.14.21   243

Sophronius of Jerusalem
Oratio 8
PG 87.3664A   405

Pseudo-Sophronius of Jerusalem
Fragmentum commentarii liturgici
13   223

Sozomen
Historia ecclesiastica
2.4   70, 135
5.9   354
7.19.3   279

Pseudo-Sphrantzes
Chronicon sive Maius (ed. Grecu)
p. 170.2   316
p. 506.3   300

Statius
Silvae
5.1,34   123n

Stephen the Deacon
Vita Stephanii Iunioris
PG 100.1076A   272

Stichoi to Charona
Vaticanus Gr. 207, f. 372r   72

Stobaeus
Eclogae
1   81

Florilegium
1.3.56   268
1.49.44   261

Strabo
Geographica
6.1.5   111

Suetonius
Claudius
44   355

Suidas
Lexicon   110, 153, 179, 250

Symeon Metaphrastes
Vita Matronae prima
49 = *Acta Sanctorum*
   Nov. 3 (1910) 811D   412
49 = *Acta Sanctorum*
   Nov. 3 (1910) 811F   406

Symmachus
Vita Abel
8   282

Synesius of Cyrene
Epistulae
157   265

Tabula Cebetis
15:2–3   242n, 243
22:1   341n
23:3   341n
24:2   341n

Tatian
Oratio ad Graecos
7.2   331
15   118

Tertullian
De anima
53   398n, 399

Apologeticum
22.8   403

De carne Christi
3.6   118
6.3–5   118

De corona militis
7   341

9. Papyri, Inscriptions

10. Ancient Near Eastern, Samaritan, Persian, Sanskrit, Arabic Sources

Index of Names and Subjects

Index of Modern Authors

2012.08.15   161.00